SEVENTH EDITION

American Social Welfare Policy
A Pluralist Approach

Howard Jacob Karger
The University of Queensland, Australia

David Stoesz
Mississippi Valley State University

Boston Columbus Indianapolis New York San Francisco Upper Saddle River
Amsterdam Cape Town Dubai London Madrid Milan Munich Paris Montréal Toronto
Delhi Mexico City São Paulo Sydney Hong Kong Seoul Singapore Taipei Tokyo

Editorial Director: Craig Campanella
Editor in Chief: Ashley Dodge
Editorial Product Manager: Carly Czech
Editorial Assistant: Nicole Suddeth
Vice President/Director of Marketing: Brandy Dawson
Executive Marketing Manager: Kelly May
Marketing Coordinator: Courtney Stewart
Managing Editor: Melissa Feimer
Senior Project Manager/Liaison: Lynne Breitfeller
Senior Operations Supervisor: Mary Fischer
Operations Specialist: Diane Peirano
Art Director: Jayne Conte

Cover Designer: Sue Behnke
Interior Design: Wee Design
Cover Image: Shutterstock
Media Director: Brian Hyland
Senior Digital Media Editor: Paul DeLuca
Media Project Manager: Tina Rudowski
Full-Service Project Management: Revathi Viswanathan, PreMediaGlobal
Composition: PreMediaGlobal
Printer/Binder: Courier Kendallville
Cover Printer: Courier Kendallville

Credits and acknowledgments borrowed from other sources and reproduced, with permission, in this textbook appear on the appropriate page within text.

Use of the trademark(s) or company name(s) implies (imply) no relationship, sponsorship, endorsement, sale, or promotion on the part of Pearson Education, Inc. or its affiliates.

Library of Congress Cataloging-in-Publication Data
Karger, Howard Jacob
   American social welfare policy : a pluralist approach / Howard Jacob Karger,
David Stoesz. — Seventh edition.
      pages cm
   Includes index.
   ISBN 13: 978-0-205-84897-3
   ISBN 10: 0-205-84897-4
 1. Public welfare—United States.   2. United States—Social policy.   3. Welfare state—
United States.   I. Stoesz, David.   II. Title.
   HV95.K354 2014
   361.973—dc23

                                                          2012048039

10 9 8 7 6 5
V011

ISBN 10:   0-205-84897-4
ISBN 13: 978-0-205-84897-3

CONTENTS

The years since the publication of the last full edition have been marked by dramatic events on the domestic and international fronts. By late 2012, the global financial crisis (GFC) that began in 2008 led to an overall unemployment rate of around 8 percent (more than 14 percent for African Americans). For workers over age 55, that unemployment rate jumped to 16 percent.

More than 12 million Americans suddenly found themselves unemployed and unable to pay their bills. Most economic predictions in 2012 called for continued high unemployment as employers were not generating a sufficient number of new jobs or replacing high numbers of unemployed workers. Approximately 1.4 million homes, or 3.3 percent of all homes with a mortgage, were scheduled for foreclosure in mid-2012. The number of mortgages with overdue payments stood approached 9 percent. Although housing prices had risen a modest 2 percent by mid-2012, they were still almost at the same price level as 2002.

These concerns were further heightened by the massive and growing U.S. debt, which reached over $16 trillion in late-2012, or about 100 percent of the nation's GDP. In addition, the GFC left large parts of Europe in economic tatters, as Portugal, Ireland, Greece, and Spain, among others, teetered on the edge of bankruptcy. While many Western economies were losing steam, the economies of China, India, Brazil and Indonesia were in a high growth mode.

The international front was equally turbulent as the Arab Spring's push for democracy toppled or destabilized governments in Tunisia, Egypt, Yemen, Libya, and Syria. By 2012, the Iraq and Afghanistan wars had dragged on for more than a decade and cost the lives of thousands of Americans, Iraqis, and Afghanis. The combination of the GFC, the cost of two simultaneous and unfunded wars, and President Obama's extension of the Bush tax cuts left the American economy in profound debt. The way forward was further stymied as the federal government was virtually paralyzed by the Republican Party's commanding majority in the House of Representatives, with the Democrats holding only a slight edge in the Senate. A divided government resulted in policy options being at a virtual standstill.

In the midst of this virtual paralysis, several important policy developments emerged in the first term of the Obama administration. Some of these achievements include the Dodd-Frank Wall Street Reform and Consumer Protection Act, one of the most significant financial reform acts since the Great Depression; the Patient Protection and Affordable Care Act of 2010 (known as Obamacare); repeal of the military's Don't Ask Don't Tell (DADT) rule; the Credit Card Accountability, Responsibility, and Disclosure Act; and the Children's Health Insurance Program Reauthorization Act of 2009 (CHIPS).

The presidential election of 2012 proved to be one of the most acrimonious in recent memory. Extreme Republican Party ideologues drove the party far to the right in areas such as contraception, abortion, health care, voter's rights, and immigration. In the end, President Obama's moderate approach triumphed as he won 303 electoral votes compared to Mitt Romney's 206 votes. While close, Obama won the popular vote by 50.4 percent to Romney's 48 percent. The election clearly illustrated the sharp divisions in American society between the more liberal Northeast, West Coast, some Western and Midwestern states, and the far more conservative South and rural areas. The voting patterns also highlighted the different priorities between young and old voters, religious and non-religious voters, white and minority voters, female and male voters. These patterns reflect differing perceptions of where America should be heading.

Despite these divisions, the current policy environment could offer social welfare advocates multiple opportunities for change. Consider several of the conservative themes driving public philosophy: "Privatization," long a part of human services in the United States, is evident in nonprofit organizations and private practitioners. "Devolution" is familiar to providers of child welfare, mental health, and corrections—traditionally state-controlled programs—to say nothing of professionals who have served as elected officials in state and local governments. "Faith-based social services" has been a cornerstone of the nonprofit sector, evident in such agencies as Catholic Charities, the Salvation Army, and Jewish community services, among others. As these examples illustrate, advocates of social justice already have substantial expertise in domains that conservatives have appropriated. In turn, this expertise could be mobilized to enhance the public interest while benefitting social work.

Several changes will be required if human service professionals are to reclaim a prominent role in social policy. Markets have been a primary means of distributing goods and services to the nonpoor, and the application of market dynamics to low-income families should be evaluated on merit, not discarded solely on ideological grounds. State and local politics have been important arenas for introducing innovations in social welfare and for providing social workers a first step on the ladder of public service; such opportunities should be celebrated, not dismissed.

If social work is to reassert its role in public policy, acceptance of privatization and devolution will be insufficient for the profession to become an influential player. Public policy involves the kind of power that occurs in three basic forms: money, votes, and networks. Although these resources have been the staple of politics, the information age requires players to possess a higher level of sophistication. To be competitive, one must have command of information systems, large data sets, and complex decision menus.

If social work can educate students about these methods and begin to insert itself into the policy environment, the profession will have to again become an influential force in social policy. On the other hand, if the profession rests on its historic laurels, it will remain a bit player. Such an eventuality would essentially waste the substantial assets that social work brings to social affairs: a distinguished legacy, the altruism of the young, and a unique moral imperative.

This edition of *American Social Welfare Policy* attempts to provide the information necessary for the reemergence of social work in social policy, nationally and internationally. In addition to discussing the basic concepts, policies, and programs that have typified the U.S. welfare state, the text includes chapters on the voluntary nonprofit sector (Chapter 6) and the for-profit corporate sector (Chapter 7). Chapter 9 directs attention to a new strategy in social policy: tax expenditures. Chapter 3 discusses the often neglected role of religion in the formation of social welfare policy. The final chapter, Chapter 18, examines the influence of global capitalism, a development that not only weds the developed nations to the undeveloped nations, but in the process shifts capital and jobs in unprecedented volumes. This edition has also put more emphasis on international social policy.

We owe many debts in completing this edition. The reviewers of this and previous editions have provided an invaluable service in identifying deficiencies. We would like to thank the reviewers of this edition for their insightful comments and suggestions. Earlier editions were aided by Dr. Stephen Thornton, Deanna Machin and Dr. Peter Kindle.

A very special thanks to Crystal Joyce for her tireless work on this edition. Without her this book would not have reached completion by the deadline. Finally, thanks to our families. In anticipation of the next edition, comments by students and faculty are welcome. The authors can be contacted via email: Howard Karger at H.karger@uq.edu.au and David Stoesz at Davestoesz@aol.com.

About the Authors

Howard Karger (right) is professor and Head of the School of Social Work and Human Services, The University of Queensland, Brisbane, Australia. David Stoesz (left) is professor, Mississippi Valley State University. Howard and David have been friends and colleagues for more than 30 years. In addition to seven editions of *American Social Welfare Policy*, they have coauthored two other books: *The Politics of Child Abuse in America* (with Lela Costin) (Oxford University Press, 1996) and *Reconstructing the American Welfare State* (Rowman and Littlefield, 1992). Howard's book, *Shortchanged: Life and Debt in the Fringe Economy* (Berret-Koehler, 2005) examines the financial practices and products that exploit millions of American families. In 2006, the book won the Independent Publishers Award in Finance/Investment/Economics. David's book, *Quixote's Ghost: The Right, the Liberati, and the Future of Social Policy* (Oxford University Press, 2005), explains how conservatives have assumed control of domestic policy and proposes a new framework for social policy. *Quixote's Ghost* won the 2006 Pro Humanitate Literary Award. Howard, Anna and their dog Mr. Fuggs live in Brisbane, Australia; David lives in Itta Bena, Mississippi.

CHAPTER 1

Social Policy and the American Welfare State

Source: The Image Works

Social welfare policy is best viewed through the lens of political economy (i.e., the interaction of economic, political, and ideological forces). This chapter provides an overview of the American welfare state through that lens. In particular, it examines various definitions of social welfare policy, the relationship between social policy and social problems, and the values and ideologies that drive social welfare in the United States. In addition, the chapter examines the effects of ideology on the U.S. welfare state, including the important roles played by conservatism and liberalism (and their variations) in shaping welfare policy. An understanding of social welfare policy requires the ability to grasp the economic justifications and consequences that underlie policy decisions. As such, this chapter contains a brief introduction to Keynesianism, free market economics, socialism, and communitarianism, among others.

American social welfare is in transition. Starting with the Social Security Act of 1935, liberals argued that federal social programs were the best way to help the disadvantaged. Now, after 70 years of experimenting with the **welfare state**, a discernible shift has occurred. The conservatism of U.S. culture—so evident in the Reagan, Bush (both Bushes), and even Clinton and Obama presidencies—has left private institutions to shoulder more of the welfare burden. For proponents of social justice, the suggestion that the private sector should assume more responsibility for welfare represents a retreat from the hard-won governmental, social legislation that provided essential benefits to millions of Americans. Justifiably, social advocates fear the loss of basic goods and services during the transition in social welfare.

The election of Barack Obama as the 44th President of the United States in 2008 not only broke a racial barrier but also promised to sweep away the strident conservatism that had defined the presidency of George W. Bush. The Obama victory, with 52 percent of the vote and increased Democratic majorities in both chambers of Congress, heartened liberals who had anticipated an expansion of government social programs. However, the euphoria among liberals soon gave way to despair as the Democratic Party lost control of the House of Representatives and barely held on to the Senate in the midterm elections of 2010.

While liberal pundits hailed the resurgence of "a vast new progressive movement,"[1] structural limits and the emergence of a strong reactive element

would restrain Obama's ambitions. Massive deficits left by the Bush administration, compounded by a severe global financial crisis and two unfunded wars, meant that economic issues would trump other priorities. Reduced tax revenues would impede the ability of the government to meet existing obligations, let alone expand social programs. Obama's centrist inclinations to build bipartisan support for his legislative agenda failed as newly elected extremist Tea Party legislators squashed most of his attempts at compromise. Instead, ideologically driven legislators focused on social issues such as abortion, and even resuscitated the previously long-dead issue of contraception. Parts of the nation had not just turned right, but hard right. Added to this was the side-show around Obama's birth certificate, doubts about whether he was Christian or Moslem, accusations that he was socialist, and various other distractions.

The 2012 presidential election was marked by the often extreme positions taken by Republican presidential contenders. Long dormant issues like access to birth control resurfaced as Republican candidates vied for the support of the religious right and Tea Partiers. This political climate led to an anti-science orientation, often reflected in wildly unsubstantiated claims. For instance, Jeanine Notter, a Republican state senator from New Hampshire, claimed that medical evidence showed that birth control pills can cause prostate cancer. Todd Akin (R-MO) stated that doctors had told him that it is extremely rare for "legitimate" rape victim to become pregnant: "If it's a 'legitimate' rape, the female body has ways to try to shut that whole thing down."[2] Despite the lack of any medical evidence, former Republican presidential candidate Michelle Bachmann (R-MN) warned that a Tampa mother told her how her little daughter suffered from mental retardation after getting the HPV (human papilloma virus) vaccine. Other former Republican candidates, like Texas governor Rick Perry, believe that evolution is a questionable theory. John Shimkus (R-Ill) cited the Book of Genesis as evidence that climate change is a hoax since God promised Noah he would not destroy the Earth due to people's wickedness. Rick Santorum cited climate change a travesty of scientific research designed to create panic that would lead to further governmental control of people's lives.[3] Nowhere is the power of conservative elements more evident than in the gun control issue. Despite the spate of mass shootings—i.e. 2007 Virginia Tech shooting that left 33 dead; 2011 Tucson shooting that killed six people and wounded former U.S. Representative Gabrielle Giffords; and the 2012 Aurora Colorado massacre—no gun legislation has been passed. The response of Obama and presidential contender Mitt Romney was to pray for the families of the deceased.

Other wild allegations and statements circulated, such as Allen West's (R-FL) charge that 78 to 81 members of the Congressional Progressive Caucus of the U.S. Congress were members of the Communist Party. That would be quite a feat since 5 percent of the total 2,000 (probably inflated) members of the U.S. Communist Party would have to make their way from a tiny office in New York City to the U.S. Congress.[4] Conservative rock and roll singer Ted Nugent's commented that if Obama were re-elected, he would either be dead or in jail. On air, country singer Hank Williams, Jr., compared Obama to Hitler. The election also illustrated the nation's regional fissures. For instance, a 2012 Public Policy poll of registered Republican voters found that 45 percent of Alabamians and 52 percent of Mississippians believed that Obama is a Muslim (the other 40 percent were not sure). Only about 25 percent of those voters believed in evolution.[5]

By August 2012, the Republican Party had settled on former Massachusetts Governor Mitt Romney as their presidential candidate. The subsequent presidential election proved to be one of the most costly and acrimonious in recent memory. All told, the 2012 presidential campaigns spent upwards of $2 billion, much of that from super PACs. However, the final list of 2012 expenditures might never be known since some of the biggest spending groups were nonprofit organizations that were permitted to hide their spending from public scrutiny.[6]

This spending spree was spurred on by the U.S. Supreme Court decision in Citizens United v. Federal Election Commission, which maintained that the First Amendment prohibited the government from restricting independent political expenditures by corporations and unions.[7] In the end, President Obama's centrist positions led to a win of 303 electoral votes compared to George Romney's 206 votes.

The 2012 election also illustrated the deep division in American society between the liberal states (e.g., the Northeast, West Coast, and some Western and Midwestern states) and the highly conservative Southern and rural areas. A breakdown of the state and country votes highlighted the vastly different

voting patterns between urban and rural voters, young and old voters, religious and non-religious voters, white and minority voters, and women and male voters.[8] These patterns reflect differing visions of American society and where it should be going.

Structural features of the American welfare state militate against a major expansion of government, per se. A pluralistic mix of private and public services is an overriding feature of U.S. social welfare. As in other realms, such as education, in social welfare private institutions coexist alongside those of the public sector. U.S. social welfare has a noble tradition of voluntary citizen groups taking the initiative to solve local problems. Today, private voluntary groups provide valuable services to AIDS patients, the homeless, immigrants, victims of domestic violence, and refugees.

Social welfare has become big business. During the last 30 years, the number of human service corporations—for-profit firms providing social welfare through the marketplace—has increased dramatically. Human service corporations are prominent in long-term nursing care, health maintenance, child day care, psychiatric and substance abuse services, and even corrections. For many welfare professionals, the privatizing of social services is troubling, occurring as it does at a time when government has reduced its commitment to social programs. Yet, human service corporations will likely continue to be prominent players in shaping the nation's social welfare policies. As long as U.S. culture is democratic and capitalistic, entrepreneurs will be free to establish social welfare services in the private sector, both as nonprofit agencies and as for-profit corporations.

The **mixed welfare economy** of the United States, in which the voluntary, governmental, and corporate sectors coexist, poses serious questions for social welfare policy. To what extent can voluntary groups be held responsible for public welfare, given their limited fiscal resources? For which groups of people, if any, should government divest itself of responsibility? Can human service corporations care for poor and multiproblem clients while continuing to generate profits? Equally important, how can welfare professionals shape coherent social welfare policies, given the fragmentation inherent in such pluralism? Clearly, the answers to these questions have much to say about how social welfare programs are perceived by human service professionals, their clients, and the taxpayers who continue to subsidize social programs.

The multitude of questions posed by the transition of social welfare is daunting. Temporarily satisfied by the 1996 welfare reform bill, conservatives have shifted their attention to advocating privatization of social insurance programs such as Social Security and Medicare. Past advocates of social justice such as Jane Addams, Whitney Young Jr., and Wilbur Cohen, to name a few, interpreted the inadequacy of social welfare provision as an opportunity to further social justice. It remains for another generation of welfare professionals to demonstrate the same imagination, perseverance, and courage to advance social welfare in the years ahead. Those accepting this challenge will need to be familiar with the various meanings of social welfare policy, differing political and economic explanations of social welfare, and the multiple interest groups that have emerged within the U.S. social welfare system.

Definitions of Social Welfare Policy

The English social scientist Richard Titmuss defined social services as "a series of collective interventions that contribute to the general welfare by assigning claims from one set of people who are said to produce or earn the national income to another set of people who may merit compassion and charity."[9] Welfare policy, whether it is the product of governmental, voluntary, or corporate institutions, is concerned with allocating goods, services, and opportunities to enhance social functioning.

William Epstein defined social policy as "social action sanctioned by society."[10] Social policy can also be defined as the formal and consistent ordering of human affairs. Social welfare policy, a subset of social policy, regulates the provision of benefits to people to meet basic life needs, such as employment, income, food, housing, health care, and relationships.

Social welfare policy is influenced by the context in which benefits are provided. For example, social welfare is often associated with legislatively mandated programs of the **governmental sector**, such as **Temporary Assistance for Needy Families (TANF)**. In the TANF program, social welfare policy consists of the rules by which the federal and state governments apportion cash benefits to an economically disadvantaged population. TANF benefits are derived from general revenue taxes (often paid by citizens who are better off). But this is a

simplification of benefits provided to those deemed needy. Benefits provided through governmental social welfare policy include cash, along with non-cash or in-kind benefits, including personal social services.[11] Cash benefits can be further divided into social insurance and public assistance grants (discussed in depth in Chapters 10 and 11).

In-kind benefits (provided as proxies for cash) include such benefits as food stamps; Medicaid; housing vouchers; Women, Infants, and Children (WIC) coupons; and low-income energy assistance. Personal social services are designed to enhance relationships between people as well as institutions, such as individual, family, and mental health treatment; child welfare services; rehabilitation counseling; and so forth. Although complicated, this classification reflects a common theme—the redistribution of resources from the better-off to the more disadvantaged. This redistributive aspect of social welfare policy is generally accepted by those who view social welfare as a legitimate function of the state. Governmental social welfare policy is often referred to as "public" policy, because it is the result of decisions reached through a legislative process intended to represent the entire population.

But social welfare is also provided by nongovernmental entities, in which case social welfare policy is a manifestation of "private" policy. For example, a nonprofit agency with a high demand for its services and limited resources may establish a waiting list as agency policy. As other agencies adopt the same strategy for rationing services, clients begin to pile up on waiting lists, and some are eventually denied services. Or consider the practice of "dumping," a policy that has been used by some private health care providers to abruptly transfer uninsured patients to public hospitals while they are suffering from traumatic injuries. Rescission refers to terminating an insurance policy due to concealment, misrepresentation, or fraud. In health insurance, it refers to terminating a policy following the diagnosis of an expensive illness, with the insurance company claiming the policyholder withheld relevant information about a pre-existing medical condition. Although partially limited by the Patient Protection and Affordable Care Act of 2010, it continues in some form by some insurance companies. Patients sometimes die as a result of private social welfare policy.

Because U.S. social welfare has been shaped by policies of governmental and nonprofit agencies, confusion exists about the role of for-profit social service firms. The distinction between the public and private sectors was traditionally marked by the boundary between governmental and nonprofit agencies. Profit-making firms are "private" nongovernmental entities that differ from the traditional private voluntary agencies because they operate on a for-profit basis. Within private social welfare, it is therefore necessary to distinguish between policies of for-profit and nonprofit organizations. A logical way to redraw the social welfare map is to adopt the following definitions: *Governmental social welfare policy* refers to decisions made by the state; *voluntary social welfare policy* refers to decisions reached by nonprofit agencies; and *corporate social welfare policy* refers to decisions made by for-profit firms.

Social Problems and Social Welfare Policy

Social welfare policy often develops in response to social problems. The relationship between social problems and social welfare policy is not linear, and not all social problems result in social welfare policies. Or, social welfare policies are funded at such low levels that they are ineffectual. For example, the Child Abuse Prevention and Treatment Act of 1974 was designed to ameliorate the problem of child abuse, yet underbudgeting left Child Protective Service (CPS) workers unable to promptly investigate the increase in child abuse reports, resulting in many children dying or undergoing serious injury.

Social welfare is an expression of social altruism that contributes to the maintenance and survival of society by helping to hold together a society that can fracture along social, political, and economic stress lines. Social welfare policy is also useful in enforcing social control, especially as a proxy for more coercive law-based measures.[12] Simply put, the poor are less likely to revolt against the unequal distribution of wealth and privilege when their basic needs are met. Social welfare benefits also subsidize employers by supplementing low and nonlivable wages, thereby maintaining a work incentive. Without social welfare benefits like earned income tax credit (EITC), employers would have to raise wages and therefore consumer prices. Social welfare benefits also support key industries, such as agriculture (food stamps), housing (e.g., Section 8), and health care (e.g., Medicaid and Medicare). If social welfare benefits were suddenly eliminated, several U.S. businesses would collapse, and prices for many goods and services would rise. In that sense, social welfare benefits help stabilize prices and maintain economic growth.

Social welfare policies also relieve the social and economic dislocations caused by the uneven nature of economic development under capitalism. For example, one of the main features of capitalism is a constantly changing economy where jobs are created in one sector and lost (or exported) in another, thereby resulting in large islands of unemployed workers. Myriad social welfare programs, such as unemployment insurance and food stamps, help soften the transition. Finally, social welfare policies are a means for rectifying past and present injustices. For example, affirmative action policies were designed to remedy the historical discrimination that denied large numbers of Americans access to economic opportunities and power. Teacher incentive pay and other educational policies are designed to help ameliorate the unequal distribution of resources between underfunded urban and better funded suburban school systems.

Social Work and Social Policy

Social work practice is driven by social policies that dictate how the work is done, with whom, for how much, and toward what ends. For example, a social worker in a public mental health center may have a caseload in excess of 200 clients. The size of that caseload makes it unlikely that the worker will engage in any kind of sustained therapeutic intervention beyond case management. Or consider the case worker who—in the midst of high unemployment—must find employment for recipient mothers about to lose benefits due to mandatory time limits. In these and other instances, economic and political factors structure the work of agencies and limit the ability of workers to succeed in their job.

An ideological preference among policymakers for private sector social services has resulted in less funding for public agencies. In response to diminishing revenues, public agencies adjust in predictable ways, such as cutting qualified staff (or replacing them with lower paid and less qualified workers) and expecting existing staff to do more with less. In addition, they promote short-term (or drug-based) interventions to more cheaply process clients. Cuts are made by freezing or reducing the salaries and benefits of professional staff. Consequently, the accomplishments of trained social workers depend, in part, on the available agency resources.

Social workers in private practice that depend on managed care experience similar constraints. For instance, managed care plans dictate how much a social worker will be paid and how many times they will be permitted to see a client. Accordingly, these plans structure the kinds of interventions that can be realistically implemented in the allotted time. In fact, these policies structure the day-to-day work of much of social work.

Values, Ideology, and Social Welfare Policy

Social welfare policies are shaped by a set of social and personal values that reflect the preferences of those in decision-making capacities. According to David Gil, "choices in social welfare policy are heavily influenced by the dominant beliefs, values, ideologies, customs, and traditions of the cultural and political elites recruited mainly from among the more powerful and privileged strata."[13] How these values are played out in the realm of social welfare is the domain of the policy analyst. As Chapter 2 illustrates, social welfare policy is rarely based on a rational set of assumptions backed up by valid research.

One view of a worthwhile social policy is that it should leave no one worse off and at least one person better off, at least as that person judges his or her needs. In the real world of policy, that rarely occurs. More often than not, policy is a zero-sum game, in which some people are advantaged at the expense of others. Or, at least they perceive themselves as being treated unfairly. For example, the upper 1 percent of Americans bring home nearly a quarter of the U.S. income every year and control 40 percent of the nation's wealth.[14] Despite their wealth and advantage, many see increased taxes and regulation as an unfair infringement on their wealth, and an attack on the most productive members of society, who also happen to be the job creators.[15]

Recent U.S. social welfare policy has been largely shaped by values around self-sufficiency, work, and the omniscience of the marketplace. As policymakers expected disadvantaged people to be more independent, support for government social programs was cut to presumably discourage dependency. Although these cuts saved money in the short run, most of them fell squarely on the shoulders of children. Eventually, these cuts in social programs may lead to greater expenditures, as the generation of children who have gone without essential services begin to require programs to remedy problems associated with poor maternal and infant health care, poverty, illiteracy, and family disorganization. Although in 2011, the International Monetary Fund (IMF) ranked the U.S. seventh internationally in purchasing power parity (what a family income can actually buy in a given country) and 32nd in public spending on family benefits, just above Lithuania, Latvia, Greece, Malta, Mexico, Chile, and Korea.[16]

Social values are organized through the lens of ideology. Simply put, an **ideology** is the framework of commonly held beliefs through which we view the world. It is a set of assumptions about how the world works: what has value, what is worth living and dying for, what is good and true, and what is right. For the most part, these beliefs are rarely examined and are simply assumed to be true. Hence, the ideological tenets around which society is organized exist as a collective social consciousness that defines the world for its members. All societies reproduce themselves partly by reproducing their ideology; in this way, each generation accepts the basic ideological suppositions of the preceding one. When widely held ideological beliefs are questioned, society often reacts with strong sanctions. Ideological trends influence social welfare when adherents of one orientation hold sway in decision-making bodies.

The hold of ideology on social policy is especially strong in times of threat, such as the current "War on Terror." In this instance, social welfare policy fades into the background as the perceived need for national security takes center stage. U.S. social history has seen periods where oppressed groups assert their rights in the face of mainstream norms. Such periods of social unrest strain the capacity of conventional ideologies to explain social problems and offer solutions. Sometimes social unrest is met with force (i.e., the labor strikes of 1877) while in other times, such as the Great Depression, it is met with the expansion of social welfare programs.

The Political Economy of American Social Welfare

The term **political economy** refers to the interaction of political and economic theories in understanding society. The political economy of the United States has been labeled **democratic capitalism**—an open and representative form of government that coexists with a market economy. In that context, social welfare policy plays an important role in stabilizing society by modifying the play of market forces and softening the social and economic inequalities generated by the marketplace.[17] To that end, two sets of activities are necessary: state provision of social services (benefits of cash, in-kind benefits, and personal social services) and state regulation of private activities to alter (and sometimes improve) the lives of citizens. Social welfare bolsters social stability by helping to mitigate the problems associated with economic dislocation, thereby allowing society to remain in a state of more or less controlled balance.

As noted earlier, the U.S. welfare state is undergirded by political economy. Ideally, the political economy of the welfare state should be an integrated fabric of politics and economics; but in reality, some schools of thought contain more political than economic content, and vice versa. For example, most economic theories contain sufficient political implications to qualify them as both economic and political. Conversely, most political schools of thought contain significant economic content. It is therefore difficult to separate political from economic schools of thought. For the purposes of this chapter, we will organize the political economy of U.S. welfare into two separate categories: (1) predominantly economic schools of thought and (2) predominantly political schools of thought. Nevertheless, the reader will find a significant overlap among and between these categories.

The U.S. Economic Continuum

In large measure, economics forms the backbone of the political system. For example, the modern welfare state would not exist without the contribution of economist John Maynard Keynes. Conversely, the conservative movement would be much weaker without the contribution of classical or free market economists such as Adam Smith and Milton Friedman. Virtually every political movement is somehow grounded in economic thought. The three major schools that have traditionally dominated American thought are Keynesian economics; classical or free market economics (and its variants); and to a lesser degree, democratic socialism.

Keynesian Economics

Keynesian economics drives liberalism and most welfare state ideologies. John Maynard Keynes' economic theories formed the substructure and

John Maynard Keynes is best known as the economic architect of the modern welfare state.

Source: CORBIS – NY

foundation of the modern welfare state, and virtually all welfare societies are built along his principles. Sometimes called demand or consumer-side economics, this model emerged from Keynes's 1936 book, *The General Theory of Employment, Interest and Money.*

An Englishman, Keynes took the classical model of economic analysis (self-regulating markets, perfect competition, the laws of supply and demand, etc.) and added the insight that macroeconomic stabilization by government is necessary to keep the economic clock ticking smoothly.[18] He rejected the idea that a perfectly competitive economy tended automatically toward full employment and that the government should not interfere in the process. Keynes argued that instead of being self-correcting and readily able to pull themselves out of recessions, modern economies were recession prone and had difficulty providing full employment.

According to Keynes, periodic and volatile economic situations that cause high unemployment are primarily caused by the instability in investment expenditures. The government can stabilize and correct recessionary or inflationary trends by increasing or decreasing total spending on output. Governments can accomplish this by increasing or decreasing taxes (thereby increasing or decreasing consumption) and by the transfer of public goods or services. For Keynes, a "good" government is an activist government in economic matters, especially when the economy gets out of full employment mode. Keynesians believe that social welfare expenditures are investments in human capital that eventually increase the national wealth (e.g., by increasing productivity) and thereby boost everyone's net income.

Keynes's doctrine emerged from his attempt to understand the nature of recessions and depressions. Specifically, he saw recessions and depressions as emerging from businesses' loss of confidence in investments (e.g., focusing on risk rather than gain), which in turn causes the hoarding of cash. This loss of confidence eventually leads to a shortage of money as everyone tries to hoard cash simultaneously. Keynes's answer to this problem was that government should make it possible for people to satisfy their economic needs without cutting their spending, which prevents the spiral of shrinking incomes and shrinking spending. Simply put, in a depression the government should print more money and get it into circulation.[19]

Keynes also understood that this monetary policy alone would not suffice if a recession spiraled out of control, as in the Great Depression of the 1930s. He pointed to a liquidity trap whereby people hoard cash because they expect deflation (a decrease—extreme in a depression—in the price of goods or services), insufficient consumer or industry demand, or some catastrophe such as war. In a depression, businesses and households fail to increase spending regardless of how much cash they have. To help an economy exit this trap, government must do what the private sector will not—namely, spend. This spending can take the form of public works projects (financed by borrowing) or direct governmental subsidization of demand (welfare entitlements). To be fair, Keynes saw public spending only as a last resort to be employed if monetary expansion failed. Moreover, he sought an economic balance: Print money and spend in a recession; stop printing and stop spending once it is over. Keynes understood that too much money in circulation, especially in times of high production and full employment, leads to inflation. Although

relatively simple, Keynes's theories represent one of the great insights of twentieth-century economic thought.[20] These ideas also formed the economic basis for the modern welfare state.

Conservative or Free Market Economics

Whereas liberalism is guided by Keynesian economics, the conservative view of social welfare is guided by free market economics. It is predicated on a belief in the existence of many small buyers and sellers who exchange homogeneous products with perfect information in a setting in which each can freely enter and exit the marketplace at will.[21] As an ideal type, none of these assumptions hold in the real world of economics. For instance, the free market model does not address the dominance of distribution networks by a single retailer like Walmart. There is nothing in the free market model that addresses the lack of equitable distribution of knowledge, experience, opportunity, and access to resources enjoyed by buyers and sellers. The free market model ignores theft, fraud, and deception in cases like Enron, and it ignores the competitive advantages that accrue through lobbying and special interest negotiations like Halliburton's no competition bids for Iraq reconstruction projects. It also ignores the power of large retailers to control the market by instituting late shopping hours or even 24/7 businesses that make it impossible for small family-owned businesses to compete. In short, an unregulated market economy becomes monopolistic as more of the market is taken over by fewer enterprises.

The ascendance of the conservative economic (and social) argument accelerated after 1973, when the rise in living standards began to slow for most Americans. Conservatives blamed this economic slowdown on governmental policies—specifically, deficit spending, high taxes, and excessive regulations.[22] In a clever sleight of hand, government went from having the responsibility to address economic problems (à la Keynes) to being the cause of them.

Milton Friedman, considered by some to be the father of modern conservative economics, was one of Keynes's more ardent critics. In opposition to Keynes, Friedman argued that using fiscal and monetary policy to smooth out the business cycle is harmful to the economy and worsens economic instability.[23] He contended that the Depression did not occur because people were hoarding money; rather, there was a fall in the quantity of money in circulation. Friedman argues that Keynesian economic policies must be replaced by simple monetary rules (hence the term *monetarism*). In effect, he believes that the role of government is to keep the money supply growing steadily at a rate consistent with stable prices and long-term economic growth.[24]

Friedman counseled against active efforts to stabilize the economy. Instead of pumping money into the economy, government should simply make sure enough cash is in circulation. He called for a relatively inactive government in economic affairs that did not try to manage or intervene in the business cycle. For Friedman, welfare spending existed only for altruistic rather than economic reasons.[25] To the right of Milton Friedman is Robert Lucas, 1994 Nobel Prize winner and developer of the "theory of rational expectations." Lucas argued that Friedman's monetary policy was still too interventionist and would invariably do more harm than good.[26]

Developing outside of conventional economics, **supply-side economics** enjoyed considerable popularity during the early 1980s. Led by Robert Barth, editorial page head of the *Wall Street Journal*, supply-siders were journalists, policymakers, and maverick economists who argued that demand-side policies and monetary policies were ineffective.[27] They maintained that the incentive effects of reduced taxation would be so large that tax cuts would dramatically increase economic activity to the point where tax revenues would rise rather than fall. (Former President George H. W. Bush referred to this as *voodoo economics* in 1980.[28]) Specifically, supply-siders argued that tax cuts would lead to a large increase in labor supply and investment and therefore to a large expansion in economic output. The budget deficit would not be problematic because taxes, increased savings, and higher economic output would offset the deficit. In the early 1980s, supply-siders seized power from the Keynesians and mainstream conservative economists, many of whom believed in the same things but wanted to move more slowly.[29]

Although some supporters preferred to think of supply-side economics as pure economics, the theory contained enough political implications to qualify as a political as well as an economic theory. Popularized by supporters such as Jack Kemp, Arthur Laffer, and Ronald Reagan, supply-side economics provided the rationale for the dramatic cuts in social programs executed under the Reagan administration.

Despite their popularity in the early years of the Reagan administration, the term "supply-side economics" fell out of favor when it became evident that massive tax cuts for the wealthy and corporations did not result in increased productivity. Instead, the wealthy spent their tax savings on luxury items, and corporations used tax savings to purchase other companies in a merger mania that took Wall Street by surprise. Some corporations took advantage of temporary tax savings to transfer their operations abroad, further reducing the supply of high-paying industrial jobs in the United States. For these and other reasons, the budget deficit grew from about $50 billion a year in the Carter term to $352 billion a year in 1992.[30]

Although the term "supply-side economics" fell out of favor by the late 1980s, its basic tenets, such as the belief that massive tax cuts for the rich would increase productivity (and the necessity of social welfare spending cuts), were adopted enthusiastically by the G.W. Bush administration in the form of the Economic Growth and Tax Relief Reconciliation Act of 2001 (EGTRRA), and the Jobs and Growth Tax Relief Reconciliation Act of 2003 (JGTRRA). Citizens for Tax Justice estimated that more than $1 trillion has been lost to the U.S. Treasury as a result of the Bush tax cuts (later continued by the Obama administration).[31] The result of these policies mirrored the effects of the earlier supply-side doctrine: huge federal and state budget shortfalls, corporate hoarding, greater economic inequality, and stagnant wages.[32] The federal budget deficit reached about $175 billion in 2007; by early 2012 that rose to $1 trillion.[33]

Conservative economists argue that large social welfare programs—including unemployment benefits and public service jobs—are detrimental to the society in two ways. First, government social programs erode the work ethic by supporting those not in the labor force. Second, because they are funded by taxes, public sector social welfare programs divert money that could otherwise be invested in the private sector. Conservative economists believe that economic growth helps everyone because overall prosperity creates more jobs, income, and goods, and these eventually filter down to the poor. For conservative economists, investment is the key to prosperity and the engine that drives the economic machine. Accordingly, many conservative economists favor tax breaks for the wealthy based on the premise that such breaks will result in more disposable after-tax income freed up for investment. High taxes are an impediment to economic progress because they channel money into "public" investments and away from "private" investments.

In the conservative paradigm, opportunity is based on one's relationship to the marketplace. Thus, legitimate rewards can occur only through marketplace participation. In contrast to liberals who emphasize mutual self-interest, interdependence, and social equity, conservative economists argue that the highest form of social good is realized by the maximization of self-interest. In the conservative view (as epitomized by author Ayn Rand[34]), the best society is one in which everyone actively— and selfishly—pursues their own good. Through a leap of faith, the maximization of self-interest is somehow transformed into a mutual good. In that sense, conservatives occupy the opposite end of the philosophical spectrum from traditional liberals.

Conservative economists maintain not only that high taxation and government regulation of business serve as disincentives to investment, but that individual claims on social insurance and public welfare grants discourage work. Together these factors lead to a decline in economic growth and an increase in the expectations of beneficiaries of welfare programs. For conservatives, the only way to correct the irrationality of governmental social programs is to eliminate them. Charles Murray has suggested that the entire federal assistance and income support structure for working-aged persons (Medicaid, the former Aid to Families with Dependent Children [AFDC], food stamps, etc.) be scrapped. This would leave working-aged persons no recourse except to actively engage in the job market or turn to family, friends, or privately funded services.[35]

Many conservative economists argue that economic insecurity is an important part of the entrepreneurial spirit. Unless people are *compelled* to work, they will choose leisure over work. Conversely, providing economic security for large numbers of people through welfare programs leads to diminished ambition and fosters an unhealthy dependence on the state. Conservatives further argue that self-realization can occur only through marketplace participation. Hence, social programs harm rather than help the most vulnerable members of society. This belief in the need for economic insecurity formed the basis for the 1996 welfare reform bill that included a maximum time limit on welfare benefits (see Chapter 11).

Some conservative economists are influenced by "public choice" theory. The public choice school gained adherents among conservative analysts as faith ebbed in supply-side theories. Not widely known outside academic circles until its major proponent, James Buchanan, was awarded the Nobel Prize for economics in 1986, the public choice model states that public sector bureaucrats are self-interested utility-maximizers, and that strong incentives exist for interest groups to make demands on government. The resulting concessions from this arrangement flow directly to the interest group and their costs are spread among all taxpayers. Initial concessions lead to demands for further concessions, which are likely to be forthcoming so long as interest groups are vociferous in their demands. Under such an incentive system, different interests are also encouraged to band together to make demands, because there is no reason for one interest group to oppose the demands of others. But while demands for goods and services increase, revenues tend to decrease. This happens because interest groups resist paying taxes directed specifically toward them and because no interest group has much incentive to support general taxes. The result of this scenario is predictable: Strong demands for government benefits accompanied by declining revenues lead to government borrowing, which in turn results in large budget deficits.[36] Adherents of public choice theory view social welfare as a series of endless concessions to disadvantaged groups that will eventually bankrupt the government. On the other hand, it would be logical also to apply public choice theory to defense industry interest groups who make similar demands on government while not paying a fair share of taxes.

The Global Financial Crisis (GFC)

Alan Greenspan, the former 18-year chairman of the Federal Reserve, admitted that he "made a mistake" in trusting free markets to regulate themselves without government oversight. Greenspan further admitted that "I made a mistake in presuming that the self-interests of organizations, specifically banks and others, were . . . capable of protecting their own shareholders and their equity in the firms."[37] This was an amazing series of admissions from the man known as the "oracle" in economic matters. More importantly, he questioned the belief that unregulated free markets inevitably yield superior economic gain.

The initial event triggering the 2008 GFC was the collapse of the U.S. housing market and the realization that domestic and foreign banks, investment houses and institutions were holding hundreds of billions of dollars of subprime mortgages (i.e., nonviable mortgages held by problematic borrowers) that were little more than toxic debt offering little hope of repayment.

It is overly simplistic to blame the GFC solely on subprime loans. Multiple factors converged to create the crisis, including the largely unregulated derivatives market and the reliance on various forms of dodgy financial instruments. Derivatives are used by banks and corporations to hedge risk or engage in speculation. They are financial instruments whose value depends on an underlying commodity, bond, equity or currency. Investors purchase derivatives to bet on the future (or as a hedge against the potential adverse impacts of an investment), to mitigate a risk associated with an underlying security, to protect against interest rate or stock market changes and so forth.

Derivatives are used in a variety of financial areas. For example, credit derivatives can involve a contract between two parties that allows one of them to transfer their credit risk to the other. The party transferring the risk pays a fee to the party that assumes it. These derivatives are risky investments because they are basically bets made in large amounts, often in the billions. Like all forms of gambling, derivatives only work if the casino has the money to meet their obligation to bettors. If the casino lacks the cash to pay winners (i.e., it has a liquidity problem), the entire system collapses. The 2008 GFC was partly based on the failure of the derivatives market.

The initial response to the GFC occurred in 2008 when former President George W. Bush signed the $168 billion stimulus package giving tax rebates to more to 130 million households.[38] Administration officials hoped the tax package would kick-start the economy and deflect it from recession. They were wrong. Afterward, federal loans and bailouts came at an almost dizzying pace. In 2008, the Federal Reserve enticed JP Morgan with a $29 billion credit line to take over the failing Bear Stearns investment house.[39] One financial institution after another failed or was taken over. In 2008 Bank of America bought Countrywide Mortgage (the largest US mortgage lender with assets of $209 billion). Fearing that Merrill Lynch was next, it quickly sold out to Bank of America. After Washington Mutual was seized by federal regulators, it was bought by JP Morgan Chase, the third largest U.S. bank. Meanwhile, Wells Fargo acquired Wachovia Bank.[40]

While the Feds let Lehman Brothers collapse (the largest bankruptcy in U.S. history), they provided American International Group (AIG) with an $85 billion line of credit. Not wanting to be left out of the party, U.S. automakers gained $25 billion in taxpayer subsidized loans.[41] Much of the money to pay for the bailouts came from foreign investors, who purchased U.S. Treasury bills. However, like all investors, they remain cautious about the early 2012 $15 trillion U.S. federal debt.[42] The GFC and the 2008 collapse of Wall Street temporarily chilled the previous debate around privatizing Social Security (see Chapter 10).

Democratic Socialism

Democratic socialism (as opposed to old Soviet-style socialism) is based on the belief that radical economic change can occur within a democratic context. This view is at odds with both Keynesianism and conservative economics. Specifically, Keynesians basically believe in the market economy but want to make it more responsive to human needs by smoothing out the rough edges. Conservatives believe that the economy should be left alone except for a few minor tweaks, such as regulating the money flow. Other conservative economists argue that the market should be left totally alone. On balance, both Keynesians and economic conservatives have a basic faith that capitalism can advance the public good. In that sense, Keynesians and economic conservatives have more in common with each other than Keynesians have with socialists.

Proponents of socialism argue that the fundamental nature of capitalism is anathema to advancing the public good. They contend that a system predicated on pursuing profit and individual self-interest can lead only to greater inequality. The creation of a just society requires a fundamental transformation of the economic system, and the pursuit of profit and self-interest must be replaced by the collective pursuit of the common good. Not surprisingly, they refute Keynes because of his belief that economic problems can be fixed by technicalities instead of sweeping institutional change. Socialists dislike conservatives for obvious reasons, such as the primary importance they place on markets and their belief in subordinating social interests to market forces.

Left-wing theorists maintain that the failure of capitalism has led to political movements that have pressured institutions to respond with increased social welfare services. They believe that real social welfare must be structural and can only be accomplished by redistributing resources. In a just society that makes goods, resources, and opportunities available to everyone, only the most basic forms of social welfare (health care, rehabilitation, counseling, etc.) would be necessary. In this radical worldview, poverty is directly linked to structural inequality: People need welfare because they are exploited and denied access to resources. In an unjust society, welfare functions as a substitute, albeit a puny one, for social justice.[43]

Some socialists argue that social welfare is an ingenious arrangement to have the public assume the costs associated with the social and economic dislocations inherent in capitalism. According to these theorists, social welfare expenditures "socialize" the costs of capitalist production by making public the costs of private enterprise. Thus, social welfare serves both the needs of people and the needs of capitalism. For other socialists, social welfare programs support an unjust economic system that continues to generate problems requiring yet more programs. These radicals argue that social welfare programs function like junk food for the impoverished: They provide just enough sustenance to discourage revolution but not enough to make a real difference. As such, social welfare is viewed as a form of social control. Frances Fox Piven and the late Richard Cloward summarize the argument:

> Relief arrangements are ancillary to economic arrangements. Their chief function is to regulate labor, and they do that in two general ways. First, when mass unemployment leads to outbreaks of turmoil, relief programs are ordinarily initiated or expanded to absorb or control enough of the unemployed to restore order; then, as turbulence subsides, the relief system contracts, expelling those who are needed to populate the labor markets.[44]

For radicals, real social welfare can occur only in a socialist economic system.

The U.S. Political Continuum

Differing views on political economy produce differing conceptions of the public good. Competition among ideas about the public good and the welfare state has long been a knotty issue in the political

economy of the United States. Since governmental policy is driven largely by an ideologically determined view of the public good, it will vary depending which political party is in power.

The major American ideologies, (neo)liberalism and (neo)conservatism, hold vastly different views of social welfare and the public good. Since conservatives believe that the public good is best served through marketplace participation, they prefer private sector approaches over governmental welfare programs. Conservatives are not anti-welfare per se; they simply believe that government should have a minimal role (through a "safety net") in ensuring the social welfare of citizens. Traditional liberals, on the other hand, view government as the primary institution capable of bringing a measure of social justice to millions of Americans who cannot fully participate because of obstacles such as racism, poverty, and sexism. Traditional liberals view government social welfare programs as a key component in promoting the public good. One of the major differences between these orientations lies in their differing perceptions of how the public good is enhanced or hurt by welfare state programs.

The understanding of "the public good" is lodged in the political and ideological continuum that makes up the U.S. political economy. An appreciation of this requires an understanding of the interaction of schools of political thought and how they evolved. These ideological tenets also shape the platforms of the major political parties and can be divided into two categories: (1) liberalism and left-of-center movements and (2) traditional conservatives and the far right.

Liberalism and Left-of-Center Movements

Liberalism   Since Franklin Delano Roosevelt's New Deal, liberal advocates have argued for advancing the public good by promoting an expanding economy coupled with the growth of universal, non-means–tested social welfare and health care programs. Traditional liberals used Keynesianism as the economic justification for expanding the welfare state, and as such, the general direction of policy from the 1930s to the early 1970s was for the federal government to assume greater amounts of responsibility for the public good.

American liberals established the welfare state with the passage of the Social Security Act of 1935. Harry Hopkins—a social worker, the head of the

Federal Emergency Relief Administration, a confidant of President Roosevelt, a co-architect of the New Deal, and a consummate political operative—developed the calculus for American liberalism: "tax, tax; spend, spend; elect, elect."[45] This approach was elegant in its simplicity: The government taxes the wealthy, thereby securing the necessary revenues to fund social programs for workers and the poor. This approach dominated social policy for almost 50 years. In fact, it was so successful that by 1980 social welfare accounted for 57 percent of all federal expenditures.[46]

By the mid-1960s, the welfare state had become a central fixture in America, and politicians sought to expand its benefits to more constituents. Focusing on the expansion of middle-class programs such as Federal Housing Administration (FHA) home mortgages, federally insured student loans, Medicare, and veterans' pensions, liberal policymakers secured the political loyalty of the middle class. Even conservative politicians respected voter support for the welfare state, and not surprisingly, the largest growth in social welfare spending occurred under Republican president, Richard M. Nixon.

Despite such support, the promise of the U.S. welfare state to provide social protection similar to Western Europe never materialized. By the mid-1970s, the hope of traditional liberals to build a welfare state mirroring those of northern Europe had been replaced by an incremental approach that narrowly focused on consolidating and fine-tuning the programs of the Social Security Act. One reason for this failure was the ambivalence of many Americans toward centralized government. "The emphasis consistently has been on the local, the pluralistic, the voluntary, and the business-like over the national, the universal, the legally entitled, and the governmental," observed policy analyst Marc Bendick.[47]

Liberalism lost ground for another reason. The Social Security Act of 1935—the hallmark of American liberalism—was primarily a self-financing social insurance program that rewarded working people. Public assistance programs that contained less political capital and were therefore a better measure of public compassion, were rigorously means tested, sparse in their benefits, and operated by the less than generous states. For example, although Social Security benefits were indexed to the cost of living in the mid-1970s, AFDC benefits deteriorated so badly that about half its value was

lost between 1975 and 1992. At the same time that Social Security reforms reduced the elderly poverty rate by 50 percent, the plight of poor non-working families worsened.

Neoliberalism   By the late 1970s, the liberal belief that the welfare state was the best mechanism to advance the public good was in retreat. What remained of traditional liberalism was replaced by a neoliberalism that was more cautious of government, less antagonistic toward big business, and more skeptical about the value of universal entitlements.

The defeat of Jimmy Carter and the election of a Republican Senate in 1980 forced many liberal Democrats to reevaluate their party's traditional position on domestic policy. This reexamination, which Charles Peters christened "neoliberalism" to differentiate it from old-style liberalism, attracted only a small following in the early 1980s.[48] By the mid-1990s, however, most leading Democrats could be classified as neoliberal. Randall Rothenberg charted signs of the influence of neoliberalism on the Democratic domestic policy platform as early as 1982, when he observed that the party's midterm convention did not endorse a large-scale federal jobs program, did not endorse a national health insurance plan, and did not submit a plan for a guaranteed annual income.[49]

In the late 1980s, a cadre of prominent mainstream Democrats established the Democratic Leadership Council (DLC). In part, their goal was to wrest control of the Democratic Party from traditional liberals and to create a new Democratic Party that was more attuned to the beliefs of traditional core voters. In 1989, the DLC released *The New Orleans Declaration: A Democratic Agenda for the 1990s,* which promised that Democratic Party politics would shift toward a middle ground combining a corporatist economic analysis with Democratic compassion. Two of the founders of the DLC were Al Gore and Bill Clinton, who chaired the DLC just before announcing his candidacy.[50]

Compared to traditional liberals, neoliberals were more forgiving of the behavior of large corporations and were opposed to economic protectionism. They were also opposed to strong financial regulation, which helps explain why the repeal of the 1933 Glass-Steagall Act (the act curbed speculation in commercial banking) was passed under the neoliberal Clinton administration. Some commentators partly attribute the 2007 global financial crisis to the repeal of Glass-Steagall.[51]

Grounded in *realpolitik*, neoliberals viewed the New Deal approach as too expensive and antiquated to address the mood of voters. Consequently, they distanced themselves from the large-scale governmental welfare programs associated with Democrats since the New Deal. Like their neoconservative counterparts, they called for reliance on personal responsibility, work and thrift as an alternative to governmental programs. Accordingly, their welfare proposals emphasized labor market participation (workfare), personal responsibility (time-limited welfare benefits), family obligations (child support enforcement), and frugality in governmental spending.

Former Secretary of Labor Robert Reich advocated a postliberal formulation that replaced social welfare entitlements with investments in **human capital.** Public spending was divided into "good" and "bad" categories: "Bad" was unproductive expenditures on welfare and price supports; "good" was investments in human capital, such as education, research, and job training.[52]

Neoliberalism altered the traditional liberal concept of the public good. Instead of viewing the interests of large corporations as antithetical to the best interests of society, they argued for free trade, less regulation, and a laissez-faire approach to social problems. They also viewed labor unions with caution. In effect, the new shapers of the public good had systematically excluded key actors of the old liberal coalition.

The neoliberal view of the public good reflects a kind of postmodern perspective. For neoliberals, the public good is elusive, and its form is fluid. Definitions of the public good change as a social order evolves and new power relationships emerge. Thus, neoliberals view the public good in the context of a postindustrial society composed of new opportunities and new institutional forms.

Neoliberalism is more of a political strategy and pragmatic mode of operation than a political philosophy embodying a firm view of the public good. This is both its strength and its weakness. Specifically, the strength of neoliberalism lies in its ability to compromise and therefore to accomplish things. Its weakness is that when faced with an ideological critique, neoliberals are incapable of formulating a cogent ideological response. President Obama fits squarely within the neoliberal orientation around pragmatism, which partly explains

President Barack Obama looks up at a campaign stop in Oakland, Calif., Monday, July 23, 2012.

Source: Paul Sakuma/AP Images

what appears to underline his refusal to enact strong banking regulations in the aftermath of the global financial crisis.

The Self-Reliance School   A perspective gaining influence in economically distressed areas and in developing countries is the **self-reliance school.**[53] This school maintains that industrial economic models are irrelevant to the economic needs of poor communities and are often damaging to the spiritual life of people.[54] Adherents of self-reliance repudiate the emphasis of Western economic philosophies on economic growth and the belief that the quality of life can be measured by material acquisitions. These political economists stress a balanced economy based on the real needs of people, production designed for internal consumption rather than export, productive technologies that are congruent with the culture and background of the population, the use of appropriate and manageable technologies, and a small-scale and decentralized form of economic organization.[55] Simply put, proponents of self-reliance postulate that more is less, and less is more. The objective of self-reliance is the creation of a no-poverty society in which economic life is organized around issues of subsistence rather than trade and economic expansion. Accepting a world of finite resources and inherent limitations to economic growth, proponents argue that the true question of social and economic development is not what people think they want or need but what they require for survival. The self-reliance school accepts the need for social welfare programs that ameliorate the dislocations caused by industrialization, but it prefers low-technology and local solutions to social problems. This contrasts with the conventional wisdom of the welfare state, which is predicated on a prescribed set of programs on a national scale, administered by large bureaucracies and sophisticated management systems.

Classical Conservatives and the Far Right

Classic Conservatism   Former conservative political leaders such as Nelson Rockefeller, Richard Nixon, and Barry Goldwater represented traditional conservatism. Few traditional conservatives now occupy important leadership positions in the Republican Party, as most have been replaced by cultural conservatives.

On one level, all conservatives agree on important values relating to social policy. They are anti-union, oppose aggressive governmental regulations, demand lower taxes and less social spending, want local control of public education, oppose extending civil rights legislation, and believe strongly in states' rights. Beneath this agreement, fundamental differences exist among various conservative factions.

Traditional conservatives part ways with cultural conservatives on a range of social issues. First, as strict constitutionalists, traditional conservatives believe strongly in the separation of church and state. They see prayer and religion as personal choices in which government has no constitutional right to intervene. Second, while classical and cultural conservatives want a weaker federal government, cultural conservatives demand that government use its power to set a religious-based agenda in areas such as abortion, contraception, and gay marriage.

Third, classical conservatives are more socially liberal than their cultural counterparts. For example, the late Barry Goldwater, a conservative icon and former U.S. senator, stated that, "I have been, and am still, a traditional conservative, focusing on three general freedoms—economic, social, and political. . . .

The conservative movement is founded on the simple tenet that people have the right to live life as they please, as long as they don't hurt anyone else in the process."[56] Following that line of reason, Goldwater's outspoken support of gays in the military was directly opposed to the tenets of cultural conservatives. Regarding reproductive freedom, classical conservatives might challenge cultural conservatives on various measures that limit or ban abortions.

From the late 1970s onward, old-style conservatives such as Nelson Rockefeller, Barry Goldwater, and William Cohen—who were more concerned with foreign policy than with domestic issues—were replaced by a new breed of cultural conservatives. These cultural conservatives were committed to reversing 50 years of liberal influence in social policy. How the cultural conservatives came to shape social policy warrants elaboration, although it is first important to examine neoconservatives, the forerunners of cultural conservatism.

Neoconservatism   Before the 1970s, conservatives were content to merely snipe at welfare programs, reserving their attention for areas more consistent with their traditional concerns such as the economy, defense spending, and foreign affairs. However, by the mid-1970s, conservative intellectuals recognized that their former stance toward social welfare was myopic as welfare was too important to be lightly dismissed. Consequently, **neoconservatives** sought to arrest the growth in governmental welfare programs while simultaneously transferring as much welfare responsibility as possible from government to the private sector.[57] They faulted government programs for a breakdown in the mutual obligation between groups; the lack of attention to how programs were operated and benefits awarded; the dependency of recipients; and the growth of the welfare industry and its special interest groups, particularly professional associations.[58] To counter the liberal goals of full employment, national health care, and a guaranteed annual income, neoconservatives maintained that high unemployment was good for the economy, that health care should remain in the private marketplace, and that competitive income structures were critical to productivity. They argued that income inequality was socially desirable because social policies that promote equality encourage coercion, limit individual freedom, and damage the economy.[59] By the late 1970s, the neoconservative position began to be usurped by the emerging cultural conservatives.

Cultural and *Social* Conservatism The neoconservative assault on liberal social policy was soon taken over by a coalition of cultural and social conservatives, who raged against governmental intrusion in the marketplace while simultaneously attempting to use the authority of government to advance their objectives in the areas of sexual abstinence, school prayer, abortion, birth control, evolution (i.e., creationism), gun rights, and antigay rights proposals. These conservatives cleverly promoted a dual attitude toward the role of government. Mimicking classical conservatives, they demanded a laissez-faire approach to economics but steadfastly refused to apply that orientation to social affairs. Instead, these conservatives argued for social conformity and a level of governmental intrusion into private affairs that most classical conservatives would find appalling. In contrast to the classical conservative position on the separation of church and state, social conservatives opportunistically embraced the rising tide of fundamentalist religion, even to the point of rewriting history by arguing that the Founding Fathers were opposed to a secular state and were guided by Christian principles.[60]

By the late 1980s, this coalition of economic conservatives, right-wing Christians, and opportunistic politicians had virtually decimated what remained of Republican liberalism, whose adherents had become an endangered species like liberal Democrats.

For liberals, the state represents the best vehicle for promoting the public good. In contrast, cultural conservatives view the state as the cause of rather than the solution to social problems. With the exception of protecting people (police and defense) and property, cultural conservatives argue that the very existence of the state is antithetical to the public good, because government interferes with the maximization of individual self-interest. Their posture toward government is adversarial, except when the state is used to further their social agenda. In tandem with this agenda, conservative presidents, such as Reagan and the two Bushes, prohibited the future growth of the welfare state by using tax policy and federal budget deficits to thwart increased public spending. For example, few responsible politicians would argue for increased social welfare spending given the 2012 federal debt of more than $15 trillion.

After hammering away at social programs, conservatives had accomplished relatively little in the area of social insurance and health programs. For instance, costs for social insurance entitle-ment programs such as Social Security and Medicare continued to soar. In the end, conservatives underestimated three key factors: (1) the resiliency of the welfare state, (2) the continued support (however ambivalent) among the middle class, and (3) the difficulty of translating rhetoric into viable reform proposals. Nevertheless, conservatives had learned from past mistakes. Instead of toying with incremental policies, they proposed bold new social initiatives that were incorporated into the Contract with America (designed to alter most of the safety net programs within a two-year period), a document signed by more than 300 House Republicans in 1994.[61] Their crowning victory occurred with the passage of the Personal Responsibility and Work Opportunity Reconciliation Act (PRWORA) in 1996.

Social and cultural conservativism flourished in the 2010 Congressional midterm elections and in the 2012 presidential race. By 2011, this conservative coalition may have pushed some Republican presidential candidates, such as Mitt Romney, into taking extreme positions on gay rights, abortion, health care and even long resolved issues like contraception.

Libertarianism **Libertarians** reflect another perspective. Specifically, this school of thought believes in little or no government regulation. Libertarians basically want the government to stay out of people's pocketbooks and their bedrooms.

> We, the members of the Libertarian Party, challenge the cult of the omnipotent state and defend the rights of the individual. We hold that all individuals . . . have the right to live in whatever manner they choose, so long as they do not forcibly interfere with the equal right of others to live in whatever manner they choose. We . . . hold that governments . . . must not violate the rights of any individual: namely, (1) the right to life—accordingly we support the prohibition of the initiation of physical force against others; (2) the right to liberty of speech and action—accordingly we oppose all attempts . . . [at] . . . government censorship in any form; and (3) . . . we oppose all government interference with private property. . . .[62]

Libertarians argue that governmental growth occurs at the expense of individual freedom. They also believe that the proper role for government is to provide a police force and a military that possesses only defensive weapons. Libertarians are highly

Former **Republican presidential candidate Rep. Ron Paul (R-TX) 2012**.

In this Feb. 11, 2012 file photo, Republican presidential candidate Rep. Ron Paul, R-Texas, speaks to his supporters following his loss in the Maine caucus to Mitt Romney.

Source: Robert F. Bukaty/AP Images

critical of taxation because it fuels governmental growth. Apart from advocating minimal taxation earmarked for defense and police activities, they oppose the income tax. Because libertarians emphasize individual freedom and personal responsibility, they advocate the decriminalization of narcotics and believe that government should intercede in social affairs only when an individual's behavior threatens the safety of another.

In 2009, social and cultural conservatives, populists and libertarians of various ilk banded together to form what is referred to as the Tea Party. This American political movement advocated a rigid interpretation of the U.S. Constitution, especially on issues like gun control. The movement also focused on reducing government spending, eliminating the national debt, cutting social programs, and dramatically reducing taxes. Although not initially a religiously-inspired movement, it soon allied itself with social and religious conservatives such as former Alaska governor Sarah Palin and U.S. Congressperson Michele Bachman (R-MN). In 2010, Bachmann formed the Tea Party Congressional Caucus, which contained 66 members in 2012.

Former presidential candidate and libertarian Ron Paul is often thought of as the "intellectual godfather" of the Tea Party movement. For many Americans, 2012 presidential contender Ron Paul embodied libertarianism, which is consonant with how he presents himself. True libertarians, however, have a problem with Paul who is against abortion rights, gay marriage, and open borders.

The Welfare Philosophers and the Neoconservative Think Tanks

Many early welfare thinkers envisioned a U.S. welfare state based on a European model.[63] This vision was shared by virtually every social welfare scholar writing in the late 1960s and early 1970s.[64] In turn, most social workers supported a liberal welfare philosophy grounded in a system of national social programs that would be deployed as more citizens demanded greater services and benefits. This framework was informed by European welfare states, especially the Scandinavian variant that spread health care, housing, income benefits, and employment opportunities equitably across the population.[65] It also led Richard Titmuss to hope that the welfare state, as an instrument of government, would eventually lead to a "welfare world."[66]

Despite the widespread acceptance of this liberal vision, an alternative vision arose that questioned the fundamental nature of welfare and social services. Throughout the 1970s and 1980s, conservatives (especially right-wing **think tanks**, or conservative policy institutes) busily made proposals for welfare reform. In fact, no conservative policy institute could prove its mettle until it produced a plan to clean up "the welfare mess." The Hoover Institution at Stanford University helped shape the early conservative position on welfare. "There is no inherent reason that Americans should look to government for those goods and services that can be individually acquired," argued Hoover's Alvin Rabushka.[67] Martin Anderson, a Hoover senior fellow and domestic policy adviser to the Reagan administration, elaborated the conservative position on welfare in terms of the need to (1) reaffirm the need-only philosophical approach to welfare and state it as explicit national policy; (2) increase efforts to eliminate fraud; (3) establish and enforce a fair, clear work requirement; (4) remove inappropriate beneficiaries from the welfare rolls; (5) enforce support of dependents by those who have the responsibility and are shirking it; (6) improve the efficiency and effectiveness of welfare administration; and (7) shift more responsibility from the federal government to state and local governments and private institutions.[68] These recommendations formed the backbone of the 1996 PRWORA.

In turn, the Heritage Foundation featured *Out of the Poverty Trap: A Conservative Strategy for Welfare Reform* by Stuart Butler and Anna Kondratas.[69] Following along the same lines, the

Free Congress Research and Education Foundation proposed reforming welfare through "cultural conservatism"—that is, by reinforcing "traditional values such as delayed gratification, work and saving, commitment to family and to the next generation, education and training, self-improvement, and rejection of crime, drugs, and casual sex."[70]

A handful of other works also served as beachheads for the conservative assault on the liberal welfare state. George Gilder's *Wealth and Poverty* argued that beneficent welfare programs represented a "moral hazard" that insulated people against risks essential to capitalism and thus contributed to dependency.[71] Martin Anderson concluded that income calculations should include the cash equivalent of in-kind benefits, such as food stamps, Medicaid, and housing vouchers, thus effectively lowering the poverty rate by 40 percent.[72] Taken together, these ideas and recommendations provided a potent critique of welfare programs.

Perhaps the most enduring change engineered by the conservative movement is what Jacob Hacker calls the "Great Risk Shift."[73] Private ownership of property and the acceptance of personal responsibility have long been core American values, which partly explains why opposition to former President Bush's "ownership society" had not materialized. In *The Great Risk Shift,* Hacker examines Bush's ownership society and the Republican Party's emphasis on personal responsibility as the code for shifting economic risk away from government and corporations and onto the back of the American family.

Hacker argues that private and public support mechanisms have fallen behind the pace of change in contemporary society. Almost half of marriages end in divorce. Over a third of employed Americans are frequently worried about losing their jobs. Structural changes in the nature of employment, primarily seen in a shift away from manufacturing to the lower-paying service sector, have left many without the skills needed for new jobs or the resources to retrain. The likelihood of family income dropping 50 percent has almost tripled since the 1970s; personal bankruptcies and home foreclosures have increased by a factor of five; and over any two-year period more than 80 million Americans go without health insurance coverage.[74] Hacker maintains that during a 30-year period in which middle-class incomes have remained stagnant, the need for economic security has been neglected by public and private institutions.[75]

The risk shift is occurring in almost all sectors. Corporate retirement programs are transitioning from defined benefit plans (i.e., retirees are guaranteed a set retirement income) to defined contribution plans whereby retirement income depends upon the savvy of the employees' investment managers. Whether these changes will help or hurt the individual depends on many factors, but it is clear that it is a shift in risk to the individual worker.

The absence of universal health care has underscored the importance of employer-provided health insurance; however, the increasing instability of employment often means that job transitions are accompanied by the failure to acquire health coverage. Conservatives have proposed Health Savings Accounts as a means of activating market forces to control health costs, but they reflect another risk shift from the corporation to the individual worker. The former Bush administration suggested the elimination of employer-provided health insurance in favor of tax deductions for health insurance premiums, yet another risk shift from corporations to the individual or family.[76] An important implication of Hacker's argument is that good social welfare policy analysis can no longer be restricted to a focus on income; it must also attend to the shifting dynamics of risk. As such, progressive social welfare policies must work to mitigate the degree of risk the individual family must bear.

Conclusion

John Judis and Michael Lind argue that, "Ultimately American economic policy must meet a single test: Does it tend to raise or depress the incomes of most Americans? A policy that impoverishes the ordinary American is a failure, no matter of its alleged benefits for U.S. corporations or for humanity as a whole."[77] We would add: "What are the effects of an economic policy on the social health of the nation?" Researchers at Fordham University's Institute for Innovation in Social Policy have argued that the nation's quality of life has become unhinged from its economic growth. "We really have to begin to reassess this notion that the gross domestic product—the overall growth of the society—necessarily is going to produce improvements in the quality of life."[78] Constructing an Index for Social Health that encompassed governmental data from 1970 to 1993, researchers found that in six categories—children in poverty, child abuse, health insurance coverage, average weekly earnings adjusted for inflation, out-of-pocket health costs for senior citizens, and the gap between rich and poor—"social health" hit its lowest point in 1993. As current poverty data suggest, these indicators have worsened since 1993.

A corollary question is, "What's the economy for, anyway?" In other words, do we exist to serve the economy or should the economy serve us? Economists often talk about the gross national product (GNP) or gross domestic product (GDP), productivity, and overall economic growth as if they were religious truths. Discussions typically revolve around how to best grow the economy, not whether the economy should grow. Meanwhile, too little of the economic discussion involves environmental sustainability or quality of life issues. John de Graaf has addressed these issues in *Affluenza* (the film and the book) as have other authors in various forms. (See Spotlight Box 1.1)

Spotlight 1.1

WHAT'S THE ECONOMY FOR, ANYWAY?

by John de Graaf

In the global economy, it seems *everyone* is dissatisfied and looking for different models. One by one, Latin American countries are moving from Right to Left. On the other hand, in Europe, the parties of social democracy have been losing ground to the Center (Europe's "right-wing" parties would be Centrist or Left in the U.S.), one after another.

All of this frenetic searching begs the fundamental question: What's the Economy for, Anyway? How much stock can we take in the Dow Jones? Is the Gross Domestic Product the measure (the grosser the better), and stuff the *stuff*, of happiness? Is the good life the *goods* life?

If so, then there's little doubt that the freer-market regimes win big. U.S. per capita GDP is still 30% higher than the average in Western Europe, just as it was a generation ago. We've got bigger homes, bigger cars, and more high-definition televisions. On the other hand if we measure success by the happiness, health, fairness and sustainability of economies, the picture looks very different.

I've been doing a little number-crunching lately, comparing data from such sources as the 2007 OECD [Organization for Economic Cooperation and Development] Fact Book, the World Health Organization and the UN [United Nations] Human Development Index, trying to see how countries are doing in real, empirical terms when it comes to health, quality of life, justice and sustainability. The results, I'm afraid, would come as a shock to those who look to the United States as the model of economic success.

Let me do a few of the numbers: compared, for example, to the western European nations, the U.S. ranks *worst* or next-to-worst when it comes to child welfare, health care, poverty, income equality, pollution, CO_2 emissions, ecological footprint, personal savings, income and pension security, balance of payments, municipal waste, development assistance, longevity, infant mortality, child abuse, depression, anxiety, obesity, murder, incarceration, motor vehicle fatalities, and leisure time. We do slightly better in education. Our unemployment rate looks pretty low, unless you count those 2.3 million people we've got behind bars, an incarceration rate 7 to 10 times as high as Europe's.

Since 1970 Europeans have traded a portion of their productivity gains for free time instead of stuff, a trade that pays off in many ways. New studies show that long working hours, the norm in the United States, contribute to poor health, weakened family and community bonds *and* environmental damage. Americans, far less healthy than Europeans, spend twice as much for health care per person. In fact, we spend nearly half the world's *total* health care budget, an amount that will reach 20% of our GDP by 2010—with the worst outcomes. Yet, all of that spending counts as a *plus* when it comes to GDP. The leisure that Europeans enjoy, the long meals and café conversations, the long walks and bike rides, count only as wasted time, adding not a single point to GDP. *La dolce vita*, by that measure, is for losers.

But which countries come out on *top* in measures of quality of life? It's the northern European nations, those that combine a strong social safety net with shorter working hours, high but progressive tax rates and strong environmental regulations. *The pattern is as clear as can be.*

I have found no one who refutes these figures. They simply explain them away by saying that the U.S. can't be like Europe. Why not?

One argument for why the United States can't even have such things as paid maternity leave—a reality in every country on the globe except the U.S., Swaziland, Lesotho, Liberia, and Papua New Guinea—is that we're so affected by *globalization*. But with its massive domestic market, the U.S. is just about the *least* affected by globalization of all industrial countries.

American conservatives argue that Europeans can't continue to compete in the global economy." But according to the World Economic Forum, over the past few years, four of the six most globally competitive countries have been in Europe. Even American businesses invest five times as much each year in Germany as they do in China and more in Belgium than in India. And they make money doing it.

When all else fails, there's the final appeal: the U.S. may not be very healthy, fair or sustainable, but it's "the land of opportunity," where *anyone* can make it big if they're willing to work hard enough. Yet a recent study finds that Americans actually have only about one-half to one-third as much chance as Europeans of escaping low-income lives and rising to the top.

The steady drone from some European business leaders about the American economic miracle masks what should be obvious—they'd like to join our CEOs in making 400 times as much as their average workers, instead of the miserable 30 to 40 times as much they now make. Their voices speak louder than those of the average European citizen, who enjoys his or her six weeks of vacation, restful meals, family leave, health care, sick pay, free college education, and secure pension plan.

Since Ronald Reagan declared that "government cannot be the solution because government is the problem," indices of American quality of life, fairness, economic security, and environmental sustainability have all fallen sharply in comparison with those in Europe. The conservative economic revolution has produced a *gush-up* instead of a "trickle-down." For most of us, the "ownership society," emphasizing privatization, deregulation and massive tax cuts for the wealthy, is really a "*you're on your owner* ship" society.

To make America better, our President tells us, we must do even *more* of these things, making tax cuts for the wealthy permanent, for example. But the working definition of insanity is to keep doing the same things hoping for a different result.

If we want to build societies that really work for people, we need to ask, "What's the Economy for, anyway?" And then we need to separate the real results from the myths, shed a little of our American hubris and start looking at how other countries are actually edging us out by providing policies that succeed. That way lies a happier, healthier, more just and sustainable world.

John De Graaf is a documentary filmmaker and co-author (with David Wann, Thomas Naylor, and Vicki Robin) of *Affluenza: The All-Consuming Epidemic* (San Francisco, CA: Berrett-Koehler, 2005).

As this chapter has demonstrated, social welfare in the United States is characterized by a high degree of diversity rather than a monolithic, highly centralized, well-coordinated system of programs. Rather, a great variety of organizations provide a wide range of benefits and services to different client populations. The vast array of social welfare organizations contributes to what is commonly called "the welfare mess." Consequently, different programs serving different groups through different procedures have created an impenetrable tangle of institutional red tape that is problematic for administrators, human service professionals, and clients.

The complexity of U.S. social welfare policy can be attributed to several influences, some of which are peculiar to the American experience. For instance, the U.S. Constitution outlines a federal system whereby states vest certain functions in the national government. Although the states have assumed primary responsibility for social welfare through much of U.S. history, this changed with Franklin Delano Roosevelt's New Deal which ushered in a raft of federal programs. Over subsequent decades, federal social welfare initiatives played a dominant role in the nation's welfare effort. Still, states continued to manage important social welfare programs, such as mental health, corrections, and social services. Over time, the relationship between the federal government and the states changed. From the New Deal of the 1930s through the Great Society of the 1960s, federal welfare programs expanded, forming the American version of the "welfare state." Beginning in the 1980s, the Reagan administration sought to return more of the responsibility for welfare to the states, a process called devolution.[79] This process was furthered by the Clinton administration with the signing of the PRWORA.

A second factor is attributed to the relatively open character of U.S. society. Often referred to as a melting pot, the national culture is a protean brew of immigrant groups that become an established part of national life.[80] A staggering influx of Europeans in the late nineteenth century gave way to waves of Hispanics and Asians a century later.[81] Historically, social welfare programs have played a prominent role in the acculturation of these groups. At the same time, many ethnic groups brought with them their own fraternal and community associations, which not only provide welfare benefits to members of the community but also serve to maintain its norms. Other groups that have exerted important influences on U.S. social welfare are African Americans, the aged, women, and Native Americans. The very pluralism of U.S. society—a diverse collection of peoples, each with somewhat different needs—contributes to the complexity of social welfare.

The economic system exacerbates the complexity of social welfare. With important exceptions, the U.S. economy is predominantly capitalist, with most goods and services being owned, produced, and distributed through the marketplace. In a capitalist economy, people are expected to meet their basic needs in the marketplace through labor force participation. When people are unable to participate fully in the labor market, like the aged or the handicapped, social programs are deployed to support these groups. These programs take various forms. Many are governmental programs. Private sector programs often complement those of the public sector. Within the private sector, two organizational forms are common—nonprofit organizations and for-profit corporations. Often these private sector organizations coexist, proximate to one another.[82] For instance, in many communities, family planning services are provided by the public health departments; Planned Parenthoods (a private nonprofit); and by for-profit health maintenance organizations.

Finally, various religious or faith-based organizations strongly influence American social welfare. This is seen most clearly in the range of faith-based agencies that offer social services, such as Jewish Family Services, Lutheran Social Services, Catholic Charities, and the Salvation Army. In many cases, religious-based agencies provide services to groups that would not otherwise receive them. Today many faith-based agencies receive federal funds for various services they provide to the public. It is likely that this trend will grow.

The pluralism of national culture is of increasing interest to social welfare policy analysts as the influence of the federal government in social policy diminishes. In light of reductions in many federal social programs and calls for the private sector to assume more responsibility for welfare, the prospect of molding the diverse entities involved in American social welfare into one unified whole under the auspices of a central federal authority seems remote. This vision of a unified social welfare system is implicit in the proposals of advocates for nationalized programs that ensure basic goods and services such as food, housing, education, health, and income as a right of citizenship. Although programs of this nature have been integral to the welfare states of northern Europe for decades, there is a serious question as to their plausibility for the United States given the complexity built into its social welfare system.[83] Given these developments, welfare professionals face a formidable challenge: How can basic goods and services be brought to vulnerable populations within a context of such complexity and uncertainty?

DISCUSSION QUESTIONS

1. According to the authors, American social welfare is undergoing a transition. Which ideologies, schools of political economy, and interest groups within social welfare stand to gain most from this transition?
2. Ideology tends to parallel schools of political economy. How would classical conservatives and liberals address current social welfare issues such as health care, long-term care for the aged, and substance abuse? How would neoconservatives and neoliberals diverge from traditional conservatives and liberals on these issues?
3. Which schools of political, social, and economic thought discussed in this chapter would come closest to being classified as moderate? Why?
4. The chapter argues that in large measure social policy dictates social work practice. Do you agree with that premise? Explain your position. Can you think of any instances (historic or otherwise) in which social work practice has led to changes in social welfare policy?
5. In your opinion, which schools of economic and political thought are the most compatible with social work practice? What are the incompatibilities in the

various schools of thought with macro- and micro-level social work and practice?

6. Chapter 1 describes the U.S. political continuum ranging from Liberalism to Libertarianism. Access the website of the National Association of Social Workers (www.naswdc.org) and read through the Advocacy and Legislative Issues links. Where would you place the NASW along the U.S. political continuum? Why?

7. The Heritage Foundation (www.heritage.org) and The Urban Institute (www.urban.org) are think tanks that deal with research on a variety of issues related to social welfare policy. Scan the topics and a few of the titles easily accessible from the home page of each website. Does either adopt a specific point of view that tends to dominate? If you were looking for a progressive position on an issue, which one would you access?

8. In their book *Economics for Social Workers: The Application of Economic Theory to Social Policy and the Human Services* (New York: Columbia University Press, 2001), Michael Anthony Lewis and Karl Widerquist identify four conditions that must hold for a free market to exist: (a) the market must contain many small buyers and sellers; (b) the goods and services sold by each firm must be largely homogeneous with all other firms; (c) all buyers and sellers must have accurate information upon which to make their decisions; and (d) buyers and sellers can enter or exit the market at will. If it is correct to assume that there is no free market without meeting these conditions, would you describe the U.S. economy as a free market? In what ways do we violate this model? In what ways do we support it?

NOTES

1. E. J. Dionne Jr., "The Opening Obama Saw," *Washington Post* (November 3, 2008), p. A21.

2. Chris Gentilviso, Todd Akin, "On Abortion: 'Legitimate Rape' Victims Have 'Ways To Try To Shut That Whole Thing Down,'" The Huffington Post, August 19, 2012. Retrieved September 2012 from, http://www.huffingtonpost.com/2012/08/19/todd-akin-abortion-legitimate-rape_n_1807381.html

3. Howard Karger, Stupid is as Stupid Does: How the US Republicans Channelled Forrest Gump, unpublished manuscript. School of Social Work and Human Services, The University of Queensland, Brisbane, Australia, May 2012.

4. Howard Karger, Stupid is as Stupid Does: How the US Republicans Channelled Forrest Gump, unpublished manuscript. School of Social Work and Human Services, The University of Queensland, Brisbane, Australia, May 2012.

5. Public Policy Polling, Other Notes from Alabama and Mississippi, March 12, 2012. Retrieved September 2012 from, http://www.publicpolicypolling.com/main/2012/03/other-notes-from-alabama-and-mississippi.html

6. Kenneth P. Vogel, "The Billion-Dollar Bust?," Politico, November 7, 2012. Retrieved November 8, 2012 from, http://www.politico.com/news/stories/1112/83534.html

7. Deborah Tedford, "Supreme Court Rips Up Campaign Finance Laws," National Public Radio, January 21, 2010. Retrieved November 8, 2012 from, http://www.npr.org/templates/story/story.php?storyId=122805666

8. HuffPost Politics Election Results, The Huffington Post, November 8, 2012. Retrieved November 2012 from, http://elections.huffingtonpost.com/2012/results

9. Richard Titmuss, *Essays on the Welfare State* (Boston: Beacon Press, 1963), p. 16.

10. Contained in personal correspondence between David Stoesz and William Epstein, April 2000.

11. See Alfred Kahn, *Social Policy and Social Services* (New York: Random House, 1979).

12. Frances Fox Piven and Richard Cloward, *Regulating the Poor* (New York: Vintage, 1971).

13. David Gil, *Unraveling Social Policy* (Boston: Shenkman, 1981), p. 32.

14. Joseph Stiglitz, "Of the 1%, by the 1%, for the 1%," *Vanity Fair*, May 2011. Retrieved February 2012 from, http://www.vanityfair.com/society/features/2011/05/top-one-percent-2011

15. Max Abelson, "Bankers Join Billionaires to Debunk 'Imbecile' Attack on Top 1%," Bloomberg News, December 20, 2011. Retrieved February 2012 from, http://www.bloomberg.com/news/2011-12-20/bankers-join-billionaires-to-debunk-imbecile-attack-on-top-1-.html

16. International Monetary Fund, World Economic Outlook Database, September 2011, New York, NY; OECD, Public policies for families and children, June 14, 2011. Retrieved February 2012 from, http://www.oecd.org/document/4/0,3746,en_2649_34819_37836996_1_1_1_1,00.html

17. Claus Offe, *Contradictions of the Welfare State* (Cambridge, MA: MIT Press, 1984).

18. John Maynard Keynes, *The General Theory of Employment, Interest and Money* (London: Macmillan, 1936).

19. Paul R. Krugman, *Peddling Prosperity: Economic Sense and Nonsense in the Age of Diminished Expectations* (New York: W.W. Norton, 1994).

20. Ibid.

21. In their book *Economics for Social Workers: The Application of Economic Theory to Social Policy and the Human Services* (New York: Columbia University Press, 2001), Michael Anthony Lewis and Karl Widerquist identify four conditions that must hold for a free market to exist.

22. Ibid.

23. Milton Friedman, *Money Mischief: Episodes in Monetary History* (New York: Harcourt Brace, 1992).

24. Milton Friedman, *Capitalism and Freedom* (Chicago, IL: University of Chicago Press, 1962).
25. Ibid.
26. Robert E. Lucas, *Studies in Business Cycle Theory* (Cambridge, MA: MIT Press, 1981).
27. Krugman, *Peddling Prosperity.*
28. Ibid.
29. Ibid.
30. Congressional Budget Office, *The Economic and Budget Outlook: Fiscal Years 1993–1997* (Washington, DC: Congressional Budget Office, 1992), p. 28.
31. Citizens for Tax Justice, Cost of Tax Cuts for the Wealthiest Americans, 2012. Retrieved February 2012 from, http://costoftaxcuts.com
32. See Beth Shulman, *The Betrayal of Work: How Low Wage Jobs Fail 35 Million Americans* (New York: The New Press, 2003); Lawrence Mishel, Jared Bernstein, and John Schmitt, *The State of Working America 2000/2001* (Ithaca, NY: Cornell University Press, 2001); and Jared Bernstein, "Economic Growth Not Reaching Middle- and Lower Wage Earners," January 28, 2004, retrieved 2004 from www.epinet.org/content.cfm/webfeatures_snapshots
33. Office of Management and Budget, "The Nation's Fiscal Outlook Fiscal Year 2008." Retrieved 2008 from www.whitehouse.gov/omb/budget/fy2008/outlook.html
34. See Ayn Rand, *The Fountainhead* (New York: New American Library, 50th Anniversary Edition, 1996); *Atlas Shrugged* (New York: Signet Book; 35th Anniversary Edition, 1996).
35. Charles Murray, *Losing Ground* (New York: Basic Books, 1984), pp. 227–228.
36. *Privatization: Toward More Effective Government* (Washington, DC: U.S. Government Printing Office, 1988), pp. 233–234.
37. Michael Grynbaum, "Greenspan Concedes Error on Regulation," *The New York Times*, October 23, 2008, p. 1.
38. CNN News, "Taxpayers Would Get Checks under Economic Stimulus Plan," January 24, 2008. Retrieved October 25, 2008 from, http://edition.cnn.com/2008/POLITICS/01/24/economic.stimulus/
39. Edmund L. Andrews, "Fed Acts to Rescue Financial Markets," *The New York Times*, March 17, 2008, p. 4.
40. Mark Landler, "U.S. Is Said to Be Urging New Mergers in Banking," *The New York Times*, October 20, 2008, p. 18.
41. Paul Wallis, "$25 Billion Fed Loan to Car Industry; It's Not a Bailout, Says Detroit," Digital Business Journal, September 29, 2008. Retrieved October 25, 2008 from, http://www.digitaljournal.com/article/260441
42. Associated Press, "2008 U.S. Budget Deficit Bleeding Red Ink First 4 Months Of Budget Year At Nearly $88B, Double Amount Recorded For Same 2007 Period," CBS News, February 12, 2008. Retrieved October 24, 2008 from, http://www.cbsnews.com/stories/2008/02/12/national/main3822385.shtml
43. Jeffry Galper, "Introduction of Radical Theory and Practice in Social Work Education: Social Policy." Mimeographed paper, Michigan State University School of Social Work, ca. 1978.
44. Piven and Cloward, *Regulating the Poor,* pp. 3–4.
45. Harry Hopkins, *Spending to Save: The Complete Story of Relief* (Seattle: University of Washington Press, 1936).
46. Neil Gilbert, Harry Specht, and Paul Terrell, *Dimensions of Social Welfare Policy* (Englewood Cliffs, NJ: Prentice Hall, 1993).
47. Marc Bendick, *Privatizing the Delivery of Social Welfare Service* (Washington, DC: National Conference on Social Welfare, 1985), p. 1.
48. Charles Peters, "A New Politics," *Public Welfare* 41, no. 2 (Spring 1983), pp. 34, 36.
49. Randall Rothenberg, *The Neoliberals* (New York: Simon & Schuster, 1984), pp. 244–245.
50. David Stoesz, *Small Change* (New York: Longman, 1995).
51. Robert Kuttner, The Alarming Parallels Between 1929 and 2007, *The American Prospect,* (October 2, 2007).
52. Robert Reich, *The Next American Frontier* (New York: Times Books, 1983).
53. Bruce Stokes, *Helping Ourselves: Local Solutions to Global Problems* (New York: W.W. Norton, 1981).
54. Sugata Dasgupta, "Towards a No-Poverty Society," *Social Development Issues* 12 (Winter 1983), pp. 85–93.
55. Some of these economic principles were addressed by E. F. Schumacher in *Small Is Beautiful* (New York: Harper & Row, 1973).
56. Barry M. Goldwater, *The Conscience of a Conservative* (New York: Putnam, 1960), pp. 109–110.
57. See Peter Steinfels, *The Neoconservatives* (New York: Simon & Schuster, 1979).
58. Interview with Stuart Butler, Director of Domestic Policy at the Heritage Foundation, October 4, 1984.
59. Alan Walker, "The Strategy of Inequality: Poverty and Income Distribution in Britain 1979–89," in I. Taylor (ed.), *The Social Effects of Free Market Policies* (Sussex, England: Harvester-Wheatsheaf, 1990), pp. 43–66.
60. James C. Mckinley Jr, "Texas Conservatives Win Curriculum Change," *The New York Times,* March 13, 2010, p. A10.
61. Kristen Geiss-Curran, Sha'ari Garfinkle, Fred Knocke, Terri Lively, and Sue McCullough, "The Contract with America and the Budget Battle," unpublished manuscript, University of Houston, Spring 1996.
62. The Libertarian Party, "Statement of Principles," Washington, DC, 1996.
63. Daniel Patrick Moynihan, *Came the Revolution* (New York: Harcourt Brace Jovanovich, 1988), p. 291.
64. See Harold Wilensky and Charles Lebeaux, *Industrial Society and Social Welfare* (New York: Free Press, 1965); and Mimi Abramovitz, "The Privatization of the Welfare State," *Social Work* 31 (July–August 1986), pp. 257–264.

65. R. Erikson, E. Hansen, S. Ringen, and H. Uusitalo, *The Scandinavian Model* (Armonk, NY: M.E. Sharpe, 1987).

66. Richard Titmuss, *Commitment to Welfare* (New York: Pantheon, 1968), p. 127.

67. Alvin Rabushka, "Tax and Spending Limits," in Peter Duignan and Alvin Rabushka (eds.), *The United States in the 1980s* (Stanford, CA: Hoover Institution, 1980), pp. 104–106.

68. Martin Anderson, "Welfare Reform," in Peter Duignan and Alvin Rabushka (eds.), *The United States in the 1980s,* pp. 171–176.

69. Stuart Butler and Anna Kondratas, *Out of the Poverty Trap: A Conservative Strategy for Welfare Reform* (New York: Free Press, 1987).

70. William Lind and William Marshner, *Cultural Conservatism: Toward a New National Agenda* (Washington, DC: Free Congress Research and Education Foundation, 1987), p. 83.

71. George Gilder, *Wealth and Poverty* (New York: Basic Books, 1981), p. 118.

72. Anderson, "Welfare Reform," p. 145.

73. Jacob. S. Hacker, *The Great Risk Shift: The Assault on American Jobs, Families, Health Care, and Retirement* (New York: Oxford University Press, 2006).

74. Ibid.

75. Lawrence Mischel, Jared Bernstein, and Sylkvia Allegretto, *The State of Working America 2004/2005* (Ithaca, NY: IRL Press, 2005).

76. Julie Appleby, "Bush Unveils Health Plan Tied to Tax Deduction," *USA Today*, January 24, 2007. Retrieved March 17, 2007, from www.usatoday.com/money/industries/health/2007-01-24-bush-health-usat_x.htm

77. John Judis and Michael Lind, "For a New Nationalism," *The New Republic* (March 27, 1995), p. 26.

78. Mitchell Landsberg, "Nation's Social Health Declined in '93," *Houston Chronicle* (October 16, 1995), p. 1C.

79. Domestic Policy Council, Up from Dependency (Washington, DC: White House Domestic Policy Council, December 1986).

80. For a classic description of the assimilation phenomenon, see Nathan Glazer and Daniel Patrick Moynihan, *Beyond the Melting Pot* (Cambridge, MA: MIT Press, 1970).

81. Thomas Muller et al., *The Fourth Wave* (Washington, DC: Urban Institute, 1985).

82. The three auspices of social welfare in the United States have been termed the "mixed economy of welfare." See Sheila Kamerman, "The New Mixed Economy of Welfare," *Social Work* 28 (January–February 1983), pp. 43–50.

83. Marc Bendick, *Privatizing the Delivery of Social Welfare Service* (Washington, DC: National Conference on Social Welfare, 1985).

CHAPTER 2

Social Welfare Policy Research

A Framework for Policy Analysis

Source: Auremar/Shutterstock

Policy analysts engage in the systematic investigation of a social policy or a set of policies. They are employed in a variety of settings, including federal, state, and local governments; think tanks; universities; social justice or public interest groups or community organizations; and larger social agencies. The goals of policy analysis can range from pure research to providing information to legislators (i.e., congressional researchers) and to advocacy research. This chapter examines one of the major tools used by the policy researcher, a systematic and structured framework for policy analysis. The authors also propose a model for policy analysis.

A **policy framework**—a systematic model for examining a specific social welfare policy or a series of policies—is one means analysts use to evaluate the congruence of a policy with the mission and goals of the welfare state. Analysts can also employ policy frameworks to assess whether key social welfare values—that is, social justice, redistribution, or equity—are incorporated within a given policy. Moreover, a policy framework can help determine if a policy is consistent with established social welfare values or historical precedents. For example, consider the proposal that foster care should be abolished and that all children suspected of being abused or neglected should be placed in orphanages. The use of a policy framework would illustrate that this proposal reflects a clear break with the general drift of child welfare policy since the end of the twentieth century, and that it contravenes established values such as family reunification. In addition, a systematic analysis would reveal that this policy is neither economically, politically or socially feasible.

An analytic framework can also be used for comparing existing policies. For example, comparing the mental health policies of Missouri with those of Massachusetts and Minnesota would yield valuable information for all three states. A comparative analysis of the health systems of the United States, Canada, and United Kingdom would also provide useful information for decision makers. Finally, analytic frameworks are useful in evaluating competing policies and helping analysts make a recommendation on which policy most effectively addresses a problem or remedies a need.

Policy analysis frameworks are useful for social work practitioners on several levels and can address micro and macro policies at the agency, statewide or national levels. Agency policies dictate what

a social worker will do, with whom, and for how long. They also define who is (or is not) a client and what services will be offered. Social work practitioners can analyze agency policies on issues like flextime, merit pay, agency-based day care, job sharing, and so forth. Child welfare workers can use policy analysis to evaluate impending state or federal legislation and the concomitant fiscal allocations. Social workers in health care can analyze managed care policies in terms of equity, effectiveness, and a wide range of other issues. Social work practice is clearly influenced—if not driven—by social policy.

Policy analysis is also useful in environmental scanning activities of non- and for-profit agencies. As the delivery of social services becomes more heavily located in the competitive marketplace, social agencies will be forced to replicate private sector corporate behavior. This includes being aware of changing demographics and market trends, and monitoring new legislation. In some sectors, events change so rapidly that agencies must quickly modify their operations to remain viable. Data-based environmental scanning allows agencies to make long- and short-term plans based on changing demographics, new competing organizations, or the effects of impending legislation. Environmental scanning also allows agencies to discover new markets and to protect their existing ones.[1]

Social welfare policies and programs are complex phenomena. For example, it is easy to propose a social policy such as mandatory drug testing for all governmental employees. On the surface, the policy appears simple: Illegal drug users are discovered through testing and then are forced to seek treatment. On closer scrutiny, the hidden issues become problematic. Is it constitutional to require drug treatment if a positive result is found? Is occasional use of marijuana sufficient grounds for requiring drug treatment? Because alcohol is a legal substance, drug tests do not detect it. Is alcohol less debilitating than marijuana? Can mandatory drug testing be misused by supervisors to harass employees? Will drug testing produce the desired results? Without a systematic means to analyze the effects of a policy, decisions become arbitrary and may produce consequences that are worse than the original problem.

All well-designed policy frameworks are characterized by eight key elements:

- Policy frameworks systematically analyze a social policy or program.

The policy analyst is expected to evaluate policies and make recommendations. To succeed, the analyst must accept his or her own values while basing the analysis on objective criteria.

Source: StockLite Shutterstock

- Policy frameworks reflect the understanding that social policy is context sensitive, and that there are competing priorities in all policy options.
- Policy frameworks utilize rational methods of inquiry and analysis. The data used in policy analysis is derived from scientific inquiry and legitimate sources. Data is objectively interpreted and analyzed.
- The analytic method is explicit and all succeeding policy analyses should approximate the same conclusion.
- Policy analysis is based on the commitment to derive the largest possible benefit at the least possible cost. A good social policy is one that benefits at least one person (as he or she perceives his or her own self-interest) while at the same time hurting no one (a variation of the

Pareto Optimality). Although rarely achieved in the real world of finite resources—and proliferating claims on them—policy analysts should nevertheless strive to realize that goal.
- Policy frameworks should attempt to take into account the unintended consequences of a particular policy or program.
- Policy analysts should consider alternative social policies or alternative uses of present or future resources allocated to a given policy.
- Policy frameworks should examine the potential impact of a policy (or a series of policies) on other social policies, social problems, and the public good.

A policy framework can provide decision makers and the general public with information, an understanding of the ramifications of a policy on the target problem (and other problems and policies), and alternative policies that could more effectively address the problem. Untoward consequences are more frequent when the decision-making process is not based on a systematic framework for policy analysis.

History is replete with examples of well-intentioned policies that proved catastrophic. For example, the U.S. Congress enacted a law in 1919 that prohibited the manufacture, sale, or transport of alcohol in an effort to cut down on crime, familial instability, unemployment, and sundry other alcohol-related social problems. Advocates of Prohibition, including many social workers, touted the end of alcohol as a major step forward in the social evolution of the United States. By the time Prohibition was repealed in 1932, most of the original supporters were silent. Despite their best hopes, Prohibition did not decrease crime or lead to more family stability and greater social order; instead, it encouraged the growth of an organized crime industry that fed the ongoing taste of Americans for alcohol. Instead of curbing alcohol-related nightlife, Prohibition led to the creation of illegal and well-attended speakeasies. Even many supporters conceded that alcohol was almost as abundant as before Prohibition. A systematic analysis of Prohibition done before the passage of the bill might have demonstrated the futility of this policy initiative.

A similar argument can be made for the current policy of drug interdiction and enforcement. After almost a half-century of vigorous drug enforcement, marijuana, heroin, cocaine, and other drugs continue to be readily available. While there is little hard evidence that vigilant drug enforcement has resulted in lowered drug use, it has increased the prison population. In 1980, about 220 people were incarcerated for every 100,000 Americans; by 2010 that number had more than tripled to 731 or roughly 2.27 million people.[2] This represents by far the highest rate of incarceration in the world, both in terms of actual numbers and in proportion to the population. While Americans represent only about 5 percent of the world's population, the United States has 25 percent of the world's inmates.[3] Roughly 25 percent of inmates are in U.S. prisons for drug-related crimes.[4] Since 1985, the money that states spend on prisons has risen at six times the rate of spending on higher education.[5] The drug interdiction policy has also led to the creation of international drug cartels whose wealth and power rival that of many national governments and multinational corporations—and whose impact has been staggeringly destructive. From January to September 2011, the Mexican government reported that almost 13,000 people were killed in drug-related violence, including security forces and innocent bystanders. Roughly 48,000 Mexicans were murdered or accidentally killed in drug-related violence from 2006 to early 2012.[6]

The drug policy also led to an increase in drug-related homicides in the United States and to the deterioration of inner-city neighborhoods racked by gang warfare fed by the lucrative drug trade. Drug enforcement policies have not stopped the flow of illegal drugs, but they have created a vibrant industry that includes government officials, contractors, private correctional corporations, police departments, and large segments of the legal and judicial system. All of these groups have a vested interest in maintaining the status quo, regardless of its effectiveness. In short, a social problem led to a social policy, which in turn, led to a powerful industry that depends on the continuation of an ineffective policy for its very existence.

As this example suggests, social policy is often driven by politics and rarely, if ever, systematically, analyzed. Even a cursory examination of Prohibition would have informed policy makers of the potential success of a drug interdiction policy. Policy analysis often occurs only after a bill or policy is enacted. As a result, analysts are asked to perform an autopsy to determine why a specific bill or policy failed.

The purpose of a policy framework is to provide the analyst with a model or a set of questions for systematically analyzing a policy. Consequently, the choice of a policy framework must fit the requirements of the project as well as the available resources. Every policy framework can be fine-tuned or modified, and the best policy framework is often a synthesis of existing models.[7]

A Proposed Model for Policy Analysis

Policy analysts are expected to evaluate a policy and make recommendations. As part of the process, the analyst must acknowledge their own values, while at the same time, basing the analysis on objective criteria. The proposed policy framework is divided into four sections: (1) the historical background of the policy, (2) a description of the problem(s) that necessitated the policy, (3) a description of the policy, and (4) the policy analysis (see Figure 2.1).

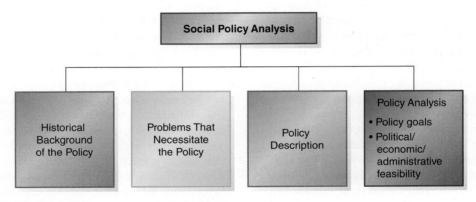

FIGURE 2.1 Proposed Framework for Policy Analysis

Historical Background of the Policy

The policy analyst should examine similar past policies and assess how they fared. Understanding the historical antecedents of a policy is important for two reasons. First, the analyst should identify the historical problems that led to the original policy. Questions might include: What historical problems led to the creation of the policy? How was the problem previously handled? When did the policy originate and how has it changed over time? What is the legislative history of the policy?

Spotlight 2.1

A MODEL FOR POLICY ANALYSIS

The model for policy analysis can be divided into four sections—the historical background of the policy, a description of the problem that necessitated the policy, a description of the policy, and the policy analysis. Each of these sections requires the policy analyst to ask specific questions.

Historical Background of the Policy

- What historical problems led to the creation of the policy?
- How important have these problems been historically?
- How was the problem previously handled?
- What is the historical background of the policy?
- When did the policy originate?
- How has the original policy changed over time?
- What is the legislative history of the policy?

Description of the Problem That Necessitated the Policy

- What is the nature of the problem?
- How widespread is it?
- How many people are affected by it?
- Who is affected and how?
- What are the causes of the problem?

Policy Description

- How is the policy expected to work?
- What are the resources or opportunities that the policy is expected to provide?
- Who will be covered by the policy and how?
- How will the policy be implemented?

- What are the short- and long-term goals and outcomes of the policy?
- What are the administrative auspices under which the policy will be lodged?
- What is the funding mechanism for the policy?
- What agencies or organizations will be charged with overseeing, evaluating, and coordinating the policy?
- What are the formal or informal criteria that will be used to determine the effectiveness of the policy?
- How long is the policy expected to be in existence?
- What is the knowledge base or scientific grounding for the policy?

Policy Analysis

- Are the goals of the policy legal?
- Are the goals of the policy just and democratic?
- Do the goals of the policy contribute to greater social equality?
- Do the goals of the policy help the redistribution of income, resources, rights, entitlements, rewards, opportunities, and status?
- Do the goals of the policy contribute to a better quality of life for the target population?
- Will the goals adversely affect the quality of life of the target population?
- Does the policy contribute to positive social relations between the target population and the overall society?
- Are the goals of the policy consistent with the values of professional social work?

Second, a historical analysis helps to curb the tendency of decision makers to reinvent the wheel. For instance, an analyst may find that circumstances have changed, and a previously unsuccessful policy may now be viable. A historical analysis also helps the analyst to understand the forces that were mobilized to support or oppose a given policy. This part of the analysis locates a policy within a historical framework, thus helping to explain its evolution.

Problems That Necessitate the Policy

The second step in policy analysis is an examination of the problems that led to the creation of the policy. To fully assess whether a proposed policy will successfully remedy a social problem, the analyst must understand the parameters of the problem. Furthermore, the analyst must be familiar with the nature, scope, and magnitude of the problem and with the affected populations. In this way, the analyst can discern early whether the policy is appropriate. Specific questions might include the following: What is the nature and cause of the problem? How widespread is it? Who and how many people are affected by it?

Policy Description

The next step is the description of the policy. This section requires a detailed explanation of the policy, including a description of (1) how the policy is expected to work; (2) the resources or opportunities the policy is expected to provide (power, cash, economic opportunity, in-kind benefits, status redistribution, goods and services, and so forth); (3) who will be covered by the policy and how (e.g., universal versus selective entitlement, means testing, and so forth); (4) how the policy will be implemented; (5) the expected short- and long-term goals and outcomes of the policy; (6) the administrative auspices under which the policy will be lodged; (7) the funding mechanism, including short- and long-term funding commitments; (8) the agencies or organizations that have overall responsibility for overseeing, evaluating, and coordinating the policy; (9) the criteria used to determine the effectiveness of the policy; (10) the length of time the policy is expected to be in existence (i.e., is it a "sunset law" designed to end at a certain date?); and (11) the knowledge base or science undergirding for the policy.

Policy Analysis

This section is the heart of any policy analysis. In this section, the analyst engages in a *systematic* analysis of the policy.

Policy Goals   The policy goals are the criteria by which all else is measured. Often the analyst must interpret the overall goals of the policy since they may not be explicitly stated. The following questions may help to explicate the goals of a particular policy:

- Are the goals legal, just, and democratic?
- Do they contribute to greater social equality?
- Do the goals positively affect the redistribution of income, resources, rights, entitlements, rewards, opportunities, and status?
- Do the goals contribute to a better quality of life for the target population? Will they adversely affect the quality of life of the target group?
- Does the policy contribute to positive social relations between the target population and the overall society?
- Are the policy goals consistent with the values of professional social work (i.e., self-determination, client rights, self-realization, and so forth)?

Analysts must understand the value premises of the policy as well as the ideological assumptions underlying it. To this end, several questions should be asked: What covert ideological assumptions are contained in the policy? How is the target population viewed in the policy? What social vision, if any, does the policy contain? Does the policy encourage the status quo or does it represent a radical departure? Who are the major beneficiaries? Is the policy designed to foster real social change or to placate a potentially insurgent group? Exposing the hidden ideological dimensions of a policy is often the most difficult task for the policy analyst.

Despite good intentions, a prospective policy must be viable. American history is littered with worthy policies that were simply not viable at the time they were proposed. For example, at the height of the Great Depression, a California physician named Francis Townsend proposed that all citizens over the age of 65 be given a flat governmental pension of $200 a month. While this proposal might have received at least a cursory hearing in prosperous times, in the midst of the Great Depression policymakers dismissed it as nonviable. The overall viability of a policy is based on three factors: political feasibility, economic feasibility, and administrative feasibility.

Political Feasibility The political feasibility of a policy is a subjective assessment. In order to evaluate a policy, the analyst must assess which group(s) will oppose or support a particular policy, and they must estimate the power and constituency base of each group. However, the size of the constituency base and its relative power are sometimes unrelated. For example, despite its relatively small numbers, the American Medical Association (AMA) is a powerful lobby. Conversely, although more than 30 million Americans are poor, they have negligible political clout.

The political viability of a policy is subject to the public's perception of its feasibility. In other words, for a policy to be feasible, it must be perceived as being feasible. For example, although a sizable portion of the public would welcome some form of national health care, none exists. The United States lacks a comprehensive national health care system partly because of the power of the health care industry, but also partly because the public believes it cannot happen. Thus, a public myth is born around what is and what is not possible.

In assessing the political feasibility of a policy, the analyst must examine the public's sentiment. Does a large segment of the public care about the policy (i.e., do they perceive they will be affected by it)? Do large numbers of people fear a policy, as in comprehensive health care? Does the policy threaten fundamental social values? Is the policy congruent with the current social and political climate? Can either side marshal substantial public support for or against the policy? The answers to these questions will help the policy analyst determine the political feasibility of the policy.

The analyst should consider the relationship between the policy and external factors in agencies and institutions. For example, which social welfare agencies, institutions, or organizations will support or oppose the policy? What is their relative strength? How strident is their support or opposition to the policy? Which federal, state, or local agencies would be affected by the policy? The world of social policy is highly political, and some governmental and private social welfare agencies have political power on par with elected officials. Groups of institutions often coalesce around policies that directly affect them, and through lobbying efforts, they can defeat legislation. In cases where they cannot defeat a policy outright, administrative units can implement a policy in ways that ensure its failure. The analyst must therefore take into account whether key administrative units support or oppose a new or existing policy.

Economic Feasibility Most social policies require some form of direct or indirect funding. In assessing the economic feasibility of a policy, the analyst must question: What is the minimum level of funding necessary for successfully implementing the policy? Is the policy adequately funded? If not, what is the public sentiment toward increased funding? What are the funding needs of the policy likely to be in the future?

Given the current political and economic climate, it appears unlikely that bold new social policy initiatives requiring large revenues will be successful. More likely, new, revenue-based policy legislation will be based on the reallocation of existing resources (budget-neutral policies) rather than on new revenue sources. This approach—taking money from one program to fund another—is called **pay-go** financing. The danger is that thinning out fiscal resources among many programs may mean that none are adequately funded. The analyst must therefore decide whether a new policy initiative should be recommended based on the funding prospects. The parameters of this decision are complex. If a new policy is recommended despite insufficient resources, the chances of its failure are greater. If a policy is not recommended, there is no possibility that future fiscal resources will be allocated to it. As a result, many policy analysts lean toward incremental approaches, tending to recommend policies in the hope that future funding will become available.

Administrative Feasibility The analyst must also be concerned with the administrative viability of a policy. Regardless of the potential value of a policy, responsible administrative and supervisory agencies must possess the personnel, resources, skills, and expertise needed to effectively implement the policy. In addition, directors and supervisors must be sympathetic to the goals of the policy, have the expertise and skill needed to implement or oversee the policy, and have an understanding of the fundamental objectives of the policy. Policy analysts focus on two key aspects of administrative feasibility: effectiveness and efficiency.

Effectiveness is based on the likelihood that the policy will accomplish what its designers intended. This encompasses several questions: Is the policy broad enough to accomplish its stated goals? Will the benefits of the policy reach the target group? Is the implementation of the policy likely to cause new or other social problems? What are the ramifications of the policy on the non-target sector (i.e., higher taxes, reduced opportunities, diminished freedom, etc.)?

Another challenge facing policy analysts is the nature and extent of a policy's unintended consequences. Virtually all policies have unforeseen consequences. One example of this is methadone, a drug legally administered to addicts as a substitute for heroin. When introduced in the 1960s, methadone was thought to be a safe way to wean addicts away from heroin. However, by the mid-1970s health experts realized that methadone was almost as addictive as heroin, and that some addicts were selling their methadone as a street drug. Despite this unintended outcome, some addicts were able to withdraw from heroin, and on balance, the methadone program was a positive development. Because policy analysts cannot see into the future, recommendations are made on the basis of available data. Nevertheless, analysts must try to anticipate the possibility of adverse future consequences.

Policy analysts look closely at *efficiency*, or the cost-effectiveness of the proposed policy compared to alternative policies, no policy, or the present policy. Social policy always involves trade-offs. Even in the best of economic times, fiscal resources are always inadequate to meet the breadth of human need. For example, virtually everyone could benefit from some form of social welfare, whether it is counseling, food stamps, or free health care. But because resources are finite, society must choose the primary beneficiaries for social allocations. Publicly financed services are often provided on the basis of two criteria: (1) the severity of the problem (those who most need it) and (2) means (those least able to afford it). As a result, adequately funding one policy can mean limiting the allocations of another. This is the essential trade-off in social welfare policy. When analysts evaluate a policy, they are cognizant that promoting one policy often means that needs in other areas may go unmet. Hence, the analyst asks, "Is the policy important enough to justify the allocation of scarce resources?" Are there other areas where scarce resources could be better used?

The policy analyst frequently compares the cost-effectiveness of a proposed policy with an alternative policy. Will the proposed policy yield better results than the present policy or no policy at all? Is it advantageous to enlarge or modify the present policy rather than create a new one? Will an alternative policy provide better results at a lower cost? Can an alternative policy achieve the same results? These questions are often addressed in a thorough policy analysis.

Researching and Analyzing a Social Policy Assignment

Students tasked with a policy analysis assignment will face two major hurdles. The first is finding and focusing on a manageable social policy, and the second is finding or generating information relevant to it.

One of the most difficult tasks the student faces is choosing the actual policy. A manageable assignment requires selecting a policy that is both specific and discrete. For example, it would be virtually impossible to do an exhaustive analysis of U.S. child welfare policy. For one thing, the U.S. lacks an integrated child welfare policy; instead, child welfare is characterized by a patchwork quilt of myriad programs. Second, differing child welfare policies on the national, state, and community levels would make such a policy analysis even more daunting. To succeed, the student would have to focus on a small segment of child welfare.

A second task involves locating policy-relevant information. There are seven major avenues for finding information. First, policy analysts may choose to generate their own data through primary research, including surveys, opinion polls, experimental research, longitudinal studies, and so forth. Although this method can yield a rich body of information, time and cost constraints may prove an impossible obstacle. Moreover, the same research may already exist in other places, in which case the replication of the effort would be unwarranted.

Second, governmental or agency records are often useful sources for relevant data. These can include archival material; memos; meeting minutes; policy manuals; and departmental records. A surprising amount of online information is available on government or agency websites.

A third avenue for policy research is the records and published minutes of legislative bodies and committees. On the federal level these sources include the *Congressional Record* and the minutes of the various House and Senate committees and subcommittees. All state legislatures have similar record-keeping procedures, and most of these records are available in regional or university libraries or online.

A fourth source of information is governmental publications. For example, the U.S. Government Printing Office maintains catalogues of all government documents published. Other documents include the Census Bureau's population studies; publications of the Departments of Labor, Commerce, Housing, and Health and Human Services; and the *Green Book* of the House Committee on Ways and

Means, a publication containing comprehensive information on social programs and participants.

A fifth source of policy-relevant information includes think tanks, advocacy organizations, and professional associations. All think tanks employ research staff who evaluate and analyze social policies. Examples of these include the Brookings Institution, the American Enterprise Institute, the Heritage Foundation, the Hoover Institute, the Urban Institute, the Center on Budget and Policy Priorities, the Reason Foundation, the Hudson Institute, the Progressive Policy Institute, and the Economic Policy Institute. Again, much of this information can be accessed through the Internet. Because most think tanks are affiliated with particular political or economic ideologies their data and policy recommendations should be viewed critically.

Many national advocacy organizations retain research staff and publish reports that are helpful to the policy analyst. Some of these organizations include the Urban League, the National Association for the Advancement of Colored People (NAACP), the Children's Defense Fund, the National Farm Organization, and the National Organization for Women. Many professional associations, such as the American Medical Association, the American Public Welfare Association, the National Association of Social Workers (NASW), and the American Psychological Association, also publish policy-relevant information.

A sixth data source is professional journals, books, and monographs. Articles or books on specific policy topics can be found in various places, including the *Social Science Index*, Google Scholar and the subject headings in library catalogues. Commercial electronic databases such as Lexis/Nexis and Westlaw are also useful. Last, policy-relevant information can be derived from interviews with principals in the policy process, advocates, recipients of services, and government officials. Personal interviews may also help gauge public opinion and assess the opposition or support for a particular policy. Taken together, these sources can be a gold mine for the student and the seasoned policy analyst.

Social Policy Research and the Internet

The Internet has made the job of the policy analyst immeasurably easier, more efficient, and even more fun. Policy analysts no longer have to wait months before their library receives the report they are seeking; no longer must they contend with lost, misplaced, or checked-out documents, or wade through library stacks filled with feet of government reports. Instead, analysts can now directly download the newest government data, legislative reports, and governmental bills. The researcher is also helped by major university libraries, which are making the full texts of articles available online. Plus, virtually all major newspapers and news services are now online.

Recruiting subjects and collecting data online for research requiring quantitative data collection has several advantages:

- Posting messages on e-mail lists or other online media (e.g., social network sites) to recruit and interview subjects is more efficient and less costly than traditional forms of data collection such as mailing questionnaires or using field researchers.
- Data obtained online do not require transcription, which lowers research costs.
- Subjects living anywhere in the world can respond to questionnaires at their convenience.
- Principal investigators living in various parts of the country or the world can quickly and conveniently communicate with each other to clarify aspects of the research, provide feedback, and share reactions to the findings.[8]
- Survey Monkey and other online web-based programs make surveys far easier to conduct than traditional mailed surveys.
- Qualitative research can even be done online using Skype, Face Time, Tango, Viber, or other video teleconferencing programs.

There are also disadvantages to online data collection. First, there is a danger that convenience and cost will drive sampling methods, resulting in a biased sample. Second, the pool of people available to the researcher is limited to those who possess (or have access to) and understand the technology.

Conclusion

The choice of a policy analysis framework depends on several factors, including (1) the kind of problem or policy that is being analyzed; (2) the resources available to the analyst, such as time, money, staff, facilities, and the availability of data; (3) the needs of the decision maker requesting the analysis; and (4) the time frame within which the analysis must be completed.

Because it is impossible to evaluate all of the data (data are essentially infinite) and to ask all of the possible questions, no policy analysis is ever complete. Policy analysis is always an approximation of the ideal, and therefore decisions are inevitably made on the basis of incomplete information. How incomplete the information is and how close an approximation to a rational decision is offered to decision makers will depend on the skills of the analyst, the available resources, and the time allotted for the project.

Despite its reliance on an analytic framework, social policy analysis is largely subjective. Because a policy is analyzed by human beings, it is always done through the lens of the analyst's value system, ideological beliefs, and their particular understanding of the goals and purposes of social welfare. Subjectivity may be evident in the omission of facts or questions or in the relative weight given to one variable over another. Other forms of subjectivity include asking the wrong questions about the policy, evaluating it on the basis of expectations that it cannot meet, or expecting it to tackle a problem the policy was not designed to remedy. Finally, political pressure can be put on the policy analyst to come up with recommendations that are acceptable to a certain interest group. Regardless of the causes of subjectivity, policy analysis always approximates the ideal and always involves an informed hunch as to the effects of a policy or a set of policies.

DISCUSSION QUESTIONS

1. What are the main advantages of using an analytic framework for social policy analysis?
   Describe the benefits of using such a framework. What, if any, are the potential drawbacks?
2. Although the *unintended* consequences of a social policy are obviously unpredictable, what can a policy analyst do to minimize the risk? Describe a social policy that has produced unintended consequences that were either positive or harmful.
3. Can a policy researcher neutralize his or her personal values when conducting a policy analysis? If so, describe ways in which this can be done.
4. What components should be added to the proposed policy framework presented in this chapter? Which of the components provided in this framework are the most important, and why?
5. Are most social policies analyzed rationally? If not, why not? Describe the factors that stand in the way of a systematic and rational analysis of social policy in the U.S. context. How much value do decision makers place on social policy research? Why?

6. Because any analysis of social policy is by nature incomplete, should decision makers minimize policy studies? What alternatives, if any, can be used in lieu of a thorough and systematic policy analysis?
7. The Brookings Institution (www.brookings.edu) and the Cato Institute (www.cato.org) are two influential policy research think tanks that often take different views on specific social problems. Access these websites and compare the materials provided by each think tank on a research topic of your choice. How would you describe the different frameworks through which the problem is approached? Which would you access first when looking for new information? Why?

NOTES

1. Thanks to Brene Brown for her ideas on environmental scanning. Dr. Brown has repeatedly pointed out that environmental scanning is a concept that successful agencies must adopt.
2. Adam Gopnik, "The Caging of America: Why do we lock up so many people?" *The New Yorker*, January 30, 2012, pp. 20–28
3. International Centre for Prison Studies, World Prison Brief, 2011. Retrieved February 2012 from, http://www.prisonstudies.org/info/worldbrief/wpb_country.php?country=190
4. Drug War Facts, Prison and Prison Offenders, 2011. Retrieved February 2012 from, http://www.drugwarfacts.org/cms/Prisons_and_Drugs#Federal-State.
5. Adam Gopnik, "The Caging of America: Why do we lock up so many people?" *The New Yorker*, January 30, 2012, pp. 20–28.
6. BBC News, "Q&A: Mexico's Drug-Related Violence," January 25, 2012. Retrieved February 2012 from, http://www.bbc.co.uk/news/world-latin-america-10681249
7. Many social policy writers have developed excellent policy frameworks, among them Elizabeth Huttman, *Introduction to Social Policy* (New York: McGraw-Hill, 1981); Neil Gilbert and Harry Specht, *Dimensions of Social Welfare Policy,* 2nd ed. (Englewood Cliffs, NJ: Prentice Hall, 1986); Gail Marker, "Guidelines for Analysis of a Social Welfare Program," in John E. Tropman et al. (eds.), *Strategic Perspectives on Social Policy* (New York: Pergamon Press, 1976); David Gil, *Unraveling Social Policy* (Boston: Shenkman, 1981); and Charles Prigmore and Charles Atherton, *Social Welfare Policy* (New York: D.C. Heath, 1979).
8. Richard Lakeman, "Using the Internet for Data Collection in Nursing Research," *Computers in Nursing* 15, no. 5 (1997), pp. 269–275.

CHAPTER 3

Religion and Social Welfare Policy

Howard Jacob Karger and Peter A. Kindle

Source: Christy Thompson/Shutterstock

Every week, more than 300,000 congregations, mosques, temples, and ashrams meet to conduct religious services across the United States.[1] Over 80 percent of the American population report a religious affiliation, over 90 percent report a personal belief in the existence of a supreme being, and more than $295 billion was donated to churches and charities in 2006.[2] Not only are the American people the most religious Western democracy in the world, the variety of religious expression in this country is unequaled.

There are more Jews practicing their faith in the United States than there are in Israel. By some estimates, there are more Muslim adherents in the United States than there are in Kuwait, Oman, Qatar, Lebanon, or the United Arab Emirates.[3] In the year 2000, there were almost 1,200 congregations practicing the Bahai faith, over 1,600 Buddhist worship centers, and over 600 Hindu temples.[4] To one accustomed to the variety of religious expressions and practices that are part of contemporary America, it may be difficult to recognize that this diversity has not always been the case.

While we understand and appreciate the important contributions made by the world's religions to U.S. social policy, the vast majority of this chapter will focus on Christianity. This is not because we are Christocentric—on the contrary. However, U.S. social welfare history has been more strongly influenced by Christianity than by any other world religion. In order to understand how religion has influenced the development of social welfare policy, it is necessary to understand the major historical trends that have shaped religion in the United States. As such, this chapter examines the religious roots of the welfare state, and how changes in religious thought have been reflected in social welfare policies.

Religious Antecedents of Welfare Statism

The roots of social welfare go deep into the soil of Judeo-Christian tradition. It was the disfavored son Cain who repudiated his responsibility to his brother with the defensive, "am I my brother's keeper?"[5] Societal structures in ancient Judaism encoded protections for the most powerless (e.g., the poor, the orphan, and the widow). The poor were allowed to glean the remains and corners of the fields at harvest time, and to avoid the destitution of widowhood, brothers-in-law were commanded to marry their brother's widow and to raise her children as his own.[6]

Christian traditions build on Jewish foundations. Jesus himself is said to value the "cup of cold water" given in faith, and early gatherings of Christians were reputedly communitarian in that they appear to have shared material provision for daily living in an egalitarian fashion.[7] "No one claimed that any of his possessions was his own, but they shared everything they had."[8] In fact, there are interpreters of religious history that attribute the survival of Jewish and Christian sects during the first and second centuries to this communitarian impulse.

There are other traditions of compassion that could be related to the development of welfare statism, but the dominance of Judeo-Christian influence is without peer in Western societies. For instance, the dominance of Christian tradition in Europe, and the identification of church with state government during the medieval period, led to the gradual assumption of government responsibility for social welfare.

Church, State, and Social Welfare in Colonial America

Most settlers in colonial America were poor; however, unlike their European ancestors, they were not destitute.[9] According to Robert Morris, less than 1 percent of American colonists received help from outside sources.[10] The new frontier provided ample opportunity for work.

European Protestants valued work. Martin Luther viewed work as a responsibility to God. Furthermore, work conferred dignity and was a "calling" by God. In Luther's view, a person served God by doing the work of his vocation. Therefore, those who are able-bodied and yet unemployed are sinners. John Calvin took Luther's argument one step further by claiming that work carried out the will of God and, as such, would ultimately help to create God's kingdom on earth. According to both Luther and Calvin, God-fearing people must work regardless of their wage or type of employment.[11] God commanded work, America provided opportunity, and economic success became a sign of divine favor. This Protestant ethic (Roman Catholics were less than 2 percent of the population in 1776) fueled the creation of a work-oriented society and provided a religious foundation for the condemnation of the poor.[12] If prosperity was a sign of God's favor, then poverty was a sign of God's displeasure. When assistance was required, it was provided on a case-by-case basis in town meetings. When the number of cases increased as a result of indentured servants and abandoned children, the English system of overseers was introduced. It was not uncommon for the town council to auction off the poor to neighboring farmers, apprentice out children, place the poor in private homes at public expense, or send them to privately operated almshouses. Settlers believed that children should be part of a family unit, and thus the practice of indenture became widespread.[13] It was inconceivable until the mid-1800s that there could be any federal responsibility for social welfare.

The Second Great Awakening

The nineteenth century opened (1800–1830) with a period of unusually intense religious fervor termed the Second Great Awakening. The religiosity sparked by the Second Great Awakening contributed to the general spirit of reform.[14] The Puritans' vision of America as "a city set on a hill" was renewed across the nation: America's destiny was to be a pure and holy nation.

Church attendance doubled in comparison to the revolutionary era,[15] but the organizational structure of most denominations was still quite rudimentary. Similar to today, those denominations with the most adherents in 1776 were in serious decline, and the more evangelistic denominations were on the rise. In 1776, Congregationalists, Episcopalians, and Presbyterians made up 55.1 percent of religious adherents; by 1850 these denominations represented only 19.1 percent. The Baptists and Methodists, who made up 19 percent of adherents in 1776, had grown to 55 percent by 1850. Catholics, who encompassed less than 2 percent of the population in 1776—in spite of western expansion into Texas and French Catholic lands to the Mississippi River—remained a modest minority of 14 percent in 1850.[16] Voluntary associations were formed to promote causes the existing denominational structures could not support. For example, the American Board for Foreign Missions (1810), the American Tract Society (1814), the American Bible Society (1816), and the American Sunday School Union (1824) were organized.[17] However, this kind of religious fervor was not contained solely within the churches and religious endeavors, but was also channeled into moral and social reform.

From his pulpit at Hanover Street Congregational Church in Boston, Lyman Beecher (1775–1863) railed against moral license. Largely due to his efforts, the Connecticut Society for the Reformation of Morals (1823) and later the American Temperance Union (1836) were formed.[18] Casual and heavy drinking of alcohol that had been the American custom since the time of the first colonists came under attack. Abstinence from all strong drink became the new moral standard, if not the actual practice, of the average American citizen. It would be more than a century before the temperance movement would culminate in the 18th Amendment prohibiting the manufacturing, transportation, or sale of alcoholic beverages.[19]

The tone was set for future clashes between church and state by the New England Sabbatarian campaign (1828–1832). Although ultimately unsuccessful, the clergy-led campaign to end mail delivery on Sunday did "recruit moral reformers and give them their political baptism.[20] "They raised funds, held rallies, published tracts, signed petitions, and failed. . . ."[21] This experience was to prove invaluable for abolitionists that followed, and according to James A. Morone, established a new institutional symbiosis between private organizations and the public bureaucracy that was instrumental in melding local and national interests in this geographically dispersed nation.[22] Perhaps no reform movement shows more clearly the intricate interweaving of religion and politics than the abolition movement. While the former editor of a small Baptist temperance journal, William Lloyd Garrison (1805–1879), thundered against the evils of slavery in his *Public Liberator and Journal of the Times* (in press from 1831 to 1843), Charles G. Finney (1792–1875) led religious revivals throughout the northern states that led converts to support the abolition movement. Many, if not the majority, of these converts were women who stepped forward with Garrison's support to take an active role in the leadership of the movement.[23] Even though there was little sympathy for the abolitionists in the southern states, the religious fervor of the Second Great Awakening had its influence. The Cane Ridge camp meeting in Kentucky (1801) is often cited as the beginning of the awakening, and its influence was felt in both Tennessee and Ohio.[24] The Baptists and Methodists were quick to adopt the revival patterns that fueled their rapid growth. For the first time, conversion efforts were directed toward the slave population of the South with considerable success. Sydney Ahlstrom notes that "the evangelization of the slaves was prosecuted with increased vigor" as though it was a direct response to northern abolitionists.[25] Three products of the Second Great Awakening had a lasting influence on what was to become social welfare policy. First, the religious impulse for reform was channeled into private organizations attempting to effect public change. Second, a cadre of female leaders were mobilized and trained. Third, an African American clergy began to form to lead the African American converts. Even though the egalitarianism associated with the religious revival had produced tumult, social welfare reform proceeded at a slower pace.

The Civil War Era

Those denominations with national constituencies split over the slavery issue prior to the beginning of the Civil War. In 1845, the Methodists and Baptists divided into autonomous northern and southern denominations. The Presbyterians followed in 1857. Those denominations without national membership (e.g., Congregationalists, Unitarians, and Universalists), those whose congregational polity had yet to produce denominational structures (e.g., Jews and Disciples of Christ), and those who were withdrawn or isolated from public life (e.g., Latter Day Saints and Mennonites) did not separate into distinct denominations. Lutherans, Episcopalians, and Catholics did not take a denominational stand on slavery prior to the outbreak of war in 1860. They did not split into distinct national churches until there were two separate nations—the United States and the Confederate States of America.[26]

During the course of the Civil War (1861–1865), the evangelistic fervor of the Second Great Awakening was rekindled. Soldiers on both sides of the conflict required assistance, and the existing churches and private organizations were generous in meeting these needs. In the North, the Christian Commission raised more than $3 million in cash and millions more in supplies and services, and recruited over 5,000 volunteers to assist Northern soldiers. The work of the Southern churches is less well documented, but the religious support was no less fervent. Linus P. Brockett wrote in his 1864 book, *The Philanthropic Results of the War in America*, "neither in ancient nor modern times has there been so vast an outpouring of a nation's wealth for the care, the comfort, and the physical

and moral welfare of those who have fought the nation's battles or been the sufferers from its condition of war."[27] This philanthropic impulse was to continue to influence America's early social welfare for some time.

For example, Dorothea Dix, a Sunday school teacher, led a campaign to reform the care of the mentally ill. She was successful in lobbying for state actions but became convinced that federal assistance was needed due to the large expenditures required. In 1854, both houses of Congress passed a bill to assist the mentally ill. It was vetoed by President Franklin Pierce with these words, "If Congress has the power to make provisions for the indigent insane . . . it has the same power for the indigent who are not insane. . . . I cannot find any authority in the Constitution for making the Federal Government the great almoner of public charity throughout the United States."[28] Federal responsibility for social welfare was to develop slowly and gradually.

However, the Civil War ushered in a new period for relief activities. Families who had lost a breadwinner or who had a breadwinner return from the war permanently disabled could not be blamed for their misfortunes. As a response to this hardship, localities passed laws that raised funds for the sick and needy and, in some instances, for the founding of homes for disabled soldiers. Another concern was the increasing numbers of freed slaves, and freedman relief societies with religious ties were organized in most northern cities during the first year of the war.[29] Other welfare issues during the Civil War included the disease and filth rampant in army camps and hospitals and the shortage of trained medical personnel. In an effort to remedy this situation, in 1861 Unitarian minister Henry W. Bellows and a group of citizens (mainly women) organized the U.S. Sanitary Commission, the first important national public health group. Functioning as a quasi-governmental body, the commission was financed and directed by the private voluntary sector. Working initially in the area of preventive health education, the commission eventually became involved in serving the needs of soldiers.[30] Another social welfare institution that emerged from the Civil War was the Freedmen's Bureau. By the close of the war, political leaders realized that the emancipation of millions of slaves would create serious social problems. Former slaves having no occupational training, land, or jobs would require assistance. In 1865, following the earlier example of local freedman's relief societies, Congress established the

Bureau of Refugees, Freedmen, and Abandoned Lands. The Freedmen's Bureau, as it was commonly called, was responsible for directing a program of temporary relief for the duration of the war and one year afterward. After a bitter struggle, Congress extended the Freedmen's Bureau for an additional six years.

Under General Oliver Howard, the bureau performed a variety of services designed to help African Americans make the transition from slavery to freedom. For example, the bureau served as an emergency relief center that distributed 22 million rations to needy Southerners. The bureau also functioned as an African American employment agency, a settlement agency, a health center that employed doctors and operated hospitals, an educational agency that encouraged the funding of African American colleges and provided financial aid, and finally, as a legal agency that maintained courts in which civil and criminal cases involving African Americans were heard. The Freedmen's Bureau set an important precedent for federal involvement in a variety of human services. In 1872, the bureau was dissolved by Congress.[31] Northern denominations continued the work, sponsoring thousands of educational missionaries to teach in African American schools, and founding Lincoln University in Pennsylvania, Morehouse College and Atlanta University in Georgia, Talladega College in Alabama, Tougaloo University in Mississippi, Hampton Institute in Virginia, and Fisk University in Tennessee.[32]

The Late Nineteenth and Early Twentieth Centuries

Although immigration increased the size of the Catholic denomination until it was the largest in America by 1890, the Protestant hegemony over America was unchallenged. Protestant discrimination contributed to Catholic and Jewish sectarianism. Parochial schools, Catholic versions of professional organizations and semiprofessional guilds, and even a Catholic alternative to fraternal lodges, "created a parallel society within which [Catholics] were protected from Protestant insults as well as from Protestant influences."[33] Jewish sectarianism was no less isolated from the Protestant mainstream. As late as 1866, white American Protestant denominations were capable of forming into a single ecumenical association called the Evangelical Alliance to assert "the claim that Protestantism

was the only true religion of the republic."[34] This alliance was short-lived but provided the development of a Protestant confidence in large-scale organizations and affirmed the "optimism about realizing God's kingdom in this world."[35] Other—social, philosophical, and theological—in the late nineteenth century would cause this optimism to crumble.

Immigration and industrialization made significant impacts on Protestant optimism. Prior to industrialization, most people lived in small, rural communities with an array of institutions that afforded a high degree of self-sufficiency. Chief among these institutions were the local churches. Survival necessitated a degree of solidarity, or interdependence, and the local churches were an apt institution to fill this need. From 1890 to 1920, 22 million immigrants came to the United States. At the same time, the American people became more urban. Seventy-five percent of foreign immigrants lived in the cities and, during the decade following 1920, 6 million people moved from farms to cities.[36] Community solidarity was no longer the norm. Millions of the new immigrants were Catholic, and tens of thousands were Jewish. Numerical increases alone threatened Protestant hegemony.

Philosophically, many people looked to the developing social sciences for guidance in redefining social policy. There, prominent scholars drew lessons from the natural sciences that could be used for purposes of social engineering. Borrowing from biology, some American proponents of the new science of sociology applied the idea of natural selection to social affairs.

Social Darwinism was a bastard outgrowth of Charles Darwin's theory of evolution as described in his 1859 classic, *The Origin of Species*.[37] Social theorists such as Herbert Spencer and America's William Graham Sumner reasoned that if Darwin's laws of evolution determined the origin and development of species, then they might also be applied to understanding the laws of society.[38] Applying Darwin's rules to society and then adapting laissez-faire principles of economics to sociology led to a problematic set of assumptions. First, if the "survival of the fittest" (a term coined by Spencer) was a law governing the lower species, then it must also govern the higher species. Because subsidizing the poor allowed them to survive, this circumvented the law of nature, and because the poor reproduced more rapidly than the middle classes, society was thus subsidizing its own demise. Social Darwinists believed essentially that the poor would eventually overrun society and bring down the general level of civilization.

Conservative, evangelical theologians asserted that poverty was related to improvidence: People were poor because they engaged in drinking, slothfulness, licentious behavior, and gambling. An opposition movement known as the Social Gospel emerged. Composed of theologians concerned with the abuses created by industrialization and the excesses of capitalism, Social Gospelists believed that the church should recapture the militant spirit of Christ by taking on the issues of social justice and poverty. The critique posed by the Social Gospelists called for fair play and simple justice for the worker.[39] Lack of unanimity led to lack of a coordinated Protestant response to human need. By 1920, evangelical Protestants had discontinued most social relief work, at least in part, as a means of distinguishing themselves from the more public and liberal theology of the mainline Protestants.[40]

Meanwhile Catholic charities developed to serve the immigrant poor in the North. Jewish social services expanded nationwide to provide assistance to Jewish eastern European and Russian immigrants.[41] In the South, no comparable institutional relief was afforded the freedman who would remain marginalized until the latter half of the twentieth century.

The Rise of Social Work as a Profession

Religion and social welfare in nineteenth-century America were inextricably linked. Almost all forms of relief emanated from church groups, and all major denominations had some mechanism for providing social welfare, at least until the early twentieth century.[42] For example, as early as 1880 there were 500 private, church-related social welfare organizations in New York City alone, with the largest network of social services provided by Protestant churches. Christian charity suffused the Charity Organization Societies (COSs) and Settlement Houses that assumed a major share of the responsibility for urban social welfare during the late nineteenth century.

It was thought that in order to reclaim providence, the poor must be taught to live a moral and self-disciplined life. Although early religious social workers clung tenaciously to their desire to teach

the moral life, they also understood the need to provide material assistance.[43] On balance, the early social worker was often more concerned with spiritual guidance than material aid.

The relief assistance provided by these religious social workers was often linked to harsh criteria. For example, it was not uncommon for social workers to appraise the worth of the family's possessions and then instruct them to sell off everything in order to qualify for relief. Nor was it uncommon for social workers to deny relief because they felt that the poor family was intemperate and insufficiently contrite. Although social workers dispensed relief, they were basically opposed to the concept of it. In effect, they believed that distributing relief was imprudent because a reliance on charity weakens the moral fabric of the poor and provide a disincentive for work.

Urban Needs during Industrialization

Life in late nineteenth-century America was hard. The dream of milk and honey that motivated many immigrants to leave their homelands became, for many, a nightmare. The streets of American cities were overcrowded, rampant with disease and crime, and economically destitute. Many tenement houses in the larger cities had no windows or indoor plumbing. Tuberculosis was widespread, and among some groups, infant mortality ran as high as 50 percent. Scant medical care existed for the poor; there was no public education; and insanity and prostitution rates among immigrants were high.[44] Industrial and economic prospects were equally bleak. Factory conditions were deplorable: Workers were expected to labor six or seven days a week (often on Sunday), and 18-hour days were not uncommon, especially in summer.[45] Factories were poorly lit and unsanitary, easily turned into fire traps, and offered almost no job security. Moreover, homework (taking piecework home, usually for assembly by whole families in one- or two-room tenements) was common. Women were forced to work night shifts and then take care of their homes and children by day.[46] No special protective legislation for women existed until the early 1900s, and child labor was legal.

Charity Organization Societies

First evident in the 1870s, Charity Organization Societies (COSs) had offices in most American cities by 1900.[47] With the exception of meager state-sponsored indoor and outdoor relief, the COS movement was the major provider of care to the destitute. COSs varied in their structures and methods. In general, they coordinated relief giving by operating community-wide registration bureaus, providing direct relief, and "educating" both the upper and lower classes as to their mutual obligations.

The work of the COSs was carried out by a committee of volunteers and agency representatives who examined "cases" of needy applicants and decided on a course of action. The agent of the COS was the "friendly visitor," whose task was to conduct an investigation of the circumstances surrounding the cases and to instruct the poor in ways of better managing their lives. Friendly visitors, drawn from the upper classes, often held a morally superior attitude toward their clientele, and their intervention in the lives of the poor was interpreted by some observers as a form of social control as well as a means of providing assistance.[48] In any case, the charity provided by these organizations was often less than generous. Leaders of the movement drew an important lesson from Social Darwinism and the Protestant work ethic in believing that beneficent charity was counterproductive because it contributed to sloth and dependency. Josephine Shaw Lowell, president of the New York Charity Organization Society, believed that charity should be dispensed "only when starvation was imminent."[49]

One of the best-known settlement houses, Hull House was established by Jane Addams in 1889.

Source: AP Wide World Photos

Settlement Houses

Begun in the 1880s, the settlement house movement had emerged in most of the big cities over the next two decades. Settlement houses were primarily set up in immigrant neighborhoods by wealthy people, college students, unattached women, teachers, doctors, and lawyers, who themselves moved into the slums as residents. Rather than simply engaging in friendly visiting, the upper- and middle-class settlement leaders tried to bridge class differences and to develop a less patronizing form of charity. Rather than coordinating the existing charities like the COS movement, they sought to help the people in the neighborhoods to organize themselves.

Jane Addams established Hull House in 1889 (Spotlight box 3.1). She approached the project and the Chicago ethnic community in which it was based with a sense of Christian Socialism that

was derived from a "rather strenuous moral purgation"[50] rather than a sense of *noblesse oblige*. By 1915, this altruism was shared by enough settlement workers so that more than 300 settlements had been established, and most large American cities boasted at least one or more settlement houses.[51] Even though the larger settlements provided individual services to the poor, they were essentially reform oriented. These reforms were achieved not only by organizing the poor to press for change but also by using interest groups formed by elite citizens, as well as by the formation of national alliances. Settlement-pioneered reforms included tuberculosis prevention, the establishment of well-baby clinics, the implementation of housing codes, the construction of outdoor playgrounds, and the enactment of child labor and industrial safety legislation. Settlements also promoted some of the first studies of the urban black in America, such as W. E. B. Du Bois's *The Philadelphia Negro*.

The Social Casework Agency

It was during the "Progressive Era" (1890s to the beginning of World War I) that the social casework agency emerged. COSs and settlement houses served as models for the delivery of social welfare services. Both were of modest size in terms of staff, both were located in the communities of the clientele they served, both served a predominantly poor population, both relied on contributions from a variety of sources for private donations, and both contained religious undercurrents.[52] Typically, workers in these agencies were female volunteers. COS techniques for investigation were refined, with their aim being the identification of a "social diagnosis" as the basis for case intervention.[53] Subsequently, these activities, along with the community-oriented work of the settlement reformers, gave birth to the profession of social work.

As predominant service delivery forms, COSs and settlement houses were shaped by two influences: the need for scientifically based techniques and the socialization of charity. Together, these contributed to the emergence of the social casework agency. COSs and settlement houses had provided meaningful activity for upper- and middle-class women who found it necessary to ground their work in techniques derived from science. This necessity had been driven home in 1915 during the National Conference of Charities and Correction, when Abraham Flexner, a renowned authority on medical education, was asked to address the question of whether social work was a profession. Much to the disappointment of the audience, Flexner stated that social work lacked many of the basic requirements of a profession, particularly a scientifically derived knowledge base that was transmittable.[54]

The Progressive Movement

A reaction to the heartlessness that characterized a large segment of American society came in the form of the Progressive movement. Progressive Era philosophy injected a measure of public credibility and Christian morality into social, political, and economic affairs, which resulted in a unique blend of social reform encompassing anti–big business attitudes, a belief that government should regulate the public good, a strong emphasis on ethics in business and personal life, a commitment to social justice, a concern for the "common man," and a strong sense of paternalism. Progressives believed that the state had a responsibility to protect the interests of the vulnerable public. Supported by the nation's most respected social workers, including Jane Addams, Lillian Wald, and Paul U. Kellogg, the Progressive Party presented a presidential ticket in 1912. The advent of World War I diminished the liberal fervor that had characterized the Progressive Era of the late 1800s and early 1900s. In the wake of the disillusionment that followed the war, the mood of the country became conservative. Progressive ideas were treated skeptically by the 1920s, and activists were often accused of being communists.

Prohibition and the Twenties

On January 16, 1920, the 18th Amendment went into effect, and Prohibition became the law of the land. This single event, the culmination of religious and moral reforms that had begun more than a century before, signaled the high point of Protestant dominance in the United States, but this was to be short-lived.

Theologically, mainline Protestantism had evolved to embrace the findings of the natural

Spotlight 3.1

JANE ADDAMS AND HULL HOUSE

In 1889, Jane Addams established Hull House to serve residents of the Chicago community in which she lived. To learn more about Jane Addams and Hull House, go to www.uic.edu/jaddams/hull/urbanexp. Using historical photos and narrative, this website presents a comprehensive overview of Hull House and its surrounding neighborhoods.

sciences and the new social sciences in preference to biblical and historical traditions. Hence, the Protestantism of the 1920s held little resemblance to its nineteenth century predecessor. Postwar patriotism was bolstered by economic prosperity—despite the one-third of Americans living in poverty—leading to the uncritical conclusion that capitalism and the Protestant work ethic had divine favor.[55] Although the Social Gospel had waned, it continued in the larger urban congregations that were most proximate to those living in urban poverty and in the voices of social conscience best personified by Reinhold Niebuhr of Union Theological Seminary in New York.[56]

The prosperous twenties abruptly ended in late 1929 as stock market values crashed. Within four years, over a quarter of Americans were unemployed, Prohibition had been repealed, and Franklin D. Roosevelt was elected president.

The Great Depression and New Deal

The Great Depression called for emergency measures, and Roosevelt's New Deal programs were the response. Social and policy changes took place with blinding speed as the federal government became "the great almoner of public charity."[57] Billions were spent on relief efforts to provide food, clothing, and shelter. Public works projects employed as many as 3.2 million a month by 1938. A minimum wage, a maximum work week, collective bargaining, and the abolishment of child labor were enacted in 1937. The apogee of the New Deal was the Social Security Act of 1935 that included a national old-age retirement system; federal grants to states for maternal, child, and disabled welfare services; and a federal-state unemployment system.[58]

Protestant churchmen could not keep pace, and even the liberal mainline churches tended to withdraw into a quiescent spirituality. At best, the mainline waged an ineffective post hoc critique of the New Deal, while the conservative and evangelical groups became more isolated and sectarian. In contrast to the Protestant denominations, the Roman Catholic Church strongly supported the New Deal because its social teaching was largely unaffected by Social Darwinism. Pius XI's encyclical *On the Reconstruction of the Social Order* (1931) advanced Pope Leo XIII's ideas expressed in *On Capital and Labor* (1891), which promoted labor over capital, supported labor unions and minimum wage legislation, and positioned the Catholic Church

as a champion of the poor.[59] Unfortunately, the denominational support for labor and the poor was not replicated within the Protestant establishment.

Social workers and others with tenancy experience in a settlement house stepped to the forefront to provide the moral leadership previously provided by religion. Edith Abbott, president of the National Conference of Social Welfare and Dean of the University of Chicago School of Social Service Administration, participated in drafting the Social Security Act. Both Frances Perkins (the first Secretary of Labor) and Harry Hopkins (credited as the primary architect of the New Deal) were identified as social workers. The National Association for the Advancement of Colored People (NAACP) and the National Urban League also included key social workers in their early formation.[60]

The Reawakening of a Religious Social Conscience and the Great Society

The liberal, moral leadership provided during the New Deal yielded the framework for the modern social welfare state. Income disparities were mitigated, and federal responsibility for social welfare was well established. Despite this progress, irreligious liberal thinkers recognized the disadvantages reason held in comparison with the conservatives' appeal to traditional faith. None attempted to face this disadvantage with more honesty than John Dewey in *A Common Faith* (1934) and *Liberalism and Social Action* (1935). His attempt to dislodge the "impulses of generosity and self-sacrifice, of humility and communal solidarity" from religious roots proved unsuccessful.[61] Liberal social action grinded to a halt following World War II until it was re-energized by a prophetic religious voice.

On December 1, 1955, Rosa Parks refused to give up her seat to a white man on a Montgomery, Alabama, city bus. Female coworkers at the local NAACP office and some local students distributed bus boycott leaflets to Montgomery's African American clergy that very day. Martin Luther King Jr. was elected president of the hastily organized Montgomery Improvement Association.[62] A prophet had been found.

Rejecting liberal, white leadership and, in most cases, counsel, King led a nonviolent activist movement confronting discrimination and segregation that was opposed by white southerners and his own African American denomination. Northern, white liberal churchmen offered weak support.[63] Recent scholarship has challenged the typical classification of this movement as mere civil protest:

> Participants often recalled the movement years as a heady, life-transforming era touched with divine significance. . . . Such testimony suggests that it may be misleading to view the civil rights movement as a social and political event that had religious overtones. . . . To take the testimony of intense religious transformation seriously is to consider the civil rights movement as part of the historical tradition of religious revivals.[64]

Lyndon B. Johnson, who became president following John F. Kennedy's assassination in 1963, tapped into the religious and moral ideals sparked by King and the sacrifices made in the name of desegregation. He declared a "War on Poverty" in his State of the Union address on January 8, 1964.[65] Over 1,000 pieces of legislation were passed as part of Johnson's Great Society including the Civil Rights Act in 1964 and the Voting Rights Act in 1965.[66] White churchmen continued to lag behind the waves of social change, and social workers were among those who stepped forward to lead. For example, the Secretary of Health, Education, and Welfare, Wilbur Cohen, played a major role in the passage of the Medicare and Medicaid Acts of 1965, only two of his 65 innovations in social welfare policy.[67] Even though the Vietnam War was to prove a fatal distraction, Johnson's War on Poverty and Great Society had some success. By 1969 the number of Americans living below the poverty line had fallen by more than half.[68] Much of that drop, however, could be attributed to the Social Security cost of living adjustments rather than the success of the anti-poverty programs.

The Continuing Decline of Mainline Influence

White religious leadership, in comparison to the courage and conviction of the African American churches, proved to be distracted by internal issues or radical irrelevancy. Roman Catholics were preoccupied with Vatican II (1962–1965). This reform movement, led by Pope John XXIII, ended the last vestiges of isolation and parochialism for American Catholics.

In 1950, twenty-nine Protestant and Orthodox denominations had reorganized the mainline into the National Council of Churches, largely because the delivery of social services—formerly within the domain of religions—had now become the responsibility of

government after the New Deal. The new focus was on ecumenism. The Methodist Church and Evangelical United Brethren became the United Methodists in 1968. The Civil War breach between Presbyterian groups ended with the Presbyterian Church in the United States of America in 1984, and several Lutheran bodies created the Evangelical Lutheran Church in America in 1988.[69] Despite claims to the contrary, the National Council of Churches never represented a majority of religious adherents in the country, and the embrace of liberation theologies did little to maintain public influence or lay support. Developed in the class struggles and economic disparities of Latin America, "liberation theology employs a Marxist-style class analysis, which divides the culture between oppressors and oppressed. . . . But unlike Marxism, liberation theology turns to the Christian faith for bringing about liberation."[70] The goal is the radical transformation of society. James Cone applied the insights of liberation theology to the African American struggle for civil rights in his *Black Theology of Liberation* (1970), and Mary Daly did the same for women in her *Beyond God the Father* (1973).

The influence of liberation theology on mainline thought was evident as early as 1964 when the National Council of Churches criticized Great Society reforms as inadequate.[71] President Richard M. Nixon took office in 1968 and became an unlikely champion of the mainline goal—a guaranteed annual income as a fundamental right of citizenship. National Council of Churches' support quickly turned to opposition when Nixon refused to triple the proposed benefit level.[72] Nixon's Family Assistance Plan was ultimately to fail in the Senate. Former President Jimmy Carter (1976–1980) was to court mainline support for his own watered-down version that also failed.[73] Mainline church influence has yet to recover. Martin Marty, a leading church historian, has written that "everybody knows that when the mainline churches take a position, it is only six people in a room on Riverside Drive."[74] Riverside Drive is the local address of the National Council offices in New York, and, hyperbole aside, political events since the presidential election in 1980 indicate that there is some truth in Marty's observation.

The New Christian Right

In 1965, the late Jerry Falwell, senior minister at Thomas Road Baptist Church in Lynchburg, Virginia, preached that "believing the Bible as I do,

Jerry Falwell founded the Moral Majority, a political action group that supports prayer and the teaching of creationism in public schools and opposes abortion, the Equal Rights Amendment, and gay and lesbian rights.

Source: AP Wide World Photos

I would find it impossible to stop preaching the pure saving gospel of Jesus Christ and begin doing anything else—including fighting Communism, or participating in Civil Rights reforms."[75] By 1979 he had changed his mind and founded the Moral Majority, a political action group committed to overturning the secular trends Falwell interpreted as moral deterioration. The Moral Majority was for prayer and the teaching of creationism in public schools but was opposed to abortion, feminist issues such as the Equal Rights Amendment, homosexual rights, and even peace talks with the Soviet Union.[76]

Falwell had picked an opportune time to organize the Moral Majority. The two largest conservative evangelical denominations, Southern Baptists and Missouri-Synod Lutherans, had largely remained aloof from the fundamentalist controversy in the 1920s, but each had recently begun internal struggles over the challenges of theological liberalism. Each rejected liberalism in favor of a traditional

conservative theology.[77] Lay support for theological conservatism was easily converted into sympathy for Falwell's political agenda.

Beginning with Ronald Reagan's elections in 1980 and 1984 through the election of George H. W. Bush in 1988, and again in George W. Bush's elections in 2000 and 2004, the Christian Right has been quick to claim credit for each victory. Even though a consensus has yet to develop among religious scholars, preliminary studies seem to indicate that the influence of the Christian Right on social policy and politics is not so simply determined. Analyses of the National Election Studies indicate that with the exception of conservative and evangelical support in 1976 for the Southern Baptist candidate, Jimmy Carter, there has been no significant change in the voting patterns of white, conservative Protestants. This group comprised 20 percent of the Democratic voters in 1972 and 18 percent in 1996, and it comprised 27 percent and 30 percent of Republican voters in 1972 and 1996, respectively. In comparison, the largest change was noted among white, mainline Protestants who were 45 percent of the Republican voters in 1972 but fell significantly to only 33 percent of the Republicans in 1996.[78] Other studies support a more limited political orientation, especially during congregational activities, for white conservative Protestants.[79] If the Christian Right has influenced national elections since 1980, it has not been by changing the pattern of voting among white conservative evangelicals.

Since the 2006 midterm elections, commentators on religion and politics have often heralded the decline of the Christian Right.[80] In general, it is clear that America's tolerance for extreme religious voices has its limits. John McCain, the Republican candidate for the 2008 presidential election, rejected the endorsement of televangelists John Hagee and Rod Parsley,[81] and Barack Obama, the Democratic candidate, resigned from his two-decade-long church membership over comments made by his former pastor, Jeremiah Wright.[82]

The other movement that is shaping conservative Christianity is the prosperity gospel, which is based on the belief idea that God rewards the faithful with health and wealth. It teaches that financial blessing—i.e., material wealth—is the will of God for Christians, and this is realized through faith, positive speech, and donations to Christian ministries. The message to followers is that the road to future prosperity begins with sowing a "faith seed" through donations to the ministry.[83]

Emerging from early twentieth-century revival meetings, the prosperity gospel grew in popularity with the rise of television preachers in the 1980s (despite the revelation that many were using donations to support a lavish lifestyle). The gospel spread among large and small churches, and the through the ministries of televangelists such as Creflo Dollar, Joyce Meyer, Paul Couch, and T.D. Jakes. Many mainstream Christian leaders condemn the prosperity gospel as bad theology.[84]

Perhaps a greater threat to the political influence of the Christian Right is developing from within the ranks of conservative evangelical leaders, especially the younger generation of megachurch leaders, many who have begun to question their close association with the Republican Party and the reduction of religious values to issues of personal morality, such as opposition to abortion and gay marriage.[85] This growing concern among conservative evangelicals ranks with poverty, war, environmentalism, and the harsh economic consequences often associated with globalization reflect a Catholic-like interpretation of biblical themes that extend to economic, environmental and social justice issues. The extent to which issues of justice may trump issues of personal morality has yet to be determined in national elections.

Religion and Social Policy

A University of Michigan study found that the United States is one of the most highly religious countries in the industrialized world. Roughly 46 percent of American adults claim to attend church at least once a week compared with 14 percent in Great Britain, 8 percent in France, 7 percent in Sweden, and 4 percent in Japan.[86] In terms of religious adherence, the United States is closer to developing nations such as India, Brazil, and Lebanon than to other western nations.[87] Of the 27 states in the European Union, only Denmark (Church of Denmark), Greece (Church of Greece), Malta (Roman Catholic Church), and England in the United Kingdom (Church of England) have state religions. Except for Malta, religion plays a far lesser role in politics in these countries than the United States.

Religion also impacts politics, and Americans are comfortable with public displays of faith. In fact, despite the constitutional barrier between church and state, the vast majority of Americans want their leaders to be religious. A poll conducted by the Pew Forum on Religion and Public Life found that 72 percent of Americans agreed with the statement that "the president should have strong religious beliefs."[88] In contrast, a UK study by the Richard Dawkins Foundation for Reason and Science posed the statement that: "Religion should be a private matter and should not have special influence on public policy." Seventy-four percent of the respondents (who recorded or would have recorded themselves as Christian in the 2011 UK Census) strongly agreed or tended to agree with that statement.[89]

By the end of former president Bill Clinton's first term, many liberals were disillusioned because the important policy successes of the Clinton administration were tinged with conservatism. For example, the Personal Responsibility and Work Opportunity Reconciliation Act of 1996 (PRWORA) capped public assistance benefits, replaced Aid to Families with Dependent Children (AFDC) with Temporary Assistance for Needy Families (TANF), and eliminated recipients' entitlement to public assistance. Equally important, Section 104 of the PRWORA contained the Charitable Choice provision:

> The purpose of this section is to allow States to contract with religious organizations, or to allow religious organizations to accept certificates, vouchers, or other forms of disbursement . . . on the same basis as any other non-governmental provider without impairing the religious character of such organizations, and with diminishing the religious freedom of beneficiaries of assistance funded under such program. [Section 104(b)]

Former president George W. Bush was a strong advocate of Charitable Choice. In his second week in office, Bush established the White House Office of Faith-Based and Community Initiatives with units in the Departments of Labor, Justice, Housing and Urban Development, and Education, and Health and Human Services.[90] Executive orders later expanded faith-based involvement to the Department of Agriculture and the U.S. Agency for International Development.[91] Federal funding became available for faith-based organizations (FBOs) through state channels.[92] Federal-level FBO funding is available through TANF, the Emergency Food and Shelter Program, the Emergency Shelter Grant program, and the Community Development Block Grant program. Educational funding is more problematic due to a long history of Supreme Court limitations on tax support for private schools.[93] Michigan, Ohio, and Texas have been most aggressive in facilitating funding for FBOs, but the research indicates that most of this funding is directed to older, established nonprofit agencies with religious roots (e.g., Catholic Charities, Catholic Social Services, Jewish Family Services, Lutheran Social Services, Salvation Army, and Young Women's Christian Association).[94] Congregations of all denominations have been reluctant to pursue Charitable Choice funding. Even though more than half of all congregations provide some type of social service, primarily emergency food and shelter, only 3 percent receive public funds.[95]

Marvin Olasky was among the first to advocate for faith-based provision of social services.[96] His rationale was clear: "holistic service delivery that focuses on personal transformation and provides long-term, lasting solutions to poor people's problems are best provided in a faith context."[97] Besides, churches were awash in well-intentioned volunteers. The problem is that neither of these assumptions is correct. The National Congregations Study indicates that congregation-based social services are advanced by the smallest handful of volunteers, and that these services are overwhelmingly dispensed at arm's length. "If congregations' social services are imagined to be more effective than secular social services because they are more holistic, neither quantitative nor qualitative evidence supports the idea."[98] In fact, quantitative studies suggest that that FBOs may underperform in comparison to public agencies.[99] Charitable Choice will likely remain a permanent part of the federal provision of social services, but it is unlikely that FBOs have the capacity and commitment to sustain comprehensive and long-term services on a level comparable to federal and state bureaucracies.

Conclusion

Despite some positive signs, the tension between religion and social and public policy continues to dominate American political life in areas of women's health, the environment, education and science. These issues came to a head in 2011 and 2012 as Republican presidential contenders Rick Santorum, Rick Perry, Newt Gingrich, and Michelle Bachman vied for Tea Party support by trying to outdo each other in terms of their conservatism. As such, they agreed that environmental concerns were based on "junk science." Santorum stated that the notion of global warming is not climate science but "political science." He went on to state that those who believe that man should protect the earth are wrong. Instead, "We're not here to serve the earth. That is not the objective, man is the objective."[100]

One of the most potent areas for religious intervention involves women's health, including abortion, contraception, administering the human papilloma virus (HPV) vaccine (i.e., it prevents genital infections associated with increased risk of cervical cancer, thought to be caused by multiple sexual partners), and even prenatal amniocentesis testing that Santorum maintained was a means of "culling out" disabled children in America.[101]

The election of rightwing Tea Party candidates in state governments spurred on the culture wars surrounding women's health. One of the foremost targets was the right to abortion. To end abortions, some state legislatures passed "personhood" laws. The Virginia bill stated that life begins when sperm fertilizes an egg, and an unborn child at any stage of development had all the rights, privileges, and immunities available to all citizens of the state. Most personhood bills offered no exceptions in the case of a pregnancy resulting from rape or incest. Strictly interpreted, personhood bills would outlaw some forms of contraception, such as the "morning after pill," since they terminate a pregnancy after fertilization. Doctors who perform in vitro fertilization procedures would risk prosecution, and stem cell research would be prohibited.[102]

The Virginia legislature briefly entertained another GOP-sponsored bill that would have required women to undergo a physically invasive transvaginal ultrasound procedure before having an abortion. The final bill was modified to require a less-invasive pre-abortion abdominal ultrasound. Thus, Virginia became the eighth state, including North Dakota and Texas, to enact a mandatory ultrasound law. Texas began enforcing some of the most strident anti-abortion laws in the country by requiring women seeking abortions to hear their doctors describe the development of a fetus while viewing a sonogram. They were then required to wait 24 hours before undergoing an abortion. Other states, such as Georgia, are considering prohibiting abortions after 20 weeks (the current legal limit is 26 weeks) on the spurious grounds that by then the fetus has the neural pathways necessary to experience pain. Rick Santorum went so far as to advocate the right of states to ban contraception.[103]

The legalization of gay marriage and the military's rescinded "don't ask, don't tell" rule are also important issues for the religious right. These conservatives believe in creationism (i.e., intelligent design) rather than an evolutionary theory thought to be incomplete or pseudo-scientific. Religious conservatives fear that teaching evolution promotes an atheistic worldview.

In addition to the traditional lightning rod issues, some religious conservatives have declared war on the separation of church and state. These conservatives—including radio commentator Rush Limbaugh—maintain that the Constitution does not require the separation of church and state. In the process, they disavow Thomas Jefferson, who coined the phrase "separation of church and state." These and other issues continue to drive and divide much of American social policy.

DISCUSSION QUESTIONS

1. How has the Protestant work ethic affected U.S. social welfare policy? Is there any recent evidence that suggests that this theological perspective has a continuing influence today?
2. There is a division of American Protestantism into mainline and evangelical camps. Describe the form of social welfare each camp is most likely to promote.
3. Religion has had an important role in the development of professional social work. Does religion continue to have a significant influence on social work policies, values, and practice? If so, how is that manifested?
4. How would social welfare policy change if the theological movements of the Protestant mainline (the Social Gospel and liberation theology) were the dominant influences?
5. Are Charitable Choice and faith-based initiatives likely to solve U.S. social welfare problems? Why?

NOTES

1. American Religion Data Archive. Retrieved November 2004, from www.thearda.com
2. "U.S. Charitable Giving Reaches $285.02 Billion in 2006." Retrieved from the Planned Giving Design Center website at www.pgdc.com/pgdc/news-story/2007/06/26/u-s-charitable-giving-reaches-295-02-billion-2006
3. Authors' conclusion based on comparison of Allied Media Corp. demographic information (at www. allied-media. com) with population statistics reported in the *CIA World Factbook* (at https://www.cia.gov/library/publications/the-world-factbook/index.html).
4. American Religion Data Archive. Retrieved November 2004, from www.thearda.com
5. Genesis 4:7 (New International Version).
6. Gary V. Smith, "Poor, Orphan, Widow," in *Holman Bible Dictionary* (Nashville, TN: Holman Bible Publishers, 1991), pp. 1124–1125.
7. Matthew 10:41 (New International Version).
8. Acts of the Apostles 4:32 (New International Version).
9. David Rothman and Sheila Rothman (eds.), *On Their Own: The Poor in Modern America* (Reading, MA: Addison-Wesley, 1972).
10. Robert Morris, *Rethinking Social Welfare* (New York: Ketev Press, 1972), p. 143.
11. David Macarov, *The Design of Social Welfare* (New York: Holt, Rinehart and Winston, 1978).
12. Roger Finke and Rodney Stark, *The Churching of America. 1776–1990: Winners and Losers in Our Religious Economy* (New Brunswick, NJ: Rutgers University Press, 1992).
13. Nathan Edward Cohen, *Social Work in the American Tradition* (New York: Holt, Rinehart and Winston, 1958), pp. 23–24.
14. Peter W. Williams, *American's Religions: From Their Origins to the Twenty-First Century* (Urbana, IL: University of Illinois Press, 2002), pp. 181–190.
15. Finke and Stark, *The Churching of America*, p. 16.
16. Ibid., p. 55.
17. Sydney E. Ahlstrom, *A Religious History of the American People* (New Haven, CT: Yale University Press, 1972), pp. 423–425.
18. Ibid., p. 426.
19. James Morone, *Hellfire Nation* (New York: Knopf, 2001), pp. 311–317.
20. Ibid., p. 189.
21. Ibid., p. 25.
22. Ibid., pp. 186–189.
23. Ibid., pp. 159–168.
24. Ahlstrom, *A Religious History*, pp. 432–435.
25. Ibid., p. 659.
26. Ibid., pp. 659–668.
27. Quoted in Ahlstrom, *A Religious History*, p. 681.
28. Quoted in Walter Trattner, *From Poor Law to Welfare State* (New York: Free Press, 1974), p. 62.
29. Ahlstrom, *A Religious History*, p. 680.
30. Trattner, *From Poor Law to Welfare State*, p. 63.
31. Ibid., p. 87.
32. Ahlstrom, *A Religious History*, pp. 694–695.
33. Finke and Stark, *The Churching of America*, p. 139.
34. Thuesen, "The Logic of Mainline Churches," p. 35.
35. Ibid., p. 35.
36. June Axinn and Herman Levin, *Social Welfare* (New York: Dodd, Mead, 1975), p. 129.
37. Charles Darwin, *On the Origin of Species by Means of Natural Selection* (London: John Murray, 1859).

38. See Herbert Spencer, *An Autobiography,* 2 vols. (New York: D. Appleton, 1904); William Graham Sumner, *Social Darwinism* (Englewood Cliffs, NJ: Prentice Hall, 1963); and Richard Hofstadter, *Social Darwinism in American Thought* (Boston: Beacon Press, 1959).

39. Charles Howard Hopkins, *The Rise of the Social Gospel in American Protestantism, 1865–1915* (New Haven, CT: Yale University Press, 1940).

40. George M. Marsden, *Fundamentalism and American Culture: The Shaping of Twentieth Century Evangelicalism, 1870–1925* (New York: Oxford University Press, 1980).

41. Robert Morris and Michael Freund (eds.), *Trends and Issues in Jewish Social Welfare in the United States, 1899–1952* (Philadelphia: The Jewish Publication Society of America, 1966), p. 15.

42. Macarov, *The Design of Social Welfare.*

43. Roy Lubove, *The Professional Altruist: The Emergence of Social Work as a Career, 1880–1930* (New York: Atheneum Books, 1975).

44. Robert Bremner, *From the Depths: The Discovery of Poverty in the United States* (New York: New York University Press, 1956).

45. David Montgomery, *Workers' Control in America* (Cambridge, UK: Cambridge University Press, 1979).

46. Ibid.

47. Lubove, *The Professional Altruist,* pp. 1–21.

48. Ibid., p. 14.

49. Axinn and Levin, *Social Welfare,* p. 100.

50. Hofstadter, *The Age of Reform,* p. 211.

51. Ibid., p. 92.

52. H. L. Weissman, "Settlements and Community Centers," *Encyclopedia of Social Work,* 18th ed. (Silver Spring, MD: NASW Press, 1987), p. 21.

53. Mary Richmond, *Social Diagnosis* (New York: Russell Sage Foundation, 1917).

54. Maryann Syers, "Abraham Flexner," *Encyclopedia of Social Work,* 18th ed. (Silver Spring, MD: NASW Press, 1987), p. 923.

55. Clark Chambers, *Seedtime of Reform* (Ann Arbor, MI: University of Michigan Press, 1967), p. 211.

56. Ahlstrom, *A Religious History,* pp. 939–943.

57. President Franklin Pierce quoted in Trattner, *From Poor Law to Welfare State,* p. 62.

58. Cohen, *Social Work in the American Tradition,* p. 169.

59. Chester Gillis, *Roman Catholicism in America* (New York: Columbia University Press, 1999), p. 72.

60. Biographical information from *Encyclopedia of Social Work,* 18th ed.

61. David L. Chappell, *A Stone of Hope: Prophetic Religion and the Death of Jim Crow* (Chapel Hill, NC: University of North Carolina Press, 2004), pp. 12–18.

62. Allitt, *Religion in America since 1945,* pp. 47–48.

63. Chappell, *A Stone of Hope,* pp. 26–43.

64. Ibid., p. 87.

65. Michael B. Katz, *The Undeserving Poor: From the War on Poverty to the War on Welfare* (New York: Pantheon Books, 1989), p. 80.

66. New York Public Library, *American History Desk Reference,* pp. 112–113.

67. Charles Schottland, "Wilbur Joseph Cohen: Some Recollections," *Social Work* 32, no. 5 (September/October 1987), pp. 371–372.

68. Katz, *The Undeserving Poor,* pp. 113–114.

69. Williams, *America's Religions,* pp. 352–356.

70. See Gustavo Gutierrez, *A Theology of Liberatio* (Maryknoll, NY: Orbis, 1973). Quoted in D. D. Webster, "Liberation Theology," *Evangelical Dictionary of Theology* (Grand Rapids, MI: Baker Book House, 1984), p. 636.

71. Brian Steensland, "The Hydra and the Swords," in Robert Wuthnow and John H. Evans (eds.), *The Quiet Hand of God: Faith-Based Activism and the Public Role of Mainline Protestantism* (Berkeley, CA: University of California Press), p. 214.

72. Ibid., pp. 215–217.

73. Ibid., pp. 217–218.

74. Quoted in Finke and Stark, *The Churching of America,* p. 224.

75. Quoted in Allitt, *Religion in America since 1945,* p. 151.

76. "Moral Majority," *The Columbia Encyclopedia.* Retrieved November 2004, from www.bartleby.com/65/e-/E-MoralMajo.html

77. Finke and Stark, *The Churching of America,* pp. 187–198.

78. Jeff Manza and Clem Brooks, "The Changing Political Fortunes of Mainline Protestants," in Robert Wuthnow and John H. Evans (eds.), *The Quiet Hand of God: Faith-Based Activism and the Public Role of Mainline Protestantism* (Berkeley, CA: University of California Press), pp. 163–167.

79. Mark Chaves, *Congregations in America* (Cambridge, MA: Harvard University Press, 2004), pp. 94–126.

80. For examples, see Dionne, *Souled Out;* Amy Sulivan, *The Party Faithful: How and Why Democrats Are Closing the God Gap* (New York: Scribner, 2008); Jim Wallis, *The Great Awakening: Reviving Faith and Politics in a Post-Religious Right America* (New York: HarperCollins, 2008); and Christine Wicker, *The Fall of the Evangelical Nation: The Surprising Crisis Inside the Church* (New York: HarperCollins, 2008).

81. Neela Banerjee and Michael Luo, "McCain Cuts Ties to Pastors Whose Talks Drew Fire," *New York Times* (May 23, 2008).

82. Michael Powell, "Following Months of Criticism, Obama Quits His Church," *New York Times* (June 1, 2008).

83. Religious Link, "Is the 'Prosperity Gospel' Prospering?," 2012. Retrieved February 2012 from http://www.religion-link.com/tip_060227.php.

84. Ibid.

85. David D. Kirkpatrick, "The Evangelical Crackup," *New York Times* (October 7, 2007).

86. Ram A. Cnaan and Stephanie C. Boddie, "Charitable Choice and Faith-Based Welfare: A Call for Social Work," *Social Work* 47, no. 3 (July 2002), p. 225.

87. Lisa M. Montiel, "The Use of Public Funds for Delivery of Faith-Based Human Services." The Roundtable on

Religion and Social Welfare Policy, 2003, p. 18. Retrieved December 2004, from www. religionandsocialpolicy.org

88. Diane Swanbrow, U.S. One of the Most Religious Countries, The University Record Online, University of Michigan, November 24, 2003. Retrieved September 2012 from, http://www.ur.umich.edu/0304/Nov24_03/15.shtml.

89. Charles Blow, Why Is America So Religious? The New York Times, September 29, 2008, B5.

90. Richard Allen Greene, "Religion and Politics in America," BBC News, September 15, 2004. Retrieved September 2012 from, http://news.bbc.co.uk/2/hi/americas/3658172.stm.

91. Richard Dawkins Foundation for Reason and Science (UK), Religious and Social Attitudes of UK Christians in 2011, Topline results, February 15, 2012. Retrieved September 2012 from, http://c3414097.r97.cf0.rackcdn.com/IpsosMORI_RDFRS-UK_Survey_Topline_15-02-2012.pdf.

92. Mark Ragan, Lisa M. Montiel, and David J. Wright, "Scanning the Policy Environment for Faith-Based Social Services in the United States." The Roundtable on Religion and Social Welfare Policy, 2003, p. 18. Retrieved December 2004, from www.religionandsocialpolicy.org

93. Montiel, "The Use of Public Funds," pp. 4–11.

94. Ibid., p. 13.

95. Chaves, Congregations in America, p. 66.

96. Marvin Olasky, The Tragedy of American Compassion (Washington, DC: Regnery Gateway, 1992).

97. Chaves, Congregations in America, p. 58.

98. Ibid., p. 65.

99. S. S. Kennedy and W. Bielefeld, Charitable Choice at Work: Evaluating Faith-Based Job Programs in the States (Washington, DC: Georgetown University Press, 2006).

100. Huffington Post, "Alice Stewart, Rick Santorum Aide, Explains Offensive Obama Gaffe," February 20, 2012. Retrieved February 2012 from http://www.huffingtonpost.com/2012/02/20/alice-stewart-rick-santorum-obama-_n_1289335.html?ref=politics

101. Newsmax, "Santorum: Obamacare Prenatal Testing Will Cull Ranks of Disabled," February 22, 2010. Retrieved February 2012 from, http://www.newsmax.com/Politics/santorum-prenatal-testing-obamacare/2012/02/22/id/430137

102. Don Reed, "Republicans With Power: Virginia Personhood Laws a Preview of GOP Presidency? The Huffington Post, February 16, 2012. Retrieved February 2012 from, http://www.huffingtonpost.com/don-c-reed/republicans-with-power-vi_b_1282644.html

103. Ibid and Christina Wilkie, "GOP Candidates Reveal How They Would Enact Pro-Life 'Personhood' Laws," The Huffington Post, December 28, 2011. Retrieved February 2011 from, http://www.huffingtonpost.com/2011/12/28/gop-candidates-personhood_n_1172082.html

CHAPTER 4

Discrimination in American Society

Source: CORBIS – NY

Discrimination occurs in virtually all countries, and spans the spectrum from moderate to severe. Forms of discrimination include (1) religious, (2) gender, (3) sexual orientation, (4) national origin, culture or tribal; (5) racial (including "colorism" based on the skin tones), (6) class and caste, (7) political, and (8) personal characteristics such as disability, age, and appearance.

Discrimination and poverty are inextricably linked to the fabric of American social welfare. Economic, social, and political discrimination often leads to poverty, which in turn, results in the need for income maintenance and other social programs. Realizing that discrimination leads to poverty, some policymakers have tried to address this cycle by attacking discrimination. These policymakers hope that if discriminatory practices and attitudes are curtailed, the result will be equal opportunities for achievement and success. This chapter probes discrimination based on race, gender, sexual orientation, disability, and age.

Discrimination

The causes of discrimination in U.S. society are complex. The main theories reflected in the literature fall into three broad categories: psychological, normative-cultural, and economic.

Psychological interpretations attempt to explain discrimination in terms of intrapsychic variables.[1] For example, a theory called the frustration-aggression hypothesis, formulated by J. Dollard, maintains that discrimination is a form of aggression activated when individual needs become frustrated.[2] Dollard argues that when people cannot direct their aggression at the real sources of their rage, they seek a substitute target. Thus, relatively weak minority groups become an easy and safe target for the aggression and frustration of slightly stronger discontented groups. For example, poor Southern whites have been viewed as an outwardly racist group. Exploited by the rigid economic and social class system of the old South, they often focused their rage on African Americans, a group even weaker than themselves. African Americans therefore served a twin purpose for poor whites: On the one hand, they formed a lower socioeconomic group, making poor whites feel better about their own standing; on the other, they were scapegoats for the frustrations of poor whites. Women, racial minorities, homosexuals, and other disenfranchised groups often serve the same purpose for those on a slightly higher social rung.

The normative–cultural explanation suggests that individuals hold prejudicial attitudes because of their socialization. Through overt and covert messages, a society teaches discrimination and rewards those who conform to prevailing attitudes and behaviors. Because of strong societal pressures to conform to established norms, resistance to discriminatory practices becomes difficult.[3] For example, special opprobrium in the old South was reserved for liberal whites who broke the norms governing interactions with African Americans.

Some discrimination is economically based. Economic discrimination occurs when a dominant group discriminates to maintain their economic and political advantages. For instance, example, male workers may discriminate against female workers because they perceive them as encroaching on their employment prospects. Employers may promote discriminatory attitudes because as long as women workers are stigmatized, they will remain a cheap labor pool. By pitting stigmatized groups (women, racial, and ethnic minorities) against each other, employers can suppress wage demands and force wage concessions by threatening to replace relatively well-paid employees with lower-paid workers from a disenfranchised group. Simply put, discrimination partly determines who will flip the burgers and supersize the drinks.

To maintain an air of legitimacy, discrimination must have moral, social, and theological underpinnings. To that end, some have used the Bible to explain the inferiority of women, the "sin" of homosexuality, and the necessity of separating the races. For example, some people maintain that menstrual cycles cause severe mood swings that make women incapable of holding positions of power. Others believe that African Americans are descended from Ham and have committed biblical sins that justify discrimination. Some people claim that African Americans are racially inferior, based on theories supported by dodgy anthropological theories supported by dubious intelligence testing.

Social stigma and discrimination can lead to the transformation of disenfranchised groups into a lower socioeconomic class. Alternatively, as in the case of gays, lesbians, and the aged, social stigma and discrimination can result in social marginalization without triggering statistically observable economic discrimination. For example, although the individual incomes of gays and lesbians (and the assets of the elderly) are higher than the national averages, people in these groups often experience economic discrimination in the form of restricted career choices, including forced occupational clustering, limited access to upper managerial positions, discrimination in hiring practices, forced retirement, and so forth. The following sections will examine some core components of discrimination and social stigma, including racism, sexism, homophobia, ageism, and discrimination against people with disabilities.

Racism

Racism refers to discrimination against and prejudicial treatment of a racially different minority group. This prejudicial treatment may take the form of differential hiring and firing practices and promotions, differential resource allocations in health care and education, a two-tier transportation system, segregated housing policies, discriminatory behavior of judicial and law enforcement agencies, and/or stereotypical and prejudicial media images. A pattern of racial discrimination that is strongly entrenched in a society is called *institutional racism.*

Demographic data often divides society along the lines of whites and people of color. However, clumping white Americans into a single category is misleading. For example, after the Civil War vast numbers of immigrants arrived from southern and central Europe who were neither Protestant nor Anglo-Saxon. In addition, while many white Americans have an Hispanic surname, they may have no Hispanic cultural memory. Those from Arabic-speaking countries may experience discrimination, even though they are classified as white.[4]

Throughout America's history, whites have been in the majority. While whites represented 69 percent of the population in the 2000 Census, by 2010, their population had declined to 64 percent. By 2050, whites will make up only 50 percent of the population with minority groups expected to account for the other half of the population. This demographic shift is mainly attributable to low birth rates and high rates of immigration.[5] The Census Bureau projects that between 2004 and 2050, Asians and Hispanics will see the most dramatic increases, as the U.S. population grows to reach 420 million.[6] A good deal of social history in the next several decades will demonstrate how the United States addresses this changing demography and whether it will result in greater equality. Regardless, major social institutions will be transformed because of this demographic shift.

The Minority Middle Class

The Census Bureau has no official definition of the middle class. Although the idea of "middle class" is central to American life, there is no official definition of what constitutes the middle class, and no reliable income figure that connotes a middle-class lifestyle. Some analysts classify households with total annual incomes between $40,000 and $140,000 as middle class.[7] Other analysts categorize middle-class families as having annual incomes between $25,000 and $75,000. Still others use annual incomes of $50,000 as a marker. However, since the cost of living differs so much depending on location (such as geographic, urban or rural), a precise definition of "middle class" is virtually impossible.

Educational gains were significant, and in 2010, over 80 percent of blacks aged 25 and over were high school graduates; close to 20 percent had a bachelor's degree or higher.[8] In 2006, over 4 million African Americans had an advanced degree.[9] There is now no significant difference in high school graduation rates between whites and blacks, and in 2009, more than 21 percent of black women and almost 18 percent of black men had earned a college degree.[10]

African Americans have made significant gains in professional employment.

Source: Yuri Arcurs/Shutterstock

from 2001, when the Census Bureau recorded the lowest poverty rate for African Americans (22.7

Some 10 percent of non-Hispanic whites were poor in 2010, a rate less than one-third of that of blacks at 27 percent. Similarly, median household income in 2010 was more than 38 percent higher for non-Hispanic whites than for blacks.[23]

Family Structure   In 2011, 28 percent of African American households were married.[24] In 2010, 41 percent of African American households headed by a single female with no husband were living below the poverty line, a statistic which reflects the difficulties of single income women raising families.[25]

African American Businesses   In 2007, Black-owned firms constituted only 7.1 percent of all business in the United States[26] While black-owned businesses grew 46 percent between 1987 and 1992, receipts in these businesses constituted only 1 percent of total U.S. business receipts in 1992. Receipts for black-owned firms averaged $52,000 per firm compared with $193,000 for all U.S. firms. Overall, the annual combined revenue of the 25 largest U.S. black-owned businesses in 2002 was only $7.8 billion.[27]

Labor Force Participation and Income   Discrimination continues in the areas of employment and wages. Although laws and regulations addressing employment racial discrimination have had some success, they have not adequately prevented widespread discrimination against African Americans.

As noted earlier, the recession that began in 2007 hit African Americans and other minorities especially hard. According to the Bureau of Labor Statistics, while white unemployment went up from 8.6 to 8.7 percent from 2009–2010, black unemployment rose from 15.6 to 16.3 percent.[28] Unemployment rates have improved in 2012, with black unemployment at 13.6 percent and white unemployment at 7.4 percent. Nevertheless, black unemployment rates are still almost twice that of whites, reflecting significant inequality in the labor force.[29]

Discrimination influences income, and not surprisingly, the more education, the greater the income gap. In 2011, white males with an advanced degree earned $733 a week in comparison to African American males at $520 a week. This $213 difference in earnings translates into a 29 percent gap (see Table 4.1).[30]

Jared Bernstein offers several explanations for the African American wage gap, including employment discrimination (aided by the lax enforcement of antidiscrimination laws); employment in vulnerable sectors of the labor economy; lower rates of overall unionization, and the general erosion of worker rights.[31] Another explanation suggests that as middle-class African Americans advance, greater unemployment occurs among those left behind. But this explanation does not address the large African American/white unemployment differential among college-educated men. According to Franklin Wilson, the cause of this discrepancy can be found in two factors: (1) the decline during the 1980s in the number of public sector jobs traditionally filled by college-educated African American men and (2) the failure of African Americans to penetrate

TABLE 4.1 Usual Weekly Earnings of Full-Time Wage and Salary Workers Aged 25 and Over 2011

	*Asian	White		African American		Hispanic	
		Men	Women	Men	Women	Men	Women
No H.S. Diploma	$284	$301	$272	$280	$246	$294	$260
H.S. Grad	$326	$390	$328	$335	$298	$341	$302
Some College or Associate Degree	$369	$438	$368	$374	$341	$377	$338
BA Degree	$502	$587	$496	$494	$451	$460	$424
BA Degree and Higher	$575	$615	$535	$502	$489	$488	$472
Advanced Degree	$679	$733	$632	$520	$590	$606	$567

*Gender division for Asian women was not available.

Source: Adapted from U.S. Bureau of Labor Statistics, "News Release: Usual Weekly Earnings of Wage and Salary Workers Fourth Quarter 2011," January 24, 2012. Retrieved Feb 2012, from *www.bls.gov/news.release/pdf/wkyeng.pdf.*

the occupations that entail managerial or supervisory responsibilities. Regardless of the causes, African Americans continue to earn less than whites, irrespective of household composition, education, region, or religion.

Crime In 2008, 2.3 million people were held in U.S. federal or state prisons or in local jails. The annual growth rate of people incarcerated in the United States between 2000 and 2006 was 2.6 percent. The lifetime likelihood of going to state or federal prison for blacks is about twice that of Hispanics and five times higher than for whites. Based on rates of first incarceration, about 32 percent of black males will enter state or federal prison during their lifetime, compared to 17 percent of Hispanic males and 5.9 percent of white males.[32] Moreover, the racial composition of the 3,297 people on death row in 2010 was 44 percent white, 41 percent black and 12 percent Latino. Given that blacks make up only about 13 percent of the U.S. population, they are overrepresented on death row by more than three times their overall number.[33]

In 2008, blacks were almost six times more likely than whites to be murdered.[34] Although the homicide rate for blacks in the United States has fallen in recent years, it remains unacceptably high. Blacks aged 20 to 24 years old have the highest homicide rates, more than seven times that of blacks aged 13 to 16 years old. The homicide rate for blacks aged 25 to 29 is the second highest and is comparable to the 20 to 24 age bracket: 1,101 compared to 1,409 respectively. Overall, the black male homicide rate in 2007 was 39.7 percent compared to 5.4 percent for white males.[35]

Housing Housing patterns reflect the economic gulf between African Americans and whites. Minority (African American, Hispanic, and Native American) households are both poorer and more likely to be renters than white households. The home ownership rate in 2007 for whites was 68 percent, for Hispanic or Latino households the rate was 50 percent, and for African American households, 47 percent.[36] As noted earlier, many of these homes were purchased under less than desirable terms and may be subject to foreclosure.

Health The effects of racism are also evident in health issues. The 2004–2006 black infant mortality rate in the United States was 13.5 per 1,000 live births, more than twice that of whites (5.7

deaths).[37] Taken by itself, the U.S. black infant mortality rate ranks high internationally (see Table 4.2). The rate of sudden infant death syndrome (SIDS) among African Americans was 113.5 deaths per 100,000 live infant births in 2001 compared to 45.6 for whites. In 2005, black men were nearly seven times more likely than white men to be diagnosed with HIV, and black women more than 20 times more than white women.[38] Not surprisingly, life expectancy is lower for African Americans. In 2006, black males had a life expectancy of 70 years compared to 76 years for whites. For African American women, the life expectancy was 76.9 years compared to 81 years for white women.[39]

A major factor affecting infant mortality is low birth weight. Although the cause is unknown, low birth weight (less than 5.5 pounds) increases the chances of infant death during the first month by 40 percent. Overall, 7.8 percent of babies were born at low birth weight in 2002; for African Americans it was 13.4 percent.[40]

Education There is currently no significant difference in high school completion rates between African American and white students (88 percent compared to 84 percent).[41] Although roughly the same proportions of black and white students graduate from high school, college completion rates significantly differ. In 2009, 51 percent of all whites aged between 18 and 21 years old were enrolled in higher education compared with 41.5 percent of all blacks. The percentage of whites aged 25 and over holding a bachelor's degree in 2009 was 30 percent compared with 19 percent for blacks.[42] As a high school diploma becomes less valuable in the marketplace, educational upgrading can help protect workers' incomes. In 2011, both blacks and whites with a bachelor's degree earned over $100 more a week in comparison to those with only a high school diploma.[43] The strong correlation between higher education and higher salaries implies that the disparity between African American and white college completion rates will have a long-term impact on the economic well-being of minorities.[44]

Welfare Dependency Welfare dependency is another indicator of racism. Although welfare dependency is decreasing for African Americans, in 2002 7.7 percent received more than 50 percent of their total annual family income from means-tested public assistance programs compared to 1.9 percent of the non-Hispanic white population.[45]

TABLE 4.2 Infant Mortality Rates and Ranks*: Selected Countries, 2012 (Deaths per 1,000 Live Births)

Rank	Country	Rate	Rank	Country	Rate
221	Japan	2.21	180	Greece	4.92
219	Singapore	2.65	179	Taiwan	5.10
218	Sweden	2.74	178	Hungary	5.24
214	Italy	3.36	174	United States	5.98
213	Spain	3.37	173	Croatia	6.06
212	France	3.37	170	Serbia	6.40
211	Finland	3.40	169	Poland	6.42
208	Germany	3.51	168	Slovakia	6.47
202	Ireland	3.81	161	Chile	7.36
200	Switzerland	4.03	152	Costa Rica	9.20
199	Israel	4.07	148	Sri Lanka	9.47
198	South Korea	4.08			
196	Denmark	4.19	144	Botswana	10.49
195	Austria	4.26	137	Panama	11.32
189	Australia	4.55	119	Malaysia	14.57
188	United Kingdom	4.56	111	China	15.62
187	Portugal	4.60	104	Mexico	16.77
184	New Zealand	4.72	96	Venezuela	20.18
183	Cuba	4.83	94	Brazil	20.50
182	Canada	4.85	90	Peru	21.50

*Ranks are on a scale from 1 to 222, with 1 being the country with the highest infant mortality rate and 222 being the country with the lowest.

Sources: Adapted from Central Intelligence Agency, The World Factbook: Country Comparison-Infant Mortality Rate (2012). Retrieved Feb 2012, from www.cia.gov/library/publications/the-world-factbook/rankorder/2091rank.html.

Hispanic Americans

In 2002, Hispanics became the nation's largest minority community.[46] By 2010, the U.S. Hispanic population totaled 50.5 million.[47] It is projected that from 2002 to 2050, the Hispanic population will increase by 188 percent to 102.6 million, or roughly one-quarter of the U.S. population. According to the 2010 U.S. Census, Hispanics accounted for 15.2 million, or more than one-half, of the total population increase of 27.3 million from 2000 to 2010.[48]

The use of the term *Hispanic* masks a rich diversity within this group. U.S. Hispanics have roots in 22 different countries; their family histo-

ries are from Mexico, Puerto Rico, Cuba and other Caribbean islands, and Central and South America as well as the United States. Latinos pump $300 billion into the U.S. economy. Despite this fact, 26.6 percent of Hispanics lived below the poverty line in 2010, compared to just 9.9 percent of non-Hispanic whites and 27.4 percent of African Americans.[49]

Because of the large number of undocumented workers coming from Central America and Mexico, the Hispanic population of the United States is difficult to accurately measure. Some estimates of the number of undocumented workers in the United States (most of them from Spanish-speaking countries) are about 12 million.

The total Hispanic population is growing rapidly and is geographically concentrated, with over 50 percent residing in three states: California, Texas, and Florida.[50]

Hispanic Poverty and Income

The poverty status of Hispanics worsened from the 1980s onward and compares to the rate of African American poverty. Although the Latino position has improved in recent years, they still are relatively poor compared to whites. In 2010, the median income for all households in the United States was $49,445, with white median household income at $51,846. For Hispanic households, it was $37,759. About 15.1 percent of the United States was classified as living below the poverty threshold in 2010, reflecting a 2.6 percent increase from 2007. Compared with non-Hispanic whites at 9.9 percent, the Hispanic poverty rate was almost triple at 26.6 percent.[51]

Diversity in the Hispanic Population

Although for statistical purposes the Hispanic population is often considered as a single group, the various Latino subgroups have distinct social and historical backgrounds. For example, Cubans living in Florida may have little in common historically or politically with Mexican Americans living in California, and Puerto Ricans living in New York may have little understanding of the culture of either Cuban Americans or Mexican Americans. These differences are also reflected in income.

Mexican Americans constitute about 67 percent (17.1 million) of all Hispanics in the United States and are the fastest-growing Spanish-speaking subgroup. In 2000, there were 20.6 million Mexican Americans in the United States; by 2010, this number had grown to 31.8 million, comprising 75 percent of the current overall Hispanic population.[52] The poverty of Mexican Americans is correlated in part to deficits in educational attainment. In 2009, 21 percent of Hispanics aged between 18 and 24 had never completed high school compared to a 91 percent completion rate for whites. In 2010, only 11 percent of Mexican Americans had earned a college degree or higher compared to 30 percent of whites. In fact, the proportion of Hispanics with a bachelor's degree or more in 2009 was much lower than for the total population (27 percent).[53]

Although average household worth fell, the Latino community's total wealth rose. The number of Hispanic businesses increased 31 percent (from around 1.2 million to 1.57 million) from 1997 to 2002.[54] Overall, the economic data clearly suggest a difficult economic picture for most Hispanic communities in the United States, especially Mexican Americans and Puerto Ricans.

American Indians

Despite the 562 federally recognized tribes (including 223 Alaskan Native groups) and 275 American Indian reservations, there is no single definition of an American Indian.[55] The Bureau of Indian Affairs (BIA) classifies someone as American Indian if they are a member of a recognized American Indian tribe and have one-fourth or more Indian blood. The Census Bureau uses self-identification. In 2010, American Indian and Alaska Natives numbered almost 3 million people or 0.9 percent of the U.S. population.[56] According to BIA estimates, about half of American Indians live on or near reservations.[57]

American Indians, in some ways the poorest group in the United States, experience oppression similar to that of other disenfranchised populations. The history of American Indians is marked by hardship, deprivation, and injustice. Before white settlement, American Indians numbered somewhere between 900,000 and 12 million.[58] This population was decimated as a result of disease, the westward expansion of white settlers and the resulting wars and genocidal policies. By 1880, the census reported only 250,000 American Indians.[59] Moreover, American Indians were not granted citizenship until 1924; New Mexico prohibited them from voting until 1940.

The social and economic problems faced by American Indians are similar to those of other at-risk minority populations (see Table 4.3). After generations as the nation's poorest and most overlooked minority, American Indians continue to suffer from what a 2003 U.S. Commission on Civil Rights report called a "quiet crisis" of discrimination, poverty, and unmet promises. Unemployment, substance abuse, and school dropout rates are among the highest in the nation, and American Indians face staggering health problems.[60] In 2004, American Indians were 770 percent more likely to die from alcoholism, 650 percent more likely to die from tuberculosis, 420 percent more likely to die

TABLE 4.3 Selected Indicators of American Indian Social and Economic Well-Being, 2003

	Native American Indian	All Races
% of single-parent households with children	45.4	31.8
H.S. dropout rate	15.5	9.0
% of those age 16–19 not in school or working	14.8	8.0
% of children in poverty	32.8	17.0
% of married couples with children in poverty	46.6	24.0
Median income	$36,549	$43,318

Source: Adapted from Willeto, A. (2006) "Native American Kids: American Indian Children's Well-Being Indicators for the Nation and Two States", *Social Indicators Research* (2007) 83:149–176.

from diabetes, 280 percent more likely to die from accidents, and 52 percent more likely to die from pneumonia or influenza than the rest of the United States, including other minority populations. As a result of high mortality rates, the life expectancy for American Indians is 71, nearly five years less than the rest of the U.S. population.[61]

American Indian tribes are sovereign nations under federal law and states may not enforce their civil codes on reservations. The Indian Gaming Regulatory Act of 1988 allowed tribes to operate gambling operations within their borders. By 2008, there were nearly 450 gaming operations run by more than 235 tribes in 28 states. In 2008, the Indian gaming industry contributed $8.5 billion in output, over 700,000 jobs, $27 billion in wages, and $10.8 billion in federal, state, and local tax revenue. Economists William Evans and Julie Topoleski found mixed results around gaming. While more young adults moved back to reservations and adult employment increased by 26 percent, most of that growth was among non-Indians. Four years after a casino opens, communities experienced a 10 percent increase in auto thefts, larceny, and violent crime, and an increase in bankruptcies. Their presence in many states diverts funds from taxable activities.[62]

Caught in the paternalistic web of the Bureau of Indian Affairs, American Indians continue to struggle to retain their identity. Having been robbed of their land, murdered indiscriminately by encroaching white settlers (as well as by the U.S. Cavalry), and treated alternately as children and pests by the federal government, for many years American Indians were further oppressed by having their children taken away by welfare officials. This widespread abuse by welfare workers, who evaluated American Indian child-rearing practices as neglectful in the context of white middle-class family values, was partially remedied by the **Indian Child Welfare Act of 1978**, which restored child-placement decisions to the individual tribes. As a result of this act, priority in placement choices for American Indian children was given to tribal members rather than white families.[63] In an attempt to remedy historical injustices, the Indian Self-Determination Act of 1975 emphasized tribal self-government, self-sufficiency, and the establishment of independent health, education, and welfare services.[64] Despite these limited gains, the plight of American Indians serves as a reminder of the mistakes made by the United States in both past and its present policies toward disenfranchised minority groups.

Asian Americans

There are more than 25 Asian-Pacific subgroups in the United States, including Chinese, Filipino, Japanese, Asian-Indian, Korean, Vietnamese, Laotian, Thai, Cambodian, Polynesian (Hawaiian, Samoan, and Tongan), Micronesian and Melanesian. By 2000, the six largest Asian population groups in the United States are: Chinese (2.7 million), Filipino (2.4 million), Japanese (1.1 million), Asian-Indian (1.9 million), Korean (1.2 million), and Vietnamese (1.2 million).[65] In 2010, the Asian population was 14.7 million,[66] and according to the 2010 Census, Asians alone were the fastest-growing race group, increasing by 43 percent between 2000 and 2010.[67] It is projected that because of above-average birthrates and accelerating legal and illegal immigration, the Asian population will more than triple to 33 million by 2050.[68]

While the social and economic data on Asians is mixed, perhaps the most striking feature is their high median family income (see Figure 4.1). Economic and social data point to a population that has made great strides, especially in the educational area. In 2010, 89 percent of Asian and Pacific Islanders were high school graduates or higher compared with 88.6 percent of whites, 84.2 percent of African Americans, and 63 percent of Hispanics.[69] While Asians made up only 3 percent of the population in 1990, they represented 12 percent of the students at Harvard University; 20 percent at Stanford; and in 2003, 45 percent at the University of California.[70] In 2010, 30 percent of all males had a college degree or higher. Of those, 31 percent were white, 18 percent were African American, 13 percent were Hispanic, and 56 percent were Asian and Pacific Islander.[71]

Impressive as these economic statistics are, they conceal several phenomena:

- most Asians live in expensive urban areas where salaries are higher than the U.S. average;
- many recent Asian immigrants work in low-wage sweatshops in urban Chinatowns;
- although many Chinese and Japanese Americans have achieved economic success, Southeast Asians are at higher risk of poverty than whites;
- Asians are underrepresented in the higher-salaried public and private career positions and their salaries tend to be lower than whites;
- and although a large number of Asian immigrants have become successful entrepreneurs and own and operate their own small businesses, for some this role was forced on them as a result of discrimination.

Asians in the United States have also experienced more subtle forms of discrimination. For example, because of their economic and educational achievements, Asians are often thought of as a "model minority." Because of this status, many Asians experience severe internal and external pressure regarding achievement and success. Some Asian Americans complain that they are discriminated against in colleges and universities because of their strong academic performance. Facing this backlash, some Asians have redoubled their efforts to become mainstream U.S. citizens—to be in the center of the society rather than on the margins as "hyphenated Americans."

Many Asians point to contributions resulting from Asian cultural values that include an emphasis on frugality, greater consideration for the feelings of others, and a balance between group and individual welfare. According to sociologist Tu Weiming, the less individualistic culture of Asians, their lower sense of self-interest, their less adversarial nature, and their less legalistic approach have valuable lessons for the United States.[72]

Immigrants and Immigration

At current rates, the U.S. Census Bureau estimates that immigration will help swell the U.S. population from 310 million in 2010 to more than 420 million in 2050.[73] It is difficult to determine exactly how many illegal immigrants are in the United States, although current estimates place the number at 11 million.[74] In 2004, Mexicans made up over half of undocumented immigrants (57 percent), with another 23 percent coming from other Latin American countries. Almost two-thirds (65 percent) of the undocumented population live in just six states: California, Texas, New York, Florida, and New Jersey. However, much of the rapid growth in the undocumented population since the mid-1990s has been outside these states.[75] In 2009, the foreign-born population of the United States was 38.5 million, equal to 12.5 percent of the U.S. population.[76] While poverty rates are higher for immigrants, they are lower than naturalized citizens (10 percent) than native-born Americans (12 percent).

The pace of economic growth in the 1990s would have been impossible without the influx of immigrants who contributed to job growth in three ways: (1) by filling an increasing share of jobs, (2) by taking jobs in labor-scarce regions, and (3) by filling the types of jobs shunned by native workers. In fact, immigrants filled four of every 10 job openings at a time when the unemployment rate hit record lows in the mid-1990s.[77]

Not only is the number of jobs filled by immigrants important, but the location and kind of jobs is also important. In earlier years, most new immigrants from Latin America and Asia clustered in a few large cities, such as Los Angeles, New York, and Chicago. However, the 1990s witnessed a spread to the western Midwest, New England, and the Mid- and South Atlantic regions. In some parts of the country, almost all labor force growth between 1996 and 2000 was due to immigration.

Because a large number of new immigrants have less than a high school education, new immigrants commonly fill low-skill, blue-collar jobs. About 33 percent of immigrants have not finished high school compared with 13 percent of natives. Many immigrants are not only lower-skilled than native workers, but their skills do not translate into the U.S. workplace. Although immigrants overwhelmingly fill blue-collar jobs, they also account for as much as half the growth in categories such as administrative support and services.[78]

Legal immigration to the United States has undergone several important changes since the mid-1980s. For one, while the number of immigrants remained relatively constant from 1985 to 1988, it rose sharply from 1988 to 1991 due to the impact of the Immigration Reform and Control Act of 1986 (IRCA) which granted legal status to undocumented immigrants who had been in the United States continuously since 1982 or had worked in agriculture. But by 1995, the total number of immigrants admitted to the United States was less than half of those admitted in 1991.[79]

Other changes have occurred in U.S. immigration since the 1950s. The most notable was the shift in immigration from Europe to Asia. In 2009, Asians represented 37 percent of persons obtaining permanent legal resident status in the United States, compared to only 9 percent of Europeans. After Asians, the next highest was from North America (33 percent), followed by Africa (11 percent), and South America (9 percent).[80] (See Figure 4.2.) In 1996, Congress passed the **Personal Responsibility and Work Opportunity Reconciliation Act (PRWORA)** which contained important implications for legal and illegal immigration (PRWORA will be discussed more fully in Chapter 11).[81] Specifically, the bill disentitled most legal immigrants (including many who had been living in the United States for years but were not citizens) from food stamps, public assistance, and Supplemental Security Income (SSI). (Illegal immigrants were never entitled to these benefits.) The only immigrants still entitled to benefits were (1) those

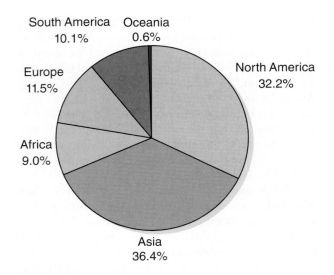

FIGURE 4.2 Immigrants by Place of origin, 2007

Sources: U.S. Department of Homeland Security, *Yearbook of Immigration Statistics: 2007,* "Persons Obtaining Legal Permanent Resident Status by Region and Country of Birth: Fiscal Years 1998 to 2007." Retrieved June 2008, from HYPERLINK "http://www.dhs.gov/xlibrary/assets/statistics/yearbook/2007/table03d.xls"

who had become citizens or who had worked in the United States and paid Social Security taxes for 10 years or more and (2) veterans of the U.S. Army who were noncitizens. In addition, states were allowed to deny Medicaid benefits to immigrants.[82] While some of the harsher provisions were later rescinded, anti-immigration sentiment remained.

In 1996, Congress revisited immigration, this time voting to double the size of the Border Patrol, stiffen penalties for document fraud and immigrant smuggling, bar illegal immigrants from qualifying for Social Security benefits or public housing, give states the right to deny illegal immigrants drivers' licenses, and increase the earnings requirements for U.S. residents wishing to sponsor foreign family members.[83]

Immigration policy changed dramatically since the World Trade Center attacks of September 11, 2001. After 9/11, three important acts were passed: (1) the USA Patriot Act, (2) the Enhanced Border Security Act, and (3) the Homeland Security Act of 2002. While these acts do not directly shape immigration policy per se, they impact it by more carefully screening and monitoring foreigners who temporarily visit (and sometimes wish to settle in) the United States. Moreover, surveillance also intensified. For instance, 9/11 and various foiled attempts at terrorist acts in the New York

Foreign students have been especially affected by stricter immigration procedures.

Source: Carlos E. Santa Maria/Shutterstock

area led the New York Police Department (NYPD) to secretly infiltrate and spy on Muslim university students in the Northeast. The NYPD defended their actions by citing convicted terrorists worldwide who had once been affiliated with Muslim student groups.[84] The question brought up by these and other tactics is just how much freedom a democratic society is willing to forego for presumed security benefits.

In April 2010, Arizona adopted the nation's toughest bill on illegal immigration into law. Its aim was to identify, prosecute and deport illegal immigrants. The law made the failure to carry immigration documents a crime and gave the police broad power to detain anyone suspected of being in the country illegally. For many, it signaled an open invitation for harassment and discrimination against Hispanics regardless of their citizenship status. In 2011, the federal government filed a Supreme Court case around the legality of a state instituting its own immigration policies.[85]

Guest Workers

From 1942 until 1964, Mexican nationals were recruited to enter the United States, primarily for agricultural work, under a treaty between Mexico and the United States. This "Bracero" program employed almost 450,000 workers at its peak in 1956,[86] with more than 4.5 million participating during the program period. The treaty provisions[87] provided significant protections for the guest worker, from standards for housing, compensation, and even the savings of a portion of earnings to be remitted once the worker returned to Mexico. However, these provisions were better known for their violation than for their enforcement.[88] Housing was clearly substandard for the migrant workers, wage guarantees were rarely implemented, and the withheld savings were distributed to only a small proportion of the workers.

The abuse of guest workers continues today. Current immigration law permits the recruitment of temporary foreign workers, and 388,000 temporary worker visas were granted in 2009. Of those, 60,000 were seasonal workers in agricultural services, and 45,000 were seasonal workers in nonagricultural services.[89]

Home country recruiters often require substantial payment for services for low-skill employment in forestry, fishery, and agriculture, areas that frequently escape federal oversight. The lack of education and English proficiency also severely limits the guest worker's ability to assert his or her legal rights. To solicit the economic contribution of foreign nationals through employment without extending the same legal protections and services available to citizen employees is discriminatory. How the country chooses to rectify the structural inequities of a guest worker program may be the most important issue facing immigration reform. The dramatic growth in immigration is a problem faced by most Western industrialized countries.

Immigration-Based Discrimination in Europe

Recent wars, repression and dislocations in Iran, Iraq, Afghanistan, Libya, Syria, Yemen, Somalia, Zimbabwe, and Sri Lanka, to name a few, have set into motion a powerful wave of immigration into developed and developing countries. This migration has created untold problems for European nations accustomed to homogenous populations.

Most forms of discrimination are characterized by social exclusion. While Western Europe prides itself on tolerance and multiculturalism, recent events challenge that perception. Post-World War II Europe experienced an economic boom that required large numbers of workers, which in turn, led to high levels of immigration. The increase in immigration was also fueled by large numbers of migrants arriving from former European colonies or territories, such as the Caribbean, Algeria, and parts of Africa. Germany adopted a guest worker program based on the belief that Turkish workers would return home once their labor was no longer needed. After several generations, many Turkish immigrants viewed Germany as their home. Similarly, large numbers of immigrants came to the United Kingdom (UK) from former colonies, including India, Pakistan, the Caribbean, South Africa, Kenya, and Hong Kong.

One of the largest immigrant groups in Europe came from Muslim countries, which resulted in a Muslim population of about 20 million, out of 500 million European Union (EU) residents. A 2008 Brookings study found that the EU countries with the largest Muslim populations are France (8 percent), Netherlands (6 percent), Germany (4 percent), and the United Kingdom (3 percent). Muslims living in the EU are more likely to be poor and live in segregated high crime neighborhoods.[90] Some analysts suggest that Muslims may self-segregate due to language and different cultural norms (i.e., prohibitions against drinking).

There are also calls—especially in the United Kingdom—for the formal institution of Sharia law in ethnic Muslim neighborhoods.[91] Parallel to the British legal system, Sharia or Muslim religious law has been operated by local Muslim councils since 1982 and is growing in use as thousands of Muslims use it to settle civil disputes, as well as family, financial and commercial problems. Plaintiffs and defendants voluntarily choose to accept the court's rulings because the courts have no legal powers and cannot impose penalties. Despite its growth, women's groups and others oppose Sharia courts because they argue that they are male-dominated and discriminate against women.[92] By 2011, the leaders of western Europe's three largest countries—Germany, France and the United Kingdom—acknowledged that multiculturalism had failed. German Chancellor Andrea Merkel was disillusioned by the slow pace of Turkish immigration; British Prime Minister David Cameron by the tolerant attitude toward extreme Islam; and France's Nicholas Sarkozy by Muslim prayer in the street. Right-wing Dutch parties had long denigrated multicultural policies.[93]

Anti-Islamic sentiment in Western Europe has been fueled by several events, including the 2004 Madrid commuter train bombings that killed 191 people and wounded 1,800. A subsequent investigation revealed these bombings were directed by an al-Qaeda-inspired terrorist cell. One year later, four coordinated terrorist suicide attacks on the London subway and bus system killed 52 people and injured more than 700. Still another event was the murder of Theo van Gogh, who had worked with Somali-born Ayaan Hirsi Ali to produce *Submission*, a controversial film criticizing the treatment of women under Islam. Shortly afterward, a Danish newspaper published cartoons depicting Muhammad, which resulted in worldwide riots and the deaths of 100 people. While supporters saw this as free speech, opponents viewed it as Islamophobic and racist. In 2007, Lars Vilk published a caricature (later reprinted by some Swedish newspapers) of a dog with the head of Mohammed. Vilk became the target of several assassination attempts based on a Fatwa (a death sentence issued by Muslim clerics) and had a bounty placed on his head.[94] The above events (and others) highlighted the cultural differences between how secular rights (i.e., free speech and freedom of the press) were viewed in the West compared to the sacred in religious Islamic thinking.

The anti-Muslim sentiment was further aggravated by the rise in honor killings within Europe's

Middle Eastern and Asian immigrant communities. Estimated at 5,000 deaths a year worldwide, honor killings typically involve the murder of a woman, usually by brothers and fathers (often with the collusion of mothers, sisters, aunts, or grandmothers), for acts perceived as dishonoring the family. These acts can include refusing an arranged marriage; having sex outside marriage; rebellious behavior (e.g., wearing Western clothes); disobeying male family members; dating someone the family disapproves of; attending the university; or even having been raped.[95,96,97]

In 2003–2004, the French government passed a law banning all clothing that indicates a student's religious affiliation from public schools. While the law was written in a religion-neutral way, its aim was to prohibit Muslim girls from wearing headscarves to class. In 2011, France took one step further by prohibiting the burqa (Muslim headgear that hides the full face) from being worn in public. (Belgium had passed a similar law in 2010, while other European countries like Germany and Italy were debating it). Apart from security reasons (i.e., not being able to identify the wearer), the argument was that the burqa undermined the minimal demands of social life, degraded women, and was an affront to equality. Opponents of the burqa ban argue that the law is unjust and violates individual liberty. Moreover, the law prevents veiled Muslim women from leaving home, thereby further isolating them. No reliable data exists as to how many Muslim women support or oppose the burqa ban.[98,99]

Still another negative reaction to the growth of Islam in Europe was expressed by Swiss voters who approved a ban on building new minarets on the top of mosques.[100]

The European Union maintains that successfully integrating immigrants is critical to maximizing their potential for development. Curbing illegal or irregular migration is tackled by targeting employers who hire undocumented workers and by seeking to set up a humane and effective return policy. The humane treatment of immigrants and the importance of human rights in the European Union are reflected in the 1997 Amsterdam Treaty. Specifically the treaty reinforces the right to non-discrimination and provides for the suspension of a member state where there is a serious breach of human rights.[101]

Women and Society

Hilary Clinton, Secretary of State in the Obama administration, shattered an important glass ceiling for women. Although former Democratic Congresswoman Geraldine Ferraro ran for vice president with Walter Mondale in 1984, her candidacy was short-lived, as Mondale lost to Ronald Reagan in a landslide election. It took another 23 years for a woman to run as a serious candidate for the U.S. presidency. In a tightly contested primary race, Hillary Clinton lost to Barack Obama, the first African American president.

Sexism denotes the discriminatory and prejudicial treatment of women based on their gender. It is also a problem U.S. society has wrestled with since the beginning of the nation. Sexism can manifest itself in a myriad of ways. For example, women may be kept out of military academies (and combat duty), private clubs, and certain sports. Occupational boundaries can keep women from operating heavy construction machinery, or being involved in skilled trades such as bricklaying. Or, women reach a glass ceiling from where they cannot rise any higher. Sexism can take political forms, like appointing or electing token women to offices or cabinet positions or creating "special appointments" to placate feminist groups.

Sexism reared its head especially high in the 2011–2012 Republican presidential primary, where candidates such as Rick Santorum, Newt Gingrich, and Mitt Romney attacked women's health in areas such as abortion, the right to amniocentesis, and even the right to birth control covered by health insurance.[102]

Violence and Sexism

Sexism can also manifest itself in crime and family violence.[103] According to a study by Patricia Tjaden and Nancy Thoennes, nearly 25 percent of surveyed women said they were raped and/or physically assaulted by a current or former spouse, cohabiting partner, or date at some time in their lifetime. Approximately five percent (1.5 million) of U.S. women are raped and/or physically assaulted annually by an intimate partner.

The U.S. medical community treats millions of intimate partner rapes and physical assaults annually. Of the estimated 4.9 million intimate partner rapes and physical assaults perpetrated against women annually, about 2 million will result in an injury to the victim, and one-half-million will result in some type of medical treatment. Most intimate partner victimizations are not reported to the police. Only one-fifth of all rapes, one-quarter of all physical assaults, and one-half of all stalkings against women by intimates are reported to the police.[104]

In 1994, Congress passed the Violence against Women Act (VAWA) which represents a comprehensive approach to domestic violence and sexual assault by combining a broad array of legal and other reforms. Specifically, the law was designed to improve the response of police, prosecutors, and judges; force sex offenders to pay restitution to their victims; and increase funding for battered women's shelters. VAWA mandates a nationwide enforcement of protection orders and provides penalties for crossing state lines to abuse a spouse or violate a protection order. It also prohibits anyone facing a restraining order for domestic abuse from possessing a firearm.[105] VAWA was funded at $412 million in 2012.[106]

The Feminization of Poverty

Sexism also has an economic face. The median amount that a full-time female worker loses in wages over a 40-year period due to the gender or "career wage gap" is $434,000, rising to $713,000 if they have a bachelor's degree or higher. Not only are women's wages lower, but one-quarter to one-third of working women also lack basic benefits. Four in ten working women work evenings, nights, or weekends on a regular basis, and one-third work shifts different than their spouses or partners. Thirty-one percent of working women have no sick leave, and 34 percent do not have access to these benefits through their employers.[107]

Because women's wages are generally lower than those of men, women more often have to resort to public welfare programs. The term *feminization of poverty* was coined by Diana Pearce in a 1978 article in *Urban and Social Change Review* in which she argued that poverty was rapidly becoming a female phenomenon as women accounted for an increasingly larger proportion of the economically disadvantaged.[108]

In 2010, 6.6 million women lived below the poverty line. The effects of poverty also impact families. Between 2009 and 2010, the poverty rate for children under the age of 18 increased from 21 to 22 percent. Of particular significance is the disparity in income between single female and single male householders who are raising families. A single female householder's median annual income is $32,031 in comparison to a single male householder at $49,718. This wage gap means that it is

more difficult for single women to support a family than it is for single men.[109]

The causes of the feminization of poverty are complex. When women are deserted or divorced, many must find jobs immediately or go on public assistance. Those who choose welfare are held in poverty by the low benefits; those who opt to work are kept in poverty by the low wages that characterize service jobs. Low-paying service employment, such as fast-food outlets and retail stores, make welfare benefits seem attractive because staying at home involves no child care costs, transportation, clothing, and lunch costs.

Women frequently enter the workforce through the service and retail trades, clerical jobs, cleaning, food preparation or service, personal service work, or auxiliary health service work. These occupations are marked by low pay, a low level of unionization, little status, meager workplace benefits, and limited prospects for job advancement. Thus, much of the increase of women in the workforce is in the "secondary labor market" (see Chapter 5), a marginal area of employment.

The economics of low-wage service work are gloomy. For instance, if a single mother with one child in day care chooses to avoid the stigma of welfare and finds work at near the minimum wage, her prospects for economic survival are bleak.[110,111] The mock budget in Table 4.4 illustrates the dilemma of a single mother who finds full-time employment at $6.00 an hour.

A 2010 USDA report found that an average middle class family spent about $12,000 on child-related expenses in their baby's first year; by age two, they spent more than $12,500 a year.[112] Hence, a single mother with two children earning $8 an hour (75 cents above the federal minimum wage) would have a gross annual income of $15,360, about $9,000 below the $24,000 a year in estimated expenses for two young children. The low minimum wage combined with inflation makes a single mother's plight even more dire. In short, neither welfare nor low-income work provides single female-headed households with viable economic choices.

Inequities in **public transfer programs** also aggravate the economic problems of low-income women. For example, Social Security and public assistance are often the only viable options for women. Although median transfers to women are lower than to men, they constitute a higher share of the recipients' total income: about one-third for female-headed households compared to one-tenth

TABLE 4.4 Monthly Budget for a Working Mother with One Child in School and One Infant in Day Care (Gross Monthly Income for a Full-Time Worker at $7.25 an hour: $1,160)

Expenses	Monthly Total
Day care for 1 child	$ 611.00[a]
Rent	$ 650.00[b]
Health care	$ 93.75[c]
Utilities	$ 60.00[c]
Food	$ 367.00[d]
Clothing	$ 62.00[a]
Transportation	$ 200.00[c]
Entertainment	$ 50.00
Sundry items (e.g., soap, cleaners, repairs, sheets, blankets, etc.)	$ 100.00[c]
Total approximate cost	$2,193.75[c]
Monthly deficit between income and budget	–$ 1087.75

a. Child care costs are calculated based on the average of the most and least expensive cities for child care according to the. Child Care Aware® of America, Press Releases Despite Weak Economy, Child Care Costs Continue to Rise, August 15, 2012, Retrieved October 2012 from, http://www.naccrra.org/newsroom/press-releases/2012/8/despite-weak-economy-child-care-costs-continue-to-rise.

b. Rent was calculated on the basis of the average of HUD—determined fair market rents for a 2-bedroom. See HUD 2012 Fair Market Rents (FMR) Effective October 1, 2011, Retrieved October 2012 from, http://www.ohiohome.org/compliance/fairmarket-rents_12.pdf

c. Calculated from the Bureau of Labor Statistics, Consumer Expenditures, September 25, 2012. Retrieved December 2012 from, http://www.bls.gov/news.release/cesan.nr0.htm

d. The amount for food is based on the maximum SNAP allocation that this mother would receive in 2012 if she had 1 child and no countable income.

for male-headed households. Moreover, Social Security is often the only source of income for elderly women. However, Social Security is riddled with pitfalls: (A) because women's wages are lower than men's, their retirement benefits are also lower; (B) homemakers are not covered on their own unless they held a job in the past; (C) widows do not qualify for benefits unless they are 60 years old or have a minor in the house; (D) divorced women are entitled to only one-half of their ex-husband's benefits, which is inadequate if it is their only source of income; and (E) because of child care responsibilities, women typically spend less time in the workforce than men, and their benefits are therefore usually lower.[113]

Myths Around Women and Work

Myths abound in attempting to explain why women consistently earn less than men:[114]

Myth 1. A working mother's wages are not necessary to her family's survival; her job is a secondary activity that usually ceases with marriage or childbirth.

Fact. Most families require two paychecks to maintain the same standard of living as their parents. Twenty percent of working mothers are heads of households; two out of three working mothers report that they cannot decrease their working hours because of economic need. According to a 2004 AFL-CIO study, three in ten working women reported making all or almost all of their families' incomes. Three in five earned half or more of their family's income.[115] The only families that realized an increase in their real incomes and living standards in the last two decades had two college-educated working parents. Three-fourths of these gains came from the longer hours women added to the labor force.[116]

Myth 2. A working mother is unreliable, because her family is her primary concern.

Fact. Although some working mothers choose the "mommy track" (flexible and/or shorter work hours), others are forced into it by a lack of affordable quality day care. Seventy-five percent of mothers return to work within a year after childbirth.

Myth 3. Large numbers of working women leave the workforce to return home to raise their children.

Fact. Statistics show an opposite trend. In 1978, mothers of infants had a labor force participation rate of 36 percent; by 2011 that number rose to 64 percent.[117] The choice to become full-time homemakers is now the exception rather than the rule (see Figure 4.3).

Myth 4. Small businesses cannot afford to provide benefits and services such as child care, maternity leave, and flextime. For large businesses, such costs decrease their international competitiveness.

In 2006, approximately 59 percent of women were in the labor force. The unemployment rate for women in 2006 was 4.6 percent. Asian women had the lowest rate (3.1 percent), with white (4 percent), Hispanic (5.9 percent), and African American women (8.4 percent) following. From 1975 to 2006, the labor force participation rate of mothers with children under age 18 rose from 47 percent to 71 percent. Mothers with older children are more likely to be working than mothers with children under 6 years old. Unmarried mothers (76 percent) have higher participation rates than married mothers (68 percent). Only 7 percent of women were engineering managers and 33 percent lawyers, but 91 percent were registered nurses and 83 percent were social workers. Hispanic and African American women are more likely than white and Asian women to work in service occupations. Women who worked full time in 2006 had median weekly earnings of $600. This was 80.8 percent of the $743 median weekly earnings of men. The average workweek for women has increased by about 2 hours since 1976.

FIGURE 4.3 Who Is in the Work Force?

Source: Bureau of Labor Statistics, *Women in the Labor Force: A Databook, 2007*

Fact.   Family assistance programs raise productivity, increase worker loyalty, decrease turnover, and curb absenteeism. The majority of employers report no change in costs owing to family leave legislation.[118] An AFL-CIO study found that 64 percent of working women reported having no control over their work hours; 79 percent lacked child care benefits.[119]

Myth 5.   Women are doing better economically and rapidly closing the wage gap.

Fact.   In 1979, women earned 64 percent of a male wage; by 1993 it was 71 percent; and by 1999, 77 percent. In 2010, the rate was the same as it was in 1999.[120]

Income and Job Disparities Between Men and Women

Some of the income disparity between men and women can be traced to **occupational segregation.** Occupations such as cashier, receptionist, and home health aides are traditional female jobs in which 75 percent or more of the workers are women. But they are also typically among the lowest paying jobs. Women have gained ground in acquiring more managerial and professional positions, but the clerical and teaching fields are still among the most heavily female occupations.

The largest category of women workers in 2006 were teachers (3.2 million, excluding those in colleges and universities), and female secretaries and administrative assistants. About half of all working women are in pink collar ghettos where 80 percent of coworkers are women. In 2006, almost 97 percent of secretaries were women, as were 90 percent of bookkeepers, 89 percent of nurses, and 84 percent of librarians. In 2006, women still made up only 2 percent of electricians; 6 percent of mechanical engineers; 12 percent of civil engineers; and 13 percent of police.[121]

The women with the highest earnings in 2006 were those employed as pharmacists, CEOs, lawyers, physicians and surgeons, and financial services salespersons. Women's wages lag behind men's even in most female-dominated professions (see Tables 4.5, 4.6, and 4.7). As Table 4.7 illustrates, overall earnings in most professions are considerably lower for females (even with the same education) than for males. There is also a significant wage gap and underemployment of women in what are perceived as traditionally male occupations. In 2010, there were only 391,000 women reported as employed in natural resources, construction, and maintenance occupations in contrast to over 9 million men. The average weekly wages for women in these occupations was $515, and for men, $740. Similar patterns can be seen in production, transportation, and repair and installation occupations, suggesting that there is a glass ceiling in male-dominated industries that women are struggling to break.[122]

Many women face extraordinary challenges in finding and securing employment at fair wages. Some of these obstacles include difficulty in finding high-quality and affordable day care, inadequate family leave policies, inflexible working conditions, poor or non-existent health insurance, and sexual harassment.

Day Care: A Barrier to Female Employment

A major barrier to female employment involves day care and subsidized child care leaves, which are a

TABLE 4.5 Median Usual Weekly Earnings of Full-Time Wage and Salary Workers By Occupation and Sex, 2011 Annual Averages

Weekly Earnings Selected Occupations	Women	Men
Management, Professional and Related Occupations	$941	$1,269
Management, Business and Financial Operations	$977	$1,370
Service Occupations	$433	$551
Sales and Office Occupations	$602	$738
Office and Administrative Support Occupations	$615	$668
Natural Resources, Construction, and Maintenance Occupations	$515	$740
Installation, Maintenance, and Repair Occupations	$751	$807
Production, Transportation and Material Moving Occupations	$485	$651
Number of Workers (in thousands) Selected Occupations	**Women**	**Men**
Management, Professional and Related Occupations	20,524	19,267
Management, Business and Financial Operations	7,386	8,676
Service Occupations	6,991	7,387
Sales and Office Occupations	13,977	9,012
Office and Administrative Support Occupations	9,908	3,787
Natural Resources, Construction, and Maintenance Occupations	391	9,574
Installation, Maintenance, and Repair Occupations	146	4,013
Production, Transportation and Material Moving Occupations	2,603	10,730

Source: Adapted from U.S. Bureau of Labor Statistics, "News Release: Usual Weekly Earnings of Wage and Salary Workers Fourth Quarter 2011," January 24, 2012. Retrieved Feb 2012, from www.bls.gov/news.release/pdf/wkyeng.pdf.

TABLE 4.6 Median Weekly Earnings, Selected Traditionally Female Occupations, 2007

Occupation	Earnings	
	Women	Men
Registered nurses	$976	$1,098
Elementary school teachers	847	938
Cashiers	344	409
General office clerks	550	584
Health aides, except nursing	373	434

Source: Based on data from U.S. Department of Labor, Bureau of Labor Statistics, Median weekly earnings of full-time wage and salary workers by detailed occupation and sex: 2007. Retrieved April 2008 from http://www.bls.gov/cps/cpsaat39.pdf.

TABLE 4.7 Annual Median Earnings of Persons by Educational Attainment and Sex, Year-Round, Full-Time Workers, 2010

Level of Education	Women	Men
9th to 12th grade (non-graduate)	$20,883	$29,435
High school graduate	$29,857	$40,055
Some college, no degree	$33,401	$46,434
Associate degree	$37,773	$50,282
Bachelor's degree or more	$51,942	$71,778

Source: U.S. Census Bureau, "Income, Poverty, and Health Insurance Coverage in the United States: 2010," September 2011. Retrieved Feb 2012, from www.census.gov/prod/2011pubs/p60-239.pdf.

necessity for most working families. The availability of day care has increased rapidly. By the early 1990s, there were three times as many child care centers as in the mid-1970s, and four times as many children were enrolled.[123] By 2007, there were 118,947 child care centers (excluding family child care homes) offering 7.65 million spaces.[124]

The average annual fee for full-time child care varies dramatically from state to state and depends on the age of a child. In some of the more expensive states like New York, the cost of yearly care for an infant was $13,437 in 2007 and $10,473 for a 4 year old. In Massachusetts, the cost was $14,591 for an infant and $10,787 for a 4 year old. In less expensive states like Mississippi, the cost for an infant was $4,542 and $3,380 for a 4 year old; in Louisiana it was $5,096 for an infant and $4,610 for a 4 year old.[125] These costs can put a severe financial strain on both single and two-parent families. As shown in Table 4.8, in 2007 a single mother in New York earning $6.00 an hour would have to spend her entire salary just to pay for day care for one child.

First instituted in the 1970s, the Title XX Social Services Block Grant program is the largest federal program for child care services. In 1990, the U.S. Congress passed additional legislation that increased the supply of child care and expanded early childhood education. Through child care, development block grants, and amendments to Title IV-A of the Social Security Act, Congress provided new funds to help families with child care costs and to help states improve the quality and supply of these services.[126]

More than 120 countries provide paid maternity leave. *The United States is the only industrialized country in the world without paid maternity leave.*[127] While the 1993 Family and Medical Leave Act (FMLA) allow for maternity leave, it is unpaid. The American child care system is two-tiered: Those with means receive first-rate child care, or they can stay at home; those without the means are dependent on the ebb and flow of funding for publicly supported day care.[128]

Other Obstacles Faced by Working Women

Many working mothers also require flexible family leave arrangements. Although 30 states had some form of parental or medical leave law on their books, no such law existed on the national level until 1993. With the election of former president Bill Clinton, the FMLA was rushed through Congress and was signed into law in 1993.

The FMLA requires public employers, and private employers with 50 or more workers, to offer job-protected family or medical leave for up to 12 weeks to qualifying employees (i.e., worked for the employer at least 1,250 hours in the previous year) who need to be absent from work for reasons covered by the law. Reasons include an employee's illness (including maternity-related), or the need to care for an ill family member. While the law does not mandate paid leave, it allows for health coverage to continue during the leave period. A worker who uses the FMLA is guaranteed the same or a comparable job upon returning to work. Many workers fail to take advantage of the FMLA because it is only unpaid leave.

Women working in traditionally female occupations (the largest share of working women) have the lowest rate of health care coverage. More than 15 million women of childbearing age in the United States have no public or private medical coverage

TABLE 4.8 States with the Most and Least Expensive Child Care Costs, 2007

Most Expensive States	4 Year Old Child
Massachusetts	$10,787
Wisconsin	10,524
New York	10,473
Colorado	9,765
Minnesota	9,350
Connecticut	9,111
Washington	8,804
Least Expensive States	
Mississippi	$3,380
Arkansas	4,475
Louisiana	4,610
South Carolina	5,460
Alabama	4,888
Missouri	4,836
West Virginia	4,560

Source: The National Association of Child Care Resource & Referral Agencies "2007 Price of Child Care". Retrieved June 2008 http://www.naccrra.org/randd/docs/2007_Price_of_Child_Care.pdf.

for maternity care, even though the average cost of having a baby is more than $5,000, which does not include the costs of prenatal visits, ultrasounds, and other lab charges. Half of all women earning $7.25 an hour or less lack health care coverage, and divorced and separated women are twice as likely to be uninsured as married women. Of the 4 million births each year in the United States, 500,000 are not covered by any health insurance plan. Moreover, basic health insurance frequently does not cover important women's health services, such as family planning, reproductive care, elective, and maternity care, and childbirth.[129] If women are to participate more fully in the labor force, comprehensive health care insurance needs to be made available to everyone.

Another issue affecting working women is sexual harassment, which is defined as unwelcome sexual behaviors, including jokes, teasing, remarks, questions, and deliberate touching; letters, telephone calls, or materials of a sexual nature; pressure for sexual favors; and sexual assault. Although sexual harassment is illegal (Title VII of the 1964 Civil Rights Act has been interpreted as prohibiting sexual harassment) it remains all too common in the workplace.[130]

The Nineteenth Amendment to the U.S. Constitution gave women the right to vote in 1920. That alone did not end their economic and social plight, and shortly after winning the vote, the Women's Party proposed the first Equal Rights Amendment (ERA) to the Constitution. In 1972, Congress passed a newly drafted ERA, finally extending the ratification deadline to 1982. Despite the endorsement of 450 organizations representing 50 million members, the ERA was defeated in 1982, just three states short of the 38 required for ratification. Despite the heated rhetoric, the ERA read as follows: "Equality of rights under the law shall not be denied or abridged by the United States or any other State on account of sex. . . . The Congress shall have the power to enforce, by appropriate legislation, the provisions of this article. . . . This amendment shall take effect two years after the date of ratification."[131]

The battle for women's rights was also fought around **comparable worth**—the idea that workers should be paid equally for different types of work, if those jobs require the same levels of skill, education, knowledge, training, responsibility, and effort. The desire to equalize incomes through comparable worth is based on the belief that the **dual labor**

TABLE 4.9 Comparable Worth and Average Annual Income, 2006

	2006 Mean Annual Income
Child care workers	$ 18,820
Teacher assistants	21,860
Nursing aides	22,960
Hairdressers and cosmetologists	24,550
Preschool teachers	25,900
Home health aides	20,100
Social and human services assistants	27,200
Fitness trainers	31,710
Auto mechanics	36,070
Truck drivers	36,320
Maintenance and repair workers	39,060
Machinists	35,810
Auto body mechanics	38,230

Source: U.S. Department of Labor, Bureau of Labor Statistics, National Occupational Employment and Wage Estimates, All Occupations, May 2006. Retrieved April 2008 from http://data.bls.gov/oes/datatype.do#oes.f.5.

market has created a situation whereby "women's work" (e.g., secretarial, teaching, social work, nursing, child care) is valued less than traditional male occupations.

An illustration of the debate around comparable worth is provided in Table 4.9 which lists average wages for jobs typically occupied by women and men. Although controversial, 20 states have passed laws making comparable worth a requirement or goal of state employment. Nevertheless, comparable worth brings up a difficult question: What criteria should determine the comparability of different jobs? Some critics have rejected the idea of comparable worth on the grounds that the economic costs would be catastrophic.

In 1963, Congress passed the Equal Pay Act, requiring employers to compensate male and female workers equally for performing the same job under the same conditions (not all jobs were covered by the bill). Another protective measure was Title VII of the Civil Rights Act of 1964 that prohibited sex discrimination in employment and provided the right of redress in the courts. In 1972, Presidential Executive Order 11375 mandated that employers practicing sex discrimination be prohibited from receiving federal contracts. Title IX of the Educational Amendments of 1972 prohibited discrimination in educational institutions receiving federal funds. Finally, the Equal Credit Act of 1975 prohibited discrimination by lending institutions on the basis of sex or marital status.

Abortion and Women's Rights

Feminists often point to the abortion issue as another area where women's rights are threatened. Pro-choice advocates argue that where abortion is concerned, some male legislators and judges have promulgated laws and regulations to control the behavior of women by denying them full reproductive freedom. They argue that the choice of an abortion is a personal matter involving a woman and her conscience. Anti-abortion forces claim that life begins at conception and that abortion is murder. Moreover, they point to the 1.21 million legal abortions performed in the United States in 2008, while at the same time pointing to the scarcity of adoptable infants.[132]

In 1973, Sarah Weddington, a young attorney from Austin, Texas, argued *Roe v. Wade* before the U.S. Supreme Court. Though her client had long since relinquished her child for adoption, Weddington argued that a state could not unduly burden a woman's right to choose an abortion by making regulations that prohibited her from carrying out that decision. The Court ruled in favor of Weddington, and abortion was legalized in the United States, thereby nullifying all state laws that made abortion illegal during the first trimester of pregnancy. (Before 1970, four states—New York, Alaska, Hawaii, and Washington—had already made abortion legal contingent upon a physician's agreement.) Within a decade after *Roe v. Wade*, almost 500 bills were introduced in Congress, most of which sought to restrict abortions through a constitutional amendment outlawing abortion, by transferring the power to regulate abortion decisions to the states, or by limiting or terminating federal funding of abortions.[133]

The abortion debate has also been marked by Byzantine maneuvers and complex twists. In 1977, the Hyde Amendment prohibited the federal government from funding abortions except to save the life of a mother. Also in 1977, the federal

government lifted its ban on funding abortions for promptly reported cases of rape and incest and in cases where childbirth would result in severe and long-lasting harm to a woman. The 1980 Supreme Court decision in *Harris v. McRae* upheld the constitutionality of the Hyde Amendment. In 1981, the government again reversed its position, this time cutting federal funding of abortions except to save the life of the mother. By 1990, federal funds paid for only 165 abortions, a dramatic drop from the almost 300,000 federally funded abortions in 1977.[134] In 1994, the Freedom of Access to Clinic Entrances Act was signed into law which expanded the civil liberty of persons to have unobstructed access to any abortion or reproductive health services clinic. Any person or group that interferes with the right of such persons is subject to legal penalties, which range from a high fine to imprisonment.

The strategy of the anti-abortion movement has been to whittle away at *Roe v. Wade* by attempting to restrict abortions on the state level. For example, in a 1989 landmark decision, the Supreme Court upheld a Missouri law that prohibited public hospitals and public employees from performing an abortion (except to save the life of the mother), required physicians to determine whether a woman who is at least 20 weeks pregnant is carrying a fetus able to survive outside the womb, and declared that life starts at conception. In 1991, the Court ruled in *Rust v. Sullivan* that the United States can prohibit federally financed family planning programs from giving out abortion information (i.e., the gag rule). On former President Clinton's second day in office, he signed a bill overturning this "gag rule."

Despite the rise in population, the U.S. abortion rate has remained steady at about 1.2 million abortions a year. A substantial proportion of this was due to the use of emergency contraception. Medication abortion accounted for 17 percent of all abortions performed in 2008 and 25 percent of all eligible abortions. Sixty-one percent of women who have abortions are already mothers, and more than half have two or more children.[135] Many women want to be responsible and take care of their existing children, and many are concerned that having another child would compromise the care available to existing children. Two-thirds of women who feel this way are at or below the poverty line and received little help from their partners.

Since 1973, abortion has proved to be one of the most divisive issues in American public life with a roughly even split of opinion. For instance, a 2011 Gallup poll found that 47 percent of Americans identify as pro-choice (a 9 point drop from 1995) while 47 percent identify as pro-life.[136]

The 2010 midyear election ushered in a number of highly conservative state and federal legislators whose agenda partly centered on outlawing abortions. Their strategy was to impose a web of restrictions on women, doctors, and clinics designed to discourage abortion. For instance, a 2011 Texas law required women seeking an abortion to make two visits to the abortion clinic, the first one was to receive an ultrasound. After the ultrasound, she has to wait 24 hours before getting an abortion. Another Texas law requires physicians to give women seeking abortions state-mandated information about medical risks, adoption alternatives, and developmental stages of the fetus. In 2009, North Dakota passed a similar law that required doctors to show an ultrasound to a pregnant woman before being going through with the procedure. Similarly, a bill was introduced in North Dakota that required an abortion provider to tell a woman considering an abortion that it "will destroy the life of an unborn child, a unique human being." In 2012, the Virginia legislature passed a draconian law that would have required a woman seeking an abortion to have a transvaginal ultrasound before an abortion. She would also have been required to listen to the heartbeat of the fetus. After much state and national pressure, the governor refused to sign the bill, and it was referred back to the legislature. The revised bill was similar to the Texas legislation.[137]

The most aggressive anti-abortion tactic came in the form of a "personhood amendment," which defines a person as beginning at the moment the sperm fertilizes the egg. "Personhood" does not discriminate in terms of rape, incest, or saving the life of the mother, because the fertilized egg would have the same legal rights as the mother. This amendment would have not only made abortion illegal from the moment of conception, but also certain forms of birth control such as the morning after pill and intrauterine devices. Most physicians would likely abstain from performing in vitro fertilization because they feared criminal charges if an embryo doesn't survive. Personhood referendums appeared in both Colorado and Mississippi and were defeated in both states. Proponents have vowed to return with a slightly modified amendment.[138] All of these laws are part of an unprecedented surge of anti-abortion legislation that has advanced through Republican-controlled legislatures since 2010.

Discrimination against women is problematic in much of the developed and developing world. For instance, women's rights go from relatively high levels of protection in some Western nations to extreme oppression and danger in others. Women also frequently face multiple forms of discrimination based on gender, religion, ethnicity, class or caste, and race.

Gender Discrimination in an International Context

One of the more extreme forms of gender discrimination is manifested in female genital mutilation (FGM), which involves injury or removal of parts of the external female genitalia for cultural or religious reasons. According to the World Health Organization, about 140 million girls and women worldwide are currently living with the consequences of FGM. This non-medical procedure is mostly carried out on young girls between infancy and age 15, and approximately 92 million girls 10 years of age and older have undergone FGM in Africa. This procedure (also practiced among some immigrant groups in industrialized nations) has no health benefits and can cause severe bleeding, urination problems, cysts, infections, infertility, childbirth complications, and the increased risk of post-natal deaths. Internationally recognized as a human rights violation, FGM has been documented in 28 African countries and several in Asia and the Middle East (see Table 4.10).[139]

Women face other forms of discrimination in patriarchal societies. For instance, Saudi Arabian women have fewer rights than men and face widespread discrimination. Their freedom of movement is restricted, and their actions frequently require permission from a husband or close male relative. For instance, Saudi women are not permitted to leave their neighborhood without the company of their husband or nearest male relative, nor are they permitted to drive cars. They require permission to travel by airplane, check into hotels, or rent apartments. Saudi Arabia has strict gender separation whereby women are forbidden to be in physical contact with unrelated males. Consequently, they have only limited access to employment, parks, museums, and libraries.[140] Discrimination is also evident in family law as Saudi children legally belong to their father. In a divorce or the death of a husband, the wife is granted custody of daughters until the age of 9 and sons until they are 7. Older

TABLE 4.10 Countries Where Female Genital Mutilation Has Been Documented

Country	Year	Estimated Prevalence of Female Genital Mutilation 15-49 Years (%)
Benin	2006	12.9
Burkina Faso	2006	72.5
Cameroon	2004	1.4
Central African Republic	2008	25.7
Chad	2004	44.9
Côte d'Ivoire	2006	36.4
Djibouti	2006	93.1
Egypt	2008	91.1
Eritrea	2002	88.7
Ethiopia	2005	74.3
Gambia	2005/6	78.3
Ghana	2006	3.8
Guinea	2005	95.6
Guinea-Bissau	2006	44.5
Kenya	2008/9	27.1
Liberia	2007	58.2
Mali	2006	85.2
Mauritania	2007	72.2
Niger	2006	2.2
Nigeria	2008	29.6
Senegal	2005	28.2
Sierra Leone	2006	94
Somalia	2006	97.9
Sudan, northern (approx. 80% of the total population in survey)	2000	90
Togo	2006	5.8
Uganda	2006	0.8
Tanzania	2004	14.6
Yemen	2003	38.2

Source: World Health Organization, Female genital mutilation and other harmful practices, 2012. Retrieved March 2012 from, http://www.who.int/reproductivehealth/topics/fgm/prevalence/en/index.html.

children are typically awarded to the father or the paternal grandparents. Although Saudi women can inherit from family members, their share is generally smaller than for men.[141]

One of the most extreme examples of gender oppression took place in Afghanistan from 1996 to 2001, when the ruling Taliban government implemented a strict interpretation of Sharia law. Before the Taliban, Afghanistan was under Russian influence and gender discrimination—especially in urban areas—was less pronounced. Before the Taliban, women constituted 70 percent of school teachers;

50 percent of government workers; 60 percent of university teachers; 50 percent of students at Kabul University; and 40 percent of doctors.

By 1996, the Taliban had excluded women from government and public life. It implemented a severe system of gender apartheid that severely restricted women's access to education, health care, and employment. Women were effectively put under house arrest and prohibited from working or attending school, and they could not leave their homes without being accompanied by a husband or close male relative. The windows of their homes were painted, and they could only appear in public wearing the sanctioned full-body covering. Those with no male relatives were trapped in their homes. Moreover, women could not be heard and were beaten for showing a bit of ankle or wearing noisy shoes. They could not speak in public or to men who were not relatives; they were beaten or killed for minor infractions of these rules.

Because female doctors were generally prohibited from employment, and male doctors were forbidden to treat women, most Afghan women had no access to basic medical care, which led to a dramatic increase in preventable deaths. Although a few female doctors were allowed to work in a handful of female-only hospitals, most eventually fled the country. Those who stayed could not operate properly while wearing the burqa.

Women accused of prostitution or infidelity were hung in public squares or stoned to death. Those accused of homosexuality were buried alive. Brothels proliferated since educated women had few means of survival. Not surprisingly, the Taliban emphasis on modesty did not preclude the use of rape to terrorize the population and dishonor entire villages. Suicide rates and depression for women and girls skyrocketed under these conditions.[142]

The U.S. invasion that overthrew the Taliban in 2001 raised hopes that Afghani women would soon regain their human rights. Although women now have greater rights than before, the government did not overturn all of the Taliban's edicts. Nor have they been able to provide the necessary security for women to attend school and participate in public life, especially in Taliban-controlled areas. In some areas, young girls who tried to attend school had acid thrown in their faces.[143,144]

There are relief and aid organizations, such as the Afghanistan Relief Organization and Green Village Schools, that focus on teacher training and building schools for children. As a result, 2.5 million girls, or 42 percent of girls of school age, now attend school. This is a dramatic increase over the Taliban period where virtually no girls attended school.[145]

Yet another form of gender discrimination and oppression occurs through trafficking—typically for sexual purposes—of women or young girls (or boys) within or outside of a specific country. These women or girls are commonly recruited from poor, oppressed, or stigmatized communities; and are often homeless or drug addicts. Tourists, widows, and job-seekers are also falsely lured abroad by promises of a steady income and a better life.

Traffickers may promise citizenship, employment, marriage, education, and a better quality of life. They may promise high wages that can be sent home to families or children. They may promise domestic employment with sufficient income to allow the victim to save money for education or buy a home in their native country. Or, they may threaten to harm or kill the women's family in their home country if they don't comply. In the end, victims are forced to become prostitutes or do other work in the sex industry. Domestic servants can be held in involuntary servitude with no pay, no passport, and no means of escape. They are sometimes sexually abused by their employers or lent out as prostitutes to acquaintances.

International trafficking in human beings requires complex business and organizational arrangements that include travel agents to arrange transit, brokers, or agents to secure immigration clearances, real estate agents to find the property, accountants to ensure the business appears legal, and others to ensure the business functions smoothly. Although the exact number of victims of sex trafficking is unknown, it could be in the hundreds of thousands worldwide.[146]

Gays and Lesbians: Two Populations at Risk

In today's culture wars, one of the most intense controversies surrounds the issue of whether homosexuality is an acceptable lifestyle and whether those who are openly gay and lesbian should enjoy protected status under civil rights and all civil laws. Forty years ago few people in public or religious life would have dared to raise the possibility that it is acceptable to be gay. In 1960, all 50 states had laws criminalizing (on a felony level) sodomy by consenting adults.

In recent decades, there has been a slow but dramatic shift in public attitudes toward homosexuality. In 1993, after years of concerted pressure by gay activists, the American Psychiatric Association removed homosexuality from its *DSM-III* list of "objective disorders" and declared it "a normal, if divergent lifestyle." Laws forbidding sodomy were repealed in state after state throughout the 1970s and 1980s. Although there is no federal law against discrimination based on sexual orientation by private sector employers, 14 states, the District of Columbia, and over 140 cities and counties have enacted antidiscrimination laws. Many of these laws also ban discrimination in housing and public accommodation.[147] In 2003, the U.S. Supreme Court in *Lawrence v. Texas* ruled Texas' sodomy statute was unconstitutional, which then invalidated any remaining state sodomy laws. In 2008, the California Supreme Court struck down two state laws that had limited marriage to be only between a man and a woman, making California the second state after Massachusetts to allow same-sex marriages.[148] These policies and polls reflect a significant shift in public opinion about homosexuality.

Despite these limited successes, many homosexuals continue to be forced to live in the closet, concealing their sexual orientation in order to survive in a hostile world. Often the objects of ridicule and bullying, homosexuals have been denied housing and employment, harassed on the job, assaulted, and even killed because of their sexual orientation. Discrimination and violence remains commonplace.

In his 1999 State of the Union address, former President Clinton referred to the murder of Matthew Shepard: "We saw a young man murdered in Wyoming just because he was gay."[149] In 2009, President Obama signed into law the Matthew Shepard and James Byrd, Jr. Hate Crimes Prevention Act (known as the Matthew Shepard Act). This act expands the 1969 federal hate-crime law to include crimes motivated by a victim's actual or perceived gender, sexual orientation, gender identity, or disability. This is also the first federal law to extend legal protections to transgender persons. According to the National Coalition of Anti-Violence Programs, there were 1,393 anti-LGBT incidents in 2006.[150] Represented in all occupations and socioeconomic strata, gays and lesbians make up anywhere from 1 to 10 percent of the population.

Gay Rights

The self-perception of gays and lesbians has undergone a dramatic shift since the 1960s. Gays and lesbians have begun to identify themselves as members of an oppressed minority, similar to other oppressed minority groups. As gays and lesbians have become more visible, they have organized support groups; religious groups, social service organizations; subchapters of professional associations; and political action groups. The political power of gays and lesbians had grown to the point that by 1984, activists were successful in inserting a gay civil rights plank in the Democratic Party platform.

However, when gays and lesbians have demanded equal rights under the law, the result has been mixed—and generally negative. During the 1970s, Miami gays tried to pass a civil rights amendment that would have prevented discrimination based on sexual orientation. This referendum failed, and similar efforts were defeated in St. Paul and other cities. Houston voters defeated two gay rights proposals in 1986, one calling for an end to discrimination in city employment practices based on sexual orientation, and the other calling for an end to the maintenance of sexual orientation data in city employment records. In Tampa, Florida, and in Portland, Maine, voters in the 1990s overturned city ordinances protecting gays and lesbians.[151] Conversely, 13 states had antidiscrimination laws by the late 1990s. Municipalities across the country have also adopted civil rights ordinances to cover lesbians and gay men in areas such as employment, public accommodations, housing, and credit.[152]

For almost 20 years, the Supreme Court refused to hear cases concerning gay rights, but in 1985 it heard *Oklahoma City Board of Education v. The National Gay Task Force*. The Supreme Court ruled that public schoolteachers cannot be forbidden to advocate homosexuality (e.g., by way of public demonstrations), but they can be prohibited from engaging in homosexual acts in public. In 1988, the Supreme Court ruled that the Central Intelligence Agency could not dismiss a homosexual without justifying the dismissal. In 1992, Colorado voters passed a referendum (Amendment 2) that prevented any law banning discrimination against gays. This amendment nullified gay rights laws that already existed in Aspen, Denver, and Boulder. On May 20, 1996, the U.S. Supreme Court ruled that Colorado's Amendment 2 was unconstitutional.

Gays and Lesbians in the Military

The U.S. armed forces have generally not tolerated homosexuality in their ranks. Draft board physicians in 1940 were ordered to screen out homosexuals on the basis of such characteristics as a man's lisp or a woman's deep voice. Because World War II created a desperate need for soldiers, these instructions were often overlooked. After the war, however, gay and lesbian military personnel were discharged, and exclusionary policies were again enforced. A similar situation occurred during the Vietnam War; once the conflict ended, gays and lesbians were again persecuted, and their careers terminated.[153] The policy of the U.S. armed forces that excluded gays and lesbians from military service read as follows: "Homosexuality is incompatible with military service. The presence in the military environment of persons who engage in homosexual conduct or who, by their statements, demonstrate a propensity to engage in homosexual conduct, seriously impairs the accomplishment of the military mission."[154] Those who admitted to homosexuality at the time of enlistment were rejected; if homosexuality came to light later on, the individual was separated. Although more liberal policies were put into effect during the 1970s and 1980s, they were directed at the type of separation, not the legitimacy of the separation.[155]

One campaign promise of former president Bill Clinton was to end discrimination against homosexuals in the military. As one of his first official acts, Clinton signed an order that prohibited military recruiters from inquiring about the sexual orientation of potential recruits. Shortly afterward, he proposed wide-ranging reforms aimed at ensuring equal rights for gays and lesbians serving in the military. Facing criticism from the Joint Chiefs of Staff and many influential members of Congress, Clinton retreated from his earlier position and instead supported a "Don't Ask, Don't Tell, Don't Pursue, and Don't Harass" (DADT) policy that prohibited the military from asking questions as long as homosexuals behaved discreetly. However, under this rule, service people can be discharged if they state they are gay, lesbian, or bisexual or make a statement that indicates a propensity to engage in a homosexual act.

A 1999 report by the Service members Legal Defense Network (SLDN), a gay rights group, noted that in the first five years of the DADT policy, there was a 92 percent increase in gay-related discharges.

The Log Cabin Republicans claim that 13,000 men and women have been expelled from the military since the DADT rule came into effect. In a momentous event, DADT was repealed on September 20, 2011. In turn, the Department of Defense deleted the statutes around "homosexual conduct" being grounds for administrative separation. The acceptance of gays and lesbians in the military puts the United States in line with other countries, including Australia, Austria, Belgium, Canada, Czech Republic, Denmark, Estonia, Finland, France, Germany, Ireland, Israel, Italy, Lithuania, Luxembourg, Netherlands, New Zealand, Norway, Slovenia, South Africa, Spain, Sweden, Switzerland, United Kingdom, and Uruguay.

Gay and Lesbian Family Life

A long-standing issue for gays and lesbians has been the recognition of gay unions. In 2001, the Netherlands became the first country to recognize same-sex marriages (SSM). Belgium followed suit. By 2012, Argentina, Canada, Iceland, Norway, Portugal, South Africa, Spain, and Sweden had legalized gay marriages. In the United States, Connecticut, Iowa, Massachusetts, New Hampshire, New York, Vermont, Washington, D.C., and Oregon's Coquille and Washington State's Suquamish Indian tribes have legalized gay marriages. In 2012, Washington and Maryland legalized same-sex marriage, which may be derailed by referendum votes. Among other countries, Finland, Greenland, Iceland, Germany, and France allow same-sex couples to enter into legal partnerships, and although they have many of the benefits and protections of civil marriage, they are not legally married. Conversely, 30 states have changed their constitution to specifically forbid SSMs.

The question of gay marriages became an issue in 1996 when it appeared that Hawaii might soon recognize such marriages. Conservative states feared that a same-sex couple could relocate to a state that allowed gay marriages, then move to their state and demand that it be recognized. By 1996, one-third of states had passed legislation prohibiting the recognition of SSMs from another state. The federal government entered the fray by passing the Defense of Marriage Act (DOMA), which effectively established that the only legitimate marriage was with a member of the opposite sex.

In 1999, the Vermont Supreme Court found no compelling reason not to recognize a civil union for same-sex couples and ruled that they should be granted the same rights and responsibilities as married Vermonters. The Vermont governor signed into law a "civil union" bill in 2002 that granted Vermont gay and lesbian couples most of the rights and benefits available to married couples under the law.[156] These protections included insurance benefits, inheritance, medical decision-making rights, and state tax benefits and obligations. The one exception was the right to have a same-sex union legally called a marriage. The concept of civil union has been criticized because it creates a separate and thereby unequal set of rights.[157]

In California, same-sex marriages were performed for a short time in 2008 after the California Supreme Court ruled that limiting marriage to opposite-sex couples violated the state constitution.

A long-standing issue for gays and lesbians has been the recognition of gay unions.

Source: Lisa F. Young/Shutterstock

However, in 2008 the California electorate approved Proposition 8, which made a gay marriage ban part of California's constitution. As of early 2012, the legality of Proposition 8 continues to be battled out in the courts.

The question of parental rights is linked to the recognition of same-sex unions. Specifically, sexual orientation is often a factor in issues of family law, including custody, visitation, and foster/adoptive parent eligibility. Because homosexuality does not enjoy a constitutionally protected status, it can be considered in legal actions surrounding the rights of parents and would-be parents. In some jurisdictions, it effectively blocks adoption and foster care placement. Although most states have no statute explicitly prohibiting gay and lesbian adoption or foster care placement, several states unofficially do not permit it.[158] Gay marriage rights also affect inheritances, hospital visitation rights, end-of-life decisions, and many other aspects of marriage unions taken for granted by heterosexual couples.

AIDS and the Gay Community

The AIDS crisis has been used to justify homophobic attitudes. In the early days of the epidemic (i.e., the 1980s), there were recommendations for quarantining AIDS victims, renewed attempts at punishing homosexual behavior, increased job discrimination, and a generally hostile climate for both gays and lesbians. At the federal level, former senator Jesse Helms successfully introduced a bill that prevented the Centers for Disease Control and Prevention from using AIDS education funds in ways that could foster homosexuality. Although in the United States, AIDS still predominantly affects gay and bisexual men, intravenous drug users, and African American women, the movement of AIDS into the heterosexual community has fueled some sympathy toward the gay population. But positive change has come only after the documentation of more than a million AIDS cases in the United States, resulting in about 500,000 deaths.[159]

The AIDS crisis has had a devastating effect on the lives of gay men. There are few older gays in larger cities who have not lost either a lover or close friends to the disease.

Homophobia—the irrational fear of homosexuality—continues to limit the civil rights and legal protections of gays and lesbians. Justifications for this attitude have been found in religious texts that view homosexuality as a sin against God, and in psychological explanations that view homosexuality as a disease or symptom of arrested development or a fear of intimacy. Some forms of Christian counseling are based on "praying away the gay," or reorientation, which claims that by using prayer and effort, the client can learn to be attracted to the opposite sex and rid themselves of gay urges. The practice of trying to change sexual orientation was discredited by the American Psychological Association in 2009 as ineffective and potentially harmful.[160]

The self-perception of gays and lesbians has undergone a dramatic shift since the 1960s, as they began to identify as members of an oppressed minority. As they have become more visible, they have organized political action organizations and religious groups such as Dignity (Roman Catholics), Integrity (Episcopalians), Mishpachat Am (Jews), and Lutherans Concerned. These changing attitudes have encouraged some political leaders to openly court the gay vote. The Clinton administration was the first to openly (albeit erratically) endorse gay rights. For example, Clinton backed the Employment Non-Discrimination Act (a gay civil rights bill); appointed more than 100 openly gay and lesbians to administrative jobs; nominated the first-ever open lesbian to the U.S. District Court; and mandated that all federal agencies add sexual orientation to their affirmative action policies. Clinton also stopped the denial of security clearance based on sexual orientation; granted political asylum to gays and lesbians at risk of persecution in their home countries based on their sexual orientation; and increased public health spending on AIDS.[161] Unfortunately, much of this progress was reversed in the two terms of the G.W. Bush administration.

Lesbian, gay, bisexual, and transgendered rights are an area of worldwide discrimination. On the positive side, seven of the ten countries that have legalized same-sex marriage are in Europe, where another 14 have legalized civil unions. The laws of the European Union guarantee equal treatment in employment and vocational training, regardless of one's sexual orientation. EU policies and regulations not only guarantee equality and non-discrimination for all LGBT people, they also require EU member states to proactively fight discrimination. In general, the gay and lesbian community is likely to enjoy far greater rights and protections in the European Union than in many other parts of the world.[162]

An International Perspective on LGBT Rights

Laws around gay and lesbian rights differ around the world, going from complete legality in most Western European countries to the death penalty in Saudi Arabia, Sudan, Mauritania, Somaliland, United Arab Emirates, Yemen, and Iran. The laws around gay and lesbian rights also differ in Africa, ranging from severe illegality (38 of 53 African nations criminalize it) to full legal protection (South Africa allows same-sex marriages with a wide-ranging ban on discrimination). But even in South Africa, "corrective rape" (raping lesbians to "cure" their homosexuality) occurs.

In 2009, Ugandan parliamentary member David Bahati introduced a bill that would make certain forms of homosexuality punishable by death. This bill would have transformed the Ugandan maximum 14-year prison sentence for same-sex relations into two categories: aggravated homosexuality (resulting in the death penalty) and "the offense of homosexuality" (life imprisonment). The bill would have also allowed for the extradition of Ugandans who engaged in homosexual acts outside the country. Penalties were included for individuals, companies, or organizations that support LGBT rights.

It is believed that Bahati was inspired by three U.S. evangelical Christians (Scott Lively, Caleb Lee Brundidge, and Don Schmierer) who held a two-day anti-gay conference in Uganda a month before the bill was introduced.[163] Not surprisingly, Bahati's bill (which enjoyed popular support in Uganda) caused a commotion in the West, with some countries threatening to cut off aid. In response, a revised bill reduced the severest penalties to life imprisonment.[164]

On October 9, 2010, a Uganda newspaper published a front-page article titled "100 Pictures of Uganda's Top Homos Leak." In addition to their photographs, the paper listed the names and addresses of 100 gays and lesbians alongside a yellow banner that read "Hang Them." The newspaper alleged that they were trying to recruit Ugandan children into their ranks, a charge that Bahati and others made in defense of the bill. David Kato, a Ugandan gay activist, was beaten to death shortly after the paper came out, and one woman was almost killed when neighbors stoned her house. A Ugandan court later ordered the paper to stop outing gays.[165]

Ageism

Ageism is a problem in a consumer-oriented society that idolizes youth. Like other minority groups, the aged face significant social and economic barriers. For example, workers over 50 often find it difficult to find equivalent employment if they lose their jobs, something that has received wide publicity since the recession that began in 2007. The aged in the United States are seldom respected for their wisdom and experience; nor do they occupy high social positions protected by tradition. Instead, once they have lost their earning potential, the aged are often perceived as a financial albatross around the neck of an economically productive society. Socially isolated in retirement communities, low-income housing, or other old-age ghettos, the aged often become invisible.

America is getting older—nearly 21 percent of the U.S. population will be 65 or older by 2050, compared with 13 percent in 2009. For the first 99 percent of human history, the average life expectancy was approximately 18 years. Life expectancy rose from age 47 in 1900 to 78.4 by 2008.[166] Due largely to the aging of the Baby Boom generation (those born between 1946 and 1964), the growth rate was especially rapid among those aged 55 to 65. While those aged 65 and older also increased 5 percent in this five year period, those aged 85 and older increased by 20 percent to 5.1 million.[167]

This aging trend will have significant consequences for health care costs, since disabilities increase with age. For example, while only about 20 percent of people aged 65 to 74 need help with daily activities such as eating, bathing, and dressing, 53 percent of those over age 85 need assistance with daily activities.[168] Similarly, although only a small percentage (4 percent) of all elderly people live in nursing homes, these numbers vary dramatically with age.[169]

Elderly Poverty and Social Programs

The proportion of older people living in poverty and low income has been declining in recent decades. In 1959, 35 percent of people aged 65 and over lived below the poverty threshold. In 2008, 10 percent lived in poverty, 26 percent were in the low-income group, 36 percent in the middle-income group, and 29 percent in the high-income group.[170] As of 2010, the poverty rate for the 65 year age bracket had remained consistent at 9 percent, and the median annual income was $31,408. In fact, between 2007 and 2010, all age groups experienced a decline in income except for the 65 plus age group, whose income increased by 5.5 percent.[171]

Poverty rates differ by age and sex in the older population. Older women (12 percent) were more likely than older men (7 percent) to live in poverty in 2006. Race and ethnicity are also related to poverty among the elderly. Older non-Hispanic whites (7 percent) were less likely than older blacks (23 percent) and older Hispanics (19 percent) to be living in poverty. As such, policymakers must calculate the impact of increasing numbers of minority elderly in determining the future funding needs of health and income-based social programs.

Total income for those over 65 comes largely from four sources: Social Security; earnings; pensions; and asset income. Most of the elderly rely—some heavily—on Social Security. Nine out of ten people age 65 and over live in families with Social Security income, 60 percent are in families with income from assets, and almost one-half (45 percent) with income from pensions. Only 1 in 20 live in families receiving public assistance.[172] Other than the very poor, seniors are the only group with universal health coverage and the only group to receive non-means–tested government assistance.[173]

Health Care and the Elderly

These aging trends have significant implications for social welfare policy. For one, as the numbers of elderly increase, their demands on society for housing, health, and recreational services become greater. The stresses put on the health care system by an increasingly aging population are already evident in the near insolvency of Medicare. For example, the hospitalization rate increased from 306 hospital stays per 1,000 Medicare enrollees in 1992 to 350 in 2005, although the average length of a hospital stay decreased from 8.4 days to 5.7 days. Also, the number of Medicare funded physician visits and consultations increased from 11,359 per 1,000 Medicare enrollees in 1992 to 13,914 in 2005.[174] As the population ages in the coming decades, and as the group aged 85 and over grows rapidly, the burden of health care expenses will become even more problematic.

While elderly women live longer than men, they have only 58 percent of their income. Hence, more of elderly women's health care costs will have to be borne by the government or by their families, putting increasing burdens on both. In addition, as people live longer and require more care—especially in-home care—more pressure will be put on family members to provide or pay for that care. Since families are already stressed by increasing workloads, other family pressures, and the often large geographic distances between children and parents, the state may be pressed to provide even more care for greater numbers of the elderly.

The elderly vote in large numbers, and over the years their voices have been heard more clearly by politicians than those of minorities. In the 1960s, policymakers responded to the needs of the elderly by passing the Older Americans Act (OAA) of 1965. The objectives of the OAA included (1) an adequate retirement income that corresponds to the general standard of living; (2) the promotion of good physical and mental health, regardless of economic status; (3) the provision of centrally located, adequate, and affordable housing; (4) the availability of meaningful employment, with the elimination of age-specific and discriminatory employment practices; (5) the provision of civic, cultural, and recreational opportunities; and (6) adequate community services, including low-cost transportation and supported living arrangements.[175]

Negative stereotypes of elderly persons continue to be perpetuated by the media and the film industry. Moreover, the elderly continue to be victimized by crime, domestic violence by family members, and job discrimination. Perhaps the clearest expression of continuing ageism is seen in employment policies. The 1967 Age Discrimination in Employment Act (ADEA) protected most workers age 40 to 69 from discrimination in hiring, job retention, and promotion. However, for most workers the protection of the ADEA stops when they reach age 70. Legislation to remove the "70 cap" has consistently failed in Congress, as employer lobbies have argued that they require a free hand in personnel policies.

People with Disabilities

People with disabilities also experience the effects of discrimination. (See Tables 4.11 and 4.12.) In 2010, 9.5 percent of householders aged between 18 and 64 (8.8 million) reported having a disability.[176]

Disability is a difficult term to define. One medical definition is based on the assumption that a disability is a chronic disease requiring various forms of

TABLE 4.11 Disabled Persons, Age 21–64

Disability	Percent Employed*
Difficulty hearing	68.1
Difficulty seeing	55.3
Mental disability	47.2
Difficulty walking	40.8

*Persons may have more than one type of disability.

Source: U.S. Census Bureau, Americans With Disabilities: 2002 (Washington, DC: U.S. Department of Commerce, Economics, and Statistics Administration, May 2006). Retrieved April 2008 from http://www.census.gov/prod/2006pubs/p70-107.pdf.

TABLE 4.12 Characteristics of the Civilian Noninstitutionalized Population by Age, Disability Status, and Type of Disability, 2010

	Number (in thousands)	Percent
Total all ages	303,858	100
With any disability	66,672	18.7
With severe disability	38,284	12.6
Total population 6 years and older	278,222	100.00
Needed personal assistance	13,349	4.4
Total population 15 years and older	241,682	100
With any disability	451,454	21.3
visual	10,087	4.1
hearing	8668	4.1
mental	14,329	6.4
Total population 25 to 64 years	177,925	100
With any disability	29,479	16.6
Severe disability	20,286	11.4
Total population 65 years & older	38,599	100
With any disability	19,234	49.8
With a severe disability	14,138	36.6

Source: Matthew W. Brault, Americans With Disabilities: 2010, U.S. Census Bureau, P70-131, July 2012. Retrieved August 2012 from, Current Population Reports http://www.census.gov/prod/2012pubs/p70-131.pdf.

treatment. Another definition derived from the medical model—a definition used as a basis for determining eligibility in the Social Security Disability Insurance program—characterizes people with disabilities as those unable to work (or unable to work as frequently) in the same range of jobs as nondisabled people.[177] People with disabilities are viewed as inherently less productive than other members of society. A third model defines disability based on what those with disabilities cannot do, seeing the disabled in terms of their inability to perform certain functions expected of the able-bodied population. As William Roth maintains, "the functional limitation, economic, and medical models all define disability by what a person is not—the medical model as not healthy, the economic model as not productive, the functional limitation model as not capable."[178]

A newer definition—the psychosocial model—views disability as a socially defined category. In other words, people with disabilities constitute a minority group, and if a person with disabilities is poor, it is because of discrimination rather than personal inadequacy. This definition locates the problem in the interaction between disabled people and the social environment. Therefore, the adjustment to disability is not a personal problem but a social challenge requiring the adjustment of society. This definition requires that society reevaluate its attitudes and remove the physical and transportation barriers placed in the way of people with disabilities. It also requires the elimination of stereotypes. In part, this newer definition of disability was expressed in Section 504 of the Rehabilitation Act of 1973 (PL 93-112).

Although the potential range of disabilities is vast, people with disabilities share a central experience rooted in stigmatization, discrimination, and oppression. Like other stigmatized groups, those with disabilities experience poverty in numbers disproportionately larger than the general population. Perhaps not surprisingly, rates of disability are greatest among the aged, African Americans, the poor, and blue-collar workers.[179] Compared to the able-bodied, people with disabilities tend to be more frequently unemployed and underemployed and, as a consequence, often fall below the poverty line. In 2010, the median income of households containing a person with a disability was $25,550, which is less than half that of households without a person with a disability ($58,736 respectively).[180] Because disability is often correlated with poor education, age, and poverty, it is not surprising that African Americans are twice as likely as whites to

have some level of disability (their representation is even greater in the fully disabled population), and that more women are disabled than men. The problems of low wages and unemployment are exacerbated because people with disabilities often need more medical and hospital care than others, are less likely to have health insurance, and spend three times more of their own money on medical care than do the able-bodied.[181] In fact, the uninsured rate for people with a disability increased from 16 percent in 2009 to 17.3 percent in 2010.[182]

√ The greatest stride in disability rights occurred on July 26, 1990, when former president George Bush signed the Americans with Disabilities Act (ADA) (PL 101-336) into law (see Figure 4.4). This act is the most comprehensive legislation for people with disabilities ever passed in the United States. The ADA lays a foundation of equality for people with disabilities, and it extends to disabled people civil rights similar to those made available on the basis of race, sex, color, national origin, and religion through the Civil Rights Act of 1964. For example, the ADA prohibits discrimination on the basis of disability in private sector employment; in state and local government activities; and in public accommodations and services, including transportation provided by both public and private entities.[183]

In spite of some serious loopholes, the ADA is an important step forward for disabled people. Nevertheless, some argue that while the ADA is a good law in principle, abuses are stirring up widespread resistance. Specifically, disability is often defined so broadly that virtually anyone with a problem, regardless of its extent, can claim protection under the ADA. Despite the ADA and other federal laws, discrimination is still widespread against people with disabilities. For instance, most buildings still do not meet the needs of the physically handicapped in terms of access, exits, restrooms, parking lots, warning systems, and so forth. Many apartment complexes and stores continue to be built without allowing for the needs of people with disabilities. The struggle for full social, political, and economic integration of the disabled remains an ongoing battle.

Legal Attempts to Remedy Discrimination

Attempts to eliminate discrimination are a relatively recent development. Although the Fourteenth Amendment of the Constitution guaranteed

I. Employment
   A. Employers may not discriminate against an individual with a disability in hiring or promotion if the person is otherwise qualified for the job.
   B. Employers can ask about one's ability to perform a job but cannot inquire if someone has a disability; nor can employers subject a person to tests that tend to screen out people with disabilities.
   C. Employers must provide "reasonable accommodation" to employees with disabilities. This includes job restructuring and modification of equipment. Employers are not required to provide accommodations that impose an "undue hardship" on business operations.
   D. All employers with 15 or more employees must comply with the ADA.

II. Transportation
   A. New public transit buses and rail cars must be accessible to individuals with disabilities.
   B. Transit authorities must provide comparable para-transit or other special transportation services to individuals with disabilities who cannot use fixed bus services, unless an undue burden would result.
   C. Existing rail systems must have one accessible car per train.
   D. New bus and train stations must be accessible. Key stations in rapid, light, and commuter rail systems must be made accessible. All existing Amtrak stations must be accessible by July 26, 2010.

III. Public Accommodations
   A. Private entities such as restaurants, hotels, and retail stores may not discriminate against individuals with disabilities.
   B. Auxiliary aids and services must be provided to individuals with vision or hearing impairments, unless an undue burden would result.
   C. If removal is readily achievable, physical barriers in existing facilities must be removed. All new construction and alterations of facilities must be accessible.

IV. State and Local Government
   A. State and local governments may not discriminate against individuals with disabilities.
   B. All government facilities, services, and communications must be accessible, consistent with the requirements of Section 504 of the Rehabilitation Act of 1973.

V. Telecommunications
   A. Companies offering telephone service to the general public must offer telephone relay services to individuals who use telecommunications services for the deaf (TDDs) or similar devices.

FIGURE 4.4 A Summary of the Americans with Disabilities Act

all citizens equal protection under the law, it was also used to perpetuate discrimination on the basis of "separate but equal" treatment. Overt segregation existed in the South until the middle of the twentieth century, and separate but (supposedly) equal public facilities characterized much of the social and economic activity of the Southern United States. The extensive system of Southern segregation included public transportation, schools, private economic activities, and even public drinking foun-

tains. It was only in the mid-1950s that the U.S. Supreme Court overturned the *Plessy v. Ferguson* (1896) decision that had formed the basis for the separate but equal doctrine.

Desegregation and the Civil Rights Movement

In a landmark decision on *Brown v. Board of Education of Topeka, Kansas,* the U.S. Supreme

Court ruled in 1954 that separate but equal facilities in education were inherently unequal. The Court ruled that separating the races was a way of denoting the inferiority of African Americans. In addition, the Court ruled that segregation hindered the educational and mental development of black children. Although the Supreme Court ruled against officially sanctioned segregation in public schools, **de facto segregation** was not addressed until the *Swann v. Charlotte-Mecklenburg Board of Education* ruling of 1971. This ruling approved court-ordered busing to achieve racial integration of school districts with a history of discrimination.

The gains made by African Americans were won through bitter struggle. Until the middle 1960s, Southern blacks enjoyed few rights, with total segregation enforced in almost all spheres of social, economic, political, and public life. Segregation in the North occurred through de facto, or unofficial, rather than de jure, or legal means. The net effect was almost the same.

In 1955 Rosa Parks, too tired to stand in the "colored" section in the back of a bus in Montgomery, Alabama, sparked a nonviolent bus boycott led by Martin Luther King Jr. Still another protest was begun when African American students in North Carolina were refused service at an all-white lunch counter. The Civil Rights movement grew rapidly and resulted in widespread demonstrations (in Selma, Alabama, one march drew more than 100,000 people), picket lines, sit-ins, and other forms of political protest. Gaining international publicity, the protests of the late 1950s and early 1960s attracted Northern religious leaders, students, and white liberals—some of whom would lose their lives. By the time the Reverend Martin Luther King Jr. was assassinated in 1968, many demands of the Civil Rights movement had been incorporated in the Civil Rights Act of 1964. Ironically, Congress exempted itself from complying with the act until 1988. The 1964 Civil Rights Act had not lived up to its promise. Power had not shifted, and African American and other minority groups continued to be disenfranchised economically, politically, and socially. It soon became apparent that other remedies were required. One of those was affirmative action, a set of policies designed to provide equal opportunities for minorities and women.

Affirmative Action

Two basic strategies have been employed to address racial, economic, and other injustices. The first is non-discrimination, in which no preferential treatment is given to selected groups. The second is **affirmative action**, whose overall goal is to ensure that women and minorities are admitted, hired, and promoted in direct proportion to their numbers in the population. Affirmative action policies and legislation represent an aggressive step beyond the largely reactive stance taken by simple non-discrimination policies. As such, affirmative action policies give preferential treatment to minority and female applicants. Its ostensible goal is to correct past wrongs done to groups of people throughout the country's history.

There are three types of affirmative action programs: (1) employers and schools can adopt voluntary programs to increase the hiring of minorities and women; (2) the courts can order an employer or school to create an affirmative action plan; and (3) federal, state, and local governments can require contractors to adopt affirmative action plans to remain eligible for government contracts.[184]

As Table 4.13 illustrates, affirmative action and civil rights legislation affect a much wider group of Americans than minorities. Moreover, as demonstrated by the table, rulings on affirmative action and civil rights cases have been inconsistent, characterized by two steps forward and one or two steps backward.

Opponents of affirmative action argue that it leads to racial quota systems, preferential treatment, and reverse discrimination. They argue that it violates the equal protection under the laws guaranteed in the Fourteenth Amendment. Still others argue that affirmative action benefits minority group members who do not need the help while placing whites who are innocent of any wrongdoing at a disadvantage. These critics maintain that rights inhere in individuals, not in groups. Other conservatives, such as Supreme Court Justice Antonin Scalia, argue that there never was a justification for affirmative action because the Constitution is "colorblind."[185] Moderates such as former president Bill Clinton note that "affirmative action has been good for America. Affirmative action has not always been perfect, and affirmative action should not go on forever. . . . We should reaffirm the principle of affirmative action and fix the practices. We should have a simple slogan: Mend it, but don't end it."[186]

TABLE 4.13 Milestones in Civil Rights and Affirmative Action Rulings

Legislation or Court Ruling	Summary
Plessy v. Ferguson (1896)	The U.S. Supreme Court established the "separate but equal" doctrine.
Fair Employment Practices Committee (1935)	Employers are directed to not discriminate in hiring based on race.
Brown v. Board of Education of Topeka, Kansas (1954)	The Supreme Court ruled that "separate but equal" facilities in education were inherently unequal.
Equal Pay Act of 1963	Men and women have a right to equal pay for doing the same work
Civil Rights Act of 1964, including amendments added in 1972, 1978, and 1991	1. Voter registration is a legal right that cannot be tampered with. 2. It is unlawful to discriminate or segregate based on race, color, religion, or national origin in any public accommodation, including hotels, motels, theaters, and other public places. 3. The attorney general will undertake civil action on the part of any person who is denied access to a public accommodation. If the owner continues to discriminate, a court fine and imprisonment will result. 4. The attorney general must represent anyone who undertakes the desegregation of a public school. 5. Each federal department must take action to end discrimination in all programs or activities receiving federal assistance. 6. Public or private employers, employment agencies, or labor unions with more than 15 employees cannot discriminate against an individual because of their race, color, religion, national origin, or sex. An Equal Opportunity Commission will be established to enforce this provision. A 1968 amendment to this act prohibited discrimination in housing.
Age Discrimination Act of 1967	Persons over 40 may not be discriminated against in any terms or conditions of their employment.
Griggs v. Duke Power Co. (1971)	The Court prohibited discriminatory employment practices. It put the burden of proof on the employer to show that hiring criteria have a direct relationship to the job. Griggs was overturned by *Wards Cove Packing Co. Inc. v. Atonio* (1989), in which the Court imposed tougher standards for proving discrimination and shifted the burden of proof onto the employee.
Swann v. Charlotte-Mecklenburg Board of Education (1971)	The Court ruled in favor of court-ordered busing to achieve racial integration of school districts with a history of discrimination.
Title IX of Education Amendments of 1972	Institutions receiving federal financial assistance may not discriminate based on sex.

(Continued)

TABLE 4.13 *(Continued)*

Legislation or Court Ruling	Summary
Rehabilitation Act of 1973	Discrimination on the basis of mental or physical disability is prohibited.
Vietnam Era Veterans Readjustment Act of 1974	Employers with federal contracts must take steps to employ and advance qualified disabled veterans.
Milliken v. Brady (1974)	The Court ruled that mandatory school busing across city-suburban boundaries to achieve racial integration was not required unless segregation had resulted from an official action.
Marco DeFunis v. University of Washington Law School (1974)	DeFunis claimed that he was denied admission to law school even though his grades and test scores were higher than those of minorities who were admitted. The Supreme Court ruled in his favor.
Age Discrimination Act of 1975	Employers who receive federal financial assistance cannot discriminate based on age.
Regents of the University of California v. Bakke (1978)	The Supreme Court ruled that Alan Bakke was unfairly denied admission to the University of California-Davis Medical School. Like DeFunis, Bakke argued that his qualifications were stronger than those of many of the minority candidates who were admitted.
United Steelworkers v. Weber (1979)	The Court upheld an affirmative action plan to erase entrenched racial biases in employment.
Fullilove v. Klutznick (1980)	The Court ruled that federal public works contracts may require 10 percent of the work to go to minority firms.
Firefighters Local Union No. 1784 v. Stotts (1984)	The Court ruled that an employer may use seniority rules in laying off employees, even when those rules adversely affect minority employees. This ruling was a blow to affirmative action, because it perpetuated the dilemma that minorities are the last to be hired and the first to be fired. The Department of Justice used this decision to force Indianapolis and 49 other jurisdictions to abandon their use of hiring quotas.
Wyatt v. Jackson Board of Education (1986)	An affirmative action plan must have a strong basis in evidence for remedial action.
United States v. Paradise (1987)	The Court found that a judge may order racial quotas in promoting and hiring to address "egregious" past discrimination.
Johnson v. Transportation Agency (1987)	The Court permitted the use of gender as a factor in hiring and promotion.
City of Richmond v. J. A. Croson (1989)	The Court imposed standards of "strict scrutiny." Racial or ethnic classifications must serve a compelling interest and be narrowly tailored.
Martin v. Wilks (1989)	The Court imposed tougher standards for Asian Americans to be included in affirmative action plans and made it easier to challenge settlements of those plans.
Metro Broadcasting Inc. v. FCC (1990)	The Court allowed minority preferences to promote diverse viewpoints across the airwaves.

TABLE 4.13 *(Continued)*

Legislation or Court Ruling	Summary
Adarand Constructors Inc. v. Pena (1995)	The Court ruled that federal affirmative measures using racial and ethnic criteria in decision making must meet the same standards of strict scrutiny imposed in *Croson*.
Hopwood v. State of Texas (1996 5th Cir.)	The appeals court ruled that the University of Texas's goal of achieving a diverse student body did not justify its affirmative action program, -suggesting that achieving diversity does not represent a compelling state interest.
California Proposition 209 (California Civil Rights Initiative) (1996). Now Article I, Section 31 of the California Constitution	Racial or gender preferences in public education, employment, and state contracting are prohibited. In 1997, a three-judge panel of the Ninth Circuit Court of Appeals upheld the referendum passed by -California voters. The U.S. Supreme Court refused to consider the appeal.[a] The passage of the CCRI effectively put an end to affirmative action in California.
Washington State I-200 (1998)	"Preferences" in state and municipal hiring and recruitment to the state university system are prohibited. This 1998 ballot measure effectively repealed affirmative action in Washington state.
One Florida Plan (1999)	Racial preferences in university admissions and state contracting are prohibited. In November 1999, Florida Gov. Jeb Bush ordered an end to racial preference programs in agencies under his control. The One Florida plan replaces race and ethnicity with criteria such as a student's socioeconomic background, geographical diversity, status as a first generation college student, or preparation in a low-performing D or F school.
Grutter v. Bollinger and *Gratz v. Bollinger* (2003)	The U.S. Supreme Court ruled that race can be a factor in university admission decisions but limited the extent of it. In two separate but related decisions, the Court ruled that the University of Michigan's law school affirmative action policy (*Grutter v. Bollinger*) that favors minorities is legal. In the second decision (*Gratz v. Bollinger*) it ruled that the University of Michigan's undergraduate admissions, which awards 20 points on a 100 point scale to blacks, Hispanics, and Native Americans, violated equal protection provisions of the Constitution.

[a]D.D. Gehring (ed.), *Responding to the New Affirmative Actions Climate: New Directions for Student Services* (San Francisco: Jossey-Bass, 1998).

Sources: Adapted from ACLU, "Affirmative Action," ACLU Briefing Paper No. 17 (New York: ACLU, n.d.); American Council on Education, "Major Civil Rights and Equal Opportunity Legislation Since 1963," retrieved from www.berkshire-aap.com/ace; Winnie Chen, Vilma Hernandez, Erin Townsend, and Carol Wyatt, "Affirmative Action," unpublished class paper, Graduate School of Social Work, University of Houston, 1996; Marjorie Blythe and Anna Conaty, "Affirmative Action and the State of America's Minorities," unpublished paper, Graduate School of Social Work, University of Houston, 2000; and National Public Radio, "Split Ruling on Affirmative Action High Court Rules on Race as Factor in University Admissions," June 23, 2003, retrieved October 2004 from www.npr.org/news/specials/michigan.

William Julius Wilson, an African American sociologist, criticizes the ability of affirmative action strategies to help the most disadvantaged members of society:

> Programs based solely on [race-specific solutions] are inadequate . . . to deal with the complex problems of race in America. . . . This is because the most disadvantaged members of racial minority groups, who suffer the cumulative effects of both race and class subjugation . . . are disproportionately represented amongst the segment of the general population that has been denied the resources to compete effectively in a free and open market. . . . On the other hand, the competitive resources developed by the advantaged minority members . . . result in their benefitting disproportionately from policies that promote the rights of minority individuals by removing artificial barriers to valued positions. . . . [If] policies of preferential . . . treatment are developed in terms of racial group membership rather than real disadvantages suffered by individuals, then these policies will further improve the opportunities of the advantaged without necessarily addressing the problems of the truly disadvantaged such as the ghetto underclass.[187]

Affirmative action is one of the most controversial aspects of U.S. social policy. Moreover, it is open to a wide array of moral conundrums. For example, although Asian Americans encounter significant discrimination, do their income levels and educational attainment mitigate against the need for preferential treatment? Moreover, if historical social discrimination were a basis for affirmative action, Jews, Catholics, Irish, Eastern Europeans, and other groups who were for a time squeezed out of the U.S. social mainstream should also be eligible. Should poor whites be covered under affirmative action because they face class-based prejudice? Should women who grow up in upper-class families and attend Ivy League universities be covered under affirmative action based on their gender?

Conclusion

Discrimination takes many forms in the United States and elsewhere. It can be targeted against African Americans, Hispanics, Native Americans, Asians, women, gays and lesbians, people with disabilities, and poor whites. Ironically, the majority of the U.S. population experiences discrimination: 51 percent of the population are women; almost 13 percent are over age 65; almost 20 percent are disabled; and roughly one in three Americans is either Hispanic, African American, or Asian. Hence, discrimination in U.S. society is not about numbers per se, but reflects the relative lack of political, social, and economic power of marginalized groups.

Because discrimination can lead to poverty, it often results in the creation of income maintenance and poverty programs designed to curb its effects. Those who become beneficiaries of these programs soon find themselves with a second handicap—the stigma of being on public assistance, or just plain needing help.

Some policymakers have tried to reduce the need for long-term and expensive social welfare programs by arresting the cycle of discrimination and stigma. They often undertake this effort by advocating for policies designed to attack discrimination at its roots. These can include antidiscrimination legislation, affirmative action policies, women's rights legislation, city and state pro-gay and lesbian ordinances, and legislation to protect the rights of the physically and mentally challenged. It is hoped that by curtailing discrimination, U.S. society can offer at-risk populations equal opportunities for achievement and success. Similar efforts to curb discrimination, beginning with anti-employment legislation, have been instituted by the European Union as well as by some member nations and cities. At best, the scorecard on these well-intentioned antidiscrimination policies, both in the United States and abroad, has been mixed. Despite a strong start, affirmative action programs in the United States have not led to widespread economic success for women and minorities. Gays and lesbians continue to be discriminated against, even in places that have passed civil rights ordinances. Although women have made significant gains over the past few decades, they still earn less than males in comparable jobs. Transnationally, poverty rates for minority groups are higher than for majority populations. For instance, in the United States, the poverty rates for ethnic and racial minorities are three times higher than for whites; in the United Kingdom, the rates average twice that of whites.

Discrimination has profoundly negative effects—not just on the human rights and economic well-being of a large number of affected groups—but on the character, culture, and economy of societies as a whole. Analysts and policymakers in the United States and globally have the challenging task of developing new strategies that effectively fight discrimination in all its forms.

DISCUSSION QUESTIONS

1. Racism can be manifested in many forms, including poverty, housing problems, underemployment, unemployment, wage differences, lowered educational opportunities, high crime rates, and welfare dependency. What are the causes of racism. Describe the primary causes of individual and institutional racism. How are these factors dealt with by society?
2. Over the past four decades, numerous legal and judicial decisions have attempted to eradicate racism, including the 1964 Civil Rights Act and various Supreme Court rulings. Were these attempts successful? Why or why not?
3. Sexism is a powerful and pervasive force permeating much of U.S. society. How is it manifested? What strategies can be employed to lessen the impact of sexism in society?
4. Most women in U.S. society work to either provide a necessary second income or as the family's primary wage earner. Describe some of the major obstacles faced by working women. What can be done to eliminate some of these obstacles?
5. What are some of the most important social, political, and economic hurdles standing in the way of full equality for gays and lesbians? What can be done to ameliorate them?
6. Being elderly in U.S. society is in many ways a social handicap. Why might that be true?
7. People with disabilities face significant discrimination. What is the evidence to support this belief?
8. The Americans with Disabilities Act (ADA) is the most important piece of legislation affecting people with disabilities. Why? What are its loopholes?
9. Based on the information you have read in this chapter, what are the major causes of discrimination? Why?

NOTES

1. Billy J. Tidwell, "Racial Discrimination and Inequality," Encyclopedia of Social Work, 18th ed. (Silver Spring, MD: NASW, 1987), p. 450.
2. J. Dollard et al., *Frustration and Aggression* (New Haven, CT: Yale University Press, 1939).
3. Tidwell, "*Racial Discrimination and Inequality.*"
4. Stephanie Bernardo, *The Ethnic Almanac* (Garden City, NY: Doubleday, 1981).
5. U.S. Census Bureau, "Overview of Race and Hispanic Origin: 2010," March 2011. Retrieved Feb 2012, from www.census.gov/prod/cen2010/briefs/c2010br-02.pdf
6. V. Dion Haynes, "Movement Aims to Explain and Deflate White Power," *Daily Titan,* 1999. Retrieved 2000 from http://dailytitan.fullerton.edu/issues/spring_98/dti_03_04/movementaims.html
7. U.S. Census Bureau, "Population Profile of the United States: Dynamic Version by Race and Hispanic Origin in 2005", Retrieved April 2008 from http://www.census.gov/population/pop-profile/dynamic/RACEHO.pdf
8. U.S. Census Bureau, "Statistical Abstract of the United States: 2012," Washington, D.C, 131st edition. Retrieved Feb 2012, from www.census.gov/compendia/statab/
9. U.S. Census Bureau, "The Black Population in the United States: Population CPS Reports 2001–2004", Retrieved May 2008 http://www.census.gov/population/www/socdemo/race/black.html
10. U.S. Census Bureau, "Statistical Abstract of the United States: 2012," Washington, D.C, 131st edition. Retrieved Feb 2012, from www.census.gov/compendia/statab
11. U.S. Census Bureau, "Income, Poverty, and Health Insurance Coverage in the United States: 2010," September 2011. Retrieved Feb 2012, from www.census.gov/prod/2011pubs/p60-239.pdf
12. See Andrew Cassel, "Black Middle Class Continues to Grow, but Gaps Remain," Philadelphia Inquirer (July 12, 2004), p. B6.
13. U.S. Census Bureau, "Income, Poverty, and Health Insurance Coverage in the United States: 2010," September 2011. Retrieved Feb 2012, from www.census.gov/prod/2011pubs/p60-239.pdf
14. U.S. Census Bureau, "Income, Poverty, and Health Insurance Coverage in the United States: 2010," September 2011. Retrieved Feb 2012, from www.census.gov/prod/2011pubs/p60-239.pdf
15. U.S. Census Bureau, "Current Population Survey: 2011 For the Annual Social and Economic Supplement," Washington, DC. Retrieved Feb 2012, from www.census.gov/hhes/www/cpstc/cps_table_creator.html
16. U.S. Census Bureau, "Housing Vacancies and Home Ownership: Annual Statistics 2007." Retrieved June 2008, from www.census.gov/hhes/www/housing/hvs/annual07/ann07t20.html
17. U.S. Census Bureau, "USA Quick Facts", Jan 2012. Retrieved March 2012, from http://quickfacts.census.gov/qfd/states/00000.html
18. U.S. Census Bureau, "Income, Poverty, and Health Insurance Coverage in the United States: 2010," September 2011. Retrieved Feb 2012, from www.census.gov/prod/2011pubs/p60-239.pdf
19. U.S. Census Bureau, "The Black Population: 2010," September 2011. Retrieved Feb 2012, from http://www.census.gov/prod/cen2010/briefs/c2010br-06.pdf
20. U.S. Census Bureau, "The Black Population: 2010," September 2011. Retrieved Feb 2012, from http://www.census.gov/prod/cen2010/briefs/c2010br-06.pdf
21. U.S. Census Bureau, "Income, Poverty, and Health Insurance Coverage in the United States: 2010," September 2011. Retrieved Feb 2012, from www.census.gov/prod/2011pubs/p60-239.pdf
22. See "Family Income Finally Rises," *New York Times* (September 27, 1996), p. 18; and U.S. Census Bureau, "The Black Population in the United States, March 2002." Retrieved July 2004, from www.census.gov/prod/2003pubs/p20-541.pdf
23. U.S. Census Bureau, "Income, Poverty, and Health Insurance Coverage in the United States: 2010," September 2011. Retrieved Feb 2012, from www.census.gov/prod/2011pubs/p60-239.pdf

24. U.S. Census Bureau, "Current Population Survey: 2011 For the Annual Social and Economic Supplement," Washington, DC. Retrieved Feb 2012, from www.census.gov/hhes/www/cpstc/cps_table_creator.html

25. U.S. Census Bureau, "Income, Poverty, and Health Insurance Coverage in the United States: 2010," September 2011. Retrieved Feb 2012, from www.census.gov/prod/2011pubs/p60-239.pdf]

26. U.S. Census Bureau, "USA Quick Facts", Jan 2012. Retrieved March 2012, from http://quickfacts.census.gov/qfd/states/00000.html

27. U.S. Census Bureau, "Current Population Survey: 2006", Washington, D.C., Revised August 2007. Retrieved April 2008 from http://pubdb3.census.gov/macro/032007/perinc/new03_009.htm.

28. Boyce Watkins, "Black Unemployment Rate Increases 700% More than White," Black Voices, September 6, 2010. Retrieved October 2010, from www.bvonmoney.com/2010/09/06/black-unemployment-rate-increases-700-more-than-white/

29. U.S. Bureau of Labor Statistics, "Employment Status of the Civilian Population by Race, Sex, and Age," Feb 2012. Retrieved Feb 2012, from www.bls.gov/news.release/empsit.t02.htm

30. U.S. Bureau of Labor Statistics, "News Release: Usual Weekly Earnings of Wage and Salary Workers Fourth Quarter 2011," January 24, 2012. Retrieved Feb 2012, from www.bls.gov/news.release/pdf/wkyeng.pdf

31. Bernstein, *Where's the Payoff?*

32. Bureau of Justice Statistics, "Criminal Offender Statistics." Retrieved June 2008, from www.ojp.usdoj.gov/bjs/crimoff.htm#inmates

33. See American Bar Association, "A Statistical Look at Criminal Justice and Injustice," Human Rights Magazine (Winter 2004), p. 19; and Matthew Klein, "Death Row in Black and White," American Demographics 20, no. 5, pp. 39–40.

34. U.S. Census Bureau, "Statistical Abstract of the United States: 2012," Washington, D.C, 131st edition. Retrieved Feb 2012, from www.census.gov/compendia/statab/

35. U.S. Census Bureau, "Statistical Abstract of the United States: 2012," Washington, D.C, 131st edition. Retrieved Feb 2012, from www.census.gov/compendia/statab/

36. U.S. Census Bureau, "Projected Population of the United States, by Race and Hispanic Origin: 2000 to 2050," March 18, 2004. Retrieved July 2004 from www.census.gov/ipc/www/usintermproj/natprojtab01a.pdf

37. U.S. Department of Health and Human Services, Center for Disease Control and Prevention, "Health, United States, 2010: With Special Feature on Death and Dying," Washington, D.C, Feb 2011. Retrieved Feb 2012, from www.cdc.gov/nchs/data/hus/hus10.pdf

38. Centers for Disease Control and Prevention, CDC Features, "CDC Addresses the HIV/AIDS Epidemic among African Americans," February 2008. Retrieved April 2008, from www.cdc.gov/Features/BlackHIVAIDSAwareness

39. National Vital Statistics Reports, "Deaths: Preliminary Data for 2006," June 2008. Retrieved June 2008, from www.cdc.gov/nchs/data/nvsr/nvsr56/nvsr56_16.pdf

40. U.S. Census Bureau, "Census Bureau Facts for Features, African American History Month, 2004."

41. U.S. Census Bureau, "Statistical Abstract of the United States: 2012," Washington, D.C, 131st edition. Retrieved Feb 2012, from www.census.gov/compendia/statab/

42. U.S. Census Bureau, "Statistical Abstract of the United States: 2012," Washington, D.C, 131st edition. Retrieved Feb 2012, from www.census.gov/compendia/statab/

43. U.S. Bureau of Labor Statistics, "News Release: Usual Weekly Earnings of Wage and Salary Workers Fourth Quarter 2011," January 24, 2012. Retrieved Feb 2012, from www.bls.gov/news.release/pdf/wkyeng.pdf

44. U.S. Census Bureau, "Statistical Abstract of the United States: 2012," Washington, D.C, 131st edition. Retrieved Feb 2012, from www.census.gov/compendia/statab/

45. See U.S. Department of Health and Human Services, Indicators of Welfare Dependence: Annual Report to Congress, 2003, HHS, Washington, DC.

46. Department of Commerce, "Young, Diverse, Urban: Hispanic Population Reaches All-Time High of 38.8 Million."

47. U.S. Census Bureau, "Overview of Race and Hispanic Origin: 2010," March 2011. Retrieved Feb 2012, from www.census.gov/prod/cen2010/briefs/c2010br-02.pdf

48. U.S. Census Bureau, "Overview of Race and Hispanic Origin: 2010," March 2011. Retrieved Feb 2012, from www.census.gov/prod/cen2010/briefs/c2010br-02.pdf

49. U.S. Census Bureau, "Income, Poverty, and Health Insurance Coverage in the United States: 2010," September 2011. Retrieved Feb 2012, from www.census.gov/prod/2011pubs/p60-239.pdf

50. U.S. Census Bureau, "The Hispanic Population: 2010," May 2011. Retrieved March 2012, from http://www.census.gov/prod/cen2010/briefs/c2010br-04.pdf

51. U.S. Census Bureau, "Income, Poverty, and Health Insurance Coverage in the United States: 2010," September 2011. Retrieved Feb 2012, from www.census.gov/prod/2011pubs/p60-239.pdf

52. U.S. Census Bureau, "The Hispanic Population: 2010," May 2011. Retrieved March 2012, from http://www.census.gov/prod/cen2010/briefs/c2010br-04.pdf

53. U.S. Census Bureau, "Statistical Abstract of the United States: 2012," Washington, D.C, 131st edition. Retrieved Feb 2012, from www.census.gov/compendia/statab/

54. U.S. Census Bureau, "Summary Statistics for Changes in the Number of Hispanic-Owned Businesses and Their Receipts: 1997 to 2002." Retrieved June 2008, from www.census.gov/csd/sbo/summarychangehispanic.pdf

55. Compiled from Bureau of Indian Affairs, Answers to Frequently Asked Questions, 2001. Retrieved August 2004, from http://usa.usembassy.de/etexts/soc/bia.pdf. See also U.S. Department of the Interior. Retrieved October 21, 2008, from www.doi.gov/bia

56. U.S. Census Bureau, "Overview of Race and Hispanic Origin: 2010," March 2011. Retrieved Feb 2012, from www.census.gov/prod/cen2010/briefs/c2010br-02.pdf

57. See Evelyn Lance Blanchard, "American Indians and Alaska Natives," *Encyclopedia of Social Work,* 18th ed. (Silver Spring, MD: NASW, 1987), p. 61; U.S. Bureau of the Census, *Census of Population and Housing Summary* (Washington, DC: U.S. Government Printing Office, 1990), p. 93; and U.S. Department of the Interior, Bureau of Indian Affairs, "Statistical Abstract on the Web."

58. H. F. Dobyns, *Native American Historical Demography: A Critical Bibliography* (Bloomington, IN: Indiana University Press, 1976), p. 32.

59. H. E. Fey and D. McNickle, *Indians and Other Americans: Two Ways of Life Meet* (New York: Harper & Row, 1970), pp. 9–12.

60. Thomas Hayden, "A Modern Life: After Decades of Discrimination, Poverty, and Despair, American Indians Can Finally Look Toward a Better Future," *U.S. News and World Report* (October 4, 2004), p. 20.

61. U.S. Commission on Civil Rights, Office of the General Counsel, "Broken Promises: Evaluating the Native American Health Care System," Draft Report for Commissioners' Review, Washington, DC, July 2, 2004.

62. William N. Evans and Julie H. Topoleski, "The Social and Economic Impact of Native American Casinos," *NBER Working Paper No. w9198*, National Bureau of Economic Research, September 2002. Retrieved October 2004, from www.bsos.umd.edu/econ/evans/wpapers/evans_topoleski_casinos.pdf

63. B. J. Jones, "The Indian Child Welfare Act: The Need for a Separate Law," American Bar Association, 1995. Retrieved October 2004, from www.abanet.org/genpractice/compleat/f95child.html

64. U.S. Department of Justice, "Coverage Issues under the Indian Self-Determination Act," Memorandum for the Assistant Attorney General Civil Division, April 22, 1998. Retrieved October 2004, from www.usdoj.gov/olc/isdafin.htm

65. U.S. Census Bureau, "The Asian Population, 2000," February 2002. Retrieved September 2004, from www.census.gov/prod/2002pubs/c2kbr01-16.pdf

66. U.S. Census Bureau, "Overview of Race and Hispanic Origin: 2010," March 2011. Retrieved Feb 2012, from www.census.gov/prod/cen2010/briefs/c2010br-02.pdf

67. U.S. Census Bureau, "Overview of Race and Hispanic Origin: 2010," March 2011. Retrieved Feb 2012, from www.census.gov/prod/cen2010/briefs/c2010br-02.pdf

68. Felicity Barringer, "U.S. Asian Population Up 70% in 80's," *New York Times* (March 2, 1990), p. 1.

69. U.S. Census Bureau, "Statistical Abstract of the United States: 2012," Washington, D.C, 131st edition. Retrieved Feb 2012, from www.census.gov/compendia/statab/

70. Daniel Goleman, "Probing School Success of Asian-Americans," *New York Times*, September 11, 1990, p. A8.

71. U.S. Census Bureau, "Statistical Abstract of the United States: 2012," Washington, D.C., 131st edition. Retrieved Feb 2012, from www.census.gov/compendia/statab/

72. Ibid.

73. Population Resource Center, Immigration: Key Facts & Trends, 2012. Retrieved March 2012 from, http://www.prcdc.org/300million/Immigration/

74. G.H. Hansen, "Immigration and Economic Growth," *Cato Journal* 32:1 (Winter 2012), pp.25–34.

75. Jeffrey S. Passel, Randy Capps, and Michael Fix, "Undocumented Immigrants: Facts and Figures," Urban Institute Immigration Studies Program, Washington, DC, January 12, 2004.

76. Population Resource Center, Immigration: Key Facts & Trends, 2012. Retrieved March 2012 from, http://www.prcdc.org/300million/Immigration/

77. Pia M. Orrenius, Federal Reserve Bank of Dallas, "U.S. Immigration and Economic Growth: Putting Policy on Hold," *Southwest Economy* (6), (November/December 2003), p. 3.

78. Ibid.

79. U.S. Department of Justice, Immigration and Naturalization Service, "Immigration to the United States in Fiscal Year 1995" (Washington, DC: USDOJ, August 5, 1996).

80. Congressional Budget Office, "Immigration Policy in the United States: An Update 1" (December 2010). Retrieved Feb 2012, from American State Papers at http://heinonline.org/HOL/Page?handle=hein.congrec/cbo9397&id=1&collection=congrec&index=cbo/cbohs

81. HR 3734: Personal Responsibility and Work Opportunity Reconciliation Act (Immigration Provisions)—Conference Committee Version: Title IV, Restricting Welfare and Public Benefits for Aliens (Washington, DC: U.S. House of Representatives, Conference Committee, August 5, 1996), p. 16.

82. Patty Reinert, "Federal Welfare Plan Hits Legal Immigrants," *Houston Chronicle* (August 2, 1996), pp. 1A and 16A.

83. Greg McDonald, "House Passes $600 Billion Spending Bill," *Houston Chronicle* (September 29, 1996), pp. 1A and 32A.

84. *The Wall Street Journal*, "NYPD surveillance of students called 'disgusting'," February 26, 2012, p. 5.

85. Mike Sacks, "Arizona Immigration Law's Supreme Court Oral Argument Set For April," *The Huffington Post*, February 3, 2012. Retrieved March 2012 from, http://www.huffingtonpost.com/2012/02/03/arizona-immigration-law-_n_1253502.html

86. "Mexican Migration to the United States." Retrieved March 20, 2007, from www.farmworkers.org/migrdata.html

87. "The Official Bracero Agreement." Retrieved March 20, 2007, from www.farmworkers.org/bpaccord.html

88. Dick Meister, "Give Braceros Their Money," 2001. Retrieved March 20, 2007, from www.labornet.org/viewpoints/meister/braceros.htm

89. Congressional Budget Office, "Immigration Policy in the United States: An Update 1" (December 2010). Retrieved Feb 2012, from American State Papers at http://heinonline.org/HOL/Page?handle=hein.congrec/cbo9397&id=1&collection=congrec&index=cbo/cbohs

90. Justin Vaisse, Muslims in Europe: A short Introduction, US – Europe Analysis Series, The Brookings Institution, Center on the United States and Europe, September 2008. Retrieved March 2012 from, http://www.brookings.edu/~/media/Files/rc/papers/2008/09_europe_muslims_vaisse/09_europe_muslims_vaisse.pdf

91. Toni Johnson, Europe: Integrating Islam, Council on Foreign Relations, July 25, 2011. Retrieved March 2012 from http://www.cfr.org/religion/europe-integrating-islam/p8252

92. Divya Talwar, "Growing Use of Sharia by UK Muslims," BBC Asian Network, January 16, 2012. Retrieved March 2012 from, http://www.bbc.co.uk/news/uk-16522447

93. John R. Bowen, "Europeans against Multiculturalism," Boston Review, July/August 2011. Retrieved March 2012 from, http://bostonreview.net/BR36.4/john_r_bowen_european_multiculturalism_islam.php

94. Sify News, "Swedish Newspapers Reprint Prophet Mohammed Cartoon," March 10, 2010. Retrieved March 2012 from, http://www.sify.com/news/swedish-newspapers-reprint-prophet-mohammed-cartoon-news-international-kdktEpgbdic.html

95. Deutsche Welle, Europe Grapples with "Honor Killings," 2012. Retrieved March 2012 from, http://www.dw.de/dw/article/0,,1244406,00.html

96. BBC News, "Europe Tackles Honour Killings," June 22, 2004. Retrieved March 2012 from, http://news.bbc.co.uk/2/hi/europe/3828675.stm

97. Paula Newton, "Guilty Verdict in 'Honor' Murders," CNN, January 29, 2012. Retrieved March 2012 from, http://articles.cnn.com/2012-01-29/americas/world_americas_canada-honor-murder_1_honor-murder-verdicts-family-car?_s=PM:AMERICAS

98. Amiel Ungar, "Muslims see French Anti-Burqa Law as Veiled Threat," Israel National News, April 11, 2011. Retrieved March 2012 from, http://www.israelnationalnews.com/News/News.aspx/143503#.T1Fhf3ncCSp

99. Tzvi Ben Gedalyahu, "Ban the Burqa, Muslim Veil Trend Spreads to Italy," Israel National News, August 5, 2011. Retrieved March 2012 from, http://www.israelnationalnews.com/News/News.aspx/146406#.T1GclXncCSo

100. Toni Johnson, Europe: Integrating Islam, Council on Foreign Relations, July 25, 2011. Retrieved March 2012 from http://www.cfr.org/religion/europe-integrating-islam/p8252

101. Treaty of Amsterdam Amending the Treaty on European Union, the Treaties Establishing the European Communities and Related Acts. Official Journal C 340, November 10, 1997. Retrieved March 2012 from, http://eur-lex.europa.eu/en/treaties/dat/11997D/htm/11997D.html

102. Diane Roberts, "The Republican Party Declares War on Women," The Guardian, March 5, 2012, p. 16.

103. U.S. Department of Justice, "National Crime Victimization Survey," August 1995. Quoted in U.S. Department of Justice, "The Violence against Women Act," September 23, 1996. Retrieved 2000, from www.ovw.usdoj.gov/index.html

104. Patricia Tjaden and Nancy Thoennes, "Extent, Nature, and Consequences of Intimate Partner Violence: Findings from the National Violence against Women Survey," National Institute of Justice, NCJ 181867, July 2000. Retrieved October 2004, from http://ncjrs.org/txtfiles1/nij/181867.txt

105. U.S. Department of Justice, National Crime Victimization Survey.

106. Campaign for Funding to End Domestic and Sexual Violence, VAWA Appropriations For Fiscal Years '10, '11, '12 and '13, 2012. Retrieved March 2012 from, http://www.nnedv.org/docs/Policy/FY13Approps_Chart.pdf

107. AFL-CIO, "Ask a Working Woman Survey Report."

108. Diana Pearce, quoted in S. Bianchi, "Feminization and Juvenilization of Poverty: Trends, Relative Risks, Causes and Consequences," Annual Review of Sociology 25 (1999), pp. 307–333.

109. U.S. Census Bureau, "Income, Poverty, and Health Insurance Coverage in the United States: 2010," September 2011. Retrieved Feb 2012, from www.census.gov/prod/2011pubs/p60-239.pdf

110. Although we have stressed single female-headed families here, it is important to acknowledge that single male-headed families are growing even more rapidly. From 1959 to 1989, single male-headed families grew from 350,000 to 1.4 million, compared with 7.4 million mother-only and 25.5 million two-parent households. From 1960 to 1990, the percentage of father-only households increased 300 percent. See Daniel R. Mayer and Steven Garasky, "Custodial Fathers: Myths, Realities, and Child Support Policy," Institute for Research on Poverty, Madison, WI, August 1992, Discussion Paper no. 982-992, pp. 8–9.

111. National Commission on Children, Poverty, Welfare and America's Families, p. 3.

112. Diane Harris, "The Cost of Raising a Baby," Parenting, 2010. Retrieved October 2012 from, http://www.parenting.com/article/the-cost-of-raising-a-baby.

113. Martha N. Ozawa, "Gender and Ethnicity in Social Security," Conference Proceedings, Nelson A. Rockefeller Institute of Government, State University of New York at Albany, November 1985, pp. 2–6.

114. Much of the following section is based on information found in Wider Opportunities for Women, Making Both Ends Meet (Washington, DC: Wider Opportunities for Women, 1991), pp. 4–9.

115. AFL-CIO, "Ask a Working Woman Survey Report," Washington, DC, 2004.

116. Thomas A. Kochan, "Bringing Family Values to the Workplace," The Boston Globe, (August 29, 2004), p. 18.

117. Bureau of Labor Statistics, Employment Characteristics of Families Summary, Employment Characteristics of Families—2011. Retrieved October 2012 from, http://www.bls.gov/news.release/famee.nr0.htm

118. Family assistance was one of the major thrusts of the former Clinton administration. It is also an issue that crosses racial and social class lines.

119. AFL-CIO, "Ask a Working Woman Survey Report."

120. U.S. Census Bureau, "Income, Poverty, and Health Insurance Coverage in the United States: 2010," September 2011. Retrieved Feb 2012, from www.census.gov/prod/2011pubs/p60-239.pdf

121. Department of Labor, Bureau of Labor Statistics, *Women in the Labor Force—A Databook*, 2007. Retrieved June 2008, from www.bls.gov/cps/wlfdatabook-2007.pdf

122. U.S. Bureau of Labor Statistics, "News Release: Usual Weekly Earnings of Wage and Salary Workers Fourth Quarter 2011," January 24, 2012. Retrieved Feb 2012, from www.bls.gov/news.release/pdf/wkyeng.pdf

123. S. Hofferth, "Childcare, Maternal Employment and Public Policy," *Annals of the American Academy of Political and Social Sciences* 563 (May 1999), pp. 20–38.

124. The National Association of Child Care Resource & Referral Agencies "2007 Child Care Capacity." Retrieved June 2008, fromwww.naccrra.org/randd/program.php?Page_1

125. The National Association of Child Care Resource & Referral Agencies, "2007 Price of Child Care." Retrieved June 2008, fromwww.naccrra.org/randd/docs/2007_Price_of_Child_Care.pdf

126. Children's Defense Fund, "The State of America's Children," p. 37.

127. Sarah Fass, Paid Leave in the States: A Critical Support for Low-wage Workers and Their Families, National Center for Children in Poverty, March 2009. Malman School of Public Health, Columbia University.

128. Sidel, *Women and Children Last,* p. 123.

129. National Commission on Working Women of Wider Opportunities for Women, "Women, Work and Health Insurance" (Washington, DC: Wider Opportunities for Women, n.d.).

130. National Commission on Working Women, "Women and Nontraditional Work."

131. Jim Harris, *The Complete Text of the Equal Rights Amendment* (New York: Ganis & Harris, 1980), p. 7.

132. Guttmacher Institute, "An Overview of Abortion in the United States." Retrieved June 2008, from www.guttmacher.org/media/presskits/2005/06/28/abortionoverview.html

133. Nanneska Magee, "Should the Federal Government Fund Abortions? No," in Howard Jacob Karger and James Midgley (eds.), *Controversial Issues in Social Policy* (Boston: Allyn & Bacon, 1993).

134. Tanya Albert, "Abortion, Legal since 1973, Still Shapes, Divides Doctors," *AMNews,* January 27, 2003, p. 30.

135. Guttmacher Institute, Facts on Induced Abortion in the United States, August 2011. Retrieved March 2012 from, http://www.guttmacher.org/pubs/fb_induced_abortion.html

136. Gallup, Abortion, 2012. Retrieved March 2012 from, http://www.gallup.com/poll/1576/abortion.aspx

137. Guttmacher Institute, State Policies in Brief: An Overview of Abortion Laws, March 1, 2012. Retrieved March 2012, from http://www.guttmacher.org/statecenter/spibs/spib_OAL.pdf

138. Chris McGreal, "Personhood Amendment Campaigners Vow to Fight on after Mississippi Defeat," *The Guardian,* November 9, 2011, p. 8.

139. World health Organization, Female genital mutilation, Fact sheet N°241, February 2012. Retrieved March 2012 from, http://www.who.int/mediacentre/factsheets/fs241/en/index.html

140. OECD, Gender Equality and Social Institutions in Saudi Arabia, Social institutions and Gender Index, nd. Retrieved March 2012 from, http://genderindex.org/country/saudi-arabia

141. OECD, Gender Equality and Social Institutions in Saudi Arabia, Social institutions and Gender Index, nd. Retrieved March 2012 from, http://genderindex.org/country/saudi-arabia

142. Cindy Hanford, Women's Lives Under the Taliban: a Background Report on the Condition of Women in Afghanistan since 1996. National Organization of Women, November 2001. Retrieved March 2012 from, http://www.now.org/issues/global/afghanwomen1.html

143. Homa Khaleeli, "Afghan Women Fear for the Future," The Guardian, February 4, 2011, p. 16, G2.

144. Atia Abawi, "Afghan Girls Maimed by Acid Vow to Go to School," CNN News, January 22, 2009. Retrieved March 2012 from, http://articles.cnn.com/2009-01-22/world/acid.attacks_1_kandahar-taliban-afghan-government?_s=PM:WORLD

145. Lianne Gutcher, "Fears and Blessings at Kabul Girls' School in Vanguard of Progress," The Guardian, July 19, 2011, p. 12.

146. U.S. Department of State, Trafficking in Persons Report 2011. Retrieved March 2012 from, http://www.state.gov/j/tip/rls/tiprpt/2011/index.htm

147. Margaret S. Stockdale, "Patchwork Protections: Progress and Problems in Battling Sexual Orientation Discrimination in Employment," Southern Illinois University Carbondale, Society for Industrial Psychology. Retrieved October 2008, from, www.siop.org/tip/Jan08/02stockdale.aspx

148. "California Court Affirms Right to Gay Marriage," *New York Times,* May 16, 2008.

149. "State of the Union Address 2000," *Washington Post.* Retrieved November 2001, from www.washingtonpost.com/wp-srv/politics/special/states/docs/sou00.htm

150. National Coalition of Anti-Violence Programs, "Annual Report on Anti-LGBT Hate Violence Released," May 07, 2007. Retrieved April 2008, from www.ncavp.org/media/MediaReleaseDetail.aspx?p_2285&d_2409

151. Kent Kilpatrick, "Oregon Voters Reject Stigmatizing Homosexuals," *The Advocate* (November 5, 1992), p. 2C.

152. Human Rights and Equal Opportunity Commission, "Federal and State Anti-Discrimination Law." Retrieved

October 2008, from www.hreoc.gov.au/info_for_employers/law/index.html

153. Much of the section on gays and lesbians in the military was derived from Rivette Vullo, "Homosexuals in the Military," unpublished paper, Louisiana State University School of Social Work, Baton Rouge, LA, December 4, 1991. See also K. Dyer (ed.), *Gays in Uniform: The Pentagon's Secret Reports* (Boston: Alyson, 1990).

154. Dyer, *Gays in Uniform,* p. xiv.

155. Joseph Harry, "Homosexual Men and Women Who Served Their Country," *Journal of Homosexuality* 10 (1984), pp. 117–125.

156. R. Sneyd, "Same-Sex Bill Not about Marriage, Legislators Say," *Patriot Ledger* (March 18, 2000), p. 18.

157. Ibid.

158. See J. J. Sampson et al., *Texas Family Code Annotated* (Eagan, MN: West Group, August 1999); and N. D. Hunter et al., *The Rights of Lesbians and Gay Men: The Basic ACLU Guide to a Gay Person's Rights,* 3rd ed. (Carbondale & Edwardsville, IL: Southern Illinois University Press, 1992).

159. National Institute of Allergy and Infectious Diseases, "HIV/AIDS Statistics," National Institutes of Health, July 2004. Retrieved October 2004, from www.niaid.nih.gov/factsheets/aidsstat.htm

160. Mariah Blake, "God Has Created You for Heterosexuality': Clinics Owned by Michele Bachmann's Husband Practice Ex-Gay Therapy, The Nation, July 8, 2011, p. 17

161. Joann Szabo, Phyllis Tonkin, Veronique Vaillancourt, Philip Winston, and Deidre Wright, "The Clinton Scorecard," unpublished paper, University of Houston Graduate School of Social Work, Houston, TX, April 25, 1996.

162. European Union Agency for Fundamental Rights, Lesbian, Gay, Bisexual and Transgender Rights, 2011. Retrieved March 2012 from,http://fra.europa.eu/fraWebsite/lgbt-rights/lgbt-rights_en.htm

163. Jeffrey Gettleman, "Americans' Role Seen in Uganda Anti-gay Push," The New York Times, January 3, 2010, p. A9.

164. Josh Kron, "Resentment Toward the West Bolsters Uganda's New Anti-Gay Bill," The New York Times, February 28, 2012, p. B6.

165. BBC News, "Uganda's Rolling Stone Paper Told to Stop Outing Gays," November 1, 2010. Retrieved March 2012 from, http://www.bbc.co.uk/news/world-africa-11666789

166. Federal Interagency Forum on Aging Related Statistics, Older Americans 2010: Key Indicators of Well-Being, 2010. Retrieved March 2012 from, http://www.agingstats.gov/agingstatsdotnet/Main_Site/Data/2010_Documents/Docs/OA_2010.pdf

167. U.S. Census Bureau "Older Adults in 2005." Retrieved June 2008, from www.census.gov/population/pop-profile/dynamic/OLDER.pdf

168. Ibid.

169. C. Cozic (ed.), *An Aging Population: Opposing Viewpoints* (San Diego, CA: Greenhaven Press, 1996).

170. Agingstats.gov "Older Americans 2008: Key Indicators of Well-Being". Retrieved June 2008 from http://agingstats.gov/Agingstatsdotnet/Main_Site/Data/2008_Documents/Economics.aspx

171. U.S. Census Bureau, "Income, Poverty, and Health Insurance Coverage in the United States: 2010," September 2011. Retrieved Feb 2012, from www.census.gov/prod/2011pubs/p60-239.pdf

172. Agingstats.gov, "Older Americans 2008: Key Indicators of Well-Being." Retrieved June 2008, from http://agingstats.gov/Agingstatsdotnet/Main_Site/Data/2008_Documents/Economics.aspx

173. Cozic, *An Aging Population.*

174. Agingstats.gov, "Use of Healthcare Services."Retrieved June 2008, from http://agingstats.gov/agingstatsdotnet/Main_Site/Data/2008_Documents/Health_Care.pdf

175. Agingstats.gov, "Use of Healthcare Services.". Retrieved June 2008, from http://agingstats.gov/agingstatsdotnet/Main_Site/Data/2008_Documents/Health_Care.pdf Haber, "Trends and Demographic Studies on Programs for Disabled Persons," in L. G. Perlman and G. Austin (eds.), *A Report of the Ninth Annual Mary E. Switzer Memorial Seminar* (Alexandria, VA, 1985), pp. 27–29.

176. U.S. Census Bureau, "Income, Poverty, and Health Insurance Coverage in the United States: 2010," September 2011. Retrieved Feb 2012, from www.census.gov/prod/2011pubs/p60-239.pdf

177. William Roth, "Disabilities: Physical," *Encyclopedia of Social Work,* 18th ed. (Silver Spring, MD: NASW, 1987), p. 86.

178. Ibid.

179. Haber, "Trends and Demographic Studies," p. 32.

180. U.S. Census Bureau, "Income, Poverty, and Health Insurance Coverage in the United States: 2010," September 2011. Retrieved Feb 2012, from www.census.gov/prod/2011pubs/p60-239.pdf

181. Winifred Bell, *Contemporary Social Welfare,* New York: MacMillan, 1983, p. 174.

182. U.S. Census Bureau, "Income, Poverty, and Health Insurance Coverage in the United States: 2010," September 2011. Retrieved Feb 2012, from www.census.gov/prod/2011pubs/p60-239.pdf

183. Administration on Developmental Disabilities, *Fact Sheet* (Washington, DC: Administration on Developmental Disabilities, n.d.).

184. Kathy Brown, "Mend It, Don't End It," *Outlook* 90, no. 3 (Fall 1996), p. 9.

185. Ibid., p. 11.

186. Bill Clinton, "Mend, Don't End, Affirmative Action," *Congressional Quarterly Weekly Report* 53 (July 22, 1995), pp. 2208–2209.

187. Wilson, *The Truly Disadvantaged,* pp. 146–147.

Poverty in America

Source: Brian Eichhorn/Shutterstock

This chapter examines the characteristics of poverty in the United States, focusing particular attention on demographic aspects and ways of measuring poverty; family constitution and poverty; child poverty and elderly poverty; the urban and rural poor; and the connections between poverty and work-related issues such as the minimum wage, structural unemployment, dual labor markets, job training programs, and the alternative financial sector or the fringe economy. Last, key strategies developed to combat poverty will be surveyed.

Poverty can be defined as deprivation—either absolute or relative. Absolute poverty refers to an unequivocal standard necessary for survival (e.g., the calories necessary for physical survival, adequate shelter for protection against the elements, and proper clothing). Relative poverty refers to deprivation that is relative to the standard of living enjoyed by other members of society. Although basic needs are met, citizens may be considered poor if they possess fewer resources, opportunities, or goods than others. Relative poverty (or deprivation) is inequality in the distribution of income, goods, or opportunities.

The Culture of Poverty

Poverty theories sometimes cycle in and out of fashion, albeit modified. One such theory is the Culture of Poverty (COP) which maintains that poverty and poverty traits are transmitted intergenerationally in a self-perpetuating cycle. According to this theory, the COP transcends regional, rural/urban, and national differences and everywhere shows striking similarities in family structure, interpersonal relations, time orientation, value systems, and patterns of spending.

Writing in the 1960s, Oscar Lewis argued that the COP is characterized by hopelessness, indifference, alienation, apathy, and a lack of effective participation in or integration into the social and economic fabric of society. Key elements are a present-tense time orientation; cynicism and mistrust of those in authority; feelings of marginality, helplessness, dependence, and inferiority; a high incidence of maternal deprivation; lack of impulse control and the inability to defer gratification; a sense of resignation and fatalism; a widespread belief in male superiority; a high tolerance for psychological pathology; a high incidence of abandonment of wives and children; and a matriarchal family structure.[1]

By the late 1960s, cultural explanations of poverty became a taboo subject among sociologists since it placed the blame for poverty squarely on the character of the poor. It was also seen in many quarters are being inherently racist. However, the older culture debate around poverty has resurfaced, albeit different form. Contemporary social scientists reject the notion of a monolithic and fixed COP. Instead, they attribute destructive attitudes

Spotlight 5.1

POVERTY

People living in poverty fall into three general categories:
1. Those making only minimum wage (the working poor)
2. The unemployed
3. Those with poor health or an occupational disability (e.g., a deficit in human capital such as poor education or a low quality and quantity of training and skills)

RESULTS is a nonprofit grassroots advocacy organization committed to creating the political will to end hunger and the worst aspects of poverty. RESULTS members lobby elected officials for effective solutions and key policies that affect hunger and poverty. To learn more about RESULTS, go to the organization's website at www.results.org.

and behavior to racism and isolation rather than the flawed moral character of the poor.

The critique of the old COP theory is grounded in the realization that many aspects of a poverty culture observed by Lewis are now commonplace among the middle class, such as high divorce rates, cohabitation outside of marriage, single-motherhood, and relaxed sexual mores. The prism by which the poor are viewed continues to vacillate between the poor as causes of their own poverty or as victims of a racist, market society.

Eugenics and Poverty

Theories based on genetic inferiority have been used as explanations for poverty, crime, and disease. Henry Goddard's *The Kallikak Family* was an account of a Revolutionary War soldier who had an affair with a feebleminded servant girl before marrying a "respectable" woman.[2] Goddard meticulously listed the disreputable descendants of the servant girl and compared them with the respectable achievers of the wife's descendants. Generations of students were taught the dogma of eugenics. For a time, the eugenics movement lost favor when these theories were used by Hitler to justify genocide. However, the movement reemerged with the publication of Arthur Jensen's 1969 article "How Much Can We Boost IQ and Scholastic Achievement?"[3] Jensen concluded that compensatory education was doomed to failure since 80 percent of intelligence (measured by IQ tests) was inherited.[4]

The eugenics argument was rekindled in 1994 by Richard Herrnstein and Charles Murray's *The Bell Curve*, in which the authors argued that inequality in the United States was due to the lack of genetic intelligence.[5] Armed with statistics, tables, and charts, Herrnstein and Murray tried to demonstrate that those in the lower socioeconomic classes have lower IQ scores, which explains why white males (who test higher) control society's institutions.[6] They argue that affirmative action programs overlook intellectual meritocracy, and spending money to educate the poor is wasteful given their innate deficiencies.

The scholarship in *The Bell Curve* has been attacked by a wide range of critics in the scientific and educational communities.[7] Critics argue that Herrnstein and Murray exaggerate IQ as a predictor of job performance, attribute inaccurate validities to IQ scores, and substitute hypotheticals for reality.[8] Despite its resilience in popular culture,

theories of genetic inferiority have been repudiated by scores of educators, psychologists, sociologists, and anthropologists.[9]

The Radical or Socialist View of Poverty

For radicals, poverty results from exploitation by the ruling capitalist class. According to socialists (see Chapter 1), poverty provides capitalists with an army of surplus laborers who depress the wages of other workers. In an oversupply of labor, employers can easily threaten recalcitrant workers with dismissal given the intense competition for jobs.

David Gil observes that poverty can be understood in terms of status, resource allocation, and the division of labor.[10] For instance, societies must develop resources—symbolic, material, life-sustaining, and life-enhancing goods and services. They must also develop a division of labor and must assign individuals or groups to specific tasks related to developing, producing, or distributing societal resources. This division of labor is used to assign status to individuals and groups; that is, the more highly the societal elite prize the function an individual or group performs, the higher the status reward. This often has little to do with the actual value of a job. For instance, while teachers are far more important to most of us than Wall Street stockbrokers who craft risky financial instruments, the pay difference between them is staggering. By manipulating the division of labor, a society is able to assign individuals to specific statuses. In turn, poverty is correlated to the status a group or occupation occupies within a society.

The assignment of status roles is complemented by the distribution of rights. Higher-status roles implicitly involve greater compensation than lower-status roles, and such rewards come by way of the distribution of rights. Higher-status groups are also rewarded more entitlements and rights to material and symbolic resources, goods, and services than their lower-status cohorts. Conversely, lower-status groups are denied these resources or privileges by formal and informal constraints. For example, all things being equal, rich children have a greater chance of being admitted into elite Ivy League schools than those from a low-income family. Capitalist societies rationalize this status and goods allocation by an expressed belief in the omniscience of the marketplace. In other words, rewards are based on the value of one's contribution to the market. This ideology is rarely questioned. Socialists argue that poverty will exist as long as wealth and privileges are based solely on market values. For radicals, the abolition of poverty cannot occur without fundamentally altering the economic fabric of society.

Who Makes Up the Poor?

For most Americans, poverty is a fluid (rather than static) condition in which people cycle in and out. The University of Michigan's Panel Study of Income Dynamics (PSID) has followed thousands of U.S. families (9,000 in 2010) since 1968. The study has found that as people gained (or lost) jobs, as marriages were created (or dissolved), or as offspring were born (or left home), people were either pushed into poverty or escaped from it.[11]

PSID data points to a constellation of events that push people in and out of poverty. Some of these events include changes in household composition (divorce, abandonment, single-motherhood), loss of employment, and disability status. The shift from a two-adult household to a female-headed household and vice versa are the most likely causes for a transition into or an exit from poverty. While family composition was traditionally though to be the most salient factor in entering poverty, an even more important variable seems to be a loss or gain of employment. Some data suggests that the loss of a spouse's employment leads to short-term rather than long-term poverty spells, while employment gains of other household members are more important for exiting long-term poverty. In short, changes in employment rather than household composition may be the most important factors in who enters and exits poverty.[12]

An urban institute report by Gregory Acs and Seth Zimmerman found that intragenerational mobility rates have changed little since the 1980s and is considerable immobility at the bottom of the income distribution. More than 50 percent of individuals on the bottom economic rung will remain there ten years later, and less than seven in ten will make it to the American middle class. The report also observes that educational attainment continues to be the primary factor in upward economic mobility, while race and gender as indicators of upward mobility have diminished over time.[13]

Bradley Schiller found that upward mobility is experienced by the poor—one-third of minimum wage workers had received a raise within a year, and 60 percent were beyond the minimum wage within two years. "The longitudinal experiences of minimum-wage youth . . . refute the notion of a

'minimum-wage trap,'" he concluded. "Youth who started at the minimum wage in 1980 recorded impressive wage gains over the subsequent seven years both in absolute and relative terms."[14]

The following statistics from 2010 suggest some notable trends in poverty in the United States:

- The poverty rate was 15.1 percent (46.2 million people), up from 14.3 percent in 2009. This is the third year in a row that the poverty rate has increased.
- The poverty rate for children under 18 was 22 percent, up from 20.7 percent in 2009. The poverty rate for people over 65 was 9 percent.
- Beginning in 2001, the poverty rates also grew for nearly every racial and ethnic group. The poverty rate for blacks was 27.4 percent in 2010, almost three times higher than the poverty rate for whites (9.9 percent). For Hispanics, the poverty rate was 26.6 percent, but for children under the age of 18 it was 35 percent. The poverty rate for Asians was 12.1 percent. These numbers represent an important shift since poverty rates had edged downward throughout the 1990s; by 2001 the cycle was reversing and poverty rates began to climb.
- Poverty rates were 12.8 percent in the Northeast, 13.9 percent in the Midwest, 16.9 percent in the South, and 15.3 percent in the West.
- Not surprisingly, poverty rates were the lowest in suburbs and high within urban areas (19.7 percent) and outside metropolitan areas (16.5 percent).[15]

Table 5.1 describes the characteristics and numbers of the poor over a 50-year period.

Measuring Poverty

There are two versions of the federal poverty measure: (1) the poverty threshold and (2) the poverty guideline. The poverty threshold, also called the **poverty line,** is the official federal poverty measure and is used primarily for statistical purposes, such as estimating the number of Americans in poverty each year. All official population figures are calculated using the poverty threshold. The poverty guideline uses a slightly lower poverty level than the weighted poverty threshold. For example, the poverty threshold for a family of four in 2010 was $22,314,[16] while the poverty guideline was $22,050 for the same family.[17] The poverty guideline is used for determining eligibility for federal programs such

TABLE 5.1 Persons below the Poverty Line, Selected Years and Characteristics, 1959–2010 (number and percentage below poverty, in thousands)

Year	Overall	Aged	Children[a]	Individuals in Female-Headed Families[b]	Blacks	Hispanic[c]	White
2010	46,180	3,520	16,401	15,895	10,675	13,243	31,650
	15.1%	9.0%	22.0%	34.2%	27.4%	26.6%	13.0%
2006	36,460	3,394	12,827	13,199	9,048	9,243	24,416
	12.3%	9.4	17.4	30.5	24.3	20.6	10.3
+2002	34,570	3,578	12,133	11,667	8,884	8,556	24,074
	12.1%	10.4	16.7	26.5	24.1	21.8	10.3
1999	32,258	3,167	12,109	12,687	9,091	7,439	21,922
	11.8%	9.7	18.9	27.8	22.7	22.8	9.8
1995	36,425	3,318	13,999	12,315	9,872	8,574	24,423
	13.8%	10.5	20.2	32.4	29.3	30.3	11.2
1990	33,585	3,658	14,431	12,578	9,837	6,006	22,326
	13.5%	12.2	20.6	37.2	31.9	28.1	10.7
1986	32,370	3,477	12,876	11,944	8,983	5,117	22,183
	13.6%	12.4	20.5	38.3	31.3	27.3	11.0
1980	29,272	3,871	11,543	10,120	8,579	3,491	19,699
	13.0%	15.7	18.3	36.7	32.5	25.7	10.2
1978	24,497	3,233	9,931	9,269	7,626	2,607	16,259
	11.4%	14.0	15.9	35.6	30.6	21.6	8.7
1969	21,147	4,787	9,961	6,879	7,095	NA	16,659
	12.1%	25.3	14.0	38.2	32.2	NA	9.5
1959	39,490	5,481	17,552	7,014	9,927	NA	28,484
	22.4%	35.2	27.3	49.4	55.1	NA	18.1

+These numbers may appear inconsistent because the U.S. Census Bureau changed the classification of races in the 2000 and 2010 census to include the designation of more than one race. In addition, the statistics were calculated slightly differently in different years.

[a]All children, including unrelated children.

[b]Does not include females living alone.

[c]People of Hispanic origin may be of any race; it is an overlapping category.

Sources: Compiled from Committee on Ways and Means, U.S. House of Representatives, Overview of Entitlement Programs: 1992 Green Book (Washington, DC: U.S. Government Printing Office, 1992), Tables 2 and 3, pp. 1274–1275; and U.S. Census Bureau, "Poverty 1995," September 26, 1996, retrieved from www.census.gov/hhes/poverty/pov95/thresh95.html; Joseph Dalaker and Bernadette D. Proctor, U.S. Census Bureau, "Poverty in the United States: 1999," Current Population Reports, Ser. P60-210 (Washington, DC: U.S. Government Printing Office, 2000); and Bernadette D. Proctor and Joseph Dalaker, U.S. Census Bureau, "Poverty in the United States: 2002, Demographic Programs," Current Population Reports: Consumer Income, U.S. Department of Commerce, Economics and Statistics Administration (Washington, DC: U.S. Government Printing Office, September 2003); Carmen DeNavas-Walt, Bernadette D. Proctor, and Jessica Smith "Income, Poverty, and Health Insurance Coverage in the United States: 2006" Economics and Statistics Administration U.S. Census Bureau, Issued August 2007, Retrieved June 2008 from "http://www.census.gov/prod/2007pubs/p60-233.pdf" http://www.census.gov/prod/2007pubs/p60-233.pdf; U.S. Census Bureau, "Income, Poverty, and Health Insurance Coverage in the United States: 2010," September 2011. Retrieved Feb 2012, from www.census.gov/prod/2011pubs/p60-239.pdf.

TABLE 5.2 Changes in the Poverty Line Based on Income and Family Size, 1975–2010

Family Size	Income, Selected Years						
	1975	1980	1985	1990	2003	2007	2010
1	$2,724	$4,190	$5,250	$6,652	$9,393	$10,787	$11,139
2	3,506	5,363	7,050	8,509	12,015	13,884	14,218
3	4,293	6,565	8,850	10,419	14,680	16,218	17,374
4	5,500	8,414	10,650	13,359	18,810	21,386	22,314
5	6,499	9,966	12,450	15,572	22,245	25,791	26,439
6	7,316	11,269	14,250	17,839	25,122	29,664	29,897
7	9,022	13,955	16,050	20,241	28,544	34,132	34,009

Source: Compiled from U.S. Census Bureau, Technical Paper 56, ser. P-60, nos. 134 and 149 (Washington, DC: U.S. Government Printing Office, 1992); U.S. Census Bureau, "Poverty 1995," retrieved September 1996 from www.census.gov/hhes/poverty/pov95/thresh95.html; and Carmen DeNavas-Walt, Bernadette D. Proctor, and Robert J. Mills, U.S. Census Bureau, "Income, Poverty and Health Insurance Coverage in the United States: 2003," Current Population Reports, ser. p. 60–226, retrieved October 2004 from www.census.gov/prod/2004pubs/p60-226.pdf. U.S. Census Bureau, "Poverty Thresholds 2007". Retrieved June 2008 from http://www.census.gov/hhes/www/poverty/threshld/thresh07. html; U.S. Census Bureau, "Income, Poverty, and Health Insurance Coverage in the United States: 2010," September 2011. Retrieved Feb 2012, from www.census.gov/prod/2011pubs/p60-239.pdf.

as Head Start, Food Stamps, the School Lunch Program, and Low-Income Home Energy Assistance Program. Other federal programs, including TANF and Supplemental Security Income, use the poverty threshold. As noted earlier, the federal poverty index for a family of four was $22,314 in 2010, up from $8,414 in 1980.[18] (See Table 5.2.) These increases are due solely to the effects of inflation.

The poverty threshold used by the federal government was developed by taking the cost of the least expensive food plan (the Thrifty Food Plan developed by the Department of Agriculture) and multiplying that number by three. This formula was based on 1955 survey data showing that the average family spent about one-third of its budget on food. Formally adopted by the Social Security Administration (SSA) in 1969, the official poverty measure provides a set of income cutoffs adjusted for household size, the number of children under age 18, and the age of the household head. To ensure constant purchasing power, the SSA adjusts the poverty line yearly, using the consumer price index (CPI).

The poverty index is plagued by a variety of structural problems. A National Academy of Sciences (NAS) report noted that the poverty threshold disregards various in-kind benefits when counting family income,[19] including the costs (i.e., clothing, transportation, etc.) of employment; regional variations in living costs (i.e., housing and food); sales, payroll, and property taxes; the value (and costs)

of health care coverage and out-of-pocket medical expenses; and the change in consumption patterns (food costs now account for only one-seventh of household expenditures).[20]

Roosa et al., support this critique and raise the following issues around the poverty threshold:

- It does not reflect family structure and type (e.g., working mothers contributing to the household income or the healthcare costs of raising a child with a disability).
- It does not account for how families' needs change across lifespans (e.g. the different costs associated with children at various ages and the costs of having one or more elderly parents requiring full-time care).
- It does not account for recent changes such as the casualization of the workforce (which has increased job and income insecurity).
- It is arbitrary for those close to the limit. For instance, there is no significant difference between a family living below the poverty line and one that earns $1 more than the threshold.[21]

To partially offset the inherent flaws in the poverty index, Obama administration officials developed a new formula, the Supplementary Poverty Measure (SPM) that considers a wider range of factors in determining the poverty threshold. The SPM does not simply calculate a family's income and cost of food; instead, the new measure factors in modern expenses (e.g., high cost of healthcare, childcare, housing, utilities and in-kind benefits), plus "a little more," a new category that provides a little extra padding. The new formula will also adjust for geographic location (a major flaw in the existing poverty measure) and take into account benefits like food stamps, housing subsidies, and tax credits. Consequently, the new poverty measure will likely increase the percentage of people classified as poor, especially among the elderly Americans who are subject to high medical expenses. Although the SPM will be used in Census Bureau reports, it will not replace the existing poverty measure in determining eligibility for government programs since it would substantially increase the costs of those programs.[22] Among other variables, an accurate poverty threshold would take into account important changes (and additional costs) in family structure and labor force participation.

Families and Poverty

Family composition is strongly correlated to poverty, and families at greatest risk of poverty in the United States are those headed by single females. In 2010, the poverty rate for all families was 13.2 percent; for female-headed households with no husband present, it was 34.2 percent. These figures become even starker when disaggregated. Families headed by non-Hispanic white women had a poverty rate of 24.8 percent; families headed by African American and Hispanic women had poverty rates of 41 percent and 44.5 percent, respectively.[23]

More than 1 million American children see their parents divorce or separate each year, and more than half will spend some time in a single-parent family. Using six nationally representative data sets tracking more than 25,000 children, Sara McLanahan and Gary Sandefur found that children raised with only one biological parent are disadvantaged in myriad ways. Compared to children who grow up in two-parent families, they are (1) twice as likely to drop out of school; (2) 2.5 times as likely to become teen mothers; (3) 1.4 times as likely to be idle—out of work and out of school; (4) likely to have lower grade point averages, lower college aspirations, poorer academic attendance records; and (5) higher rates of divorce. These patterns persist even after adjustments for differences in race, the education of parents, the number of siblings, and the child's geographic location.[24] On the other hand, studies have found that children who live in two-parent families where one parent is abusive (or has a high level of antisocial behavior) fare less well than children whose parents divorce and the child lives in a single-parent family with a nonabusive parent.[25]

The families at greatest risk of poverty in the United States are those headed by single females. This poverty is compounded when child support payments are withheld.

Source: The Image Works

Child Support Enforcement

According to the Census Bureau, 60 percent of mothers in 2008 had child support orders or agreements in place compared to 40 percent of fathers. Of those with orders, just under half received full payment and over half received partial or no payment.[26]

Child support is important for families with only one custodial parent. According to the Census Bureau, 76.3 percent of custodial parents received some child support in 2007. The proportion of custodial parents receiving every payment they were due was 47 percent in 2007. Of the almost 14 million custodial parents in 2008, 7.4 million (54 percent) had some type of formal child support agreement in place. The most commonly cited reasons for custodial parents not entering into any formal agreement were that they did not feel the need to go to court and make a formal agreement (35.1 percent), they felt that the other parent provided what they could in support (35 percent) or they felt that the other parent could not afford child support (32.4 percent).[27]

Child support is very important for low-income families, and in 2004, it constituted 26 to 29 percent of the income of divorced families and reduced their poverty rate by 7 to 11 percent.[28] It is also a key income source for poverty-level families, since child support for parents who received full child support payments constituted 48 percent of their average income.[29] In 2004, child support payments lifted 500,000 children out of poverty.[30] One study of welfare leavers found that those with regular child support payments had a slower rate of welfare reentry, a faster rate of finding work, and a slower rate of job loss compared to families without steady child support income.[31]

In 1996, former President Clinton signed into law the Personal Responsibility and Work Opportunity Reconciliation Act (PRWORA), which also addressed child support enforcement. Specifically, failure to meet child support obligations could result in the revocation of driver's and professional licenses; wage garnishment; liens; and/or denial, revocation, or limitation of passports. Delinquent support obligations could also be collected through unemployment and disability insurance benefits.

Children in Poverty

In 2010 there were 16.4 million poor children in the United States, whose poverty rate is higher than for any other age group—22 percent compared to the overall poverty rate of 15.1 percent. For children under age six, the poverty rate was even higher at 25.3 percent (6,343,000 children).[32] In 2007, more than 7 percent of U.S. children lived in extreme (family incomes below 50 percent of the poverty line) poverty and 39 percent of children lived in or near poverty (family incomes below 200 percent of the poverty line).[33] Compared to poverty in later childhood, research indicates that extreme poverty during a child's first five years is especially deleterious to their future life chances.[34]

Minority children experience more instances of poverty: in 2010, 40 percent of African American and 35 percent of Hispanic children lived below the poverty line compared to 12.4 percent of non-Hispanic white children.[35]

Poverty and the Elderly

On the surface, the poverty picture for the elderly (once the poorest group in the country) seems to be growing less bleak. In 1959 the poverty rate for those over 65 was 35 percent, which decreased to 9 percent by 2010.[36]

Elderly poverty is higher within minority groups. In 2010 18 percent of elderly African Americans and Hispanics were poor compared to 6.8 percent of elderly non-Hispanics.[37]

The federal government's estimate of the elderly poor is questionable, especially since the poverty line is calculated using two formulas: (1) families headed by persons under age 65 and (2) families headed by persons 65 or older, for whom the poverty line is set lower. For example, the poverty line in 2010 for an unrelated individual 65 or older was $10,458 compared to $11,344 for those under 65, a difference of $886 or 8 percent.[38] This difference is based on the assumption that the elderly spend less on food since they require less food to absorb the same amount of nutrients. It does not take into account that the aged often have higher medical expenses. The National Academy of Science (NAS) has devised its own poverty index which estimates the elderly poverty population to be closer to 18.6 percent than to the government's claim of around 10 percent.[39]

The Rural Poor

About 7.8 million rural Americans live in poverty. Those working in farming, fishing, and forestry have a poverty rate of 16.8 percent, which is higher than any other occupations profiled by the U.S. Bureau of Labor Statistics.[40]

Many rural areas have poverty rates exceeding those of central cities, and in 2010 the rural poverty rate of 16.5 percent was higher than the urban poverty rate of 14.9 percent. Broken down, the poverty rate of the South was 16.9 percent; 15.3 percent in the West; 13.9 percent in the Midwest, and 12.8 percent in the Northeast.[41] In 2009, 14 Southern and Western (heavily rural) states had poverty levels of 16 percent or more; Mississippi's poverty rate was almost 22 percent. Since the farming population accounts for only 10 percent of the rural population, the rural poor are therefore mostly nonfarmers.[42]

Rural minority members experience considerable poverty, and in 2010 the non-metro poverty rates for blacks and Hispanics were more than double the poverty rate of non-metro whites. Broken down, the 2010 non-metro poverty rate for blacks was 33 percent; 30 percent for non-metro Hispanics; and 13 percent for non-metro whites.[43]

The rural poor are more likely than the urban poor to live in chronic long-term poverty. Despite higher unemployment in rural areas, the rural poor rely less on public assistance than the urban poor. Lack of information and access to services, fear of stigma, and reliance on informal employment may help explain some of this difference.[44]

Family structure also has a significant bearing on poverty, with the highest poverty among single female-headed, non-metro families. In 2010, 41 percent of female-headed, non-metro families were poor compared to 21 percent of male-headed, non-metro families. For non-metro families headed by both husband and wife, the poverty rate was only 7.4 percent. In 2010 the child poverty rate in non-metro areas was 24.4 percent.[45]

Several factors contribute to chronic rural poverty, including high levels of illiteracy, low levels of education, a shortage of highly trained workers, high numbers of low-skill and low-paying jobs, high levels of underemployment and unemployment, and a poor physical infrastructure. Since rural areas have difficulty in attracting major industries, it is not surprising that the lack of economic opportunity has resulted in the outmigration of many educated and skilled rural families.[46]

Work and Poverty

Almost one in four U.S. workers lives in or around the edges of poverty. Thirty-five million Americans work full time but fail to make an adequate living. They are the nursing home aides, poultry processors, pharmacy assistants, child care workers, data entry keyers, janitors, and other employees of the secondary and tertiary labor markets.

A Profile of the Working Poor

The working poor are defined as individuals who spend at least 27 weeks in the labor force (working or looking for work) but whose family or personal incomes fall below the poverty line. In 2010, about 10.6 million persons were classified as the working poor, a group that represents a growing segment of the poverty population.[47] In 2009, 15 percent of part-time and 4 percent of full-time workers were classified as the working poor. The likelihood of being among the working poor decreases with educational levels, and in 2009, only 2 percent of college graduates (in the work force for 27 weeks) were counted as the working poor compared to 20 percent of those with less than a high school diploma. Whites and Asians accounted for only 11 percent of the working poor, while African Americans accounted for 15 percent and Hispanics for 18 percent.[48]

Why Are There Working Poor?

The large numbers of working poor are related to several factors, including the replacement of high-paying industrial jobs with low-paying service jobs. Millions of Americans who were working full time, year-round earned less than the official poverty level. In 2009, almost 5 million full-time workers (4.2 percent) were classified as the working poor.[49] This employment trend reflects a clear movement away from higher-paying manufacturing jobs to low-wage service employment. In the 1950s, 33 percent of all workers were employed in primary manufacturing industries (e.g., cars, radios, refrigerators, and clothing). By 1992 only 17 percent were employed in those industries. From 2001 to 2009, 2.5 million manufacturing jobs disappeared from the United States. In fact, General Motors employed about half as many workers in 2009 as it did at the end of 2000. Many economists and forecasters predict that this trend will intensify as increased international competition leads to more outsourcing of industrial and white-collar jobs. This competition will also lower wages for lesser-skilled occupations, and thus increase income inequality and the numbers of the working poor. In line with this, real wages have stagnated since the mid-1990s while productivity has grown rapidly. The Economic Policy Institute reports wages in the industries in which jobs are being created are, on average, 21 percent lower than wages in those industries in which jobs are disappearing. In addition, expanding industries are less likely to provide workers with health insurance than industries cutting jobs.[50]

Underemployment and Unemployment

The failure of the labor market to meet the economic needs of the population has been the source of important distinctions in employment policy. For example, those over 16 who are looking for work are counted by the Department of Labor as unemployed. But the **unemployment** rate does not assess the adequacy of employment. For example, part-time workers who wish to work full time are counted as employed; and workers holding jobs below their skill levels are not identified, even though such workers are **underemployed.** Finally, **discouraged workers** who simply give up and stop looking for work, relying on other methods to support themselves, do not appear in the unemployment statistics because they are not actively seeking work.

A second set of distinctions relates to economic performance. In a robust economy, businesses start up and close down in significant numbers, leaving workers temporarily out of work until they find other employment. Such **frictional unemployment** is considered unavoidable and reflects the cost of a constantly changing economy. **Structural unemployment** refers to "deeper and longer-lasting maladjustments in the labor market," such as changes in the technical skills required for new forms of production.[51] Because of swings in economic performance, some unemployment may be cyclical, as when recessions pitch the rate upward; but because certain groups of workers in certain regions have persistent difficulty finding work owing to an absence of jobs, some unemployment may be chronic.

These distinctions are noteworthy, because when people are out of work, they frequently rely on welfare benefits to tide them over. Thus, welfare programs are often designed to complement the labor market, which is why some observers refer to welfare as a **social wage,** or the amount government pays to workers through welfare programs when they are unable to participate in the labor market. Logically, much of welfare could be eliminated if well-paying jobs were plentiful, but such has not been the case in the United States. Policymakers have tacitly accepted an unemployment rate of between 4 and 5 percent as normative, which means that at any given time 5 to 8 million workers are unemployed.[52] Yet in 1978, Congress enacted the Humphrey–Hawkins Full Employment Act, which set an unemployment rate of 3 percent—equivalent to frictional unemployment—as a national goal. Since then, many government programs to aid unemployed, underemployed, and discouraged workers have been reduced or eliminated, leaving many Americans dependent on welfare programs for support.

The outsourcing of U.S. jobs to low-wage countries, such as India and China, may also exacerbate unemployment. A report by the U.S. Department of Labor (DOL) found that in 2010, a total of 7,247 mass layoff events resulted in a loss of 1.3 million jobs. (Extended mass layoffs refer to layoffs of at least 31 days duration that involve the filing of initial claims for unemployment insurance by 50 or more individuals from a single establishment during a consecutive five week period.) While officially 5,336 workers were laid off due to out-of-country relocations, it is difficult to determine how many workers actually lost employment due to outsourcing since employers may report reasons for layoffs in different terms (i.e., cost-cutting, changes in demand, etc.). The DOL report also notes that the number of mass layoff events has significantly decreased from the 2009 number total of 11,824.[53] Nonetheless, the trend of outsourcing work overseas raises concerns about the potential loss of the high-wage, white-collar jobs (especially in information technology) that were once considered safe from global competition. It also raises the specter that competition from less expensive overseas workers will slow the wage growth of American workers.[54]

The absence of employment opportunities contributes to other social problems. Research by M. Harvey Brenner shows that a seemingly small increase in the unemployment rate is associated with an increase in several social problems. During the 1973–1974 recession, for example, the unemployment rate increased by 14.3 percent, a change associated with the pathologies shown in Table 5.3. Brenner calculated that the combination of the 1973–1974 increase in the unemployment rate, the decrease in real per capita income, and an increase in the business failure rate was related to "an overall increase of more than 165,000 deaths [from cardiovascular disease] over a ten-year period (the greatest proportion of which occurs within three years)."[55] Overall, the total economic, social, and health care costs of this seemingly slight increase in unemployment cost $24 billion.[56]

The impact of the high unemployment rate that began in 2008 is particularly difficult for older workers in search of new employment. By mid-2011, the typical length of time a jobless worker in the United States was unemployed fell to 38.3 weeks. But the outlook was bleaker for older workers. While older workers are less likely to be unemployed, when they are, their spells are longer. In 2011, the average jobless person over age 65 was looking for work for

TABLE 5.3 Consequences of Increases in Unemployment

Pathological Indicator	Percentage Increase Due to Rise in Unemployment Increase	Rise in Incidence of Pathology
Total mortality	2.3	45,936
Cardiovascular mortality	2.8	28,510
Cirrhosis mortality	1.4	430
Suicide	1.0	270
Population in mental hospitals	6.0	8,416
Total arrests	6.0	577,477
Arrests for fraud and embezzlement	4.0	11,552
Assaults reported to police	1.1	7,035
Homicide	1.7	403

Source: Reprinted from M. Harvey Brenner, Estimating the Effects of Economic Change on National Health and Social Well-Being (Washington, DC: U.S. Government Printing Office, 1984), p. 2.

43.9 weeks; for those between 55 and 64 it was 44.6 weeks. The longer that a worker is out of the workforce, the less employable they become.[57]

Dual Labor Markets

According to Piore, the labor market can be divided into two segments, or "dual labor markets"—a **primary labor market** and a **secondary labor market:**

> The primary market offers jobs which possess several of the following traits: high wages, good working conditions, employment stability and job security, equity and due process in the administration of work rules, and chances for advancement. The other, secondary sector, has jobs which, relative to those in the primary sector, are decidedly less attractive. They tend to involve low wages, poor working conditions, considerable variability in employment, harsh and often arbitrary discipline, and little opportunity to advance. The poor are confined to the secondary labor market.[58]

Researchers calculated that in 1970 36.2 percent of workers fell into the secondary labor market, a modest increase over 1950s 35 percent.[59] By the 2000s, however, two factors increased the proportion of workers in the secondary labor market. First, membership in labor unions—the best security for nonprofessional workers—fell from 31 percent of nonagricultural workers in 1970 to under 12 percent in 2010 (the lowest rate in 70 years),

The minimum wage has been criticized by both conservatives and liberals.

Source: imageegami/Shutterstock

leaving millions of workers vulnerable to the vicissitudes of the secondary labor market. Second, a higher proportion of the new jobs created were in the service sector, which consists largely of secondary labor market jobs.[60]

Wages and Poverty

The Minimum Wage   The low minimum wage is another factor that explains the growth of the working poor. In 2007 Congress passed the Fair Minimum Wage Act which increased the minimum wage in three incremental steps from $5.15 an hour (which it had been stuck since 1997) to $7.25 an hour in 2009.[61]

Despite the recent increases, it is difficult for minimum wage employment to provide an adequate household income. Under the 2012 minimum wage of $7.25 an hour, a single parent with two children working full time would earn $13,920 a year and be at 73 percent of the $19,090 poverty line. A four-person, two-parent family where both adults are working full time and earning the minimum wage would gross $27,840 a year, or only $4,790 above the poverty line. About 286,000 workers earned exactly the prevailing federal minimum wage in 2008 while 1.9 million had wages below the minimum. Together, these 2.2 million workers made up 3.0 percent of all hourly-paid workers in 2008.[62]

Traditional labor economists argue that minimum wage increases result in inflation and significant job losses for low-wage workers,[63] an argument disputed by the Economic Policy Institute which did not find an increase in unemployment following the federal minimum wage increase in 1996–1997.[64] The Fiscal Policy Institute concluded that states that enacted minimum wage increases higher than the federal standard experienced stronger small business and retail sector growth as a result.[65] The following

TABLE 5.4 Value of the Minimum Wage, Selected Years

Year	Percent of Poverty Line for a Family of Three	Percent of Average Wage	Value of the Minimum Wage, 1995 Dollars	Minimum Wage, Nominal Dollars
1955	73	44	$3.94	$0.75
1960	88	48	4.75	1.00
1965	103	51	5.59	1.25
1968	120	56	6.49	1.60
1970	107	50	5.92	1.60
1975	101	46	5.71	2.10
1980	98	47	5.76	3.10
1985	81	39	4.76	3.35
1988	73	36	4.33	3.35
1989	71	35	4.13	3.35
1990	79	38	4.44	3.80
1993	75	39	4.50	4.25
1995	72	37	4.25	4.25
1997	83	42	4.89	5.15
2007	73	30	4.30	5.85

Sources: Based on data from Isaac Shapiro, The Minimum Wage and Job Loss (Washington, DC: Center on Budget and Policy Priorities, 1988), p. 3; U.S. Census Bureau, "Income 1995" (Washington, DC: U.S. Government Printing Office, September 26, 1996); and Center on Budget and Policy Priorities, "Assessing the $5.15 an Hour Minimum Wage," March 1996, retrieved from http://epn.org/cpbb/cbwage.html.; Bureau of Labor Statistics, "May 2007 National Occupation Employment and Wage Estimates". Retrieved July 2008 from http://www.bls.gov/oes/current/oes_nat.htm#b00-0000, U.S. Census Bureau, "Income, Poverty, and Health Insurance Coverage in the United States".

employment sectors have the highest proportion of minimum wage jobs:

Food service workers (26.6%)
Sales occupations (18.7%)
Office and administration support workers (13%)
Transportation and material moving
 workers (8.2%)
Cleaning and building service workers (8.2%)
Personal care workers (7.5%)[66]

Unlike countries, such as Australia, the U.S. minimum wage is not automatically adjusted to the cost of living. Congress must pass a bill, and the president must sign it into law for the minimum wage to rise. The minimum wage has risen only slightly during the past 18 years, increasing to $4.25 an hour by 1991 and then remaining at that

level for more than five years. By 1996 approximately 10 million American workers were earning between $4.25 and $5.14 per hour. In 1997, the federal minimum wage was again raised, this time to $5.15 an hour. The minimum wage was frozen from 1997 to 2007.

In 1950, the minimum wage brought a worker to 56 percent of the median wage. Throughout the 1950s and 1960s (see Table 5.4), the minimum wage hovered between 44 and 56 percent of the average wage. Even the higher minimum wage of $7.25 in 2009 brought a worker to only 34 percent of the $40,711 U.S. national wage. An increased minimum wage can result in a spillover effect, since some metropolitan businesses use a "real" minimum wage that is $1 to $2 above the federal level.

The Living Wage Movement These kinds of campaigns seek to pass local ordinances requiring private businesses that benefit from public money to pay their workers a living wage. Commonly, these ordinances cover employers who hold large city or county service contracts or receive substantial financial assistance from the city in the form of grants, loans, bond financing, tax abatements, or other economic development subsidies. Since 1994, community, labor, and religious coalitions have fought for and won similar ordinances in St. Louis, Boston, Los Angeles, Tucson, San Jose, Portland, Milwaukee, Detroit, Minneapolis, and Oakland. By 2000, there were more than 75 living wage campaigns under way in cities, counties, and states.

The justification for these campaigns is that when subsidized employers pay workers less than a living wage, taxpayers pay a double bill in the increased taxes necessary to pay for food stamps and other income support services required by low-wage earners to support themselves and their families. Many citywide campaigns have defined the living wage as equivalent to the poverty line for a family of four, although ordinances that have passed stipulate a wide range of wages. Increasingly, living wage coalitions are proposing other community standards in addition to a wage requirement, such as health benefits, vacation days, and language that supports union organizing.[67]

In addition to the federal minimum wage, states can institute their own higher minimum wage (see Table 5.5). As of 2012, 18 states and the District of Columbia set their minimum wages at rates higher than the federal level.[68] This represents a decrease from 2008, where 29 states and the

TABLE 5.5 States with Minimum Wages above the Federal Rate, 2012

State	Minimum Wage ($)
Alaska	$7.75
Arizona	7.65
California	8.00
Colorado	7.64
Connecticut	8.25
District of Columbia	8.25
Florida	7.67
Illinois	8.25
Maine	7.50
Massachusetts	8.00
Michigan	7.40
Montana	7.65
New Mexico	7.50
Nevada	8.25
Ohio	7.70
Oregon	8.80
Rhode Island	7.40
Vermont	8.46
Washington	9.04

Source: U.S. Department of Labor, Division of Communications Wage and Hour Division, Minimum Wage Laws in the States – January 1, 2012. Retrieved March 2012, from http://www.dol.gov/whd/minwage/america.htm.

District of Columbia had higher minimum wages than the federal wage rate[69] Arizona, Colorado, Florida, Missouri, Montana, and Nevada annually adjust their wage rates according to changes in the cost of living.[70]

Strategies Developed to Combat Poverty

For the vast majority of households, the road to ending poverty involves savings and accumulation of assets. These are important prerequisites for purchasing a home, sending a child to college, starting a small business, and reaching other economic goals. Moreover, when people begin to accumulate assets, their thinking and behavior changes, leading to important psychological and social effects that are not achieved when simply receiving and spending regular income.[71] Despite its importance, asset accumulation for the poor has been virtually ignored in welfare state policies. Moreover, the tax system does not reward asset accumulation for the poor in two primary areas: tax benefits for home equity and for retirement pensions go largely to the better-off. In these two areas alone, the federal government spends well over $100 billion each year, and the total is rising rapidly.[72] Even worse, many means-tested welfare programs count assets and savings as income when calculating eligibility. Hence, the poor who have accumulated assets or savings must spend these down to qualify for assistance.

IDAs

The concept of individual development accounts (IDAs) was introduced in 1991 by Michael Sherraden in *Assets and the Poor*.[73] IDAs are part of an asset-building policy strategy designed to reduce wealth inequality by enabling asset-poor individuals to accumulate assets. Low-income individuals establish savings accounts matched by public and private resources, which are then used for home purchases, business capitalization, and post-secondary education.[74]

In Sherraden's framework, IDA accounts would be established for all low-income individuals, and would be tax benefitted to foster asset accumulation. Depending on the financial circumstances of the depositor, individual savings would be matched by federal, state, or private contributions at varying rates. The matching system would be flexible and permit the government to supplement savings as the economic circumstances of individuals change. Despite the flexibility, IDA withdrawals would be restricted to approved purposes such as home purchases, education, retirement, or the creation of a business. IDA assets could be transferred to children at death or prior to death.[75]

Three Approaches to Combat Poverty

Policy analysts have identified three basic strategies for combating poverty. The first strategy (used in the War on Poverty and Great Society programs) was to apply a curative or rehabilitative strategy to the problems of the poor. The **curative approach to poverty** aims to end chronic and persistent poverty by helping the poor to become self-supporting through changes in their personal lives and in their environment. By breaking the cycle of poverty, the curative approach strives to initiate the poor into employment and, later, the middle class. The second strategy is the **alleviative approach to poverty,** which is exemplified by public assistance programs that focus on easing the suffering of the poor rather than attacking the causes of poverty. The third strategy is the **preventive approach to poverty,** exemplified by social insurance programs such as Social Security. In this approach, people are required to utilize social insurance to insure against the costs of accidents, sickness, death, old age, unemployment, and disability. The preventive strategy sees the state as a large insurance company whose umbrella shelters its members against the vicissitudes of life.

John Kenneth Galbraith's *The Affluent Society* identified two kinds of poverty: **case poverty** and **area poverty.** According to Galbraith, case poverty was the outgrowth of personal deficiencies (i.e., deficits in human capital). Area poverty was related to economic problems endemic to a region. "Pockets of poverty" or "depressed areas" resulted from a lack of industrialization or the inability of an area to adjust to technological change. This kind of poverty was a function of the changing nature of the marketplace.[76]

One example of a case poverty approach is the federal government's attempt to promote education as a means of increasing human capital. Poverty is highly correlated with educational deficits, and adolescent parenthood is strongly associated with low levels of basic skills and high school dropout rates.[77] To help address these educational deficits,

TABLE 5.6 Percentage of Persons in Poverty by State, Comparison between 2006 and 2010

State	Poverty % 2006	Poverty % 2010	State	Poverty % 2006	Poverty % 2010
United States	12.3	15.3	Missouri	11.4	15.3
Alabama	14.3	19.0	Montana	13.5	14.6
Alaska	8.9	9.9	Nebraska	10.2	12.9
Arizona	14.4	17.4	Nevada	9.5	14.9
Arkansas	17.7	18.8	New Hampshire	5.4	8.3
California	12.2	15.8	New Jersey	8.8	10.3
Colorado	9.7	13.4	New Mexico	16.9	20.4
Connecticut	8.0	10.1	New York	14.0	14.9
Delaware	9.3	11.8	North Carolina	13.8	17.5
Dist. Of Columbia	18.3	19.2	North Dakota	11.4	13.0
Florida	11.5	16.5	Ohio	12.1	15.8
Georgia	12.6	17.9	Oklahoma	15.2	16.9
Hawaii	9.2	10.7	Oregon	11.8	15.8
Idaho	9.5	15.7	Pennsylvania	11.3	13.4
Illinois	10.6	13.8	Rhode Island	10.5	14.0
Indiana	10.6	15.3	South Carolina	11.2	18.2
Iowa	10.3	12.6	South Dakota	10.7	14.4
Kansas	12.8	13.6	Tennessee	14.9	17.7
Kentucky	16.8	19.0	Texas	16.4	17.9
Louisiana	17.0	18.7	Utah	9.3	13.2
Maine	10.2	12.9	Vermont	7.8	12.7
Maryland	8.4	9.9	Virginia	8.6	11.1
Massachusetts	12.0	11.4	Washington	8.0	13.4
Michigan	13.3	16.8	West Virginia	15.3	18.1
Minnesota	8.2	11.6	Wisconsin	10.1	13.2
Mississippi	20.6	22.4	Wyoming	10.0	11.2

Sources: U.S. Census Bureau "POV46: Poverty Status by State: 2006". U.S. Census Bureau, Current Population Survey, 2007 Annual Social and Economic Supplement. Retrieved July 2008 from http://pubdb3.census.gov/macro/032007/pov/new46_100125_01.htm; U.S. Census Bureau, "Poverty: 2009 and 2010". October 2011. Retrieved March 2012, from http://www.census.gov/prod/2011pubs/acsbr10-01.pdf.

the federal government initiated the Head Start program, targeted at poor children age three to five and their families.[78]

Area poverty is illustrated by reviewing poverty rates on a state-by-state basis (see Table 5.6). While the 2010 national poverty rate was 15.3 percent, some states with extensive poverty pockets had much higher rates, including Mississippi (22.4 percent); New Mexico (20.4 percent); District of Columbia, Alabama, Kentucky, Arkansas and Louisiana (19 percent); and South Carolina and West Virginia (18 percent). By contrast, states like New Hampshire (8 percent); Maryland, Alaska, Connecticut, and New Jersey (10 percent); Hawaii, Virginia, and Wyoming (11 percent); and Massachusetts (11.4 percent) had poverty rates below the national average.[79]

The various approaches to poverty are not merely hypothetical formulations; they form the basis for social welfare policy. Between 1965 and 1980, social welfare policies were grounded in the view that public expenditures should be used to stimulate opportunities for the poor. As a result, major social welfare legislation was enacted, and billions of dollars were earmarked for the remediation of poverty. However, beginning with the Reagan administration in 1980, there was a move away from reliance on social welfare expenditures and toward an emphasis on ending poverty through economic overall growth and tax transfers.

Consequently, public expenditures for poverty programs decreased and tax cuts—intended to give people incentives to work and save money—increased. The Reagan approach maintained that the poor should wait for gains coming from increased economic activity rather than relying on welfare programs. This perspective assumed that the trickle-down effect of economic growth would benefit the poor more than direct economic subsidies. According to analyst Kevin Phillips, "Low-income families, especially the working poor, lost appreciably more by cuts in government services than they gained in tax reductions."[80] Despite the nation's long-standing belief in eradicating poverty through labor market participation, the main factor responsible for the decrease in poverty rates from the 1960s to the late 1970s were governmental cash and in-kind transfers.[81]

To gain perspective on U.S. poverty, it is helpful to locate it within a wider international context. While the U.S. poverty rate is lower than in most developing countries, it is more than double the 2011 4.5 percent poverty rate in Norway and the significantly higher than the 6.3 percent rate in France, the 7 percent in Switzerland and Austria and the 9.3 percent in Canada. Social workers and policymakers need to look at successful strategies that other countries have used to address poverty, including generous social welfare benefits and policies that curb income inequality.[82]

World Poverty

The good news about world poverty is that between 1990 and 2008, the number of people in developing countries living below the extreme poverty line of $1.25 per day (22 percent of the developing world) fell from 1.82 billion to 1.29 billion. Despite higher food and fuel prices, the World Bank noted that extreme global poverty continued to fall from 2008 to 2010. They predict that by 2015, the number of people living in extreme poverty will drop to 883 million. These projections will obviously prove false if food prices rise and the global economic crisis cuts deeper into the ability of rich nations to offer foreign aid and charitable giving.

One indicator of severe poverty is the infant mortality rate, which is measured by the number of infant deaths per 100,000 live births. Developed countries with less than 10 deaths per 100,000 births include Austria, Belgium, Denmark, Iceland, Italy, Sweden, Switzerland, Spain, Slovak Republic, Singapore, Serbia, Qatar, Portugal, Poland, Norway, Netherlands, Malta, Macedonia, Kuwait, Japan, Israel, Ireland, Germany, France, Finland, Czech Republic, Bosnia-Herzegovina, and Australia. In comparison, some of the poorer countries have extraordinarily high levels of infant deaths. Countries with more than 500 deaths per 100,00 live births include Afghanistan (1,400); Chad (1,200); Somalia (1,200); Guinea-Bissau (1,000); Liberia (990); Burundi (970); Central African Republic (850); Nigeria (840); Mali (830); Niger (820); Tanzania (790); Zimbabwe (790); Guinea (680); Angola (610); Cameroon (600); Lao (580); Burkina Faso (560); Mauritania (550); Mozambique (550); Kenya (530); Rwanda (540); and Malawi (510).

Still another indicator of poverty is life expectancy, which ranges from a high of 83.3 years in Japan to a low of less than 49 years old in Guinea-Bissau, Sierra Leone, Afghanistan, and the Central African Republic. The average life expectancy in Sub-Saharan Africa is only 54 years old.[83]

Global poverty is influenced by multiple factors. For one, most poor countries were part of the empires of European colonial powers. When the Europeans granted independence to their colonies, they often left nations with diminished resources and geographical boundaries based on political concessions or the self-interest of the colonizer.

Global poverty is often marked by food insecurity. The agricultural self-sufficiency of poor nations is hampered by cheap food imports from the United States, Europe, and Australia, which is partly driven by the subsidies given to Western farmers. This food problem is further exacerbated by the much touted "Green Revolution," a series of agricultural technology transfers that began in the late 1960s. While the Green Revolution has helped feed much of the world, it has also led to the monocultural farming of cereals and grains (frequently used for livestock, export, and ethanol) rather than the traditional polyculture farming based on crop variety. While fewer people in the world die of starvation, many suffer from malnutrition and vitamin deficiencies as a result of a high starch and low protein diet. The reliance on pesticides has also had a major impact on the ecology of farming areas and the quality of drinking water supplies.[84]

Climate change in the form of droughts, floods, extreme heat, and violent storms, is having a major impact on already marginal farming and grazing areas in the developing world. This change affects poor nations more than the richer ones, since the very poor tend to live in highly vulnerable locations with little means or resources to adapt to change. For example, the population of Bangladesh and Burma live in densely populated deltas subject to flooding from storm and tidal surges. Sub-Saharan African countries—some of the poorest in the world—have populations that are highly dependent on unstable rains for their crops and grazing areas. Droughts have a devastating impact on these already semiarid areas. Although the poorest countries contribute the least to pollution and greenhouse gas emissions, they appear to suffer the harshest effects of climate change, such as the floods in Bangladesh and the droughts in large parts of Africa.[85]

Another factor that drives world poverty is the graft and corruption that marks some governments in developing countries. This corruption drains economic growth and leads to bureaucratic institutions where bribery—often on multiple levels—is required to accomplish anything. Corruption also discourages foreign investment and ensures that resources and wealth remain in the hands of the small elite that run the country, thus diminishing the prospects for wider development. This system is reinforced by weak democratic structures that prevent an equitable distribution of resources and deny the poor a voice.

Attempts to remedy world poverty center around two major approaches to international development: the pro-growth and the pro-poor growth models. The pro-growth model maintains that aid strategies should focus exclusively on economic growth since poverty reduction will naturally occur as the economy expands. The latter model considers an economic policy as pro-poor if its main focus is on lessening inequality and reducing poverty. There is a debate about whether pro-growth policies skew income and inevitably lead to more inequality and higher poverty.[86] Some development economists, like Martin Ravillion, have integrated both approaches by adopting a pro-growth policy as the center of a poverty reduction strategy.[87]

Foreign or development aid is given by wealthier Western governments to assist poorer countries to alleviate poverty or for economic development. It is sometimes used as a cover to sell or provide arms to poorer countries. While humanitarian aid is one-time emergency assistance to address a natural catastrophe, the longer-term goal of foreign aid is used to alleviate structural poverty-related problems.

The largest donor nations in 2010 were (in billions): USA ($30); UK ($13); Germany, ($13); EU ($13); Japan ($11); Netherlands ($6); and Canada ($5).[88] The largest recipient nations were (in billions) were: Afghanistan ($6); Ethiopia ($4); Democratic Republic of the Congo ($3); Haiti ($3); Tanzania ($3); Vietnam ($3); India ($3); Iraq ($2); Nigeria ($2); Sudan ($2); Mozambique ($2); Uganda ($2); Kenya ($2); and Rwanda ($1).[89]

Numerous secular and religious nonprofit organizations are also actively fighting world poverty. Some of these include the Bill and Melinda Gates Foundation, Christian Aid, Habitat for Humanity, Oxfam, World Vision, Save the Children, Heifer International, and Doctors without Borders. These organizations are classified as non-governmental organizations (NGO), nonprofit organizations which are independent of governmental control. NGOs try to achieve social, economic, and humanitarian goals within a nonpolitical environment. Although supposedly purely humanitarian, some religiously-based NGOs proselytize and/or promote a conservative political and social agenda. There are an estimated 40,000 small and large NGOs (non-governmental organizations) that operate worldwide, some of which originate within a developing country.[90]

NGOs are typically involved in activities focused on health, farming, economic development, and education. For instance, the work of the Bill and Melinda Gates Foundation (gave almost $3 billion in grants in 2010) includes support for developing a malaria vaccine, and support for organizations such as the Alliance for a Green Revolution in Africa, World Food Programme, TechnoServe (helping small coffee farmers improve crops), Alliance for Financial Inclusion, Consultative Group to Assist the Poor (microfinance), and Opportunity International (aiding and developing commercial banks in Africa).[91]

Numerous strategies have been proposed to curb or eliminate global poverty. For instance, at the 2000 United Nations Millennium Summit, world leaders agreed to eight development goals—now called the Millennium Development Goals (MDGs)—to be achieved by 2015. The MDGs are supported by major international organizations, such as the International Monetary Fund (IMF) the International Labour Organization (ILO), and the World Trade Organization (WTO), to name a few. The eight MDGs for poverty reduction were approved by all 193 UN member states and 23 international organizations. These goals include:

1. Eradication of extreme poverty and hunger
2. Provision of universal primary education
3. Promotion of gender equality and the empowerment of women
4. Reduction of child mortality rates
5. The improvement of maternal health
6. The reduction in the instance of HIV/AIDS, malaria, and other diseases
7. Achieving environmental sustainability
8. Developing a global partnership for development, including targets for aid, trade, and debt relief.[92]

Microcredit or "microfinance" is another poverty reduction strategy that centers around providing financial services to low-income people who lack access to mainstream banking services. Microfinance is based on the idea that the poor can better their lives—and even leave poverty—if they are given access to low-cost financial services and products. Like everyone else, those living in poverty need a wide range of financial services to start or manage their businesses, to build assets, and to smooth them over in hard times.[93] While it is a useful tool in the poverty reduction battle, microfinance is sometimes oversold as a panacea for eradicating poverty.

Given the pressing problems that remain, it is far too early to celebrate the decline in the number of people living in extreme poverty. For example, the global financial crisis remains a salient feature of economic life, and while food prices were somewhat lower in 2011, they remain high relative to income in the developing world. Writing in *The Observer*, John Vidal wonders how the world will feed an additional 2.5 billion people—an extra China and India—in 2050.[94] The UN suggests that food production will have to nearly double to meet that need. At the same time, there are already one billion chronically hungry people in the world, a

problem exacerbated by the limited land left for agriculture. Climate change is also making food production more tenuous in marginal farming or grazing areas, especially those in already semiarid regions. Drinking water is also becoming increasingly scarce in some regions of the world, while overfishing is rapidly depleting an important food source. Vidal points out that while food production has nearly doubled in a generation, water use has increased three fold. He argues that unless dramatic changes occur, the current method of water and energy-intensive farming will exhaust the earth's resources before the world is able to feed the additional people.[95] These challenges will hopefully lead us to something more than despair. Human beings have the intellectual capacity—if not always the will—to find our way out of dilemmas.

America's Fringe Economy[96]

In 2008, America—and much of the world—experienced an economic crash not seen since the Great Depression of the 1930s. A massive credit bubble allowed Americans to spend more than they earned, and rising home prices and a robust stock market made it seem like the party would never end.[97] From 1960 to 2008 the ratio of household debt to personal disposable income more than doubled as Americans went on the longest sustained spending spree in history.[98] By 2009, more than 83 percent of all consumer debt was secured by residential property that was rapidly declining in value.[99] In short, many average American middle-class households became accustomed to a lifestyle that could not be sustained by their income alone.

While much of the economic life of the middle class is rooted in credit tied to their house or credit cards,[100] many poor people encounter obstacles to basic credit and are vulnerable to exploitation by fringe businesses. The often shoddy storefronts of fringe financial businesses hide the true scope of this economic sector. For instance, 90 percent of payday lending revenues are based on fees from trapped borrowers. The typical payday borrower pays back $793 for a $325 loan. In 2010, payday lending fees cost poor American families upwards of $4.7 billion a year in fees.[101]

The past decade has been a good one for check cashers, payday lenders, pawnshops, rent-to-own stores, and the like. The number of payday loan outlets increased significantly from just 2,000 in 1995 to 20,600 in 2009. The total loan volume in 2009 was $29.2 billion.[102] Ten large companies, including listed companies, own or operate about 40 percent of payday loan stores in the United States.[103]

In short, America's fringe economy is not a mom-and-pop operation composed of small storefronts that generate moderate family incomes; instead, it is a multi-billion parallel economy that provides low-income consumers with a full range of cash, commodities, and credit lines. While pawnshops, check cashers, and payday lenders are a major part of the fringe economy, they are only the tip of the iceberg. This subeconomy also includes mainstream banks issuing high-interest credit cards and expensive check overdraft protection, high-interest home financing and refinancing loans, and deferred interest retail payments. Fringe economic services exist in every sector where people borrow or spend money.

The prices of commodities and financial services in the fringe economy have little relationship to their real value in the mainstream marketplace. Within this economic bubble, used cars can cost twice their book value, housing prices are determined by the financial desperation of home buyers rather than the home's value, a 14-day $200 payday loan can cost $40 in interest/fees, and credit cards come with yearly and monthly service fees plus annual percentage rates (APR) of 30 percent or more. In the fringe economy, economic distress and low credit scores translate into high costs that are justified by the supposedly higher risk of serving a poor or credit-challenged population.

The Unbanked and the Functionally Poor

The unbanked (e.g., individuals and families without accounts at deposit institutions) make up an important part of the fringe economy. About 12 million U.S. households (one-fourth of all low-income families) have no relationship with mainstream financial services, such as a bank, savings institution or credit union.[104] The unbanked report they lack checking accounts because (1) they do not write enough checks to warrant one, (2) they have almost no month-to-month financial savings to deposit, (3) they cannot afford high bank fees, (4) they cannot meet minimum bank balance requirements, (5) they want to keep their financial records private, and/or (6) they are uncomfortable dealing with banks. Almost 85 percent of the unbanked have yearly incomes below $25,000.[105]

One industry-funded study found that the average payday loan customer was female with children living at home, was between 24 and 44, earned less than $40,000 a year, was a high school graduate, was a renter, was transient (most had lived in the same home for less than five years), and had little job tenure.[106] This group represents the lower-and-moderate-income working class rather than the poorest of the poor.

The misconception that only the poor use the fringe economy overlooks the convergence of the traditional poor with growing segments of the middle class that is functionally poor. The functionally poor can include homeowners who are "over under" in their mortgages (i.e., they owe more than their house is worth), have huge credit card debt, have tarnished credit histories that precludes them from moderate interest loans, carry high-interest-rate credit cards, or finance their purchases through tricky time-deferred payments. In that sense, a burgeoning sector of the middle class is economically closer to the traditional poor than to the traditional middle class.

Credit and the Poor

Credit is a bridge between real household earnings and consumption decisions, offering relief during periods of economic distress and uncertainty.[107] Payment options are flexible for those with good credit and collateral is not required. Hence, the middle class can purchase goods, services or borrow cash without losing their possessions. On the other hand, neither trust nor the presumption of goodwill exists in the fringe economy. A borrower with compromised credit typically must provide collateral such as a secured bank account, a post-dated check, household goods, or a car title. Those who manage to find unsecured credit are often charged high interest rates and face onerous loan terms.

Credit card use has become almost mandatory in the United States. Renting a car or reserving a hotel room or flight is almost impossible without a credit card. The average American credit card holder has ten cards—four retail cards, three bank cards, one phone card, almost one gasoline card, and one travel and entertainment card. Not surprisingly, bank write-offs for uncollectible credit card debt was $75 billion in 2010.[108]

There are two basic types of credit cards: unsecured and secured cards. Unsecured credit cards are based on the cardholder's creditworthiness, past use of credit, and ability to repay debt. Conversely, secured credit cards require cardholders to guarantee their credit line by providing cash collateral, thereby making it almost impossible for the borrower to default.

Preloaded or Stored Value Debit Cards   A variation of the secured credit card is the preloaded debit card, sometimes called a stored value card (SVC). Using a Visa or MasterCard logo, SVCs are similar to pre-paid phone cards in that they are preloaded with funds. When the funds are exhausted, the card must be reloaded, or it becomes invalid. Unlike secured credit cards, pre-paid cards are not dependent on credit or banking history since they are not linked to a bank account. (Customers can use the entire amount loaded onto the card.) There is also no debt to repay. Like any fringe economy transaction there are downsides. Usage fees are high. They also do not build credit history since there is no extension of credit.

Telecommunications and the Alternative Services Market   Consumer telecommunications are divided into two groups: post- and pre-paid services. For post-paid (i.e., paying *after* a charge is accrued) telephone services, customers are required to undergo credit checks and those without an acceptable credit score are denied service and forced into the more expensive pre-paid sector.

Post-paid cell phone service is also dependent on good credit scores—clients with problematic credit are a lucrative part of the wireless industry. Like regular telephone service, pre-paid cell phone plans are always hugely more expensive than post-paid plans.[109] The large difference in pricing between pre- and post-paid plans is perplexing since prepaying customers cannot default. The sole reason for the higher prices is the customer's economic vulnerability. Prepayment plans are also unfair because they allow corporations to use a customer's money without paying interest. Pre-paid customers are therefore penalized twice—once by paying higher prices and then again when the company uses their money without paying interest. Consumers trying to build or rebuild their credit history also derive little benefit from prepaying because no credit is extended, and therefore there is nothing to report to a credit agency.

The Furniture and Appliance Rental Industry
The rent-to-own (RTO) sector targets low- and moderate-income consumers. RTOs advertise no credit

checks, weekly or monthly payments, and a choice of appliances, furniture, and jewelry that would otherwise be unaffordable for these customers if bought outright.[110] The $6.8 billion a year RTO industry served over 3 million customers in 2007 and is a major player in the fringe economy.[111] The RTO industry employs two approaches to transactions: (1) customers rent goods and pay weekly or monthly fees or (2) they rent-to-own with payments extending from 12 to 24 months. In either case, customers can usually cancel the agreement without further cost or obligation. Customers take ownership of the property if the contract is renewed a prescribed number of times (usually 12 to 24 months) or if they complete the lease agreement. No credit bureau reports are filed because RTO customers make advanced payments.[112] RTOs make money in other ways. For one, RTOs retailers offer merchandise at a "cash price and carry" price. According to a 1997 PIRG study, the typical RTO cash price on an item was $389 compared with the average department store price of $217.[113] Successful fringe businesses long ago realized the importance of treating low-income customers well. Good customer service is important to poor consumers, especially those who have been humiliated by mainstream merchants after bad credit checks. Some poor consumers are so sensitive to poor treatment that they will pay more, sometimes much more, just to feel they are being respected. As one former Rent-A-Center manager stated it succinctly, "If you treat the customer like royalty, you can bleed them through the nose."[114]

Pawnshops   Pawnshops are a high-growth industry, and at least five chains are publicly traded (i.e., EZ Pawn, Cash America Pawn, Express Cash, Famous Pawn and First Cash Pawn). According to the National Pawnbrokers Association, the number of pawnshops in the United States has nearly doubled in the past ten years from 6,900 in 1988 to 13,000 in 2008, a reflection of the present tough economic times.[115]

A pawnshop loan is a relatively simple transaction. A pawnbroker makes a fixed-term loan that is guaranteed by collateral. The customer is given a pawn ticket that includes their name, address, a description of the pledged good, the amount lent, the maturity date, and the amount that must be repaid to reclaim the property. The property is returned when the customer presents the ticket and pays the loan and fees in full by the agreed-on time. If the loan is not repaid, the collateral becomes the property of the pawnbroker, and the customer's debt is extinguished. Customers can repay a loan at any time during the loan term and redeem the collateral. However, many pawnshops have an open-ended policy whereby the customer can extend the pawn indefinitely by paying only the loan interest. Pawnshops are typically regulated by state and sometimes by local governments; interest rates can range from 1.5 percent to 25 percent a month, depending upon the state regulation. While some state laws cap interest rates, loopholes often allow "lease back" agreements to add fees, sometimes effectively doubling interest rates.[116] The average pawn shop loan is about $75 but can go as low as $15.[117]

Car Title Pawns   Car title pawns (vehicle title lenders) operate similarly to pawnshops. A customer needs a short-term loan, but instead of using his or her television or stereo as collateral, they use their vehicle title. In most cases, this substantially increases the amount that can be borrowed since vehicles generally have more value than televisions, stereos or microwaves. Unlike pawnshop transactions, the borrower does not forego the use of their property during the course of the loan, even though the vehicle is technically owned by the lender until the loan is repaid.

Car title pawns operate in the following way. A borrower provides the lender with a free and paid-up vehicle title and an extra set of keys. In return for a 30-day loan, the borrower either allows the title lender to keep the title or puts a lien on the vehicle.

The vehicle is appraised based on the lowest possible value, which is the wholesale or trade-in price in rough condition. For example, the NADA used car guide lists a 2004 Ford Crown Victoria as having a retail value of $6,250 if bought from a dealer in March 2012. The dealer trade-in on that car in rough condition would be $2,235. Since car title pawn companies generally lend up to 50 percent of the value of a vehicle, the maximum loan would be $1,118. A loan default would therefore provide the lender with a car worth at minimum $2,235 (and much likely more) for $1,118 plus any interest payments made by the borrower. If the lender repossesses the vehicle and resells it more than the loan value, the borrower receives nothing from the proceeds of the sale.

Vehicle title loans are usually for 30 days and often involve an APR of 300 percent or more. The borrower can ask for multiple 30-day extensions after paying the interest and fees. After several months, the loan will exceed the value of the vehicle.

Payday Loans   Legislation around payday loans varies widely between states, with some jurisdictions limiting the annual percentage rate (APR) that payday lenders can charge. Other jurisdictions outlaw payday lending entirely while still others have few, if any, restrictions. Payday loans (and certain other financing) offered to military personnel and their dependents must include certain protections, such as a maximum 36 percent interest rate cap.

To qualify for a payday loan, the customer must have a valid checking account from which a check is issued (or electronically debited) to cover the interest and principal for the loan. On a $300 payday loan the lender may ask for a $300 check and then deduct the interest from the amount received by the borrower. Borrowers must also provide recent pay stubs and valid identification. Many payday lenders consider benefits as income and will give loans to those on public assistance, recipients of child support or alimony, and Social Security beneficiaries.[118]

Payday loans are typically issued for a maximum of $300 ($500–$1,000 for established customers) and are usually given for 14 or 18 days. The average fees are roughly $20 per $100 borrowed (fees can be as high as $37 per hundred), or 20 percent for the two week loan period. Since the borrower repays $360 on a $300 loan, this translates into a 500 percent APR. (Nationally, the average APR for payday loans is 474 percent.[119]) Because the lender may extend the loan (called a rollover) for additional 14- or 18-day periods (after the interest is paid), a $300 payday loan extended to 42 days or three loan periods will accrue $180 in interest charges alone, elevating the full loan repayment to $480 in less than two months. Unlike pawnshop transactions where a customer loses their collateral if they default, payday loans can inflict potentially greater damage on borrowers, including criminal prosecution for writing a hot check.[120]

Collection tactics for payday loans can be aggressive. If a borrower cannot repay the loan, it may be turned over to a collection agency and result in the loss of a house, car or the garnishing of wages. In some cases, the collection agency can add additional interest to the original debt.[121] Some payday loan companies require borrowers to agree beforehand to pay all fees related to the collection of their account, including attorney fees, collection fees, and court costs.[122] A default on a payday loan involves a worthless check, and some state credit laws allow for triple damages when a bad check is used in a

TABLE 5.7 Draining EITC: 2002 Tax Preparation, RAL Fees, and Check Cashing

Type of Fee	Cost to Tax Filer	Drain on EITC Program (in millions)
RAL loan fee	$ 75	$363
Electronic filing fee	$ 40	194
Document preparation/ application/handling fee	$ 33	160
Tax preparation fee	$100	484
Check cashing fee	$ 57	110*
Total	$305	1,311

*This was based on 40 percent of low-income tax filers using a check cashing service.

Source: Based on Chi Chi Wu and Jean Ann Fox, *The High Cost of Quick Tax Money: Tax Preparation, "Instant Refund" Loans, and Check Cashing Fees Target the Working Poor.* (Washington, DC: National Consumer Law Center, Consumer Federation of America, January 2003). Reprinted with permission of the National Consumer Law Center, www.consumerlaw.org, 617-542-9595.

retail transaction. Lenders may also require that customers sign statements authorizing them to go directly to the borrower's employer and ask for the amount owed to be deducted from their paychecks.

Tax Refund Anticipation Loans   Refund anticipation loans (RALs) are short-term loans secured by an expected tax refund. RALs are expensive and similar to other forms of fringe credit with an APR ranging from 67 to 774 percent.[123] Tax preparation services earn about $1 billion dollars a year in fees from these loans.[124]

RALs are common in low-income neighborhoods where there are a large number of tax refunds associated with the federal earned income tax credit (EITC) program (see Chapter 9). Under EITC, the working poor receive refunds that exceed what they paid in taxes. In addition to EITC, low- and moderate-income families with children are also eligible for the federal Child Tax Credit (CTC), worth up to $1,000 a child. The EITC and CTC tax refunds create a powerful incentive for mainstream tax preparers to enter the poverty services market.

RALs are expensive. For example, a tax filer eligible for a $1,900 EITC refund who takes out a RAL will pay $248 (see Table 5.7), thereby reducing the original $1,900 to $1,652.[125] Most of these costs are incurred simply to get an EITC refund a few days earlier compared to filing electronically and having the IRS directly deposit the refund into a checking account. RALs are also risky for low-income tax filers. Because a RAL is a loan from a bank in partnership with a tax preparer, it must be

repaid even if the IRS denies or delays the refund, or if the refund is smaller than expected. Moreover, when tax filers apply for RALs, they give the lender the right to use the tax refund to pay for old tax preparation debts that may be owed. If low-income consumers are fleeced when they enter a tax preparation office, they are ripped off again on their way out. About 45 percent of RAL customers use commercial check cashing outlets (CCOs) to cash their refund checks, paying fees that range from 3 to 10 percent of the face value of the check. All told, EITC-eligible families can lose more than 16 percent of the value of their tax refund. High tax preparation and RAL fees hurt poor working families and substantially diminish the economic impact of the EITC and CTC. In 2010, tax filers paid almost $1 billion in RAL and other fees, which took a substantial chunk out of the $59.5 billion the EITC program had targeted for the poor.[126] Table 5.7 illustrates the impact of tax preparation fees and RALs on tax filers and the EITC program.

Check Cashing Outlets (CCOs)   Behind these 11,000 plus storefronts lies an industry that cashes upwards of 180 million checks a year with a face value of more than $55 billion. The CCO industry generates nearly $1.5 billion a year in revenues.[127] In large urban areas, from 20 to 40 percent of the unbanked pay fees to cash their paychecks through CCOs.[128] Many larger CCOs are one-stop financial service centers since they offer a wide range of services in one location: (1) check cashing; (2) utility and other bill pay services; (3) money transfers;

(4) payday loans; (5) money orders; (6) telecommunications products (e.g., pre-paid long distance calling cards, pre-paid local phone service, cell phones and beepers); and (7) other services such as fax transmissions, copy services, stamps and envelopes, notary services, mailboxes, and lottery tickets.[129]

CCOs are an expensive way to cash checks. Most check cashing fees range from 1 to 10 percent (plus a service fee in some states) of the face value of a check.[130] Check cashing charges are often based on a sliding scale, and Dollar—the second largest CCO—charges 3.5 percent, or $35, to cash a $1,000 payroll check.[131] Fees for cashing personal checks can run as high as 10 to 12 percent of the value of the check. If a customer cashes twenty $800 paychecks a year through Dollar, they will pay $560—far more than the costs of even a deluxe checking account in a mainstream bank. High check cashing fees do not correspond to high risk since about 70 to 90 percent of all checks cashed at CCOs are relatively secure payroll checks with an average value of $500 to $600.[132] Losses are also extremely low.

Transportation in the Fringe Economy

The path to car ownership for the poor is mined with high down payments, predatory financing, extortionate interest rates, and overpriced insurance. Understanding the used-car industry is necessary to appreciate the obstacles faced by the poor. Used-car lots fall into two categories: franchised dealerships and independent lots. Franchised used-car lots are part of new-car dealerships and their cars tend to be newer, cleaner, and more expensive. Independent dealers frequently sell older and less expensive vehicles and hence a large number of poor buyers end up there, many of which are "here today and gone tomorrow."

A major obstacle faced by the poor is that most mainstream lenders refuse to finance vehicles that are older than four to six years or have more than 100,000 miles on the odometer. Some lenders only finance vehicles purchased through franchise dealerships, and some further restrict that to dealerships that also sell new cars. These restrictions limit the choices for the poor since used cars sold by franchised dealers generally sell for top dollar.

Three tiers of financing exist for used-car buyers. The first is prime lending, which is offered to borrowers with a higher income and a good credit history. Interest rates are low because they are tied to the prime rate. The second tier is subprime lending, which is geared toward buyers with credit problems but who still have sufficient creditworthiness to secure a loan. Subprime loans carry higher interest rates, involve a substantial down payment, and often require that a vehicle be purchased from a franchised dealership. The third tier is nonprime lending or dealer financing, whereby vehicles are financed in-house. This type of financing often carries the highest interest rates and can require weekly payments.

Buy-Here, Pay-Here used-car lots provide in-house financing and hence do not require buyers to undergo a credit check. Dealer-financed cars require a down payment and late payments can result in immediate repossession. In some cases, the buyer is expected to hand deliver their payments to the dealership weekly.

Buy-Here, Pay-Here used-car lots are generally more profitable than franchised car dealerships. For instance, in 2002 the average retail price of used cars sold by franchised car lots was $11,793 with a gross profit of $1,741. In that same year, the average retail price of a used car in a Buy-Here, Pay-Here lot was $7,810 with a gross profit of $3,772.

Auto insurance is another area where the poor are hard hit. For example, many people with older cars insure them only for state-mandated liability rather than for collision (damage to their vehicle) coverage. It makes little sense to pay $600 a year for collision coverage on a car worth $1,000, especially with a $500 deductible. Unfortunately, consumers who finance through Buy-Here, Pay-Here dealerships or subprime lenders must insure their vehicles for liability *and* collision, regardless of whether it is cost effective.

The poor are hard hit by high auto-insurance rates. According to one study, 92 percent of large insurance companies run credit checks on potential customers, which translate into insurance scores.[133] These scores determine whether the carrier will insure an applicant and for how much. Those with poor or no credit may be denied coverage, while those with limited credit will likely pay high premiums. Although there is no evidence that residents in low-income or high minority zip codes are involved in more accidents, they pay more for basic auto insurance, even if they have been accident- and ticket-free for years.[134] Mounting consumer complaints have aroused the suspicion of some state insurance regulators that this may be a new form of redlining—a practice outlawed by the Fair Housing Act of 1968—since it discriminates against low-income, single-parent, young, and minority consumers whose credit histories may be less than perfect.[135]

While mainstream auto insurers calculate premiums based on six-month or one-year period, fringe auto insurers usually provide only monthly quotations. Many also require a sizeable down payment and a service fee. The premiums charged by fringe insurers are exorbitant compared with mainstream auto insurers. These insurers get away with charging high premiums for several reasons: (1) they have captive consumers who were rejected by large insurance carriers; (2) the insurance requirements of Buy-Here, Pay-Here dealers and subprime lenders create a steady stream of buyers desperate for insurance; (3) in some states auto insurers are minimally regulated and regulators are lax in rooting out predatory insurers, especially those serving the poor; and (4) many state vehicle inspections require a proof-of-insurance card before a vehicle can pass inspection. Some car owners pay the high monthly premium to get the card and pass inspection, after which they drop the coverage. This may explain why fringe auto-insurance rates are quoted monthly rather than biannually. Not coincidentally, fringe auto insurers take the pressure off mainstream carriers to cover the poor.

The poor pay more than the middle class for financial services in both absolute dollars and relative to their income.[136] These costs are aggravated by a dual financial system with one system for the poor and another for the middle and upper classes. This dual system leads to even greater inequality: Banks for the middle class and check cashers for the poor; access to savings tools for the middle class and barriers to savings for the poor; low-cost financial services for the middle class and high fee-based services for the poor. The fringe economy represents a financial exploitation that depletes the resources of poor families and communities. To better understand the poor, policy analysts must be aware of the myriad ways in which the poor are economically exploited.

Conclusion

Poverty is one of the most intractable problems in the United States and elsewhere in the world. Because poverty is both a political and a social issue, the policies surrounding it are often less than objective. For example, governments can halve the poverty rate simply by redefining the poverty index of threshold. In the United States, poverty rates by placing a high dollar value on in-kind benefits such as food stamps

and Medicaid. Conversely, governments can swell the ranks of the poor by moving the poverty line upward and increasing the income level at which people are defined as poor. Like all social policies, poverty-related policies exist in a context marked by political exigencies, public opinion, the economic health of a society, and the complex mask of ideology.

Although mountains of poverty-related data are available, policymakers remain uncertain as to the precise causes of poverty. What is known is that these causes are complex and involve, among other things, the effects of discrimination; the composition of family life, including the rise in single, female-headed families and teenage pregnancies; geographical location; and age. In large measure, the determination of whether a child is poor depends on chance—the family he or she was born into. Nobel Prize winning economist Joseph Stiglitz argues that "America has long prided itself on being a fair society, where everyone has an equal chance of getting ahead, but the statistics suggest otherwise: the chances of a poor citizen, or even a middle-class citizen, making it to the top in America are smaller than in many countries of Europe."[137] Policymakers know that the skewed distribution of income in society and governmental tax and investment policies have major impacts on the numbers of people in poverty and on the extent of their poverty.

Most policymakers agree that employment is the best antipoverty program. Thus, work-related factors such as the value of the minimum wage (especially its relationship to mean incomes), the level of under- and unemployment, the rise or decrease in family incomes, and the general state of the economy all have a major impact on the level and extent of poverty. The availability of job training programs and the regulation of the dual labor market help determine the salaries workers will make. Taken together, these factors have caused poverty rates to remain higher in the United States than in many other industrialized nations. They have also helped make poverty seem like an intractable problem with few viable solutions.

DISCUSSION QUESTIONS

1. The measurement of poverty is both complex and controversial. Nevertheless, the way that poverty is measured has important consequences for the development of social policy in the United States. Describe some of the potential pitfalls in measuring poverty rates and discuss how the calculation of poverty rates affects the creation of social policy.

2. Working families make up an important and growing segment of the poor. What is causing the increase in the numbers of working poor? What specific policies should be implemented to reduce the number of working poor families?

3. Several theories have been advanced to explain why some individuals and groups of people are persistently poor while others are not. Theorists who have tried to tackle this problem include Daniel Patrick Moynihan, Oscar Lewis, and Edward Banfield, among others. Although all theories of poverty have intrinsic flaws, which theory or combination of theories described in this book (or elsewhere) do you think best explains the dynamics of poverty?

4. Many strategies have been developed to fight poverty, including the curative approach, the alleviative approach, and the preventive approach. Of these strategies, which is the most effective in fighting poverty and why? What alternative strategies, if any, could be developed that would be more effective in combating poverty?

5. Policy analysts have traditionally argued that jobs are preferable to welfare and that the lack of employment opportunities results in increasing needs for social welfare. Is this relationship apparent in your community? What is the evidence?

6. A commonly held belief is that government make-work jobs are inferior to private sector employment. Yet many New Deal jobs programs have made important contributions to the infrastructure of the nation's cities. What New Deal projects are evident in your community? If a new governmental jobs program were initiated, what community needs might it address?

7. The fringe economy is a high-growth sector that is adversely affecting the economic lives of the poor. What policies or programs would you propose that could regulate, constrain or abolish the fringe economic sector? What legislative or policy reforms are needed?

NOTES

1. See Edward C. Banfield, *The Unheavenly City* (Boston: Little, Brown, 1966) and Oscar Lewis, *La Vida* (New York: Harper & Row, 1965).

2. Henry Goddard, *The Kallikak Family* (New York: Arno Publishers, 1911).

3. Arthur R. Jensen, "How Much Can We Boost IQ and Scholastic Achievement?" *Harvard Educational Review* 39 (Winter 1969), pp. 1–23.

4. Winifred Bell, *Contemporary Social Welfare* (New York: Macmillan, 1983), p. 261.

5. Richard Herrnstein and Charles Murray, *The Bell Curve* (New York: Free Press, 1994).

6. Winnie Chen, Vilma Hernandez, Erin Townsend, and Carol Wyatt, "Affirmative Action," unpublished paper, University of Houston Graduate School of Social Work, Houston, TX, May 1, 1996.

7. T. Beardsley, "For Whom the Bell Curve Really Tolls," *Scientific American* 272, no. 1 (1995), pp. 14–17; Stephen Gould, "Ghosts of Bell Curves Past," *Natural History* 104, no. 2 (1995), pp. 12–19; and C. Lane, "The Tainted Sources of the Bell Curve," *The New York Review of Books* 41, no. 20 (1994), pp. 14–19.

8. Gould, "Ghosts of Bell Curves Past," p. 14.

9. Bell, *Contemporary Social Welfare*, p. 264.

10. David Gil, *Unraveling Social Policy* (Boston: Shenkman, 1981).

11. Blanche Bernstein, "Welfare Dependency," in Lee D. Bawden (ed.), *The Social Contract Revisited* (Washington, DC: Urban Institute Press, 1984), p. 129.

12. Greg J. Duncan et al., *Years of Poverty, Years of Plenty* (Ann Arbor, MI: Institute for Social Research, 1984).

13. Daniel McMurer and Isabel Sawhill, *Getting Ahead* (Washington, DC: Urban Institute, 1998), p. 33.

14. Bradley Schiller, "Relative Earnings Redux." Review of Income and Wealth 40, no. 4 (1994), p. 629.

15. U.S. Census Bureau, "Income, Poverty, and Health Insurance Coverage in the United States: 2010," September 2011. Retrieved Feb 2012, from www.census.gov/prod/2011pubs/p60-239.pdf

16. U.S. Census Bureau, "Income, Poverty, and Health Insurance Coverage in the United States: 2010," September 2011. Retrieved Feb 2012, from www.census.gov/prod/2011pubs/p60-239.pdf

17. U.S. Department of Health and Human Services, "Prior HHS Poverty Guidelines and Federal Register References," March 2012. Retrieved March 2012, from http://aspe.hhs.gov/poverty/figures-fed-reg.shtml

18. U.S. Census Bureau, "Income, Poverty, and Health Insurance Coverage in the United States: 2010," September 2011. Retrieved Feb 2012, from www.census.gov/prod/2011pubs/p60-239.pdf

19. Institute for Research on Poverty, "Improving the Measurement of American Poverty," *Focus* 19, no. 2 (Spring 1998), p. 2.

20. Ibid.

21. M.W. Roosa, S. Deng, R.L. Nair, G.L. Burrell, "Measures for Studying Poverty in Family and Child Research," *Journal of Marriage and Family*, 67:4 (2005), pp. 971–988.

22. U.S. Senate, "Introduction of the Poverty Data Correction Act of 1999," p. 1. Retrieved 2008, from www.govtrack.us/congress/bill.xpd?bill=s106-204

23. U.S. Census Bureau, "Income, Poverty, and Health Insurance Coverage in the United States: 2010," September 2011. Retrieved Feb 2012, from www.census.gov/prod/2011pubs/p60-239.pdf

24. Sara McLanahan and Gary Sandefur, *Growing Up with a Single Parent* (Cambridge, MA: Harvard University Press, 1997).

25. Sara McLanahan and Gary Sandefur, *Growing Up with a Single Parent* (Cambridge, MA: Harvard University Press, 1997).

26. U.S. Census Bureau, "Custodial Mothers and Fathers and Their Child Support: 2007," November 2009. Retrieved March 2012, from http://www.census.gov/prod/2009pubs/p60-237.pdf

27. U.S. Census Bureau, "Custodial Mothers and Fathers and Their Child Support: 2007," November 2009. Retrieved March 2012, from http://www.census.gov/prod/2009pubs/p60-237.pdf

28. Center for Law and Social Policy, "Child Support Substantially Increases Economic Well-Being of Lowand Moderate-Income Families," Washington, DC, 2004.

29. U.S. Census Bureau, "Custodial Mothers and Fathers and Their Child Support: 2007," November 2009. Retrieved March 2012, from http://www.census.gov/prod/2009pubs/p60-237.pdf

30. Center for Law and Social Policy, "Child Support Substantially Increases Economic Well-Being of Lowand Moderate-Income Families," Washington, DC, 2004.

31. Center for Law and Social Policy, "Child Support Substantially Increases Economic Well-Being of Low- and Moderate-Income Families," Washington, DC, 2004.

32. U.S. Census Bureau, "Income, Poverty, and Health Insurance Coverage in the United States: 2010," September 2011. Retrieved Feb 2012, from www.census.gov/prod/2011pubs/p60-239.pdf

33. Carmen DeNavas-Walt, Bernadette D. Proctor, and Jessica Smith "Income, Poverty, and Health Insurance Coverage in the United States: 2006" Economics and Statistics Administration U.S. Census Bureau, Issued August 2007 Retrieved May 2008 from http://www.census.gov/prod/2007pubs/p60-233.pdf

34. Bennett, Li, Song, and Yang, "Young Children in Poverty."

35. U.S. Census Bureau, "Income, Poverty, and Health Insurance Coverage in the United States: 2010," September 2011. Retrieved Feb 2012, from www.census.gov/prod/2011pubs/p60-239.pdf

36. U.S. Census Bureau, "Income, Poverty, and Health Insurance Coverage in the United States: 2010," September 2011. Retrieved Feb 2012, from www.census.gov/prod/2011pubs/p60-239.pdf

37. U.S. Census Bureau, "Income, Poverty, and Health Insurance Coverage in the United States: 2010," September 2011. Retrieved Feb 2012, from www.census.gov/prod/2011pubs/p60-239.pdf

38. U.S. Census Bureau, "Income, Poverty, and Health Insurance Coverage in the United States: 2010," September 2011. Retrieved Feb 2012, from www.census.gov/prod/2011pubs/p60-239.pdf

39. Cliff Pinckard, "New Formula Shows Poverty Rate Among Elderly Believed to be Higher than First Thought," Cleveland.com, September 4, 2009. Retrieved March 2012 from, http://www.cleveland.com/nation/index.ssf/2009/09/new_formula_shows_poverty_rate.html

40. U.S. Bureau of Labor Statistics, "A Profile of the Working Poor, 2009". March 2011. Retrieved March 2012, from http://www.bls.gov/cps/cpswp2009.pdf

41. U.S. Census Bureau, "Income, Poverty, and Health Insurance Coverage in the United States: 2010," September 2011. Retrieved Feb 2012, from www.census.gov/prod/2011pubs/p60-239.pdf

42. DeNavas-Walt, Proctor, and Smith "Income, Poverty, and Health Insurance Coverage in the United States: 2006."

43. U.S. Department of Agriculture, Economic Research Service, Rural Income, Poverty and Welfare: Poverty Demographics. 17 September 2011. Retrieved March 2012, from http://www.ers.usda.gov/Briefing/IncomePovertyWelfare/PovertyDemographics.htm

44. Porter, *Poverty*.

45. U.S. Department of Agriculture, Economic Research Service, Rural Income, Poverty and Welfare: Poverty Demographics. 17 September 2011. Retrieved March 2012, from http://www.ers.usda.gov/Briefing/IncomePovertyWelfare/PovertyDemographics.htm

46. See Economic Research Service, "Rural America at a Glance," USDA, Rural Development Briefing Room, retrieved 1999 from www.ers.usda.gov/briefing/rural/Ruralecn/index.htm#pov; and Ohio State University Extension, "Poverty Fact Sheet Series—Rural Poverty," Family and Consumer Sciences, retrieved 2000 from http://ohioline.ag.ohio-state.edu/hyg-fact/5000/5709.html

47. U.S. Census Bureau, "Income, Poverty, and Health Insurance Coverage in the United States: 2010," September 2011. Retrieved Feb 2012, from www.census.gov/prod/2011pubs/p60-239.pdf

48. U.S. Bureau of Labor Statistics, "A Profile of the Working Poor, 2009". March 2011. Retrieved March 2012, from http://www.bls.gov/cps/cpswp2009.pdf

49. U.S. Bureau of Labor Statistics, "A Profile of the Working Poor, 2009". March 2011. Retrieved March 2012, from http://www.bls.gov/cps/cpswp2009.pdf

50. Robert E. Scott, Growing U.S. Trade Deficit With China Cost 2.8 Million Jobs Between 2001, Economic Policy Institute, Washington, DC, September 20, 2011

51. Michael Sherraden, "Chronic Unemployment: A Social Work Perspective," *Social Work* (September–October 1985), p. 403.

52. As Sherraden notes, the common understanding that an unemployment rate of 5 is "normal" is not supported by economists, who calculate that structural and frictional unemployment can be reduced to 3 percent through astute social policies.

53. U.S. Bureau of Labor Statistics, "Extended Mass Layoffs in 2010". November 2011. Retrieved March 2012, from http://www.bls.gov/mls/mlsreport1038.pdf

54. *New York Times*, "Not Many Jobs Are Sent Abroad, U.S. Report Says" (June 11, 2004).

55. M. Harvey Brenner, *Estimating the Effects of Economic Change on National Health and Social Well-Being* (Washington, DC: U.S. Government Printing Office, 1984), pp. 2–4.

56. Ibid.

57. Catherine Rampell, "Older Workers Without Jobs Face Longest Time Out of Work," *The New York Times*, May 6, 2011, p. 10B.

58. Michael Piore, "The Dual Labor Market," in David Gordon (ed.), *Problems in Political Economy* (Lexington, MA: D. C. Heath, 1977), p. 94.

59. David Gordon, Richard Edwards, and Michael Reich, *Segmented Work, Divided Workers* (New York: Cambridge University Press, 1982), p. 211.

60. Harrington, *Who Are the Poor?* p. 10.

61. James Parks, "Kennedy, Pelosi Promise Quick Action on Minimum Wage if Democrats Win Congress", October 24, 2006. Retrieved March 20, 2007 from http://blog.aflcio.org/2006/10/24/kennedy-pelosi-promise-quick-action-on-minimum-wage-if-democrats-win-congress/

62. Bureau of Labor Statistics, "Characteristics of Minimum Wage Workers: 2008," Labor Force Statistics from the Current Population Survey. Retrieved November 2010 from, http://www.bls.gov/cps/minwage2008.htm

63. George. J. Borjas, *Labor Economics.* (Boston: McGraw Hill, 2005)

64. "Minimum Wage: Facts at a Glance".

65. "Sates with Minimum Wages above the Federal Level have had Faster Small Business and Retail Job Growth", Fiscal Policy Institute, March 30, 2006. Retrieved March 20, 2007 from http://fiscalpolicy.org/FPISmallBusinessMinWage.pdf

66. The Bureau of Labor Statistics, "Characteristics of Minimum Wage Workers: 2007", Table 4. Retrieved July 2008 from http://www.bls.gov/cps/minwage2007tbls.htm#5

67. Acorn, National Living Wage Resource Center, "Introduction to ACORN's Living Wage Web Site." Retrieved 2000 from www.livingwagecampaign.org

68. U.S. Department of Labor, Division of Communications Wage and Hour Division, Minimum Wage Laws in the States – January 1, 2012. Retrieved March 2012, from http://www.dol.gov/whd/minwage/america.htm

69. U.S. Department of Labor, Employment Standards Administration Wage and Hour Division, Minimum Wage Laws in the States – January 1, 2008. Retrieved 12 May, 2008 from http://www/dol.gov/esa/minwage/america.htm

70. U.S. Department of Labor, Division of Communications Wage and Hour Division, Minimum Wage Laws in the States – January 1, 2012. Retrieved March 2012, from http://www.dol.gov/whd/minwage/america.htm

71. Ibid.

72. Ibid.

73. Michael Sherraden, *Assets and the Poor: A New American Welfare Policy* (Armonk, NY: M. E. Sharpe, 1991).

74. Ibid.

75. Ibid.

76. John Kenneth Galbraith, *The Affluent Society* (Boston: Houghton Mifflin, 1958).

77. Harrington, *Who Are the Poor?* p. 17.

78. Ibid., p. 22.

79. U.S. Census Bureau, "Poverty: 2009 and 2010". October 2011. Retrieved March 2012, from http://www.census.gov/prod/2011pubs/acsbr10-01.pdf

80. Kevin Phillips, *The Politics of Rich and Poor* (New York: Random House, 1990), p. 87.

81. Sheldon Danziger, "Poverty," *Encyclopedia of Social Work,* 18th ed. (Silver Spring, MD: NASW Press, 1987), pp. 301–302.

82. News in English, "Poverty hits 10 percent in Oslo," May 4, 2011. Retrieved July 28, 2012 from http://www.newsinenglish.no/2011/05/04/poverty-hits-10-percent-in-oslo/ Index Mundi, Population below poverty line – World. Retrieved July 28, 2012 from http://www.indexmundi.com/map/?v=69]

83. United Nations, Human Development Report 2011. Sustainability and Equity: A Better Future for All, 2011. Retrieved March 2012, from http://hdr.undp.org/en/media/HDR_2011_EN_Complete.pdf

84. Frances Moore Lappé, Joseph Collins, Peter Rosset, and Luis Esparza, *World Hunger: Twelve Myths* (2nd ed.) (New York: Grove Press, 1998).

85. OneWorld, Global Poverty Guide, December 2011. Retrieved October 2012 from, http://uk.oneworld.net/guides/poverty

86. J. Humberto Lopez, Pro-Growth, Pro-Poor: Is there a Trade-Off? The World Bank (PRMPR), Washington, DC, July 10, 2010.

87. Martin Ravallion, Pro-Poor Growth: A Primer, Development Research Group, World Bank, Washington, DC., 2010.

88. OECD, Aid Statistics, Donor Aid Charts, Development Co-operation Directorate (DCD-DAC), 2011. Retrieved March 2012 from,http://www.oecd.org/countrylist/0,3349,en_2649_34447_1783495_1_1_1_1,00.html

89. OECD, Aid Statistics, Recipient Aid Charts, Development Co-operation Directorate (DCD-DAC), 2011. Retrieved March 2012, from http://www.oecd.org/countrylist/0,3349,en_2649_34447_25602317_1_1_1_1,00.html

90. Helmut Anheier, "Measuring Global Civil Society." In Helmut Anheier, Marlies Glasius, and Mary Kaldor (Eds.) *Global Civil Society* (Oxford: Oxford University Press, 2001)

91. Bill and Melinda Gates Foundation, Foundation Fact Sheet, 2012. Retrieved March 2012 from, http://www.gatesfoundation.org/about/Pages/foundation-fact-sheet.aspx

92. United Nations, 2015 Millennium Development Goals, 2012. Retrieved March 2012 from, http://www.un.org/millenniumgoals/bkgd.shtml

93. Kiva, About Microfinance

94. John Vidal, "The Future of Food," *The Observer,* January 22, 2012, p. B15.

95. John Vidal, "The Future of Food," *The Observer,* January 22, 2012, p. A16.

96. For a fuller examination of the fringe economy see Howard Karger, *Shortchanged: Life and Debt in the Fringe Economy* (San Francisco: Berrett-Koehler, 2005).

97. Kenneth J. Lansing, "Spendthrift Nation," *FRBSF Economic Letter,* November 10, 2005. Retrieved March 22, 2007, from www.frbsf.org/publications/economics/letter/2005/el2005-30.html

98. Ibid.

99. Brian K. Bucks, Arthur B. Kennickell, Kevin B. Moore, Gerhard Fries, and A. Michael Neal, "Recent Changes

in U.S. Families Finances: Evidence from the 2001 and 2001 Survey of Consumer Finances," *Federal Reserve Bulletin,* 2006. Retrieved March 22, 2007, from www.federalreserve.gov/pubs/oss/oss2/2004/bull0206.pdf

100. Robert D. Manning, *Credit Card Nation* (New York: Basic Books, 2000).

101. Center for Responsible Lending, "Financial Quicksand: Payday Lending Sinks Borrowers in Debt with $4.2 Billion in Predatory Fees Every Year", November 30, 2006. Retrieved July 2008, from www.responsiblelending.org/pdfs/rr012-Financial_Quicksand-1106.pdf

102. Consumer Federation of America, Payday Loan consumer Information, circa 2011. Retrieved March 2012 from, http://www.paydayloaninfo.org/facts. National Consumer Law Center, "Utilities and Payday Lenders: Convenient Payments, Killer Loans." Retrieved July 2008, from www.consumerlaw.org/reports/content/payday_utility.pdf

103. Ibid.

104. Fannie Mae Foundation, 2001.

105. Federal Reserve Board, 2002; IO Data Corporation, Payday Advance Customer Research: Cumulative State Research Report, September 2002. IO Data Corporation, Salt Lake City, UT.

106. Io Data Corporation, 2002.

107. Manning, *Credit Card Nation.*

108. Yepoka Yeebo, "Decrease In Credit Card Debt All Down To Write-Offs, Report Says," *The Huffington Post,* March 20, 2011. Retrieved March 2012 from, http://www.huffingtonpost.com/2011/03/20/decrease-in-credit-card-debt_n_837806.html

109. See Sprint PCS. Retrieved 2004, from www.sprintpcs.com; and AT&T Wireless. Retrieved 2004, from www.attwireless.com

110. See APRO 2003; and James M. Lacko, Signe-Mary McKernan, and Manoj Hastak, *Survey of Rent-to-Own Customers, Federal Trade Commission* (Bureau of Economics, Washington, DC, 1999).

111. APRO, "About Rent-to-Own: Rent-to-Own Industry Overview." Retrieved July 2008, from www.rtohq.org/apro-rto-industry-overview.html

112. Rent-A-Center. Retrieved January 2, 2004, from www.rentacenter.com; ColorTyme. Retrieved January 2, 2004, from www.colortyme.com; Aaron Rents. Retrieved 2004, from www.aaronrents.com; RentWay. Retrieved 2004, from www.rentway.com; Rent Rite. Retrieved 2003, from www.rentrite.com

113. Public Interest Research Group (PIRG), "Don't Rent to Own: The 1997 PIRG Rent-to-Own Survey," U.S. Public Interest Research Group, Washington, DC, June 11, 1997.

114. Quoted in Freedman, 1993, p. D16.

115. UPI.com, "Tough Times Send Many to Pawnshops," June 16, 2008. Retrieved July 2008, from www.upi.com/Business_News/2008/06/16/

Tough_times_send_many_to_pawn_shops/UPI-47261213629989/

116. Caskey, 1994.

117. American Financial Services Association, "Pawnshops Struggle, 2002." Retrieved 2002, from www.spotlightonfinance.org/issues/August/Stories/story13.htm/

118. American Financial Services Association, 2002.

119. Consumer Federation of America, 2002.

120. AARP, "Payday Loans Don't Pay." Retrieved 2008, from www.aarp.org/money/wise_consumer/smartshopping/a2002-10-02-FraudsPaydayLoans.html

121. AARP, "Payday Loans Don't Pay." Retrieved 2008, from www.aarp.org/money/wise_consumer/smartshopping/a2002-10-02-FraudsPaydayLoans.html

122. Quik Payday, "APR Disclosure, 2002." Retrieved 2002, from ww.quikpayday.com/ apr-disclosure.html

123. Consumer Federation of America, 2002.

124. Daniel P. McKernan, *The Monitor,* "The Real Cost of Tax Refund Anticipation Loans," December 20, 2007. Retrieved July 2008, from www.fbmonitor.com/2007/12december/122007/pdf/122007part5.pdf

125. See Karger, *Shortchanged,* p. 98.

126. Internal Revenue Service, About EITC, 2011. Retrieved March 2012 from, http://www.eitc.irs.gov/central/abouteitc/

127. See Anne Kim, "The Unbanked and the Alternative Financial Sector. Discussion Comments to the Changing Financial Markets and Community Development Conference." Federal Reserve Bank of Chicago, transcript, April 5, 2001. Retrieved 2002, from www.ppionline.org/ppi_ci.cfm?cp_3&knlgAreaID_114&subsecid=236&contentid=3843; and Financial Service Centers of America, 2003.

128. John Caskey, "Bringing Unbanked Households into the Banking System," *Capitol Xchange,* The Brookings Institution, January 2002. Retrieved 2002 from, www.brookings.edu/articles/2002/01metropolitanpolicy_caskey.aspx

129. ACE Cash Express, "ACE Store Services, 2002." Retrieved 2002, from www.acecashexpress.com/general/services.html

130. Mukherjee, 1997, p. 25.

131. Kim, 2001, op cit.

132. Financial Service Centers of America (FiSCA), 2003.

133. "Conning & Co. Study Says Auto Insurers Are Paying Closer Attention to Credit Scores," *Insurance Journal* (August 2, 2001).

134. Consumers Union, "Reducing the Number of Uninsured Motorists," *Consumers Union SWRO Issue Pages for the 77th Texas Legislature* (January 2001).

135. A.M. Best Company, Inc., "Insurers Expect Battle on Use of Credit Scores in About Half the United States," *BestWire* (January 30, 2002).

136. *Caskey,* 1997.

137. Joseph Stiglitz, "Of the 1%, by the 1%, for the 1%," *Vanity Fair,* May 2011, p. 19.

CHAPTER 6

The Voluntary Sector Today

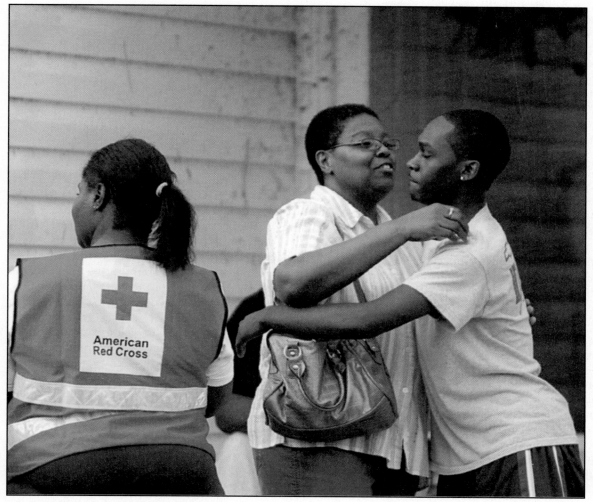

Source: The Wilson Times, Brad Coville/AP Images

This chapter locates the voluntary sector with respect to the other institutions involved in social welfare in the United States. The heart of the **voluntary sector** is made up of private, nonprofit organizations, which are ubiquitous at the local level. Supporting the voluntary sector are philanthropic contributions that have been a mainstay for social service initiatives. In this chapter, the work of prominent human service agencies is described, and the role of voluntary agencies in advocating social justice is examined. The fiscal crisis of the voluntary sector is discussed, providing historical and economic context to the ongoing funding problems of nonprofit service agencies. Finally, the responses of the voluntary sector to September 11, 2001, and Hurricane Katrina in 2005, as well as the emerging trends in the voluntary sector are considered.

During the last decade, welfare professionals have been reassessing the capacity of the voluntary sector to meet the nation's social welfare needs. As governmental expenditures for social welfare fail to increase in the face of rising demand for human services, the voluntary sector has been called on to shoulder more of the welfare burden. This shift in responsibilities was stated explicitly by former president Reagan, in the early 1980s when he appealed to the charitable impulses of Americans as a way for the nation to address human needs while reducing federal appropriations to social programs. The idea was restated by George H. W. Bush, and affirmed by his reference to "a thousand points of light" during his 1988 presidential campaign. Although former president Clinton made no comparable gesture to the nonprofit sector, his statement that "the era of big government is over" had enormous implications for nonprofit agencies. The emergence of "compassionate conservatism" and its corollary, "faith-based social services," promoted by former president George W. Bush restated the conservative case for a reinvigorated voluntary sector. President Obama's continuation and expansion of the Office of Faith-Based and Community Service continue this trend initiative as does the Republican repudiation of federal government programs in the wake of the 2010 midterm elections.

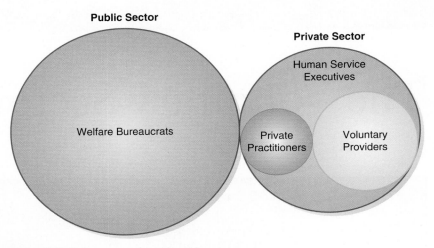

FIGURE 6.1 Dynamics of Structural Interests

Structural Interests within Social Welfare

Organized responses to the needs of Americans have undergone fundamental change since European settlement. In a sense, the voluntary sector is the first modern welfare institution; it has a long legacy in American social welfare. Over the centuries, the voluntary sector has witnessed the emergence of competing institutions: the state and federal governmental programs of the public sector, the private practices of professional entrepreneurs, and a corporate sector accountable to chief executive officers and stockholders. Reflecting on this transformation, David Stoesz posited that four groups can be identified within U.S. social welfare: traditional providers, welfare bureaucrats, clinical entrepreneurs, and human service executives.[1] Because these groups have become integrated into the nation's political economy, they are termed *structural interests*.

Traditional Providers

The heart of the voluntary sector consists of professionals and laypersons who seek to maintain and enhance traditional relations, values, and structures in their communities through private, nonprofit agencies. **Traditional providers** see social welfare as tightly interwoven with other community institutions. According to traditional providers, voluntary nonprofit agencies offer the advantages of neighborliness, a reaffirmation of community values, a concern for community as opposed to personal gain, and freedom to alter programming to conform to changes in local priorities.

Much of the heritage of social welfare can be traced to early proponents of this structural interest—people such as Mary Richmond of the **Charity Organization Society (COS)** movement and Jane Addams of the settlement house movement.

Voluntary agencies routinized philanthropic contributions by socializing charity. Beginning with Denver's Associated Charities in 1887, the concept of a community appeal spread so rapidly that by the 1920s more than 200 cities had "community chests." The needs of social workers for effective treatment techniques and the economic imperatives for organizational survival functioned together to standardize the social agency. Perhaps the best description of the casework agency is found in the 1923 Milford Conference Report, *Social Casework: Generic and Specific*, which comprehensively outlined the organization through which professional caseworkers delivered services.[2] By the 1940s, the social casework agency had become a predominant form of service delivery. Today, much social service provision exists in the form of United Way—subsidized sectarian and nonsectarian agencies, whose member groups collected $5.09 billion in 2010.[3]

Welfare Bureaucrats

Welfare bureaucrats are public functionaries who maintain the welfare state in much the same form in which it was conceived during the New Deal. "Their ideology stresses a rational, efficient, cost-conscious, coordinated delivery system."[4] Welfare bureaucrats view federal government intervention vis-à-vis social problems as legitimate and necessary, considering the apparent lack of concern by the private sector and local governments. Moreover, they contend that federal intervention is more effective than other forms, because authority is centralized, guidelines are standardized, and benefits are allocated according to principles of equity and equality.

The influence of welfare bureaucrats grew as a result of the Social Security Act of 1935. To a limited extent, the larger community chests "exerted a pressure toward rationalization of the professional welfare machinery,"[5] but this did not diminish the effect of the governmental welfare bureaucracy, which soon eclipsed the authority of traditional providers. Actually, a unilinear evolution between these interests could have occurred had Harry Hopkins, head of the Federal Emergency Relief Administration in the 1930s, not prohibited states from turning federal welfare funds over to private agencies.[6] Private agencies lapsed into a secondary role when they were denied the resources to significantly address the massive social problems caused by the

Great Depression, while federal and state agencies ascended in importance. An array of welfare legislation followed the Social Security Act, including:

- the Housing Act of 1937,
- the G.I. Bill of 1944,
- the Community Mental Health Centers Act of 1963,
- the Civil Rights Act of 1964,
- the Food Stamp Act of 1964,
- the Economic Opportunity Act of 1964,
- the Elementary and Secondary Education Act of 1965,
- the Medicare and Medicaid Acts of 1965,
- Supplemental Security Income in 1974,
- Title XX of the Social Security Act of 1975,
- the Full Employment Act of 1978,
- the Americans with Disabilities Act of 1980,
- the No Child Left Behind Act of 2001, and
- the Medicare Modernization Act of 2003.

Implicit in the methods advocated by welfare bureaucrats is an expectation, if not an assumption, that the social welfare administration should be centralized, that eligibility for benefits should be universalized, and that social welfare should be firmly anchored in the institutional fabric of society. The influence of welfare bureaucrats had been curtailed somewhat since the mid-1980s. The Reagan administration all but capped the growth of public social welfare expenditures as a percentage of gross domestic product (GDP). The presidency of George W. Bush transmitted a mixed message to welfare bureaucrats: While a series of tax cuts reduced federal revenues for social programs, the addition of a prescription benefit to Medicare and the augmentation of payments for managed care strengthened their relations to the pharmaceutical industry and health insurance companies. Smarting from election losses in the 1980s and 2000, liberal Democrats had begun to reconsider their objections to private sector solutions to social problems. Evidence of this can be seen in the 2010 Affordable Care Act, health care reform legislation promoted by President Obama, which relies heavily on the private sector. Still, the volume of resources and the number of people dependent on public welfare and social insurance assure welfare bureaucrats of a dominant and continuing role in the foreseeable future.

Clinical Entrepreneurs

Clinical entrepreneurs are professional service providers, chiefly social workers, psychologists, and physicians, who work for themselves instead of being salaried employees. Important to clinical entrepreneurs in each specialty is the establishment of a **professional monopoly**, the evolution of which represents a concern on the part of practitioners that their occupational activity not be subject to political interference from the state or the ignorance of the lay public. As an extension of the entrepreneurial model of service delivery, professional monopoly offers privacy in practice, freedom to establish one's worth by setting fees, and the security ensured by membership in the professional monopoly.

The social worker as a clinical entrepreneur is a relatively recent phenomenon, and the **National Association of Social Workers (NASW)** did not officially sanction this form of service delivery until 1964. By the 1970s, **private practice** in social work was developing as an important form of service delivery. By 1985, a large portion of psychotherapy was being done by social workers, and the *New York Times* noted that "growing numbers of social workers are treating more affluent private clients, thus moving into the traditional preserve of the elite psychiatrists and clinical psychologists."[7] Yet, in the early 1990s, NASW reported that only about 15,000 of its members (11.1 percent) were in solo or partnership practice as private practitioners, compared to about one-third of NASW members employed in for-profit firms.[8] A 2009 survey conducted by the National Association of Social Worker revealed that the median income of MSW private practitioners was $52,000 per year, while those with doctorates earned an average of $78,000.[9]

Human Service Executives

Unlike clinical entrepreneurs, **human service executives** are salaried employees of for-profit firms and, as such, have less autonomy. As administrators or chief executive officers of large corporations, human service executives advance market strategies for promoting social welfare. While welfare bureaucrats emphasize the planning and regulatory functions of the state, human service executives favor the rationality of the marketplace in allocating resources and evaluating programs.

For-profit firms became prominent in social welfare in the United States during the 1960s, when Medicaid and Medicare funds were paid to private nursing homes and hospitals.[10] Since then, human service executives have been rapidly creating independent, for-profit human service corporations that provide an extensive range of nationwide services. Human service corporations have established prominent, if not dominant, positions in several human service markets, including nursing home care, hospital management, health maintenance, child care, home care, and even corrections and welfare. Most recently, human service corporations have aggressively exploited the managed care market.

No longer passively dependent on government appropriations, human service corporations are in a strong position to shape the very markets they serve, influencing not only consumer demand but also governmental policy through establishing and maintaining a **human services industrial complex.** This capacity to determine or control a market qualitatively distinguishes corporate welfare, the health, vacation, and retirement benefits attached to employment from the earlier form of business involvement in social welfare—that is, from philanthropic contributions to nonprofit agencies of the voluntary sector. For these reasons, human service executives are now well positioned to challenge the power of welfare bureaucrats.

Marginal Interests

Social welfare in the United States is also populated by numerous groups that have not become as symbiotically attached to the social structure as have the structural interests just described. These marginal interest groups usually represent special populations that have been ignored, excluded, or oppressed by mainstream society. A partial list of marginal interest groups includes African Americans, poor women, Native Americans, homosexuals, the disabled, residents of isolated rural areas, and Hispanic Americans. These groups are of concern to welfare professionals because typically they have not had the same opportunities as mainstream populations; in other words, they have been denied social justice. Within the context of democratic capitalism, elevating marginal interests remains extraordinarily difficult.

In U.S. culture, groups excluded from the mainstream are expected to gather their resources and identify leaders who will mount programs to serve their particular group. Although this expectation is congruent with traditional values such as self-sufficiency and community cohesion, the solidarity approach does not necessarily ensure success. Programs to aid victims of domestic violence and the homeless, for example, have often struggled to mount and sustain minimal services, because the United Way often has funding priorities consonant with the needs of clientele more highly regarded in the community.

√ In a democratic polity, marginal groups can also make claims on the social order by seeking benefits through governmental programs; but doing so presents other problems. Government programs are likely to be managed by welfare bureaucrats, who have their own understanding of what is best for the marginal interest. For example, during the 1980s, the effort to combat AIDS was plagued by volatile disagreements between gay advocacy organizations, such as Act Up! and the public health bureaucrats who run the Centers for Disease Control and Prevention.

Despite such obstacles, members of marginal groups have powerful incentives to work within existing structures if their needs are to be met. Usually, their success in this regard is mixed. As a result of affirmative action, African Americans have been able to secure positions within the welfare bureaucracy in relatively significant numbers and are now well established among welfare bureaucrats. White women have found in private practice a desirable framework within which to provide services and they are well represented among clinical entrepreneurs. In contrast, many marginal groups continue to struggle against a welfare industry that is controlled by structural interests indifferent to minority concerns. The structural interest of human service executives, for example, remains a bastion of white patriarchy.

Activists from the African American community struggle to contain gang violence, reduce the number of teen pregnancies, and halt the scourge of illegal drugs, often with inadequate resources. Indeed, one of the most glaring contradictions of U.S. social welfare are the state-of-the-art medical centers controlled by human service executives located right next to inner-city ghettoes inhabited by the poorest and most neglected Americans. How has the U.S. welfare state come to assure wealth for health and human service executives while generating, at the same time, an underclass?

The Independent Sector

When policymakers turned to the voluntary sector in the 1980s to compensate for reductions in the governmental welfare effort, little was known about nonprofit social service agencies. Such agencies√ include tens of thousands of organizations, many of which are not associated with any national umbrella association (see Table 6.1). Lester Salamon and Alan Abramson, authorities on the voluntary sector, observed that "despite their importance, these organizations have tended to be ignored in both public policy debates and scholarly research."[11] As government assumed a dominant role in U.S. social welfare, the voluntary sector receded in importance. If the Reagan and Bush presidencies rekindled interest in the voluntary sector, the 1994 Republican takeover of Congress created a small firestorm. As part

TABLE 6.1 Nonprofits Earning More Than $25,000/Year

Field of Activity	Revenues (billions)	%	Number	%
Arts, culture, humanities	37,841	11	32.5	2.3
Education	61,970	18.1	260.8	18.6
Environment & animals	14,528	4.2	13.5	1.0
Health	42,880	12.5	788.7	56.3
Human services	115,267	33.6	175.1	12.5
International and foreign	6,407	1.9	28.4	2.0
Public & societal benefit	42,633	12.4	88.1	6.3
Religion related	21,469	6.3	12.5	0.9
Total	**342,995**	**100**	**1,399.7**	**100**

Source: Kennard Wing, Katie Roeger, and Thomas Pollak, "Non-Profit Sector in Brief," (Washington, DC: Urban Institute, 2009), p. 4.

of their "Contract with America," congressional Republicans promised to reform welfare as part of an extensive overhaul of the whole welfare state. Government, they argued, had induced the dependency of millions of families on public assistance; welfare programs largely benefited the welfare professionals who worked in them; and all of this diminished the influence of community institutions. Congressional conservatives had a strategy in mind when they critiqued federal social programs, however: Replace governmental welfare programs with private, voluntary sector initiatives. "The crisis of the modern welfare state is not just a crisis of government," contended conservative scholar Marvin Olasky. "The more effective provision of social services will ultimately depend on their return to private and especially religious institutions."[12]

Beginning in the 1970s, researchers had begun to investigate the scope of the voluntary sector. Their task has not been easy. The picture emerging from preliminary investigations reveals a sector that, if small compared to government and corporate entities, is extraordinarily rich socially. Perhaps the most convenient measure of the scale of the voluntary sector is to count the voluntary and philanthropic associations that received tax-exempt status as social service agencies from the IRS—1.5 million in 2007.

The vast majority of nonprofit organizations are small, reporting less than $25,000 per year. Of more affluent nonprofits, several attributes are noteworthy. Elite philanthropy, often associated with symphonies, operas, and ballets (known by consultants as SOBs), has visibility far beyond its share of revenues. By far, the largest components consist of colleges and universities (education) and hospitals (health). While human services shows the largest number of nonprofits, their total revenue is far less than education and health, indicative of organizations with much smaller budgets.

Although nonprofits focusing on foreign affairs represent the smallest cohort of American voluntary sector organizations, their value is far greater than this number represents. According to the Hudson Institute's Index of Global Philanthropy, international aid through voluntary sector organizations eclipses direct federal aid by a significant margin (see Table 6.2).

Generally, the expansion of the voluntary sector has paralleled economic growth. However, the Great Recession has reduced charitable contributions. In 2009 $303.8 billion was contributed to nonprofit activities, down $4 billion from 2007.

TABLE 6.2 Total Net Engagement by U.S. in Developing Countries

Component	$Billions	%
U.S. official development assistance	30.4	9
U.S. private philanthropy	39.0	12
Foundations	4.6	12
Corporations	7.6	19
Voluntary organizations	14.0	36
Volunteerism	3.7	9
Universities and colleges	1.9	5
Religious organizations	7.2	18
U.S. remittances	95.8	29
U.S. private capital flows	161.2	49
Total	326.4	100

Source: Carol Adelman, "Global Philanthropy," (Washington, DC: Hudson Institute, 2012), p. 8.

Consistently, individual contributions account for most of charitable giving, 75 percent, with corporate, foundations, and corporations accounting for 25 percent.[13]

Public support for nonprofit organizations has suffered somewhat from controversies affecting a number of prominent nonprofits. A dispute about the use of contributions to aid victims of 9/11 led to the resignation of the director of the American Red Cross. Questionable practices in response to 9/11 were compounded by the Gulf Coast disaster of Hurricane Katrina. (Ultimately, the Red Cross would go through seven executives in as many years and have to cut up to one-third of its headquarter staff to address a $200 million deficit.[14]) And victims of the Oklahoma City bombing questioned why they were not able to get assistance for their losses comparable to that provided to victims of 9/11.[15] Even though profound questions were raised during the last decades of the twentieth century about whether the voluntary sector could replace government social programs, there is little doubt that philanthropy will expand significantly during the twenty-first century. Aside from normal economic growth, the value of the four tax cuts enacted by the Bush administration is expected to have significant philanthropic consequences. According to Paul Schervish,

We estimate that an unprecedented $45 to $150 trillion in wealth transfer is in the offing over the next five decades, that this will produce at least $21 trillion to $55 trillion of charitable giving, and that between 52 percent and 65 percent of this amount will be contributed by households with $1 million in net worth.[16]

The extent to which such unprecedented wealth will be used to amplify *moral citizenship*—fulfilling the inclinations and obligations of caring—will be one of the challenges of the twenty-first century.[17]

Advancing Social Justice

In addition to providing social services, the voluntary sector has been important in U.S. social welfare because it has been the source of efforts to advance the rights of disenfranchised populations. In this respect, the voluntary sector is essential to the nation's culture, in that it is a correcting influence to the indifference often shown to marginal populations by governmental and corporate bureaucracies. This case was argued vigorously by the late John W. Gardner, former secretary of Health, Education, and Welfare and chairman of the board of Independent Sector. According to Gardner, the voluntary sector fosters much of the pluralism in the life of this country, taking on those concerns that do not attract the broad spectrum of public support necessary for the legislation that mandates governmental programs, and concerns that do not represent the commercial prospects necessary to attract the interests of the business community. Indeed, much of what Americans would identify as central to their culture can be attributed to organizations of the voluntary sector: hospitals, schools, religious institutions, welfare agencies, fraternal associations, symphonies, and museums, to name a few. According to Gardner,

> Institutions of the nonprofit sector are in a position to serve as the guardians of intellectual and artistic freedom. Both the commercial and political marketplaces are subject to leveling forces that may threaten standards of excellence. In the nonprofit sector, the fiercest champions of excellence may have their say. So may the champions of liberty and justice.[18]

Gardner's last reference here is not merely rhetorical but has its basis in history. Gardner noted that ". . . virtually every far-reaching social change

in our history has come up in the private sector: the abolition of slavery, the reforms of populism, child labor laws, the vote for women, civil rights, and so on."[19]

Important social welfare initiatives have also originated in the voluntary sector. For instance, services to battered women, patients with AIDS, and the homeless have been pioneered by voluntary sector organizations. Given the public apathy toward these groups, for many years the voluntary sector was the only source of service for these groups.

That social change begins in the voluntary sector has a particular lesson for human service professionals: The openness of democratic American culture means that anyone is free to organize for purposes of rectifying past injustices. Wendy Kopp's Teach for America (TFA) is a good illustration. In 1988, armed with a vision of a Peace Corps–like program for inner cities and rural areas, the then 23-year-old Kopp began to hustle corporate contributions to match idealistic professionals to disadvantaged communities. In 1996, TFA boasted a $5.5 million budget and was graduating 500 volunteers annually;[20] by 2012 9,000 volunteers were teaching 600,000 students through a TFA budget augmented by a $100 million endowment.[21] In one of the most distressed communities in America, Harlem, Jeoffrey Canada established the Harlem Children's Zone, in the process becoming an exemplar for the Obama administration's America's Promise initiative.[22]

The United Way

Perhaps the best recognized of voluntary sector organizations is the United Way. Local United Ways, as well as the United Way of America, are nonprofit organizations. The purpose of local United Ways is to raise funds that are then disbursed to nonprofit agencies in the community, most of which are United Way members. Local United Ways also contribute a small percentage of funds to the national headquarters, the United Way of America. Because the United Way is a confederation of organizations, power resides within the local United Ways. The United Way of America provides support services nationwide but has no direct authority over local United Ways.

United Way contributions have oscillated over time. Revelations of managerial improprieties on the part of United Way CEO William Aramony in the early 1990s precipitated a reduction in

One of the most well-known nonprofit human service organizations is the United Way.

Source: PhotoEdit Inc.

donations (adjusted for inflation) to United Ways. Aramony was found to have misappropriated $1.2 million in United Way funds, was sentenced to seven years in federal prison, and was fined $522,000.[23] After the Aramony scandal, administrative problems within the United Way continued. In 2003, Oral Suer, head of the United Way of the National Capital Area (Washington, DC), was found to have misappropriated $1.5 million through various financial arrangements. Suer was subsequently sentenced to 27 months in prison, but the credibility of the United Way serving the nation's capital had been severely damaged. In 2001, the United Way of the National Capital Area had raised $90 million; after the Suer scandal, contributions fell to $19 million, causing the organization to lay off half of its staff, close several satellite offices, and forfeit its lucrative fundraising contract with federal employees.[24] In a sector where credibility is a virtue, such damage requires years to repair. Fortunately for the United Way, contributions have modestly rebounded in the last number of years, despite the effects of the Great Recession.[25]

Elite Philanthropy

The United Way offices that dot the nation's landscape, which pursue relatively modest goals, can be classified as "bourgeois" philanthropy. "Elite" philanthropy, on the other hand, has much grander expectations. Originally, defined as support to the

"SOBs"—symphonies, operas, and ballets[26]—elite philanthropy morphed to issues far beyond the fine arts. During the late 1990s, Ted Turner announced an unprecedented $1 billion contribution to the United Nations; this gift was matched by Bill Gates, whose foundation pledged $1 billion for various disease prevention initiatives in the Third World, notably work on HIV/AIDS in sub-Saharan Africa.[27] By 2004, the Gates Foundation was investing $600 million annually for prevention of diseases that ravaged developing nations, significantly outspending other charities.[28] In 2006 Warren Buffett, reluctant to establish his own foundation, donated over $6 billion to the Gates Foundation, raising its assets to $44 billion.[29] As a result of their collaboration, Gates and Buffett announced an initiative to encourage the wealthiest Americans to commit half of their wealth to philanthropy; by 2010 40 families had subscribed, representing $600 billion;[30] a year later the number had grown to 69. The major philanthropic foundations are identified by the names of the titans of U.S. capitalism (see Table 6.3).

Despite the substantial philanthropic activity of foundations—gifts of $43 billion in 2007[31]—critics questioned their generosity. Accusations of impropriety, fraudulent activity, and stinginess have plagued the foundation world. In addition to criticisms of fund misuse, many people question the motives of large philanthropies and the individuals who support these organizations. "Elite American philanthropy serves the interests of the rich to a greater extent than it does the interests of the poor, disadvantaged, or disabled," argues Teresa Odendahl; it is "a system of 'generosity' by which the wealthy exercise social control and help themselves more than they do others."[32] Odendahl calculated that about one-half of all gifts itemized on income tax returns were made by the wealthy.[33] For what purposes do the rich demonstrate such beneficence? They give to institutions that "sustain their culture, their education, their policy formulation, their status—in short, their interests."[34] In other words, wealthy Americans usually use the tax code to maintain institutions of elite culture, such as private schools, museums, symphony orchestras, and opera companies. The use of funds that have been withdrawn from public use by the tax code in order to reproduce the social institutions of the rich is unacceptable to Odendahl, who proposes reforms that would require philanthropy to be put to public benefit in different ways.

TABLE 6.3 Largest Philanthropic Foundations

Rank	Name/(State)	Assets	As of Fiscal Year End Date
1.	Bill & Melinda Gates Foundation (WA)	$33,120,381,000	12/31/06
2.	The Ford Foundation (NY)	11,615,906,693	09/30/05
3.	J. Paul Getty Trust (CA)	9,618,627,974	06/30/05
4.	The Robert Wood Johnson Foundation (NJ)	9,367,614,774	12/31/05
5.	The William and Flora Hewlett Foundation (CA)	8,520,765,000	12/31/06
6.	Lilly Endowment, Inc. (IN)	8,360,760,584	12/31/05
7.	W. K. Kellogg Foundation (MI)	7,799,270,734	08/31/06
8.	The David and Lucile Packard Foundation (CA)	6,351,000,000	12/31/06
9.	The Andrew W. Mellon Foundation (NY)	5,586,112,102	12/31/05
10.	John D. and Catherine T. MacArthur Foundation (IL)	5,492,269,240	12/31/05
11.	Gordon and Betty Moore Foundation (CA)	5,308,627,945	12/31/05
12.	The California Endowment (CA)	4,405,938,934	02/28/06
13.	The Rockefeller Foundation (NY)	3,417,557,613	12/31/05
14.	The Starr Foundation (NY)	3,344,801,753	12/31/05
15.	The Annie E. Casey Foundation (MD)	3,265,655,271	12/31/06
16.	The Kresge Foundation (MI)	3,032,422,497	12/31/05
17.	The Duke Endowment (NC)	2,708,834,085	12/31/05
18.	The Annenberg Foundation (PA)	2,539,268,854	06/30/06
19.	Carnegie Corporation of New York (NY)	2,530,191,576	09/30/06
20.	Charles Stewart Mott Foundation (MI)	2,480,562,766	12/31/05

Source: "Top 20 U.S. Foundations by Asset Size," The World Bank Group. Retrieved December 12, 2008, from http://go.worldbank.org/5M7C7NGCMO.

The Future of the Voluntary Sector

Despite the visibility of elite philanthropy, most Americans voiced preference for voluntary efforts to address social problems. Of respondents to a poll of the public's perception of problem solving, 56 percent ranked sectarian agencies as important for "solving social problems in their communities," compared to 53 percent for local nonprofits, 39 percent for the United Way, 33 percent for state government, and 28 percent for the federal government.[35] The ability of the nonprofit sector to meet these public expectations is problematic, however. Several forces have transformed the nonprofit sector, including the intrusion of commercial firms, the rise of faith-based social services, and the emergence of social entrepreneurship.

Commercialization

In the mixed welfare economy, the voluntary sector coexists with government but also competes with commercial providers. This places nonprofit organizations in an odd position: Having secured a tax-exempt status from government in order to provide charity care, many voluntary sector agencies find themselves competing with for-profit corporations in the same market. The commercialization of health care, described in Chapter 7, is a case in point. The **commercialization** issue is particularly important for nonprofit agencies desiring to enhance their incomes. Faced with static, if not declining, revenues, some voluntary sector agencies have experimented with commercial activities in order to supplement income derived from traditional sources (contracts, contributions, grants, and fees). That nonprofit organizations should be allowed to engage in commercial endeavors without restriction is "unfair competition," according to business operators, who note that nonprofits do not ordinarily pay taxes on their income. Business operators fear that, exempt from taxation, nonprofits could lower their prices, increasing pressure on tax-paying businesses operating in the same market, eventually driving them out of business. This issue was resolved by a celebrated legal case involving the alumni of the New York University Law School purchasing the Mueller Macaroni Company as a subsidiary of the law school in order to claim company profits as alumni contributions. Since the law school was a nonprofit, competing pasta companies feared that their prices could be undercut and challenged the purchase. They won, and Congress quickly established the Unrelated Business Income Tax in order to regulate unfair competition.[36] As a result, in 2004, 38,000 nonprofits collectively were required to pay $368 million in federal taxes on unrelated business income of $9.5 billion.[37]

Such new tax regulations open the possibility of further restrictions on the revenue base of voluntary sector agencies. For example, some YMCAs have stopped advertising their programs for fear that local authorities may interpret those programs as commercial and thereby attempt to tax their income.

Finally, the unfair competition issue presents other disturbing questions for administrators of nonprofit organizations. "We can't ask nonprofits to be more like for-profits in the ways that we like—efficient, responsive, aggressive—without expecting that they will also become more like for-profits in the ways that we don't: rapacious, hardheaded and, yes, sometimes selfish," noted Jacob Hacker.[38]

Faith-Based Social Services

The idea of government's contracting with voluntary sector agencies is not a novel concept; through purchase-of-service agreements dating to the late 1960s, government has negotiated arrangements for delivery of a range of social services, often with sectarian agencies. This liberal mechanism for decentralization, however, has given conservatives an entrée to pose more fundamental questions about the proper role of government in social welfare. Since the 1980s, conservative think tanks have, with increasing urgency, sought an alternative to federal social programs.

A primary proponent of sectarian nonprofit agencies has been Marvin Olasky, a journalist who has argued that voluntary religious agencies provided efficient and effective services to the needy well before the New Deal and the deployment of the welfare state.[39] Another source of support has come from evangelical Christians, who have objected to the absence of moral standards that they see as characterizing traditional social service agencies managed by liberal welfare professionals. Since its resurgence with the 1980 election of Ronald Reagan, conservatism had been in opposition to liberal social policy; however, it lacked a positive stance with respect to a large segment of the electorate—the middle class, the elderly, and the ill, among others. Invoking the virtues of the voluntary sector provided a way to address this ideological deficit, an approach that George W. Bush enthusiastically proclaimed during his 2000 presidential campaign as "compassionate conservatism."[40] Eventually, Bush proposed a five-year, $5 billion federal program for faith-based organizations; however, Democrats objected because of the possibility of discrimination in hiring, and the proposal failed (see Table 6.4). Undaunted, Bush instituted part of the

TABLE 6.4 Federal Grants to Faith-Based Organizations

Agency	Money for Grant Programs (in millions)	Money for FBOs (in millions)	Percentage for FBOs
HHS	$10,874.3	$567.9	5
HUD	2,197.7	532.1	24
Justice	791.7	51.6	7
Labor	512.4	11.3	2
Education	134.7	6.8	5

Source: Adapted from Alan Cooperman, "Grants to Religious Groups Top $1.1 Billion," *Washington Post* (March 10, 2004), p. A27.

plan through executive order. The Bush administration's designs for faith-based services received a boost when a federal judge determined that sectarian agencies could dismiss employees who refused to adhere to religious precepts of their sectarian employers.[41] Ultimately, even conservatives expressed reservations about the "faith-based" policy initiative. David Kuo, deputy director of the White House Office of Faith-Based and Community Initiatives, questioned the sincerity of the Bush administration in *Tempting Faith: An Inside Story of Political Seduction*, a book that noted the manipulation of initiative in order to curry the support of religious conservatives.[42] Regardless, the Bush faith-based initiative diverted $10.6 billion to religious organizations.[43] President Obama continues Bush's faith-based social policy under the renamed Office of Faith-based and Neighborhood Partnerships.

Enthusiasm for faith-based initiatives notwithstanding, the approach had yet to demonstrate its superiority through research. Indiana researchers evaluated 2,830 people who enrolled in 27 employment programs and found no difference between sectarian and secular organizations with respect to placement rates and beginning wages; graduates of faith-based organizations tended to work fewer hours and were less likely to receive health insurance.[44]

Regardless, proponents of faith-based social services, including many traditional sectarian agencies with a long history of helping the needy, such as the Salvation Army, insisted that government programs were too bureaucratic and impersonal, and that secular nonprofit agencies were populated by welfare professionals who failed to infuse services with adequate moral content to be effective. Although Bush's "faith-based" policy initiative may not have generated the revenue promised, it not only demonstrates how appeals to the voluntary sector resonate with conservative Republicans, but Obama's continuation of the policy shows how important nonprofit organizations are to Democrats as well.

Social Entrepreneurship

Many theologically inclined liberals endorsed the idea of faith-based social services, but others pursued innovations through capital and technology. A new generation of social entrepreneurs has emerged as experiments with markets reveal untapped opportunities for program innovation, both locally and nationally. For example, the Ben & Jerry's ice cream company and Working Assets Long Distance (WALD) [now CREDO] represent an ethic in which business praxis is inextricably suffused with social consciousness.[45] In 2007, CREDO contributed $3.5 million to progressive organizations advocating in several areas: social justice, the environment, civil rights, and international justice.[46] Realizing that there was a minimal return on the time invested in securing foundation grants, Peter Samuelson, founder of Starlight Starbright, an organization serving critically ill children, approached the marketing department of Colgate-Palmolive and convinced them to incorporate cause-related marketing in their products. "The results were astonishing," Samuelson reported. "Instead of receiving $25,000 from the corporation's foundation, we were suddenly receiving $250,000 from a cause-related marketing campaign."[47]

Concerned about the decline of civic institutions, particularly in urban areas, sociologists proposed "social capital" as a vehicle for revitalization. For Robert Putnam, the term *social capital* referred to "features of social organization, such as

Former President George W. Bush advanced faith-based social services as an alternative to traditional social programs.

Source: Tony Gutierrez/AP Images

networks, norms, and trust, which facilitate coordination and cooperation for mutual benefit. Social capital enhances the benefits of investment in physical and human capital."[48] At the nexus of social capital, community-based nonprofit organizations can facilitate the development of poor neighborhoods, provided they exploit new markets and technologies. An illustration of the social capital approach to community development is the work of former congressman Floyd Flake, pastor of the Allen African Methodist Episcopal Cathedral in Jamaica, New York.[49] Flake has used his position as church pastor to construct a $34 million network of community development ventures. Seeing the future as a social entrepreneur, Flake recognizes the ideological implications of recent changes in social policy: "Those of us who have made a commitment to stay in an urban community have decided that *this* is our paradise," he observed. "We are going to rebuild that paradise—and we understand that it means some paradigm shifts, even politically, because the majority of statehouses today are in the hands of Republican governors and the majority of the assemblies are in the hands of Republicans. So we can either continue in a protest mode or we find ways to have entrée to deal with who is in power now."[50]

Although the social entrepreneur movement has been slow to evolve in relation to social welfare, it has captured the imagination of international development advocates. David Bornstein championed their cause in his best-selling book, *How to Change the World: Social Entrepreneurs and the Power of New Ideas*.[51] The latent capacity of the commercial sector to provide micro-credit loans to low-income families has spawned financial institutions worldwide.[52] The Grameen Bank, described in Chapter 18, has become an iconic institution melding a business ethic with social responsibility and leveraging the upward mobility of peasant families in the Third World.

As the social entrepreneur gospel spread, its proponents characterized it as qualitatively different from traditional nonprofit or commercial organizations. David Bornstein and Susan Davis argue that social entrepreneurship represents a new generation of organizational activity, the use of collective agency to address pressing social problems:

> Social entrepreneurship represents a fundamental reorganization of the problem-solving work of society: a shift from control-oriented, top-down policy implementation to responsive, decentralized institution building. It draws on

a core insight of the twentieth century: namely, that a dynamic marketplace of ideas and initiative is the basis of a thriving economy.[53]

Within social entrepreneurship lurks a critique of government. Public social programs may anchor the welfare state, but they are hardly champions of innovation; legislated by a majority of elected representatives, government social programs, of necessity, are the product of a cultural consensus. Invariably, public policies take decades to be enacted, and many suffer from inadequate resources upon implementation. Finally, public programs evolve stakeholders who become dependent upon them. "Once a program is rolled out, with a budget and a constituency to defend it, it will remain there almost regardless of its effectiveness."[54] By contrast, social entrepreneurs are opportunistic, flexible, innovative, and accountable.

In contrast to the skepticism of traditional welfare advocates toward capitalism, social entrepreneurs embrace its advantages. "The new breed of philanthropic and social entrepreneurs want to see measurable results, and soon; they embrace business and businesslike methods; they want projects to be sustainable and scalable, capable of living and growing on their own."[55]

Issues Facing the Voluntary Sector

Minimal IRS requirements for nonprofit status coupled with the openness of American society have placed the voluntary sector under scrutiny for what many perceive as abusive practices.

Frivolity Stanford University's Center on Philanthropy and Civil Society has taken the IRS to task for indiscriminate approval of nonprofit applications, authorizing tax exemption for organizations such as The Sisters of Perpetual Indulgence (an organization of drag nuns), Ghostface Ryderz (family oriented motorcyclists), and the Metempyrion Foundation (encouraging telepathic communication).[56]

Politicization Loosening of regulations around campaign contributions have resulted in private groups using nonprofit provisions of the tax code, such as section 527, to allow unlimited, although indirect, candidate advocacy. While the IRS rejected nonprofit status for organizations training candidates for office, it failed to take action on Super-PACs which expanded after the *Citizens United* decision rendered by the United States Supreme Court.[57]

Property tax exemptions Tax-exempt institutions, particularly churches, colleges, and hospitals, fail to pay local taxes to reimburse cities for essential services, such as water, sanitation, and public safety.[58] For example, an analysis of the New York City budget revealed that $13.5 billion was forfeited due to nonprofit exemptions from paying the property tax.[59]

Charitable aid One justification for granting hospitals tax-exempt status is their provision of charitable aid to the indigent; however, competition within healthcare has caused nonprofit health providers to minimize unreimbursed care. Not only have nonprofit hospitals billed the poor for healthcare, but they have also contracted with debt collection agencies that use aggressive debt collection practices. Since $1 billion of charitable care is provided annually, the issue is not academic.[60]

Religious precepts A primary motive for sectarian nonprofits is to promote religious values; however, these may conflict with public policy. Catholic Charities, for example, has terminated services in several jurisdictions rather than comply with rules to which it objects, such as allowing homosexuals to adopt children.[61]

Celebrity philanthropy Seeking public visibility, nonprofits often solicit support from celebrities, some of whom adopt a signature cause, such as Bono and African development and George Clooney and Sudan. Global Philanthropy Group has developed this as a business model, charging celebrities $25,000 per month to promote their causes.[62] Doubtless, nonprofits appreciate benefiting from such exposure, yet celebrity philanthropy raises the prospect that its real value is less social welfare and more entertainment.

Salaries Large nonprofits, such as universities and hospitals, have paid executives salaries comparable to those managing corporations of comparable size. The adoption of a business model for executive compensation raises questions when the purpose of the nonprofit is clearly social welfare. If the CEOs of the American Cancer Society and the American Heart Association claim salaries of $1 million, should the leader of Boys & Girls Clubs be similarly compensated?[63] A journalist investigating care of the disabled in New York, uncovered a network controlled by two brothers whose nonprofits earned them million dollar salaries, paid primarily by Medicaid.[64] Certainly, management of nonprofit organizations can be lucrative for CEOs, as evident Table 6.5.

Conclusion

There are a number of important challenges facing the voluntary sector: How will the nonprofit preserve its mission of caring for the disenfranchised without succumbing to the bottom-line ethos of the corporate sector? How will it respond to the range of diverse populations without favoring the mainstream? How

TABLE 6.5 Salaries of Nonprofit Executives

Category	2010 Median Salary	2010 Maximum Salary
Animals	$100,000	$554,751
Arts, Culture, Humanities	162,263	1,350,000
Education	177,734	1,916,143
Environment	115,734	493,332
Health	150,986	745,251
Human Services	117,875	787,300
International	128,187	879,591
Public Benefit	151,197	1,204,968
Religion	88,021	500,450

Reference: "Charity Navigator: 2012 CEO Compensation Study, November, p. 5.

will it adapt to the latest innovations in technology while putting forth a human face on social welfare? Finally, how the nonprofit sector responds to the Great Recession poses the greatest economic challenge since its creation over a century ago.

DISCUSSION QUESTIONS

1. What are the most prominent nonprofit human service agencies in your community? Are they members of the United Way? What do agencies perceive to be the advantages of United Way membership? Do they perceive disadvantages to United Way membership?

2. Has the United Way in your community failed to achieve its goals in contributions in recent years? If so, what are the causes? The proposed solutions?

3. What are the newer nonprofit agencies in your community? What populations do they serve? Are these agencies members of the United Way? If not, how do they attract the necessary resources? What is their perception of the United Way?

4. If there are unmet needs in your community, how would you create a nonprofit agency to meet them? Whom would you recruit for your board of directors? Where would you solicit resources, both cash and in-kind? Whom would you recruit for staff? What would you name your agency? Would your agency focus on providing services or on advancing social change?

5. In response to diminishing resources, many nonprofit social agencies have resorted to entrepreneurial strategies to raise money. What innovative projects have agencies deployed in your community? What entrepreneurial strategies can you think of that might be successful for nonprofit agencies in your community?

6. What are the most prominent foundations in your community? What has been the source of revenues for their activities? How would you rank them with respect to the volume of their gifts versus assets? Which foundations have been most active with respect to social welfare? Have their gifts increased or decreased in recent years?

7. Thinking as a social entrepreneur, how would you apply a business ethic to address a social problem in your community? Are there local nonprofits that have undertaken commercial ventures to increase their revenues? How successful have they been?

NOTES

1. David Stoesz, "A Structural Interest Theory of Social Welfare," *Social Development Issues* 10 (Winter 1985), pp. 73–85.

2. National Association of Social Workers, *Social Casework: Generic and Specific* (Silver Spring, MD: NASW, 1974).

3. http://unway.3cdn.net/65baa8073da0505c36_mlbrwvl93.pdf

4. Robert Alford, *Health Care Politics* (Chicago: University of Chicago Press, 1975), p. 204.

5. Roy Lubove, *The Professional Altruist* (New York: Atheneum, 1969), p. 197.

6. Walter Trattner, *From Poor Law to Welfare State* (New York: Macmillan, 1974), p. 237; and "The First Days of Social Security," *Public Welfare* 43 (Fall 1985), pp. 112–119.

7. Goleman, "Social Workers Vault into a Leading Role in Psychotherapy," *New York Times* (April 3, 1985), p. C-1.

8. Per conversation with NASW staff, November 16, 1992.

9. http://workforce.socialworkers.org/studies/profiles/Private%20Practice%20Solo%20and%20Group.pdf

10. Donald Light, "Corporate Medicine for Profit," *Scientific American* 255 (December 1986), pp. 81–89.

11. Alan Abramson and Lester Salamon, *The Nonprofit Sector and the New Federal Budget* (Washington, DC: Urban Institute, 1986), p. xi. See also Waldemar Nielsen, *The Third Sector: Keystone of a Caring Society* (Washington, DC: Independent Sector, 1980).

12. Marvin Olasky, "Beyond the Stingy Welfare State," *Policy Review* (Fall 1990), p. 14.

13. http://www.census.gov/compendia/statab/2012/tables/12s0580.pdf

14. Stephanie Strom, "Short on Fund-Raising, Red Cross Will Cut Jobs," *New York Times* (January 16, 2008), p. A13; Philip Rucker, "Corporate Leader Named Red Cross CEO," *Washington Post* (April 9, 2008), p. A3.

15. Lisa Belkin, "The Grief Payout," *New York Times Magazine* (December 8, 2002).

16. Paul Schervish, "The Cultural Horizons of Charitable Giving in an Age of Affluence" (Cambridge, MA: Boston College Social Welfare Research Institute, September 23, 2003), p. 1.

17. Paul Schervish, "The Sense and Sensibility of Philanthropy as a Moral Citizenship of Care" (Cambridge, MA: Boston College and Indiana University Center on Philanthropy, January 2004).

18. Gardner quoted in O'Connell, Origins, Dimensions and Impact of America's Voluntary Spirit, p. 6.

19. John W. Gardner, *Keynote Address* (Washington, DC: Independent Sector; 1978), p. 13.

20. Irene Lacher, "Teaching America a Lesson," *Los Angeles Times* (November 11, 1990), E1; personal communication, Teach for America, October 7, 1996.

21. http://www.teachforamerica.org/our-organization

22. Paul Tough, Whatever It Takes (New York: Houghton Mifflin, 2008).

23. "Key Dates in the Adjudication of Former Management" (Fairfax, VA: United Way of America, 1996).

24. Jerry Markon, "Ex-Chief of Local United Way Sentenced," *Washington Post* (May 15, 2004), p. A1.

25. http://www.thenonprofittimes.com/article/detail/united-way-revenue-up-2-4-percent-in-2010-4079

26. David La Piana, "Are There Too Many Nonprofits," Washington, DC: Urban Institute, April 3, 2012).

27. Jean Strouse, "How to Give Away $21.8 Billion," *New York Times Magazine* (April 16, 2000).

28. Sebastian Mallaby, "Opening the Gates," *Washington Post* (April 5, 2004), p. A17.

29. Yuki Nogouchi, "Gates Foundation to Get Bulk of Buffett's Fortune," *Washington Post* (June 26, 2006), p. A1.

30. Stephanie Strom, "The Pledge," *New York Times*, November 11,2010, p. F1.

31. Stephanie Strom, "Foundations Set Record for Giving in '07," *New York Times* (May 2, 2008), p. A13.

32. Teresa Odendahl, *Charity Begins at Home.* (New York: Basic Books, 1990), pp. 3, 245.

33. Ibid., p. 49.

34. Ibid., p. 232.

35. Richard Morin, "Nonprofit, Faith-Based Groups Near Top of Poll on Solving Social Woes," *Washington Post* (February 1, 2001), p. A19.

36. Sebastian Mallaby, "Opening the Gates," Washington Post, April 5, 2004, p. A17.

37. http://www.irs.gov/pub/irs-soi/04eoub.pdf

38. Jonathan Cohn, "Uncharitable?" *New York Times Magazine* (December 19, 2004), p. 55.

39. Marvin Olasky, *The Tragedy of American Compassion* (Washington, DC: Regenery Gateway, 1992); *Renewing American Compassion* (New York: Free Press, 1996).

40. Hanna Rosin, "Putting Faith in a Social Service Role," *Washington Post* (May 5, 2000), p. A1.

41. Alan Cooperman, "Bush's Faith Plan Faces Judgment," *Washington Post* (October 20, 2005), p. A25.

42. David Kuo and John DiIulio, "The Faith to Outlast Politics," *New York Times* (January 29, 2008), p. A27.

43. Michelle Boorstein and Kimberly Kindy, "Faith-Based Office to Expand Its Reach," *Washington Post*, February 6, 2009, p. A2.

44. Alan Cooperman, "Faith-Based Charities May Not Be Better, Study Indicates," *Washington Post* (May 25, 2003), p. A7.

45. Bill Shore, *The Cathedral Within.* (New York: Random House, 1999).

46. "Our Donations at Work," (San Francisco, CREDO, March 20, 2008).

47. Peter Samuelson, "The Robin Hood Effect," *Privilege* (November 2004), p. 1.

48. Robert Putnam, "The Prosperous Community," *The American Prospect* no. 13 (Spring 1993), p. 1.

49. Terry Neal, "Ex-Lawmaker Refuses to Be Boxed In," *Washington Post* (January 10, 1998), p. A8.

50. R. Baker, "The Ecumenist," *The American Prospect* (January 17, 2000), p. 28.

51. David Bornstein, *How to Change the World* (New York: Oxford University Press, 2004).

52. Elizabeth Malkin, "Microloans, Big Profits," *New York Times* (April 5, 2008), p. B1.

53. David Bornstein and Susan Davis, *Social Entrepreneurship* (New York: Oxford University Press, 2010), p. 94.

54. Bornstein and David, op cit, p. 36.

55. Jonathan Rauch, "'This is Not Charity'," *The Atlantic* (October 2007), p. 76.

56. Rob Reich, Lacey Dorn, Stefanie Sutton, "Anything Goes," (Stanford, CA: Stanford University, 2009), pp. 17-24.

57. Stephanie Strom, Political Advocacy Groups Denied Tax-Exempt Status," Washington Post, July 20, 2011, p. B8; Mike McIntire, "Under Tax-Exempt Cloak, Political Dollars Flow," *New York Times*, September 24, 2010, p. A1; Jonathan Weisman, "Scrutiny of political Nonprofits Sets Off Claim of Harassment," *New York Times*, March 12, 2012, p. A20.

58. Pat Read, "Are Their Too Many Nonprofits," seminar at the Urban Institute April 3, 2012.

59. http://ibo.nyc.ny.us/cgi-park/?p=365

60. Nina Bernstein, "Hospitals Flout Charity Aid Law," *New York Times*, February 13, 2012, p. A1.

61. Laurie Goodstein, "Illinois Bishops Drop Program Over Bias Rule," *New York Times*, December 29, 2011, p. A1; Dan Frosch, "Catholic Fund Cuts Off Groups Over Ties Unsettling to Church," *New York Times*, April 6, 2012, p. A1.

62. John Colapinto, "Looking Good," *New Yorker*, March 26, 2012, p. 58; Laura Holson, "Charity Fixer for the Stars, " *New York Times*, December 5, 2010, p. ST8.

63. Stephanie Strom, "Nonprofit Salaries Under the Microscope," *New York Times*, July 27, 2010, p. A12.

64. Russ Buettner, "Reaping Millions from Medicaid in Nonprofit Care for the Disabled," *New York Times*, August 2, 2011, p. A1.

CHAPTER 7

Privatization and Human Service Corporations

Source: John Marshall Mantel/AP Images

This chapter reviews the privatization of social welfare, a dynamic that has accelerated in recent decades. As a function of public dissatisfaction with governmental social programs, increasing reliance on the private sector to finance and deliver social services has emerged as an important theme in American social welfare. **Privatization,** as this idea has been termed, addresses the problem of the proper relationship between the public and private spheres of the national culture. In this case, the concept of privatization has come to involve "the idea that private is invariably more efficient than public, that government ought to stay out of as many realms as possible, and that government should contract out tasks to private firms or give people vouchers rather than provide them services directly."[1]

Historically, much social welfare has been provided by the private nonprofit sector, and many nonprofits contract with government to provide social services. Since the 1980s, however, conservatives have called for downsizing government, in the process shifting service responsibility to the private sector, providing opportunities to the for-profit sector. Increasing demand for services has further propelled the commercial social welfare sector.

Proprietary firms have become well established in several other **human services** markets: nursing care, hospital management, managed medical care, childcare, and corrections. Finally, in this chapter we consider collective bargaining as a response to privatization. Health and human service professionals have been reluctant to join unions, primarily because they fear that doing so would taint their professional status. Yet, continuing privatization means that unions may be the only aggregate defense for professionals who have become employees of profit-making health and human service corporations.

That government should not hold a monopoly on social welfare is not a novel idea. Even liberal policy analysts entertained ways in which the private sector could complement governmental welfare initiatives.[2] Liberal proponents of social programs are often willing to concede a viable role to the private sector—even an innovative role—but insist that government must be the primary instrument to institutionalize social justice. Conservatives see the proper balance as one in which the private sector is the primary source of protection against social and economic calamity, and the government activity should be held in reserve as the secondary source. According to conservative doctrine, government can deploy the "safety net" of social programs, but these should provide benefits only as a last resort.

In *Reinventing Government*, David Osborne proposed a more integrated and dynamic relationship between the public and private sectors: Government should establish the objectives of public policy, assigning the execution to the private sector.[3] Osborne tapped into a theme that had been integral to U.S. social programs: reliance on the private sector to deliver the goods. Nowhere had this been more evident than in health care. When the social engineers of the War on Poverty crafted Medicare and Medicaid, they elected to reimburse private providers rather than deploy government-owned health care systems such as the Veterans Administration. The result, as we shall see momentarily, was the emergence of a for-profit industry in health care that

Spotlight 7.1

TECHNIQUES FOR THE PRIVATIZATION OF SERVICE DELIVERY

The President's Commission on Privatization identifies three techniques for the privatization of service delivery:

1. Selling government assets
2. Contracting with private firms to provide goods and services previously offered by the government
3. Using vouchers, whereby the government would distribute coupons authorizing private providers to receive reimbursement from the government for the goods and services they have provided

was uniquely American. Indeed, when the Clinton administration presented its Health Security Act, it not only conceded the existence of commercial health providers but structured the plan to amplify their position in the market, which also occurred with the passage of the Patient Protection and Affordable Care Act signed by President Obama.

Thus, views of privatization vary. On the one hand, privatization can be viewed as "load-shedding," and on the other, as a contractual relationship between the public and private sectors. In either event, there is no question that this relationship is being reassessed. "Governments in the United States spend roughly half a trillion dollars per year paying public workers to deliver goods and services directly," observed John Donahue. "If only one-quarter of this total turned out to be suitable for privatization, at an average savings of, say, 25 percent—and neither figure is recklessly optimistic—the public would save over $30 billion."[4] Such savings could be used to lower taxes or to extend existing programs. As state and local jurisdictions struggle to justify increasing service demand with static resources, privatization is an option that many local officials pursue.

Privatization Issues

Many health and human service professionals have trepidations about privatization. Liberal social activists have objected to privatization, citing research that identifies risks in relying on the private sector for certain activities. The irony in such a critical stance toward privatization is that many professionals opt for private practice as a method of service delivery, an arrangement through which government subsidizes entrepreneurs. Thus, private practice is condoned, but privatization of governmental activities is met with skepticism. This issue raises a profound concern for the social work profession: To the extent that social workers engage in private practice, there are fewer human service professionals in the public sector to work with people presenting more serious disorders. As a result, what limited influence social work possesses is invested in promoting its self-interest at the expense of the poor—a point underscored by the late Harry Specht and Mark Courtney in *Unfaithful Angels*:

> . . . there has been an increasing tendency of the [social work] profession to use its political power to support licensing of clinical social workers and third-party payments for social workers who are so licensed, to the relative neglect of efforts to improve the lot of social workers employed in the public social services and their clients.[5]

For many human service professionals, then, private practice represents a retreat from a service ethic that transcends self-interest: the public's welfare.

Opponents to welfare privatization voice several criticisms. First, if a corporation's profits are linked to reducing the welfare rolls, the incentive to deny aid will be significant. According to Henry Freedman of the Center for Social Welfare Policy and Law, "No company can be expected to protect the interests of the needy at the expense of its bottom line, least of all a publicly traded corporation with a fiduciary duty to maximize shareholder profits."[6] Clearly, corporations will have strong incentives to use the letter of the law to ration services to improve their profits and performance.[7] Much of this fiscal incentive will be based on the fixed-price nature of government contracts, which will include penalties for a failure to perform. Second, corporations are apt to reduce personnel costs. They may cut staff and replace full-time professionals and managers with contingent, lower-wage workers. As a way to control salaries, corporations may try to dislodge public sector unions where they exist and prohibit them where they do not. Third, privatization could encourage corporations to save money by using technology such as automated service centers to replace staff, which would have enormous implications for people who are not technologically sophisticated or who would benefit from face-to-face services. Fourth, government would find itself in a quandary if commercial providers bailed out of contracts. At worst, corporations could declare bankruptcy, effectively voiding their contractual obligations, or commercial providers could reduce the availability of services as a way to leverage more resources. Finally, corporations with a major presence in a given market are in a strong position to shape social policy, defining such factors as eligibility for program benefits and allocations. All of these corporate strategies would have a major impact on the quality of services delivered.

A new question in the debate on the balance between private and public responsibilities for welfare was introduced with the recent emergence of health and human service corporations: If government is to contract out its social welfare obligations, can the business sector pick up the slack? Logically, proponents of privatization have two options: the nonprofit, voluntary sector (Chapter 6) and the for-profit, **corporate sector.** Both sectors are well established in U.S. social welfare. Since the advent of former president Lyndon Johnson's Great Society programs, government has been contracting out services through both nonprofit and for-profit providers. The for-profit corporate sector capitalized on the contracting-out provisions of the Medicare and Medicaid programs (Table 7.1). At the same time, through the purchase-of-service concept introduced in Title Social Services Block Grant, nonprofit agencies became contractors, providing a range of social services on behalf of public welfare departments.

Unfortunately, studies comparing the performance of these sectors have been few and their findings debatable.[8] In the absence of definitive results showing the advantages of one sector over another, the privatization debate has become heated. Advocates of *voluntarization*, or reliance on the voluntary sector to assume more of the responsibility for welfare, point to the voluntary sector's historical contribution to the national culture, the rootedness of its agencies in the community, and the altruistic motives behind its programs. Advocates of voluntarization received a boost when the second Bush presidency advocated "faith-based" initiatives in social welfare. Proponents of *corporatization*, or dependence on the corporate sector to provide welfare, argue that corporations offer more cost-effective administration, are more responsive to consumer demand, and pay taxes, a strategy endorsed by the Obama administration. Corporatists scored a major victory in the 2003 Medicare reforms that introduced the prescription drug benefit that designated pharmaceutical companies as the conduit for medicines for the elderly. Whether voluntarists or corporatists prevail in the privatization debate rests largely on the ability of each party to manipulate the social policy process in their favor. Whatever the outcome, this process is certain to be lengthy and complex, as one might expect with the remaking of an institutional structure that has become as essential as social welfare is in the United States. And whether voluntarization or corporatization defines the future of social welfare, privatization has already highlighted several important issues.

Commercialization

For welfare professionals, the idea of subjecting human need to the economic marketplace is often problematic. In one of the earliest treatments of

the matter, Richard Titmuss' *The Gift Relationship* explored the differences in the ways nations manage their blood banks. Unlike the United Kingdom, blood in the United States is "treated in laws as an article of commerce"; that is, rules of the market affect the supply and quality of blood. Titmuss observed the growth of blood and plasma businesses with alarm, because these businesses bought blood from a population that was often characterized by poverty and poor health. Quite apart from the health hazard posed by a blood supply derived from such a population—a hazard highlighted by AIDS— Titmuss was concerned that the profit motive would disrupt the voluntary impulses of community life. "There is growing disquiet in the United States," he observed, that "expanding blood programs are driving out the voluntary system."[9] Indeed, a majority of blood banks in the United States are commercial. Theodore Marmor, Mark Schlesinger, and Richard Smithey, "A New Look at Nonprofits: Health Care Policy in a Competitive Age," *Yale Journal of Regulation* 3 (Spring 1986), p. 320.[10]

With the passage of Medicare and Medicaid in 1965, the federal government was placed in the position of reimbursing and regulating a private industry that evolved rapidly. In both programs, scandals involving fraudulent billing of billions of dollars and neglecting of patients, sometimes with fatal consequences, were exposed.[11] Once for-profit providers gain a significant share of a market, even nonprofit providers are likely to adopt commercial practices. In 2006, Congress convened hearings about some nonprofit hospitals which, instead of providing charity care congruent with their tax exempt status, hired collection agencies to harass former patients into paying for their care.

A poignant problem with commercialization relates to those tax-exempt providers who transition from nonprofit to for-profit status. Before the commercialization of health care, the largest health insurer was Blue Cross–Blue Shield; however, many state Blue Cross–Blue Shield plans have converted to commercial status. The transition from nonprofit to for-profit status requires the approval of state regulators, often elected officials who are concerned that low-income citizens might be left uninsured. Consequently, states often require such companies to establish health care foundations as a condition for becoming corporate. When Wellpoint and Anthem merged in California, for example, the companies offered $265 million, much of it to assure the continuation of health care to underserved communities.[12] Such foundations become an important resource for those who wish to reduce inequities in health care.

Preferential Selection

The application of market principles to client service introduces strong incentives for providers to differentiate clients according to their effect on organizational performance. Such selection can be at variance with professional standards, which emphasize the client's need for service over organizational considerations. But the marketplace tends to penalize providers that are imprudent about client selection, at the same time rewarding providers that are more discriminating. The practice of choosing clients according to criteria of organizational performance—as opposed to client need—is known as **preferential selection.** Under marketplace conditions, providers that do not practice preferential selection are bound to serve a disproportionate number of clients with serious problems and with less ability to pay the cost of care, thereby running deficits. By contrast, providers that select clients who have less serious problems and who can cover the cost of care often claim surpluses. For example, an analysis of psychiatric patients admitted to a public and a private hospital found that the latter selected patients of higher social status. The researchers concluded that "patients in the marginal/uncredentialed social class were comparatively more likely to be admitted to state mental hospitals than to private hospitals."[13]

Critics of privatization complain that creaming the client population through preferential selection is unethical and should be prohibited. Simply ruling out the practice is, however, easier said than done. Accusations of preferential selection are not new; private nonprofit agencies were accused of denying services to welfare recipients long before proprietary firms became established.[14] In Denver, where public hospitals have sustained heavy deficits by caring for a disproportionate burden of the medically indigent, the problem has become critical. Jane Collins, director of clinical social work for the Denver Department of Health and Hospitals, described public hospitals in the city as having become "social dumps."[15] Reports of dumping when life-threatening injuries are evident have drawn the ire of many human service professionals. In some cases, private hospitals have transferred indigent patients with traumatic injuries to public facilities without providing proper medical care, thus contributing to the deaths of several patients. When the federal government prohibited such transfers, many hospitals responded by closing their emergency rooms rather than incur the cost of uncompensated care.

Preferential selection on the part of a large number of providers is likely to be adopted by others who wish to remain competitive. In analyzing the practice in health care, a team of researchers from Harvard University and the American Medical Association noted that "in the same way that competition from for-profit providers leads to reduction in access, the more competitive the market for hospital services generally, the more likely are all hospitals in that market to discourage admissions of Medicaid and uninsured patients."[16] In other words, even nonprofit providers—who are exempt from taxes because they contribute to the community's welfare—are compelled to adopt the discriminatory practices of for-profit providers in a competitive market, unless the nonprofits are willing to underwrite the losses that more costly clients represent to for-profit providers.

Cost-Effectiveness

Proponents of privatization frequently cite the discipline imposed on organizational performance by a competitive environment as a rationale for market reforms in social welfare. A competitive environment provides strong incentives for organizations to adopt cost-effective practices that reduce waste. This claim has led to a handful of studies of for-profit versus nonprofit service providers. In a comprehensive review of the issue, the Institute of Medicine of the National Academy of Sciences concluded that there was "no evidence to support the common belief that investor-owned organizations are less costly or more efficient than are nonprofit organizations."[17] Later, Robert Kuttner summarized analyses conducted by an association of nonprofit hospitals and found that "investor-owned hospitals . . . were 13.7 percent more expensive on a charge basis than nonprofit and public hospitals." Again, not only were for-profit hospitals more expensive, but they also provided less care to the poor, admitting only half as many Medicaid patients as nonprofit hospitals. Another analysis of proprietary hospitals by the same association of nonprofit hospitals found that investor-owned hospitals were 30 percent more expensive than nonprofit hospitals.[18] A study of 14,423 nursing homes found that even though public facilities had a significantly higher proportion of Medicaid patients, they, along with nonprofit providers, performed better than their for-profit counterparts.[19]

A competitive environment provides strong incentive for organizations to adopt cost-effective practices that reduce waste.

Source: Gromovataya/Shutterstock

Moreover, the promise of cost containment through privatization has not been borne out, and this presents an enormous problem for the governmental sector. A good example is provided by the Medicare program. Through Medicare the government subsidizes health care for elderly people, most of which is provided by the private sector. In response to runaway Medicare costs, in 1983 Congress enacted the **Diagnostic Related Groups (DRGs)** prospective payment plan, whereby hospitals are reimbursed fixed amounts for medical procedures. Adopted by private health insurers, DRGs would prove a successful cost containment strategy, contributing to passage of the Affordable Care Act in 2010."[20]

Standardization

While commercial provision of human services allows the wealthy to purchase concierge care, that is timely and individualized care, the less affluent are often consigned to substandard services because government reimbursements are at such low levels that they encourage standardization. In this way, privatization can induce human service organizations to adopt an industrial mode of provision in which the accepted measure of success is not necessarily high quality of service rendered but the maximum number of people processed at the lowest cost. Thus, corporations can generate surpluses, essential for investor-owned facilities, by reducing the quality of care and lowering labor costs. Because the logic of the market dictates that the goal of production is to process the largest

number of people at the lowest possible cost, the **standardization** of services is an important method for lowering organizational expenses.

Under these circumstances, life care—the service offered by the continuing-care retirement community—has emerged as an attractive alternative to traditional nursing home care that has been standardized to reduce costs. Under life-care plans, residents can purchase cottages or apartments in self-contained communities, at prices comparable to that of a new home, which provide a range of human services. In many respects, the life-care community provides more affluent residents an opportunity to purchase a higher level of long-term care. Many continuing-care facilities boast such amenities as wall-to-wall carpeting, maid service, and designer landscaping. The prospect of extensive proprietary involvement in life-care troubles some analysts. Lloyd Lewis, director of a nonprofit life-care community, feared that "well-funded proprietary interests" would "drain off the more financially able segment of our older population, widening the gap between the 'haves' and the 'have nots'."[21] To a significant extent this has already occurred. The late Robert Ball, former commissioner of the Social Security Administration, noted that even life-care communities operating under nonprofit auspices are often beyond the means of "the poor, the near poor, or even the low-income elderly."[22] As human service corporations divert capital to care for those who represent profit margins, economic and political support for the care of those less fortunate diminishes. "Those who cannot gain admission to [a private] institution will be forced into boarding homes or bootleg boarding homes," suggested one critic. "These boarding homes will be filled with what are literally social rejects. We're reverting back to the way the industry was in the fifties and sixties."[23] Left unchecked, this pattern is likely to divide long-term care into two clearly demarcated systems, with the affluent enjoying the generous care of completely—some would say excessively—provisioned life-care communities and the elderly poor dependent on the squalid institutions willing to accept government payment for their care.

Oligopolization

The privatization of human services invites **oligopolization**—the control of a market by few providers as organizations seek to reduce competition by buying their competitors. Within the corporate sector, three waves of acquisition can be identified: acquisitions affecting long-term care, hospital management, and health maintenance organizations (HMOs). As firms gain control of major shares of markets, they are in a strong position to leverage influence through trade associations to shape social policy. For instance, debate about prescription drug benefits and universal health care funneled tens of millions of dollars into lobbying; of the top 20 lobbying organizations in 2007 focused on health care: Pharmaceutical Research and Manufacturers of America, $22.7 million; American Medical Association, $22.1 million; American Hospital Association, $19.7 million; Amgen, $16.3 million; and Pfizer, $13.8 million.[24] Oligopolization of human services presents a daunting specter in that a small number of wealthy and powerful trade associations are in a strong position to shape social policy to conform to their interests. Within health care, this development led Arnold Relman, former editor of *The New England Journal of Medicine*, to voice alarm at the growing influence of the "new medical-industrial complex" in defining health policy in the United States.[25]

One provision of the Affordable Care Act of 2010 called for the creation of accountable care organizations, regional networks of providers that would provide high quality of care at lower costs by integrating services. Within a year of the passage of health reform, "there is a growing frenzy of mergers involving hospitals, clinics and doctor groups eager to share costs and savings, and cash in on the incentives," noted a journalist. In Baltimore, for example, Johns Hopkins Medicine acquired Sibley Memorial Hospital in Washington, DC and Suburban Hospital in Bethesda, Maryland, an exurb of Washington.[26]

The Challenge of Privatization

For many health and human service professionals, privatization is contrary to social welfare. Advocates of government's responsibility for ensuring social and economic equality contend that privatization is nothing less than a retreat from a century of hard-won gains in social programs. This case is argued cogently by Pulitzer Prize–winning sociologist Paul Starr:

> A large-scale shift of public services to private providers would contribute to further isolating the least advantaged, since private firms have strong incentives to skim off the best clients and most profitable services. The result would often be a residual, poorer public sector providing services of last resort. Such institutions would

be even less attractive as places to work than they are today. And their worsening difficulties would no doubt be cited as confirmation of the irremediable incompetence of public managers and inferiority of public services. Public institutions already suffer from this vicious circle; most forms of privatization would intensify it.[27]

Most profoundly, privatization reinforces a tendency in market economies to evolve dual structures of benefits, services, and opportunities: adequate and varied services for the affluent, substandard and uniform services for the poor. As Robert Kuttner has pointed out, "in a purely for-profit enterprise or system, there is no place for uncompensated care, unprofitable admissions, research, education, or public health activities—all chronic money losers from a strictly business viewpoint."[28] For many human service advocates, the purpose of social welfare is to correct for the inherent tendency of markets to direct resources toward the affluent and away from the poor. From this left-leaning perspective, the idea of privatization of social welfare violates the essential meaning of social welfare because it is a government function.

Yet, increased reliance on the private sector at a time when public social programs are under assault is a reality that must be faced by those concerned about social welfare. In the absence of a politically effective Left and the diminishing influence of a progressive labor movement, there appears little chance of launching new government social programs that conform to traditional liberal priorities. Insofar as corporations have assumed ever-larger responsibilities for social program activities, such as Medicaid, State Children's Health Insurance Program (SCHIP), child welfare, and mental health, welfare professionals have little choice but to concede privatization as a basis for welfare provision.

In some instances, for-profit organizations have reported success with long-term public welfare recipients. Celebrating its twenty-fifth anniversary, America Works places TANF recipients, ex-felons, and the long-term unemployed in jobs that pay on average $15,000 to $18,000 per year. America Works has won awards for its entrepreneurial model: Its placement fee of $5,000 is paid only after a client has been a successful employee for four months. Since its inception, America Works claims to have saved taxpayers millions of dollars in welfare benefits.[29] In some instances, private sector analogues to public services have demonstrated surprising success. In New York and Connecticut, an innovative program called America Works has evolved through the private sector:

Each year the company finds jobs for more than 700 of the state's hard-core unemployed, 68 percent of whom are (as a result) permanently weaned from the welfare rolls. The company gets paid only after the former welfare recipient has been working for four months and its $5,000 fee is less than half of what it costs New York State to support an average welfare family of three. All told, America Works is saving taxpayers approximately $4.5 million annually and providing many of the state's hard-core unemployed with meaningful work.[30]

Upon closer inspection, there are strong arguments in favor of privatization as a strategy for promoting social welfare. Through commercial loans and issuance of stock, for-profit organizations have faster access to capital than does the governmental sector (which requires a lengthy public expenditure authorization process) or the voluntary sector (which relies on arduous fundraising campaigns) for purposes of program expansion. The private sector has also been the source of important program innovation;[31] thus, welfare administrators have missed opportunities for promoting social welfare by ignoring privatization. How health and human service professionals choose to respond to the challenge of privatization—whether reactively or innovatively—will be critical for the future of U.S. social welfare.

Unions and the Private Sector

Unions of health and welfare professionals are one response to privatization. Since the Great Depression, social welfare professionals have organized collectively in order to obtain better wages and benefits, to enhance working conditions, and to improve services to clients. Social workers in the public sector often hold memberships in unions—most often in the American Federation of State, County, and Municipal Employees (AFSCME), with 1.6 million members in 2012, or in the Service Employees International Union (SEIU), with 2.1 million members in 2012. Altogether, about one in four social workers belong to a collective bargaining unit.[32] Because of the dispersion of social work activities, however, social workers have been less successful than nurses or teachers in using unions to achieve their ends.

Collective bargaining is the foundation of the union process, face-to-face negotiation between unionized employees and management for the purpose of arriving at a union contract. Such bargaining is supposed to be done in good faith, and the legal rights of workers are protected by the National Labor Relations Act. If these rights are attenuated, workers can petition the National Labor Relations Board to address grievances. The ultimate power of unions is to exercise the right to strike when the bargaining process breaks down. Theoretically, both parties have an interest in a successful collective bargaining process, because strikes hurt both union members and their employers. Collective bargaining can also address professional issues such as caseload size, educational benefits like tuition reimbursement, conference release time and reimbursements, payment for professional dues and subscriptions, and flexible work hours. One union leader noted, "To the professional—the teacher or caseworker—things like class size and caseload size become as important as the number of hours in a shift is to the blue collar worker."[33]

A significant question before human service professionals has been the extent to which union objectives are consistent with professional values. Despite the constructive influence that unions could potentially exert in response to workplace problems in social welfare, social workers have approached unions with great apprehension. Opponents to collective bargaining contend that (1) unions cost employees money; (2) strike losses are never retrieved; (3) even when they are not purposely kept uninformed by union leadership, members have little voice in union affairs; (4) bureaucratic union hierarchies control the economic destiny of members; (5) union corruption is rampant; (6) union opposition to management attempts to increase productivity arrests organizational growth; (7) union featherbedding results in unneeded employees and unnecessary payroll expenses; (8) union activities foster conflict rather than collaboration; and (9) unions fail to extrapolate the effects of wage increases on future employment, inflation, and taxes.

A fundamental concern among social welfare professionals revolves around the ultimate tactic that unions can bring to employer–employee relations: job actions, particularly strikes. For social workers pledged to make client welfare a priority, the prospect of denying services as a result of job actions makes union membership and professional commitment contradictory. In covering a strike by

Local 1199 of the Retail Drug Employees Union, which included the social work staffs of more than 50 hospitals and nursing homes, Dena Fisher wrote:

> Standards for professional practice conflict with the [NASW] Code of Ethics with regard to behavior during a labor strike when the prescribed behavior includes withholding service, failing to terminate clients properly, and picketing activity directed toward consumers. The problem is that participation in a strike is a nonprofessional activity. Standards of professional behavior conflict with union membership requirements.[34]

Yet, proponents of union membership cite ways in which collective bargaining can complement professional objectives. In an attempt to encourage a better relationship with professional social workers, Jerry Wurf, former AFSCME president, explained that to improve public services and programs, the commitment of AFSCME is important to show how labor organizations are tied to social work. AFSCME, as a social missionary, grew over the last decade as a result of more social workers in the field.[35]

As unions have lost membership, dropping to its lowest level in 70 years at 11.9 percent of the labor force, they have become more receptive to non-confrontational methods to advance their objectives.[36]

Andy Stern, a caseworker who rose to the Presidency of SEIU, found job actions against employers inferior to alternative methods to advance his union's agenda. After losing a strike with the Beverly nursing home corporation, Stern convinced the company to sign a contract improving staff working conditions if SEIU convinced government to increase reimbursement to patients cared for by Beverly. In New Jersey, SEIU negotiated novel contracts with employers that were not binding until a majority of employers had also agreed, spreading the contract costs across a wide spectrum of companies.[37]

The few studies that examined the issue found little incongruity between the loyalties of social workers who belong to unions. Leslie Alexander and his colleagues studied 84 union members with MSW degrees and found that "they view their work as solidly professional and, for the most part, do not see unionism and professionalism as incompatible."[38] Ernie Lightman reported similar findings when studying 121 randomly chosen professional social workers in Toronto, Canada. According to Lightman, "the vast majority saw no incompatibility; indeed, many felt unionization may facilitate

service goals, offsetting workplace bureaucracy."[39] Reporting on child welfare agencies in Pennsylvania and Illinois, Gary Shaffer found that "workers did not find unionism incompatible with their educational or professional goals."[40]

Such complementarity notwithstanding, the concept of social work "exceptionalism" pervades the debate about professionalism and unions. The exceptionalism premise implies that tasks performed by social workers are more important than those performed by many other workers, especially nonprofessionals, and that normal labor relations principles are therefore not applicable. Proponents of social work exceptionalism must address two matters: First, how is it that other semiprofessionals, such as teachers and nurses, have reconciled their professional priorities with union activities and become more powerful in the contexts of their work as a result? Are social service activities to be considered more essential than education or health care? Second, does the idea of social work exceptionalism contribute to the powerlessness of social workers? If social work places such value on the empowerment of clients, why should social workers not also be so empowered?

While social workers in the United States procrastinate about an alliance with unions, events such as privatization and government cuts in funding make the issue ever more urgent. In recent years, conservative governors in Indiana and Wisconsin convinced legislators to reduce union influence, to the detriment of social workers employed in those states. As these adverse developments suggest, social workers and unions should be able to collaborate in problem solving, fostering a public debate on social issues and promoting practical solutions.

Welfare Capitalism

The business community in the United States influences social welfare in several important ways. Benefit packages for employees, which are usually available to dependents, provide important health and welfare benefits to a large segment of the working population. Historically, this form of "welfare capitalism" has been an important complement to public social programs. "For much of the 20th century, indeed, the development of U.S. social policy has followed an identifiable second track of intervention, one to which scholars of the welfare state, orthodox or revisionist, have paid only limited attention," noted Jacob Hacker. "The legislative milestones along this track have not been large and highly prominent social programs, but public policies of diverse form—tax breaks, regulations, credit subsidies, and government insurance—designed to encourage and shape private responses to public social problems."[41] The implications of welfare capitalism are momentous. Once private sector activities are calculated as part of the national welfare effort, provision of welfare services in the United States is similar in scale to that of European nations. Politically, any welfare state with competing public and private sectors can develop separate solutions to citizens' needs, evident in the liberal defense of Social Security contemporaneous with conservative preference for private alternatives, such as 401(k) plans.[42]

Among welfare theorists, however, corporate sponsorship of social welfare initiatives activities tends to be underappreciated. Welfare state ideology, as it evolved, left little room for the corporation, viewing it as the source of much suffering and as generally unwilling to pay its share of the tax burden to remediate the problems it had spawned. For example, advocacy groups, such as the public interest research groups (PIRGs) associated with Ralph Nader and Citizens for Tax Justice, regularly criticize the corporate sector for pursuing economic and political self-interest, sacrificing the general welfare in the process. Notorious examples of the sacrifice of civic values in pursuit of profits have been chronicled by liberal advocacy groups. These include the disruption, then abandonment, of Love Canal because of improper disposal of toxic waste; the exploitation of Mexican agricultural workers in the Southwest; the extortion of huge sums from New York City housing officials by landlords who provide single-room occupancy lodgings for the homeless; and the deceit of tobacco companies about the harmful effects of smoking. To corporate critics, CEOs flaunt their positions by commanding salaries way out of proportion to their productivity. When super-rich CEOs downsize production, lay off thousands of workers, and thereby decimate a local economy,[43] they become cultural pariahs. At the same time, few would doubt that wealth and status are enormously influential when wealthy executives leave private life and run for public office. "It's no accident that the Senate is a citadel of multi-millionaires," observed one longtime Washington journalist.[44]

Power and wealth notwithstanding, the corporate sector has made contributions to the **commonweal,** or public good. During the industrial era, major foundations were established that instituted important benchmarks in the development of the U.S. welfare state, and by the end of the twentieth century, minority Americans were making their mark in corporate philanthropy. Native American tribes contributed $35 million for the new Museum of the American Indian that opened in Washington, DC, in 2004. Jeong Kim used the sale proceeds from Yurie Systems for millions of dollars to aid higher education. In 2003, African American publishing tycoon John Johnson contributed $4 million to Howard University's School of Communication.[45]

At this point, many welfare theorists began to reexamine the role of the corporate sector in U.S. social welfare. The concept of the "mixed welfare economy" combines the corporate proprietary sector with the governmental and voluntary sectors as primary actors in social welfare.[46] And the issue of privatization provoked a vigorous argument about the proper balance between the public and private (including corporate) welfare sectors.[47] Although Neil Gilbert's *Capitalism and the Welfare State* provided a timely review of the issues posed by "welfare capitalism,"[48] empirical investigations of for-profit human service corporations are in their infancy.[49]

Corporate Social Responsibility

The corporation has also influenced U.S. social welfare as a result of accusations that it has been insensitive to the needs of minorities, the poor, women, and consumers. During the 1960s, criticism of the corporation focused on business's neglect of minorities and on urban blight. A decade later, issues relating to affirmative action, environmental pollution, and consumer rip-offs were added to the list. These problems contributed to a public relations crisis, as a leading business administration text noted:

The corporation is being attacked and criticized on various fronts by a great number of political and citizens' organizations. Many young people accuse the corporation of failing to seek solutions to our varied social problems. Minority groups, and women, contend that many corporations have been guilty of discrimination in hiring and in pay scales.[50]

Melvin Anshen, a professor of public policy and business responsibility at Columbia University's Graduate School of Business bemoaned the fact that "profit-oriented private decisions are now often seen as antisocial."[51]

In order to improve their public image, many businesses established policies on **corporate social responsibility**. Corporations that were reluctant to take seriously the social implications of their operations ran the risk of inviting the surveillance of public interest groups. As an example, the Council on Economic Priorities (CEP), founded in 1969, developed a reputation for investigating the social responsibility of U.S. corporations. CEP released *Rating America's Corporate Conscience*, which evaluated 125 large corporations based on their standing with respect to seven issues: charitable contributions; representation of women on boards of directors and among top corporate officers; representation of minorities on boards of directors and among top corporate officers; disclosure of social information; involvement in South Africa; conventional weapons-related contracting; and nuclear weapons-related contracting.[52] Subsequently, CEP served as the platform to launch Social Accountability International, which established workplace standards and monitored factories in developing nations.[53] In 2010, Human Rights Campaign published its report, *Corporate Equality: Rating American Workplaces on Lesbian, Gay, Bisexual and Transgender Equality*, calculating that 338 businesses achieved a rating of 11 percent.[54]

Although public relations facades frequently gloss over businesses' substantive abuses, specific corporate social responsibility policies have advanced social welfare. During the late 1960s, General Electric and IBM instituted strong policies on equal opportunity for and affirmative action toward minorities and women. Under the title, Public Interest Director, Leon Sullivan assumed a position on the General Motors board of directors, from which he presented principles governing ethical practices for U.S. corporations doing business in South Africa.[55] Ultimately, U.S. firms' adherence to the "Sullivan principles" contributed to the fall of apartheid in South Africa. More recently, financial consultants pioneered the concept of socially responsible investing. The practice of excluding certain industries from mutual fund portfolios because their activities are contrary to those of investors gained considerable ground during the 1980s. An illustration of socially responsible investing is the Domini Social Index (DSI), an investment strategy that screens out businesses in five areas: military contracting, alcohol and tobacco, gambling, nuclear power, and, prior to the end of apartheid, South Africa.[56]

Corporate practices have also been applied directly to social problems, as evident in initiatives undertaken by the Enterprise Foundation and the Ford Foundation. In 1981, developer James Rouse established the Enterprise Foundation, a foundation that supported charitable projects. In 2009 Enterprise announced a $4 billion investment in retrofitting multi-family housing units to make them more energy efficient.[57] Recognizing the tendency of community institutions in poor areas to become dependent on government or philanthropy for continuing operations, the Ford Foundation sought contributions from corporations for a program to apply business principles to social problems. By 2010, the Local Initiatives Support Corporation (LISC) had invested $1.1 billion through its sustainable communities initiative.[58] In the light of such ventures, some business leaders have become enthusiastic about the activist responses to social problems on the part of the corporation.

Corporate Influence on Social Welfare Policy

Corporate social responsibility notwithstanding, it would be naive to think that the corporate sector is above self-interest in its orientation toward social welfare. The conservative political economist Irving Kristol stated as much when he wrote that "corporate philanthropy is not obligatory. It is desirable if and only if it serves a corporate purpose. It is expressly and candidly a self-serving activity, and is only legitimate to the degree that it is ancillary to a larger corporate purpose. To put it bluntly: There is nothing noble or even moral about corporate philanthropy."[59] And corporate influence in social welfare is not exerted simply through myriad corporations acting independently. Special interest organizations, such as the National Association of Manufacturers and the United States Chamber of Commerce, have routinely pressed for public policies that clearly reflect the priorities of the business community. The influence that the business community brings to public policy is discussed in greater detail in Chapter 8. Since the 1970s, certain foundations have made sizable contributions to conservative policy institutes, constructing the ideological infrastructure that would challenge liberalism in social policy.

At the turn of the twentieth century, conservative foundations continued to support think tanks

associated with the Right. By the end of the twentieth century, such contributions placed conservative
policy institutes at the center of the social policy
debate. Not only were conservative think tanks
well endowed with resources but they were dispersed throughout the United States. As a result of
these investments in the "marketplace of ideas," the
conservative imprint on social policy has become
indelible, and many of the most prominent conservative think tanks—American Enterprise Institute
for Public Policy Research (AEI), Heritage, and
Cato—have become household names.

Prominent conservative policy institutes favored
by the business community have been the AEI and
the Heritage Foundation. Established as nonpartisan
institutions for the purpose of enhancing the public's
understanding of social policy, these policy institutes
distanced themselves from the special interest
connotations of earlier business advocacy groups.
At the same time, conservative think tanks served
as vehicles through which the business community
could take a less reactive stance regarding social
policy. Conservative policy institutes, then, addressed
the complaint voiced by Lawrence Fouraker and
Graham Allison of Harvard's Graduate School of
Business Administration: "Public policy suffers
not simply from a lack of business confidence on
issues of major national import, but from a lack of
sophisticated and balanced contribution by both
business and government in the process of policy
development."[60]

Corporate influence in social welfare is
dynamic, involving a range of organizations, evident in crafting the 2003 Medicare reforms. Central to the passage of Medicare reform was Thomas
A. Scully, the Director of the Centers for Medicare
and Medicaid Services (CMS). Before taking the
helm of CMS, Scully was president of the Federation of American Hospitals (FAH), a trade association of for-profit hospitals, for which he was paid
$675,000 per year. At CMS, his salary was only
$134,000 per year, so it is not surprising that Scully
announced a swift exit after two-and-a-half years
of federal service during which he helped pass the
2003 Medicare reforms,[61] battening the act with
subsidies to health care corporations. Immediately
after passage of the legislation, he left the government to work for Alston & Bird, an Atlanta law
firm specializing in health care. Within a year, Scully
was back on Capitol Hill lobbying on behalf of the
Renal Leadership Council, a kidney dialysis trade
association. Joining him were other Alston & Bird

acquisitions: Colin Roskey, former adviser to the
Senate Finance Committee, and Marc Scheineson,
former associate commissioner of the Food and
Drug Administration. Alston & Bird's head of DC
operations and former Clinton White House official, Marilyn Yeager, stated, "It's a very nice team
here. They have a lot of expertise."[62]

The 2003 Medicare reforms would have been
chalked up as just another Republican maneuver to
co-opt a Democratic issue had the program's chief
actuary, Richard Foster, not revealed that his attempts
to inform Congress of the program's true costs—
$551.5 billion over 10 years—had been suppressed by
Scully. Foster's exposé was newsworthy because the
Medicare reforms had passed by a close margin, and
many members of Congress voted in favor only after
being assured that the health reforms were within the
$400 billion parameter stated by the White House.
Federal law prohibits the obstruction of communication between federal employees and Congress,[63]
but that did not stop Scully from blocking access to
Foster's memo explicating the more realistic costs of
Medicare reform. "If Rick Foster gives that to you," a
House Democratic aide who had requested the memo
was told by Scully, "I'll fire him so fast his head will
spin."[64] Foster, a career civil servant, stuck to his story,
accusing the White House of having full knowledge
of his projections, but favoring lower estimates generated by other agencies.[65] A subsequent House inquiry
failed to clarify the matter, in large part because the
Republican leadership was unwilling to grant sub-
poena power to the committee, making testimony
voluntary. When the House committee asked Scully
to testify about the suppression of Foster's projection, he said he was "unable to appear" because he
was traveling.[66] Lacking a majority in the House at
the time, Democrats were unable to get a full hearing on the scandal. By the time Democrats regained
control of Congress, the prescription drug benefit had
been introduced, millions of Medicare recipients were
receiving medication, and the pharmaceutical trade
associations were prepared to oppose any reforms to
Part D. Its tawdry passage notwithstanding, the Medicare prescription drug benefit was a done deal.

In anticipation of the Obama administration's
health reform initiative, health care organizations
unleashed a legion of lobbyists on lawmakers. By
one count, an unprecedented $200 million was spent
on attempts to influence members of Congress who
found themselves confronted with 4,500 lobbyists.
Prominent among them were the representatives from
for-profit hospitals, the pharmaceutical industry, and

the health insurance industry.[67] When Obama's first choice as Secretary of Health and Human Services, former Senator Tom Daschle, removed himself from consideration due to financial improprieties, his services were quickly acquired by Alston & Bird.[68]

The Future of Corporate Involvement in Social Welfare

Corporations will continue to influence social welfare policy, reflecting the preference of business leaders that businesses assume a primary role in activities of both the voluntary and governmental sectors. It follows that human service advocates, rather than outright rejecting corporate involvement in social policy and programming, should engage the business community proactively. A creative illustration of this kind of engagement appears in the "Decency Principles" proposed by Nancy Amidei, a social worker and syndicated columnist. Her standards for responsible business practices included the following:

1. Equitable wages. Wages should be high enough to allow workers to escape poverty; there should be comparability across lines of race, age, sex, and handicapping conditions.
2. Employee rights. Employees should be provided equal opportunity, the right to organize for collective bargaining, affordable child care, safe working conditions, and health coverage.
3. Housing. Businesses should work for more affordable housing and help relocated or migrant workers obtain affordable housing.
4. Environmental responsibility. Business practices should include responsible use of resources, sound handling of dangerous substances, and conformance with environmental protection laws.

Amidei suggested that a corporation's adherence to the "Decency Principles" be a basis for government decisions on such matters as providing tax abatements to corporations to attract new industry or awarding government contracts.[69] Incorporating the corporate sector in social policy has been the objective of advocates of **industrial policy**—periodic meetings of representatives of business, labor, and government to define mutually agreed objectives." One advocate of industrial policy is former secretary of Labor Robert Reich. Reich attributed much of the industrial malaise of the United States to underinvestment in human capital. However, human capital investments can be wasteful, leading to nonproductive dependency, when not coupled with the needs of industry. "Underlying many of the inadequacies of American social programs, in short, is the fact that they have not been directed in any explicit or coherent way toward the large task of adapting America's labor force."[70] The attachment of social needs to industrial productivity would fundamentally alter social welfare. "Government bureaucracies that now administer these programs to individuals will be supplanted, to a large extent, by companies that administer them to their employees," suggested Reich. "Companies, rather than state and local governments, will be the agents through which such assistance is provided."[71]

Significantly, industrial policy attracted conservative adherents as well. Influential analyst Kevin Phillips proposed a "business–government partnership" through which labor and business would agree to work cooperatively with government so that the United States could regain its dominant role in the international economy. Such business-government partnerships are commonplace within the European welfare states. For Phillips, however, industrial policy conflicted with the traditional liberal orientation to social welfare:

Political liberals must accept that there is little support for bringing back federal agencies based on New Deal models to run the U.S. economy, and that much of the new business-government cooperation will back economic development and nationalist (export, trade competition) agendas rather than abstractions like social justice or social welfare.[72]

The primacy of business interests in public policy has not been accepted by many social welfare advocates. Their argument has been that even though "corporatism" may seem plausible to corporate executives, government officials, and labor unions, it offers little to the unemployed or to the welfare or working poor.[73] Another reason to reject corporate involvement in social welfare has been its inefficiency. Currently, the United States spends 16 percent of GDP on health care, yet 47 million Americans lack health insurance. Liberals who have advocated universal health care as public policy have pointed their fingers at the commercialization of health care as a primary factor for this paradox. As a result of the fragmentation of U.S. health care, simply managing the complexity of such an incoherent arrangement imposes administrative costs of $1,059 per capita in the United States, compared to $307 in Canada.[74]

David Himmelstein, a Harvard physician and universal health advocate, estimated that the administrative savings if the United States were to adopt a single-payer system, similar to Canada's, would realize annual savings of $375 billion, sufficient to provide health insurance to every American.[75]

Other instances of privatizing government services demonstrate that anticipated cost savings often don't materialize. The Internal Revenue Service contracted out tax collection only to discover it lost $37 million.[76] An analysis of private prisons in Arizona revealed that they were more costly than traditional state operated facilities.[77] Similarly, a study of the $320 billion that the federal government contracts out annually found that contractors charged federal agencies twice the cost of using internal employees.[78]

Any program that reimburses third parties invites the possibility of improper payments. The GAO, for example, suspects that Medicaid and Medicare incur $70 billion in improper payments annually.[79] In 2011, the Justice Department announced charges against 91 people for defrauding Medicare for $300 million in eight cities.[80] This pales in comparison to the penalties charged HCA for improper billing of Medicare and Medicaid, noted below.

Despite the critique of corporate involvement in health and human services, commercial providers are likely to play an active role in defining social welfare. The economy of the United States is, after all, capitalist, and entrepreneurs are free to establish businesses in whatever markets they consider profitable. Unless government strictly regulates—or prohibits—the for-profit provision of human services, human service corporations will influence U.S. social welfare to an even greater extent in the future. Skeptics of the commercialization of social welfare may take comfort in holding the moral high ground, but practically speaking, they are losing territory with accelerating speed to for-profit entrepreneurs. If the expansion of health and human service corporations during the latter decades of the twentieth century is not sufficient evidence, then consider the Medicare reforms of 2003 that subsidized the pharmaceutical industry, to say nothing of the Affordable Care Act, which complements the commercialization of health care.

Human Service Corporations

Continued demand for human services in the postindustrial period has drawn the corporate sector directly into social welfare in the United States.

Corporate exploration of the growing human services market has proceeded at pace. In contrast, shackled by debt and denied revenue because of tax cuts, government social programs struggle to keep up with demand for services. Dependent on government support and on contributions of middle-income Americans who have experienced a continual erosion of their economic position, the voluntary sector is unlikely to meet future service demands. Relatively unfettered by government regulation and with easy access to capital from commercial sources, the corporate sector has made dramatic inroads into service areas previously reserved for governmental and voluntary sector organizations.

Significantly, the incentives for corporate entry into human services were initially provided through government social programs, especially with passage of Medicare and Medicaid in 1965. As a percentage of gross domestic product, public welfare expenditures more than doubled, from 8.8 percent in 1970 to 20.5 percent in 1991. Health care allocations figured prominently in the expansion of public welfare expenditures over this period. In 1970, government spent $24.9 billion on health care; by 1991 that figure had grown to $317.0 billion,[81] and $2.6 *trillion* in 2010.[82] The potential profits for corporations entering the rapidly expanding health and human services market were unmistakable.

Concomitantly, public policy decisions encouraged proprietary firms to provide health and human services. By using a market approach to ensure the availability of health care for the medically indigent and the elderly, Medicaid and Medicare avoided the costs of constructing a system of public sector facilities and, in so doing, contributed to the restructuring of health care in the United States. What was essentially a haphazard collection of mom-and-pop nursing homes and small private hospitals was transformed, in a short period, into a system of corporate franchises, complete with stocks traded on Wall Street. And almost a decade later, incentives offered through Medicaid and Medicare to encourage the corporate sector to become involved in hospital care were replicated in the health maintenance industry. The Health Maintenance Organization Act of 1973 stimulated a sluggish health maintenance industry that has since grown at an explosive rate. As Pulitzer Prize–winning journalists Donald Barlett and James Steele noted, "Wall Street reasoned that a portion of America's hospitals could be assembled into national chains, much like department stores and auto-parts distributors, and investors could make a fortune."[83]

TABLE 7.1 Prominent Human Service Corporations

Company	Revenues 2007	Revenues 2011	Market	Employees 2011
UnitedHealth	$75.4 billion	$102 billion	HMO	99,000
Wellpoint	61.1 billion	60.7 billion	Health care	37,700
Aetna	27.6 billion	8.5 billion	Health insurance	33,300
HCA	25.5 billion	29.5 billion	Hospital management	150,000
Humana	25.3 billion	36.8 billion	HMO	40,000
CIGNA	17.6 billion	22.0 billion	HMO	31,400
Universal Health	N/A	7.5 billion	Psychiatric care	46,500
Health Net	14.1 billion	11.9 billion	Health care	7,351
Coventry	9.9 billion	12.1 billion	HMO	14,400
Tenet Healthcare	8.9 billion	8.8 billion	Hospital management	43,856
CCA	1.5 billion	1.7 billion	Corrections	16,750
Sunrise	1.6 billion	1.3 billion	Assisted living	31,600
MAXIMUS	738.7 million	929.6 million	Consulting	7,102

Initially dependent on government welfare programs, the corporate sector developed a life of its own. Exploitation of the nursing home, hospital management, and health maintenance markets has led to corporate interest in other markets. By the 1980s, human service corporations had established prominence in child care, ambulatory health care, substance abuse, psychiatric care, and home health care, as well as in life care and continuing care. By the 1990s, managed care firms were restructuring health and mental health services so as to batten corporate profits; by the end of the twentieth century, they had established beachheads in welfare and corrections, as well. Increasingly, proprietary firms were able to obtain funds for facilities through commercial loans or sales of stock, and to meet ongoing costs by charging fees to individuals, companies, and nongovernmental third parties. Insofar as resources for human service corporations are not financed by the state, firms are free to function relatively independent of government intervention.

How big is the corporate sector in U.S. social welfare? Early in the twenty-first century, more than 20 of the largest firms reported annual revenues that were far greater than *all* contributions to the United Ways of America.[84] These corporations employed thousands of workers, some more than the number of state and local workers for public welfare programs in any state in the union.[85] Some salient statistics on the larger human service corporations are listed in Table 7.1.

Consolidation and Growth in New Human Service Markets[1]

Human service corporations have become prominent, if not dominant, in several areas of social welfare: nursing homes, hospital management, HMOs, child care, and home care. More recently, proprietary firms established beachheads in other markets, notably life and continuing care, corrections, and welfare. The descriptions of the following subsectors are somewhat arbitrary because many companies diversify their operations, functioning across several subsectors. In health care, for example, a hospital management firm will operate nursing homes as well as an HMO. Over time, these holdings can change significantly, reflecting the dynamic nature of the evolving health and human services market. Human service markets have also become global; Sunrise Senior Living generated $1.4 billion for elder care services in Britain, Canada, and the United States; the GEO

[1]Financial information on corporations is from Yahoo! Finance: http://finance.yahoo.com/q/pr?s=MMS+Profile

Group earned $1.6 billion providing correctional services in Australia, Canada, South Africa, and the United Kingdom as well as the United States.

Nursing Homes

Among corporate initiatives in social welfare, expansion into the nursing home industry is unparalleled. Between 1965 and 1978, expenditures for nursing home care increased 16.9 percent *annually*.[86] By the early 1980s, nursing homes had become a $25-billion-a-year industry, and the number of nursing home beds exceeded those in acute care facilities for the first time.[87] At that time, 70 percent of nursing homes were under proprietary management. Market conditions such as these led a writer in *Forbes* magazine to observe, "This is a guaranteed opportunity for someone. How the nursing home industry can exploit it is the real question."[88]

Given this trend, one industry analyst believed that the industry would eventually fall into the hands of "five or six corporations."[89] A decade later, Beverly continued as the largest corporation focusing on long-term care, managing 703 nursing homes, 30 assisted living centers, 6 hospices, 11 transitional hospitals, and 4 home health centers. Yet, Beverly's share of the nursing home market did not go unchallenged. On March 1, 1995, Beverly's primary competitor, NME, merged with American Medical International to form Tenet Healthcare Corporation, a $5.5 billion company.[90] Yet, Tenet would falter. In response to an FBI investigation into unnecessary heart surgeries performed at a California hospital, Tenet agreed to a $54 million penalty. Under new management, Tenet opted to sell one-third of its hospitals.[91]

Meanwhile labor costs and regulatory problems beset Beverly which, on the verge of bankruptcy, was sold to Fillmore Strategic Investors in 2005 for $1.6 billion. The nursing care industry would be shaped largely by Manor Care, which owned 500 nursing homes and had been acquired by the Carlyle Group for $6.3 billion.[92] By 2011, Tenet had rebounded from its legal difficulties, posting revenues of $8.8 billion, but had divested most of its nursing homes.

2003 Medicare Reforms

The Medicare Modernization Act of 2003 included two provisions that were favored by corporate health providers: a prescription drug benefit and an 11 percent augmentation for Medicare beneficiaries who enrolled in managed care plans, Medicare Advantage. Immediately, pharmaceutical companies floated plans to attract subscribers; in many states as many as 50 plans vied to sign-up seniors.[93] Among the most aggressive are UnitedHealth and Wellpoint (see Table 7.1). The fortunes of managed care companies have varied considerably. In a bid to gain access to the market, drugstore chain CVS purchased the Medicare prescription from Universal American for $1.25 billion, summing the number of beneficiaries to 3.1 million.[94] A year later, CVS was ordered by the Federal Trade Commission to reimburse seniors $5 million for overpriced medications.[95]

By gaining such a large share of recipients who need prescription drugs and desire managed care just a few years after passage of Medicare reform, UnitedHealth and Humana are well positioned to exploit the 77 million baby boomers who began retiring in 2008. That managed care companies have so quickly addressed the needs of seniors makes alteration of the Medicare drug provisions from which they have profited less likely.

Hospital Management

The growth of the nursing home industry has been matched by corporate involvement in hospital management. Between 1976 and 1982, the number of investor-owned or investor-managed hospitals increased from 533 to 1,040, accruing gross revenues of approximately $40 billion.[96] The mid-1990s witnessed the largest mergers among health care corporations that had occurred up to that point. The merger of National Medical Enterprises and American Medical International to form Tenet Healthcare Corporation effectively approximated the market share controlled by Humana. This transaction paled, however, in comparison to the acquisition of HCA by Columbia. The Columbia/HCA merger created a $20 billion behemoth that dwarfed Tenet and Humana. By the mid-1990s the holdings of Columbia/HCA included 292 general hospitals, 28 psychiatric hospitals, and 125 outpatient and auxiliary facilities.[97] Being the largest health and human service corporation was not without its problems, however. An intensely competitive health market invited irregularities, the scale of which matched the size of the perpetrator:

In June 2003, HCA agreed to pay $631 million in civil penalties and damages growing out of false claims to the government health care programs. That came on top of $840 million in criminal fines, civil restitution, and penalties the company paid in

2000. That same year, the company agreed to pay $250 million to settle other Medicare overbilling claims. In all, HCA has paid $1.7 billion as a result of its fraudulent practices.[98]

Despite such setbacks, HCA was well positioned with respect to federal programs that accounted for one-third of its revenue. The son of the company's founder, Thomas Frist Jr., was none other than Bill Frist, who would become Senate Majority Leader. After flirting with a presidential campaign, Bill Frist joined his father and brother in buying HCA for $33 billion, executing the largest purchase of a publicly held company in the nation's history.[99] In 2010, HCA was publicly traded once again; a year later the company reported revenues of $29.5 billion. By 2012, HCA was eclipsed by Humana, a company whose revenue had tripled from $12.2 billion in 2004 to $36.8 billion in 2011.

Health Maintenance Organizations

Pioneered by the nonprofit Kaiser Permanente in California, the concept of **health maintenance organizations (HMOs)** was slow to attract the interest of the corporate sector. However, from 1973 to 1981, the Health Maintenance Organization Act of 1973 authorized funds for the establishment of these membership health plans in a large number of favorable marketing areas. This funding, coupled with the growth in the nursing home and hospital management industries, reversed investor apathy. By 1983, 60 HMOs were operating on a proprietary basis.[100] By the end of the century, the HMO industry was a commercial enterprise, save Kaiser-Permanente, which had to adopt for-profit strategies in order to remain competitive.

At the beginning of the twenty-first century, the insurance giant CIGNA dominated the industry, controlling 46 HMOs in which 3 million people were subscribers.[101] CIGNA's reign was not to last, however. In November 2004, WellPoint and Anthem received permission from California regulators to consummate their merger announced a year earlier. As a condition to the merger, the health providers agreed to pay $265 million to upgrade health care in California. Combined, WellPoint and Anthem eclipse CIGNA as the nation's largest health care insurer.[102] By 2012, Wellpoint and UnitedHealth Group International vied for dominance in corporate health care. Although Wellpoint reported $60.7 billion in

Health maintenance organizations such as Kaiser Permanente offer prepaid medical services. Members pay a monthly or yearly fee for all health care, including hospitalization. Because costs to patients are fixed in advance, preventive medicine is stressed to avoid costly hospitalization. One criticism of HMOs is that patients can use only doctors and specialists who are associated with the organization.

Source: PhotoEdit Inc.

revenues compared to UnitedHealth's $102 billion, it remained the nation's largest health insurer with 78 million members. But UnitedHealth was closing in as a result of its acquisition of PacifiCare for $8.1 billion, representing 3.3 million enrollees.[103]

The largest managed care company providing behavioral health services, Magellan, emerged from bankruptcy in 2004, having consolidated its position, reporting revenues of $2.8 billion in 2011. A primary competitor is Psychiatric Solutions, which was purchased by Universal Health in 2010. Operating a number of specialty hospitals including psychiatric clinics, Universal reported revenues of $7.5 billion in 2011. Community Health Systems, which also operates psychiatric hospitals, reported revenues of $13.6 billion in 2011.

Child Care

As a human services market, child care has been exploited effectively by proprietary firms. The increasing participation of mothers in the labor market has increased the demand for child care. Between 1979 and 2000, the number of hours worked by wives increased 50.7 percent,[104] a figure that would likely increase as a function of stagnating family income and the work mandate affixed to welfare reform. Consequently, the day care market, like its largest provider, KinderCare, expanded rapidly. Begun in 1969, KinderCare demonstrated prodigious growth, claiming approximately 825 "learning centers" representing $128 million in revenue in 1983.

During the 1990s, KinderCare dominated the child care industry with more than 1,100 centers, but new competitors were emerging to serve a seemingly infinite need for organized child care. Within a few years, KinderCare's command of the child care industry would be challenged by several upstarts that showed explosive growth. Bright Horizons Family Solutions managed more than 500 workplace centers in 37 states, reported revenue of $423 million, and had 16,000 employees; La Petite Academy boasted 650 centers, $383 million in revenue, and 12,000 employees; Learning Care Group reported $206 million in revenue and 7,500 workers. By 2007, KinderCare had been acquired by Knowledge Learning Corporation, which boasted annual revenues of $1.6 billion, almost double what KinderCare had reported in 2004. Many of the smaller child care businesses were acquired by Learning Care Group, which operated 1,049 centers in the United States and abroad.

Home Health Care

Several companies in the **home health care** market replicated the success of corporations in the nursing home industry. Home Health Care of America, later renamed Caremark, began in 1979. A leader in the field, the company grew particularly quickly. By the mid-1990s Caremark was reporting annual revenues of $2.4 billion and claimed health care facilities in Canada, France, Germany, the United Kingdom, the Netherlands, and Japan.[105]

Home health care expansion continued during the early 1990s, when home health companies adjusted their services to meet earlier hospital discharges resulting from implementation of Medicare's prospective payment system: as patients went home sooner, the need for a range of specialized in-home health services grew. Quickly, home health companies began to offer a variety of these services to patients. In markets where conventional home health companies failed to offer such specialized care, new firms entered the market and expanded rapidly.

The diversification of elder care began to accelerate in anticipation of the retirement of the baby boomers, providing consumers for companies such as Apria Healthcare Group and American Home Patient. Although Caremark had been acquired by the CVS drugstore company, the home health industry was comprised of smaller providers. In 2007, the industry consisted of Tender Loving Care Health Care Services reporting $112.6 million in revenues; Assisted Living Concepts, $229.4 million; Altria Senior Living Group, $183.6 million; and National Home Health Care Corporation, $110.8 million. Odyssey, a commercial hospice, reported revenues of $404.9 million in 2007.

Corrections

Among the more ambitious of human service corporations is the Correction Corporation of America (CCA), founded in 1983 by Tom Beasely with the financial backing of Jack Massey, founder of the Hospital Corporation of America. CCA officials noted that many states were unable to contend with overcrowding of prison facilities and proposed contracting with state and local jurisdictions for the provision of correctional services. As CCA acknowledged in its 1986 annual report, court orders to upgrade facilities, coupled with governmental reluctance to finance such improvements, provided strong incentives for jurisdictions to consider contracting out correctional services:

Government response to [overcrowding] has been hampered by the administrative and budgetary problems traditionally plaguing public sector facilities. Most systems have suffered a lack of long-term leadership due to their ties to the political process, and many jurisdictions have placed a low priority on corrections funding. The outcome has been a proliferation of out-dated facilities with a lack of sufficient capacity to meet constitutional standards.[106]

By 1986, CCA operated nine correctional facilities with a total of 1,646 beds, and the company was negotiating with the Texas Department of Corrections "to build and manage two minimum security prisons which will provide an additional 1,000 beds."[107]

Most analysts expect that proprietary correctional facilities would continue to grow in popularity as governmental agencies recognize the cost savings of contracting out correctional services. CCA moved steadily ahead, capitalizing on the dire need of local and state governments for greater prison capacity. By 2012, CCA reported revenues of $1.7 billion from holdings that had expanded to 66 correctional facilities, totaling 91,000 beds. CCA's chief competitor is the GEO Group, which operates 116 prisons in the United States, the United Kingdom, South Africa, and Australia, totaling 80,000 beds and earning the company $1.6 billion in 2012. Undaunted, other firms were entering the market: Avalon Correctional Services reported revenue of $26 million in 2010 for community reentry programs for inmates. Other companies serving inmates include Correctional Medical Services and MHM Services, Inc., which provides mental health services in several state prisons.

Public Welfare

Several companies have become profitable through contracts with state and local government. The largest consulting group, MAXIMUS, increased its revenues from $738.7 million in 2007 to $930 million in 2011.

Within five years of passage of the 1996 welfare reform act, for-profit firms claimed 13 percent of $1.5 billion contracts for services, among them Lockheed Martin and MAXIMUS. Much of the profit generated by MAXIMUS was due to replacing unionized workers with less costly nonunion employees.[108] During the 1990s, MAXIMUS contracted to provide a range of welfare-related services through Wisconsin Works (W-2), the welfare waiver granted to then governor, and later Secretary of HHS, Tommy Thompson. Since W-2 mandated

work, MAXIMUS hired Financial and Employment Planners to find jobs for welfare recipients; however, their caseloads were double what had been intended and only half of recipients were referred for employment. But the $100 million contract had been intended as a national model for MAXIMUS, so the company redoubled its efforts to comply with provision of its contract. Some of these efforts were found to be suspect, such as expending $100,000 on backpacks, mugs, and other promotional objects, $3,000 to take clients roller-skating, and $2,600 for clowns to entertain MAXIMUS staff. Despite questionable expenditures, MAXIMUS met its caseload reduction objectives and was not only recognized with a $100,000 Innovation in American Government Award which was cosponsored by Harvard's Kennedy School of Government and the Ford Foundation, but used its success in W-2 to secure a $100 million welfare-to-work contract in New York City.[109]

Several companies provide managed health care for populations eligible for Medicaid, Medicare, and SCHIP. For 2011, AMERIGROUP coordinated the services of 80,000 physicians in eleven states, serving 2 million people, and claimed revenues of $6.3 billion. Centene Corporation generated $5.3 billion, and Molina Healthcare reported $4.7 billion serving low-income people receiving Medicaid and SCHIP.

Private Practice

Despite their antipathy toward privatization, many social workers engage in private practice, a commercial activity. Indeed, mental health care has been an area in which social workers have emulated the success of psychiatrists and psychologists. As a form of independent practice, private practice is influenced by the policies of the states regulating it, by professional associations, by the insurance companies that pay clinicians for their services, and by managed care companies that have become established as providers of mental health services. Private social work practice in mental health has been controversial within the social work profession, as reflected in this depiction:

> In increasing numbers, social workers are flocking to psychotherapeutic pastures, hanging out their shingles to advertise themselves as psychotherapists just as quickly as licensing laws will permit. For the most part, professional associations of social workers and schools of social

work are active participants in the great transformation of social work from a professional corps concerned with helping people deal with their social problems to a major platoon in the psycho-therapeutic armies.[110]

Despite its detractors, private practice continues to be an attractive vehicle for delivering clinical social services. In 2001, 23 percent of social workers reported that their primary activity was in solo or group private practice; another 37 percent indicated that they were "involved" in private practice. For some time, many mental health services have been delivered by psychiatrists and psychologists who work predominantly out of private offices. The upsurge of social workers' interest in private practice is such that today a large portion of students entering graduate programs in social work—as many as 80 percent[111]—do so with the expressed intent of establishing a private practice. Professional schools of social work are specifically equipped to prepare graduate students for private practice. "M.S.W. programs appear to offer more to the practitioner bound for private practice than to the social worker who would prefer to work in an agency setting," concluded researchers in a study of private and agency-based social workers.[112]

The current enthusiasm for private practice can be attributed to several factors. First, private practitioners often enjoy a prestige and an income that sets them apart from salaried professionals.[113] While the median salary of social workers in private practice is about $50,000, those with an ACSW and who specialize in family therapy can earn over twice that.[114] In addition, private practitioners work significantly fewer hours per week compared to colleagues in public and nonprofit settings.[115] In 2002, 41 percent of social workers in private practice worked between 10 and 29 hours per week, a greater number than colleagues in public and nonprofit settings who worked 30 hours or more, 32 percent.[116] It is not surprising that social workers, who are mostly female and usually underpaid—social work salaries are significantly less than those of nurses or teachers[117]—would see private practice as a way to increase their earnings and status. In fact, women are more likely to engage in private practice than to work in traditional social service agencies; two-thirds of private practitioners are women.[118]

Private practitioners also have a degree of autonomy that is not available to professionals who are bound by the personnel policies of traditional agencies.

Researchers found that "whereas 55 percent of the private practitioners report a high level of congruence between their expectations and their activities, only 18.3 percent of the agency practitioners do so."[119] This autonomy is important for experienced professionals who find continued supervision unnecessary or intrusive and who desire some flexibility in their work schedules to make room for other priorities. Finally, private practice allows professionals to specialize in activities at which they are best instead of having to conform to organizational requirements of the private agency or governmental bureaucracy. Again, 66.5 percent of private practitioners reported that they were able to do the things at which they excelled, whereas only 22.9 percent of agency practitioners said they could do so.[120]

The image of private practice that has emerged is one of freedom and opportunity, sans rules and regulations. This is somewhat misleading. Although private practice may involve comparatively fewer compliance requirements compared to salaried employment, it is anything but unfettered. In actuality, private practice involves many policies with which practitioners must be familiar if they are to be successful. The policies that affect private practice originate primarily from three sources: the professional community (a private entity); a government regulatory authority (a public entity); and, because of the role of managed care, corporate firms (commercial entities). This situation is complicated by the provision of service through the marketplace of a capitalist economy that traditionally discriminates against groups that do not participate fully in the labor market—minorities, women, elderly people, and people with disabilities. These groups frequently lack the resources to purchase the services provided by private practitioners. For this reason, private practice is not easily reconciled with the traditional values of social work, which emphasize service to the community and to the disadvantaged. So it is paradoxical that private practice has become a popular method of social work practice.

Despite the popularity of private practice, it has provoked controversy within the professional community. There are several aspects to this controversy, not the least of which is that many practitioners who have committed themselves to helping the disadvantaged by working in voluntary and governmental sectors view the popularity of private practice as antithetical to everything that is "social" about social work. One critic impugned the motives of social workers in private practice. "Over 15 years

ago, when I first had exposure to private practitioners, they were objects of envy, never of nonaccep-
tance. Obviously this envy has continued. For we
see more social workers developing private practices. But why all the sham? Let's be honest enough
to say it's usually done for the money."[121]

Defenders of private practice emphasize the benefits of the method for practitioners and clients. Why
should social workers not enjoy the same professional freedom and responsibility as other professions
that use private practice extensively, for instance, law,
medicine, and psychiatry? Moreover, "some clients
prefer the opportunity to choose their own practitioner and a service they consider more personal and
confidential."[122] Concern for the client's perceptions
means that practitioners must be concerned about
their image. This is evident in one privately practicing
social worker's description of her office:

It is decorated with comfortable chairs, built-
in book cases, soft lighting, etc., and is arranged in
such a way as to offer several different possibilities
for seating. It is commensurate with most of the
socio-cultural levels of my client group and provides him or her the opportunity for free expression
without being overheard. Dealing with only one
socio-cultural client group allows me to provide
physical surroundings which facilitate the client's
identification with the worker.[123]

On the surface, then, private practice often
provokes strong responses from human service
professionals who perceive private practitioners as
avoiding efforts by the voluntary and governmental
sectors to advance social justice. On the other hand,
some private practitioners believe that their work
offers them an opportunity not only to enhance their
status but also to provide mental health services to a
middle class that the profession has neglected.

Beneath this surface issue, there are more substantive problems raised by private practice. Perhaps the most important of these is preferential
selection. In an era of specialization, professionals
will refer to other providers those clients with problems that are inappropriate for their practice. An
important finding of research on private practice
was that private practitioners do not perceive their
clients in the same way that agency-based social
workers do. The latter "were significantly more
likely to agree with the statement that 'my personal
values and those of my clients differ greatly' than
those in private practice."[124] Preferential selection
becomes an issue when private practitioners elect
to serve less troubled clients (who are able to pay

the full cost of care) while referring multi-problem
clients (who are unable to pay the practitioner's fee
for service directly or through insurance) to agencies of the voluntary sector. Such "creaming" of the
client population places an enormous burden on
public agencies, which are left to carry a disproportionate share of chronically disturbed and indigent
clients. In effect, then, the public sector absorbs
the losses that private practitioners would suffer if
they served this population. Preferential selection
has become so pronounced that researchers have
facetiously identified it as a syndrome. According
to Franklin Chu and Sharland Trotter, the commercialization of private practice contributes to
the **YAVIS syndrome**—the tendency of clients of
private practitioners to be young, attractive, ver-
bal, intelligent, and successful. One might add W to
the syndrome, because the clients also tend to be
disproportionately white.[125] Consequently, clients
of private practitioners are less likely to be poor,
unemployed, old, and uneducated.

The Future of Private Practice

In response to the limitations imposed by traditional practice settings, many human service professionals have turned to private practice as a way
of securing their economic and professional objectives. Private practice gives program administrators a chance to maintain their direct service skills,
educators the opportunity to continue contact with
clients, and clinicians with families the freedom to
combine professional practice and attention to family life. More important, private practice may prove
an adjunct to agency activities. "By fostering part-
time practice," researchers have noted, "the profession can keep its main focus on agency services
where there is a commitment to serve persons without regard to their ability to pay and where there
can be a basis for social action and reform."[126]

As the growth of managed care illustrates, much
of private practice is a result of larger social forces.
The commercialization of social work came under
scrutiny as the profession became more immersed
in private practice. "There is concern," reported
Newsweek, "that too many social workers are turning their backs on their traditional casework among
the poor to practice therapy." *Newsweek* wondered
at the consequences of "an apparent middle-class
therapy explosion at the expense of public welfare
and grassroots service."[127] How social work will
reconcile its commitment to social justice with the

new opportunities presented by private practice remains a central question before the professional community.

Conclusion

Despite the proliferation of human service corporations, health and human service professionals have been slow to adopt the corporate sector as a setting for practice. Considering that organizations under traditional auspices—the voluntary and governmental sectors—are increasingly limited in their capacity to provide services, it is unfortunate that health and human service professionals have been loathe to consider corporations as a suitable vehicle for delivering services and benefits. Actually, for-profit firms can be advantageous for several reasons. Proprietary firms may provide access to the capital needed for expanding social services, a primary explanation for their rapid growth. And human service corporations can reduce the cost of commercially derived capital by depreciating assets and writing off interest payments against income during the first years of operation. These present obvious advantages for human service administrators who are faced with diminishing revenues derived from charitable or governmental sources.

In some instances, too, the corporate sector offers more opportunities for program innovation than are possible under other auspices. Governmental programs must be mandated by a public authority, and this requires a consensus on how to deal with particular concerns. Voluntary sector agencies are ultimately managed by boards of directors that reflect the interests of the community in organizational policy. When human service issues are controversial, welfare professionals can encounter stiff opposition to needed programs. Some of this difficulty can be obviated by a corporate structure that is not so directly wedded to the status quo. The corporate sector offers greater organizational flexibility than that usually found in governmental agencies and a level of sophistication in managerial innovation not often found in the voluntary sector. Paralleling the expansion of the healthcare market has been the growth in medical schools offering dual MD/MBA degrees, numbering 65 universities in 2011.[128] Whether or not schools of social work adopt similar programs will determine the competitiveness of their graduates in the health and human services market that is dominated by the corporate sector.

DISCUSSION QUESTIONS

1. Privatization is a hotly debated issue in social welfare. To what extent are some of the major concerns about privatization (e.g., unfair competition between nonprofit agencies and commercial firms, preferential selection and dumping of clients, superior performance of private providers, the emergence of an oligopoly of private providers) evident in your community? Should human service professionals practice in for-profit firms?

2. If you were inclined to establish a business providing a human service, what population would you focus on? How would you get capital to start the business? Would you own the business, or would you share ownership with stockholders? How would you market your service? What would you do with the profits—provide stockholders with dividends, enlarge the business, or make contributions to nonprofit agencies? What would be the name of your business?

3. Think tanks exist in Washington, DC, and in most state capitals. Obtain a copy of the annual report of a think tank. Who funds the think tank? Is there a relationship between the funding source and the ideological character of reports that the think tank publishes? What is the think tank's track record in social welfare issues?

4. In order to attain job security, many human service professionals join unions. What is the largest union to which social workers belong in your community? Do issues relating to service delivery figure in the union's negotiations with management? Under what conditions would human service professionals in your community engage in a strike?

5. The debate between private practice and agency-based practice continues as a heated issue within social work. What are the advantages and disadvantages of each? Is there a common base of social work practice? Can you foresee some ways to resolve the issue and bring private practitioners and agency-based practitioners together?

6. Private practice continues to be a focus of students in schools of social work. How many of your classmates are planning to become private practitioners? What are their motives? Do faculty members in your social work program who also have private practices serve as role models to students? Is there an opportunity in your studies to discuss the implications of private practice for social work?

7. How does your state regulate the practice of social work? What governmental unit is responsible for regulating social work? How is it constituted? Does your state have reciprocity arrangements with other states, honoring licenses granted in other jurisdictions? Has your state's social work licensing unit expelled professionals for unethical practices?

8. What is the position of your state chapter of the National Association of Social Workers on regulating professional practice? Are licensing and vendorship still high on the state chapter's priority list? If so, which social workers in your state remain concerned about the regulation of professional practice? Why?

9. What are the main concerns within your professional community about private practice—fees, misdiagnosis, licensing, image, competition with other professionals, vendorship? How are disagreements arbitrated, formally or informally?

10. Employee ownership is a way for human service professionals to attain control over their practices. Of the prominent social service agencies in your community, which ones might be candidates for employee ownership? If such a transition were accomplished, how would you ensure accountability to consumers? To the community?

NOTES

1. Paul Starr, "The Meaning of Privatization," quoted in American Federation of State, County, and Municipal Employees, *Private Profit, Public Risk: The Contracting Out of Professional Services* (Washington, DC: AFSCME, 1986), pp. 4–5.

2. Charles Schultz, *The Public Use of Private Interest* (Washington, DC: Brookings Institution, 1977); Donald Fisk, Herbert Kiesling, and Thomas Muller, *Private Provision of Public Service* (Washington, DC: Urban Institute, 1978); Harry Hatry, *A Review of Private Approaches for the Delivery of Public Services* (Washington, DC: Urban Institute, 1983).

3. David Obsborne and Ted Gaebler, *Reinventing Government* (New York: Addison Wesley, 1992).

4. John Donahue, *The Privatization Decision* (New York: Basic Books, 1989), p. 216.

5. Harry Specht and Mark Courtney, *Unfaithful Angels* (New York: Free Press, 1994), p. 107.

6. Quoted in Bernstein, "Giant Companies Entering Race to Run State Welfare Programs," p. 1.

7. Ibid.

8. See Lawrence S. Lewin, Robert A. Derzon, and Rhea Margulies, "Investor-Owned and Nonprofits Differ in Economic Performance," *Hospitals* (July 1, 1981), pp. 65–69; Robert V. Pattison and Hallie Katz, "Investor-Owned Hospitals and Not-for-Profit Hospitals," *New England Journal of Medicine* (August 11, 1983), pp. 54–65; Robin Eskoz and K. Michael Peddecord, "The Relationship of Hospital Ownership and Service Composition to Hospital Charges," *Health Care Financing Review* (Spring 1985), pp. 125–132; J. Michael Watt et al., "The Comparative Economic Performance of Investor-Owned Chain and Not-for-Profit Hospitals," *New England Journal of Medicine* (January 9, 1986), pp. 356–360; Bradford Gray and Walter McNerney, "For-Profit Enterprise in Health Care: The Institute of Medicine Study," *New England Journal of Medicine* (June 5, 1986), pp. 560–563;

Regina Herzlinger and William Kradker, "Who Profits from Nonprofits?" *Harvard Business Review* (January–February 1987), pp. 554–562.

9. Richard Titmuss, *The Gift Relationship* (New York: Pantheon, 1971), p. 223.

10. Theodore Marmor, Mark Schlesinger, and Richard Smithey, "A New Look at Nonprofits: Health Care Policy in a Competitive Age," *Yale Journal of Regulation* 3 (Spring 1986), p. 320.

11. Clifford Levy and Michael Luo, "New York Medicaid Fraud May Reach Into Billions," *New York Times* (July 18, 2005), p. A1; Clifford Gaul, "Bad Practices Net Hospitals More Money," *Washington Post* (July 24, 2005), p. A1; Charles Duhigg, "At Many Homes, More Profit and Less Nursing," *New York Times* (September 23, 2007), p. A1.

12. Milt Freudenheim, "California Backs Merger of 2 Giant Blue Cross Plans," *New York Times* (November 10, 2004), p. C1.

13. Charles Muntaner et al., "Psychotic Inpatients' Social Class and Their First Admission to State or Private Psychiatric Baltimore Hospitals," *American Journal of Public Health*, 84, no. 2 (February 1994), p. 287.

14. Richard Cloward and Irwin Epstein, "Private Social Welfare's Disengagement from the Poor," in Meyer Zald (ed.), *Social Welfare Institutions* (New York: John Wiley, 1965), pp. 628–629.

15. Emily Friedman, "The 'Dumping' Dilemma," *Hospitals* (September 1, 1982), p. 54.

16. Mark Schlesinger, "The Privatization of Health Care and Physicians' Perceptions of Access to Hospital Services," *The Milbank Quarterly* 65 (1987), p. 40.

17. Gray and McNerney, "For-Profit Enterprise in Health Care," p. 1525.

18. Robert Kuttner, "Columbia/HCA and the Resurgence of the For-Profit Hospital Business," *New England Journal of Medicine* 335, no. 5 (August 1, 1996), pp. 365–366.

19. Anna Amirkhanyan, Hyun Kim, and Kristina Lambright, "Does the Public Sector Outperform the Nonprofit and For-Profit Sectors?" *Journal of Policy Analysis and Management*, 27, 2 (Spring 2008), pp. 326–353.

20. http://www.healthreformgps.org/wp-content/uploads/he08022010_report.pdf

21. U.S. Senate Special Committee on Aging, *Discrimination against the Poor and Disabled in Nursing Homes*, (Washington, DC: U.S. GPO, 1984), p. 25.

22. Ibid., p. 10.

23. Quoted in William Spicer, "The Boom in Building," *Contemporary Administrator* (February 1982), p. 16.

24. "Big Lobbying Spenders in 2007," *Washington Post* (April 15, 2008), p. A13.

25. Arnold Relman, "The New Medical-Industrial Complex," *New England Journal of Medicine* 303, no. 17 (1980), p. 80.

26. Robert Pear, "As Health Law Spurs Mergers, Risks Are Seen," *New York Times*, November 21, 2010, p. A1.

27. Paul Starr, "The Limits of Privatization," in Steve Hanke, *Prospects for Privatization* (New York: Proceedings of the Academy of Political Science, 1987), pp. 82–107.

28. Kuttner, "Columbia/HCA," p. 363.

29. http://www.americaworks.com/index.php?option=com_content&view=article&id=18&Itemid=5

30. Reason Foundation, *Privatization 1992* (Los Angeles: Reason Foundation, 1992), p. 17.
31. David Stoesz, "Human-Service Corporations: New Opportunities in Social Work Administration," *Social Work Administration* 12 (1989), pp. 35–43.
32. Milton Tambor, "Unions," *Encyclopedia of Social Work*, 19th ed. (Washington, DC: National Association of Social Workers, 1995), pp. 2418–2419.
33. Weitzman, *The Scope of Bargaining in Public Employment* (New York: Praeger, 1975), p. 17.
34. Dena Fisher, "Problems for Social Work in a Strike Situation," *Social Work* 32 (May–June 1987), pp. 253–254.
35. Jerry Wurf, "Labor Movement, Social Work Fighting Similar Battles," *NASW News* 25, no. 12 (December 1980), p. 7.
36. http://www.nytimes.com/2011/01/22/business/22union.html?_r=1
37. Bradford Plumer, "Labor's Love Lost," *The New Republic*, 238, 4,834 (April 23, 2008), p. 27.
38. Leslie Alexander et al., "Social Workers in Unions: A Survey," *Social Work* 25 (May 1980), p. 222.
39. Ernie Lightman, "Professionalization, Bureaucratization, and Unionization in Social Work," *Social Service Review* 56, no. 1 (March 1982), p. 130.
40. Gary Shaffer, "Labor Relations and the Unionization of Professional Social Workers," *Journal of Education for Social Work* 15 (Winter 1979), p. 82.
41. Jacob Hacker, *The Divided Welfare State* (New York: Cambridge University Press, 2002), p. 22.
42. Ibid., pp. 51, 339.
43. Jinlay Lewis, "CEOs' Presence in Bush Party Draws Attention to Their Pay," *San Diego Union* (January 13, 1992), p. E3.
44. Fred Barnes, "The Zillionaires Club," *The New Republic* (January 29, 1990), p. 23.
45. Jacqueline Salmon, "Minorities Grab Fundraisers' Notice," *Washington Post* (November 7, 2004), p. F8.
46. Sheila Kamerman, "The New Mixed Economy of Welfare," *Social Work* 28 (January–February 1983), p. 76.
47. Paul Starr, "The Meaning of Privatization," and MDRC Bendick, "Privatizing the Delivery of Social Welfare Service" in *Working Paper 6* (Washington, DC: National Conference on Social Welfare, 1985); David Stoesz, "Privatization: Reforming the Welfare State," *Journal of Sociology and Social Welfare* 16 (Summer 1987), p. 139; Mimi Abramovitz, "The Privatization of the Welfare State," *Social Work* 31, no.4 (July–August 1986), pp. 257–264.
48. Neil Gilbert, *Capitalism and the Welfare State* (New Haven, CT: Yale University Press, 1983).
49. David Stoesz, "Corporate Welfare," *Social Work* 31, no. 4 (July–August 1986), p. 86; "Corporate Health Care and Social Welfare," *Health and Social Work* (Summer 1986), p. 158; "The Gray Market," *Journal of Gerontological Social Work* 16 (1989), p. 31.
50. Michael Misshauk, *Management: Theory and Practice* (Boston: Little, Brown, 1979), p. 6.
51. Melvin Anshen, *Managing the Socially Responsible Corporation* (New York: Macmillan, 1974), p. 5.
52. Steven Lydenberg, *Rating America's Corporate Conscience* (Reading, MA: Addison-Wesley, 1986).
53. http://www.sa-intl.org/index.cfm?fuseaction=Page.viewPage&pageId=472
54. Human Rights Campaign, *Corporate Equality Index* (Washington, DC: author, 2010).
55. Theodore Purcell, "Management and the 'Ethical' Investors," in S. Prakash Sethi and Carl Swanson (eds.), *Private Enterprise and Public Purpose* (New York: John Wiley, 1981), pp. 296–297.
56. Lloyd Kurtz, Steven Lydenberg, and Peter Kinder, "The Domini Social Index," in Peter Kinder, Steven Lydenberg, and Amy Domini (eds.), *The Social Investment Almanac* (New York: Henry Holt, 1992).
57. http://www.enterprisecommunity.com/solutions-and-innovation/enterprise-green-communitiescient
58. http://www.lisc.org/section/aboutus/history
59. Irving Kristol, "Charity and Business Shouldn't Mix," *The New York Times* (October 17, 1982), p. 18.
60. Lawrence Fouraker and Graham Allison, "Foreword," in John Dunlop (ed.), *Business and Public Policy* (Cambridge, MA: Harvard University Press, 1980), p. ix.
61. Robert Pear, "Health Industry Bidding to Hire Medicare Chief," *New York Times* (December 3, 2003), p. A1.
62. Judy Sarasohn, "Special Interests," *Washington Post* (June 24, 2004), p. A23.
63. Robert Pear, "Agency Sees Withholding of Medicare Data from Congress as Illegal," *New York Times* (May 4, 2004), p. A17.
64. Sheryl Stolberg and Robert Pear, "Mysterious Fax Adds to Intrigue over Drug Bill," *New York Times* (March 18, 2004), p. A1.
65. Amy Goldstein, "Foster: White House Had Role in Withholding Medicare Data," *Washington Post* (March 19, 2004), p. A2.
66. Cheryl Stolberg, "2 Decline to Testify on Drug Cost," *New York Times* (April 2, 2004), p. A15.
67. Dan Eggen," Interest Groups Rally for a Big Finish on Health-Care Reform," *Washington Post*, February 28, 2010, p. A3.
68. David Kirkpatrick, "On Health, Daschle Has Ear of White House and Industry," *New York Times*, August 23, 2009, p. A1.
69. Nancy Amidei, "How to End Poverty: Next Steps," *Food Monitor* (Winter 1988), p. 52.
70. Robert Reich, *The Next American Frontier* (New York: Times Books, 1983), p. 223.
71. Ibid., pp. 247–248.
72. Kevin Phillips, *Staying on Top: The Business Case for a National Industrial Policy* (New York: Random House, 1984), pp. 5–6.
73. Yeheskel Hasenfeld, "The Changing Context of Human-Services Administration," *Social Work* 29, no. 4 (November–December 1984), p. 524.
74. Barlett and Steele, *Critical Condition*, p. 170.
75. Steve Lohr, "The Disparate Consensus on Health Care for All," *New York Times* (December 6, 2004), p. C16.
76. Lyndsey Layton and Christopher Lee, "Collectors Cost IRS More Than They Raise," *Washington Post*, April 15, 2008, p. A1.
77. Richard Oppel, "Private Prisons Found to Offer Little in Savings," *New York Times*, May 19, 2011, p. A1.

78. Ron Nixon, "Government Pays More in Contracts, Study Finds," *New York Times*, September 13, 2011, p. A16.
79. http://www.gao.gov/products/GAO-11-409T
80. Jerry Markon, "Medicare Fraud Crackdown Naps 91 in 8 Cities Across U.S." *New York Times*, September 8, 2011, p. A3.
81. Social Security Administration, *Social Security Bulletin, Annual Statistical Supplement* (Washington, DC: U.S. Government Printing Office, 1994), p. 140.
82. http://www.cms.gov/Research-Statistics-Data-and-Systems/Statistics-Trends-and-Reports/NationalHealthExpendData/Downloads/proj2010.pdf
83. Donald Barlett and James Steele, *Critical Condition* (New York: Doubleday, 2004), p. 94.
84. David Stoesz, "Human-Service Corporations and the Welfare State," *Transaction/Society* 16 (1989), pp. 80–91.
85. Bureau of the Census, *Statistical Abstract of the United States, 1986* (Washington, DC: U.S. Government Printing Office, 1986).
86. U.S. Department of Commerce, *1982 U.S. Industrial Outlook for 200 Industries with Projections for 1986* (Washington, DC: U.S. Government Printing Office, 1982), p. 406.
87. Jerry Avorn, "Nursing Home Infections-The Context," *New England Journal of Medicine* (September 24, 1981), p. 759.
88. Blyskal, "Gray Gold," *Forbes* (November 23, 1981), p. 84.
89. Quoted in W. Spicer, "The Boom in Building," *Contemporary Administrator* (February 1982), pp. 13–14.
90. "Beverly Enterprises" and "Tenet Healthcare Corp," Standard & Poor's Stock Report (October 1995), p. 89.
91. Donald Barlett and James Steele, *Critical Condition* (New York: Doubleday, 2004), pp. 106–108.
92. http://www.hcr-manorcare.com/StockBondHolders/CarlyleClosing.aspx
93. Richard Thaler and Cass Sunstein, *Nudge* (New Haven, CT: Yale University Press, 2008).
94. Azam Ahmed, "CVS Caremark Agrees to Buy a Medicare D Unit," *New York Times*, January 1, 2011, p. B1.
95. Dina ElBoghdady, "CVS Caremark Will Refund $5 million to Medicare Customers," *New York Times*, January 13, 2012, p. A17.
96. B. Gray, "An Introduction to the New Health Care for Profit," in B. Gray (ed.), *The New Health Care for Profit* (Washington, DC: National Academy Press, 1983), p. 2.
97. "Columbia/HCA" *Standard & Poor's Stock Reports* (October 1996), p. 80.
98. Barlett and Steele, *Critical Condition*, pp. 70–71.
99. Brooke Masters, "Hospital Chain Goes Private for $33 Billion," *Washington Post* (July 25, 2006), p. D1.
100. National Industry Council for HMO Development, *Ten Year Report 1971–1983* (Washington, DC: Author, 1983).
101. "PacifiCare," "United HealthCare Corp.," and "CIGNA," *Standard & Poor's Stock Reports* (October 1996), p. 102.
102. Milt Freudenheim, "California Backs Merger of 2 Giant Blue Cross Plans," *New York Times* (November 10, 2004), p. C1.
103. Milt Freudenheim, "UnitedHealth to Buy PacifiCare in Push into Medicare," *New York Times* (July 2, 2005), p. C1.
104. Karen Kornbluh, "Americans Must Work Harder to Achieve the American Dream," (Washington, DC: New America Foundation, July 15, 2004), p. 2.
105. "Home Health Care of America," *Standard & Poor's Stock Reports* (March 1984, October 1995).
106. "Digest of Earnings Reports," *The Wall Street Journal* (August 13, 1987), p. 41.
107. Stephen Boland, "Prisons for Profit," unpublished manuscript, San Diego State University, School of Social Work, 1987, pp. 5–6.
108. Ellen Reese, *They Say Cut Back, We Say Fight Back*! (New York: Russell Sage Foundation, 2011, pp. 74–75.
109. Jason DeParle, American Dream (New York: 2004, ch. 14).
110. Specht and Courtney, *Unfaithful Angels*.
111. Philip Brown and Robert Barker, "Confronting the Threat of Private Practice," *Journal of Social Work Education* 31, no. 1 (Winter 1995), p. 106.
112. Srinika Jayaratne, Kristine Siefert, and Wayne Chess, "Private and Agency Practitioners: Some Data and Observations," *Social Service Review* 62 (June 1988), p. 331.
113. Margaret Gibelman and Philip Schervish, *What We Earn: 1993 NASW Salary Survey* (Washington, DC: NASW, 1993), pp. 25, 27.
114. http://workforce.socialworkers.org/studies/profiles/Private%20Practice%20Solo%20and%20Group.pdf
115. Diane Vinokur-Kaplan, Srinika Jayaratne, and Wayne Chess, "Job Satisfaction and Retention of Social Workers in Public Agencies, Non-Profit Agencies and Private Practice," *Administration in Social Work* 18, no. 3 (1994), p. 103.
116. Practice Research Network, Private Practice (Washington, DC: National Association of Social Workers, 2003).
117. Gibelman and Schervish, *What We Earn*, p. 32.
118. Vinokur-Kaplan, Jayaratne, and Chess, "Job Satisfaction," p. 103.
119. Ibid., p. 329.
120. Ibid.
121. Donald Feldstein, "Debate on Private Practice," *Social Work* 22, no. 3 (1977), p. 4.
122. Patricia Kelley and Paul Alexander, "Part-Time Private Practice: Practical and Ethical Considerations," *Social Work* 30, no. 3 (May–June 1985), p. 255.
123. N. T. Edwards, "The Survival of Structure and Function in Private Practice," *Journal of the Otto Rank Association* 13 (1979), pp. 12, 15.
124. Jayaratne, Sacks, and Chess, "Private Practice May Be Good for Your Health and Well-Being," *Social Work* 36 (May 1991), pp. 228–229.
125. Franklin Chu and Sharland Trotter, *The Madness Establishment* (New York: Grossman, 1974), p. 61.
126. Kelley and Alexander, "Part-Time Private Practice," p. 254.
127. David Gelman, "Growing Pains for the Shrinks," *Newsweek* (December 14, 1987), p. 71.
128. Milt Freudenheim, "Adjusting, More MD's Add MBA," *New York Times*, September 6, 2011, p. B1).

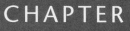
The Making of Governmental Policy

Source: J. Scott Applewhite/AP Images

This chapter describes the process by which governmental policy is made, including its phases, the importance of stratification, and the role of influential organizations. The public policy process is important because many social welfare policies are established by government, and decisions by federal and state agencies have a direct bearing on the administration and funding of social welfare programs that assist millions of Americans and employ thousands of human service professionals. Democracies vary depending on the types of representative government adopted by democratic nations. Representative democracy, as outlined in the Constitution of the United States, is often contrasted with parliamentary democracy, where the executive and legislative branches of government are integrated, expediting passage of legislation. The parliamentary system would be best approximated in America when one political party controls both houses of Congress as well as the presidency. Parliamentary forms of democracy are quite prevalent, whether they are unicameral (single legislative body) or bicameral (two-chamber bodies). Most of the welfare states of northern Europe have parliamentary forms of government, suggesting that this is more consistent with progressive values. Either form of democracy—representative or parliamentary—has an overarching benefit: As Amartya Sen has observed, there are no instances of famines within truly democratic governments, nor wars fought among them.[1]

During the early twentieth century, advocates of social justice believed that state control of all facets of society would usher in an era of true economic and social equality. However, excesses of Communist regimes spelled their demise; only North Korea and Cuba represent this form of governance. Other undemocratic forms of governance include theocracy, approximated in Iran, and monarchy, still evident in Saudi Arabia. While many nations march to adopt democratic governance, there is much debate about the outcomes with respect to social welfare.

In an open, democratic society, **public policy** should reflect the interests of all citizens to the greatest extent possible. For a variety of reasons, however, this ideal is not realized. Although many Americans have the right to participate in the establishment of public policy, they often fail to do so. Policy made and implemented by the governmental sector may be perceived as being too far removed from the daily activities of citizens, or too complicated to warrant the type of

coordinated and persistent efforts necessary to alter it. Moreover, many Americans with a direct interest in governmental policy are not in a position to shape it, as in the case of children and those with emotional impairments, who must rely on others to speak on their behalf. Consequently, governmental policy does not necessarily reflect the interests—indeed, the welfare—of the public, even though it is intended to do so. The discrepancy between what is constitutionally prescribed in making public policy and the way decisions are actually made leads to two quite different understandings of the policy process. For welfare professionals concerned with instituting change in social welfare, a technical understanding of how policy is made is essential. It is equally important for them to recognize that the policy process is skewed to favor powerful officials and their interests rather than those who lack influence, a problem that has been exacerbated by the Supreme Court's *Citizens United* decision, which permitted unlimited campaign contributions. Because social workers and their clients tend to be comparatively powerless, a critical analysis of the policy process is essential.

Technical Aspects of the Policy Process

Public policy in the United States is made through a deliberative process that involves the two bodies of elected officials that make up a legislature. This applies both to the federal government and to the states—with the singular exception of Nebraska, which has only one deliberative body, a unicameral legislature. Initially, a policy concern of a legislator is developed into a legislative proposal and usually printed in the *Congressional Record*. Because every legislator has a party affiliation and a constituency, legislators' proposals tend to reflect the priorities of those stakeholders. Often, several legislators will prepare proposals that are important to similar constituencies. Increasingly, policy institutes are instrumental in developing and vetting legislative options. Through a subtle interaction of ideas, the media, and legislative leadership, one proposal— usually a synthesis of several—is presented as a policy alternative. Other legislators are asked to sign on as cosponsors, and the measure is officially introduced. After the proposed bill is assigned to the appropriate committee, public hearings are held, and the committee convenes to "mark up" the legislation so that it incorporates the concerns of committee members who have heard the public testimony. Under propitious circumstances, the committee then forwards the legislation to the full body of the chamber that must approve it. While it is being approved by the full body of one chamber, a similar bill is often introduced in the other chamber, where it begins a parallel process. Differences between the measures approved by the two chambers are ironed out in a conference committee. The proposed legislation becomes law after it is signed by the chief executive, or, if the executive vetoes the bill, after it is passed by a two-thirds vote of each legislative chamber. This process is always tortuous and usually unsuccessful. The eventual enactment of legislation under these conditions is a true testament to legislative leadership. A third branch of government, the judiciary, assesses legal challenges to existing legislation. In the upper levels of the judiciary, members can hold their posts for life. The primary features of the policy process of the federal government are illustrated in Figure 8.1.

There are several critical junctures in a proposal's passage into legislation—or oblivion. First, most of the details in any proposal are worked out at the legislative body's committee or subcommittee level. Different versions are negotiated and reconciled at the "mark-up session," during which committee members and staff write their changes into the draft. This stage offers an important opportunity to

inject minor, and sometimes major, changes into the substance of the bill or to alter the intent of the bill's originator(s). National advocacy organizations, such as the Child Welfare League of America, often draft model bills that can be introduced in state legislatures to advance the well-being of vulnerable families. Of course, conservatives also use this method. The American Legislative Exchange Council (ALEC) writes ready-to-introduce bills that oppose unions, limit environmental regulation, and reduce taxes for corporations and the wealthy.[2] In 2011 alone, ALEC introduced 60 bills in the Virginia legislature.[3] Second, the viability of a proposal depends to a large extent on the numbers and influence of the witnesses who testify regarding its merits at subcommittee and committee hearings. Obviously, public testimony will work to the advantage of well-financed interests; such interests can afford to pay lobbyists to do this professionally, whereas advocates for the disadvantaged often rely on volunteers. Nevertheless, the public testimony stage is an important opportunity to clarify for the record the position that human service professionals may take on a given proposal. Third, budget considerations figure heavily in the likelihood of a bill's passage. Other federal spending priorities, coupled with the unwillingness of elected officials to raise taxes, increase the likelihood that legislation will be underfunded or even passed with no additional funding whatsoever. Innovative revenue "enhancers," such as earmarked taxes or

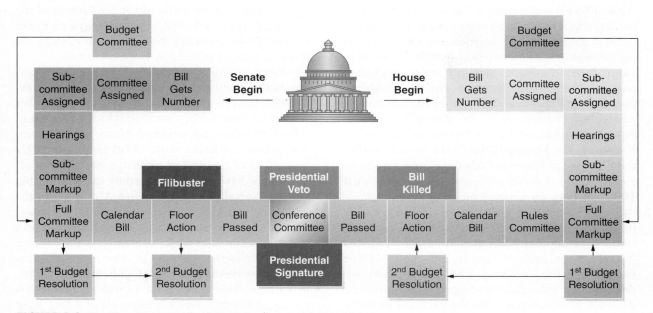

FIGURE 8.1 The Steps Necessary to Get a Policy Proposal Enacted into Law

user fees, can make a proposal more acceptable during periods of fiscal belt-tightening. The policy process, then, is not necessarily intended to facilitate the passage of a proposal into law. Of the tens of thousands of bills presented in Congress, only 10 percent were reported out of committee, and only 5 percent became law.[4]

The decision-making process is defined by *Robert's Rules of Order*,[5] a text that lays out in detail the rules for democratic deliberation. Although *Robert's Rules* can appear obtuse, its value should not be underappreciated. Those who have mastered "the means of deliberation" are one step ahead of the rest of the crowd in seeing their ideas become public policy. Social activists who are optimistic that their proposal is working its way steadily through the legislative minefield may find their hopes dashed by an adroit procedural move on the part of an opponent who sidetracks a bill until the next legislative session. The elaborate rules of decision making can be compounded by the traditions of deliberative bodies. In recent years, the U.S. Senate has effectively required a 60 vote majority to pass legislation, even though such a super-majority is not explicated in the Constitution.[6] Understandably, such procedures may tend to deter citizens from participating in the democratic process. Yet, there are means that public policy novices can employ to become better acquainted with the ways in which elected officials go about the public's business. Citizen advocate organizations, such as the League of Women Voters and Common Cause, can be helpful in making social policy more responsive to the public.

Congress and the legislatures of the larger states employ staff members as technical experts to aid in decision making. Staff reports researched as part of committee deliberations can be valuable in that they often provide the most up-to-date data on particular programs or issues. A good example of this type of resource is the *Overview of Entitlement Programs*, also known as the *Green Book*,[7] used by the U.S. House Ways and Means Committee in its consideration of social programs. Begun in the early 1980s to help committee members comprehend the vast number of social programs under their jurisdiction—Social Security, Medicare, child welfare, Temporary Assistance for Needy Families (TANF), Supplemental Security Income (SSI), and Unemployment Compensation, among others—this resource is essential reading for social program analysts. In recent years, the *Green Book* has been available online, making it more accessible.

The federal budget process begins each February when the president presents his or her proposed budget and culminates months later when he or she signs or vetoes the Congressional budget reconciliation bill that authorizes the budgets for 13 separate agencies. Typically, the ideal federal budget process is compromised in two ways: (1) a budget is not agreed upon, in which case a continuing budget resolution is passed extending funding at current levels until a complete budget is enacted; and (2) the amount of funds appropriated is less than that authorized, leaving programs with revenue shortfalls. This means that many welfare programs that receive discretionary funds are often beset with budgets that are not timely or adequately funded. The exceptions are social entitlements, such as Social Security, Medicare, and Medicaid, which are not subject to the budget cycle.[8]

A Critical Analysis of the Policy Process

The public policy process often proves frustrating for social activists. Despite the most urgent of needs, the best of intentions, and the most strategic of proposals, the social welfare program output derived from the legislative process often appears far short of what is required. Yet to conclude from this that public policy simply does not work would be an overstatement. A critical approach to public policy helps explain some of the limitations of the technical approach and suggests ways to make the legislative process a more effective strategy for those concerned with furthering social justice.

From a critical perspective, the policy process consists of a series of discrete decisions, each heavily influenced by money and connections—in other words, by power. The extent to which governmental policy reflects the concerns of one group of citizens while neglecting those of others is ultimately a question of power and influence. Several schools of thought have emerged regarding the relationship between social policy and power. According to the *elitist* orientation, individuals representing a "power structure" control social policy in order to maintain a status quo that advantages them and, in the process, excludes marginal groups. In contrast, a *pluralist* orientation assumes that social policy in a heterogeneous democratic polity is the sum total of trade-offs among different interest groups, all of which have an equal opportunity to participate. At the program level, *incrementalists* have suggested that the more important questions about social policy are the product of bit-by-bit additions to the public social infrastructure. As Charles Lindblom observed, the great bulk of legislative decision making is "incremental," representing only marginal improvements in social policy already in place.[9] Most social policy changes consist of relatively minor technical adjustments in program administration and budgeting.

As counterpoint, other scholars have focused on "paradigm shifts" through which major changes, such as the inception of Social Security in 1935 and the devolution of welfare to the states through the Personal Responsibility and Work Opportunity Reconciliation Act of 1996, have altered the very foundation of social policy. It can be argued that, in the final analysis, there are no new ideas, but there *are* new governmental policies that have enormous implications for certain groups. Few could dispute that the Social Security Act and the Civil Rights Act were radical departures from the status quo and substantially changed the circumstances of older people and African Americans, respectively. With regard to program evaluation, *rationalists* have used the methods of social science to determine objectively the extent to which policy changes bring about intended outcomes. By contrast, *social activists* use the political process as the measure of program performance, assuming that the optimum in program assessment is continued recertification and refunding by public decision makers. Most recently, *populists* who were concerned about how public policy affected typical Americans registered their influence through the Tea Party movement during the 2010 midterm elections. As might be expected in the investigation of any phenomenon as complex as social policy, a comprehensive explanation is likely to incorporate elements of more than one school of thought.

Underlying these varied approaches to interpreting social policy are assumptions about its very nature. In this regard, two orientations have become prominent. The first orientation, the *institutional conception of social welfare* holds that social policy reflects steady progress toward a desirable condition of human welfare for all. Most liberal analysts who have promoted the welfare state as an ideal have adopted an institutional perspective. Believers in the institutional conception of social welfare, liberals, expect that the national government will progressively expand social programs until, eventually, the basic needs of the entire population are guaranteed

as rights of citizenship. A competing orientation is the *residual conception of social welfare*, which holds that people in need should first rely on the labor market, then on family and friends, and next on voluntary organizations in the community, but should rely on government social programs only as a last resort and only temporarily. The residual conception, favored by conservatives, emphasizes self-sufficiency, neighborliness, and limited government assistance. To the extent that ideology is congruent with the primary political parties, the institutional conception has been advanced by Democrats, while the residual conception has been favored by Republicans.

Historically, two basic forms of rationality have served to justify social policy: bureaucratic rationality and market rationality.[10] **Bureaucratic rationality** refers to the ordering of social affairs by governmental agencies. According to bureaucratic rationality, civil servants can objectively define social problems, develop strategies to address them, and deploy programs in an equitable and nonpartisan manner. Bureaucratic rationality takes its authority from the power vested in the state, and bureaucracies have become predominant in social welfare at the federal (through the Department of Health and Human Services) and state levels. **Market rationality** refers to a reliance on the rule of "supply and demand" as a means for distributing goods and services. While on the surface this may appear to be antithetical to the meaning of rationality, a high degree of social ordering in fact occurs within capitalism. Such organization is implicit in the very idea of a market, entailing a large number of prospective consumers that businesses seek to serve. In a modern market economy, the success of a business depends on the ability of managers to survey the market, merchandise goods and services, shape consumer preferences through advertising, and reduce competition by buying or outmaneuvering competitors. Of course, market rationality is not a panacea for providing social welfare because the marketplace is not particularly responsive to those who may not fully participate in it, such as minorities, women, children, the elderly, or people with disabilities. Yet market rationality cannot be dismissed as a rationale for delivering social welfare benefits. Approximately half of Americans get their health and welfare needs met through employer-provided benefits that are ultimately derived from the market.[11]

An important aspect of governmental decision making addresses disadvantaged populations. It is entirely possible, of course, for social policy to introduce radical change that is based on data but generates mixed effects with respect to the well-being of important groups. The 1996 welfare reform legislation, for example, ended the 60-year entitlement to income for poor families on the basis of evaluations of state welfare demonstrations allegedly showing that states could provide public assistance better if the federal government were not involved. Several years later, the results of welfare reform were mixed. Those beneficiaries who had entered the labor market earned low wages, but the Earned Income Tax Credit boosted most above the poverty line. More disturbing was the subgroup that had been diverted from public assistance. Caseloads dropped more than half during the 1990s; however, most of those who left were not employed full time, leaving their fate uncertain. Unfortunately, the scanty research on "leavers" failed to clarify the matter.[12] The Great Recession had a peculiar effect on public welfare: States drove down caseloads for Temporary Assistance for Needy Families (TANF), for which they shared half the cost, leaving desperate families to make up the shortfall through food stamps, a program funded entirely by the federal government.[13] As the TANF example illustrates, the degree of change represented by any change in public policy, the extent to which it is rational with respect to bureaucratic or market criteria, and the consequences for disadvantaged populations make the social policy process a dynamic and sometimes volatile area of activity.

The Policy Process

A critical analysis of the policy process highlights the social stratification of the society, the phases through which policy is formulated, and the organizational entities that have become instrumental in the decision-making process. This section will describe and chart these factors in order to demonstrate how social policy is created in the United States.

Social Stratification

A variety of **social stratification** models differentiate groups with influence from those lacking it. A stratification familiar to Americans defines three parts: an upper class, a middle class, and a lower class. Placement of individuals in the appropriate class is usually made on the basis of income, education, and occupational status. This three-part stratification is limited in its capacity to explain very much about U.S. social welfare, however. If asked, most Americans identify themselves as middle class, even if by objective criteria they belong to another stratum. Further, the designation **lower class** is not particularly informative about the social conditions of a large portion of the population with which human service professionals are concerned.[14]

A more informative stratification consists of six social groups, which are differentiated according to wealth, internal solidarity, and control over the environment, as elaborated in Table 8.1.[15] As this stratification model indicates, some groups—the wealthy and executives—are able to influence the environment, but other groups—the working/welfare poor and the underclass—have virtually no influence. This distinction has important implications for social welfare, because those who are of lower status tend to be the recipients of welfare benefits that are the product of a social policy process in which they do not participate. The way in which these various groups influence the social policy process will be discussed in greater detail in the following section.

With these clarifications in mind, the policy process can be divided into four stages: formulation, legislation, implementation, and evaluation.

Formulation

Before the nineteenth century it would have been accurate to state that policy formulation in this country began with the legislative phase. With the advent of industrialization, many complexities were injected into the society, and in time special institutions emerged to assist the legislature in evaluating social conditions and preparing policy options. Eventually, even constitutionally established bodies, such as Congress, lapsed into a reactive role, largely responsive to other entities that formulated policy.[16] Initially, institutions of higher education provided technical intelligence to assist the legislative branch, and some still do. For example, the University of Wisconsin's Institute for Research on Poverty provides analyses on important welfare policies.[17]

TABLE 8.1 Social Stratification of the Population

Name of Group	Examples	Characteristics
The wealthy	Upper elites, the independently wealthy, large stockholders	Ownership of resources is the main source of power; control over goals is very high, but control over means is through executives.
Executives	Top administrators in business, government, the military	Organizational solidarity facilitates effective policy implementation; some control over goals and a high degree of control over means.
Professionals	Middle-level managers, technical experts, private practitioners, community leaders	Environment encourages limited solidarity; control over means is high, and goal setting can be influenced if collective action is undertaken.
Organized workers	Semiskilled workers, civic and political clubs, social action organizations	Environment encourages solidarity; groups have some control over the means by which goals are realized.
Working/welfare poor	Temporary and part-time workers earning minimum wage and who use welfare as a wage supplement	A subjugated position with no control over the environment; frustration is shared and irrational, explosive behavior results.
Underclass	Unemployables and illiterates; disabled substance abusers; itinerants, drifters, migrant workers	A subjugated position with no control over the environment; a sense of failure coupled with limited mobility reduces social interaction and leads to retreatism.

Source: Dexter C. Dunphy, *The Primary Group: A Handbook for Analysis and Field Research* (Englewood Cliffs, NJ: Prentice Hall, 1972), pp. 42–44. Copyright © 1972. Reprinted by permission of Prentice Hall, Inc.

That legislators at the federal level, as well as those in the larger states, would rely on experts to assess social conditions and develop policy options is not surprising, given the fact that each legislator must attend to multiple committee and subcommittee assignments requiring expertise in particular matters, while at the same time contend with the general concerns of a large constituency. As a result of competing demands, legislators pay somewhat less attention to the policy process than their public image would suggest, leaving much of the work to their staffs. Even then, public policy tends to get short shrift. Because reelection is a primary concern for legislators, their staffs are frequently assigned to solve the relatively minor problems presented by constituents. In fact, placating unhappy constituents has become so prominent a concern that one legislative observer notes that constituency services—called "casework" by elected officials—have become "more important than issues" for representatives.[18]

Gradually, institutions have begun to specialize in providing the social intelligence necessary for policy formulation. These policy institutes, sometimes called think tanks, now wield substantial influence in the social policy process. Not unlike prestigious colleges, think tanks maintain multidisciplinary staffs of scholars who prepare position papers on a range of social issues. With multimillion-dollar budgets and connections with national and state capitals, think tanks are well positioned to shape social policy. Generally, financial support for these institutes comes from wealthy individuals and corporations with particular ideological inclinations that are evidenced by the types of think tanks they support. Several prominent policy institutes are located on the ideological continuum in Figure 8.2.

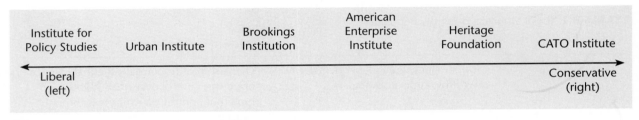

| Institute for Policy Studies | Urban Institute | Brookings Institution | American Enterprise Institute | Heritage Foundation | CATO Institute |

Liberal (left) — Conservative (right)

FIGURE 8.2 Place on the Ideological Continuum of Six Policy Institutes

Legislation

Much public policy work is conducted by federal legislators who are appointed to committees and subcommittees on the basis of their particular interests. An important and often unappreciated component of the legislative phase is the role played by the staffs of committees and subcommittees. Former legislative staffers are definitive experts in the subject area of a committee and are prized as lobbyists for special interest groups.[19] As a result of the increasing complexity of the policy process, the number of legislative staff members has multiplied. In the late 2010, 24,000 staff members served Congress, more than double the number in the late 1970s.[20] Committees are the locus of testimony on issues, and legislative hearings provide an opportunity for the official and sometimes the only input from the public on some matters. Accordingly, representatives of advocacy groups make it a point to testify before certain committees in order to ensure that their views are heard. At the federal level, the primary Senate committees are Finance, Agriculture, Appropriations, and Health, Education, Labor and Pensions, while those in the House are Ways and Means, Economic and Educational Opportunities, and Appropriations.

Throughout the process, representatives of special interests attempt to shape any given proposal so that it is more congruent with priorities of their members. Special interests can be classified according to the nature of their activities: During legislative sessions, **lobbyists** are hired to influence legislation valued by clients. As noted in Table 8.2, business interests dominated in recent decades, especially in regards to health care.

The beneficiaries are lobbying firms who have done exceedingly well during the same period, as shown in Table 8.3.

During elections, political action committees (PACs) campaign on behalf of specific candidates. Their contributions are limited and must be reported to the Federal Election Commission. In recent decades, substantial funds have been expended in order to influence elections for the purpose of shaping public policy. Contributions are made to political parties and candidates who take positions that are congruent with a donor's interests. As a result, larger contributors

Spotlight 8.1

THE POLICY PROCESS

Public policy in the United States is made through a deliberative process that involves the U.S. Senate and House of Representatives. You can learn more about each of these bodies of elected officials at their respective websites: www.senate.gov and www.house.gov. For a detailed explanation of the legislative process and how laws are made, visit http://thomas.loc.gov/home/lawsmade.toc.html. Political action committees (PACs) play an influential part in decisions on public policy. In the United States, PACs represent almost every group or interest imaginable. To review the various PACs, go to the Google search engine (www.google.com) and type in the words *political action committee*.

TABLE 8.2 Top Spenders, 1998–2012

U.S. Chamber of Commerce	$901,195,680
General Electric	$278,470,000
American Medical Assn	$277,757,500
American Hospital Assn	$229,264,136
Pharmaceutical Rsrch & Mfrs of America	$228,433,920
AARP	$220,332,064
National Assn of Realtors	$204,335,133
Blue Cross/Blue Shield	$196,908,552
Northrop Grumman	$184,925,253
Exxon Mobil	$179,292,742
Edison Electric Institute	$169,526,789
Verizon Communications	$168,877,933
Boeing Co	$167,959,310
Business Roundtable	$166,920,000
Lockheed Martin	$161,930,008
AT&T Inc	$149,019,336
Southern Co	$141,200,694
National Cable & Telecommunications Assn	$136,500,000
General Motors	$133,054,170
National Assn of Broadcasters	$129,600,000

Source: Center for Responsive Politics. Retrieved November 2012 from http://www.opensecrets.org. Used by permission.

TABLE 8.3 Top 10 Lobbying Firms, 1998–2012

Firm	Total
Patton Boggs LLP	$474,947,000
Akin, Gump et al	$384,095,000
Cassidy & Assoc	$356,922,100
Van Scoyoc Assoc	$302,228,000
Williams & Jensen	$217,704,000
Ernst & Young	$185,126,737
Holland & Knight	$171,414,544
Quinn Gillespie & Assoc	$159,548,500
Hogan & Hartson	$154,633,907
Brownstein, Hyatt et al	$148,480,000

Source: Open Secrets/Center for Responsive Politics, downloaded November 2012: http://www.opensecrets.org/lobby/top.php?indexType=I

tend to prefer one political party over another by channeling contributions through PACs, as evident in Table 8.4. In national politics, the key to influence is choreographing the resources of PACs, soft money, and lobbyists to attain party objectives.

Advocacy groups are able to influence policy indirectly by establishing 527 Committees (named for the Internal Revenue Service code that sanctions them) that advocate for specific causes. As such, 527s are prohibited from funding specific candidates or political parties (see Table 8.5).

Over time, lobbying and campaign contributions are used to redefine politics and policy. Well choreographed, significant changes in social policy have been achieved, and these have affected social welfare. For example, having secured control of the three branches of the federal government after the

2002 election, Republicans viewed consolidation of their power as the next goal. Strategists from the Right speculated that this could be achieved by bankrolling campaigns, coordinating lobbying, and investing in conservative think tanks. Ultimately, the objective was an era of political dominance that would rival—and reverse—the legislative triumphs of the New Deal coalition that engineered the American welfare state.[21] With the election of George W. Bush, the prospect of permanent conservative dominance in social policy appeared a distinct possibility. "The right has out-organized, out-fought and out-thought liberal America over the past 40 years. And the left still shows no real sign of knowing how to fight back," noted two British journalists.

> In theory, liberals have more than enough brain and brawn to match conservatives. The great liberal universities and foundations have infinitely more resources than the American Enterprise Institute and its allies. But the conservatives have always been more dogged. The Ford Foundation is as liberal as Heritage is conservative, but there is no doubt which is the more ruthless in its cause.[22]

Scrambling to regain influence in domestic policy, a group of philanthropists established the Phoenix Group to encourage innovative thinking among Progressives. Tycoons George Soros and Peter Lewis "had come to view progressive politics

TABLE 8.4 Top 20 Political Action Committee (PAC) Contributors to Federal Candidates, 2011–2012

PAC Name	Total Amount	Dem Pct	Repub Pct
National Assn of Realtors	$2,886,331	45%	54%
National Beer Wholesalers Assn	$2,721,000	41%	59%
Honeywell International	$2,671,659	39%	61%
Operating Engineers Union	$2,486,110	81%	19%
Intl Brotherhood of Electrical Workers	$2,298,850	97%	3%
American Assn for Justice	$2,264,000	96%	3%
AT&T Inc	$2,235,050	34%	65%
American Bankers Assn	$2,217,950	20%	80%
Plumbers/Pipefitters Union	$2,007,000	94%	6%
Northrop Grumman	$1,984,400	40%	60%
American Fedn of St/Cnty/Munic Employees	$1,974,725	99%	0%
Every Republican is Crucial PAC	$1,971,000	0%	100%
Lockheed Martin	$1,950,500	40%	60%
National Auto Dealers Assn	$1,894,000	28%	72%
Credit Union National Assn	$1,859,650	49%	51%
American Crystal Sugar	$1,776,000	57%	42%
International Assn of Fire Fighters	$1,748,100	85%	15%
New York Life Insurance	$1,736,750	45%	55%
Boeing Co	$1,700,000	40%	60%
Machinists/Aerospace Workers Union	$1,688,500	97%	2%

Source: Open Secrets/Center for Responsive Politics. Retrieved November 2012 from www.opensecrets.org. Used by permission.

TABLE 8.5 Top Contributors to 527 Committees, 2012 Election Cycle

Committee	Receipts ($ millions)	Expenditures ($ millions)
ActBlue	11.6	10.2
College Republicans	9.2	9.7
National Com. Citizens United	8.1	7.9
EMILY's List	7.7	6.1
SEIU	6.1	7.4
Plumbers/Pipefitters Union	4.7	3.9
Gay & Lesbian Victory Fund	3.8	3.9
GOPAC	3.3	3.3
New Conservative Coalition	3.0	2.7
Intl. Brotherhood Elec. Workers	2.8	3.2

Source: Open Secrets/Center for Responsive Politics, downloaded November 2012: http://www.opensecrets.org/outsidespending/summ.php?cycle=2012&chrt=V&type=S&ql3

as a market in need of entrepreneurship, served poorly by a giant monopoly—the Democratic Party—that is still doing business in an old, Rust Belt kind of way."[23] By the 2010 midterm elections, Armey had left Congress in order to lead FreedomWorks, an ardently conservative advocacy organization, as well as the Tea Party movement, while Soros decided not to support Democratic candidates in favor of promoting issues he favored, both evidence of the fluidity of American politics.

An open, democratic polity provides ample opportunities for groups to mobilize members to advance their cause. EMILY's List, founded by Ellen Malcolm in the mid-1980s, is illustrative. Malcolm established this PAC to increase the number of pro-choice members of Congress and to raise funds to encourage Democratic women to enter politics. Coining an acronym for "early money is like yeast, it makes the dough rise" EMILY's List focused on primaries, figuring that "if we could raise enough early money to get women started, then they could convince the traditional fundraisers that they were viable, and they could then raise the money they needed to win," Malcolm recalled. Forging strong relationships between female candidates and female donors augmented the focus on primaries and vaulted EMILY's List to the forefront of progressive politics. Three decades after its inception, EMILY's List had leveraged $86 million for pro-abortion candidates, and increased the number of Democratic women in Congress fourfold.[24]

Compared to business, labor, and lobbyists, most social advocacy groups bring few assets to bear on the political process. Limited by meager resources, social advocacy groups usually rely on volunteer lobbyists. There are several advocacy groups within social welfare that have been instrumental in advancing legislation to assist vulnerable populations—among them the American Public Human Service Association, the Child Welfare League of America, the Children's Defense Fund, the National Association for the Advancement of Colored People, the National Urban League, the National Assembly of Voluntary Health and Welfare Associations, and the National Organization for Women. Of these advocacy groups only one, AARP, ranks among the top 100 lobbyists on Capitol Hill. Despite the number of welfare advocacy organizations and their successful record in evolving more comprehensive social legislation, changes in the policy process

hamper their work. Increases in the number of governmental agencies as well as in their staffs make it difficult to track policy developments and changes in administrative procedures. Worse, the escalating cost of influencing social policy, evident in the number of paid lobbyists and in the contributions lavished by PACs, is simply beyond the means of most welfare advocacy organizations. As one Democratic candidate for the Senate lamented, "only the well-heeled have PACs—not the poor, the unemployed, the minorities or even most consumers."[25]

In 2010, the Supreme Court ruled in *Citizens United v. the Federal Election Commission* that campaign contributions in any amount were protected under the First Amendment, effectively neutralizing federal campaign finance limits. The result increased the influence of wealthy interests while diminishing those of less well endowed.[26] Almost instantly, over 1000 "super PACs" emerged and pumped unprecedented amount into the 2012 election, as shown in Table 8.6.

Perversely, Super PACs have been able to manipulate the IRS code by qualifying as "social welfare" entities in order to avoid revealing the names of contributors. In light of almost unrestricted campaign funding following the *Citizens United* ruling, the cost of the 2012 election is unprecedented, approximating $6 billion.

The increasing influence of well-heeled groups is not to say that social advocates are ineffectual. During the first two years of the Obama presidency, passage of a Stimulus Package to jump-start a flagging economy, the Patient Protection and Affordable Care Act to reform healthcare, and financial reform that included the creation of a Consumer Financial Protection Bureau, all required the choreography of a large number of disparate advocacy organizations.

Implementation

The fact that a policy has been enacted does not necessarily mean it will be implemented. Often governmental policies fail to provide for adequate authority, personnel, or funding to accomplish their stated purposes. This has been a chronic problem for social welfare programs. It is also possible that a governmental policy initiative will not be enforced even after it has been established. Many local jurisdictions have correctional and child welfare institutions now operating under court supervision

TABLE 8.6 Top 10 Super PACs

Group	Expenditures ($ millions)	Ideology
Restore Our Future	142.6	Conservative
American Crossroads	99.6	Conservative
Priorities USA Action	67.5	Liberal
Majority PAC	37.4	Liberal
House Majority PAC	30.7	Liberal
Freedomworks for America	19.1	Conservative
Winning Our Future	17.0	Conservative
Club for Growth Action	16.6	Conservative
Service Employees International Union	14.9	Liberal
Ending Spending Fund	13.0	Conservative

Source: Open Secrets/Center for Responsive Politics, downloaded November 2012: http://www.opensecrets.org/outsidespending/summ.php?cycle=2012&chrt=V&type=S&ql3

because judges have agreed with social advocates that these institutions are not in compliance with state or federal law.

Implementation, difficult enough in the normal course of events, is that much more problematic when the public is disaffected with governmental institutions. The episodic nature of public endorsement of governmental institutions has been studied extensively by Albert O. Hirschman, who investigated the relationship between "private interest and public action." According to Hirschman, public endorsement of governmental institutions is a fundamental problem for industrialized capitalist societies, which emphasize individual competitiveness while generating social and economic dislocations that require collective action. "Western societies," Hirschman observes, "appear to be condemned to long periods of privatization during which they live through an impoverished 'atrophy of public meanings,' followed by spasmodic outbursts of 'publicness' that are hardly likely to be constructive."[27] Disenchantment with governmental solutions to social problems, most recently evident in the Tea Party movement, makes public welfare programs vulnerable to their critics, leading to reductions in staff and fiscal support, often followed by an escalation in the social problem for which the social program was initially designed. Thus, the episodic nature of public support for programs designed to alleviate social problems further impedes effective implementation.

Evaluation

The expansion of governmental welfare policies has spawned a veritable industry in program evaluation. Stung by the abuses of the executive branch during Watergate and the Vietnam War, Congress established additional oversight agencies to review federal programs.[28] As a result, multiple units within the executive and legislative branches of government have the evaluation of programs as their primary mission. At the federal level, the most important of these include the Government Accountability Office (GAO), the Office of Management and Budget (OMB), the Congressional Budget Office (CBO), and the Congressional Research Service (CRS). For example, OMB developed the Program Assessment Rating Tool (PART) to evaluate federal programs, concluding that one-third are inadequate. Between 2002 and 2006 the number of programs determined to be "ineffective" or "results not demonstrated" was reduced from 55 percent to 25 percent.[29] State governments have similar units. In addition, departments have evaluation units that monitor program activities for which they are responsible. Finally, federal and state levels of government commonly contract with nongovernmental organizations for evaluations of specific programs. As a result, many universities provide important research services to government. The University of Wisconsin's Institute for Research on Poverty is distinguished for its research in social welfare, and Chapin Hall at the University of Chicago evaluates child welfare programming. In the past three decades, private consulting firms, such as MDRC, Abt Associates, MAXIMUS, and Mathematica Policy Research, have entered the field, often hiring former government officials and capitalizing on their connections in order to secure lucrative research contracts. Of course, any politicization of the research process is frowned upon, because it raises questions about the impartiality of the evaluation. On the eve of the 2012 election, for example, the Congressional Research Service released a report indicating that tax cuts for the wealthy did not contribute to economic growth, but it used language to which Republicans objected. The report was later withdrawn when it was revealed that its author had made campaign contributions to several Democratic organizations.[30] Is a former government official willing to assess rigorously and impartially a program run by an agency in which he or she was employed in the past or would like to be employed in the future? Questions about the closeness between governmental agencies, research firms, party politics, and the validity of evaluation studies have become common; indeed, the consulting firms located near the expressway surrounding Washington, DC, are often referred to as "the beltway bandits." Whether conducted in-house or contracted out to universities or commercial firms, evaluation research has become a major industry.

Investigations by program evaluation organizations can be characterized as applied (as opposed to "pure") research, the objective being to optimize program operations. As a result of this emphasis on the function of programs, evaluation studies frequently focus on waste, cost-effectiveness, and goal attainment. Owing to the contradictory objectives of many welfare policies, the constant readjustments in programs, and the limitations in the art of evaluation research, evaluations frequently conclude that any given program has mixed results. Rarely does a program evaluation provide a clear indication for future action. Often the results of a single program evaluation are used by both critics and defenders in their efforts to dismantle or to advance the program.

The very inconclusiveness of program evaluation contributes to the partisan use to which evaluation research can be put. It is not uncommon for decision makers to engage in statistical arguments that have a great influence on social welfare policy. Of the recent "stat wars," several relate directly to social welfare. One example is the question of whether underemployed and discouraged workers should be included in the unemployment rate. Currently, the Department of Labor defines unemployed as only those who are out of work and actively looking for jobs; and it considers part-time workers as employed. As a result, many African Americans, Hispanic Americans, young adults, and women are not considered unemployed, even though advocates for these groups contend that they are not fully employed. Predictably, evaluations of employment programs vary considerably. Data about the results of welfare-to-work initiatives evince a general theme: Although welfare caseloads have dropped more than 50 percent, heads of households who have found work (1) tend to remain stuck in sub-poverty-level wages, and (2) remain eligible for benefits such as food stamps and Medicaid. Such research serves varied ideological purposes. Conservatives trumpet the reduction in welfare dependency, and liberals worry about the fate of families who continue to be poor despite full-time work.

Marginalization

If the governmental decision-making process is somewhat irregular and irrational, it is also unrepresentative. As illustrated in Figure 8.3, groups in the upper levels of the social stratification populate the institutions through which policy is made. Significantly, many members of Congress are wealthy; the average net worth of Republicans in 2012 was $881,786 while that of Democrats was $862,508.[31] In the case of welfare policy, welfare beneficiaries must adjust to rules established by other social groups. The primary players in the social policy game are executives and professionals. Lower socioeconomic groups' lack of influence in the social policy process is virtually built into governmental decision making. The term *non-decision making* has been coined to describe this phenomenon—the system's capacity to keep the interests of some groups off the decision-making agenda.[32] Marginalization has a long history in the United States; generations of African Americans and women were legally excluded from decision making prior to emancipation and suffrage.

The governmental policy process also poses problems for administrators and practitioners. Policies frequently reflect assumptions about the human condition that may seem reasonable to the upper socioeconomic groups that make them but bear little resemblance to the reality of the lower socioeconomic groups that are supposed to be beneficiaries. For example, Child Support

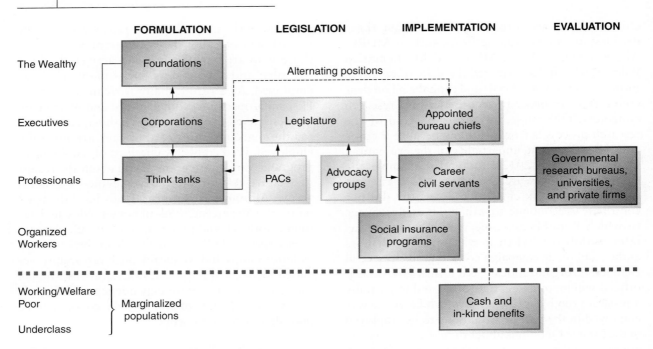

FORMULATION LEGISLATION IMPLEMENTATION EVALUATION

FIGURE 8.3 Stratification and the Public Policy Process

Enforcement policy assumes that fathers of children on TANF have the kind of regular, well-paying jobs that would allow them to meet the amounts of their court orders, whereas often their jobs are intermittent and offer low wages. Consequently, support payments to children who are dependent on welfare have been disappointing. In 2006, $21.8 billion in child support was collected through the Child Support Enforcement (CSE) program, but most of this was for non-TANF families; only $2.1 billion of TANF benefits were recovered through CSE.[33] For nonwelfare households, CSE's revenues exceeded administrative costs, but for welfare families, those for whom the program was initially justified, CSE lost money.[34]

Making the public policy process more representative is a primary concern of welfare advocates. Since the Civil Rights movement, African Americans and the poor have recognized the power of the ballot, and voter registration has become an important strategy for advancing the influence of these groups. The mobilization of marginal groups was widely understood to have vaulted Barack Obama to the White House and provided Democrats control of Congress in 2008, while their failure to vote in comparable numbers helped Republicans win an unprecedented number of victories in the midterm elections only two years later.

Political parties and campaign managers who contend with the growing ranks of independent voters have come to appreciate segmentation of the voting public. The Pew Research Center for the People and the Press has divided the electorate into nine groups, according to their affinity for different issues. In an important book, Jonathan Haidt has identified six primary values that voters articulate. These are depicted in Figure 8.4. According to Haidt, four of the six primary values held by Americans favor conservatives, leaving two to liberals.[35] On the eve of the 2012 election, conservative groups reflected 44 percent of voters, while liberals 35 percent. This means that the 2012 Presidential candidates needed to make a concerted effort to appeal to the 21 percent of independent voters in order to obtain a majority. The necessity of attracting independent voters helps explain why incumbent Obama moved away from liberal precepts and challenger Romney moved to the center despite the Rightward pull of the Tea Party. Congressional candidates have to appeal to a similarly fluid pool of voters, although the dynamic varies with each state for senators and districts for House members. Increasingly, Congressional elections are held in jurisdictions that have been balkanized into liberal or conservative enclaves, contributing to political gridlock.[36] Clearly, advocates of social and economic justice cannot afford to rest on their laurels if they wish to be competitive in the electoral marketplace.

Within the voting population, more affluent voters are more than twice as likely to exercise their

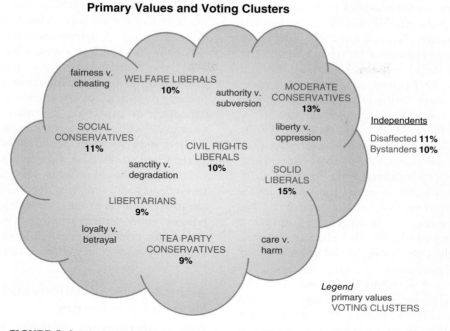

Primary Values and Voting Clusters

FIGURE 8.4 Primary Values and voting clusters

franchise as are those who are poor: In 2008, 74.9 percent of voters with incomes above $100,000 voted in the presidential election, versus only 41.3 percent of those with incomes less than $10,000.[37] In 2010, only 37.8 percent of the voting-age population voted in the national election.[38] Logically, increasing the involvement of apathetic voters would not only make inroads against marginalization but also make public social programs more responsive to their circumstances; however, the advent of voter ID laws make that more difficult. Subsequent to passage of the National Voter Registration Act in 1993—aka the motor voter law—True the Vote, founded by a Tea Party activist, worked to reverse the expansion of the number of low-income, minority voters. Alleging that voter fraud was pervasive, True the Vote disseminated a model statute, developed by the American Legislative Exchange Council, to require photo ID in order to vote. By 2011 37 states had passed voter ID laws. Former President Clinton inveighed against the requirement, likening it to poll taxes that suppressed the black vote during Jim Crow. While courts in several states postponed implementation until after the 2012 election, proponents of voter ID allied with conservative legal groups in order to challenge the legitimacy of voters in battleground states if the election is close.[39] In 2012, President Obama won reelection by mobilizing a coalition of minorities, the well educated, women, students, and blue-collar workers, leaving the Republican party with the task of appealing to a voting public that was no longer dominated by white men.

Social Work and Advocacy Organizations

The formulation of social welfare policy in the United States, as this chapter has shown, is a complicated and often arduous process. Much of this can be attributed to the nature of U.S. culture: to the competing interests inherent in a pluralistic society; to the multiple systems of government that make social policy at the same time; to public and private bureaucracies that serve large numbers of consumers; and to economic and technological developments that lead to specialization. Under these circumstances, changing social welfare policy to improve the circumstances of disadvantaged groups can be a daunting task. Regrettably, few human service professionals consider social policy advocacy an enterprise worthy of undertaking. Most social workers prefer direct service activity, in which they have little opportunity for direct involvement in social policy. Some social workers attain important positions in federal and state human service bureaucracies and are close to the policy process. Unfortunately, these managers are often administering welfare policies that have been made by legislatures and that do not necessarily represent either clients or human service professionals. Perhaps most troubling is the fact that the involvement of social workers in the formulation of social policy has been diminishing in recent years. In a provocative statement, June Hopps, former dean of the Boston College School of Social Work and former editor-in-chief of *Social Work*, acknowledged that "since the late 1960s and early 1970s, the [social work] profession has experienced a dramatic loss of influence in the arenas where policy is shaped and administered."[40] Though opportunities to enter the upper levels of the federal civil service have become available through the Presidential Management Internship and Department of Health and Human Services Emerging Leaders programs, social work has not found a way to systematically exploit these.

One indicator of good social policy is the correspondence between the policy and the social reality of its intended beneficiaries. Thus, it's clear that social welfare policy would be enhanced by the input of social workers. However, social workers have left much of the decision making about social welfare to professionals from other disciplines. "There are increasing numbers of non-social workers, including psychologists and urban planners," observed Eleanor Brilliant, "taking what might have been social work jobs in service delivery and policy analysis."[41] The consequences of welfare professionals opting to leave social policy in the hands of others are important. For direct service workers, these consequences can mean having to apply eligibility standards or procedures that, although logical in some respects, make little sense in the social context of many clients. For the public, they may mean a gradual disenchantment with social programs that do not seem to work. The causes of the retrenchment affecting social programs since the late 1970s are complex, of course; however, it is worth noting that public dissatisfaction with social programs has escalated as social welfare professionals have retreated from active involvement in public policy.

The rebuilding of a role for social workers in social policy will take concerted effort. Individual leadership is a necessary, but no longer sufficient, precondition for this objective. Essential to the undertaking will be social workers' ability to understand and manage complex organizations and programs. In fact, this skill may be the most critical for welfare professionals to acquire if they are to advance social justice, for it addresses a question central to the postindustrial era. During the Industrial Revolution, Karl Marx suggested that the central question was "who controls the means of production?" A mature industrial order and the expansion of civil bureaucracy led Max Weber to ask, "who controls the means of administration?" The evolution of a postindustrial order, in which primary economic activity occurs in a service sector dependent on processed information, raises a new question: "who controls the means of analysis?" If social workers are to shape social policy as effectively as they had in the past, they will have to learn to control the means of analysis. This means conducting research on social problems, surveying public opinion about welfare programs, analyzing existing social policy for opportunities to enhance welfare provision, and winning elected office in order to make decisions about proposed social welfare policies.

Advocacy Organizations and the New Policy Institutes

Policy analysis organizations have been instrumental in shaping social policy since the New Deal. Subsequently, policy institutes have had liberal or conservative labels ascribed to them, with the liberal organizations, such as the Brookings Institution and the Urban Institute, achieving dominance up until the late 1970s when conservative institutes, such as the American Enterprise Institute, the Heritage Foundation, and the Manhattan Institute, ascended. The failure of government social programs to expand during the Carter presidency, followed by the profoundly negative impact of the Reagan years and the two Bush presidencies, led social reformers to establish a new group of policy analysis organizations.

Children's Defense Fund Begun by Marian Wright Edelman in 1974, the Children's Defense Fund (CDF) sought to address the health, income, and educational needs of the nation's children.[42] By the mid-1980s, CDF had become a major voice in children's policy and had successfully advocated programs at the federal and state levels. In 1984, CDF helped pass the Child Health Assurance Program, which expanded Medicaid eligibility to poor women and children. It also advocated for the 1998 State Children's Health Insurance Program (SCHIP). CDF is noted for its educational publications, particularly for eye-catching posters depicting injustices inflicted on poor, minority children. Its annual report, The State of America's Children, is an authoritative compendium of issues and programs concerning children.

The Center on Budget and Policy Priorities (CBPP) Established in 1981 by Robert Greenstein, former administrator of the Food and Nutrition Service in the Agriculture Department, CBPP has fought to defend social programs for low-income people against budget cuts. With a modest staff, CBPP distributes its analyses to Congressional staffs, the media, and grassroots organizations. Despite its small size, CBPP provided much of the program analysis to refute arguments presented by conservative officials in their efforts to cut means-tested social programs. Significantly, CBPP and CDF have developed a close working relationship. CBPP regularly provides data to CDF on the health and income status of children.[43]

Economic Policy Institute (EPI) In 1986, Jeff Faux convinced labor-oriented liberals to establish a policy institute to represent "the perspective of working families and the poor."[44] During the subsequent decade, EPI expanded rapidly and published reports depicting a widening chasm between the economic circumstances of working families and the affluent. Notable among EPI publications is its annual volume *The State of Working America*, which contains current data on income, taxes, wages, wealth, and poverty.

Institute for Women's Policy Research (IWPR) Created in 1987 by Heidi Hartmann, a social program researcher and director of the Women's Studies Program at Rutgers University, IWPR quickly attained a respected position in Washington, DC. The IWPR research and advocacy agenda relating to women is extensive, including retirement, family leave, health insurance, welfare reform, and pay equity. In 1994, Hartmann received a MacArthur "genius" fellowship award for her advocacy of gender equity.

New America Foundation In 1999, Ted Halstead launched the New America Foundation in order to develop policy options congruent with the information age. With Michael Lind, Halstead wrote *The Radical Center*, a book that outlined the need for an ideological orientation that was postliberal as well as postconservative.[45]

Center for American Progress Smarting from reversals attributed to conservative think tanks, John Podesta convinced other liberals to establish the Center for American Progress in 2003. Drawing on an annual budget of $10 million and many policy experts who had served in the Clinton administration, the Center for American Progress is well positioned to compete with policy institutes from the Right.[46]

Political Practice

The capacity of social workers to reassert their role in social welfare policy depends on the willingness of individuals to consider public office as a setting for social work practice. Although many welfare pioneers began their careers advocating for social welfare policy and then assumed administrative positions managing social programs, others used elected office to advance social reform. The first woman elected to the House of Representatives was Jeannette Rankin, who won a seat in 1916 running as a Republican in Montana. As a social worker who had studied under Frances Perkins, Rankin voted for early social welfare legislation and against military expansion. More recently, social workers in **political practice** include Maryann Mahaffey, a member of the Detroit City Council, and Ruth Messinger, a former member of the New York City Council.

By 2010, five social workers had attained national office:

- Barbara Mikulski received her MSW degree in 1965 and then served on the Baltimore City Council and in the U.S. House of Representatives. In 1986, Mikulski became the first Democratic woman to be elected to the U.S. Senate in her own right. Through appointments to the powerful Appropriations and Labor and Human Resources Committees, Mikulski is well positioned to advocate programs in health and social services.[47]

Barbara Mikulski

Source: Harry Hamburg/ AP Images

- Debbie Stabenow was awarded her MSW degree from Michigan State University, after which she was elected to the Ingham County Commission, the Michigan House, and the Michigan Senate. In 1996, Stabenow ran to represent the Eighth Congressional

District of Michigan on a platform opposing the extremes of the Republican Congress elected in 1994. Having won election to the House of Representatives, in 1999 Stabenow challenged an incumbent to become the second social worker to be elected to the U.S. Senate.

Debbie Stabenow

Source: Manuel Balce Ceneta/AP Images

- Barbara Lee was elected in 1998 to fill the House seat of Ron Dellums, a social worker on whose staff she had served. Lee received her MSW from the University of California, Berkeley, and established a community mental health center while completing her graduate studies. Subsequently, she was elected to the California State Senate. Congresswoman Lee now serves on the House Committee on Banking and Financial Services and on the House Committee on International Relations, the Congressional Progressive Caucus, the Congressional Black Caucus, and the Congressional Women's Caucus.

Barbara Lee

Source: J. Scott Applewhite/ AP Images

- In 2000, Susan Davis defeated an incumbent to represent California's 49th Congressional District. Davis received her graduate degree in social services from the University of North Carolina in 1968; she subsequently moved to San Diego, where she chaired the school board. As a new member of Congress, Davis attained a coveted seat on the Armed Services Committee. Among her primary concerns are education and campaign finance reform.

Susan Davis

Source: AP Images

- Allyson Schwartz received her MSW degree from Bryn Mawr College, served in the state Senate, became a health executive, and led the effort to establish the State Child Health Insurance Program in Pennsylvania. Representing the 13th Congressional District of Pennsylvania, Representative Schwartz focuses on services to veterans as well as women and families.

Allyson Schwartz

Source: J. Scott Applewhite/ AP Images

An analysis of 250 social work elected officials—69 percent in local office, 29 percent in state office, and 2 percent in federal office—revealed that most found their social work education instrumental in their public service.[48]

Conclusion

Perhaps the best indicator of social work's potential future influence on social policy appears at the local level. For example, social workers have lobbied successfully on behalf of nonprofit agencies facing threats to their tax-exempt status,[49] encouraged students to engage in election campaigns and to become more knowledgeable about politics,[50] and managed a campaign for the election of a state senator.[51] In each of these instances, social workers were gaining the kind of experience that is essential to political involvement at higher levels. More than 200 social workers had been elected to state, county, municipal, and judicial offices. In response to increasing political activity at the state level, social work professor emeritus Bob Schneider established Influencing State Policy in order to empower human service professionals.

Social workers disinclined to engage in high-visibility activities such as campaigning for public office could make their imprint on politics through legislators' "constituent services." Pulitzer Prize–winning journalist Hedrick Smith observed that members of Congress are increasingly relying on constituent services in place of pork barrel projects as domestic expenditures dry up. Using a term familiar to most social workers, politicians call constituent services "casework"—that is, "having your staff track down missing Social Security checks, inquire about sons and husbands in the armed services, help veterans get medical care, pursue applications for small-business loans."[52] The importance of political "casework" has been noted by political scientists, who attribute up to 5 percent of the vote to such activities, a significant amount in close elections. David Himes of the National Republican Congressional Committee claimed that "our surveys have shown that constituency service, especially in the House, is more important than issues."[53]

The cultivation of practice skills in the political arena at the local level offers perhaps the most promising way for social workers to regain influence in social welfare policy. Such activity can be undertaken by virtually any professional interested in the opportunity. On a volunteer basis, social workers would find few politicians who would turn down their professional assistance in the provision of constituent services. With experience, enterprising social workers might find that political practice could be remunerative, provided that they possessed skills needed by elected officials—such as conducting surveys, maintaining data banks of contributors, organizing public meetings, and keeping current on legislation important to constituents. From another perspective, however, the prospect of political practice should be taken seriously. If social workers are sincere about making essential resources available to their clients—a responsibility stated in the NASW Code of Ethics—then some form of political practice is a professional obligation. "To do less," noted Maryann Mahaffey, "to avoid the political action necessary to provide these resources, is to fail to live up to the profession's code of ethical practice."[54]

DISCUSSION QUESTIONS

1. Clicking on the Congress.org website, select a social welfare policy and identify its primary components. Which elected members of Congress were cosponsors of the legislation? What committees were instrumental in its passage? Which special interests benefited from its passage?

2. Clicking on "Advocacy" on the policyAmerica website, identify your representative and senators. E-mail them about an issue that is important to you. Do any of your members of Congress have any important health and human service committee assignments? Do your representatives have committee assignments that could make them influential on issues important to you? Do your representatives have position statements available to constituents about specific social programs?

3. Politicians elected to your state legislature have responsibilities similar to members of Congress.

Identify your state representatives. Do they have assignments on health and human service committees? Do they have position statements they could send to you on health and human service issues?

4. Select a health and human service bill of interest to you and follow it in your state legislature. Which committees and interest groups supported or fought the proposed legislation? How was the bill changed to make it more acceptable to special interests? Have local interests, such as a major newspaper, endorsed or objected to the proposed legislation? Why?

5. Does your state chapter of the National Association of Social Workers make legislation a high priority for the professional community? What are the legislative goals of the state NASW chapter? How are those goals reflected in the resources allocated? How would you prioritize health and human services in your community?

6. If marginalization leaves many clients of social programs impotent in the public policy process, how could these people be made more influential? How could the local professional community assist in empowering beneficiaries of social programs? What could you do?

7. Identify social workers who serve in local elected offices. What led them to pursue elective office? What are their future political plans? Could you provide constituent services for these persons or help with their reelection?

NOTES

1. Amartya Sen, *The Idea of Justice* (Cambridge, MA: Belknap Harvard University Press, 2009, pp. ch. 16.

2. Paul Krugman, "Lobbyists, Guns and Money," *New York Times*, March 26, 2012, p. A23.

3. "Anita Kuman, "Howell Assails Liberal for Attack on Conservative Group," *Washington Post*, April 13, 2012, p B1.

4. U.S. Congress, *U.S. Congress Handbook 1992* (McLean, VA: Barbara Pullen, 1992), p. 184.

5. *Robert's Rules of Order* is available from several publishers.

6. David Farenthold and Paul Kane, "Senate Has Become Chamber of Failure," *Washington Post*, October 13, 2011, p. A6.

7. The latest annual edition of *Overview of Entitlement Programs* can be obtained through the Government Printing Office in Washington, DC.

8. "The Long Path to a Federal Budget," *Washington Post* (April 5, 2005), p. A21.

9. Charles Lindblom and David Braybrooke, *Strategy of Decision* (New York: Free Press, 1970).

10. For a description of these forms of rationality, see Robert Alford, "Health Care Politics," *Politics and Society* 2 (Winter 1972), pp. 127–164.

Tax policy, the use of legislation to define how revenues are generated in order to achieve social objectives, is fundamental to the structure of social welfare in the United States. Although this function may seem prosaic, in fact, tax policy has been the flash point of major historical events, as evident in the Boston Tea Party when colonists objected to taxation without representation. Massive tax cuts of the George W. Bush administration provoked dire warnings by liberals and conservatives alike about the fiscal health of the republic and contributed to the emergence of a new Tea Party movement. Although tax policy is an instrument of government, its influence is not limited solely to generating revenues for federal and state social programs: Through "tax expenditures," areas exempted from taxation, tax policy provides significant incentives not only for specific industries, but also for individual behavior, as in the mortgage interest deduction. For this reason, tax policy is of increasing interest to advocates of social justice. As support for direct benefits through traditional social programs has waned, social advocates have turned to "targeted tax expenditures"—preferably, refundable tax credits—as a means to advance economic justice. As a vehicle for funding social programs, tax policy is also an important barometer for social equity; and indeed, policy analysts have long used income distribution—and more recently wealth distribution—as an indicator of how fair the economy has been for various groups.

History of U.S. Tax Policy

All governments levy taxes to meet their legislated obligations. Because taxation appropriates income from private parties—individuals and corporations—and puts it to public use, it has been controversial and, at times, volatile. Ever since the establishment of the republic, various groups have objected to government taxation, challenging the authority to appropriate private property. Such challenges have usually been sorted out through the courts, but on occasion they have led to violent armed confrontations, as in the Whiskey Rebellion that divided the nation shortly after its creation. Although tax policy has traditionally been of professional interest primarily to the "green-eyeshade" accountants at the Internal Revenue Service, the Right also has a keen interest in it because conservatives recognize that tax money is the lifeblood that allows government to function.

A precept of American conservatism has been minimal taxation. Speaking about the American colonies, Edmund Burke observed that taxes, by their very nature, tended to be imprudent: "To tax and to please, no more than to love and to be wise, is not given to men."

Progressives and liberals understood the relationship between taxes and social programs differently, citing Oliver Wendell Holmes: "Taxes are what we pay for civilized society." Ever since the creation of the welfare state with the passage of the Social Security Act of 1935, social program expenditures have grown, and all these programs have been paid for by increasing taxes. The optimal welfare state, as liberals conceived it, would provide essential benefits as a right of citizenship. These benefits would be funded by progressive taxes—taxes that derived their revenues disproportionately from the wealthy. Implicit in this vision was the political calculus that was captured by Harry Hopkins, whose synopsis has become part of welfare folklore: "Tax, tax; spend, spend; elect, elect!" For half a century, this strategy produced solid electoral support for liberal social programs: The wealthy were taxed at higher rates, the revenues were diverted to social benefits for the middle and working classes through social programs, and social program beneficiaries expressed their gratitude by voting Democratic. Ultimately, however, liberal Democratic hegemony in social policy foundered on the shoals of its own success. As working families rose into the middle class, they tended to individualize their achievements, discounting the role of social programs and, in the process, becoming more receptive to conservative proposals to reduce social programs and their tax burden. By the 1980s, this scenario led to the election of Ronald Reagan, who had a visceral dislike for federal social programs. The Reagan presidency was revolutionary in several respects, one being profound changes in tax policy, increasing economic inequality.

While the Clinton interregnum restored a measure of fairness in tax policy, the presidency of George W. Bush viewed tax cuts as the centerpiece of its domestic agenda, achieving one cut for each year of his first term. The intent of the Bush White House was summarized by Grover Norquist, who as president of Americans for Tax Reform proposed that the Bush White House implement annual tax cuts: "I don't want to abolish government. I simply want to reduce it to the size where I can drag it into the bathroom and drown it in the bathtub."[1]

Accordingly, conservatives have viewed tax cuts as essential to rolling back social programs, "starving the beast." As Paul Krugman observed, "starving-the-beasters believe that budget deficits will lead to spending cuts that will eventually achieve their true aim: shrinking the government's role back to what it was under Calvin Coolidge."[2] For intellectuals of the Right, tax reform is ultimately the vehicle for dismantling the U.S. welfare state. "Instead of sending taxes to Washington, straining them through bureaucracies and converting what remains into a muddle of services, subsidies, in-kind support, and cash hedged with restrictions and exceptions," argued Charles Murray, "just collect the taxes, divide them up, and send the money back in cash grants to all American adults." According to Murray, a $10,000 grant to each nonincarcerated U.S. citizen, of which $3,000 would be for health care, would cost $355 billion more than current expenditures. By 2011, however, Murray's thought experiment would be revenue neutral; by 2020 it would save a half trillion dollars.[3] How this dispute between social entitlements and tax revenues will be worked out has implications far beyond beneficiaries of social welfare programs. If social program obligations exceed revenues, the only option for the federal government is to increase the national debt, a solution that had been pursued by both Democratic and Republican presidents. In 2010, the prospect of further indebtedness was effectively checked when candidates representing the Tea Party won Congressional elections on a platform that opposed to further deficit spending. Issues such as the federal deficit, global economic competition, and the fate of discretionary programs, make the resolution extraordinarily complex.

As a creation of the legislative process, tax policy is most visible in the passage of major bills. Over time, these become the basis of the state and federal tax codes, those notoriously confounding labyrinths of accounting rules. Periodically, attempts to reform tax policy emerge, such as the 1986 federal tax reform, which simplified the tax code and eliminated—at least temporarily—provisions for special interests. As this overview suggests, tax policy is dense and at the same time dynamic. Historically, three tax policies have been central to U.S. social policy: the income tax, the withholding tax, and the Earned Income Tax Credit (EITC).

- The federal income tax was instituted after approval of the sixteenth Amendment to the Constitution in 1914. A *progressive tax*, in that the wealthy were taxed at a higher rate, the income tax was initially levied on less than 1 percent of the population and had a top rate of only 7 percent. In 2009, 7.5 percent of wealthy taxpayers were affected by the highest tax rate, 35 percent, while 25.0 percent of the lowest income households were exempt from paying any federal income tax.[4]

- The Social Security withholding tax, the payroll tax, was established in 1935. For employed workers, the withholding tax was initially set at 2 percent of the first $3,000 in wages, paid equally between employers and workers. Since then Social Security withholding has increased to 12.4 percent of the first $97,500 in wages in 2007, increasing to $106,800 in 2011. The wage cap was established at the outset, under the presumption that Social Security was a public pension plan for workers who would not have recourse to retirement provisions available to the wealthy. The withholding tax is a regressive tax, in that lower-income workers pay the same rate as higher-wage employees. Most taxpayers now pay more in Social Security withholding than they do in income taxes.

- The **Earned Income Tax Credit (EITC)** was enacted in 1975 after the failure of a "negative income tax" plan advanced by the Nixon administration. A **refundable tax credit**, the EITC instructs the IRS to send a check to low-wage workers, especially those with children, whose earned income is below a certain level. In 2010, for example, a worker with two children could have received a maximum refund of $5,666.[5] Since the creation of the EITC, other tax credits have been introduced: A child care tax credit allows low-wage workers to deduct the costs of day care, and 22 states and the District of Columbia have introduced tax credits for low-income workers, some of which are refundable.

The interaction of these basic tax policies is complex. For instance, although taxpayers who fall in the top quintile (top 20 percent) of income earners, as evident in Table 9.1, claim 54.6 percent of income, they also bear the weight of paying most of the income, payroll, corporate, and estate taxes. Almost seventy percent of the federal tax burden is shouldered by the top quintile of tax payers. On the other hand, the effective tax rate of the top quintile—32.1 percent—is considerably less than its share of income. The lowest income earners often

TABLE 9.1 Federal Tax Rates, 2012

	Individual Income Tax	Payroll Tax	Corporate Income Tax	Estate Tax	All Federal Taxes
Top 0.1 %	18.4	0.7	10.9	0.6	30.6
Top 1 %	18.1	1.7	7.9	0.4	28.1
Top Quintile	14.2	6.1	4.0	0.2	24.4
Fourth Quintile	7.2	10.4	0.7	*	18.3
Middle Quintile	3.3	10.0	0.7	*	14.0
Second Quintile	−2.7	9.4	0.6	*	7.3
Bottom Quintile	−6.0	7.1	0.4	*	1.6

*less than .05 percent

Distribution of Income and Federal Taxes, 2011

	Pre-tax Income		Federal Tax Burden		Average Federal Tax
	Average $	% Total	Average $	% Total	%
Top 0.1 %	6,859,873	7.7	2,113,515	15.1	30.8
Top 1 %	1,530,773	16.8	422,727	25.6	27.6
Top Quintile	251,746	54.6	58,040	69.5	23.1
Fourth Quintile	79,524	19.9	13,168	18.2	16.6
Middle Quintile	44,639	13.5	5,592	9.3	12.5
Second Quintile	24,603	8.5	1,420	2.7	5.8
Bottom Quintile	9,187	3.8	77	0.2	0.8

Source: Table T12-0008, Tax Policy Center, Washington, D.C.: Urban Institute and the Brookings Institution, 2012.

pay "negative income tax" because of rebates paid to them through EITC for low-wage families with children.

Tax provisions fund social programs that exist within an economy that is also shaped by economic policy; thus, economic policy, through tax policy, influences social programs.

A classic example was the conservative enthusiasm about "supply-side economics" during the 1980s. As advocated by Arthur Laffer, optimal economic policy would consist of minimal taxation, so as not to impede capital formation and expansion. Given the relatively higher tax rates that preceded his presidency, Ronald Reagan endorsed tax reform that incorporated a one-third cut in the income tax, assuming that the cut would reinvigorate a sluggish economy.[6] But although the tax cut of 1981 jolted the economy out of recession, it also cut off

tax revenues to the Treasury, which then had to sell bonds to service the federal debt. Soon the federal government plunged further into debt, the depth of which was unprecedented for peacetime. By 1983, the annual deficit was $207 billion, 6.3 percent of **gross national product**, and growing. Debt service on government bonds grew commensurately, so that by the end of the 1980s, annual interest payments on the debt were $150 billion, the second largest item in the federal budget.[7]

Annual debt service overshadowed domestic policy discussions during the early 1990s. The congressional response was to impose a cap on domestic spending, an effort to stem the hemorrhaging of cash leaving the Treasury during a period when inflowing revenues had been stemmed by tax cuts. Liberal Democrats insisted that entitlement spending for social programs be exempt from the spending cap, with the result that federal budget decisions subsequently penalized discretionary programs—those with fixed budgets that are subject to the appropriation process annually—disproportionately. Because discretionary programs include research and development, student loans, public transportation, and the entire defense budget, the spending cap created intense pressure between social entitlements and discretionary programs. Thus, several years after a sharp cut in federal taxes, the effects took the form of pressure to cut an array of discretionary programs.

Looming federal deficits cast a pall over the incoming Clinton administration. After campaigning on a platform that emphasized investments in human capital, former president Clinton was confronted with the massive deficits left over from the Reagan and Bush administrations. Clinton's nascent liberal tendencies, evident in his support for public works and national health insurance, were redirected by Alan Greenspan, chair of the Federal Reserve. Greenspan argued that the economy in general, and financial markets in particular, would respond negatively to new social programs that carried high price tags, because such programs would either (1) worsen the federal debt or (2) require significant tax increases. Although Clinton balked at Greenspan's position, economic reality was making short work of the new president's campaign rhetoric. Capitulating to Greenspan's insistence on deficit reduction, Clinton put his social investment plans on hold, a decision that contributed to an unprecedented economic expansion that promised to make possible the eventual elimination of the federal debt by generating a surplus projected at $2 trillion over 10 years.

After the election of George W. Bush in 2000, and with Republicans in control of Congress, the White House was positioned to move aggressively on domestic policy; among its primary concerns was tax policy. During its first term, four tax cuts were passed, reducing federal revenues $1.9 trillion over 10 years. Because the federal government had to honor its obligation to social entitlements while increasing spending for national security and mounting a war on terrorism, the federal government not only spent the surplus inherited from the Clinton presidency but also slid rapidly back into debt. As a result, the federal debt skyrocketed. With passage of the 2004 tax cut, the federal debt was projected to increase from $4.3 trillion to $8 trillion by 2014.[8]

Conservatives minimized the fiscal consequences of the federal deficit, noting that as a percentage of gross domestic product, the Bush deficit was only 1.8 percent in 2007, while the Reagan deficits were much higher, 6 percent.[9] Adherents to supply-side economics in the Bush White House bet that economic growth would shrink the deficit—in the words of former vice president Cheney: "Reagan proved that deficits don't matter." Liberals were less sanguine. "Bush's policies may, in fact, best be explained by another, more radical agenda. Extensive tax cuts will require Congress to limit the growth of social programs and public investment and undermine other programs altogether," argued Jeff Madrick, "Rising deficits will inevitably force Congress to starve those 'wasteful' social programs. The prospective high deficits may even make it imperative to privatize Social Security and Medicare eventually."[10] In 2008, the first of 77 million baby boomers began collecting Social Security, incurring future obligations that current social insurance programs will not be able to meet. The continuation of the Bush tax cuts until the end of 2012, **when they are scheduled to expire, looms as a critical fiscal issue**; assuming continuation of tax cuts and contemporary expenditures, there will be insufficient revenues for Medicare by 2024 and Social Security by 2033.[11] Social Security will be underfunded and net interest on federal debt will approximate 15 percent of gross domestic product (GDP).[12] Deficits of the Bush presidency plunged deeper with the advent of the Great Recession in late 2007. Reductions in government revenues accompanied by increased demand for social program benefits, increased the federal deficit to 9 percent of GDP, a level not seen since World War II. Subsequently, a bipartisan commission on deficit reduction, impaneled by President Obama, proposed solutions, such as eliminating the mortgage interest deduction on second homes, increasing the retirement age for Social Security, and freezing pay increases for federal employees and military personnel for three years.[13]

Tax Policy and Special Interests

Tax policy has always contained provisions that benefit specific interests. Bending the tax code in response to lobbying is a long-standing practice in the United States, though today it is most often associated with corporate influence. Actually, the exclusion of pension plans from taxation began in 1921, and these provisions have been updated to include provisions such as individual retirement accounts. Tax expenditures that benefit individuals have now grown to the point that they exceed allocations for many prominent social welfare programs. For 2010, for example, tax expenditures for pension contributions were projected to be $117.7 billion, for health insurance $131.0 billion, and for mortgage interest deductions $88.5 billion. By comparison, in 2007 allocations for Supplemental Security Income were $41.2 billion and Temporary Assistance for Needy Families (TANF) were $16.5 billion.[14]

Realizing that the tax code can be manipulated to serve the interests of the affluent, many social justice advocates have targeted "corporate welfare," that is, the special provisions that provide advantage to specific industries, for reform. The libertarian CATO Institute reported that the federal government spends $92 billion, directly and indirectly, to subsidize private sector activities each year, including over 11,600 earmarks that members of Congress insert in bills to aid organizations in their districts in 2008.[15] Such pedestrian examples of corporate welfare were eclipsed by the creation of the Troubled Asset Relief Program (TARP) designed to fund banks and other financial institutions to prevent a depression in 2008. Funded at $700 billion, TARP generated controversy not only by the scale of assistance to investment firms, the leaders of which were largely responsible for the subprime housing bubble, but also for the seven-figure bonuses paid them while receiving the federal bailout.[16] Efforts to downsize corporate welfare have often been frustrated. As long as there is pork in politics, there is the opportunity to customize tax policy and budget bills to serve the concerns of individual legislators—who, after all, are often influenced by constituent requests. Thus, for example, tax policy is crafted both to meet the Appalachian Regional Commission's need for roads and to respond to Sonoma Valley vintners' desire to export their products to France. Tax law also has a significant influence, directly and indirectly, on the revenues of nonprofit organizations. By allowing taxpayers to deduct charitable contributions from taxable income, tax law directly encourages support of philanthropy. Lower tax rates work indirectly, at least in theory, by leaving taxpayers with more discretionary income and assets, which they may then donate to nonprofit causes. Despite changes in tax policy that prevent taxpayers who do not itemize their tax deductions to deduct charitable contributions, the charitable impulse of Americans has continued. "Giving as a percent of income has remained remarkably constant in the face of increases in the cost of giving," concluded tax policy analysts.[17]

As noted in Chapter 6, the story on charitable giving as a function of tax reduction is less unilinear than conservatives might wish. Deep tax cuts introduced during the 1980s significantly reduced federal social welfare funding; and indeed, until the early 1990s, these were made up for by increases in charitable giving. During the 1990s, however, although both private giving and federal support of nonprofits increased significantly, these sources never compensated for the total revenue losses attributed to direct federal funding cuts. After the election of George W. Bush, conservatives proposed repeal of the estate tax, the consequence of which the Congressional Budget Office predicts would be between $13 billion and $25 billion in reduced charitable contributions because the wealthy would no longer count gifts against their tax obligations.[18]

Unlike earlier economic downturns that prompted increases in charitable contributions, the Great Recession was so profound that philanthropic giving actually dropped 13 percent in 2011.[19]

Federal Tax Policy

Despite the mammoth size of the federal budget of the United States, it is predicated on a tax base that is minimal compared to those of other industrialized nations. As shown in Table 9.2, the 2011 tax burden of the United States was lower than that in most industrialized nations. The relatively low tax rate of the United States largely accounts for the nation's skewed **income distribution** (see Table 9.3). A tenet of the welfare state has been the progressive taxation of income and its redistribution to the poor through social programs. By definition, a welfare state with a low tax rate is unable to generate revenues sufficient to level the differences between rich and poor; thus, the question of income distribution has become integral to the discussion of tax policy. Income distribution changes over time; most recently, wealthier families have benefited significantly.

Economic growth during the latter decades of the twentieth century exacerbated income inequality; while

TABLE 9.2 Tax Revenue of OECD Countries as a Percent of GDP, 2009

Rank	Country	Total Tax Rate %
1	Denmark	48.1
2	Sweden	46.7
3	Italy	43.4
4	Belgium	43.2
5	Norway	42.9
6	Finland	42.6
7	France	42.4
8	Hungary	39.9
9	Netherlands	38.2
10	Luxembourg	37.6
11	Slovenia	37.4
12	Germany	37.3
13	Estonia	35.9
14	Czech Republic	34.7
15	United Kingdom	34.3
16	Iceland	33.9
17	Poland	31.8
18	New Zealand	31.5
19	Israel	31.4
20	Portugal	30.6
21	Spain	30.6
22	Greece	30.0
23	Switzerland	29.7
24	Slovak Republic	29.0
25	Ireland	27.8
26	Japan	26.9
27	Australia	25.9
28	Korea	25.5
29	United States	24.8
30	Turkey	24.6
31	Chile	18.4
32	Mexico	17.4

Source: http://www.oecd.org/document/60/0,3746,en_2649_34533_1942460_1_1_1_1,00.html#A_RevenueStatistics, downloaded February 1, 2012.

the lowest 40 percent treaded water with respect to family income, the top 20 percent fared significantly better. The fortunes of the wealthiest 20 percent of families were battened by the tax cuts during the presidency of George W. Bush, which favored the rich. By 2006, the top 10 percent of American families claimed almost half of all family income. By one calculation, the top 1 percent claimed 53 percent of the growth in income in 2004.[20]

The evidence suggests that top income earners are not "rentiers" deriving their incomes from past wealth but rather are "working rich," highly paid employees or new entrepreneurs who have not yet accumulated fortunes comparable to those accumulated during the Gilded Age. Such a pattern might not last very long. The possible repeal of the federal tax on large estates in coming years would certainly accelerate the path toward the reconstitution of the great wealth concentration that existed in the U.S. economy before the Great Depression.[21]

Income is only one component of economic justice; another measure of affluence is assets. Although considered in discussions of social policy less often than income, assets are valuable insofar as they are an indication of real wealth. Consisting of savings, real estate, stocks and bonds, and related property, assets can not only be liquidated during periods of adversity, thus offering the owner a buffer against poverty, but can also appreciate in value, thus generating additional wealth. The distribution of assets is even more skewed than income distribution, with the highest quintile owning more than 80 percent. By contrast, the wealth of the lowest quintile is negative, indicative of debt. As has been the case with income, the distribution of assets has become more skewed during 1962 to 2004, the wealthiest quintile controlling more wealth with the lowest remaining in debt. Consider the period following the Great Society efforts of the mid-1960s: Despite a major expansion of social programs for the poor, the lowest quintile still showed negative wealth, remaining mired in debt. Wealth is also skewed in relation to race and ethnicity. Between 1996 and 2002, the wealth of African Americans fell 16.1 percent, while that of Hispanics increased 14 percent (compared to an increase of 17.4 percent for non-Hispanic whites).[22]

The fact that assets are consistently negative for the lowest quintile reflects the difficulty of poorer families to buffer themselves from economic shocks. Thus, asset poverty, the wealth needed to survive for

TABLE 9.3 Changes in the Distribution of Income, 1973–2005 (Percent Change)

Quintile	1973	1979	1989	2000	2005	1973–79	1979–89	1989–2000	2000–2005
Highest	41.1	41.4	44.6	47.7	48.1	0.3	3.2	3.1	0.4
Fourth	24.0	24.1	23.7	22.7	22.9	0.1	−0.4	−1.0	0.2
Middle	17.5	17.5	16.5	15.4	15.3	0.0	−1.0	−1.1	−0.1
Second	11.9	11.6	10.6	9.8	9.6	−0.3	−1.0	−0.8	−0.2
Lowest	5.5	5.4	4.6	4.3	4.0	−0.1	−0.8	−0.3	−0.3

three months at the poverty level, exceeds income-based poverty. By 2000, the asset poverty rate was 25.5 percent, twice the conventional poverty rate of 12.7 percent.[23] The consequences of the tax cuts engineered during the second Bush presidency compounded by the Great Recession are expected to widen the chasm between rich and poor.

State Tax Policy and the Poor

Federal taxes are important in social welfare policy because they subsidize the major social entitlements, but states also levy taxes in order to meet their legislative obligations. Historically, states have held major responsibility in social programs, areas such as mental health, child welfare, and corrections; and to a great degree the adequacy of a state's social programs depends on its tax collections. Unlike federal taxation, which is uniform across the nation, state tax policy varies significantly. By way of illustration, consider the income tax. Whereas the federal income tax is uniform nationwide, 43 states have income taxes, but seven do not (Florida, Nevada, South Dakota, Alaska, Texas, Washington, and Wyoming) and two states only tax investment income (Tennessee and New Hampshire). State income taxes provide general revenues that can be used for a range of social programs, but this is not the only reason that state tax policy is important. State tax policy can establish an income floor for taxation or exempt low-income families from any tax liability altogether, thus allowing them to keep more of their income. Disparities among states are striking; in 2010, the state income threshold in Alabama was only $9,800, for example, while that of California was $34,600. Of states that levy an income tax, the more progressive jurisdictions actually provide a rebate, similar to the federal EITC.

As Table 9.4 indicates, some states have been much more generous with respect to low-income families, while others have been downright punitive.

The Efficiency of Tax Policy in Reducing Poverty

In the larger context of social policy, tax policy is one of several strategies that apportion societal resources. Within social welfare, more traditional benefits have consisted of social insurance such as Social Security, cash public assistance (means-tested cash benefits) such as TANF, in-kind public assistance (means-tested noncash benefits) such as Food Stamps, and the EITC (tax rebates). These different strategies vary in terms of their efficiency in poverty reduction over time. For elders, social insurance—compulsory contributions to social programs like Social Security and Medicare—makes the biggest dent in poverty, and means-tested in-kind benefits and tax policies are more important for children and families. Regardless, more than twice the number of elders are removed from poverty than are children and families by these different strategies (see Table 9.5).

Tax Expenditures As Poverty Policy

The use of federal tax policy to alleviate poverty and the increase in states' use of tax policy to augment the income of poor families are relatively new features of U.S. social policy. In the past quarter century, a significant shift in social welfare policy has been witnessed: Gradually, direct welfare transfers are being augmented with indirect expenditures through tax credits. While the family welfare

TABLE 9.4 State Income Tax at Poverty Line of $22,314 for Two-Parent Families of Four, 2010

Rank	State	Tax	Rank	State	Tax
1	Alabama	$ 498	16	Maine	0
2	Hawaii	292	16	North Dakota	0
3	Georgia	238	16	Pennsylvania	0
4	Oregon	234	16	South Carolina	0
5	Montana	232	16	Utah	0
6	Iowa	214	16	Virginia	0
7	Illinois	187	28	North Carolina	(63)
8	Ohio	171	29	Rhode Island	(182)
9	Missouri	102	39	Oklahoma	(243)
10	Arkansas	96	31	Nebraska	(485)
11	Kentucky	90	32	New Mexico	(485)
12	Indiana	84	33	Wisconsin	(521)
13	Mississippi	81	34	Massachusetts	(589)
14	West Virginia	47	35	Kansas	(618)
15	Louisiana	33	36	Michigan	(679)
16	Arizona	0	37	New Jersey	(728)
16	California	0	38	Maryland	(973)
16	Colorado	0	39	District of Columbia	(1445)
16	Connecticut	0	40	Vermont	(1553)
16	Delaware	0	41	Minnesota	(1762)
16	Idaho	0	42	New York	(1903)

Source: Adapted from Phil Oliff and Nicholas Johnson, *The Impact of State Income Taxes on Low-Income Families in 2010* (Washington, DC: Center on Budget and Policy Priorities, 2011), p. 12.

TABLE 9.5 Impact of Safety Net on Poverty Reduction, 2006

Category	Individuals, Over 65 (in thousands)	Percent over 65	Children Under 18 (in thousands)	Percent under 18	Persons in Unmarried Households (in thousands)	Percent in Unmarried Households
Number of poor	36,035		73,727		40,749	
Number removed due to:						
Social Insurance	13,042	77,7	1,301	8.9	1,398	8.7
Means-tested cash benefits	349	2.1	545	3.7	728	4.5
Means-tested in-kind	433	2.6	1,626	11.1	1,800	11.2
Federal taxes and refunds	−4	0	1,782	12.1	1,539	9.5
Total removed	13,820	82.3	5,254	35.8	5,465	33.9

Source: House Ways and Means Committee, Overview of Entitlement Programs (Washington, DC: U.S. GPO, 2008), adapted from Tables E-29, E-30, and E-31.

allocation was restricted to $16.5 billion when Aid to Families with Dependent Children (AFDC) was replaced by TANF, the EITC expanded to over $59.5 billion in 2010.[24] This created a major disconnect in poverty policy insofar as many of the families transitioning from welfare to work do not claim EITC benefits even though they would be eligible for them. One researcher found that while 61.6 percent of TANF/AFDC families had heard of the EITC, only 33.3 percent had received an EITC refund.[25] If welfare departments were truly concerned about poverty, as opposed to simply distributing public assistance benefits, they would make certain that all families with earned income claimed the EITC, but few welfare workers are familiar with the program. As a result, it is underutilized by the welfare poor who are entering the labor market.

Tax expenditures in the form of deductions for families' housing and health insurance costs have been enjoyed by the middle class for more than a half century, but it has not been until relatively recently that tax expenditures have been targeted for low-income families. The list of tax credits available to the poor has grown to include credits for earned income, child care, the welfare-to-work transition, care for the elderly and disabled, and adoption expenses. As the number of tax credits targeted to the poor has increased, tax credits have emerged as a contender to replace, at least partially, direct income transfers to aid the poor.

As might be expected by a transition of such magnitude, the replacement of welfare transfers with tax credits raises several policy issues:

- Tax and revenue agencies replace welfare departments as the source of benefits, a role that many departments of social services are either unprepared for or may resist outright.
- Beneficiaries of tax credits must participate in the tax system in order to claim benefits, a status that is unfamiliar for many.
- Because much tax preparation is done by commercial firms, low-income workers may fall prey to unscrupulous preparers, particularly those advancing a refund as a loan.
- Tax credit refunds are almost always paid after the fact, requiring the recipient's willingness to wait until late spring, unlike traditional welfare that arrives at monthly intervals during the year.
- As tax expenditures, tax credits are no less consequential for the federal and state treasuries than are traditional welfare transfers.

An important advantage of tax credits is that their allocations are not fixed; like open-ended entitlements, the amount awarded is determined by the volume of valid claims.

Tax credits offer new opportunities in areas historically understood as "welfare." In order to accelerate the upward mobility of the poor, for example, tax credits could be connected directly to asset-accrual strategies, such as Individual Development Accounts, by encouraging low-income taxpayers to split their refund, directing a portion to a savings instrument. The tax preparation necessary for people to access tax credits could be one of several basic services—checking, savings, financial planning—offered by community financial services that could replace current welfare departments and serve as alternatives to marginal financial outfits that exploit the poor. Integrated with other capital formation strategies such as electronic benefit transfer, deposits by commercial banks to meet their Community Reinvestment Act obligations, and deposits by government and nonprofit agencies, tax credits could be part of a broad community development initiative that would finance projects in poor neighborhoods, thereby providing jobs to residents. In this respect, tax credits may not only begin to replace traditional welfare transfers, but in so doing may well introduce a new era of basic supports for poor families.[26]

Other tax credits have been proposed to augment poverty policy. Martha Ozawa and Baeg-Eui Hong suggested using the EITC to establish a $1,000 income floor for poor children and adjusting the benefit according to family size. "The modified EITC and children's allowances combined would improve the income status of all EITC-recipient children by 23.6 percent, with black and Hispanic children benefiting more than white children," Ozawa and Hong concluded.[27] Robert Cherry and Max Sawicky proposed a universal unified child credit that would augment the EITC and child care tax credit with an additional child credit.[28] Thus, the integration of refundable tax credits and calibrating them according to family size could reduce poverty significantly.

Increasing refundable tax credits and adjusting them to family size would not only address poverty but also accelerate upward mobility for low-income households. Unfortunately, the United States lags behind other industrialized countries with respect to economic mobility; too often children born into poor households grow up to be poor, like their

TABLE 9.6 Children's Chances of Experiencing Mobility by Parents' Family Income in Percent

Quintile	Upwardly Mobile (Higher Income and Up 1 or More Quintiles)	Riding the Tide (Higher Income and Same Quintile)	Falling Despite the Tide (Higher Income and Down 1 Quintile)	Downwardly Mobile (Lower Income and Lower/Same Quintile)
Top	NA	34	10	57
Fourth	26	32	9	33
Middle	36	23	7	34
Second	52	20	1	26
Bottom	58	24	NA	18
All Families	34	27	5	33

Source: Julia Isaacs, "Economic Mobility of Families Across Generations," (Washington, DC: Brookings Institution, 2007), p 6.

parents. This is not to say that none escape poverty; indeed, some move quickly upward; the problem is that upward mobility in the United States is "sticky"—the lowest income households tend to have children who are also poor, as evident in Table 9.6. This stickiness affects minority children more than others. A pre-recession report on mobility sponsored by prominent policy institutes across the ideological spectrum concluded "it is fairly hard for children born in the bottom fifth to escape from the bottom: 42 percent remain there and another 42 percent end up in either the low-middle or middle fifth. Only 17 percent of those born to parents in the bottom quintile climb to one of the top two income groups."[29] Many minority children actually experience downward mobility. Of black children with middle class parents, 45 percent fell to the bottom of the income distribution, compared to 16 percent of white children. Poor black children fared the worst: 54 percent of children in families in the bottom quintile remained there, compared to 31 percent of white children.[30] The recession further slowed the upward mobility of minorities. A post-recession analysis of economic mobility concluded that one-fourth of middle class children had fallen out of the middle class as adults, a prospect that affected 38 percent of African American men.[31]

The Anti-Tax Movement

Proponents of publicly funded social programs assume that tax-generated revenues are prudent investments toward the public good. Within the larger policy context, there are differing views on this assumption, however. It is worth acknowledging that some of the most egregious violations of personal decency, to say nothing of civil rights, have occurred under the auspices of public programs—such as the sterilization of "feebleminded" people during the eugenics movement, the Tuskegee "experiment" on syphilitic African American men, and the warehousing of chronically mentally ill patients as well as of prison inmates.

To the extent that government enriches the powerful and mistreats citizens, a logical reform strategy is to defund the state by cutting off its tax revenues. By way of illustration, Michael Tanner of the Cato Institute calculated that $3.5 trillion has been spent on poverty programs since the Great Society period, yet with little success. "We are not going to solve our welfare problems by throwing more money at them," he concludes. "It is time to recognize that welfare cannot be reformed. It should be ended."[32]

The obvious question raised by conservatives is, why tax at all? Beyond central functions of the state, conservatives contend that citizens should be allowed to retain earned income and use it as they see fit. The liberal rebuttal to this suggestion has been that unregulated capitalism inevitably skews the distribution of resources and opportunities, leaving subgroups vulnerable to insecurity with respect to income, employment, and health. The result, liberals have contended, is that specific populations suffer disproportionate and protracted poverty, thus providing the rationale for social programs. For more than half a century, they note, social insurance and public assistance programs have buffered low-income families from poverty.

Despite support for publicly funded social programs, there are some who believe that Americans should not pay any taxes.

Source: The Richmond Times-Dispatch, Joe Mahoney/AP Images

Conservative ambitions in domestic policy are to reverse liberal dominance of government in the lives of citizens and allow them to do more for themselves. At best, the Right contends, government consumes tax revenues that could be otherwise used for personal purposes; at worst, social programs inflict not only acute damage on individuals but also long-term harm on society. The inverse relationship between citizen autonomy and government social programs is at the heart of the conservative social policy strategy. By favoring autonomy, tax cuts provide individuals with discretionary income with which they can choose the services they desire. This is shrewd politics, as Jonathan Rauch noted, "by repudiating the Washington-knows-best legacy of the New Deal, Republicans will empower the people, and the people will empower Republicans." And the consequences for welfare liberalism are equally profound:

> If the Democrats dig in their heels and fall back on stale rants against greed, inequality, and privatization, so much the better. The voters will know whom to thank for empowering choices that Republicans intend to give them. As for which is the "party of nostalgia," the voters will also remember who defended, until the last dog died, single-payer Medicare, one-size-fits-all Social Security, schools without accountability, bureaucratic government monopolies, static economics, and Mutually Assured Destruction.[33]

The success of the anti-tax movement seems evident with the relatively wide support that the Bush tax cuts have received, even if they benefit the wealthy

disproportionately. In this respect, voter support of tax cuts can be interpreted as a referendum on the welfare state; given the choice, rather than divert income to public programs through taxes, many voters prefer to keep their income for themselves.

The Debate Over Economic Inequality

Stagnant wages, growing federal debt, and the emergence of insurgent groups, such as the Tea Party and Occupy Wall Street, fueled a debate over economic inequality that raged as the recession dragged on. In February 2009, President Obama appointed a bipartisan deficit reduction committee to propose reductions in federal expenditures; however, the commission proposed reductions in social entitlements as well as popular tax expenditures, and its recommendations failed to attract the interest of Congressional leaders.[34] If federal expenditures could not be trimmed significantly, the expiration of the Bush tax cuts, scheduled for the end of 2011 promised to increase revenues, but President Obama could be criticized for overseeing a major increase in federal taxes.[35] Momentarily defusing the issue, Obama received Congressional support for continuing the Bush tax cuts, but cutting the payroll tax while continuing unemployment benefits.[36] Procrastination on tax policy not only served to invigorate the Tea Party, which sought major reductions in federal spending in order to reduce the debt, but also a nascent Occupy Wall Street movement determined to tax the wealthy at higher rates.

Public opinion found Americans divided in their understanding of how to proceed: Surveys show that while most respondents object to increasing economic inequality, they presume that such differences are inevitable given the nation's economic system.[37] Providing respondents with more data changed their perceptions, however. For example, of respondents to Pew Charitable Foundation surveys, 57 percent thought the wealthy were not paying enough in taxes, and 86 percent objected to bonuses paid to executives of investment firms.[38] In attempting to reconcile these differences, pundit Charles Lane suggested that Americans believed in the work ethic and an opportunity society, but rejected the means by which the wealthy accrued riches: "What annoys Americans is not that some of us are rich—it's that some of us get rich just through connections."[39] The possibility of such a consensus on tax policy dissolves once political party affiliation is factored into the equation. While 39 percent of Republicans and 36 percent of Democrats thought they paid more than their fair share of taxes in 2012, only 37 percent of Republicans thought the wealthy should pay more, compared to 70 percent of Democrats.[40]

Although public opinion varies considerably on tax policy, data support increasing economic inequality. While wages increased only 26 percent from 1970 to 2005, median executive compensation increased 430 percent, far above corporate profits, 250 percent.[41] If executives gained most in recent decades, professionals were not far behind, as shown in Table 9.7. By 2010, the number of American millionaires had more than five-fold since 1972, but their tax burden had almost been halved, as shown in Table 9.8. Logically, long-term income inequity affects generations; in the absence of

TABLE 9.8 Millionaires and Their Taxes, 2010 Dollars

	1972	1985	2010
$1 Million+ returns	22,887	58,603	236,893
Per 100,000 returns	30	58	162
Share of all income	1.3%	3.0%	9.5%
Average tax paid	47%	37%	25%
Average after-tax income	$1,159,595	$1,465,947	$2,319,236

Source: Andrew Hacker, "We're More Unequal Than You Think," New York Review of Books, February 23, 2012, p. 34.

TABLE 9.7 Professional Paydays, in 2010 Dollars

	1985	2010	% Increase
All Employed Americans	$39,044	$41,919	7
Radiologists	334,400	448,900	34
Urologists	226,200	380,400	43
Harvard University Professors	132,000	193,800	47
University of Chicago Professors	112,100	190,400	70
Attorneys at Wachtell Lipton	1,669,000	4,345,000	160
Attorneys at Kirkland & Ellis	850,000	3,075,000	262
CEO at Union Pacific	3,825,000	23,060,000	502
CEO at Occidental Petroleum	2,440,000	20,130,000	825

Source: Andrew Hacker, "We're More Unequal Than You Think," New York Review of Books, February 23, 2012, p. 36.

opportunity structures that assure upward mobility, economic inequality persists. Using data from Canadian economist Miles Corak, Alan Krueger, Obama's Chairman of the Council of Economic Advisors, presented the "Great Gatsby Curve;" when generational mobility is plotted in relation to economic inequality, the United States more resembles developing nations, such as Singapore and China, than those of Europe.[42]

Interpretation of data about economic inequality conforms to conventional ideology with Democrats favoring leveling the economic playing field and Republicans finding justifications for economic disparities. Liberals, such as Paul Krugman, contend that the rich should pay more, as they do in other industrialized nations, in order to upgrade America's degraded physical and social infrastructure in the process generating jobs that are badly needed during recession.[43] Indeed, billionaire Warren Buffett has complained that his tax rate of 17.4 percent is about half that of other staff in his office, including his secretary.[44] In addition to arguing that the poor are favored over time by mobility, conservatives have argued that there is much more to economic inequality, and thus poverty, than measures related to income. James Q. Wilson, for example, contends that focusing on the rich is the wrong end of the affluence continuum; the poor should be examined for self-defeating behaviors that consign them to penury. Since very few adults who finish high school, work full-time, and marry before having children are poor, the key to rectifying economic inequality is not to punish the affluent by taxing them more, but encouraging the poor to be more responsible: "the problem facing the poor is not too little money, but too few skills and opportunities to advance themselves."[45]

When the national economy hums along, ideological differences can be reconciled by taxing the wealthy moderately and diverting revenue to incremental augmentation of social programs; however, during a recession, the situation resembles a zero-sum game where the benefit to one group subtracts from the well-being of another. Five years into the Great Recession, the majority of Americans contend with at least one adverse circumstance: static wages, unemployment, or foreclosure. "This is truly a lost decade," observed Harvard economist Lawrence Katz. "We think of America as a place where every generation is doing better, but we're looking at a period when the median family is in worse shape than it was in the late 1990s."[46] Conventional welfare philosophy suggests expansion of government social benefits under these circumstances, but that option has been effectively negated by Congressional conservatives emboldened by members identified with the Tea Party. Precluding the infusion of federal support for social welfare leaves the nation contending with a "politics of austerity." According to Thomas Edsall, the current stalemate pits taxpayers, the most influential of whom are wealthy Republicans, against tax consumers, mostly lower-income minorities who tend to be Democrats. Instead of a virtuous circle through which government funds spark economic activity and minimize economic dislocation, the result is a vicious circle where federal assistance is choked-off, the needy are left to fend for themselves, and antagonism increases across class, racial, and ethnic lines.[47] How to employ tax policy in order to create a virtuous circle under conditions of significant federal debt and during a protracted recession remains a signal challenge to contemporary social policy.

Conclusion

Tax policy, often undervalued in discussions of social welfare, serves a vital function because it provides the revenues through which public programs operate. Increasing fluency in tax policy has signifi-

cant benefits for advocates of social justice. At the national level, for example, introducing progressive features to the Social Security withholding tax, adjusting the tax rate for income, and lifting the cap on taxable income, would generate significant new revenues that could make minimal Social Security benefits more adequate.

Leveraging tax policy to advance social justice requires sophistication in social policy, however. Historically, two streams of poverty policy have evolved in the United States. The first—public welfare—was legislated through the Social Security Act of 1935 and consists of TANF, SSI, Medicaid, Food Stamps, and the like. Much of public welfare is managed by HHS and parallel agencies at the state level. The second—tax credits—was enacted through the 1975 Earned Income Tax Credit and consists of an array of tax credits for individuals as well as businesses. The tax credit stream is operated by the Treasury Department and the Federal Reserve System. By understanding poverty policy exclusively through the public welfare paradigm, human service professionals omit from the realm of possibility a set of policy options that have enormous promise. Thus, if social welfare professionals are to enhance their role in the domestic policy debate, they will have to master the financial, procedural, and accounting nuances of tax policy. These are daunting fields, to be sure, but the potential payoff makes the effort worthwhile.

DISCUSSION QUESTIONS

1. Click on Congress.org and explore tax cuts that were passed during the Bush administration. Who have they benefited? Who has been disadvantaged? What changes in tax policy could advance economic justice?
2. Why has Harry Hopkins's political calculus, "Tax, tax, spend, spend, elect, elect!" lost its political currency in more recent times?
3. Should the federal government expand its spending on social programs despite the large and ongoing federal debt? What are the effects of increased spending, and what are the effects of stable or even decreasing spending, on social programs?
4. What are the positive and negative effects of increasing corporate taxation? How would it affect the poor in both the short term and the long term?
5. Should nonprofit human service corporations be required to pay taxes just as for-profit firms do? What would be the possible consequences of restructuring the tax code to mandate that nonprofits lose their nonprofit tax status?

6. Should the altruism of Americans be rewarded by tax codes that permit charitable contributions, cash as well as in-kind, to be deducted from taxes? Do the long-term effects of this tax deduction encourage or discourage real altruism?

7. Some welfare advocates concerned with income inequality argue that the function of the welfare state is to equalize incomes and assets through social welfare programs. Others believe it is unrealistic to expect that welfare state programs can do more than alleviate human suffering by providing resources to those in need. Should the goal of social welfare programs be to reduce income and asset inequality, or should that function be relegated to tax and labor policy?

8. Has the social work profession been successful in lobbying efforts and in promoting a more just society? If not, why? What strategies should social workers employ to move society toward more equitable income and asset redistribution?

NOTES

1. Paul Krugman, "Duped and Betrayed," *New York Times* (July 6, 2003), p. A31.
2. Paul Krugman, "The Tax-Cut Zombies," *New York Times* (December 23, 2005), p. A27.
3. Charles Murray, "A Plan to Replace the Welfare State," *Focus* 24, 2 (Spring–Summer 2006), p. 2.
4. Daniel Baneman and Jim Nunns, "Income Tax Paid at Each Rate, 1958–2009," (Washington, DC: Tax Policy Center, October 2011), p. 3.
5. Committee on Ways and Means, *Overview of Entitlement Programs* (Washington, DC: U.S. GPO, 2004), pp. 13–36.
6. Reynolds Farley, *The New American Reality* (New York: Russell Sage Foundation, 1996), p. 85.
7. The Economic and Budget Outlook: Fiscal Years, 1991–1995 (Washington, DC: CBO, 1990), pp. 112, 122.
8. Jonathan Weisman, "Congress Votes to Extend Tax Cuts," *Washington Post* (September 24, 2004), p. A7.
9. Lori Montgomery and Nell Henderson, "Burden Set to Shift on Balanced Budget," *Washington Post* (January 16, 2007), p. A1.
10. Jeff Madrick, "The Iraqi Time Bomb," *New York Times Magazine* (April 6, 2003), p. 50.
11. http://www.ssa.gov/oact/trsum/index.html
12. "The Bottom Line: Today's Fiscal Policy Remains Unsustainable" (Washington, DC: Government Accountability Office, September 2006).
13. Lori Montgomery, "Deficit Panelists Offer Bold Moves on Taxes, Outlays," *Washington Post*, November 11, 2010, p. A1.
14. Committee on Ways and Means, Overview of Entitlement Programs (Washington, DC: U.S. GPO, 2004), pp. 13-4–13-5.
15. http://www.cato.org/pubs/handbook/hb111/hb111-26.pdf, downloaded February 2, 2012.
16. http://troubled-asset-relief-program.net/, downloaded February 2, 2012.
17. Alan Abramson, Lester Salamon, and C. Eugene Steuerle, "The Nonprofit Sector and the Federal Budget," in Elizabeth Boris and C. Eugene Steuerle (eds.), *Nonprofits and Government* (Washington, DC: Urban Institute, 1999), p. 122.
18. David Kamin, "New CBO Study Finds That Estate Tax Repeal Would Substantially Reduce Charitable Giving," (Washington, DC: Center on Budget and Policy Priorities, 2004), p. 1.
19. http://www.philanthropyjournal.org/resources/special-reports/professional-development/post-recession-executive-director, downloaded February 2, 2012.
20. Aviva Aron-Dine and Isaac Shapiro, "New Data Show Extraordinary Jump in Income Concentration in 2004" (Washington, DC: Center on Budget and Policy Priorities, 2007), p. 3.
21. Emmanuel Saez, "Striking It Richer," *Pathways* (Winter 2008), p. 7.
22. Rakesh Kochhar, "The Wealth of Hispanic Households: 1996–2002" (Washington, DC: Pew Hispanic Center, 2004), p. 5.
23. Ray Boshara (ed.), *Building Assets* (Washington, DC: Corporation for Enterprise Development, 2001), p. 2008.
24. http://www.eitc.irs.gov/central/eitcstats/, downloaded February 3, 2012.
25. Katherin Phillips, "Who Knows about the Earned Income Tax Credit?" (Washington, DC: Urban Institute, January 2001).
26. David Stoesz and David Saunders, "Welfare Capitalism," *Social Service Review* (September 1999).
27. Martha Ozawa and Baeg-Eui Hong, "The Effects of EITC and Children's Allowances on the Economic Well-Being of Children," *Social Work* 27, no. 3 (September 2003), p. 171.
28. Robert Cherry and Max Sawicky, "Giving Tax Credit Where Credit Is Due," (Washington, DC: Economic Policy Institute, n.d.).
29. Julia Isaacs, "Economic Mobility of Families Across Generations," (Washington, DC: Brookings Institution, 2006), p. 5.
30. Julia Isaacs, "Economic Mobility of Black and White Families," (Washington, DC: Brookings Institution, 2006.
31. Gregory Acs, "Downward Mobility from the Middle Class," (Washington, DC: Pew Charitable Trusts, 2011), pp. 21, 11.
32. Michael Tanner, "Ending Welfare as We Know It" (Washington, DC: Cato Institute, 1994), p. 24.
33. Jonathan Rauch, "The Accidental Radical," *The National Journal* 35, no. 30 (July 26, 2003).
34. Jackie Calmes, "Panel Seeks cuts in Social Security and Higher Taxes," *New York Times*, November 11, 2010, p. A1.

35. David Herszenhorn, "Next Big Battle in Washington: Bush's Tax Cuts," *New York Times*, July 25, 2010, p. A1.

36. David Herszenhorn and Jackie Calmes, "Obama Reaches Accord with G.O.P. on Tax Cut; Democrats Hold Back," *New York Times*, December 7, 2010, p. A1.

37. Charles Blow, "Inconvenient Income Inequality," *New York Times*, December 17, 2011, p. A25.

38. Andrew Kohut, "Don't Mind the Gap," *New York Times*, January 27, 2012, p. A21.

39. Charles Lane, "Down with Rent," *Washington Post*, January 31, 2012, p. A17.

40. Allison Kopicki, "Americans Divided Over Tax Policy," *New York Times*, January 25, 2012, p. A16.

41. Peter Whoriskey, "Income Gap Widens as Executives Prosper," *Washington Post*, June 16, 2011, p. A1.

42. http://milescorak.com/2012/01/18/the-economics-of-the-great-gatsby-curve-a-picture-is-worth-a-thousand-words/, downloaded February 6, 2012.

43. Paul Krugman, "Taxes at the Top," *New York Times*, January 20, 2012, p. A23.

44. Warren Buffett, "Stop Coddling the Super-Rich," *New York Times*, August 15, 2011, p. A19.

45. James Q. Wilson, "Don't Blame the Rich," *Washington Post*, January 29, 2012, p. B4.

46. Sabrina Tavernise, "Soaring Poverty Casts Spotlight on 'Lost Decade'," *New York Times*, September 14, 2011, p. A1.

47. Thomas Edsall, "The Politics of Austerity," *New York Times*, November 6, 2011, p. SR8.

CHAPTER 10

Social Insurance Programs

Source: PhotoEdit Inc.

This chapter explores the major forms of social insurance in the United States: Old-Age, Survivors, and Disability Insurance (OASDI); Unemployment Insurance (UI); and Workers' Compensation. In addition, this chapter explores some of the major issues and problems surrounding social insurance programs.

Definition of Social Insurance

Social insurance is the cornerstone of U.S. social welfare policy. Specifically, it is a system whereby people are compelled—through payroll or other taxes—to insure themselves against the possibility of their own indigence, such as might result from the economic vicissitudes of retirement, the loss of a job, the death of the family breadwinner, or physical disability. Based in part on the same principles used in private insurance, social insurance sets aside a sum of money that is held in trust by the government and earmarked for use in the event of workers' retirement, death, disability, or unemployment. The major goal of social insurance is to help maintain income by replacing a portion of lost earnings. It is a pay-as-you-go system whereby the workers

and employers of today pay for those who have retired, are ill, or who have lost their jobs. Although originally designed to replicate a private insurance fund, the original Social Security program has been broadened to include a variety of programs that provide a minimal level of replacement income. Because the benefits paid to some retired workers exceed their contributions to the system, Social Security has taken on some of the characteristics of an income redistribution and/or public assistance program.

Unlike Social Security, public assistance programs are subject to **means tests** and are based entirely on need. The rationale for public assistance is grounded in the concept of *safety nets* designed to ensure that citizens receive basic services and do not fall below a given poverty level. Social insurance, on the other hand, requires beneficiaries to make contributions to the system *before* they can claim benefits. Because social insurance affects a larger number of people and benefits are generally higher, expenditures for social insurance are far greater than for public assistance. Social insurance is also universal; that is, people receive benefits as legal entitlements regardless of their personal wealth. Table 10.1

TABLE 10.1 Past and Current Federal Spending for Major Social Insurance Programs, Selected Years (expenditures in billions)

Programs	2002	2004	2006	2008	2010
OASDI	$452	$494	$539	$598	$670
Medicare	254	287	319	366	421
Unemployment Insurance	51	46	43	45	49
Total	757	827	901	1009	1140

Source: Committee on Ways and Means, U.S. House of Representatives, *2004 Green Book* (Washington, DC: U.S. Government Office, 2004), pp. I-2, I-8.

Projected Federal Spending for Social Security, Medicare and Medicaid, Selected Years (expenditures in billions)

Programs	2012	2014	2018	2020	2022
Social Security	$770	$857	$1,063	$1,197	$1,345
Medicare	560	629	769	890	1,041
Medicaid	262	330	456	522	605
Total	1,592	1,816	2,288	2,609	2,991

Source: Adapted from Congressional Budget Office (CBO), "Budget and Economic Outlook Fiscal Years 2012 to 2022," January 2012. Retrieved April 2012, from HeinOnline at http://heinonline.org/.

shows federal spending for major social insurance programs. Because social insurance benefits are linked to occupationally defined productive work, most programs are not stigmatized compared to public assistance programs. In part, this stigma occurs because public assistance programs are financed from general tax revenues and are not occupationally linked or based on a previous work record, and the eligibility for these programs is determined by means tests.

Although conservatives complain about the costs of public assistance programs, social insurance programs consume many times more resources as public welfare. In 2010, Old-Age, Survivors and Disability Insurance (OASDI) cost a total of $701.6 billion.[1] By comparison, public assistance and related programs cost $51.6 billion.[2]

The average OASDI beneficiary benefit in 2010 was $1,126 a month[3] while the median monthly Temporary Assistance for Needy Families (TANF) payment for a family of three with no income was $429.[4]

The Background of Social Insurance

The first old-age insurance program was introduced in Germany in 1889 by Chancellor Otto von Bismarck to curb the growing socialist trend in Germany. By the onset of World War I, nearly all European nations had old-age assistance programs of one sort or another. In 1920, the U.S. government began its own Federal Employees Retirement program. By 1931, 17 states had enacted old age assistance programs, although these were often harsh with stringent eligibility requirements.[5]

Spurred on by the Great Depression of the 1930s, President Franklin Roosevelt championed a government assistance program that would cover both unemployed and retired workers.[6] The result was the Social Security Act of 1935 and the establishment of the modern American welfare state.

Relatively modest compared to its present scope, the original Social Security Act of 1935 provided assistance to the elderly poor, dependent children, the blind, and some disabled children. Title VII established a Social Security Board, whose job was to monitor the fund. Title XI gave the Congress the right to alter any part of the act.[7]

The current Social Security Act provides for (1) OASDI; (2) UI programs under joint federal and state partnership; (3) federal assistance to aged, blind, and disabled under the Supplemental Security Income (SSI) program; (4) public assistance to families with dependent children (now TANF); (5) federal health insurance for the aged (Medicare); and (6) federal and state health assistance for the poor (Medicaid). Although all these programs are under the Social Security Act of 1935, not all are true social insurance programs (e.g., Medicaid, TANF, and SSI).

The Social Security Act of 1935 has been repeatedly modified, almost always in the direction of increased coverage. The original Act provided retirement and survivor benefits to only about 40 percent of workers, farm and domestic workers, the self-employed, and state and local government employees were excluded. In 1950, farmers and the self-employed were added, thereby covering more than 90 percent of the labor force. Congress made survivors and dependents of insured workers eligible for benefits in 1939, and in 1956, disability insurance was added. In 1965 Medicare—a health insurance plan for the aged—became law. In later years, workers were allowed to retire at age 62, provided they agreed to accept only 80 percent of their benefits. In 1977, an automatic cost-of-living index was attached to Social Security payments.

By 1996, more than 43 million Americans and more than one-quarter of all U.S. households depended on a Social Security check.[8] As Figure 10.1 illustrates, only 64 percent of Social Security beneficiaries were retired workers in December 2010.[9]

The Financial Organization of Social Insurance

Social insurance is relatively straightforward. Covered workers pay taxes to Social Security, and when they retire or become disabled, they (or their family) collect monthly benefits. General revenue taxes are used for Supplemental Security Income (SSI) which despite its name, is actually a means-test public assistance program.

Social Security and Medicare taxes are di among several trust funds, including (1) the O and Survivors Insurance (OASI) trust fund retirement and survivor benefits), and (2) two Disability Insurance (DI) fund (provide Insur the disabled and their families). There under Medicare trust funds: (1) the federal ance (HI) trust fund pays for servi

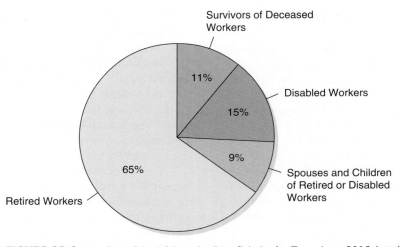

FIGURE 10.1 Number of Social Security Beneficiaries by Type, June 2012 (total 56.2 million)

Source: Social security Administration, Office of Research, Evaluation, and Statistics. "Fast Facts & Figures About Social ecurity, 2008," SSA Publication No. 13-11785, Washington, DC, August 2008

the hospital insurance (Part A) provisions of Medicare, and (2) the federal Supplementary Medical Insurance (SMI) trust fund pays for services covered under the medical insurance (Part B) provisions of Medicare.

The trust funds are governed by a board of trustees made up of the Secretary of the Treasury, the Secretary of Labor, the Secretary of Health and Human Services, the Commissioner of Social Security, and two public trustees who serve four-year terms. The board of trustees reports annually to Congress on the condition of the funds and on estimated future operations.

Before 1983, the system operated on a pay-as-you-go system, with taxes flowing into one end of the pipeline and flowing out the other end. However, since 1983 Social Security has operated under tial reserve system in which inflows exceed ws, thereby building up a reserve to help pay s to an increasingly large number of retiring omers.

lus income (i.e., income not needed to ts) is invested in U.S. government bonds he prevailing rate of interest and whose *bead* interest are guaranteed by the fed-*ing* ent. Social Security trust funds have *of it as* tical football with politicians accus- of raiding the funds. Others think noney." Social Security trust funds

are invested in sound Treasury securities similar to those held by investors across the globe. They are also considered one of the safest investments in the world. The amount of earned interest can be substantial. In 2010, the Social Security trust funds earned $108 billion in interest, nearly $28 billion more than that earned in 2002.[10]

Key Social Insurance Programs
OASDI

OASDI is a combination of Old-Age and Survivors Insurance (OASI) and Disability Insurance (DI). Commonly referred to as Social Security, it is the largest social program and covers approximately nine out of ten workers. OASDI is a federal program administered by the Social Security Administration, which in 1994 became an independent agency headed by a commissioner and a board appointed by the U.S. president for a six-year term.

Social Security is a stellar example of a program that has worked. In 2010:

- Social Security served more than 54 million people and paid out $706 billion in benefits.[11]
- Social Security provided at least half of the income for nearly two-thirds of the aged.[12]
- 85 percent of women were fully insured, up from just 63 percent in 1970.[13]

- Women accounted for 56 percent of adult Social Security beneficiaries.[14]

Before the Social Security **cost-of-living adjustments (COLAs)** took effect in 1969, the poverty rate for the elderly was double that of the general population, 25 percent versus 12 percent.[15] According to the Social Security Administration, the poverty rate for the elderly would have been 52 percent without Social Security.[16] Hence, Social Security has a strong redistributive effect, transferring resources from those with high lifetime earnings to those with lower lifetime earnings.[17]

Unlike prefunded private annuity plans, where a worker draws off money already invested, Social Security benefits are paid by today's workers rather than by the retirees. Benefits under OASDI are entitlement based; that is, they are based on the beneficiaries' earnings rather than the amount of the revenue in the trust fund. If benefits in a given period exceed revenues, the difference is made up from the reserves in the trust funds. OASDI operates in the following manner:

- On an employee's first $110,100 in earnings in 2012, the employee and the employer each pays an OASDI tax equal to 6.2 percent and a Medicare Hospital Insurance (HI) tax equal to 1.45 percent of earnings. Employees therefore pay a total of 7.65 percent. However, Congress passed a payroll tax holiday for 2011 and 2012, and employees paid only 4.2 percent of their wage earnings for the Social Security tax, instead of the normal 6.2 percent rate. Employers still pay the full 6.2 percent rate.[18] Self-employed persons pay 15.3 percent (12.4 percent for OASDI and 2.9 percent for Medicare). (Half of that tax is deductible for income tax purposes.) However, the "payroll tax holiday" temporarily reduced that to 10.4 percent.[19] In general, increases in the wage base are automatic and are based on the increase in average wages in the economy each year. For example, the highest Social Security tax a worker could pay in 2008 was $6,324 (not including the HI tax). Self-employed persons had their taxes computed on a lower base (net earnings from self-employment less 7.65 percent), and half of that tax was deductible for income tax purposes.

- Based on their age at retirement and the amount earned during their working years, workers receive a monthly benefit payment. The current full retirement age is 66 (increasing to 67 for those born after 1959), and how close a worker is to this age is significant in calculating their monthly benefits. Retired workers aged 62 receive a reduction of 5/9 of 1 percent for each month of entitlement before age 66 (depending on their year of birth), with a maximum reduction of 20 percent.[20] Benefits are modest; the average retired worker received $1,176 in 2010 if they were a current Social Security recipient, and $1,193 if they were a new recipient.[21] The maximum benefit in 2012 for a retired worker at age 66 was $2,513 a month.[22]

- Under the OASI program, a monthly payment is made to an unmarried child or eligible dependent grandchild of a retired worker or a deceased worker who was fully insured at the time of death, if the child or grandchild is (1) under age 18; (2) a full-time elementary or secondary school student under age 19; or (3) a dependent or disabled person aged 18 or over whose disability began before age 22. A grandchild is eligible only if the child was adopted by the insured grandparent.[23]

- A lump-sum benefit of $255 is payable to a spouse who was living with an insured worker at the time of his or her death, or minor children who meet certain criteria.[24]

- Under the Disability Insurance program (DI), monthly cash benefits are paid to disabled workers under the age of 65 and to their dependents. Monthly cash benefits are computed similar to the OASI program in terms of past earnings; however, the age at which the individual becomes disabled is also taken into account.[25] (Medicare benefits are treated in depth in Chapter 12.)

- In 2012, retired worker beneficiaries were required to have earned at least 40 credits (approximately ten years) before they were eligible to draw benefits.[26] For workers applying for Disability Insurance, the amount of required credits depended on the age at which the recipient became disabled.[27]

Social Security is the key social insurance program in the United States.

Source: Bradley C. Bower/AP Images

Social Security, especially OASDI, has been a heated topic for much of its history. Political conservatives and laissez-faire economists argue that Social Security socializes a portion of the national income, discourages savings, and causes retired people to become dependent on a supposedly fragile governmental system. The Social Security system, on the other hand, is extremely popular with the elderly who rely on it for much of their income, and with their grown children, for whom it helps to provide peace of mind.

Unemployment Insurance

The first line of defense for workers fired or laid off from their jobs is unemployment insurance (UI). Part of the Social Security Act of 1935, UI is a federal/state program whose objectives are (1) to provide temporary and partial wage replacement to involuntarily and recently unemployed workers, and (2) to help stimulate the economy during recessions by providing the unemployed with the necessary cash to purchase goods and services. Although the U.S. Department of Labor oversees the general program, each state administers its own UI program.[28] The current guidelines of the UI program require employers to contribute to a trust fund that is activated if an employee loses his or her job. The average weekly number of workers claiming UI in 2009 was 5.7 million at a total cost of $79.6 billion for the year. The average duration of unemployed workers in the UI program 2011 was 18.8 weeks.[29]

The Unemployment Insurance System and Benefits The UI system consists of two basic parts: (1) regular state-funded benefits, generally provided for a maximum of 26 weeks; and (2) a federal/state Extended Benefits (EB) program. The permanent EB program provides an additional 13 or 20 weeks of compensation to jobless workers who have exhausted their regular benefits in states where the unemployment situation is severe. The total number of additional weeks depends on the unemployment rate in a state and its UI laws. While the federal government and the states typically split the cost of EB, the federal government is now fully funding the program under the 2009 American Recovery and Reinvestment Act. The Act also made $7 billion available to states to modernize their UI law to expand eligibility.[30] States pay 50 percent of the benefits provided by the EB program.

In another response to the recession, Congress created the Emergency Unemployment Compensation (EUC) act in 2008. Workers who exhaust their state UI benefits can receive up to 34 weeks of additional benefits regardless of their state's unemployment rate. Those in states with high unemployment rates can receive up to 53 weeks of benefits, as well as EB benefits, if their state allows it. Some states also offer additional benefits under separate state-funded programs.

To be eligible for UI benefits, a worker must (1) be unemployed, (2) be ready and willing to work, (3) be registered for work with the state employment service, and (4) have been working in covered employment during a base eligibility period. A worker who is fired for misconduct, quits a job without a legally acceptable reason, fails to register with the state employment service, refuses a job equal to or better than the one previously held, or goes on strike is ineligible for unemployment benefits. States cannot deny benefits to workers who refuse to be strikebreakers or who refuse to work for less than the prevailing wage rate.[31]

Basic decisions concerning the amount of benefits, eligibility, and length of benefit time are made by the states. In general, state laws typically try to replace about half of a worker's previous wage up to a maximum benefit level. In 2009, the average weekly benefit was $309.60. State unemployment benefits varied widely, ranging from a weekly average of $195.63 in Mississippi to $423.02 in Hawaii.[32] Benefits are generally based on the wage earned by the beneficiary, while some states adjust that amount based on dependents.

1. States must have in place the following to receive one-third of their incentive payment:
   - A base period that includes recent wages
2. States must have in place at least two of the following four to receive two-thirds of their incentive payments:
   - No denial of benefits for seeking part-time work
   - No disqualification for separations from employment for compelling family reasons
   - Provide extended compensation to UI recipients in qualifying training programs
   - Provide dependents' allowances to UI recipients with dependents

FIGURE 10.2 Requirements for the Recovery Act Incentive Fund 2011

Source: Adapted from U.S. GAO, "Unemployment Insurance: Economic Circumstances of Individuals Who Exhausted Benefits," February 2012. Retrieved April 2012, from http://www.gao.gov/assets/590/588680.pdf

Problems in UI   Problems endemic to the UI program include:

1. *Part-time workers* were 59 percent less likely than full-time workers to collect UI benefits in 2007. In 23 states, people looking for part-time work were not considered to be looking for "suitable work" and were therefore ineligible for benefits.[33] This has changed with the introduction of the Recovery Act in 2011, which provided incentive payments to states who meet a set number of requirements (see Figure 10.2). One of the requirements is that states cannot decline benefits to unemployed persons seeking part-time work.[34]
2. *Temporary workers* are less likely than all other workers to receive UI benefits. The number of temporary workers has been increasing, and by 2003 they totaled 2.2 million. Those who work at temporary agencies face several difficulties when applying for UI benefits. First, they may not have worked enough hours or earned enough to qualify for benefits. Second, since they were employed at temporary agencies they have difficulty proving they did not voluntarily quit the job. Plus, to remain eligible for benefits, a worker cannot refuse "suitable work," or work of the same nature at or above the same pay rate that the worker was earning before. Some temporary workers have been denied benefits because they refused a different type of temporary assignment than they had previously been doing.[35]
3. *Low-wage workers.* Throughout the 1990's and early 2000's, low-wage workers were less likely to be eligible for and receive UI benefits.

This trend has persisted throughout the recession. Between 2007 and 2009, workers whose earnings were in the bottom 30 percent were half as likely to receive UI as those in the top 70 percent. This is because low-wage workers often fail to meet minimum earning requirements, particularly if they have been employed part time.[36] Another reason low-wage workers are often ineligible is that not all of their earnings are considered when determining eligibility. In most states, up to six months of a worker's earnings do not count toward the earnings requirements because the state ignores the last completed quarter and the current quarter of earnings. A number of states have adopted low-wage worker eligibility reforms based on an "alternative base period," which expands eligibility for workers who need their most recent earnings to qualify for UI.[37] By 2003, 19 states had adopted low-wage worker eligibility reforms based on an "alternative base period," which expands eligibility for workers who need their most recent earnings to qualify for UI.[38]

4. *Limited coverage.* In 1975, 75 percent of jobless workers received benefits; by 1986, it dropped to 33 percent.[39] Between 2005 and 2007, the number of UI recipients was consistent at about 36 percent; however, the recession drove that up to 49 percent by 2010.[40] Hence, just over half of the U.S. unemployed are still not receiving UI benefits. This is particularly problematic since in December 2011 the number of long-term unemployed (for 27 weeks or more) accounted for almost

43 percent of the 13 million unemployed.[41] Long-term unemployment is a particularly acute problem for older workers. While the length of unemployment for a jobless worker in the United States was 38.3 weeks in April 2011, the average jobless person from 55 to age 65 was looking for work for about 44 weeks, or just short of a year.[42]

5. *Benefit decline.* In 1986, total UI benefits were 59 percent lower than in 1976 (after adjusting for inflation). By 2010, only about half of the average worker's lost wages were replaced by UI benefits.[43] As such, many families cannot afford to live on these benefits.

6. *Longer spells of unemployment.* UI was based on the assumptions that (1) layoffs are temporary and employers will recall workers; or (2) suitable jobs would be found that match the skills and experience of the unemployed. Now, however, many people are losing their jobs because of long-term structural changes in the economy. The median duration of unemployment in July 2007 was 8.9 weeks; by 2010 it had risen to 32 weeks.[44] Temporary measures had increased unemployment to 32 weeks in all states with an additional 19 weeks in high unemployment states.

7. *Women and unemployment.* During the 2007 to 2010 recession, 2.7 million women lost their jobs. Since the recession, women have experienced less growth in employment opportunities than men. Between 2011 and 2012, men took 67 percent of the 1.9 million jobs created, and women only 33 percent. By 2012, women regained 34 percent of jobs lost during the recession, while men regained 45 percent.[45] Sixty-seven percent of part-time workers are women, and one-third of all women work part time. Women are also more likely to be employed by temporary agencies than are men, and their lower wages make them less likely to meet minimum UI earnings requirements. Finally, many women leave their jobs for voluntary reasons that are not considered "good cause" in many states. In some states, a woman is ineligible for UI benefits if she quits to escape a violent domestic partner, because of a schedule change that makes child care arrangements impossible, to take care of a sick child, or to follow a spouse to another location.

8. *Meeting the UI system's financial obligations.* The UI system has difficulty in meeting its financial obligations during economic downturns without federal aid or deficit spending. The huge increase in the number of UI recipients due to the recent recession has put enormous pressure on the UI finances. By late 2009, states had borrowed nearly $40 billion from the federal Unemployment Trust Fund to maintain their UI programs. States are required to fully repay the loans, with interest, within two to three years of borrowing the funds. If a state cannot repay the full amount, the federal government recoups its funds by effectively raising the federal tax on employers within the state.[46]

9. *Regressive Nature of UI.* Because UI benefits are capped, they replace a smaller share of previous earnings for higher-wage workers than lower-wage workers. As noted earlier, benefit levels vary widely from state to state. In addition, the federal tax is set by the Federal Unemployment Tax Act (FUTA) and is equal to 0.8 percent of the first $7,000 paid annually to each employee. This tax is regressive because most workers earn more than $7,000 per year and are effectively paying the same $56 flat tax a year regardless of their income. Hence, these taxes represent a much smaller share of the wages of high-wage workers than low-wage workers.[47]

Workers' Compensation

In 2010, the U.S. Bureau of Labor Statistics reported that 4,547 workers were killed on the job, and there were about 1.2 million non-fatal work-related injuries or illnesses that required sick leave.[48]

Workers' Compensation (WC) programs began in 1911 in Wisconsin and New Jersey. By 1948, every state operated some form of WC program. WC programs provide cash, medical assistance, rehabilitation services, and disability and death benefits to persons (or their dependents) who are victims of industrial accidents or occupational illnesses.[49] By 2009, 97 percent of all UI-covered workers were protected by Workers Compensation.[50] Although laws vary from state to state, the basic principle is that employers assume the costs of occupational disabilities without regard to fault.[51] Although most workers are covered in the majority of states, business owners and independent contractors are often excluded, as are volunteer, farm, railroad, maritime, and domestic workers. Federal employees are covered under a special program.

The specific laws governing WC vary from state to state, and there is little consistency either in benefit levels or in the administration of the programs. For example, some states require employers to carry WC insurance, some provide a state-sponsored insurance fund, others allow employers to act as self-insurers, and still others do not require compulsory WC coverage. Some state programs do not cover employees of nonprofit, charitable, or religious institutions. Because of the potential for large claims, most employers transfer their responsibility by purchasing insurance from private companies that specialize in WC.

WC programs are problematic in several ways. First, benefit levels are established on the basis of state formulas and are usually calculated as a percentage of weekly earnings (generally about 66.66 percent). As such, each state sets its own annually adjusted benefit level, and these levels vary widely across states.[52]

The cost to employers for providing WC insurance is significant, and they paid almost $74 billion in 2009 to insure their workers.[53]

There is great variability among states in the way claims are handled. Workers are often encouraged to settle out of court for attractive lump sums, even though the amounts may not equal their lost wages. Often, benefits are uneven. For example, the price attached to the loss of a body part has been interpreted differently from state to state.[54] There are often long delays between the time an injury occurs and the start of benefits. Finally, in some states employers are exempt from the Workers' Compensation tax if they can demonstrate that they are covered by private insurance. Unfortunately, private insurance coverage may prove inadequate in meeting a disability benefit. Despite receiving $58.3 billion in benefits and medical payments in 2009, injured workers or their survivors may not receive adequate protection.[55]

The Social Security Dilemma

Because of its widespread public support, Social Security was long perceived by policy analysts and legislators as the third rail of politics—touch it, and you die. For decades, the immediate focus of conservative Republicans and Democrats was on the more vulnerable public assistance programs that enjoyed less public support. Nevertheless, emboldened by the successful passage of the Personal Responsibility and Work Opportunity Reconciliation Act of 1996, conservatives increasingly turned their attention to the massive social insurance programs. Opponents argued that Social Security was depressing private savings (and thereby providing less capital for investment) by giving people a retirement check financed by the working population rather than interest on accumulated savings.

Arguments against the Current Social Security System

Social Security in the United States is a pay-as-you-go system and an intergenerational wealth transfer plan. Birthrate and longevity determine the solvency of pay-as-you-go retirement systems.

Spotlight 10.1

MAJOR SOCIAL INSURANCE PROGRAMS

In the United States, there are three major social insurance programs:
- OASDI (also known as Social Security) covers the elderly, survivors, and those people unable to work due to a disability.
- Unemployment Insurance covers workers who have been fired or laid off from their jobs.
- Workers' Compensation provides case, medical assistance, rehabilitation services, and disability and death benefits to persons (or their dependents) who are victims of industrial accidents or occupational illnesses.

The U.S. birthrate dipped below 20 per 1,000 people in 1932 (at about the time of the creation of Social Security) but rose in the 1950s and 1960s. By 2009, the birth rate had fallen to 13.5 births for every 1,000 people in 2009, the lowest recorded in the last century.

The U.S. birthrate at the time of the creation of Social Security was 2.3, but it rose to 3.0 by 1950 and continued to climb throughout that decade. Today it has dropped back to 2.1. The average life expectancy in 1935 was 63; today it is about 78. As a result of these demographic factors, the number of workers paying Social Security payroll taxes has gone from 16.5 workers for every retiree in 1950 to just 3.3 for every Social Security beneficiary in 2009. According to the Social Security Board of Trustees, that ratio is expected to decline to just 2.2 by 2025.

Social Security is fueling intergenerational tensions. Younger workers are skeptical about the ability of Social Security to support them upon retirement. They are nervous that Social Security will buckle now that the baby boomers have begun to retire. Some are also anxious because they are saving less than their parents. Ted Dimig sums up the dilemma: "So, where does this leave my generation? First of all, it leaves us with a huge resentment over the idea that our elders might saddle us with the debt for their retirement . . . while shortchanging us on our own retirement."[56]

Although OASDI is an essential part of economic security for the nation's retired, serious problems threaten its future viability. The original strategy of the Social Security Act of 1935 was to create a self-perpetuating insurance fund, with benefits to the elderly being in proportion to their contributions. That scenario did not materialize. Instead, among other things, Social Security took on some public assistance characteristics in terms of providing a minimum benefit level regardless of a worker's contribution.[57] Moreover, both the Social Security tax and the wage base upon which the tax is determined have increased so dramatically since the 1970s that many current workers may not recover their entire investment, depending on their longevity, their marital status, and whether they earned a high or low wage.

Arguments for the Current Social Security System

The Social Security program serves four main functions.

- It supports millions of survivors of deceased workers and disabled Americans.
- Social Security is the nation's most successful antipoverty program.[58] Largely because of Social Security, the nation's elderly poverty rate has fallen over the last 50 years from more than 40 percent to 9 percent.[59] By 2000, only 40 percent of elderly Americans had access to public or private pension plans or annuities.[60] Without Social Security about half of elderly Americans would live below the poverty line.
- In 2008, 88 percent of married couples and 86 percent of nonmarried persons aged 65 or older received Social Security benefits. It provided at least 50 percent of total income to 52 percent of aged beneficiary couples and 73 percent of aged nonmarried beneficiaries. Social Security benefits accounted for 90 percent or more of income for 21 percent of aged beneficiary couples and 43 percent of aged nonmarried beneficiaries.
- Social Security is important to working as well as retired Americans (about one in three Social Security recipients is not a retiree.). Financially solvent seniors are consumers and therefore good for businesses. Moreover, few children would trade the burden of payroll taxes for the onus of supporting destitute retired parents.

Social Security is a special kind of "investment" unavailable in the private sector: a lifetime retirement annuity with benefits that rise with inflation. Almost all corporate pensions (many which run out after 20 years) are not indexed to the erosion of purchasing power caused by inflation. Social Security has also been accused of overpaying the elderly, slighting younger workers (who could get a better return if they invested privately), and leading the nation to financial collapse. Merton and Joan Bernstein challenge the criticisms leveled at Social Security. They claim that rather than discouraging private savings, Social Security actually stimulates financial planning for retirement and thus encourages savings.[61] Others dispute the overpayment argument by noting that in 2010, the median income for householders aged 65 and over was $31,408, which was $18,037 below the national median household income of $49,445.[62] This would hardly suggest an elderly population growing wealthy by exploiting an overly generous Social Security system.

Social Security in Trouble Social Security began to show signs of fiscal trouble in the mid-1970s. Between 1975 and 1981, the OASI fund suffered a significant net decrease in funds and a deficit in the reserve. This imbalance between incoming and outgoing funds threatened to deplete the reserve by 1983. The prospects for Social Security seemed bleak in other ways. While the ratio of workers to supported beneficiaries (the dependency ratio) was three to one in the 1970s, it was estimated that by 2025 this ratio would approach two to one. In short, the long-term expenditures of Social Security would exceed its projected revenues. The crisis in Social Security was fueled by demographic changes (a dropping birthrate coupled with an increase in life expectancy), liberal benefits paid to retiring workers, the effects of inflation, high levels of unemployment, and the COLAs passed by Congress in the mid-1970s.

Facing these short- and long-term problems, Congress quickly passed p. 98–21, the Social Security Amendments of 1983. Among the newly legislated changes was a delay in the COLAs, such that if trust funds fell below a certain level, future benefits would be keyed to the consumer price index (CPI) or the average wage increase, whichever is lower. A second change was that Social Security benefits became taxable if taxable income plus Social Security benefits exceeded $25,000 for an individual or $32,000 for a couple. A third change increased the 2027 retirement age to 67 to collect full benefits. Although workers could retire at age 62, they would receive only 70 percent of their benefits instead of 80 percent. Finally, new federal employees were covered for the first time, as were members of Congress, the president and vice president, federal judges, and employees of nonprofit corporations. In the mid-1990s, the Social Security rules were again changed, this time easing the historic Social Security penalty for about one million beneficiaries aged 65 to 67 who are still working. The new rules meant that for those who had reached their full retirement age, the earnings limit was $36,120 with a loss of $1.00 of benefits for every $3.00 earned.[63] In addition, the retirement age for receiving full Social Security benefits was raised to 66 for those born between 1943 and 1954 and to 67 for those born after 1959.

In 2010, Congress passed a tax extension bill. Among other features was a one-year cut in Social Security payroll taxes from 6.2 to 4.2 percent. In turn, the federal government would borrow $110 billion to make up the difference. If made permanent, this would reduce the solvency of Social Security by more than a decade. Moreover, this was the first time that the Social Security payroll tax was directly used to manipulate the economy.

The Long-Term Prospects for Social Security

The long-term financial prospects for Social Security depend on several factors, including the general health of the economy, the unemployment rate, immigration, life expectancy of beneficiaries, and the birth rate. Despite the reforms noted above, the fiscal viability of the OASDI system remains in question. Some analysts suggest that Social Security is on sound footing. They point to the fact that the income and assets reserve in the combined OASDI trust funds reached $2.6 trillion in 2010. At the end of 2010, the OASDI trust fund income was $781 billion, while outgoing expenses were $712 billion. By 2020, the OASDI assets are expected to grow to $3.5 trillion.[64] However, OASDI viability represents only part of the picture, because Social Security funding also relies on additional trust funds including the Medicare HI (Hospital Insurance) Trust Fund, which pays for inpatient hospital and related care, and the SMI (Supplementary Medical Insurance) Trust Fund, which pays for physician and outpatient services, as well as the Part D prescription drug benefit (see Figures 10.3 and 10.4). Deficits in Social Security funding are expected to grow rapidly after 2014 as the baby boom generation's retirement causes the number of beneficiaries to increase more rapidly than the number of covered workers. The annual deficits will be made up by redeeming trust fund interest earnings through 2024, and then by redeeming trust fund assets until reserves are exhausted in 2037. At that point, projected OASDI tax income will be sufficient to finance about 75 percent of scheduled annual benefits from 2037 through 2084, after which the combined OASI and DI Trust Funds are projected to be exhausted (see Table 10.2).

Under the immediate assumptions of the Social Security Administration (SSA), OASDI costs

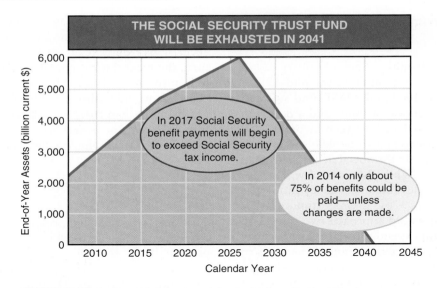

FIGURE 10.3 Projected Exhaustion of the Social Security Trust Fund

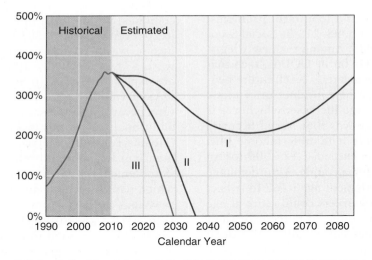

N.B. Assumption I: low cost; Assumption II: best estimate; Assumption III: high cost

FIGURE 10.4 Year of OASDI Trust Fund Exhaustion Using Social Security Estimates

Source: The 2011 Annual Report of the Board of Trustees of the Federal Old-Age and Survivors Insurance and Federal Disability Insurance Trust Funds, House Document 112-23, Washington, DC, 13 May 2011. Retrieved April 2012, from http://www.socialsecurity.gov/OACT/TR/2011/tr2011.pdf

were projected to increase faster than non-interest income in 2011, due to the increase in retiring baby boomers. After 2035, longer life expectancy and lower birth rates will continue to increase Social Security system costs relative to tax income, albeit more slowly.[65]

In actuality, annual costs of OASDI exceeded tax income in 2010, at which time the gap was covered by redeeming the Treasury bills that made up the trust fund assets.[66] By 2036, those assets will be exhausted. More specifically, the DI fund is projected to be exhausted in 2018 followed by the OASI fund in 2038.[67]

TABLE 10.2 Key Dates for the Trust Funds

	OASI	DI	OASDI	HI
First year outgo exceeds income excluding interest	2017	2005	2010	2008
First year outgo exceeds income including interest	2025	2009	2023	2008
Year trust funds are exhausted	2038	2018	2036	2024

Source: Social Security Administration, "Status of the Social Security and Medicare Programs: A Summary of the 2011 Annual Social Security and Medicare Trust Fund Reports," Last Revised May 2011. Retrieved April 2012, from http://www.socialsecurity.gov/OACT/TRSUM/index.html

For the trust funds to remain solvent for the 75-year projection period, the combined payroll tax rate must be permanently raised 2.15 percentage points, and benefits would have to be permanently reduced by 13.8 percent. Alternatively, a combination of approaches could be adopted.[68]

Medicare (Hospital Insurance and Supplementary Medical Insurance)

The outlook for Medicare has improved because of the 2010 Affordable Care Act. Despite lower revenues resulting from the recession, the HI Trust Fund is expected to remain solvent until 2029, 12 years later than earlier projected. The HI Trust Fund balance is also expected to fall below one year's projected expenditure beginning in 2012, which means it will fail the short-range financial adequacy test. More specifically, the HI trust fund is expected to be completely exhausted in 2024.[69]

Supplementary Medical Insurance

The Medicare Supplementary Medical Insurance (SMI) Trust Fund that pays for physician services and the prescription drug benefit relies heavily on general revenue funding. In 2011, the SMI program required $204.6 billion in general revenues to cover its outlays. In comparison, the HI fund required only $100 million. The amount of revenue required to fund the SMI program, along with the overall costs of HI exceeding assets, has triggered a "Medicare Funding Warning," which is issued when general revenues account for more than 45 percent of expenditures, making the program fiscally unsustainable in the long term.[70]

The DI Trust Fund

The DI fund has exceeded tax revenue since 2005 and is projected to be exhausted in 2018 unless significant changes are made to the program.[71]

According to the Trustees, the Medicare program could be made solvent over the next 75 years by an immediate percent increase in the payroll tax and/or an immediate reduction in program outlays. Part B of the Supplementary Medical Insurance (SMI) Trust Fund, which pays physician bills and other outpatient expenses, and Part D, which pays for access to prescription drug coverage, are both expected to be adequately financed since current law automatically provides financing to meet the next year's expected costs.[72]

Lingering Problems in the Social Security System

Although some Social Security reforms have provided a short-term solution, structural problems continue to plague the system. As already discussed, one problem is the "graying of America." Since 1900, the percentage of Americans 65 years and older has more than tripled (from 4.1 percent in 1900 to 12.3 percent in 2006). Between 2000 and 2010, the number of Americans aged 65 and older increased by 15.1 percent, from 35 million to 40.3 million. Older Americans now represent 13 percent of the total population.[73] Demographic projections suggest that by 2050, the number of persons over age 65 will increase to 88.5 million. In short, by 2050 the percentage of elderly is expected to climb from the current rate of 13 percent percent to 20 percent.[74] Furthermore, the elderly are living longer. Between 2000 and 2010, the 85 to 94 year old age group increased by 30 percent, and the 95 and older age group increased by 26 percent.[75,76]

These demographic trends suggest that the **dependency ratio** (the number of current workers it takes to support a retired worker) will significantly increase, as will the pressures on the Social Security system. For example, in 1960 the worker/beneficiary ratio was 5 to 1; by 2007 it had dropped to 3.4 to 1. By 2025, the dependency ratio is expected to be 2 to 1.[77] A question arises whether two workers in 2040 will be able to support one retired person, and whether the Social Security system—as presently structured—can support 20 percent of the U.S. population.

Social Security predications are predicated on the belief that certain economic and demographic factors will be in play for the foreseeable future. However, economic and demographic could easily shift, invalidating the most earnest predictions. For example, a recession (such as the one in 2007), changing demographic trends (i.e., the current low birth rate), or major changes in immigration would have profound consequences for the future of Social Security. However, there is nothing inviolate about the way Social Security is currently funded. An act of Congress could easily eliminate the self-financing social insurance feature of Social Security and replace it with general revenue taxes. Given the widespread dependence on Social Security, it seems highly unlikely that policymakers and the public will allow the system to go bankrupt.

Another issue in Social Security involves the competition between public (compulsory) and private (voluntary) pension plans. Some critics argue that private pension plans are preferable to public plans because they are not dependent on the government and have greater potential for higher returns. Private pensions originated as a means of encouraging employee loyalty and as a way of easing out aging workers. However, only about one-third of all workers and one-fourth of current employees are covered under private pension plans. Moreover, only a small fraction of these plans are indexed for inflation.

Critics of private pension plans argue that they are basically unreliable. Employees can switch jobs and thus lose their pension rights; companies can go bankrupt; corporations can raid pension funds; many are based on the vicissitudes of company stock (e.g., Enron); workers risk losing their entire retirement if the corporate stock drops; and corrupt or incompetent pension managers can wreak havoc on pension plans. Supporters of Social Security argue that unlike the riskier private pension plans, OASDI benefits are portable and indexed for inflation, and benefits are not contingent on the financial condition of the employer.

Although originally intended to supplement private pension funds and to operate as a pay-as-you-go insurance plan, OASDI has taken on many characteristics of a public welfare program. Specifically, some retirees are realizing benefits in excess of their contributions. Should social insurance be modified to reflect social assistance and income redistribution goals? If the answer is yes, then benefits must be structured to reflect the current needs of retired workers rather than their past contributions. Furthermore, if Social Security is viewed as a public welfare program, then its regressive tax structure must be modified along more progressive lines. For example, Social Security is the single largest tax paid by a low-income worker, yet that same worker receives the lowest benefits when they retire. In short, the workers hurt most by the tax receive the fewest benefits. Using that same line of reasoning, if Social Security is designed for social assistance, then should everyone, regardless of income, be eligible? More particularly, should the very wealthy be allowed to be beneficiaries? Unfortunately, there are no simple answers to these questions.

Should We Privatize Social Security?

Proposals to fully or partially privatize Social Security with individually or private fund managed accounts have emerged from several quarters, including the former Clinton administration. Supporters argue that privatization would provide individuals with control of the Social Security portion of their retirement plan, and that successful investors would likely achieve higher rates of return and higher benefits than Social Security provides.

By early 2005, the largely theoretical debate about privatizing Social Security came to a head when the former George W. Bush administration released its Social Security reform plan. In one of the greatest challenges to Social Security since its inception in 1935, the Bush plan would have diverted some payroll taxes into private accounts that workers could invest in the stock market. At the same time, the guaranteed Social Security benefit would be cut by up to 40 percent. The Bush

Critics argue that privatization would replace the guaranteed economic security of Social Security with risky stock market accounts.

Richard Drew/AP Images

administration asserted that since Social Security payroll taxes belong to the people, they should decide what to do with them. Because these accounts would be individually owned, they could be passed along to heirs. Workers would continue to get benefits from the Social Security system since the private accounts would account for only a percentage of benefits.

The Bush plan was virtually dead on arrival since even stalwart Republicans distanced themselves from such a radical departure in social policy. Most Republicans knew full well that messing with Social Security was extremely dangerous: Older people vote, and they don't like their income support fiddled with. Also, the presumed vast gains in a privatized Social Security system were predicated on a robust stock market. The 2001 stock market crash made many people wary about trusting their future retirement to the market. Discussions about privatizing Social Security were virtually extinguished by the stock market crash of 2007–2008.

Critics contended that even limited privatization would open the door to full privatization, thereby creating a voluntary system that would destroy Social Security. Critics claimed that privatization was a draconian solution to the problems of Social Security. Moreover, supporters argued that the economic system must be robust for privatization to succeed, which meant that the current Social Security system would also be doing well because more revenues would be flowing into the system.[78]

Retirement income and other forms of social insurance are addressed differently in different nations. Social insurance in some countries—similar to the U.S. system—largely depends on a guaranteed governmental benefit to compensate for lost wages due to retirement or disability. Other countries relegate social insurance benefits to a private insurance market model or a combination of private and public. The following section will examine how several industrial countries manage retirement-based social insurance benefits.

Pension Systems in Selected Industrialized Countries
Canada's Retirement Income System

The Canadian retirement system is a multifaceted system that includes tax-funded benefits, low-income benefits, employment-based pensions, and private tax-subsidized retirement savings. The following make up Canada's retirement system:

1. Old-Age Security (OAS) provides the first level of Canadian retirement income. An eligible applicant needs to be a resident and 65 years or older. Monthly payments are modest: In 2012, the average payment was $510 while the maximum was $540.
2. The Guaranteed Income Supplement (GIS) provides additional money on top of the OAS pension. In 2012, a single eligible retiree received a minimum of $492 and a maximum of $732 on top of their OAS pensions.[79]
3. The Canada Pension Plan (CPP) is another level of the system and operates similarly to U.S. Social Security in that it is universal and contributory (i.e., based on mandatory employer/employee contributions to the system). The

CPP is a joint federal and provincial scheme that is administered at the federal level. Like U.S. Social Security, the CPP is designed to be self-financing. At retirement age (65) in 2012, the minimum CPP payment was $527.96 with a maximum of $986.67.[80]

4. Yet another level consists of private pension plans and savings. The Canadian public pension system was designed to provide a modest base to augment private savings and employer pension plans. The self-employed or those with no employer pension plan can supplement their retirement income through the Registered Retirement Savings Plans (RRSPs) and Registered Pension Plans (RPPs), which assist retirement savings.

The Canadian system initially appears more complex than the U.S. system of retirement income based on Social Security, private pension plans, and tax-deferred savings (e.g., IRAs).

Retirement in the United Kingdom

The United Kingdom (UK) has a workforce of 29 million people, of which 23 million are employed in the private sector. Only 3.2 million of these workers contribute to a workplace pension plan that includes an employer contribution. (Like in the United States, many private employers have dropped employee pension plans because of the cost and future obligations to the worker.) Most of the six million UK public sector workers are enrolled in a workplace pension plan. There are also 6.4 million self-employed people paying into personal pensions, which have no employer contribution. Thirty-two percent of private sector workers (including the self-employed) contribute to a personal pension plan that lacks a guaranteed level of retirement income.[81]

Similar to Canada, the UK publicly-funded pension system is based on a two-tiered framework: Basic State Pension (BSP) and the Additional Pension (AP). The BSP is a flat-rate pension paid to anyone who has accrued sufficient National Insurance Contributions (NI). A retiree receives the full rate if they have 30 qualifying years on their NI record. Those with fewer years receive a proportionately lower payment. Spouses and civil partners without sufficient contributions can receive a pension based on the contribution of their partners, which could total 60 percent of their respective partner's BSP.

The State Second Pension (S2P) is paid to certain groups in addition to the BSP. In 2002, it was modified to provide more generous assistance for low and moderate earners, caretakers and those with a long-term illness or disability. In effect, the S2P is a top-up to the BSP based on actual or assumed earnings. All employees contribute to the AP unless they contribute instead to an alternative pension plan that has contracted out of S2P.

Pension Credit (PC) is a means-tested social security benefit designed to provide qualifying moderate income elderly with a minimum income level. PC is composed of two parts (a recipient can receive one or both): the Guarantee Credit (GC) and the Savings Credit (SC). The GC provides a guaranteed minimum level of weekly income for elderly singles and couples. The SC functions as a monetary reward for modest income retirees who have made additional plans for their retirement beyond the BSP. Some people may be eligible for the PC if they or their spouse are severely disabled, are caretakers for someone who is severely disabled, or if they have excessive housing costs.[82,83]

In 1984, Margaret Thatcher's conservative government was swept into power for a second term. Thatcher viewed the victory as a mandate to address what she saw as the last vestige of socialism—social insurance for the elderly. The Thatcher administration began the assault by declaring that the social insurance system would be unaffordable in the future. Instead, she proposed privatizing a portion of old-age benefits. Workers were asked to forego some future benefits in exchange for a tax rebate that could put into a retirement-based investment account. The result was a shrinking state pension system and a partly privatized retirement system. Unfortunately, fund management costs could reduce lump-sum pensions by up to 30 percent.[84]

Many British retirees were sold dodgy and poorly designed retirement plans on false pretenses. In turn, guilty companies were forced to return about $20 billion to investors. Britain's Pensions Commission also warned that 75 percent of those with private investment accounts will not have sufficient savings for retirement.[85]

Policymakers and legislators opposed to privatizing the U.S. Social Security would have acquired a potent critique by observing the abuses resulting from privatizing Britain's system.

The Chilean Experiment in Privatizing Social Security

In 1924, Chile was the first country in the Americas to enact a social security system that provided coverage for old-age, survivors; disability benefits; and cash sickness and medical benefits. Chile's original plan was similar to the U.S. system enacted 11 years later.

By the 1970s, Chile's public pension program was foundering for several reasons, including being overly complex with more than 100 different retirement programs with various contribution rates, retirement ages, and benefits. The predictable result was administrative inefficiency.

The funding for the system was similarly bleak. Despite high payroll taxes, Chile's social security system was generating insufficient income to pay retirees and they received fewer benefits than promised. For instance, while some workers expected to receive benefits that would replace 70 percent of their wages, their actual replacement rate was closer to 20 percent. These problems were heightened by widespread tax evasion, employers who skirted contribution requirements, and workers in the gray or underground economy who were paid in cash.[86]

By the late 1970s, the Chilean social security system was effectively broke. In 1981, military dictator Augusto Pinochet replaced Chile's publicly-funded social security program with a mandatory system of privately managed individual accounts. Under this scheme, workers contributed 10 percent of their salary (up to a specified ceiling) to a government-approved investment fund. Employees were required to pay another 3 percent to cover term life and disability insurance. The self-employed were required to set up investment accounts with the same basic features. These accounts were managed by private investment firms. On retirement, workers could purchase an annuity or withdraw their money based on a schedule.[87]

By 2005, the first generation of Chilean workers enrolled in the new system began to retire and found that Pinochet's promises fell far short of expectations. Some middle-class workers who regularly contributed to a pension fund found that hidden fees ate up almost 30 percent of their original investment. Many felt that they would be better off in the old system. Moreover, the government was forced to direct billions of dollars into a safety net for retirees whose contributions did not even reach the minimum $140 monthly pension. In 2005, pension spending made up more than a quarter of Chile's national budget, and accounted for almost as much as health and education spending combined. In addition, many workers remained outside of the system, including those in the underground economy, the self-employed, and seasonal workers. (These groups make up about half of the Chilean workforce.) Another factor was the vulnerability of retirement accounts to extreme market fluctuations.[88]

Like the British reforms, the expectations of retired Chilean workers in their retirement pension fell far short of the reality.

Germany's Social Security System

The German retirement system is built on governmental social security pensions, occupational pensions, and individual retirement accounts (relatively minor). Similar to the U.S. system, German social security provides survivor and disability benefits, and is mandatory and universal (about 85 percent of German workers are enrolled). Civil Servants (about 9 percent of the work force) have their own pension system while the self-employed (also about 9 percent of the work force) are mostly self-insured but can also participate in the public pension system.

Contributions are based on annual earnings, and the 19.9 percent contribution rate is split evenly between workers and employers, with low-wage earners paying less. The government subsidizes contributions for a worker raising a child (for up to three years) or providing care to a relative. Also similar to the U.S. system, it is a pay-as-you-go system whereby retirement benefits are paid for by current workers. Not surprisingly, the German system is financially stressed by an aging population, unemployment, workers having fewer years in the labor force (partly due to more years of education), and early retirements. Minimum retirement age is set to increase from 65 to 67.[89]

About three-fifths of Germany's working population is covered by occupational pension plans which augment Social Security. Employer-sponsored pension plans are a long-term fixture in German industry, and more than 17 million people are covered under these agreements.[90]

The Greek Pension System

Until recently, Greece had one of the most liberal pension systems in Europe. For instance, the Greek government had identified at least 580 job categories thought to be sufficiently hazardous to merit early retirement (age 50 for women and 55 for men). These hazardous industries included radio and television presenters (presumed at risk from the bacteria on their microphones) and musicians playing wind instruments (at risk for gastric reflux). All told, the Greek government had promised about 700,000 employees (14 percent of its work force) early retirement, which would give the country an average retirement age of 61.[91] The conservative business press was particularly critical in analyzing the Greek retirement system:

- Years of work to earn a full pension – Greece 35, Germany 45
- Proportion of wages as pension – Greece 80%, Germany 46%
- Number of pension payments a year – Greece, 14 (bonus payments); Germany 12
- Pension increase in 2006 – Greece 3%, Germany 0%
- Maximum Payment – Greece $3,333, Germany $2,758
- Minimum pension age for men – Greece 65, Germany 65–67
- Minimum pension age for women – Greece 60, Germany 65–67
- Average pension entrance age – Greece 62.4, Germany 63.2[92]

In its 2009 annual report on Greece, the International Monetary Fund warned that left unchecked, the government's excessive old-age pension and health payments would result in a debt level of 800 percent of Greece's total output by 2050.[93] In part, Greece's generous retirement is assumed to be accountable for its massive debt and near-bankruptcy status.

The Australian Retirement System

The Australian retirement system is based on superannuation (Super) and differs from the U.S. and other European systems because of its heavy reliance on privately managed investment funds. The compulsory superannuation (private investment funds) system was introduced as part of a reform package arising from the fear that an aging population would stress an Australian economy facing low birth rates coupled with high pension responsibilities. The solution was a three-pronged approach:

- A modest means-tested governmental pension system designed as a safety net for low-income workers who fell through the superannuation cracks.
- Compulsory contributions to a superannuation fund that would force private savings.
- The promotion of voluntary savings through the use of superannuation-based tax breaks. Superannuation forms part of an overall employment package whereby employers are required to deposit contributions calculated at least 9 percent of an employee's wages into a retirement account. (Some employers, like universities, can deposit as much as 17.5 percent into an employee's Super account.) The government offers tax breaks and other incentives to help grow Super accounts. Super funds invest in stocks, bonds, and other investments.

A worker's Super is quarantined until retirement and cannot be withdrawn before a certain age, usually 55 or over. In some cases, employees can choose their own super fund. Workers over age 55 can save an additional limited amount without accruing a tax liability.[94]

Perhaps the most compelling criticism leveled against superannuation is that it exposes the retirement income of Australians to the vicissitudes of the stock market. This was particularly problematic when stock markets plummeted in the global financial crisis, and Australia's superannuation funds lost about $430 billion.[95] Consequently, workers who planned to retire had to forestall their plans and remain in the workforce. Others were forced back into work as their Super accounts rapidly depleted.

In addition to superannuation, approximately 80 percent of retired Australians also receive a part or full age pension from the government. The pension is a governmentally-funded retirement income scheme for people who cannot fully support themselves. The single rate pension is set at roughly 28 percent of male average weekly earnings. In early 2012, the maximum amount was approximately $1,511 a month for a single and $2,278 for a couple.[96]

Conclusion

When compared to several others systems in industrialized nations, the U.S. Social Security stands out as one of the best in the world for protecting workers and retirees from the economic vicissitudes that could dramatically reduce a lifetime of contributions. While retirement benefits for American workers may be initially lower than for workers in privatized pension systems, the benefits are more predictable which allows U.S. workers to better plan for their retirement.

Social insurance programs, especially OASDI, have become a mainstay of the American social welfare state. Despite the original intent of its architects, Social Security has become a primary source of financial support for elderly Americans. Moreover, OASDI has demonstrated the ability to not only curb the poverty rate for its constituents, but to actually reduce it. A majority of Americans have come to view Social Security as a right and to count on its benefits.

Social insurance programs represent a major source of security for both elderly Americans and present-day workers. Over the past 50 years, Americans have come to believe that regardless of the ebb and flow of economic life, Social Security and Unemployment Insurance embody a firm governmental commitment to care for workers and the elderly. Economic gains made by elderly people since the mid-1960s have validated this belief. Because Social Security is clearly linked to past contributions, beneficiaries experience little stigma. This is not true for the highly stigmatized beneficiaries of public assistance programs, and it is to this population that we will turn in Chapter 11.

DISCUSSION QUESTIONS

1. Social Security is the most popular social program in the nation. Part of the reason for this popularity is that unlike income maintenance programs, it is not stigmatized. What are other reasons for its popularity?

2. There are serious concerns about the future of Social Security. Some critics argue that Social Security is doomed since the trust funds are expected to be depleted within the next 30 years. Other observers argue that Social Security is sound, because the federal government is backing it. Is Social Security on solid ground? What can we expect in the future? What can be done to make the system more stable?

3. The Social Security system is currently plagued by several different problems. What are the three most important problems facing the system?

NOTES

1. Social Security Administration, Office of Research, Evaluation and Statistics, "Annual Statistical Supplement to the Social Security Bulletin, 2011," SSA Publication No.13-11700, Washington, DC, February 2012. Retrieved April 2012, from http://www.socialsecurity.gov/policy/docs/statcomps/supplement/2011/supplement11.pdf

2. U.S. Department of Health and Human Services, Administration for Children and Families, "Administration for Children and Families All Purpose Table, Fiscal Year 2009-2011". Retrieved April 2012, from http://www.acf.hhs.gov/programs/olab/budget/fy2011apt_07D8.pdf

3. Social Security Administration, Office of Research, Evaluation and Statistics, "Annual Statistical Supplement to the Social Security Bulletin, 2011," SSA Publication No.13-11700, Washington, DC, February 2012. Retrieved April 2012, from http://www.socialsecurity.gov/policy/docs/statcomps/supplement/2011/supplement11.pdf

4. D. Kassabian, T. Vericker, D. Searle & M. Murphy, "Welfare Rules Databook: State TANF Policies as of July 2010," The Urban Institute, August 2011. Retrieved April 2012, from http://www.acf.hhs.gov/programs/opre/welfare_employ/state_tanf/databook10/databook10.pdf

5. David P. Beverly and Edward A. McSweeney, *Social Welfare and Social Justice* (Englewood Cliffs, NJ: Prentice Hall, 1987).

6. Ibid., p. 100.

7. W. Andrew Achenbaum, "Social Security: Yesterday, Today and Tomorrow," The Leon and Josephine Winkelman Lecture, School of Social Work, University of Michigan, March 12, 1996.

8. Ibid.

9. Social Security Administration, Office of Research, Evaluation and Statistics, "Fast Facts and Figures About Social Security, 2011," SSA Publication No.13-11785, Washington, DC, August 2011. Retrieved April 2012, from http://www.socialsecurity.gov/policy/docs/chartbooks/fast_facts/2011/fast_facts11.pdf

10. U.S. Social Security Administration, "Status of the Social Security and Medicare Programs." Retrieved July 2008, from www.ssa.gov/OACT/TRSUM/index.html

11. Social Security Administration, Office of Research, Evaluation and Statistics, "Annual Statistical Supplement to the Social Security Bulletin, 2011," SSA Publication No.13-11700, Washington, DC, February 2012. Retrieved April 2012, from http://www.socialsecurity.gov/policy/docs/statcomps/supplement/2011/supplement11.pdf

12. B.A. Butricia and K.E. Smith, "Racial and Ethnic Differences in the Retirement Prospects of Divorced Women in the Baby Boom and Generation X Cohorts," *Social Security Bulletin, 2011*, vol.72, no.1, Washington, DC, February 2012. Retrieved April 2012, from http://www.socialsecurity.gov/policy/docs/ssb/v72n1/ssb-v72n1.pdf

13. Social Security Administration, Office of Research, Evaluation and Statistics, "Fast Facts and Figures About

Social Security, 2011," SSA Publication No.13-11785, Washington, DC, August 2011. Retrieved April 2012, from http://www.socialsecurity.gov/policy/docs/chartbooks/fast_facts/2011/fast_facts11.pdf

14. Social Security Administration, Office of Research, Evaluation and Statistics, "Fast Facts and Figures About Social Security, 2011," SSA Publication No.13-11785, Washington, DC, August 2011. Retrieved April 2012, from http://www.socialsecurity.gov/policy/docs/chart-books/fast_facts/2011/fast_facts11.pdf]

15. Department of the Census, *Current Population Reports, 1981,* Series P-60, No. 125 (Washington, DC: U.S. Government Printing Office, 1981).

16. Social Security Administration, "Fast Facts: SSI." Retrieved November 2001 from www.ssa.gov:80/statistics/fastfacts/pageii.html

17. Ibid.

18. Social Security Administration, Office of Research, Evaluation and Statistics, "Social Security Bulletin, 2011," vol.72, no.1, Washington, DC, February 2012. Retrieved April 2012, from http://www.socialsecurity.gov/policy/docs/ssb/v72n1/ssb-v72n1.pdf

19. Social Security Administration, Office of Research, Evaluation and Statistics, "Social Security Bulletin, 2011," vol.72, no.1, Washington, DC, February 2012. Retrieved April 2012, from http://www.socialsecurity.gov/policy/docs/ssb/v72n1/ssb-v72n1.pdf

20. U.S. Social Security Administration, "When to Start Receiving Retirement Benefits," SSA Publication No. 05-10147, July 2008. Last Revised 4 January, 2012. Retrieved April 2012, from http://www.socialsecurity.gov/pubs/10147.html#a0=1]

21. Social Security Administration, Office of Research, Evaluation and Statistics, "Fast Facts and Figures About Social Security, 2011," SSA Publication No.13-11785, Washington, DC, August 2011. Retrieved April 2012, from http://www.socialsecurity.gov/policy/docs/chartbooks/fast_facts/2011/fast_facts11.pdf

22. Social Security Administration, Office of Research, Evaluation and Statistics, "Social Security Bulletin, 2011," vol.72, no.1, Washington, DC, February 2012. Retrieved April 2012, from http://www.socialsecurity.gov/policy/docs/ssb/v72n1/ssb-v72n1.pdf

23. U.S. Social Security Administration, "Survivors Planner: Survivors Benefits For Your Children," Last Revised 30 March, 2012. Retrieved April 2012, from http://www.socialsecurity.gov/survivorplan/onyourown4.htm

24. U.S. Social Security Administration, "Survivors Planner: A Special Lump Sum Death Benefit," Last Revised 21 March, 2012. Retrieved April 2012, from http://www.socialsecurity.gov/survivorplan/ifyou7.htm

25. U.S. Social Security Administration, "Benefits Planner: Number of Credits Needed for Disability Benefits," Last Revised 9 April, 2012. Retrieved April 2012, from http://www.socialsecurity.gov/retire2/credits3.htm

26. U.S. Social Security Administration, "Benefits Planner: Number of Credits Needed for Retirement Benefits," Last Revised 9 April, 2012. Retrieved April 2012, from http://www.socialsecurity.gov/retire2/credits2.htm

27. http://www.socialsecurity.gov/policy/docs/ssb/v72n1/ssb-v72n1.pdf

28. U.S. House of Representatives, Committee on Ways and Means; *Overview of Entitlement Programs, 1992 Green Book* (Washington, DC: U.S. Government Printing Office, 1992), p. 485.

29. Social Security Administration, Office of Research, Evaluation and Statistics, "Annual Statistical Supplement to the Social Security Bulletin, 2011," SSA Publication No.13-11700, Washington, DC, February 2012. Retrieved April 2012, from http://www.socialsecurity.gov/policy/docs/statcomps/supplement/2011/supplement11.pdf

30. Isaac Shapiro and Marion Nichols, *Far From Fixed: An Analysis of the Unemployment Insurance System* (Washington, DC: Center on Budget and Policy Priorities, March 1992), p. viii; and Center on Budget and Policy Priorities, Introduction to Unemployment Insurance, April 16, 2010, Washington, DC. Retrieved November 20, 2010 from, http://www.cbpp.org/cms/index.cfm?fa=view&id=1466

31. Diana M. DiNitto, *Social Welfare: Politics and Public Policy* (Englewood Cliffs, NJ: Prentice-Hall, 1991), p. 87.

32. Social Security Administration, Office of Research, Evaluation and Statistics, "Annual Statistical Supplement to the Social Security Bulletin, 2011," SSA Publication No.13-11700, Washington, DC, February 2012. Retrieved April 2012, from http://www.socialsecurity.gov/policy/docs/statcomps/supplement/2011/supplement11.pdf

33. U.S. GAO, "Unemployment Insurance—Low Wage and Part-time Workers Continue to Experience Low Rates of Receipt," September 2007. Retrieved July 2008, from www.gao.gov/new.items/d071147.pdf

34. U.S. GAO, "Unemployment Insurance: Economic Circumstances of Individuals Who Exhausted Benefits," February 2012. Retrieved April 2012, from http://www.gao.gov/assets/590/588680.pdf

35. Economic Policy Institute, "EPI Issue Guide, Unemployment Insurance."

36. U.S. GAO, "Unemployment Insurance: Economic Circumstances of Individuals Who Exhausted Benefits," February 2012. Retrieved April 2012, from http://www.gao.gov/assets/590/588680.pdf

37. Economic Policy Institute, "EPI Issue Guide: Unemployment Insurance, Washington, DC. 2010.

38. Economic Policy Institute, "EPI Issue Guide, Unemployment Insurance."

39. Center on Budget and Policy Priorities, "Addressing Long-standing Gaps in Unemployment Insurance Coverage", August 7, 2007. Retrieved July 2008 from http://www.cbpp.org/7-20-07ui.pdf

40. U.S. GAO, "Unemployment Insurance: Economic Circumstances of Individuals Who Exhausted Benefits," February 2012. Retrieved April 2012, from http://www.gao.gov/assets/590/588680.pdf

41. Simon Rogers, US Jobless Data: How Has Unemployment Changed Under Obama?, *The Guardian*, October 7, 2011

42. Catherine Rampell, "Older Workers without Jobs Face Longest Time Out of Work," *New York Times*, May 6, 2011, p. B5.

43. National Center for Children in Poverty, "Unemployment Insurance." Retrieved July 2008, from www.nccp.org/profiles/index_37.html

44. U.S. GAO, "Unemployment Insurance: Economic Circumstances of Individuals Who Exhausted Benefits," February 2012. Retrieved April 2012, from http://www.gao.gov/assets/590/588680.pdf

45. Institute for Women's Policy Research, "Job Growth Slows for Women and Men in March," No. Q008, April 2012. Retrieved April 2012, from http://www.iwpr.org/

46. Center on Budget and Policy Priorities, Introduction to Unemployment Insurance, April 16, 2010, Washington, DC. Retrieved November 20, 2010 from, http://www.cbpp.org/cms/index.cfm?fa=view&id=1466

47. Center on Budget and Policy Priorities, Introduction to Unemployment Insurance, April 16, 2010, Washington, DC. Retrieved November 20, 2010 from, http://www.cbpp.org/cms/index.cfm?fa=view&id=1466

48. U.S. Bureau of Labor Statistics, "Census of Fatal Occupational Injuries Summary, 2010," 25 August 2011. Retrieved April 2012, from http://www.bls.gov/news.release/cfoi.nr0.htm

49. DiNitto, *Social Welfare.*

50. National Academy of Social Insurance, "Worker's Compensation: Benefits, Coverage, and Costs, 2009," August 2011. Retrieved April 2012, from http://www.nasi.org/sites/default/files/research/Workers_Comp_Report_2009.pdf

51. Ways and Means Committee, *1992 Green Book*, pp. 1707–1709.

52. National Academy of Social Insurance, "Worker's Compensation: Benefits, Coverage, and Costs, 2009," August 2011. Retrieved April 2012, from http://www.nasi.org/sites/default/files/research/Workers_Comp_Report_2009.pdf

53. National Academy of Social Insurance, "Worker's Compensation: Benefits, Coverage, and Costs, 2009," August 2011. Retrieved April 2012, from http://www.nasi.org/sites/default/files/research/Workers_Comp_Report_2009.pdf

54. Charles Prigmore and Charles Atherton, *Social Welfare Policy* (Lexington, MA: D.C. Heath, 1979) pp. 66–67.

55. Social Security Administration, Office of Research, Evaluation and Statistics, "Annual Statistical Supplement to the Social Security Bulletin, 2011," SSA Publication No.13-11700, Washington, DC, February 2012. Retrieved April 2012, from http://www.socialsecurity.gov/policy/docs/statcomps/supplement/2011/supplement11.pdf

56. Ted Dimig, "Social Security on the Brink," *Houston Chronicle* (August 4, 1996), pp. 1F and 4F.

57. Joseph F. Quinn and Olivia S. Mitchell, "Social Security on the Table," The American Prospect 26 (May–June 1996), pp. 76–81.

58. AARP, *A Profile of Older Persons: 2003*, 2004. Retrieved September 2004, from http://assets.aarp.org/rgcenter/general/profile_2003.pdf

59. U.S Census Bureau, "Income, Poverty, and Health Insurance Coverage in the United States: 2010," September 2011. Retrieved Feb 2012, from www.census.gov/prod/2011pubs/p60-239.pdf

60. AARP, *AARP Profile of Older Persons: 2003*, 2004. Retrieved September 2004 from research.aarp.org/general/profile_2003.pdf

61. C. Merton and Joan Broadshaug Bernstein, *Social Security: The System That Works* (New York: Basic Books, 1987).

62. U.S Census Bureau, "Income, Poverty, and Health Insurance Coverage in the United States: 2010," September 2011. Retrieved Feb 2012, from www.census.gov/prod/2011pubs/p60-239.pdf

63. Social Security Administration, "How Much Can I Earn and Still Receive Social Security Benefits?" Retrieved July 2008 from http://ssa-custhelp.ssa.gov

64. Social Security Administration, Office of Research, Evaluation and Statistics, "Social Security Bulletin, 2011," vol.72, no.1, Washington, DC, February 2012. Retrieved April 2012, from http://www.socialsecurity.gov/policy/docs/ssb/v72n1/ssb-v72n1.pdf

65. The 2011 Annual Report of the Board of Trustees of the Federal Old-Age and Survivors Insurance and Federal Disability Insurance Trust Funds, House Document 112-23, Washington, DC, 13 May 2011. Retrieved April 2012, from http://www.socialsecurity.gov/OACT/TR/2011/tr2011.pdf

66. Social Security Administration, "Status of the Social Security and Medicare Programs: A Summary of the 2011 Annual Social Security and Medicare Trust Fund Reports," Last Revised May 2011. Retrieved April 2012, from http://www.socialsecurity.gov/OACT/TRSUM/index.html

67. The 2011 Annual Report of the Board of Trustees of the Federal Old- Age and Survivors Insurance and Federal Disability Insurance Trust Funds, House Document 112-23, Washington, DC, 13 May 2011. Retrieved April 2012, from http://www.socialsecurity.gov/OACT/TR/2011/tr2011.pdf

68. The 2011 Annual Report of the Board of Trustees of the Federal Old- Age and Survivors Insurance and Federal Disability Insurance Trust Funds, House Document 112-23, Washington, DC, 13 May 2011. Retrieved April 2012, from http://www.socialsecurity.gov/OACT/TR/2011/tr2011.pdf

69. Social Security Administration, "Status of the Social Security and Medicare Programs: A Summary of the 2011 Annual Reports," Last Revised May 2011. Retrieved April 2012, from http://www.socialsecurity.gov/OACT/TRSUM/index.html

70. Social Security Administration, "Status of the Social Security and Medicare Programs: A Summary of the 2011 Annual Reports," Last Revised May 2011. Retrieved April 2012, from http://www.socialsecurity.gov/OACT/TRSUM/index.html

71. Social Security and Medicare Boards of Trustees, Status of the Social Security and Medicare Programs, A Summary of the 2010 Annual Reports, August 5, 2010. Retrieved on November 21, 2010 from http://www.socialsecurity.gov/OACT/TRSUM/index.html

72. Ibid.

73. U.S. Census Bureau, "The Older Population: 2010," November 2011. Retrieved April 2012, from http://www.census.gov/prod/cen2010/briefs/c2010br-09.pdf

74. U.S. Census Bureau, "Newsroom - Profile America Facts for Features: Older Americans Month May 2012," Last Revised March 2012. Retrieved April 2012, from http://www.census.gov/newsroom/releases/archives/facts_for_features_special_editions/cb12-ff07.html

75. U.S. Census Bureau, "The Older Population: 2010," November 2011. Retrieved April 2012, from http://www.census.gov/prod/cen2010/briefs/c2010br-09.pdf

76. Committee on Ways and Means, 2004 Green Book.

77. Ibid.

78. Bernstein and Bernstein, Social Security.

79. Service Canada, Old Age Security Payment Amounts, April – June 2012. Retrieved April 2012 from http://www.servicecanada.gc.ca/eng/isp/oas/oasrates.shtml

80. Service Canada, Canada Pension Plan - Payment Amounts January - December 2012. Retrieved April 2012 from, http://www.servicecanada.gc.ca/eng/isp/pub/factsheets/rates.shtml

81. BBC, "Public and Private Sector Pensions Compared," November 28, 2011. Retrieved April 2012 from, http://www.bbc.co.uk/news/business-15925017

82. The Pensions Advisory Service, State Pensions: How Does it Work, 2009. Retrieved April 2012 from, http://www.pensionsadvisoryservice.org.uk/state-pensions/how-does-it-work

83. Department for Work and Pensions. 2012. Retrieved April 2012 from,http://www.dwp.gov.uk

84. Norma Cohen, "A Bloody Mess," The American Prospect, January 14, 2005, pp. 24-27.

85. Paul Krugman, "The British Evasion," New York Times, January 14, 2005, p. A8.

86. Barbara E. Kritzer, "Privatizing Social Security: The Chilean Experience," Social Security Bulletin (59)3 Fall 1996, pp. 45-55.

87. Steve Idemoto, Social Security Privatization in Chile: A Case for Caution. Economic Opportunity Institute, September 29, 2000. Retrieved April 2012 from, http://www.eoionline.org/retirement_security/reports/SSPrivatizationChileCaseCaution-Sep00.pdf

88. Larry Rohter, "Chile's Retirees Find Shortfall in Private Plan," New York Times, January 27, 2005, pp. B3-4.

89. Towers Watson, The German Pension System in Brief, January 2009. Retrieved April 2012 from, http://www.watsonwyatt.com/us/pubs/insider/showarticle.asp?ArticleID=20358

90. How to Germany, The German Retirement and Pension System - Basic Facts, 2012. Retrieved April 2012 from, http://www.howtogermany.com/pages/german-retirement.html

91. New York Times, "Patchwork Pension Plan Adds to Greek Debt Woes," March 11, 2010, p. C 6.

92. Business Insider, 10 Facts about the Greek Pension System Destroying any Hope of a Bailout, 2012. Retrieved April 2012 from, http://www.businessinsider.com/greece-germany-pensions-2010-4#years-of-work-to-earn-a-full-pension-greece-35-germany-45-1

93. New York Times, "Patchwork Pension Plan Adds to Greek Debt Woes," March 11, 2010, p. C 6.

94. Australian Government, Superannuation, 2012. Retrieved April 2012 from, http://australia.gov.au/topics/economy-money-and-tax/superannuation

95. Karina Barrymore, Super Funds Almost Back to Pre-GFC Levels, Herald Sun, April 20, 2012, p. 15.

96. Trish Power, "Age Pension: March 2012 Rates Now Available," SuperGuide, March 14, 2012. Retrieved April 2012 from, http://www.superguide.com.au/superannuation-basics/age-pension-march-2012-rates

CHAPTER 11

Public Assistance Programs

Source: J. Pat Carter/AP Images

This chapter examines key public assistance programs, including the former Aid to Families with Dependent Children (AFDC); AFDC's replacement, Temporary Assistance to Needy Families (TANF); Supplemental Security Income (SSI); and general assistance (GA). The chapter also investigates and analyzes the problems and issues inherent in public assistance programs.

The U.S. social welfare state is a complex mix of programs, policies, and services. Perhaps few people, including many policymakers, fully appreciate the complexity of the welfare system. One reason is that unlike many European countries that operate under a comprehensive and integrated welfare plan, the United States relies on a patchwork quilt of social welfare programs and policies. Hence, public assistance in the United States is a disorganized mix of programs and policies, rather than a comprehensive, integrated, and non-redundant system of social welfare services.

Public assistance programs are one of the most misunderstood components of the U.S. welfare state. Although expenditures for public assistance programs are far less than for social insurance programs, they tend to be more controversial. Unlike social insurance, public assistance programs are based entirely on need and are means tested (see Figure 11.1).

Public assistance programs that offer cash, medical, and other forms of assistance are based on the concept of safety nets—that is, plans designed to ensure that citizens receive basic services to keep

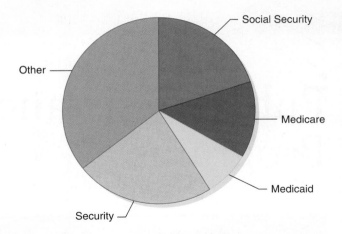

FIGURE 11.1 2011 Budget Outlays by Category (in billions of dollars)

Source: Office of Management and Budget, "Budget of the United States Government, Fiscal Year 2013," February 2012. Retrieved May 2012, from http://www.whitehouse.gov/sites/default/files/omb/budget/fy2013/assets/budget.pdf

them above a certain poverty level. There are 51 separate safety nets—one in each state and in the District of Columbia. States differ with respect to benefit levels, and the vast majority lack an adequate safety net to help the poor and the jobless.[3] In short, public assistance programs are based on a minimalist approach designed to ensure that families or individuals receive the necessary resources to meet their subsistence needs, but not enough to lift them out of poverty.

Spotlight 11.1

KEY PUBLIC ASSISTANCE PROGRAMS IN THE UNITED STATES

In the United States, there are four major public assistance programs:

1. Temporary Assistance to Needy Families (TANF): a block grant based on workfare, time-limited benefits (a maximum of 5 years), and strict work participation rates
2. Supplemental Security Income (SSI): provides cash assistance to the elderly and to disabled poor people, including children
3. General Assistance (GA): state or locally run programs designed to provide basic benefits to low-income people who are ineligible for federally funded public assistance programs
4. Supplemental Nutrition Assistance Program (SNAP): Originally known as the Food Stamp Program and renamed in 2008.[1] The program provides benefits to very low-income households for food assistance.[2]

Assumptions and Myths about Public Assistance

American attitudes toward public assistance can be characterized as a mixture of compassion and hostility. This ambivalence plays out in a series of harsh and often conflicting assumptions about public assistance recipients. The struggle around public assistance programs is symbolic, reflecting the tensions in Americans' ideas about wealth, opportunity, and privilege.

On the hostility side, the argument goes like this: If privilege is earned by hard work, then people are poor because they are lazy and lack ambition. Those driven by competitiveness see the inability of the poor to compete as a serious character flaw. On the other hand, only a few paychecks separate the welfare recipient from the average citizen—thus the compassion.

Although democratic capitalism is rooted in the belief that hard work guarantees success, real life often tells a different story. The following assumptions, among others, underlie much of the discussion around public assistance: (1) Since generous benefits create a disincentive to work; recipients must always receive lower cash benefits than the minimum wage. (2) Welfare recipients need prodding to work because they lack internal motivation. (3) Work is the best antipoverty program. (4) Public assistance programs must be highly stigmatized lest people will too readily embrace them. (5) Women receiving public assistance should work, and their children should not have the luxury of being raised by a full-time homemaker. These assumptions about public assistance—many of which are remarkably similar to those found in the Elizabethan Poor Laws—are rife with serious misconceptions.

The many myths surrounding public assistance make it imperative to discriminate between fact and fiction. (Note that in the items that follow, AFDC and TANF are used interchangeably since they served, and continue to serve, the same clientele.)

Myth 1.   Many families on the public assistance rolls include an able-bodied father who refuses to work.

Fact.   In 2011, only 100,052 of the monthly average 1.8 million TANF families were two-parent families.[4] This was a significant drop from the 342,000 two-parent TANF families in 1995.[5] The majority of TANF families are headed by mothers who are unmarried, divorced, widowed or separated.[6] About 90 percent of TANF children live with their mothers and 10 percent with their fathers.[7]

Myth 2.   Most poor people are on public assistance, and the number is growing.

Fact.   In 2011, only 1.8 million families were receiving TANF assistance on average in any given month.[8] This represents less than one-fifth of the 9.2 million families living below the poverty line in 2010.[9] Clearly, many low-income families do not turn to TANF for support. Also, states are responsible for meeting funding targets in relation to how much they distribute in TANF payments. They focus their efforts on decreasing caseloads, as well as encouraging families to become self-sufficient.

Many states have developed policies that attempt to divert assistance from applicants needing the least amount of state help to encourage them to become self-sufficient. As of July 2008, 42 states had created formal "diversion programs" that included job search requirements for eligibility or provided a one-off, lump-sum payment to deal with immediate needs instead of providing applicants a monthly TANF benefit.[10] Families that accept diversion payments are typically barred from applying for monthly TANF benefits for a stated period of time.[11]

Myth 3.   Recipient mothers have more children in order to collect greater benefits; therefore, families on public assistance are large and steadily growing in size.

Fact.   The average size of families receiving TANF benefits in 2009 was three persons.[12] This represents a decrease from 2005, where the average size

One of the most commonly held myths about public assistance is that recipients don't want to work.

Source: Albert H. Teich/Shutterstock

of TANF families was 3.8 persons.[13] In 2009, over 50 percent of TANF families had only one child, with 30 percent of child recipients between 6 and 11 years of age and 27 percent between 2 and 5 years of age.[14] In 2010, 17 states had family cap limitations that prohibited TANF families from receiving additional assistance for any child born after the mother has enrolled in the program.[15]

Myth 4. Once on welfare, always on welfare.

Fact. This has become a moot point, since the 1996 TANF regulations instituted a five-year lifetime benefit cap for recipients.[16] The number of welfare recipients who return after a period of employment is relatively modest: In 2002, 25 percent of people who received welfare between 2000 and 2002 had returned by 2002.[17] Even before TANF, more than half of all AFDC recipients left the rolls within one year of going on welfare; by the end of two years, the percentage increased to 70 percent. However, over the course of seven years, more than 75 percent of those who left welfare returned at some point.[18]

Myth 5. Welfare programs create intergenerational dependency.

Fact. Given the lifetime cap on cash assistance, the dependency issue has become less relevant. Nevertheless, even before TANF the vast majority of AFDC recipients stayed on public assistance less than four years, and those who stayed eight years or more accounted for half the number of people on the rolls at any given point in time.[19] The research is inconclusive regarding the existence of welfare dependency.

Myth 6. Most welfare recipients are African Americans and Hispanic Americans.

Fact. In FY2009, whites constituted 31.2 percent of recipients, while 33.3 percent were black, and 28.8 percent Hispanic. The remaining recipients were Asian, American Indian, or of another ethnicity.[20] Although the percentages of African Americans and Hispanics on the welfare rolls were larger than these groups' representation in the population, this is not surprising, since people of color are statistically poorer than whites.

Myth 7. Public assistance benefits provide a disincentive to work; people on welfare either do not want to work or are too lazy to work.

Fact. In 2008, 26 percent of TANF recipients were employed, 47 percent were unemployed, and 27 percent were not in the labor force. Of those who worked, 33 percent worked for 11 to more than 30 hours a week.[21]

Myth 8. Public assistance recipients are doing better than ever.

Fact. The reverse is true. Four states had lower TANF benefit levels in 2010 than in 1996; 16 states had the same benefit levels as in 1996. Even those states that raised TANF benefits have generally not kept pace with inflation. When adjusted for inflation, 48 states have lower real-dollar benefit levels in 2010 than in 1996.[22] Today, the maximum benefit amount in 30 states comprises 30 percent or less of the federal poverty level.[23]

Myth 9. Never-married teen mothers constitute the bulk of welfare recipients.

Fact. In 2008, teen parents made up slightly less than 10 percent of the TANF caseload. Of the overall TANF caseload, only 7.3 percent of adult beneficiaries were under age 20; 50 percent were aged 20–29 years; and 26 percent were aged 30–39 years.[24] According to Duncan and Hoffman, the most prominent causes for beginning AFDC spells were (1) divorce or separation (45 percent), (2) an unmarried woman becoming a pregnant household head (30 percent), and (3) a drop in earnings of the female head of the household (12 percent). Conversely, the predominant reasons for terminating public assistance spells were (1) remarriage (35 percent), (2) an increase in the earnings of a female householder (21 percent), and (3) children leaving the parental home (11 percent).[25]

Myth 10. It is easy to get on public assistance and too many undeserving people are receiving benefits.

Fact. David Morris states that: "In the early 1990s about 75 percent of those who walked into the welfare office to apply ended up on welfare rolls. Today it is closer to 25 percent. A growing number of states (13 at last count) now drop entire families from the welfare rolls after the first instance of non-compliance (e.g., the refusal to accept an assigned job or identify a paternal parent) by the adult recipient."[26]

In 2011, applicants for SNAP (food stamps) could only qualify if the household had less than $2,000 in disposable assets ($3,000 if one member was aged 60 or older); gross income below 130 percent of the official poverty guidelines for the household size; and net income below 100 percent of the poverty guidelines. Households with a person aged 60 or older, or a disabled person receiving SSI, Social Security, state general assistance, or veterans' disability benefits could have gross income exceeding 130 percent of the poverty guidelines. Households are certified for varying lengths of time, depending upon their income sources and individual circumstances.[27]

Myth 11. Public assistance recipients migrate to states where benefits are high.

Fact. Although research by the Wisconsin's Institute for Research on Poverty concluded that some poor people migrate across state lines to receive higher benefits,[28] it failed to demonstrate that high benefits per se cause migration. According to Henry Freedman of the Center for Social Policy, "Census data on migration show that poor people move in the same direction as those who are not poor, usually toward states with jobs and booming economies rather than those offering higher welfare benefits."[29] Economist Bruce Meyer concluded that "The different methods all point toward the same result: there is welfare induced migration, but it is modest in magnitude."[30]

Myth 12. Welfare spending consumes a large portion of state budgets.

Fact. Despite the recession and increase in poverty, there was a 47 percent decrease overall in TANF caseloads between FY 1997 and 2008. This suggests that not every family that needs public assistance is receiving it.[31]

Although states are heavily burdened with debt, the cause is not high levels of welfare spending; instead, it is a direct result of the worst recession since the 1930s and the steepest decline in state revenues on record. State revenues were 11.5 percent lower in 2010 than in 2008, resulting in significant cuts in state-funded services. These revenue deficits were expected to reach $140 billion by 2012, leading to even more cuts in state services.[32]

Myth 13. TANF benefits influence decisions relating to family composition (i.e., childbearing, marriage, divorce, and living arrangements) by encouraging women to head their own households.

Fact. Under the TANF guidelines, teenage mothers under age 18 are not entitled to benefits unless they are living at home or in a supervised facility. Although some empirical studies found a small correlation between public assistance benefits and the number of women who choose to head households or remarry, most researchers believe that the evidence does not support the view that generous benefits are responsible for high illegitimacy rates or the growth of single female-headed households. For example, although total welfare benefits have declined since 1975, the number of single female-headed households has remained relatively constant.[33]

Aid to Families with Dependent Children

Replaced by TANF, AFDC was arguably the most controversial program in the U.S. welfare system. It was designed to provide financial assistance and care to needy dependent children in their own homes or in the homes of responsible caregivers. Despite these modest goals, AFDC served as a symbol in the ideological battle between liberals and conservatives and caused recipients to be victimized in two ways: (1) by their own poverty, and (2) by ideologically motivated assaults against their character and motives.

The requirement for receiving AFDC was that a child be deprived of the parental support of one parent because of death, desertion, separation, or divorce. (In the case of the AFDC-Unemployed Parent program, the criterion was deprivation of parental economic support because of unemployment or illness.)

Originally called Aid to Dependent Children (ADC), the AFDC program was part of the Social Security Act of 1935 and was designed to provide support for children by dispensing aid to their mothers. In 1950, the adult caregiver (usually the mother) was made eligible for ADC benefits.[34] Also in the 1950s, medical services paid for in part by the federal government were made available for ADC recipients. Beginning in the late 1950s, some critics argued that ADC rules led to desertion by fathers, because only families without an able-bodied father were eligible. In 1961, a new component was added that allowed families to receive assistance in the event of a father's incapacity or unemployment. The new program, Aid to Families with Dependent Children-Unemployed Parent (AFDC-UP), was not made mandatory for the states, and until the welfare reform act of 1988, only 25 states and the District of Columbia had adopted it. In 1962, ADC was changed to AFDC to emphasize the family unit.

By 1962, the focus of the AFDC program had shifted to rehabilitation and new policies mandated casework and treatment services. Beginning in 1972, federal policy dictated that the AFDC program be divided into social services and **income maintenance programs.** As AFDC rules became more liberalized, the number of AFDC recipients tripled from 1960 to 1970. From 1971 to 1981 that number rose another 50 percent, and in 1992 it reached 13.6 million recipients. In 1950, AFDC recipients constituted 1.5 percent of the population; by 1992 it was 5 percent.

One notorious chapter in AFDC history involved the man-in-the-house rule. This policy mandated that any woman with an able-bodied man in the house would be terminated from AFDC because, regardless of whether the man was the father of her children, it was his responsibility to support the family. This policy was manifested in "midnight raids" whereby social workers made late-night calls to determine if a man was present. Even a piece of male clothing found on the premises could justify cutting off aid. In some states, the man-in-the-house rule was extended to include rules on dating. In 1968, the U.S. Supreme Court struck down the rule in Alabama, and the Court later reinforced its decision in a California case.[35]

The Family Support Act (FSA) of 1988 was an important piece of welfare legislation.[36] The FSA (budgeted at only $3.3 billion over a five-year period) attempted to change AFDC from an income support to a mandatory work and training program. To accomplish this, the bill established the **Job Opportunities and Basic Skills (JOBS)** program that required recipient women with children under age three (or, at state option, age one) to participate in a work or training program. By 1990, each state was to enroll at least 7 percent of its recipients (increasing to 20 percent by 1993) in a basic state education program, job training, a work experience program, or a job search program.[37]

Adoption of the AFDC-UP program became mandatory for all states, although they could choose to limit enrollment for two-parent families to 6 out of 12 calendar months in a year. Moreover, one family member of an AFDC-UP household was required to participate at least 16 hours a week in a community or make-work job in return for benefits. In addition, the FSA called for mandatory child support payments to be automatically deducted from the paycheck of an absent parent.[38]

The FSA's promise soon faded. Instead of declining, AFDC caseloads actually rose by 2.1 million from 1990 to 1992. By the end of 1991, the states had spent less than half of the available federal JOBS funds. Underappreciated at the time was the FSA component that permitted states to request waivers to existing AFDC rules, an option that opened the door for the radical welfare reforms that emerged in 1996.[39] In his 1992 presidential campaign, Bill Clinton promised to "end welfare as we know it." In 1993, he appointed a high-profile working group on welfare reform that came up with far-ranging suggestions for reforming AFDC. Unbeknownst to him at the time, this rallying cry would get out of hand and lead to the most comprehensive reform of public welfare since its inception in 1935.

The Personal Responsibility and Work Opportunity Reconciliation Act of 1996

In 1996, former President Bill Clinton signed the Personal Responsibility and Work Opportunity Reconciliation Act (PRWORA) (H.R. 3734), a complex 900-page document that confused even seasoned welfare administrators.[40] In effect, the PRWORA replaced AFDC, JOBS, and the **Emergency Assistance Program** with the Temporary Aid for Needy Families (TANF) program.

One of the most radical features of the PRWORA was among the least understood. Under the PRWORA, federal **entitlement** to public assistance was ended. In contrast, the former AFDC program operated under the principle of entitlement, which meant that states must provide assistance to anyone eligible under the law. This did not mean that states were required to provide something for nothing. In fact, states could have required recipients to participate in work, education, training, or job search programs as a condition for receiving aid. Under TANF, no family or child is *entitled* to assistance.[41] In effect, the TANF **disentitlement** rescinded the 60-year-old federal entitlement for support to poor children and families.

- In order to receive a TANF grant, each state must submit a plan to the Department of Health and Human Services (HHS). In turn, HHS determines whether the plan conforms to the law.
- TANF provides lump-sum federal **block grants** for states to operate their own welfare and work programs. A minority of states receive annual adjustments in the form of supplemental grants; but for most states the amount of the TANF block grant is frozen, except for adjustments due to bonuses or penalties. Under limited circumstances, a state experiencing an economic downturn may qualify for additional federal funding.

- Maintenance of effort provisions require that to receive a full block assistance grant the state must spend nonfederal funds at no less than 80 percent of a historic spending level based on 1994 spending. This requirement is reduced to 75 percent for a state that meets the act's **work participation rate** (percentage of TANF recipients in the workforce) requirements. A state that does not maintain the required spending level risks a dollar-for-dollar reduction in its block grant funding.

- States are prohibited from using TANF funds to assist certain categories of families and individuals. The most notable prohibition involves the use of TANF funds to assist families in which an adult has received assistance for 60 months or more. (States can, however, choose to pay beneficiaries with their own monies.) States can provide exceptions for up to 20 percent of their caseloads. Although the PRWORA mandates a maximum five-year lifetime limit on cash assistance, it allows states to set a shorter time limit. Other restrictions include a prohibition on assisting minor parents unless they are attending school and living at home or in an adult-supervised living arrangement (subject to limited exceptions), and a requirement to reduce or eliminate assistance if an individual does not cooperate with child support-related requirements, such as identifying the father.

- The TANF block grant has four specific work requirements. First, a state must require non-exempt unemployed parents or caregivers to participate in community service after receiving assistance for two months. Second, states must outline how they will require a parent or caregiver receiving benefits to engage in work not later than 24 months after they receive assistance. Third, a state must meet a work participation rate for all families of 50 percent. Fourth, states must meet a 90 percent work participation rate for two-parent families. Failure to comply with the last two work requirements results in fiscal penalties to the states. (See Table 11.1.)

- States can spend their block grants on cash assistance, noncash assistance, services, and administrative costs in connection with assistance to needy families with children. States can also choose to spend up to 30 percent of their TANF funds to operate programs under

TABLE 11.1 TANF Work Participation Rates

Fiscal Year	Percentages
Work Participation for All Families	
1997	25
1998	30
1999	35
2000	40
2001	45
2002 and beyond	50
Work Participation for Two-Parent Families	
1997	75
1998	75
1999 and beyond	90

Source: Mark Greenberg and Sharon Parrott, Summary of TANF Work Participation Provisions in the Budget Reconciliation Bill, Center on Budget and Policy Priorities and Center for Law and Social Policy, January 9, 2006.

the Child Care and Development Block Grant and the Title XX Social Services Block Grant.

- When parents participate in required work activities, the state may (but is not required to) provide child care assistance. However, a state may not reduce or terminate a family's assistance if a single parent of a child under age 6 refuses to comply with work requirements because of a demonstrated inability of the state to provide needed child care.

- Recipients are not automatically eligible for Medicaid. However, states are required to provide Medicaid coverage for single-parent families and qualifying two-parent families with children if they meet the income and resource eligibility guidelines that were in effect in the state's AFDC Program on July 16, 1996. (States may modify these guidelines to a limited extent.)

- The TANF program attempted to address the dramatic increase in non-marital births (especially teen births). First, state TANF plans must demonstrate how they will establish goals and take action to prevent and reduce out-of-wedlock pregnancies. Second, the act provides financial incentives to states to reduce their out-of-wedlock birth rates, while at the same time lowering their abortion rates. In addition, child support collection efforts were strengthened through a number of provisions.[42]

- The PRWORA allows states to impose a family cap that denies assistance to children born into families already receiving public assistance.
- States must permanently deny all Title IV-A cash assistance and Food Stamp Program benefits to recipients convicted of felony drug possession, use, or distribution. Other members of the family can continue to receive benefits. States may opt out of this provision or limit the period of denial by passing legislation. In addition to TANF, the PRWORA included other reforms, as shown below.
- Immigrants who arrived after 1996 were barred from all means-tested, federally funded public benefits for the first five years they are in the country. After five years, states can offer Medicaid to immigrants. Illegal immigrants are barred from the following federal public benefits: (a) grants, contracts, loans, and licenses; and (b) retirement, welfare, health, disability, public or assisted housing, postsecondary education, food assistance, and unemployment benefits. States cannot deny coverage of emergency medical services to either illegal or legal aliens.
- The Food Stamp Program retained its structure as an uncapped individual entitlement. However, Food Stamp Program benefits were limited to three months every three years for unemployed able-bodied single adults aged 18 to 50. An additional three months of eligibility was granted to adults who were laid off from their jobs.
- Child support collection efforts were strengthened through a number of provisions: recipient families must assign child support collection rights to the state; states must operate centralized collections units; noncustodial parents who have $5,000 or more in arrears are subject to passport revocation; states must accept out-of-state child support orders and liens; states must have laws in effect that establish authority to withhold, suspend, or restrict drivers and professional, occupational, and recreational licenses of individuals who owe overdue support.[43]

Responding to concerns about intergenerational welfare dependency, states began implementing "diversion" programs to keep families whose needs could be met through other means from ever entering the welfare rolls. In response to higher effective work participation rates that followed the reauthorization of the TANF program in 2005, states added new policies and programs that divert TANF-eligible families from the TANF system. Three kinds of diversion strategies are employed: (1) Lump-sum payment programs provide applicants who are employed or have a job offer with the option of accepting a one-time cash or voucher payment, in lieu of receiving TANF; (2) applicant work requirements target applicants likely to be subject to the TANF work requirements and require them to participate in work-related activities during the 30–45-day application certification period; and (3) temporary support programs provide TANF applicants with up to four months of assistance, which do not count toward TANF time limits or work participation rates. All but three states have implemented at least one diversion strategy, with 35 states adopting a lump-sum payment program.[44]

As opposed to strict means-tested programs like TANF, some industrialized countries have opted for other ways to transfer money to low-income families. In countries like France, Denmark, Sweden, and Germany, family benefits are universal, while in others like the United States, Canada, Czech Republic, and Italy, they are means-tested (e.g., the EITC and Child Tax Credit). The majority of large Western industrialized countries have universal family benefits and some form of single-parent assistance. For instance, Australia has a Baby Bonus that is paid to families following the birth (including stillborn) or adoption of a child. About half of the industrialized countries require some form of employment activity (i.e., workfare or welfare-to-work) as a condition for receiving public assistance benefits.

Since the 1940s, all Canadian provinces have maintained a program of social assistance or income support for low-income families, although eligibility rules and benefits vary widely between the provinces. Canada's social welfare safety net covers a broad spectrum of programs, many of which are run by the provinces. Provincial and federal government transfer programs totaled almost $177 billion in 2009.[45]

The Canadian Social Transfer (CST) program is a federal block transfer to provinces and territories to support postsecondary education, social assistance and social services, and early childhood development and childcare. The CST is designed to ensure that conditional transfers provide equal support for all Canadians, and the cash transfer to the provinces totaled almost $12 billion in 2012–13.[46]

The American Recovery and Reinvestment Act of 2009

Due to the impact of the recession, the American Recovery and Reinvestment Act (ARRA) was passed in 2009 to strengthen safety net programs such as TANF and SNAP. As part of the act:

- The federal government provided states with additional TANF funding to cope with the expansion of caseloads. This funding could be used for the provision of short or long-term cash payments, or to create new job programs.[47]
- ARRA increased SNAP benefits by 13.6 percent, provided additional funding to states for program administrative costs, and temporarily suspended the 3 month limit attached to SNAP benefits for unemployed workers.[48]
- The Child Care and Development Fund (CCDF) was provided with additional funding in order to support low-income families struggling to pay for the costs of childcare.
- Unemployed families who had only earned income for part of the year were now eligible for the Earned Income Tax Credit scheme (EITC) as annual income thresholds were reduced.[49]

A Congressional Budget Office Report that assessed the impact of ARRA during the third quarter of 2011 found that it lowered the unemployment rate and boosted employment, with between 0.4 million and 2.4 million people entering the labor force.[50]

Has the PRWORA Worked?

By 2000, Democrats and Republicans had pronounced the PRWORA a raging success. They pointed to the dramatic decline in welfare caseloads—60 percent for individuals and 53 percent for families—since the passage of the PRWORA in 1996. The number of white families on welfare showed the steepest decline, falling by 63 percent; the number of African American families fell by 52 percent; and the number of Hispanic families by 44 percent.[51] Nevertheless, important questions remain. First, caseloads had already begun to shrink—from a high of 5 million in 1994 to 4.5 million in 1996. These declines occurred before the PRWORA was fully in effect. Second, other factors such as the strong labor market in the 1990s and changes in welfare policy helped explain the drop. In the late 1990s, the nation was in the midst of the longest

peacetime expansion in its history, with low unemployment and rising wages.

Consequently, gains in employment and wages were experienced by all groups, including those with typically high rates of welfare use. Given that the PRWORA was conceived and passed by Congress in a strong economy with rising wages and low unemployment, its real test would occur in the global financial crisis that began in 2007. In 2006, there were 1.78 million families, 4.2 million recipients, and 3.2 million children receiving TANF. By 2010, there were 1.84 million families, 4.3 million recipients, and 3.2 million kids on TANF. Significantly, the poverty rate in 2006 was 12.5 percent with 37 million poor people; by 2009 that rate had increased to 14.3 percent (the highest level recorded since 1994) with some 44 million people in poverty. Surprisingly, the 7 million increase in the number of people in poverty—plus the higher number of poor children—was not reflected in dramatically higher TANF caseloads. By contrast, food stamp caseloads rose by 50 percent from December 2007 to March 2010.[52]

The modest increase in TANF caseloads hides considerable variation between states. For instance, Nevada had a 14.4 percent unemployment rate in 2010 and its TANF caseloads rose by nearly 40 percent. Michigan had an unemployment rate of 13.1 percent but its TANF caseload rose by only 2 percent. Despite an 11.8 percent unemployment rate, Rhode Island's TANF caseload fell by 10 percent as it cut children and adults when they reached their benefit time limits.[53]

Recognizing TANF's vulnerability in a recession, Congress created a $5 billion TANF Emergency Fund as part of the American Recovery and Reinvestment Act of 2009. The act provided a clause that allowed states with caseload increases to receive the same caseload reduction credit toward the work participation requirement as they had in 2007 or 2008. The provisions were designed to remove the disincentives for states to allow additional needy families to receive cash assistance. The TANF Emergency Fund provided states with 80 percent of the funding for spending increases in three categories: basic assistance, non-recurrent short-term benefits, and subsidized employment. Much to the consternation of welfare advocates, the emergency program ended in 2010 with states having drawn down the full $5 billion.

Welfare reform was grounded in the belief that recipients of public assistance could support their families through work. However, unemployment rates for single mothers have been a third higher than for all adult women and hit a high of 13.4 percent in late 2009.[54]

When the TANF block grant was created, Congress required states to spend at least 75 percent of what they had spent under AFDC. However, this requirement became increasingly ineffective as states realized that spending on a large number of existing programs—including the portion of non-means-tested programs that benefits low-income families—can be claimed as part of the block grant requirements. As a result, states have reduced their total spending on non-medical social services since 2001. As the above clearly suggests, TANF has failed to protect poor women and children from the vicissitudes of hard economic times.

There are three primary avenues for leaving TANF: (1) voluntary termination because of employment, marriage, and so forth; (2) reaching the end of the federal or state time limit; and (3) being terminated for failure to comply with work or administrative rules. According to a U.S. Census report, 36.5 percent of former welfare recipients surveyed in 2009 cited that their reason for leaving TANF was due to their income becoming too high. A further 20 percent of participants stated that they no longer needed to receive benefits. However, 12.3 percent of participants reported that they no longer received benefits because they had exceeded their time limit, and 5 percent had received the maximum amount of assistance they were allowed.[55]

Most recipients leaving public assistance (50 to 60 percent) take jobs that pay just over minimum wage. Because of this, many low-income families continue to receive some form of public assistance, such as food stamps. Between 2001 and 2006, the percentage of households receiving food stamps increased from 47.4 percent to 55.6 percent.[56]

Former TANF recipient families have not done well when it comes to average family income. In 2009, the total median monthly income for TANF families was $1,027, or just $256.75 a week.[57]

The United States Census Bureau data shows that there is a significant percentage of TANF families experiencing health barriers to work. In 2009, 34 percent of TANF families had a parent with a work-limiting disability, and 21 percent of TANF families received SSI for one or more months. The majority of TANF families have no private health insurance, a trend that has worsened during the recession. In 2006, 62.4 percent of TANF families were uninsured; by 2009, it was 69 percent.[58]

Measuring the success of a program by decreases in caseloads may not be as effective as measuring the take-up rate among families in need. For example, in 2005, TANF served only 40 percent of all eligible families in contrast to the 84 percent the AFDC program served in 1995.[59] The take-up rate among low-income families with children has also been particularly low, which is problematic given the high unemployment rates of these groups. In 2009, 38 percent of low-income single parents and over 40 percent of low-income two-parent families were unemployed. Despite the fact that many did not receive unemployment benefits, relatively few families in these groups received TANF—only 27.5 percent of single-parent families defined as "low-work" (less than 26 weeks in a year) received public assistance, a rate that was even less for two-parent low-work families (18 percent).[60] This data suggests the limitations of TANF in reaching vulnerable families during an economic downturn.

Supplemental Security Income (SSI)

SSI is designed to provide cash assistance to the elderly and to disabled poor individuals, including children. Although a public assistance program, SSI is administered by the Social Security Administration.

In 2010, the SSI program served approximately 7.9 million people at a cost of more than $48 billion.[61] SSI is a means-tested, federally-administered public assistance program funded through general revenue taxes. Unlike TANF, the basic SSI payment level is adjusted annually for inflation. A portion of elderly people receive SSI in conjunction with Social Security. Age is not an eligibility criterion for SSI, and children may receive benefits under the disabled or blind portion of the act.[62] Among others, the following people are eligible for SSI: (1) mentally retarded individuals, (2) individuals at least 65 years old who have little or no income, (3) the legally blind, (4) disabled adults with a physical or mental impairment expected to last for at least 12 months, (5) the visually impaired who do not meet the criteria for blindness, (6) drug addicts and alcoholics entering treatment, and (7) children under age 18 who have a severe impairment comparable to that of an eligible adult.

Of those receiving federally-administered SSI payments in 2010, approximately 2 million were over the age of 65. The majority of recipients (85 percent) had some form of disability, and six out of ten recipients under the age of 65 had a mental disorder. Of those recipients who had a disability in 2010, 319,000 were working.[63]

To qualify for SSI, an applicant must have limited resources. In 2010, SSI applicants were allowed to own resources valued at $2,000 or less for an individual and $3,000 for a couple (excluding, e.g., a house, a car, depending on use and value; burial plots; and certain forms of insurance). These resource limits are set by statute and have not changed since 1989. SSI benefits are not generous, although they can be higher than TANF. The average monthly SSI benefit in 2010 was $501.[64]

The SSI program began during the Nixon presidency as a substitute for a number of state-operated disability programs. When Richard Nixon took office in 1972, he attempted to streamline the welfare system by proposing a guaranteed annual income that would replace various income maintenance and disability programs. Although Congress rejected the overall plan, various disability programs were federalized in 1972 under a new program—SSI— with the federal government taking over the operation of those programs from state governments. In 1974, there were 3.25 million SSI recipients; by 2009 that number had more than doubled to almost 8 million. Concomitantly, SSI expenditures increased from $5 billion in 1974 to more than $48 billion in 2010.[65] The number of SSI recipients grew by 14 percent from 2000 to 2008 alone.[66] In large part these increases resulted from the rapid growth in the numbers of disabled persons receiving SSI, a population that grew from 2.4 million in 1984 to over 6.5 million in 2010.[67]

Two groups of SSI recipients that have shown dramatic growth in their numbers are children with disabilities and adults with disabilities related to drug addiction and alcoholism. One reason for this growth was the Supreme Court's decision in the 1990 *Sullivan v. Zebley* case that made children eligible for SSI if they had a disability that was comparable to that of an eligible adult.[68] Children are now the fastest-growing population on SSI, and by 2010, 1.2 million children had become recipients. Of those children, over 66 percent (827,128 children) had some type of mental or developmental disorder.[69]

Major concerns regarding SSI involve the low level of income and the stringent requirements for eligibility. SSI payments are so low that, as of 2008, all but seven states and jurisdictions provide some form of optional state supplementation. States may choose to set their own requirements for supplementary SSI payments, thereby including only certain beneficiaries or limiting disabilities. Stringent eligibility requirements and red tape have kept many people off the SSI rolls. For example, SSI cases are reviewed every three years (a process that usually involves a medical review), and "continuing disability reviews" may be required. Some critics believe that the federal government has purposely made entrance and continued maintenance in SSI difficult to discourage participation. Moreover, only couples receiving a combination of SSI, Social Security, and food stamps are raised to or above the poverty line. An individual who received SSI in 2008 was raised to only 73.5 percent of the poverty threshold, and couples were raised to 81.9 percent.

General Assistance

General assistance (GA) programs, also known as General Relief programs in some states, are cash and in-kind assistance programs financed and administered entirely by the state, county, or locality in which they are located. The programs are designed to meet the short-term or ongoing needs of low-income people ineligible for (or awaiting approval for) federally funded assistance such as TANF or SSI. Most states limit GA eligibility to the severely poor, without children. Although income eligibility varies across states, a majority of state GA programs limit assistance to only those with incomes less than half the poverty level.[70]

In 2008, Minnesota's GA program was a safety net for single adults and childless couples. It provided monthly cash grants for the extremely poor whose net income was less than $203 a month for singles and $260 for couples and whose resources were less than $1000. Special funding was also made available for emergency situations when a person or family lacks basic necessity items, such as shelter or food, that threatens their health or safety.[71]

Although states are generally responsible for GA, some devolve responsibility and administration to their counties. For instance, GA in each one of California's counties is established and 100 percent funded by its own board of supervisors. Hence, benefits, payment levels, and eligibility requirements vary among each of the 58 counties.[72]

Some states fund GA programs but delegate administration to counties, municipalities, or towns. This is the case in Maine where each town has a GA program to help people in emergencies. Skyrocketing oil prices in 2008 led to a huge increase in people seeking GA. In recent years, demand for GA has increased by 300 to 500 percent,[73] and in 2007, Maine disbursed $6.45 million for GA, an increase of almost $1 million from the previous year.[74]

Trends and Issues in Public Assistance

The basic principle underlying the PRWORA was transferring the responsibility for managing social programs from Washington to the states. Promoted early by the Reagan administration, this ideological perspective has been labeled the "devolution revolution" or the "new federalism."[75] Energized by the cry of "states' rights," the new federalism trades off long-term stable federal funding for increased state control through block grants.

The responsibility of states to care for their poor is not new. In part, it was the failure of states to meet that responsibility that originally led to the creation of the 1935 Social Security Act, legislation that federalized most state public assistance and social insurance programs. Devolving welfare responsibility to the states is neither new nor novel. Nevertheless, the question remains: If states were unable to mount compassionate social welfare programs before 1935, why should they do so today, especially in difficult economic times?

Transforming Public Assistance Policy into Labor Policy

Beginning almost 30 years ago, the transformation of public assistance policy into labor policy reached fruition with the passage of the PRWORA, essentially a labor policy clothed in welfare terminology.

AFDC had been a sore spot for conservatives since its inception. This antagonism persisted even though in 1995 combined AFDC and food stamps costs accounted for only 3 percent of the federal budget compared to 22 percent for Social Security, 18 percent for defense, and 10 percent for Medicare.[76] The real concern about public assistance was not about excessive spending; instead, it was a reaction to AFDC as a symbol of governmental responsibility to provide cash proxies for labor market earnings. The very existence of AFDC was a thorn in the side of economic conservatives since it implied that the marketplace was incapable of meeting the needs of all Americans.

Early federal attempts to transition recipients into the labor force were stillborn for several reasons. For one, high unemployment rates in the late 1970s and early 1980s led to an oversupply of labor resulting in little incentive to drive more workers into the labor market. On the contrary, sound public policy dictated that more people be kept out of the workforce to not further aggravate unemployment. Hence, the conservative preference for labor market employment over public assistance was therefore held in abeyance by the economic realities of the period.

A unique confluence of events came together in 1996 to complete the transformation of public assistance into labor policy. Frustrated by repeated failures of federal welfare-to-work efforts and the ignominious death of the FSA, the newly elected conservative 104th Congress was determined not to repeat past mistakes. First and foremost was to disentitle public assistance. Second, the PRWORA removed the fiscal responsibility of government to provide income support to public assistance recipients beyond a five-year lifetime cap. Under the PRWORA, the only option for those who exhaust their benefits is labor market participation or penury.

The PRWORA was passed in a period of robust economic growth. By 1996, the unemployment rate had dropped to 4.5 percent and the economy was growing at more than 2.5 percent a year.[77] The low unemployment rate combined with a strong economy meant that the 138-million-member U.S. labor force could easily absorb the 4.2 million AFDC recipients without driving down wages or increasing unemployment. The economic giddiness of the middle 1990s reinforced the conservative belief that a job existed for anyone that wanted it. It was in this climate that the PRWORA was passed.

Removing the federal responsibility for providing long-term cash assistance to the poor shifted the problem of poor support away from social welfare and into labor policy. The PRWORA represented the culmination of the long-standing conservative goal of deracinating public assistance: When the poor exhaust time-limited public assistance benefits they become a labor market rather than a welfare problem. With that change, U.S. public assistance policy became a short-term, transitional step in the march toward the full labor market participation of the poor.

The conservative push toward labor policy is not entirely without merit. First, one would be hard-pressed to argue that a well-paying job with full benefits is not the best antipoverty program. Moreover, Sweden—historically considered a progressive welfare state—has frequently used labor policy as a proxy for aggressive public assistance programs.[78] Second, the push toward workforce participation is congruent with current labor market trends for women. For instance, in 1955 only 18 percent of all U.S. mothers with children under 6 were in the labor force. By 2010, that number had risen to 64 percent. By 2011, almost 61 percent of U.S. mothers with children younger than 3 years old were in the labor force full or part-time.[79] Given these trends, welfare advocates were hard-pressed to justify non-employment- based public assistance programs when the majority of all mothers with children under age 6 are in the labor force. Despite these conservative arguments, the absence of sound federal labor policy, the historic lack of guaranteed health care insurance, and few workplace protections have resulted in most former recipients going from the frying pan into the fire. Many former recipients now occupying secondary labor market jobs face an even shakier economic future than under tainted AFDC policies.

Despite some positive gains, the substitution of labor policy for public assistance policy has led to serious problems. For one, the absence of sound labor policy rewards low-wage employers while punishing low-income workers forced into poorly paid dead-end jobs that provide little, if any, benefits. Specifically, low-wage employers are rewarded by not being required to provide employees with a minimum number of hours, benefits or employment perks. These employers are subsidized by not having to pay the requisite salary to support a worker and his or her family. In effect, low-wage employers are subsidized by taxpayers through the Earned Income Tax Credit (EITC), child tax credit, food stamps, Medicaid, and the Child Health Insurance Program (CHIPs), which partially makes up the shortfall between low salaries and the real cost of living. Moreover, compelling former recipients to become engaged in the workforce by way of a lifetime benefit cap will not ensure permanent labor force attachment, especially if the economy exhibits weakness. According to the U.S. Census Bureau, the poverty rate rose from 11.3 percent in 2000 to 12.3 percent in 2006, after dropping for four consecutive years.

The transition from public assistance to labor policy does not bode well for the "hard to employ," a group of recipients that has significant barriers to employment and difficulty in finding and sustaining work. Some of these barriers include substance abuse, physical disabilities, domestic violence, learning disabilities, mental health issues, language problems, chronic health problems, and multiple other barriers.[80] No single policy will ensure that former recipients maintain a viable attachment to the workforce. Nor can any single measure compensate for the lack of a comprehensive labor policy for low-income workers. David Stoesz sums up the dilemma: "Welfare reform that offers the welfare-poor an opportunity to become the working-poor is no *real* reform at all. The challenge that remains is to devise policies that will accelerate the upward mobility of welfare families so that they can partake in the American dream."[81]

Internationally, Sweden is viewed as a stellar example of the merger of employment and welfare policy. Swedish policymakers have long maintained that people must have a job to feel productive and unemployment leads to social and personal problems. Instead of focusing welfare policies on the provision of cash benefits to the poor, Sweden has concentrated its efforts on employment-based activities.

Sweden uses several different kinds of employment-based strategies to promote full employment. To partially mitigate the effects of frictional and other kinds of unemployment, Swedish universities are free (for Swedes), and student loans allow the unemployed to study and retrain to enter or reenter the workforce. This employment-based strategy is complemented by a system of relief work, apprenticeships, and other governmental work-sponsored programs. However, despite the emphasis on full employment, Sweden's 2012 unemployment rate stood at a relatively high 7.2 percent in mid-2012 compared to 8.1 percent in the United States.

To encourage workplace participation, maternity and parental benefits include 450 days at 75 percent of income. A housing allowance (based on income and family size) is provided for wage earners making below a certain wage. Rent—usually the single largest expenditure for a low-income family—is regulated by the state. Sweden spends about 50 percent of its GDP on welfare-related expenditures, which is financed by high income and sales taxes. Consequently, child poverty in Sweden was 6.7 percent in 2011 compared to roughly 20 percent in the United States.[82]

Teenage Pregnancy

Teenage pregnancy has been strongly associated with public assistance and welfare dependency. By 2010, teen birthrates in the United States had declined by more than 35 percent since 1991, reaching a historic low at 39.1 births per 1,000 teens aged 15–19 years in 2010. Teen birthrates in the United States nevertheless remain high, exceeding those in most developed countries. For example, U.S. rates are nearly twice as high as those in England and Wales or Canada, and nine times as high as those in the Netherlands or Japan:

Ten percent of all U.S. births in 2009 were to mothers under the age of 20.[83]

- In 2010, 367,752 infants were born to adolescent women aged between 15 and 19 years.
- The teenage birth rate is declining. Between 2009 and 2010, teenage pregnancy decreased by 9 percent for women aged between 15 and 19 years. The current rate for this age group is 34.3 live births per 10,000 women. This represents a substantial decline from the 1991 rate of 61.8 per 1,000 women.[84]
- Between 20 to 37 percent of teenage mothers have a second child within 24 months. The risk for preterm labor and low birth weight also increases for second children born to teenage mothers.[85]
- Teen mothers are more likely than mothers over age 20 to give birth prematurely (before 37 completed weeks of pregnancy). Between 2002 and 2004, preterm birth rates averaged 14.3 percent for women under age 20 compared to 11.7 percent for women aged 20 to 29. Babies born too soon face an increased risk of newborn health problems, long-term disabilities and even death.
- Teen mothers are more likely to drop out of high school than girls who delay childbearing. In 2010, only 50 percent of teenagers who had children received a high school diploma by the age of 22, compared to 90 percent of teenagers who did not give birth until age 20 or over.[86]
- Teen mothers are more likely to live in poverty than women who delay childbearing, and more than 75 percent of all unmarried teen mothers go on welfare within five years of the birth of their first child.[87]

Out-of-wedlock births have grave economic consequences. For one, teenage mothers are twice as likely to be poor as are non-teen mothers, and a teenage mother earns only half the lifetime wage of a woman who waits until 20 to have her first child. Second, as mentioned above, a strong correlation exists between young single motherhood and welfare dependency. Teen mothers who grew up on

Although teenage birthrates in the United States have declined, they still remain high, exceeding those in most developed countries.

Source: S. Borisov/Shutterstock

public assistance were more than twice as likely to be dependent on welfare themselves.[88] According to the Brookings Institute, teenage childbearing costs U.S. taxpayers $7 billion a year.[89]

The costs of developing and running teen pregnancy and prevention programs can also be substantial. In 2011, nine states reported a total cost of almost $13 billion in outlays for teen pregnancy programs. California's 'Cal-Learn case management' had the highest expenditure at $8,849,306.[90]

Although numerous programs have been developed to reduce teenage pregnancy, evaluations of these attempts have shown mixed results. One early teen pregnancy prevention program was Project Redirection. From 1980 to 1982, 805 AFDC- eligible mothers aged 17 or younger received intensive services to optimize educational, employment, and life management skills. The outcome after one, two, and five years was mixed and Project Redirection teens fared no better than the control group in obtaining a high school diploma or GED certificate. Their weekly earnings five years later were only $23 more than those in the control group. Five years later, the household income of the control group exceeded that of the Project Redirection group by $19. Two years after participation, 7 percent of Project Redirection teens were on welfare; five years later, 10 percent fewer of the control group were on welfare. Regarding childbearing, Project Redirection teens reported fewer pregnancies in the first and second years after the program; yet five years later they exceeded the control group in their number of pregnancies and live births. Researchers concluded that "the program impacts were largely transitory."[91]

From 1989 to 1992 researchers randomly assigned 2,322 poor young mothers, ages 16 to 22, either to New Chance—a program through which the women received health, education, and welfare assistance coordinated by a case manager—or to a control group that received no special services. At the 18-month follow-up, the experimental group fared worse than the control group in two important respects. First, New Chance mothers were less likely to be using contraception, were more likely to become pregnant, and were more likely to abort their pregnancies than the control group. Second, participants were less likely to be working after entering the program; were earning less; and, during the fourth to the sixth months, were more likely to be on public assistance.[92] To compound matters, New Chance cost $5,073 per participant, excluding child care.[93]

Not surprisingly, the anti-teen pregnancy movement is highly politicized. On one side are those who support comprehensive sex education that includes information about contraception. On the other side are those who favor abstinence-only-until-marriage programs, which provide no information about contraception beyond failure rates. Proponents of abstinence-only programs believe that providing information about contraception contradicts and undermines the message. The 1996 PRWORA had a provision (later set out in Title V of the Social Security Act) that appropriated $250 million over five years for state initiatives that promote abstinence. From 1998 to 2003, almost a half billion dollars in state and federal funds were used to support this initiative. The findings of eleven states whose evaluations were available in 2003 showed few short-term benefits and no

lasting, positive impact. Specifically, abstinence-only programs showed little evidence of sustained (long-term) impact on attitudes and intentions. Worse, they showed some negative impacts on the willingness of participants to use contraception, including condoms, to prevent untoward sexual health outcomes.[94] The apparent failure of abstinence-based programs illustrates how little policymakers understand the motivation and the behaviors associated with teenage pregnancy. It also illustrates how little is known about the interpersonal, social, and cultural components that lead to teenage pregnancy.

Welfare Behaviorism

Behavioral Poverty The TANF program is predicated on a form of **welfare behaviorism**—an attempt to reprogram the behaviors of the poor. Despite data demonstrating the marginal economic benefits of making welfare conditional, conservatives effectively leveraged a moral argument that public policy should change the behavior of the welfare poor. By the mid-1980s, conservative theorists had arrived at a new consensus on poverty; namely, that although the liberally inspired public assistance programs might once have been appropriate for the "cash poor," they were counterproductive for the "behaviorally poor."[95] As poverty programs expanded, conservatives contended, the social dysfunctions of the behaviorally poor metastasized: Beginning as teen mothers, women dominated family life, ultimately becoming generationally dependent on welfare; young men dropped out of school, failed to pursue legitimate employment, and resorted to sexual escapades and repetitive crime to demonstrate prowess; children lacking adult role models of effective parents promised to further populate the underclass.

Conservatives differed in how to respond to behavioral poverty. In *Losing Ground*, Charles Murray suggested "scrapping the entire federal welfare and income support structure for working-aged persons."[96] Lawrence Mead argued for making public aid contingent on conventional behaviors, particularly work.[97] Eventually, both prescriptions were incorporated in welfare policy. Following Mead's admonition, states secured federal waivers for "experiments" that required welfare mothers to meet a number of requirements or risk losing aid: (1) Through "Learnfare," children on public assistance had to have regular school attendance. (2) Through the family cap, additional assistance for children born after a mother became eligible for assistance would be denied benefits. (3) The establishment of paternity was required before a child could receive benefits (to enable the state to pursue child support). (4) As a method for protecting public health, recipient children were required to have immunizations. And (5) to dissuade teenagers from becoming pregnant, states required teen mothers to live with their parents in order to get welfare.[98]

Die-hard conservatives justified the termination of entitlement under TANF by adopting George Gilder's view that the poor needed "the spur of their own poverty,"[99] and "compassionate conservatives" found a rationale in "tough love." Either way, conservative welfare reformers conceded that terminating benefits would probably worsen deprivation but argued that stopping benefits was necessary.

Personal and Parental Responsibility The welfare behaviorism inherent in TANF reflects a belief in the importance of personal and parental responsibility. This philosophy harks back to supposedly traditional "main street" values of self-reliance, independence, and individual responsibility. It also includes a de facto belief in the limited role of government.

The view of parental responsibility reflected in the PRWORA focuses on several themes: (1) fathers have a responsibility to financially support their children; (2) mothers have a responsibility to disclose paternity before receiving public assistance; (3) mothers who have physical custody of their children have a responsibility to financially provide for them through work efforts; (4) custodial parents are responsible for ensuring that their children receive educational opportunities; and (5) custodial parents are responsible for providing basic public health protection for their children, including immunizations. Significant controversy surrounds the question of whether attempts at engineering appropriate social behaviors are successful or whether they simply function as punishment.

Another issue underlying the welfare reforms involves (re)marriage. According to several studies, no more than a fifth of mothers voluntarily leave public assistance due to earnings increases; most exits result from a change in marital status.[100] Yet public assistance programs punish marriage in two ways: (1) by how they treat a married couple with children, and (2) by how they treat families with stepparents. First, a needy two-parent family with children is less likely to be eligible for aid than a one-parent family. Although the non-incapacitated two-parent family can

apply for TANF, many states require work expectation and time limits that make the program inaccessible to many poor families. Second, a stepparent has no legal obligation to support the children of his or her spouse in most states. Nevertheless, TANF cuts or limits benefits when a woman remarries by counting much of the stepparent's income when calculating the family's countable income, thus jeopardizing the mother's eligibility status.[101] This creates a strong economic disincentive for a low-income woman to marry a low-earning male. According to Robert Rector:

> The current welfare system has made marriage economically irrational for most low-income parents. Welfare has converted the low-income working husband from a necessary breadwinner into a net financial handicap. It has transformed marriage from a legal institution designed to protect and nurture children into an institution which financially penalizes nearly all low-income parents who enter into it. Across the nation, the current welfare system has all but destroyed family structure in the inner city. Welfare establishes strong financial disincentives, effectively blocking the formation of intact, two-parent families.[102]

Welfare to Work

TANF is predicated on the long-standing belief that recipients should be moved off public assistance and into private employment as quickly as possible. Whereas conservatives argue that paid work is the best antipoverty program, some liberals have asserted that child rearing is also a productive form of work. Welfare advocates have contended that while it is socially acceptable for middle-class mothers to stay at home with young children, poor mothers are considered lazy and unmotivated if they do the same.

Workfare programs have been a constant feature of the welfare landscape since 1967, when new AFDC amendments were added to pressure recipient mothers into working. As part of those new rules, work requirements became mandatory for unemployed fathers, mothers, and certain teenagers. AFDC recipients who were deemed employable and yet refused to work could be terminated. Partly because of a lackluster federal commitment, the performance of work programs was generally disappointing. In addition, many states were reluctant to enact mandatory job requirements, because they believed that enforcing them would prove more costly than simply maintaining families on public assistance. Workfare again resurfaced in 1988 when it formed the backbone of the Family Support Act.

Often, former welfare recipients who get jobs join the ranks of the working poor. If the reality of welfare-to-work diverges from the rhetoric of welfare reform, it is because of the assumption that TANF mothers are so welfare dependent that they have no experience with the labor market. In fact, many mothers have worked and have, as a result, come to see welfare benefits as a form of unemployment or underemployment assistance. To explain the relationship between work and welfare, labor economist Michael Piore split workers into primary and secondary labor markets: Workers in the primary labor market hold down salaried jobs that include health and vacation benefits, are full time, and incorporate a career track; workers in the secondary labor market work for hourly wages—often at the minimum wage—without benefits in jobs that are part time or seasonal and are not part of a career track.

The trick of welfare reform is to catapult TANF mothers into the primary labor market. The sticking point is that substantial investments are necessary to achieve such program performance. But to do so creates two problems: First, a "moral hazard" emerges as welfare beneficiaries become recipients of benefits unavailable to the working poor not on welfare. Second, a "political hazard" is created for any elected official who states a willingness to support welfare recipients over the working poor. In such circumstances, the prudent politician favors the most expedient option—push welfare recipients into the labor market and celebrate doing so with paeans to the work ethic. These moral and political hazards thus prescribe the boundaries of plausibility: perforce, welfare reform is limited to elevating the welfare poor up to the level of the working poor.

Finally, TANF work-to-welfare programs fail to take into account barriers to employment. A study of welfare recipients by Sandra Danziger and her colleagues found high levels of barriers to work, such as physical and mental problems, domestic violence, and lack of transportation, but relatively low levels of other barriers, such as drug or alcohol dependence or a lack of understanding of work norms. Their study also found that recipients commonly have multiple barriers and that the number of barriers is strongly and negatively associated with employment status. Almost two-thirds of the study respondents had two or more potential barriers to work, and more than one-quarter had four or more.[103]

An important public assistance trend in some Western industrialized countries has been the widespread adoption of U.S.-style welfare-to-work or workfare programs. According to Asghar Zaidi, there are two main types of welfare-to-work programs: (1) those that focus on direct employment by immediately driving people off the welfare rolls and into the workforce, and (2) those that focus on increasing human capital by providing training and education to enhance the employability of recipients. In 1998, the United Kingdom adopted a New Deal (renamed Flexible New Deal in 2009) program partially based on a welfare-to-work model.[104]

The Flexible New Deal (ND) was a series of workfare and labor market policies designed to reduce unemployment by providing training, subsidized employment and voluntary work. The ND allowed the government to withdraw benefits from those who refuse "reasonable employment." Although designed to address youth unemployment, ND programs later encompassed older long-term unemployed workers, single parents, the disabled, and other groups.[105]

In 2011, the Tory government replaced the ND programs with the Work Programme (WP), a pay-by-results jobs program. Specifically, the WP uses a series of contractors—most of them private corporations rather than voluntary sector organizations—to find jobs for the unemployed. After a small initial payment, WP contractors are only paid if they can show that their clients have found and kept a job. Since the WP is based on payment by results, contractors carry the initial risk. Hence, a danger exists that private contractors will focus on places where they are more likely to get people into work rather than into long-term sustainable employment.[106]

The Australian government began a workfare-based "Work for the Dole" program in 1998. This program was designed to help job seekers improve their employment prospects by providing work experiences in local community projects. Placements encompassed a wide range of projects, including heritage and/or history, the environment, community care, tourism, sport, and community services. At the discretion of the caseworker, the long-term unemployed could be required to engage in "Full Time Work for the Dole."[107]

In 2006, a more strident U.S.-style welfare-to-work program was introduced in Australia to increase workforce participation and reduce welfare dependency among recipients in four target groups: principal caregivers, people with disabilities, older unemployed people, and the long-term unemployed. According to Adele Horin, the welfare-to-work policy failed to achieve its objectives, leaving three of the four target groups (disability pensioners, the long-term unemployed, and the older unemployed) with little or no positive gains.[108]

Australia is also testing an Income Management (IM) policy for welfare recipients. According to the government, IM is designed to ensure that money provided for welfare is spent on priority needs and expenses, such as food, housing, clothing, education, and health care. In turn, a portion of welfare payments is quarantined, and recipients cannot use it to purchase alcohol, tobacco, pornography, gambling products or gambling services. Recipients can spend the remaining money as they choose. The IM system includes a pin-protected BasicsCard that allows beneficiaries to access their income managed money using existing ATM facilities at approved stores and businesses. In addition, the IM system incorporates a Matched Savings Payment of up to $500. Each dollar a recipient saves in their personal bank account is matched up to a maximum of $500.[109]

The Evolution of Public Assistance

There are myriad ways to provide social assistance to the poor. One way is through universal benefits, which is less stigmatizing since everyone receives the same benefits. Table 11.2 illustrates how benefits are distributed to the poor in various countries.

For a half century, AFDC did little more than dispense checks; not until relatively recently has recipient behavior been a target for systematic intervention. Because of its lack of direction, AFDC became the source for derogatory colloquialisms such as "welfare mess" and "welfare queen." Instilling some order in welfare was bound to produce some desirable outcomes. It is the extent of positive outcomes that is questionable.

Welfare analysts suspect that most of the improvement in welfare program performance is attributable to those recipients who are relatively well educated, have employment experience, and are upwardly mobile. Such welfare beneficiaries are good candidates for the secondary labor market, and some will even find secure employment in the primary labor market. Of the remaining welfare families, most may be socially mainstreamed with adequate inducements and supports. But many—perhaps 20 percent—will fail to negotiate the pro-

cedural thicket imposed by the welfare reforms of the mid-1990s. While the PRWORA allows states to exempt 20 percent of families from time limits, there is no requirement that those on the lowest social stratum be allowed to stay on aid indefinitely. And indeed, there is no assurance that states will exempt the most troubled families from time limits. It is just as plausible that savvy state welfare administrators will exempt mothers who are in lengthy educational/training programs, on the basis that they represent a better long-term investment of public resources. Even some conservatives are opposed to time limits. At a 1996 conference on welfare reform, Lawrence Mead stated his opposition to time limits, primarily on the basis that virtually no research had been done to determine the consequences of terminating poor families from public assistance.[110]

A core question involves the extent to which states can be expected to comply with the federal work requirements, especially given the severe economic downturn. Fractures in TANF were obvious in 2008–2009 as many states had either exhausted their TANF funds or were approaching the need to augment federal funds with state.

In the event of a continuing economic downswing, this will produce an enormous compression effect on the states. Squeezed between static resources and increasing demands for job placement, the initial response will be to remove families from welfare or to discourage new families from enrolling.

Whenever possible, states will attempt to transfer the most troubled families to SSI, a program that is fully federally funded. This, however, will require certification of disability, and the federal government will resist SSI's becoming a dumping ground for the states' welfare reform failures. Without the SSI transfer option, states will be induced to reduce the number of cases not in compliance with work requirements. Given difficulties in operationalizing the federal five-year lifetime limit, states will be induced to consider ever shorter limits. Terminating families as soon as possible on the basis of non-compliance will ultimately screen out those families least likely to become employed. Eventually such families will cease seeking aid; and to the extent that large numbers of the more disorganized families disappear from state welfare rolls, states will avoid federal penalties for failing to meet employment requirements.

The future of families dumped from state welfare programs is bleak. Many have ended up in the tertiary job market, or worse, in shelters or on the streets. Like the deinstitutionalized, some former

TABLE 11.2 Sample of Non-Contributory Social Transfer Programs, 2004

	Guaranteed Minimum Income	Housing benefits	Family Benefits Universal	Means-tested	Lone-parent benefit	Employment conditional benefits	Childcare benefits Non-parental care	Parental care
Australia	Y	Y	–	Y	Y	Y	Y	Y
Canada	Y	GMI	–	Y	Y	Y	Y	–
Czech Republic	Y	Y	–	Y	–	–	–	Y
France	Y	Y	Y	Y	Y	Y	Y	Y
Denmark	Y	Y	Y	–	FB	–	Y	–
Finland	Y	Y	Y	–	FB	Y	Y	–
Germany	Y	Y	Y	–	T	Y	Y	Y
Sweden	Y	Y	Y	–	Y	–	–	–
Greece	–	Y	Y	–	–	–	–	–
Hungary	Y	Y	Y	–	FB	–	–	Y
Iceland	Y	Y	Y	Y	Y	Y	–	–
Ireland	Y	GMI	Y	–	Y	Y	–	Y
Italy	–	Y	–	Y	–	–	–	–
Japan	Y	GMI	–	Y	Y	Y	–	–
Korea	Y	GMI	–	–	–	Y	Y	–
Luxembourg	Y	GMI	Y	–	T	–	Y	Y
Netherlands	Y	Y	Y	–	T	Y	Y	–
New Zealand	–	Y	–	Y	Y	Y	–	–
Norway	Y	Y	Y	–	Y	–	Y	–
Poland	Y	Y	–	Y	CCB	–	–	Y
Portugal	Y	–	–	Y	T	–	–	–
Slovak Republic	Y	Y	Y	Y	Y	– –	–	Y
Spain	Y	–	–	Y	Y	T –	–	–
Sweden	Y	Y	Y	–	Y	–	–	–
Switzerland	Y	GMI	Y	–	–	–	–	–
United Kingdom	Y	Y	Y	–	–	Y	Y	–
United States	–	Y	–	Y	–	Y	Y	–

Notes: "Y" indicates that the existence of a specific benefit or tax credit. "GMI" (guaranteed minimum income), "FB" (family benefit), or "CCB" (childcare benefit) indicate that housing or lone-parent specific provisions exist as part of these schemes. "T" indicates different tax provisions or specific tax allowances for lone parents where no other benefits are available.

Source: Chris de Neubourg, Julie Castonguay and Keetie Roelen (2007). Social safety nets and targeted assistance: Lessons from the European experience, The World Bank, November.

For various historical, political and social reasons, the U.S. has opted for a strict means-tested approach to public assistance.

TANF families have been swallowed up in the urban landscape and have become virtually invisible, leading lives of quiet desperation. Conservative scholars, such as Marvin Olasky, have promised that private, especially religious, agencies will pick up the slack,[111] but this has not happened. Contributions to nonprofit agencies such as the United Way have stagnated in recent years. Ineligible for state aid and unable to get necessary assistance from the nonprofit sector, former welfare families have turned to metropolitan government as the last resort. Big-city mayors are already dreading the impact that such families will have on their already overburdened city budgets.[112]

The many positive aspects of welfare reform are outweighed by the negatives. For instance PRWORA benefits are denied for life to parents convicted of felony drug offenses unless they are participating in a drug treatment program, even though family-oriented drug treatment for addicts who are also mothers is rare. Several of the PRWORA provisions target teenagers on welfare: Teen mothers are required to live with their parents and stay in school to receive benefits; HHS is required to mount a teen pregnancy prevention initiative; and the Justice Department is required to identify older men (some of whom may be only a few years older than the mother) who impregnate female teenagers and prosecute them for statutory rape. Several provisions address child support, including the requirement that states establish registries for child support and streamline the process for establishing paternity. States are encouraged to be more aggressive in withholding income from noncustodial parents in arrears for child support. Furthermore, more vigorous penalties are directed at noncustodial parents to encourage them to pay up, such as revocation of professional, drivers, occupational, and recreational licenses.[113]

Given the track record of demonstration programs designed to prevent teen pregnancy and increase child support, the stiff penalties directed at adolescents and deadbeat dads would seem to be more of rhetorical value to elected officials than of practical use to save the public revenues now allocated to welfare programs. No one seems to have taken the trouble to calculate the ultimate cost of deploying a state-administered welfare apparatus with tracking, surveillance, and sanction capacities designed to reprogram the behavior of the millions of families on public assistance.

Recipients of public assistance programs fare less well than as those covered under the social insurances. Public assistance programs include a large dose of stigma, and the character of recipients is often maligned because of their need. Moreover, the relative success of Social Security in arresting poverty among the elderly has not been replicated in public assistance programs. In fact, the reverse is true; the poorest of the poor have endured greater levels of poverty from 1980 onward. Indeed, the legacy of welfare reform signed by former President Clinton bodes badly for the future prospects of America's poor.

Conclusion

The U.S. welfare system has undergone a dramatic transformation over the past 20 years marked by several important themes: (1) the conversion of public assistance policy into labor policy, (2) the conversion of public assistance policy into tax policy, and (3) the increased privatization of social welfare services. By converting AFDC into workfare through TANF, the PRWORA eliminated the boundary between public assistance and labor policy and became a feeder system to supply the secondary labor market with manpower. The result is fewer protected islands left for those who cannot compete in the labor market.

The conversion of public assistance policy into labor policy is shored up by tax policy through the expansion of EITC benefits, the only public assistance program that has been purposely enlarged in the past 20 years. By expanding EITC benefits through the tax code while at the same time eliminating the entitlement to AFDC, the Congress shifted the focus from the nonworking poor to the working poor, a group more marginally acceptable to conservatives and the larger society. If the past trajectory continues, public assistance benefits will be increasingly routed through tax policy for low-income workers rather than through direct cash or in-kind subsidies for the nonworking poor.

Privatized social services have encroached upon most welfare domains, including health care, public education, mental health and chemical dependency services, nursing home care, corrections, and child care. Many of these markets are already glutted by the influx of corporations seeking to increase their profits and their corporate reach.

All developed economies have some form of income support for poor families and individuals. Within the range of income transfer approaches, some countries opt for separate means-tested programs like TANF; others choose a more far-ranging (often universal) approach. Still other industrial countries use a Guaranteed Minimum Income (GMI) which guarantees that all families will have sufficient income provided they meet certain conditions, such as citizenship and/or a means test. To receive benefits, other countries require recipients to be part of the labor market and/or perform community services. While the United States is one of the few industrialized countries without a GMI, the tax system—largely through the Earned Income Tax Credit (EITC) and other tax-related programs—provides some assistance to low-income working families.

Several U.S. approaches to public assistance have been adopted by other countries. Notably, welfare-to-work policies and strict means tests were taken on board in the United Kingdom, Australia, Ireland, and other countries faced with fiscal difficulties. Given the persistence of the European economic crisis, it is likely that more countries will opt to limit public assistance and other social spending.

This is clearly a difficult time for the American welfare state. Even after huge expenditures on social welfare services, basic human needs remain unmet. Given the present economic trend—in which vast numbers of service jobs are produced, many of which are part time, have few if any benefits, and pay the minimum wage—long-term welfare benefit packages will likely be required for an increasing number of citizens. How much help these income benefit packages will contain, and at what cost, will be a matter for future discourse in public policy.

DISCUSSION QUESTIONS

1. Public assistance programs are arguably the most controversial programs in the U.S. welfare state. Critics frequently lambaste them for encouraging everything from welfare dependency to teenage pregnancy. Supporters argue that public assistance programs are poorly funded and barely allow recipients to survive. Why is public assistance so controversial? What, if anything, can be done to make the TANF program less controversial?

2. Numerous myths have arisen around the TANF program. In your opinion, what myths have been the most harmful to the programs and to recipients? Why?

3. Since the 1970s, most strategies for reforming public assistance have revolved around implementing mandatory work requirements. This strategy was evident in the programs of Presidents Carter and Reagan and was the centerpiece of the 1988 Family Support Act. The TANF program mandated that benefits should last for a maximum of five years, after which a recipient would be ineligible for continuing public assistance. Is establishing a mandatory work requirement a viable strategy for reforming public assistance? Why? Why not? What would be a better strategy for reforming public assistance?

4. TANF benefit levels vary widely from state to state because the federal government has refused to establish a national minimum benefit level. Moreover, there is little federal pressure on states to increase benefit levels and thereby curtail the erosion of public assistance benefits that has taken place since the 1970s. Should the federal government establish a minimum national benefit level for TANF and compel states to meet that level? If not, why not? If you agree, what should that level be?

5. Public assistance programs are increasingly being designed to change the behavior of poor recipients. Can and should the behavior of poor people be changed through social policy legislation? Will this legislation work? If not, why?

6. Although administered by the Social Security Administration, the SSI program carries a stigma similar to public assistance programs like food stamps or the TANF. Why does this stigma exist? What can be done to diminish it?

NOTES

1. U.S. Census Bureau, "Comparing Program Participation of TANF and Non-TANF Families Before and During a Time of Recession," November 2011. Retrieved May 2012, from http://www.census.gov/prod/2011pubs/p70-127.pdf

2. L. Pavetti & D. Rosenbaum, "Reducing Poverty and Economic Distress After ARRA," The Urban Institute, July 2010. Retrieved May 2012, from http://www.urban.org/url.cfm?ID=412150

3. Isaac Shapiro and Robert Greenstein, *Holes in the Safety Nets* (Washington, DC: Center on Budget and Policy Priorities, 1988).

4. U.S. Administration for Children and Families, "Caseload Data 2011," Last Updated 1 May 2012. Retrieved May 2012, from http://www.acf.hhs.gov/programs/ofa/data-reports/caseload/caseload_current.htm#2011

5. "Welfare Reform Issue Paper," Working Group on Welfare Reform, Family Support and Independence,U.S. Department of Health and Human Services, February 26, 1994; and Peter Gottschalk, "Achieving Self-Sufficiency for Welfare Recipients—The Good and Bad News," in *Select Committee on Hunger, Beyond Public Assistance: Where Do We Go From Here?* Serial No. 102-123 (Washington, DC: U.S. Government Printing Office, 1992), p. 56.

6. U.S. Census Bureau, "Comparing Program Participation of TANF and Non-TANF Families Before and During a Time of Recession," November 2011. Retrieved May 2012, from http://www.census.gov/prod/2011pubs/p70-127.pdf

7. U.S. Administration for Children and Families, "Caseload Data 2011," Last Updated 1 May 2012. Retrieved May 2012, from http://www.acf.hhs.gov/programs/ofa/data-reports/caseload/caseload_current.htm#2011

8. U.S. Administration for Children and Families, "Caseload Data 2011," Last Updated 1 May 2012. Retrieved May 2012, from http://www.acf.hhs.gov/programs/ofa/data-reports/caseload/caseload_current.htm#2011

9. U.S Census Bureau, "Income, Poverty, and Health Insurance Coverage in the United States: 2010," September 2011. Retrieved Feb 2012, from www.census.gov/prod/2011pubs/p60-239.pdf

10. S. Zedlewski and O. Golden, "Next Steps for Temporary Assistance for Needy Families," The Urban Institute, Brief 11, Feb 2010. Retrieved May 2012 from http://www.urban.org/uploadedpdf/412047_next_steps_brief11.pdf

11. The Urban Institute, "Welfare Rules Databook: State TANF Policies as of July 2006", September 2006. Retrieved July 2008 from http://www.urban.org/UploadedPDF/411686_welfare_databook06.pdf

12. Administration for Children and Families, "Characteristics and Financial Circumstances of TANF Recipients Fiscal Year 2009," Retrieved May 2012, from http://www.acf.hhs.gov/programs/ofa/character/fy2009/indexfy09.htm

13. U.S. Department of Health and Human Services, Characteristics and Financial Circumstances of TANF Recipients, Fiscal Year 2008, Administration for Children and Families 2009, Washington, DC. Retrieved November 21, 2010 from, http://www.acf.hhs.gov/programs/ofa/character/FY2008/indexfy08.htm

14. Administration for Children and Families, "Characteristics and Financial Circumstances of TANF Recipients Fiscal Year 2009," Retrieved May 2012, from http://www.acf.hhs.gov/programs/ofa/character/fy2009/indexfy09.htm

15. The Urban Institute, "Welfare Rules Databook: State TANF Policies as of July 2010," August 2011. Retrieved May 2012, from http://www.acf.hhs.gov/programs/opre/welfare_employ/state_tanf/databook10/databook10.pdf

16. Liz Schott and Ife Finch, TANF Benefits Are Low and Have Not Kept Pace With Inflation, Benefits Are Not Enough to Meet Families' Basic Needs, October 14, 2010, Center on Budget and Policy Priorities, Washington, DC.

17. G. Adams, R. Koralek & K. Martinson, "Child Care Subsidies and Leaving Welfare: Policy Issues and Strategies," The Urban Institute, 10 April 2006. Retrieved May 2012 from http://www.urban.org/UploadedPDF/311304_policy_issues.pdf

18. "Welfare Reform Issue Paper," Working Group on Welfare Reform, Family Support and Independence, U.S. Department of Health and Human Services, February 26, 1994; and Peter Gottschalk, "Achieving Self-Sufficiency for Welfare Recipients—The Good and Bad News," in Select Committee on Hunger, Beyond Public Assistance: Where Do We Go From Here? Serial No. 102-123 (Washington, DC: U.S. Government Printing Office, 1992), p. 56.

19. Mary Jo Bane and David T. Ellwood, Welfare Realities: From Rhetoric to Reform (Cambridge, MA: Harvard University Press, 1994).

20. Administration for Children and Families, "Characteristics and Financial Circumstances of TANF Recipients Fiscal Year 2009," Retrieved May 2012, from http://www.acf.hhs.gov/programs/ofa/character/fy2009/indexfy09.htm

21. U.S. Department of Health and Human Services, Characteristics and Financial Circumstances of TANF Recipients, Fiscal Year 2008, Administration for Children and Families, 2009, Washington, DC. Retrieved November 21, 2010 from, http://www.acf.hhs.gov/programs/ofa/character/FY2008/indexfy08.htm

22. Liz Schott and Ife Finch, TANF Benefits Are Low and Have Not Kept Pace With Inflation, Benefits Are Not Enough to Meet Families' Basic Needs, October 14, 2010, Center on Budget and Policy Priorities, Washington, DC.

23. S. Zedlewski and O. Golden, "Next Steps for Temporary Assistance for Needy Families," The Urban Institute, Brief 11, Feb 2010. Retrieved May 2012 from http://www.urban.org/uploadedpdf/412047_next_steps_brief11.pdf

24. U.S. Department of Health and Human Services, Characteristics and Financial Circumstances of TANF Recipients, Fiscal Year 2008.

25. Duncan and Hoffman, "Welfare Dynamics."

26. David Morris, "Ask Dr. Dave," 2003.

27. U.S Census Bureau, "Statistical Abstract of the United States: 2012," 2011. Retrieved May 2012 from http://www.census.gov/prod/2011pubs/12statab/socins.pdf

28. Thomas Corbett, "The Wisconsin Welfare Magnet: What Is an Ordinary Member of the Tribe to Do When the Witch Doctors Disagree?" Focus 13, no. 3 (Fall/Winter 1991), pp. 2–4.

29. Quoted in Diane Rose, Terri Sachnik, Josie Salazar, Eunice Sealey, and Virginia Wall, "Welfare Reform II," unpublished paper, University of Houston Graduate School of Social Work, Houston, TX, 1996.

30. Bruce D. Meyer, Do the Poor Move to Receive Higher Welfare Benefits? Department of Economics and Institute for Policy Research, Northwestern University and NBER, September 14, 2000, p. 1.

31. S. Zedlewski and O. Golden, "Next Steps for Temporary Assistance for Needy Families," The Urban Institute, Brief 11, Feb 2010. Retrieved May 2012 from http://www.urban.org/uploadedpdf/412047_next_steps_brief11.pdf

32. Elizabeth McNichol, Phil Oliff and Nicholas Johnson, States Continue to Feel Recession's Impact, Center on Budget and Policy Priorities, October 7, 2010, Washington DC. Retrieved November 22, 2010 from, http://www.cbpp.org/cms/index.cfm?fa=view&id=711

33. Robert Moffitt, "Incentive Effects of the U.S. Welfare System: A Review," Journal of Economic Literature 30 (March 1992), pp. 1–61; see also Barbara Vobejda, "Decline in Birth Rates for Teens May Reflect Major Social Changes," Houston Chronicle (October 29, 1996), p. 13A.

34. W. Joseph Heffernan, *Introduction to Social Welfare Policy* (Itasca, IL: F.E. Peacock, 1979).

35. Elizabeth D. Huttman, *Introduction to Social Policy* (New York: McGraw-Hill, 1981), p. 168.

36. William Eaton, "Major Welfare Reform Compromise Reached," *Los Angeles Times* (September 27, 1988), p. 15.

37. American Public Welfare Association, *Conference Agreement on Welfare Reform* (Washington, DC: American Public Welfare Association, September 28, 1988), pp. 1–3.

38. See David Stoesz and Howard Karger, "Welfare Reform: From Illusion to Reality," *Social Work* 35, no. 2 (March 1990), pp. 141–147; and Spencer Rich, "Panel Clears Welfare Bill," *Washington Post* (September 28, 1988), p. A6.

39. See David T. Ellwood, "Welfare Reform as I Knew It: When Bad Things Happen to Good Policies," *The American Prospect* 26 (May–June 1996), p. 240.

40. "Legal Immigrants to Carry Burden of Welfare Reform," *El Paso Times* (August 3, 1996), p. B1.

41. Mark H. Greenberg, "No Duty, No Floor: The Real Meaning of 'Ending Entitlements,'" Washington, DC: Center for Law and Social Policy, 1996. Retrieved 1997 from http://epn.org/clasp/clduty-2.html.

42. Paula Roberts, "Relationship between TANF and Child Support Requirements," Washington, DC: Center for Law and Social Policy, September 1996. Retrieved 1997 from http://epn.org/clasp/cltcsr.html

43. NACo Legislative Priority Fact Sheet, New Welfare Reform Law, "The Personal Responsibility and Work Opportunity Reconciliation Act of 1996," Washington, DC: NACo, 1996.

44. Linda Rosenberg, Michelle Derr, LaDonna Pavetti, Subuhi Asheer, Megan Hague Angus, Samina Sattar and Jeffrey Max, A Study of States' TANF Diversion Programs: Final Report, December 8, 2008, Mathematica Policy Research, Inc., Princeton, NJ.

45. Government of Canada, Benefits Finder, 2012. Retrieved September 2012 from, http://www.canadabenefits.gc.ca/f.1.2ch.4m.2@.jsp?lang=eng

46. Department of Finance Canada, Canada Social Transfer: What is the Canada Social Transfer (CST)? 2011. Retrieved May 2012 from, http://www.fin.gc.ca/fedprov/cst-eng.asp

47. A. Nichols & S. Zedlewski, "Is the Safety Net Catching Unemployed Families?," The Urban Institute, Brief 21, September 2011. Retrieved May 2012, from http://www.urban.org/url.cfm?ID=412397

48. L. Pavetti & D. Rosenbaum, "Reducing Poverty and Economic Distress After ARRA," The Urban Institute, July 2010. Retrieved May 2012, from http://www.urban.org/url.cfm?ID=412150

49. A. Nichols & S. Zedlewski, "Is the Safety Net Catching Unemployed Families?," The Urban Institute, Brief 21, September 2011. Retrieved May 2012, from http://www.urban.org/url.cfm?ID=412397

50. Congressional Budget Office, "Estimated Impact of the American Recovery and Reinvestment Act on Employment and Economic Output from July 2011 Through September 2011," November 2011. Retrieved May 2012 from http://heinonline.org/

51. Douglas J. Besharov, "The Past and Future of Welfare Reform," *Public Interest* (Winter 2003), pp. 18–25.

52. Elizabeth Lower-Basch, Testimony for the Record, Hearing on Welfare Reform: A New Conversation on Women and Poverty September 21, 2010, Committee on Finance, U.S. Senate Center for Law and Social Policy. Retrieved November 22, 2010 from, http://www.clasp.org/admin/site/publications/files/CLASP-Finance-Committee-testimony-for-the-record.pdf

53. Ibid., Basch

54. Ibid., Basch

55. U.S. Census Bureau, "Comparing Program Participation of TANF and Non-TANF Families Before and During a Time of Recession," November 2011. Retrieved May 2012, from http://www.census.gov/prod/2011pubs/p70-127.pdf

56. U.S. Social Security Administration, "The Food Stamp Program and Supplemental Security Income", 67(4), 2007. Retrieved July 2008 from http://www.socialsecurity.gov/policy/docs/ssb/v67n4/67n4p71.html

57. U.S. Census Bureau, "Comparing Program Participation of TANF and Non-TANF Families Before and During a Time of Recession," November 2011. Retrieved May 2012, from http://www.census.gov/prod/2011pubs/p70-127.pdf

58. U.S. Census Bureau, "Comparing Program Participation of TANF and Non-TANF Families Before and During a Time of Recession," November 2011. Retrieved May 2012, from http://www.census.gov/prod/2011pubs/p70-127.pdf

59. Pavetti & D. Rosenbaum, "Reducing Poverty and Economic Distress After ARRA," The Urban Institute, July 2010. Retrieved May 2012, from http://www.urban.org/url.cfm?ID=412150

60. A. Nichols & S. Zedlewski, "Is the Safety Net Catching Unemployed Families?," The Urban Institute, Brief 21, September 2011. Retrieved May 2012, from http://www.urban.org/url.cfm?ID=412397

61. U.S. Social Security Administration, "SSI Annual Statistical Report, 2010," SSA Publication No. 13-11827, August 2011. Retrieved May 2012 from http://www.socialsecurity.gov/policy/docs/statcomps/ssi_asr/2010/ssi_asr10.pdf

62. M. Wiseman, "Supplemental Security Income for the Second Decade," The Urban Institute, August 2010. Retrieved May 2012, from http://www.urban.org/url.cfm?ID=412266

63. U.S. Social Security Administration, "SSI Annual Statistical Report, 2010," SSA Publication No. 13-11827, August 2011. Retrieved May 2012 from http://www.socialsecurity.gov/policy/docs/statcomps/ssi_asr/2010/ssi_asr10.pdf

64. U.S. Social Security Administration, "SSI Annual Statistical Report, 2010," SSA Publication No. 13-11827, August 2011. Retrieved May 2012 from http://www.socialsecurity.gov/policy/docs/statcomps/ssi_asr/2010/ssi_asr10.pdf

65. U.S. Social Security Administration, "SSI Annual Statistical Report, 2010," SSA Publication No. 13-11827, August 2011. Retrieved May 2012 from http://www.socialsecurity.gov/policy/docs/statcomps/ssi_asr/2010/ssi_asr10.pdf

66. M. Wiseman, "Supplemental Security Income for the Second Decade," The Urban Institute, August 2010. Retrieved May 2012, from http://www.urban.org/url.cfm?ID=412266

67. M. Wiseman, "Supplemental Security Income for the Second Decade," The Urban Institute, August 2010. Retrieved May 2012, from http://www.urban.org/url.cfm?ID=412266

68. M. Wiseman, "Supplemental Security Income for the Second Decade," The Urban Institute, August 2010. Retrieved May 2012, from http://www.urban.org/url.cfm?ID=412266

69. U.S. Social Security Administration, "SSI Annual Statistical Report, 2010," SSA Publication No. 13-11827, August 2011. Retrieved May 2012 from http://www.socialsecurity.gov/policy/docs/statcomps/ssi_asr/2010/ssi_asr10.pdf

70. L. Jerome Gallagher, Cori E. Uccello, Alicia B. Pierce, and Erin B. Reidy, "State General Assistance Programs 1998," Washington, DC: The Urban Institute, April 1999. Retrieved from http://newfederalism.urban.org/html/ga_programs/ga_full.html#exesum

71. Minnesota Department of Human Services, "General Assistance Program". Retrieved July 2008 from http://www.dhs.state.mn.us/main/idcplg?IdcService=GET_DYNAMIC_CONVERSION&RevisionSelectionMethod=LatestReleased&dDocName=id_002558

72. California Department of Social Services, "General Assistance or General Relief". Retrieved July 2008 from http://www.cdss.ca.gov/cdssweb/PG132.htm.

73. Maine Emergency Management Agency, "Knox County EMA Taking on a Different Kind of Emergency", March 7, 2008. Retrieved July 2008 from http://www.maine.gov/mema/mema_news_display.shtml?id=52174

74. Maine State Legislature, "Summary of Major State Funding Disbursed to Municipalities and Counties", October 2007. Retrieved July 2008 from http://mainegov-images.informe.org/legis/ofpr/Municipal07/2007_full_report.pdf

75. Thomas Corbett, "The New Federalism: Monitoring Consequences," *Focus* 18, no. 1 (1996), pp. 3–6.

76. *Economic Report of the President*, (Washington, DC: U.S. Government Printing Office, 1995).

77. Public Broadcasting System, "Transcript of Economic Growth 101" (October 1996), Washington, D.C. Retrieved 2004 from www.pbs.org/newshour/bb/economy/october96/growth_10-30.html

78. Richard Friedmann, Neil Gilbert, and Moshe Sherer (eds.), *Modern Welfare States* (New York: New York University Press, 1987).

79. U.S. Bureau of Labor Statistics, "Economic News Release: Employment Characteristics of Families Summary," 26 April 2012. Retrieved May 2012 from http://www.bls.gov/news.release/famee.nr0.htm

80. Office of Inspector General, "State Strategies for Working with Hard-to-Employ TANF Recipients," July 2002. Department of Health and Human Services, OEI-02-00-00630, Washington, D.C.

81. David Stoesz, *A Poverty of Imagination: Bootstrap Capitalism, Sequel to Welfare Reform* (New York: Oxford University Press, 2004), p. 106.

82. *The Local*, "Poverty Drops in Sweden," March 16, 2012. Retrieved September 2012 from, http://www.thelocal.se/39720/20120316

83. U.S. Census Bureau, "Percent of Births to Teenage Mothers, Unmarried Women, and Births with Low Birth Rate by State and Island Areas: 2000 to 2009," Statistical Abstract of the United States: 2012, September 2011. Retrieved May 2012, from http://www.census.gov/compendia/statab/2012/tables/12s0089.pdf

84. Center for Disease Control and Prevention, "About Teen Pregnancy," Last updated 12 March 2012. Retrieved May 2012, from http://www.cdc.gov/TeenPregnancy/AboutTeenPreg.htm#a

85. S.N. Partington, D.L. Steber, K.A. Blair & R.A. Cisler, "Second Births to Teenage Mothers: Risk Factors for Low Birth Weight and Preterm Birth," Perspectives on Sexual and Reproductive Health, vol.41, no.2, June 2009. Retrieved May 2012, from http://search.proquest.com/pqrl/docview/224370417/fulltextPDF/136AFCD3D3A350A7C9F/2?accountid=14723

86. Center for Disease Control and Prevention, "About Teen Pregnancy," Last updated 12 March 2012. Retrieved May 2012, from http://www.cdc.gov/TeenPregnancy/AboutTeenPreg.htm#a

87. March of Dimes, "Teenage Pregnancy". Retrieved July 2008 from http://www.marchofdimes.com/professionals/14332_1159.asp

88. U.S. House of Representatives, *Overview of Entitlement Programs, 1994* (Washington, DC: U.S. Government Printing Office, 1994), p. 448.

89. See Ibid., p. 1100; and Children's Aid Society, "Adolescent Pregnancy Prevention Program, 2004." Retrieved October 2004 from www.stopteenpregnancy.com/news/news_wsj.html

90. Department of Health and Human Services, "Engagement in Additional Work Activities and Expenditures for Other Benefits and Services, April-June 2011: A TANF Report to Congress," April-June 2011. Retrieved May 2012 from http://www.acf.hhs.gov/programs/ofa/data-reports/cra/2011/june2011/cra-june2011.html

91. Denise Polit, Janet Quint, and James Riccio, "The Challenge of Serving Teenage Mothers," New York: Manpower Demonstration Research Corporation, 1988, Tables 2 & 3, p. 17.

92. Janet Quint, Denise Polit, Hans Bos, and George Cave, *New Chance* (New York: Manpower Demonstration Research Corporation, 1994), Tables 5 and 6.

93. Quint et al., *New Chance*, p. xxxi.

94. Debra Hauser, "Five Years of Abstinence-Only-Until-Marriage Education: Assessing the Impact, Advocates for Youth," October 26, 2004. Retrieved October 2004 from www.advocatesforyouth.org/publications/stateevaluations/index.htm

95. Michael Novak, *The New Consensus on Family and Welfare* (Washington, DC: American Enterprise Institute, 1987).

96. Charles Murray, *Losing Ground* (New York: Basic Books, 1984), pp. 227–228.

97. Lawrence Mead, *Beyond Entitlement* (New York: Free Press, 1986).

98. Center on Budget and Policy Priorities, "The New Welfare Law," Washington, DC: Center on Budget and Policy Priorities, 1996.

99. George Gilder, *Wealth and Poverty* (New York: Basic Books, 1981), p. 118.

100. Robert Moffitt, "Incentive Effects of the U.S. Welfare System: A Review," *Journal of Economic Literature* (March 1992) p. 30.

101. Mark Greenberg, testimony before the Domestic Task Force, Select Committee on Hunger, U.S. House of Representatives, April 9, 1992, in *Federal Policy Perspectives on Welfare Reform: Rhetoric, Reality and Opportunities,* Serial No. 102-25 (Washington, DC: U.S. Government Printing Office, 1992), pp. 52–53.

102. Robert Rector, "Strategies for Welfare Reform," Testimony before the Domestic Task Force, Select Committee on Hunger, U.S. House of Representatives, April 9, 1992, in "Federal Policy Perspectives on Welfare Reform: Rhetoric, Reality and Opportunities," Serial No. 102-25, Washington, DC: U.S. Government Printing Office, 1992, pp. 67–68.

103. Sandra Danziger, Mary Corcoran, Sheldon Danziger, Colleen Heflin, Ariel Kalil, Judith Levine, Daniel Rosne, Kristin Seefeldt, Kristine Siefert, and Richard Tolman, "Barriers to the Employment of Welfare Recipients," Poverty Research and Training Center, University of Michigan, January 1999.

104. Asghar Zaidi, Welfare-to-Work Programmes in the UK and Lessons for Other Countries, European Centre for Social Welfare, Policy Brief, October 2009, Vienna Austria.

105. Wesley Stephenson, "Jobless Training Courses 'Demoralising" *BBC News*, April 5, 2009. Retrieved May 2012 from, http://news.bbc.co.uk/2/hi/uk_news/7982550.stm

106. Channel 4 News, Fingers Crossed for Welfare-to-Work Gamble, June 10, 2011. Retrieved May 2012 from, http://www.channel4.com/news/fingers-crossed-for-welfare-to-work-gamble

107. Centrelink, Work for the Dole, 2009. Retrieved May 2012 from, http://www.centrelink.gov.au/internet/internet.nsf/services/work_dole.htm

108. Adele Horin,"Welfare Crackdown Misses Targets," *Sydney Morning Herald*, March 11, 2010, p. 4.

109. Centrelink, Income Management, Australian Government, Department of Human Services, February 17, 2012. Retrieved May 2012 from, http://www.centrelink.gov.au/internet/internet.nsf/individuals/income_mgt_customer.htm

110. Personal discussion at a conference on welfare reform, the Jerome Levy Economics Institute, Bard College, Annandale-on-Hudson, N.Y., July 12, 1996.

111. Marvin Olasky, "Beyond the Stingy Welfare State," *Policy Review* (Fall 1990), p. 14.

112. Robert Pear, "Giuliani Battles Congress on Welfare Bill," *New York Times* (July 27, 1996), p. A7.

113. *Personal Responsibility and Work Opportunity Reconciliation Act of 1996* (Washington, DC: National Association of Social Workers, 1996).

CHAPTER 12

The American Health Care System

Source: PRNewsFoto/The Children's Hospital of Philadelphia/AP Images

Fifty-five percent of Americans surveyed in February 2007 said that the most important domestic policy for the President and Congress to focus on is making health insurance available for everyone. In the same survey, 90 percent said that the present health care system requires fundamental changes or needs to be completely rebuilt.[1]

This chapter examines the U.S. health care system—specifically, the organization of medical services; key governmental health programs such as Medicare and Medicaid; the crisis in health care, including attempts to curb health care costs; the large numbers of uninsured people; the impact of the American Medical Association on health care; and that of managed care in the American health care system. The chapter also surveys various proposals designed to ameliorate the problems in U.S. health care and considers how medical services are organized in Great Britain, Canada and Australia.

The Uninsured

Health care in the United States is marked by several contradictions. According to Census Bureau data, the number of people *with* health insurance rose to 256.2 million in 2010, up from 242.9 million in 2000. Meanwhile, the number *without* such coverage rose from 36.5 million to 49.9 million in the same period. The percentage of the nation's population without health care coverage was 16.3 percent in 2010, while the percentage of people covered by government health insurance programs (Military, Medicaid, and Medicare) was 31 percent. The proportion of uninsured children in 2010 was 9.8 percent of all children, or 7.3 million.[2] Although the vast majority of Americans have easy access to a wide range of health care services through employment-based or public insurance programs, more than 49 million people remain without coverage. The medically uninsured have the following characteristics:

The uninsured are more likely than the privately insured to not receive needed medical care, and more likely to need hospitalization for avoidable acute conditions like pneumonia or uncontrolled diabetes, and more likely to rely on emergency room services or to have no regular source of care.[3] Millions of Americans seeking medical care are turned away each year because they cannot pay; millions more forego preventive services.[4] This exists even though every major city has at least one major medical center.[5] The uninsured face other problems:

- Uninsured children have a higher instance of developmental delays than those with health coverage.[6]
- They are more likely to put off seeking care; to not receive care when needed; and to not fill a prescription or get a recommended treatment because of the expense. In 2011, 28 percent of uninsured adults aged between 19 and 25 delayed seeking medical care due to expense. This is in comparison to 7.6 percent of adults within the same age bracket with private health insurance.[7]
- They are more likely to be contacted by a collection agency for overdue medical bills.
- Uninsured adults hospitalized for heart attacks are 25 percent more likely to die while in the hospital than privately insured adults. Even after controlling for the severity of the injury, uninsured adults hospitalized for a traumatic injury are more than twice as likely to die in the hospital as insured adults.
- The diagnosis of a serious new health condition, including cancer, diabetes, heart attack, chronic lung disease, or stroke, reduced the wealth of uninsured households by 20 percent. Insured households with a similar diagnosis suffered a 2 percent decline in overall wealth.
- Insured households paid about $26,957 in total medical spending after the diagnosis of a serious new health condition; uninsured households paid $42,166.
- Americans who lack health insurance cost the economy billion a year in lost productivity.[8] The cost of medical care for the uninsured totaled around $125 billion in 2004.[9]

The Organization of Medical Services

Most health care costs in the United States are paid for by private insurers, public plans, and the direct public provision of health care. Only 28 percent of health care costs was paid for directly by consumer households in 2009, a significant decline from the 1987 rate of 37 percent. Although the dominant form of health care coverage in the United States is private insurance, employer-based health care accounted for only 21 percent of national health care spending in 2009. Conversely, government spending has increased significantly, from 32 percent in 1987 to 44 percent in 2009.[10]

Spotlight 12.1

THE NATIONAL CENTER FOR HEALTH STATISTICS

The National Center for Health Statistics (NCHS) is a key resource of information about the health of Americans. As the principal health statistics agency in the United States, the organization compiles statistical information to guide action and policies to improve the health of people living within the United States. The information provided by NCHS helps to:

- Document the health status of the population and of important subgroups
- Identify disparities in health status and use of health care by race/ethnicity, socioeconomic status, region, and other population characteristics
- Describe various experiences with the health care system
- Monitor trends in health status and health care delivery
- Identify health problems
- Support biomedical and health services research
- Provide information for making changes in public policies and programs

Evaluate the impact of health policies and programs. To learn more about NCHS, go to its website at www.cdc.gov/nchs.

- Children under 18 in poverty were more likely to be uninsured—15.4 percent in 2010 compared to 9.8 percent of all children. Adults between the ages of 19 and 44 made up approximately three-quarters (75 percent) of the uninsured.
- Young adults (19 to 25 years old) were the least likely of any age group to have health insurance in 2010. Nearly 30 percent of uninsured persons were in this six year age bracket.
- The poor are three times more likely to be uninsured as those who are not poor. Just over one-quarter (26.9 percent) of people in households with annual incomes under $25,000 had no

health insurance in 2010 compared with only 8 percent for those with incomes over $75,000.

- The uninsured rate for African Americans in 2010 was 20.8 percent; for Asians, 18.1 percent; for non-Hispanic whites, 11.7 percent; for Hispanics, 30.7 percent.
- The proportion of the foreign-born population without health insurance (34.1 percent) was about two-and-a-half times that of the native population (13.8 percent) in 2010.
- The South (19.1 percent) and West (17.9 percent) have a higher uninsured rate than either the Northeast (12.4 percent) or the Midwest (13 percent).
- The number of people who received health insurance coverage through their employers fell slightly from 56.1 percent in 2009 to 55.3 percent in 2010, while the number of people covered by government health insurance programs (e.g. Medicare and Medicaid) was 95 million or 31 percent.[11] The relatively high number of uninsured Americans is not surprising, given that family employer-based health insurance premiums cost on average $13,871 annually in 2010—a high cost for a family trying to make ends meet, especially in a deep economic recession.[12] In 35 states average premium costs for workers had risen three times faster than average earnings from 2000 to 2004.[13] Purchasing affordable, accessible insurance is a particular challenge for many older people not eligible for Medicare, for workers in transition between jobs, and for small businesses and their employees. For example, premiums for COBRA (transitional health insurance allowed a worker when they terminate employment) average almost $1000 a month for family coverage and $400 for individual coverage, a huge expenditure given the average monthly unemployment check.[14]

Medical services in the United States consist of five major components:

1. Physicians in solo practice (e.g., traditional physicians who may employ a nurse and receptionist), which is becoming increasingly rare in light of group practices and managed care.
2. Group practice settings, including physicians that share facilities. This setting is becoming common as physicians are forced to pool resources—capital, equipment, office staff, and so forth—in order to compete in the health care marketplace. Group outpatient settings may also include health maintenance organizations (HMOs), physicians in industrial Employee Assistance Plan (EAP) settings, or doctors operating under university auspices. During the past few decades, physicians have increasingly worked in group practices or other organized settings.[15]
3. Physicians employed in corporate-owned for-profit clinics or in nonprofit clinics.
4. Hospitals—private, nonprofit, or public.
5. Public health services delivered on the state, local, regional, national, or international level. These services include health counseling; family planning; prenatal and postnatal care; school health services; disease prevention and control; immunization; referral agencies; STD (sexually transmitted diseases) services; environmental sanitation; health education; and maintenance of indexes on births, deaths, and communicable diseases. Government-sponsored health services include the Veterans Administration Hospitals (the largest network of hospitals in the United States), Community and Migrant Health Centers, etc.
6. Corollary health services, which includes home health services, physical rehabilitation, group homes, nursing homes, and so forth.

Major Public Health Programs: Medicare, Medicaid, and S-CHIP

Health care spending is the second fastest-growing component of the federal budget, overshadowed only by the growth in the public debt.[16] In 2010, 44.3 million people were enrolled in Medicare (14.5 percent) and 48.5 million (15.9 percent) were covered by Medicaid.[17]

Medicare

After Social Security, Medicare is the largest social insurance program in the United States with expenditures of $522.8 billion in 2010. It is also the largest public payer of health care, financing close to 20 percent of all health care spending. When Medicare began in July 1966, approximately 19 million people were enrolled;[18] by 2010, over 47 million people were enrolled in Part A, almost 44 million in Part B, and 34 million in Part D. Beneficiaries in Part A and B can choose to participate in the Medicare+Choice plan (renamed the Medicare Advantage plan and otherwise known as Part C).[19] In 2007, 8 million chose to participate in Part C.[20] In 2010, Part A benefits totaled $244.5 billion.[21]

Medicare was added to the Social Security Act in 1965 and was designed to provide elderly people with prepaid hospital and optional medical insurance. The modern Medicare system is composed of four parts: compulsory Hospital Insurance (HI), known as Part A; Supplemental Medical Insurance (SMI), known as Part B; the Medicare Advantage program, known as Part C; and the Medicare Prescription Drug, Improvement, and Modernization Act of 2003, known as MMA or Part D. Although traditionally consisting of two parts (HI and SMI), Part C (established by the Balanced Budget Act of 1997) expanded beneficiaries' options for participation in private-sector health care plans. The MMA or Part D was added in 2003.

Surrounded by controversy, the MMA was signed into law in 2003. As a 700-page document, this complex bill proved difficult for Medicare beneficiaries to understand. Apart from prescription drug coverage, Part D also includes changes for beneficiaries such as increases in the Part B deductible, increased income standards relating to the Part B premium, and new preventive health benefits. Like SMI, participation in the MMA is voluntary.

Part D provides subsidized access to prescription drug insurance coverage on a voluntary basis, upon payment of a premium, to individuals entitled to Part A or enrolled in Part B. Premium and cost-sharing subsidies are available for low-income enrollees. People may enroll in either a stand-alone prescription drug plan (PDP) or an integrated Medicare Advantage plan that offers Part D coverage.[22]

The standard benefits for the MMA include:

- In 2012, beneficiaries paid about $30 a month in premiums for basic drug coverage (these are likely to vary across plans) in addition to the Part B premium. In 2011, beneficiaries whose income was above $85,000 paid a monthly amount on top of their premiums, adjusted according to specific income brackets. All beneficiaries enrolled in the standard Part D coverage pay a $320 annual deductible and 25 percent (or approximate flat copay) of full drug costs up to $2,930. With the Health Care and Education Reconciliation Act of 2010 (called the Affordable Care Act) beneficiaries who were enrolled in Part D in 2010 received a $250 rebate, and beneficiaries enrolled in 2011 received a 50 percent discount on brand-name prescription drugs and a 7 percent discount for generic drugs. For beneficiaries enrolled in 2012 and beyond, there is the same 50 percent discount for brand-name drugs, but the generic discount is increased to 14 percent. Once the beneficiary reaches the out-of-pocket expense of $4,700, they pay only 5 percent of their total drug costs or a co-payment amount ($2.60 for generic or multi-source drugs and $6.50 for other drugs).[23]

- Beneficiaries can enroll in a stand-alone prescription drug plan for Part D (PDP) or a Medicare Advantage plan that includes Part D coverage. Most beneficiaries choose to enroll in an alternative Part D coverage plan. These alternative plans can provide lower or no deductibles, lower set payments for drugs and additional coverage for gaps in cost.[24]
- Medicare beneficiaries receive preventive benefits, including an initial routine physical examination, cardiovascular blood screening tests, and diabetes screening tests and services.
- Medicare provides additional assistance to beneficiaries who qualify based on low incomes and limited assets. For example, approved low-income Part D beneficiaries may pay reduced or no premiums, and be eligible for further cost-sharing subsidies. For Social Security beneficiaries enrolled in Part B, a "hold harmless" provision was introduced whereby the premium cannot be increased beyond Social Security cost-of-living increases. Since there was no Social Security cost-of-living increase for 2010, eligible Part B beneficiaries continued to pay the 2009 premium amount, which meant that non-eligible beneficiaries absorbed the increases to premiums.[25]
- MMA plan providers are permitted to offer an alternative benefit design provided it is equivalent and does not raise the Part D deductible or out-of-pocket limit. Plan providers are also required to provide drugs

in each therapeutic category but have flexibility to establish preferred drug lists. In addition, companies offering drug plans can change formularies at any time, while a beneficiary can only change providers once a year. Plans may utilize a preferred network of pharmacies to reduce beneficiary cost-sharing, or offer supplemental benefits for an additional premium. While Medicare has guidelines for the type of drugs the plans must cover, they do not require all plans to offer the same drugs. Beneficiaries are required to ascertain whether a plan covers the drugs they need.

Critics charge that the MMA does not curb skyrocketing drug costs. In fact, it may actually increase costs by prohibiting Medicare from using its purchasing power to negotiate lower drug prices. While private plan providers seek discounts for enrollees, they lack Medicare's purchasing power. This stands in contrast to the Veterans Administration which has successfully negotiated lower prices with drug companies. In effect, the "no negotiation" clause increases program costs, which in turn adds to the overall costs of Part D. The bill also prohibits consumers from benefiting from cheaper drugs sold in Canada and Mexico. Under the Medicare legislation, drugs can only be reimported from Canada, and then only if the Secretary of Health and Human Services certifies that the re-importation is necessary, safe and would significantly reduce costs.

Drug companies and the managed care industry are reaping huge profits from this legislation. Not only are there no mechanisms to effectively control rising drug costs, but the new drug benefit means much larger sales volume. Private insurance companies that participate in the Medicare program also realize profits as they attempt to enroll the healthiest and youngest seniors, thereby lowering their costs.[26]

Perhaps the most important part of the MMA is a little-noticed component called health savings accounts (HSAs), which offers a tax free shelter for those with high-deductible insurance. When a person puts money into an HSA, it is not taxed. Nor is it taxed when the money is removed to pay for medical costs. Critics argue that this adds to the federal budget deficit while the plan removes the owners of these accounts from the shared risk that is at the core of the health insurance system. Conservatives claim HSAs will encourage people to more closely monitor their health care spending and bring down medical costs. Critics call the accounts a tax shelter that benefits the wealthy and draws young, healthy workers out of health care plans, potentially doubling the cost of insurance for everyone else. [27]

Medicare Coverage   HI or Part A is provided free to persons age 65 or over who are eligible for Social Security or Railroad Retirement benefits. Workers and their spouses with a sufficient period of Medicare-only coverage in federal, state, or local government employment are also eligible beginning at age 65. HI is a compulsory **inpatient care** (hospital) insurance plan (it also includes some nursing and home health care) with premiums derived from a payroll tax that is part of the Social Security deduction. In 2010, the HI program covered about 47 million people (over 39 million aged and almost 8 million disabled participants).[28] The following health care services are covered under Medicare's HI program:

- Inpatient hospital includes the costs of a semi-private room, meals, regular nursing services, operating and recovery rooms, intensive care, inpatient prescription drugs, laboratory tests, X-rays, psychiatric hospitals, inpatient rehabilitation, long-term care hospitalization, and all other medically necessary services and supplies.
- Skilled nursing facility (SNF) care is covered if the treatment occurs within 30 days of a hospital stay of three days or more, and if it is deemed a medical necessity. Covered services are similar to those for hospitalized patients but also include rehabilitation services and medical appliances.
- Home health agency (HHA) care may be provided for a home-bound beneficiary if deemed medically necessary. Certain medical supplies and durable medical equipment may also be provided requiring a co-payment. Full-time nursing care, food, blood, and drugs are not provided as HHA services. Home health agency (HHA) care is covered by both HI and SMI and requires no co-payment or deductible.
- Hospice care is available to terminally ill persons with life expectancies of six months or less who refuse standard Medicare benefits. Hospice care includes pain relief, supportive medical and social services, physical therapy, nursing services, and symptom management. Medicare also covers treatment for conditions unrelated to the terminal illness. Beneficiaries pay no deductible for the hospice program, but they do pay a small coinsurance for drugs and inpatient respite care.[29]

By paying a monthly premium, U.S. citizens (and approved legal aliens) over age 65 and all disabled persons entitled to HI are eligible to enroll in the SMI program. Almost all persons entitled to HI enroll in SMI. In 2010, the SMI program covered about 44 million people (almost 37 million aged and over 7 million disabled participants) with benefits totaling $209.7 billion.[30] The SMI program covers the following:

- Physicians' and surgeons' services are covered, including some covered services furnished by chiropractors, podiatrists, dentists, and optometrists. Also covered are services provided by non-Medicare approved health care practitioners such as nurses in collaboration with a physician, clinical psychologists, clinical social workers (other than in a hospital or skilled nursing facility), and physician assistants.
- Services in an emergency room or outpatient clinic, including same-day surgery, and ambulance services.
- Laboratory tests, X-rays and other diagnostic radiology services, as well as certain preventive care screening tests.
- Ambulatory surgical center services in a Medicare-approved facility.
- Most physical and occupational therapy and speech pathology services.
- Outpatient rehabilitation facility services, and mental health treatment in a partial hospitalization psychiatric program.
- Radiation therapy, renal dialysis, and certain organ transplants.
- Approved durable medical equipment for home use, such as oxygen equipment, wheelchairs, prosthetic devices, and surgical dressings, splints, and casts.
- Drugs that cannot be self-administered.[31]

Gaps in Medicare Coverage   Fee-for-service beneficiaries pay for charges not covered by Medicare and for various cost-sharing aspects of both HI and SMI. These liabilities may be paid by beneficiaries out-of-pocket, by a third party (an employer-sponsored retiree health plan or private "Medigap" insurance), or by Medicaid (if the person is eligible). "Medigap" insurance refers to private insurance plans that pay most of the charges not covered by Medicare.

For HI hospital care, a fee-for-service beneficiary's payment share includes a one-time deductible at the beginning of each benefit period ($1,156 in 2012), which covers the beneficiary's expenses for the first 60 days of each instance of inpatient hospital care. If inpatient care is needed beyond the 60 days, additional coinsurance payments ($289 a day in 2012) are required through the 90th day of a benefit period. Each HI beneficiary also has a one-time lifetime reserve of 60 additional hospital days that may be used when the covered days have been exhausted.

While Medicare covers the first 20 days of skilled nursing facility (SNF) care, a co-payment is required ($144.50 per day in 2012) for days 21 to 100. Medicare's obligation ends after 100 days of SNF care per benefit period. Home health care has no deductible or coinsurance payment.

For SMI, the beneficiary's payment share includes one annual deductible ($140 in 2012), the monthly premiums, and the coinsurance payments for services, which is usually 20 percent of the allowed charges, less the deductible.[32]

Reimbursements to Providers Medicare payments for most inpatient hospital services are made under a reimbursement mechanism known as the prospective payment system (PPS). Under PPS, a predetermined amount is paid for each inpatient hospital stay based on a diagnosis-related group classification. In some cases the payment to the hospital is less than the actual costs, while in other cases it is more. The hospital absorbs the loss or makes a profit. Adjustments are made for unusual or costly hospital stays. Payments for skilled nursing care, home health care, inpatient rehabilitation, long-term hospital care, psychiatric hospitalization, and hospice care are made under separate PPSs.[33]

If a doctor or medical supplier agrees to accept the Medicare-approved rate as payment in full (which they often refuse to do), they may not request any additional payments from the beneficiary. If the provider does not take the assignment, the beneficiary is charged for the excess (sometimes paid by Medigap insurance). Limits exist on the excess that doctors or suppliers can charge. Medicare reimbursements to health care providers are subject to maximum payments by level of service, which are often less than some physicians will accept. In these cases, patients pay the difference between the physician's charge and the Medicare reimbursement. Patients are entitled to choose their own doctor, and consequently may elect to go to

a "participating physician" who will accept the Medicare rate as payment in full. However, due to paperwork and limited reimbursement, the number of physicians who choose to participate is lower than patient demand.[34]

Although Medicare provides important services, the gaps in coverage are extensive, which is why many beneficiaries opt for HMOs or supplement Medicare with private **Medigap** insurance.

Funding Medicare finances are handled by two trust funds in the U.S. Treasury, one for the HI program (Part A) and the other for SMI (Parts B and D). The HI program is financed primarily through a mandatory payroll tax for all employed and self-employed people. In 2012, the HI tax rate was 1.45 percent of earnings (paid by each employee with a matching amount paid by the employer) and 2.90 percent for the self-employed. An additional HI tax of 0.9 percent was added in 2013 for those with annual incomes above $200,000. Unlike Social Security, there is no earnings cap on taxable wages. The SMI program is financed by beneficiary payments ($99.90 per month in 2012) and contributions from general tax revenues. Beneficiary premiums are generally set at a level that covers 25 percent of the average expenditures for aged beneficiaries; general fund payments are calculated to match estimated program costs for the next year.[35]

Total Medicare expenditures more than doubled from 1989 to 1998, and are rising faster than the wages on which the payroll tax is based.[36] Medicare's annual cost in 2011 equaled 3.7 percent of the gross domestic product (GDP), but is expected to reach almost 6.7 percent by 2086. In turn, the projected date of the HI trust fund exhaustion is 2024. Part B of the SMI trust fund and the MMA are both expected to remain adequately funded into the future because current law automatically sets financing to meet the next year's expected costs (not true for the HI program). The outlook for Medicare improved substantially in 2010 because of program changes made in the 2010 Patient Protection and Affordable Care Act (ACA). As a result of the ACA, the Hospital Insurance (HI) Trust Fund is expected to remain solvent until 2029, 12 years longer than projected. The ACA is also expected to substantially reduce costs for the SMI program. Despite this potential improvement in Medicare's short-term future, further reforms will be needed given the retirement

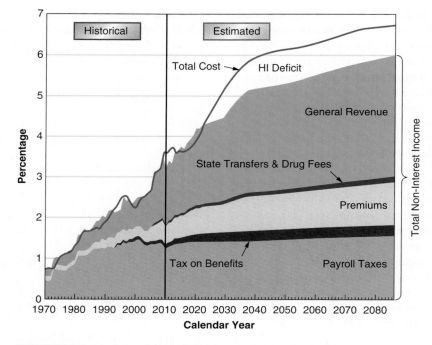

FIGURE 12.1 Medicare Cost and Non-Interest Income by Source as a Percentage of GDP

Source: Social Security Administration, "A Summary of the 2012 Annual Social Security and Medicare Trust Fund Reports," Last Revised 4th of June 2012. Retrieved June 2012 from http://www.socialsecurity.gov/OACT/TRSUM/index.html.

of the baby boomer generation that began in 2010.[37] See Figure 12.1 for Medicare program costs as a percentage of the GDP).[38]

Medicaid

Before 1965, medical care for those unable to afford it was primarily a responsibility of charitable institutions and state and local governments. In 1950, the federal government authorized states to use federal/state funds under the Social Security Act of 1935 to provide medical care for the indigent. In 1957, the Kerr-Mills Act provided for a federal/state matching program to provide health care for the elderly and the poor. However, Kerr-Mills was not mandatory, and many states chose not to participate. As a compromise to ward off more far-reaching health reforms, former President Lyndon Johnson signed the Medicaid and Medicare programs into law in 1965.[39] Replacing all previous governmental health programs, Medicaid became the largest public assistance program in the nation.[40] In 2010, Medicaid served 48.5 million

beneficiaries.[41] Total 2010 expenditures for the Medicaid program were $404.1 billion.[42]

Medicaid is a means-tested public assistance program. Eligible people receive services from physicians who accept Medicaid patients (in many places a minority of physicians) and other health care providers. These providers are reimbursed by the federal government on a per-patient basis. To contain costs, several states require Medicaid recipients to enroll in state-contracted HMOs.

Medicaid is a federal/state program. States determine eligibility within broad federal guidelines. For instance, each state establishes its own eligibility standards; determines the type, amount, duration, and scope of services; sets the rate of payment for services; and administers its own program. Medicaid policies can be complex and vary widely among states. For instance, a person eligible for Medicaid in one state may be ineligible in another, and the services provided by one state may differ in the amount, duration, or scope of services compared to other states. State legislatures may change Medicaid eligibility, services, and/or reimbursement during the year. To be eligible for federal funds, states are required to provide Medicaid coverage for most individuals who receive federally assisted income maintenance payments, as well as for related groups not receiving cash payments. Some examples of the mandatory Medicaid eligibility groups are:

- Limited and low-income families with children who meet certain eligibility requirements as set out in the state's AFDC plan in effect on July 16, 1996.
- Supplemental Security Income (SSI) recipients
- Infants born to Medicaid-eligible pregnant women. Medicaid eligibility continues throughout the first year of life, as long as the infant remains in the mother's household and she remains eligible, or would be eligible if she were still pregnant.
- Children under age 6 and pregnant women whose family income is at or below 133 percent of the federal poverty level. The maximum mandatory income level for pregnant women and infants in certain states may be higher than 133 percent if the state has established a higher percentage for covering those groups. All poor children under age 19 are covered.
- Recipients of adoption assistance and foster care under Title IV-E of the Social Security Act
- Certain Medicare beneficiaries and special protected groups; for example, those who lose SSI payments due to earnings from work or increased Social Security benefits.

- Other "categorically needy" groups as decided by the state.[43] (Table 12.1 shows the numbers and eligibility categories of the Medicaid population).

The medically needy (MN) option allows states to extend Medicaid eligibility to additional persons who would be eligible under one of the mandatory or optional groups, except that their income and/or resources are above the state's eligibility level. People may qualify immediately or may "spend down" by incurring medical expenses that reduce their income to or below their state's medically needy level. By 2009, 33 states and the District of Columbia had elected to have a program for the medically needy. All remaining states utilize the "special income level" option to extend Medicaid to the "near poor" in medical institutional settings.

Medicaid is funded by federal/state matching funds. In every state, the federal government pays at least half, and in some states far more, of state Medicaid spending. The following services are covered:

- Inpatient and outpatient hospital services
- Prenatal care and 60 days postpartum pregnancy services
- Vaccines for children
- Physician services
- Nursing facility services for persons aged 21 or older
- Family planning services and supplies
- Rural health clinic services

TABLE 12.1 Medicaid Recipients by Category, 1985–2009, Selected Years (in thousands)

Year	Total	Age 65 or Older	Blind/Disabled	Children	Adults	Other
1985	21,814	3,061	3,017	9,757	5,518	1,214
1988	22,907	3,159	3,487	10,037	5,503	1,343
1990	25,255	3,202	3,718	11,220	6,010	1,105
1993	33,432	3,863	5,016	16,285	7,505	763
1997	34,872	3,955	6,129	15,791	6,803	2,195
2000	42,886	4,289	7,479	21,086	10,543	862
2005	57,643	4,396	8,210	26,337	12,529	6,171
2007	56,825	4,043	8,424	26,584	12,371	5,402
2009	62,458	4,188	8,998	28,634	13,907	6,731

Source: Social Security Administration, *Annual Statistical Supplement, 2011,* "Unduplicated number of recipients, total vendor payments, and average payment by type of eligibility category, fiscal years 1985-2009," Released February 2012. Retrieved June 2012, from https://www.socialsecurity.gov/policy/docs/statcomps/supplement/2011/8e.pdf.

- Home health care for persons eligible for skilled nursing services
- Laboratory and X-ray services
- Pediatric and family nurse practitioner services
- Nurse midwife services
- Early and periodic screening, diagnostic, and treatment (EPSDT) services for children under 21 years.[44]

States may also receive federal matching funds to provide certain optional services, such as:

- Diagnostic and clinic services
- Intermediate care facilities for the mentally handicapped (ICFs/MR)
- Prescribed drugs and prosthetic devices
- Optometrist services and eyeglasses
- Nursing facility services for children under age 21
- Transportation services
- Rehabilitation and physical therapy services
- Home and community-based care to eligible people with chronic impairments.[45]

Program expenditures differ for different groups. For example, in 2008 children comprised nearly half of all Medicaid beneficiaries (22.8 million) and payments averaged $2,643 per child. Non-disabled adults were the second largest group, (comprising 23 percent of all beneficiaries) and averaging $3,968 in per capita costs. The greatest single outlay of funds goes to the smallest group, the elderly, who represent only 10 percent of all Medicaid beneficiaries (4.6 million), but whose costs average $15,869 per recipient. This is significantly higher than the calculated average for all Medicaid beneficiaries, which was $6,702 per person in 2010.[46]

Payment for long-term nursing home care alone accounted for more than one-third of the Medicaid budget in 2012.[47] Although Medicaid paid only 41 percent of the cost of nursing home care nationally in 2008, the program covered 1.6 million nursing home residents, averaging $29,533 per person. This equated to a total cost of $47.7 billion. A further $6.6 billion was spent on 1.1 million elderly beneficiaries using home health services.[48]

Not surprisingly, the growth of the nursing home industry parallels the creation of Medicaid. From 1965 (the year Medicaid was created) to 1970, the number of nursing home residents rose by 18 percent. Because 75 percent of nursing homes are for-profit facilities, Medicaid is a de facto subsidy for the nursing home industry. Medicaid also

functions as a subsidy for the middle class. Namely, when elderly parents spend down their assets they become eligible for Medicaid. Without Medicaid the middle-class children of elderly parents would be responsible for paying the average national rate of $150 a day for nursing home care. Since a nursing home resident lives on average 2.4 years, the total cost to a middle-class family would be more than $128,000.[49]

Despite federal guidelines, four important gaps exist in Medicaid coverage: (1) the low eligibility limits set for Medicaid; (2) the refusal of many states to adopt most or all of the Medicaid options; (3) the gaps in coverage for the elderly and disabled; (4) the general ineligibility of poor single persons and childless couples for Medicaid unless they are elderly or disabled; and (5) state cutbacks in Medicaid coverage due to lower state revenues.[50] While Medicaid covered 48.5 million beneficiaries in 2010, it did not provide health care services for some very poor persons who were not in a designated group.[51]

For all its shortcomings, the Medicaid program has led to important gains in the nation's health. In 1963, 54 percent of poor people did not see a physician and only 63 percent of poor pregnant women received prenatal care (by 1976 that number had increased to 76 percent). Between 1964 and 1975 the use of physicians' services by poor children increased 74 percent. The increased health care utilization helped bring about a 49 percent drop in infant mortality between 1965 and 1988. For African American infants, the drop in mortality was even sharper: Infant mortality dropped by only 5 percent in the 15 years before Medicaid, but by 49 percent in the 15 years after the program began. Ongoing preventive care also cut program costs for Medicaid-eligible children.[52] Medicaid is one of the most significant governmental health programs in the United States.

The Children's Health Insurance Program (CHIP)

As part of the Balanced Budget Act of 1997, Congress created the State Children's Health Insurance Program (S-CHIP), a federal-state partnership that allocated $48 billion over 10 years to expand health care coverage to low-income, uninsured children under age 19 who are ineligible for Medicaid.[53] Legislation such as the Children's Health Insurance Program Reauthorization Act (CHIPRA) of 2009 and the ACA have enabled funding for CHIP to continue to 2015. As part of the eligibility requirements, children generally must be below 200 percent of the federal poverty level. In 2010, 11.4 billion was spent on CHIP.[54] By 2011, over 7 million children were enrolled in the CHIP program.[55]

The CHIP program gives states three options for covering uninsured children: design a new children's health insurance program; expand current Medicaid programs; or a combination of both. By 2011, 17 states had chosen to implement a separate children's health insurance program; seven states and five territories had chosen to expand the Medicaid program and 26 states had elected to combine both options. CHIP is a block grant program financed by federal/state matching funds. Each state with an approved plan receives enhanced federal matching payments for its S-CHIP expenditures up to a fixed state allotment. As a further incentive for states to increase their enrolment rates, the federal matching fund for CHIP is usually 15 percent higher than for Medicaid.[56] The largest share of CHIP funds come from the federal government, and in 2011, federal matching funds averaged 71 percent.[57] The CHIPRA 2009 legislation also instituted performance bonuses for states that provide outreach measures to eligible, uninsured children and annually increase enrolment in CHIP above set quotas.[58]

Before CHIP, Medicaid eligibility was largely linked to welfare receipt. In large measure, Medicaid-eligible children had to be in an SSI or a TANF-eligible family. Perhaps the most important policy change in CHIP is that it delinked state-subsidized child health care from welfare receipt, and from working families with incomes too high to qualify for Medicaid but too low to afford private health insurance.[59] By 2011, 46 states and the District of Columbia covered children in families with incomes up to 200 percent of the federal poverty line ($44,700 for a family of four in 2011), and 24 of those states and the District of Columbia covered children in families up to 250 percent of the federal poverty line. States have also expanded eligibility categories; 22 states cover legal immigrant children and/or pregnant women.[60]

The Tobacco Settlement

Public policy is occasionally made by the court system rather than the legislature. This was the case in the 1998 tobacco industry settlement. For 40 years, tobacco companies had won every lawsuit brought against them. The long march toward a national tobacco settlement began in April 1994, when representatives from seven of the leading American tobacco companies stood before Congress and swore that nicotine was not an addictive substance. The presentation was provocative even in the eyes of people who were neutral toward cigarette companies.

In 1998, the tobacco companies were forced to accept a 600-page Master Settlement Agreement requiring them to pay $206 billion to 46 states over a 25-year period. (That amount did not include $40 billion in separate settlements reached by four other states.) From 2000 to 2004, states realized $37.5 billion in tobacco company payments. The agreement was the largest civil settlement in U.S. history. Payments are based on states' shares of the cost of smoking-related illnesses paid for through the Medicaid program. In exchange for the fine levied by the agreement, 39 states with pending individual lawsuits agreed to drop their cases. Some highlights of the MSA include:

- End youth targeting in advertising and promotion; ban the use of cartoon characters in advertising; restrict sponsorship by brand names; ban outdoor advertising; ban sales of merchandise with tobacco brand names; ban free samples to youth; and set minimum pack size at 20 cigarettes.
- The MSA disbands tobacco trade associations and creates regulations and oversight for any new trade organizations.
- The settlement limits industry lobbying by prohibiting tobacco companies from opposing legislation aimed at restricting youth access and reducing consumption.
- It included a $1.45 billion anti-smoking public education fund.[61]

States accrued significant revenues from the tobacco settlement: $9.3 billion in 2002, $7.5 billion in 2003, and $7.4 billion in 2010.[62] Contrary to the hopes of many public health advocates, there were no restrictions on the use of MSA funds by the states. Some criticism of the tobacco settlement has included:

- Between 1998 and 2010, states collected $243.8 billion in tobacco tax and settlement payments; only $8.1 billion was spent on anti-smoking and health care programs. This is also less than a third of what the Centers for Disease Control and Prevention recommended (i.e., $29.2 billion).[63] Only six states earned "A" grades from the American Lung Association in its 2004 report card for their anti-smoking programs.

- California, Connecticut, New Jersey, New York, Oregon, Rhode Island, Washington, and Wisconsin have cashed in a big chunk of their share of the settlement, selling future tobacco payments to investors for an upfront lump sum, known as securitization.
- Fewer people are smoking and hence states receive less because their yearly allotment from the settlement fund is based on the number of cigarettes sold in the state. Nationwide, the number of smokers has dropped by around 50 percent (less than 20 percent of adults and teens now smoke) since the settlement and continues to decline annually, albeit more slowly. [64] Given the fiscal crunch experienced by states, many are turning to raising cigarette taxes since studies have shown they often cause people to stop smoking.[65]

Instead of curbing advertising, the tobacco industry spends almost $10 billion a year on marketing cigarettes, with many advertisements and marketing campaigns still targeted at youth. It is clearly a conflict of interest for tobacco companies to prevent youth smoking.[66]

(For some facts on the U.S. tobacco industry, see Figure 12.2.)

To combat smoking advertisements, the Australian Parliament passed a "Plain Packaging" bill in 2011 that prohibited brand labels on cigarette boxes. Cigarettes are now sold in boxes with plain olive covers, no mention of the brand, and graphic pictures of smoking related diseases. Philip Morris has taken legal action to overturn the bill.[67] The Australian state of New South Wales will ban smoking at outdoor public places including bus stops, taxi ranks, and near the doorways of public buildings; public playgrounds (within 30 feet of children's play equipment); at major sporting grounds; and within 12 feet of any building open to the public. Non-compliance fines are expected to cost about $550.[68]

The Health Care Crisis

Health care in the United States is plagued with problems such as eroding coverage, rising and shifting costs, and an increasing number of anxious citizens fearful about getting and keeping health insurance. The following two sections will explore some parameters of the health care crisis, including health care spending and cost efficiency, the effectiveness of the U.S. health care system, attempts at cost cutting, the growing role of managed care, and the impact of AIDS on the health care budget.

Cigarettes account for over 90 percent of spending on tobacco products in the United States; in 1998 Americans smoked 24 billion packs. In 1995, U.S. spending for all tobacco products totalled about $49 billion.

Five American companies—Philip Morris, R.J. Reynolds, Brown and Williamson, Lorillard, and Liggett—produce almost all of the cigarettes sold in the United States. Two companies, Philip Morris and R.J. Reynolds, account for more than 70 percent of industry sales. About 36 billion packs of cigarettes were produced by U.S. firms in 1997; about 12 billion packs were exported to other countries and about 280 million shipped to U.S. territories and to U.S. armed forces stationed overseas. The rest were consumed by domestic smokers. Smokeless tobacco products are also produced by only five domestic manufacturers: U.S. Tobacco, Conwood, Pinkerton, National, and Swisher. Over 120 million pounds of chewing tobacco and snuff were produced in the United States in 1996; in 1995, smokeless tobacco companies posted revenues of $1.7 billion. About 2.5 billion large cigars and cigarillos and 14.2 million pounds of pipe and roll-your-own tobacco were produced by U.S. companies in 1995.

The United States is the second largest tobacco producer in the world, well below China. In 1996, tobacco was grown on over 124,000 U.S. farms, with a crop value of $2.9 billion. The tobacco industry supports more than 600,000 jobs.

FIGURE 12.2 Tobacco at a Glance

Source: CNN, "A Brief History of Tobacco." Retrieved 2001 from www.cnn.com/US/9705/tobacco/history/index.html.

Overview of U.S. Health Care Expenditures

U.S. health care cost $2.5 trillion in 2009, up from $27.4 billion in 1960. This translates into 17.6 percent of the total gross domestic product (GDP). (Health expenditures as a percentage of the GDP measure the proportion of all resources devoted to health care.) It is projected that by 2020, health care spending will rise to $4.6 trillion and account for almost 20 percent of the GDP. In comparison, health care spending in 1960 was only 5.2 percent of the GDP.[69] From 1970 to 2007, per capita health care costs rose from $341 to $7,439, an increase of more than 2,200.[70] As of 2009, health expenditure equated to $8,086 per person[71] (see Figure 12.3).

Health care spending accounted for about 14 percent of the GDP in 2001 compared to education which was only 4.8 percent. Moreover, the costs of providing health care have risen faster than the rate of inflation. From 1980 to 1992, annual increases in per capita expenditures on health care were approximately 5 points above the yearly inflation rate. While the growth rate in health care expenditures decelerated somewhat in 1992, (registering less than 3 points above the rate of inflation)[72]—it accelerated again in the late 1990s. In 2002, health care expenditures had risen by 9.5 percent, or more than four times the rate of inflation.

When health care expenditures are broken down, the largest share (31.4 percent) goes to hospitals.[73] (See Figure 12.4.) An increase in the cost of hospital care has been a key factor in driving up health care costs and between 2006 and 2007 that rose 7.5 percent.[74] In 1965, the average cost per hospital stay was $315; by 2007 it had risen to $22,596 for an average 5-day stay.[75]

Of the total amount spent on healthcare in 2009, 21 percent was sponsored by private businesses; 44 percent came from the government (federal, state, and local); and 28 percent from out-of-pocket. What this means is that household and private business spending has declined since 1987, and spending by government has increased from 32 percent in 1987 to its current share of 44 percent. This is largely due to Medicare, Medicaid, and CHIP, which comprise more than one-third of total national health care expenditure ($887.3 billion).[76]

The increase in health care insurance premiums paid by companies has been significant. From 2009 to 2010, U.S. health insurance costs had risen by 9 percent, or nine times the 1 percent inflation rate. In line with this rise, average employee out-of-pocket costs (i.e., copayments, coinsurance, and deductibles) jumped to $2,200 in 2011, a 12.5 percent increase ($1,900) from 2010. There are few workers whose salaries would have increased by that much. Total health care premiums will have more than doubled in a single decade, going from $4,100 in 2001 to $9,800 in 2011. What employees pay for medical costs will have more than tripled (from $1,200 in 2001 to $4,400 in 2011) in just a decade.[77]

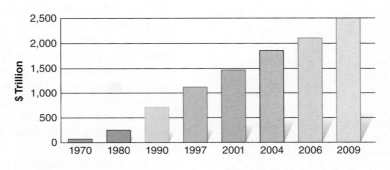

FIGURE 12.3 National Health Care Expenditures Selected Years, 1970–2009 (dollar amount in billions)

Sources: HHS, Centers for Medicare & Medicaid Services, "National Health Expenditures Aggregate, Per Capita Amounts, Percent Distribution, and Average Annual Percent Growth, by Source of Funds: Selected Calendar Years 1960 – 2006". Retrieved July 2008 from http://www.cms.hhs.gov/NationalHealthExpendData/downloads/tables.pdf; and Centers for Medicare and Medicaid Services, "Brief Summaries of Medicare and Medicaid," 1st November, 2011. Retrieved May 2012 from http://www.cms.gov/Research-Statistics-Data-and-Systems/Statistics-Trends-and-Reports/MedicareMedicaidStatSupp/downloads//2011BriefSummaries.pdf.

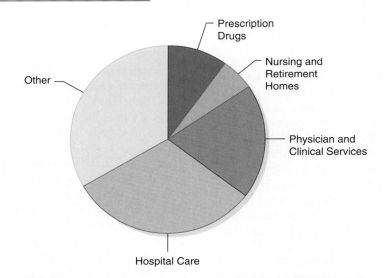

FIGURE 12.4 The Nation's Health Expenditure By Percentage, 2010

Note: "Other" includes dentist services, other professional services, home health, durable medical products, over-the-counter medicines and sundries, government administration, public health, other personal health care, research and structures and equipment.

Source: HHS, Centers for Medicare and Medicaid Services, "National Health Expenditures Aggregate, Per Capita Amounts, Percent Distribution, and Average Annual Percent Change, by Type of Expenditure: Selected Calendar Years 1960 – 2010," Retrieved June 2012 from http://www.cms.gov/Research-Statistics-Data-and-Systems/Statistics-Trends-and-Reports/NationalHealthExpendData/downloads/tables.pdf

U.S. Health Care in International Perspective

Health care costs are higher in the United States than in any other industrialized nation. The United States spends more than other countries on health care, both in absolute dollars and in the share of total economic activity. Per capita health spending in the United States was $7,160 in 2008, more than twice the average for the other industrial nations in the Organization for Economic Cooperation and Development (OECD).[78]

Specifically, health spending in the United States in 2010 was 17.3 percent of the GDP, nearly twice the percentage of Australia and the United Kingdom and by far the highest of 30 OECD countries.[79] (See Table 12.2.) Although high expenditures are often equated with excellent medical treatment, the health of the average American—as measured by life expectancy and infant mortality—is below that of other major industrialized nations. In a devastating assessment of the American health care system, the Commonwealth Fund (a healthcare-based foundation) issued a report in 2010 (based on 2008 OECD data) that compared the U.S. health care system to economically comparable countries. The report found that the U.S. has a relatively low number of hospital beds and physicians per capita, and patients in the U.S. have fewer hospital and physician visits than in most other industrial countries. At the same time, spending per hospital visit is highest in the U.S., and American patients are among the most likely to receive procedures requiring complex technology. The nation now ranks in the bottom quartile in life expectancy among OECD countries and has seen the smallest improvement in this metric over the past 20 years. According to one recent analysis, the U.S. had the highest rate of mortality amenable to health care among 19 OECD countries in 2002–03.[80] Problematic indicators for American health care revolve around a variety of factors, including diet, obesity, low levels of physical activity, high levels of births to teenage mothers, and the large number of violent deaths.[81]

Moreover, the United States is the only major industrialized country that fails to provide health

TABLE 12.2 Total Health Care Expenditures as a Percentage of GDP, 2009

Country	1975	2009	Percentage Point Change
United States	7.9	17.4	9.5
France	6.4	11.8	5.4
New Zealand	6.7	10.3	3.6
Germany	8.4	11.6	3.2
Canada	7.0	11.4	4.4
Australia	6.5	8.7	2.2
United Kingdom	5.5	9.8	4.3

Source: OECD Health Data, 2008; and OECD, Health at a Glance, 2011: OECD Indicators, 6th edition, "Health Expenditure in Relation to GDP," 23rd November, 2011. Retrieved June 2012, from http://www.oecd-ilibrary.org/docserver/download/fulltext/8111101ec061.pdf?expires=1338963221&id=id&accname=guest&checksum=5CB99C4E2B94EFC115F9792641B03E9C.

coverage for all its citizens, yet spending on health care is extremely high compared to other nations. The U.S. strategy emphasizes the role of the private market in cost containment, yet health care costs are growing more rapidly in America than in more governmentally regulated health care environments, such as Britain and Australia. Private spending as a share of total health care expenditures is far higher in the United States than in other industrialized nations. In addition, out-of-pocket per capita health care spending in the United States is more than twice that of other industrialized nations.[82]

A common perception is that other industrialized countries control costs by rationing patient care. As noted above, Americans receive fewer days of hospital care than residents of other industrialized nations and have about the same number of physician visits.[83]

Infant mortality rates also illustrate troubling trends. In 2010, the U.S. infant mortality rate of 6.1 deaths per 1,000 live births put the nation under 46 other nations, including Cuba, Hungary, Greece, Canada, Portugal, Slovenia, Israel, Czech Republic, and Singapore.[84]

In short, Americans are neither healthier, nor do they live longer than people in similar industrial nations where health care spending is 50 percent lower.

Explaining the High Cost of U.S. Health Care

Although accounting for the enormous costs of the U.S. health care system is complicated, some policy analysts attribute at least some of these costs to the following factors.

- High costs of medical malpractice. In 2008, the estimated cost of medical malpractice suits was $54.4 billion, or 2.4 percent of national health care spending for that year. The high incidence of medical malpractice also results in doctors practicing "defensive medicine" by ordering unnecessary tests for patients to avoid a possible lawsuit. The former Bush administration maintained that malpractice suits could be eliminated by passing legislation that limited what injured patients could collect in lawsuits. The Obama administration declined to pass the "cap" legislation, and instead chose to take a preventative approach by supporting research into the provision of better medical care and reduced incidents of malpractice.[85]
- The United States leads the world in the development and use of medical technology, but these advances have come at a high price. For example, by 2009, doctors performed 500,000 coronary artery bypass operations each year, and the number of stent operations (an alternative to bypasses) were well over a million.[86]
- Expensive new pharmaceutical drugs drive up costs considerably. The higher prevalence and treatment of chronic diseases, such as diabetes, has also driven up health care. Longer life spans for chronically ill patients means more care and treatment, which helps to drive up medical costs.
- The administrative costs involved in processing millions of insurance claims and complex billing procedures also adds to rising health care expenditures. Government health care administration costs in 2010 totaled $30.1 billion, a $27.3 billion increase from 1980.[87] A conservative estimate by the U.S. Centers for Medicare and Medicaid Services estimates that 7 percent of the $2.5 trillion 2010 health dollar ($175 billion) went to administrative costs.[88] Administrative costs also impact physician practices; one study of a ten physician practice found that around $250,000 a year was spent on administration, largely around dealing with health care plans and billing requirements.[89]

Hospital Costs

As noted earlier, 31.4 percent of all health care expenditures in 2010 went toward hospital costs.[90] The total costs of hospital care reached $814 billion in 2010, up from $27.2 billion in 1970.[91] According to the American Hospital Association, nearly 60 percent of hospital costs go to wages and benefits of caregivers and others. Labor costs account for the largest share of spending growth for hospital services from 2001 to 2003. In addition, the costs of technology, construction, and regulatory compliance accounts for a growing share of hospital costs. Predictions from the Centers for Medicare and Medicaid Services suggest that hospitals' share of national health expenditures will decline to less than 28 percent in 2012. However, much of this decline may be attributable to cuts in federal and state health programs.[92]

Physicians' Salaries

The fifth largest health care expenditure is physician services.[93] From 1970 to 1999, the cost of physicians' services rose by almost 1,800 percent. From 1980 to 1990 alone, the cost of physicians' services rose by 300 percent.[94] By 2008, the average salary for a number of specialist physicians, such as orthopaedic surgeons, was approaching $400,000.[95] Since then, physician salaries have experienced an overall general decline; for example, top earning specialists such as radiologists and orthopaedic surgeons earned $350,000 in 2010. By 2011, this had

The increasing costs of malpractice suits against health care providers are felt most directly by consumers, who must pay higher medical costs to offset these suits.

Source: Julie Smith/Jefferson City News Tribune/AP Images

decreased to $315,000.[96] (See Table 12.3.) Nevertheless, U.S. physician salaries are significantly higher than their counterparts in most OECD countries, such as the United Kingdom, Canada, and Switzerland. This is true even when taking purchasing-power parity into account.[97,98]

Physician organizations argue that high salaries are necessary to repay the huge debts incurred by medical students. Roughly 87 percent of medical students carry outstanding loans, with the average educational debt of 2009 medical school graduates at $156,456. Added to that is the substantial difference between private and public medical school tuition fees: the 2009 average annual fee for public medical school was $26,814 compared to $45,448 for private colleges.[99]

Despite this debt, the American Medical Association claims that "Even though the cost of medical school has risen faster than physician salaries, physicians still earn a decent return on their investment, roughly 6 percent for the $1.2 million a physician bears for the assorted costs of a public education and the wages lost while in school. Also, becoming a doctor is typically a higher paying investment when comparing average educational costs and salaries of business and law school graduates."[100] The problem of high physician salaries is aggravated by the growth in the number

TABLE 12.3 Average Salaries of Selected U.S. Practicing Physicians, 2011

Specialty	Salary
Radiology	$315,000
Orthopaedic surgery	$315,000
Cardiology	$314,000
Anesthesiology	$309,000
Urology	$309,000
Gastroenterology	$303,000
General surgery	$265,000
Emergency medicine	$237,000
Obstetrics/gynecology	$220,000
Internal medicine	$165,000
Family medicine	$158,000
Pediatrics	$156,000

Source: Medscape, Web MD, "Medscape Physician Compensation Report, 2012 Results." Retrieved June 2012 from http://www.medscape.com/features/slideshow/compensation/2012/public.

of expensive medical specialists. Although primary care physicians declined steadily as a percentage of the total physician population from 1970 to 2006 (from 40 to 33 percent), there was nevertheless a growth of 124 percent in absolute numbers. By 2009, approximately 70 percent of physicians were specialists and 30 percent primary care (12.3 percent in family medicine and general practice)—a reversal of the ratio that existed 30 years ago.[101]

The problem of high physician salaries is aggravated by the growth in the number of medical specialists. By 2002, 20 percent fewer medical students were in a primary care track compared to 1997.[102] By 2012, 19.1 percent (59 million people) of the U.S. population were living in one of the 5,796 regions that were experiencing a primary care physician shortage.[103]

The Pharmaceutical Industry

The high cost of prescription drugs is also driving up health care costs. From 1997 to 2010 the share of health care expenditures spent on prescription drugs in the United States increased from 6.8 percent in to 10 percent.[104] Although prescription drugs account for only 10 percent of total health care expenditures, their high cost is helping to drive up health care costs. From 1996 to 2005 pharmaceutical drug costs outstripped the general inflation rate and the overall rise in hospitals and physician's services, sometimes by a margin of two to three times. A 2010 study by the Association for Retired Persons (AARP) found that despite the recession, drug prices had risen an average of 8.3 percent in 2009, eight times higher than the inflation rate and faster than in preceding years. Moreover, the average retail cost of brand-name medications in 2005 (the year before Medicare Part D) was $1,049; by 2009 it had jumped 32 percent to $1,382.[105] There is scant evidence that Medicare Part D pharmaceutical plans were able to negotiate better prices.

The United States is the largest pharmaceutical drug market in the world, representing 43 percent of global sales and promotions. Despite the size of the market, American consumers pay more for medicine than consumers in any other country. In 2011, Americans spent $947 per person on drugs, followed by Canada, Greece, and Ireland.[106] Two-thirds of doctor visits result in a drug being prescribed, and overreliance on drugs is a major factor contributing to medical care being the third leading cause of death in the United States.[107] While many

low-income consumers are exposed to financial catastrophe as a result of highly inflated drug prices, manufacturers of the top 20 drugs have increased their profits at rates much higher than the Fortune 500 average, and in 2008, the industry ranked third with after-tax profits of roughly 19 percent.[108]

Harvard physician Marcia Angell disputes the drug industry's reputation as an "engine of innovation," arguing that the top U.S. drug makers spend 2.5 times as much on marketing and administration as they do on research. In contrast to the carefully cultivated image of the drug industry as a research-driven, lifesaving enterprise, a 2008 study estimated that the U.S. pharmaceutical industry spends almost twice as much on promotion as on research and development. The study estimated that of the $235 billion in drug sales in 2004, the pharmaceutical industry spent 24 percent on promotion versus 13 percent on research and development. Moreover, the authors maintain that in 2004 the drug industry spent roughly $61,000 per physician on promotions.[109] According to Marcia Angell, at least a third of the drugs marketed by the industry are discovered by universities or small biotech companies but are sold to the public at inflated prices. Angell attacks the pharmaceutical industry—whose top ten companies make more in profits than the rest of the Fortune 500 combined—for using free market rhetoric while opposing competition.

Between 2006 and 2007, PRIME Institute researchers found that the cost of commonly used brand-name drugs increased on average by 7.4 percent, outpacing inflation which was 2.9 percent. To put this into perspective, Cosmegon is a made by Ovation Pharmaceuticals for patients with Wilms' Tumor. Originally priced at $16.79 per dose, Ovation increased the price to $593.75 per dose, which represented a 3,436 percent increase.[110]

Direct-to-consumer advertising (DTCA) is the promotion of prescription drugs through newspaper and magazine ads, brochures, videos, television commercials, and internet marketing targeted at consumers and doctors. By 2008, spending on advertising had plateaued at $4.7 billion.[111]

The only two developed countries where DTCA is currently legal are the United States and New Zealand, and in limited form in Canada. While banned elsewhere, the drug industry is mounting major lobbying campaigns to have DTCA allowed in Europe and Canada.

Drug companies also aggressively market their wares to doctors by advertising and placing favorable studies in medical journals, frequent visits by sales representatives, organizing junkets, subsidizing conferences, providing free lunches and dinners, and by giving doctors free drug samples for their patients. While the drug industry maintains that DTCA helps educate consumers, critics argue that the ads are emotional and are misleading since they understate adverse side-effects by including them in fine-print or announcing them so quickly that an auctioneer would be stymied. Studies reveal that consumers who have watched DTCA ads will often request (and be prescribed) the expensive brand-name drug. As a result, DTCA unnecessarily drives up the cost of health care without improving the health of the consumer or the efficiency of the system.[112]

There is strong evidence to suggest that DTCA is also partially responsible for an overreliance on drugs. According to one study, 71 percent of American Academy of Family Physician members believed that direct-to-consumer advertising created more pressure on physicians to prescribe unnecessary medication.[113]

Cutting Health Care Costs

There are two aspects to cutting health care costs. The first involves cutting costs for governmental health care programs; the second involves lowering health care costs in the insurance, physician, pharmaceutical and hospital sectors.[114] The rising costs of Medicare have led the federal government to seek alternative ways to lower hospital costs, including the Diagnostic Related Group system (DRG). In 1983, Congress enacted the DRG form of medical payment. Although earlier Medicare rules had restricted the fees hospitals could charge, the government generally reimbursed them for the entire bill. This style of reimbursement was called retrospective (after-the-fact) payment. By contrast, DRGs are a form of **prospective payment system**, or payment before the fact, whereby the federal government specifies in advance what it will pay for the treatment of 468 classified illnesses or DRGs.[115]

Developed by health researchers at the Yale-New Haven Hospital, the DRG system was designed to enforce the economy of the health care system by defining expected lengths of hospital stays. This system provides a treatment and diagnostic classification scheme, using the patient's medical diagnosis, prescribed treatment, and age as a means for categorizing and defining hospital services. In other words,

the DRG system determines the length of a typical patient's hospital stay and reimburses the hospital only for that period of time. (Exceptions to the DRG classification system are made for long hospital stays, certain kinds of hospital facilities, hospitals that are the only facility in a community, and hospitals that serve large numbers of low-income people.) Additional costs beyond the DRG allotment must be borne by the hospital. Conversely, if a patient requires less hospitalization than the maximum DRG allocation, the hospital keeps the difference. Hence, patients not yet ready for discharge (e.g., patients who do not have appropriate aftercare services available) may be discharged—a situation that can result in patient dumping.

Managed Care

Managed care became a household word in the 1990s. By 2010, more than 68 million Americans were enrolled in HMOs.[116] (See Figure 12.5.) This represents a significant increase from the 3.3 million enrolled in 1990.[117] Managed care and HMOs have been touted by the nation's large employers as a way to control health care costs. However, while managed care cut costs for most of the 1990s, by the end of the decade costs started climbing again, increasing by more than 7 percent in 2000.[118] By 2009, managed costs rose 7 percent above 2008 levels as profits in managed care companies plummeted as a result of the recession.

Proponents of managed care argue that the system has effectively lowered health care costs without reducing the quality of health care services. They maintain that it encourages more efficient and less expensive medical care and that it can stress prevention over treatment. Because doctors reimbursed by managed care companies have little incentive to overtreat patients or recommend unnecessary medical care, the health care system is predicted to be more efficient.

Critics of managed care (including HMOs) point out serious problems. For one, managed care has not won the hearts and minds of the public. The 2010 Commonwealth Fund survey found that out of eleven countries, the United States experienced the most difficulties with their health insurance providers, with 31 percent of participants reporting that they spent a lot of time on paperwork or disputes, and/or their insurance provider declined to pay for treatment, or did not pay as much as was expected. Only 58 percent of Americans were confident that they would be able to afford needed health care.[119]

- **Health Maintenance Organizations (HMO)**—a prepaid or capitated insurance plan in which individuals or their employers pay a fixed monthly fee for services rather than a separate charge for each visit or service.

- **Preferred Provider Organizations (PPO)**—a type of HMO whereby an employer or insurance company contracts with a selected group of health care delivery providers for services at pre-established reimbursement rates. Consumers have the choice of who to contact to provide the service. If a doctor is not on the provider list, higher out of pocket expenses will result.

- **Exclusive Provider Organization (EPO)**—a type of HMO where members must get care only from the EPO doctors who may only treat members of the plan.

- **The Independent Practice Association (IPA)**—a type of HMO which has large numbers of independent doctors in private practice. Physicians are paid a fixed fee for treating IPA members but can also treat patients who are not members of the plan.

- **The Network Model**—multispeciality groups of doctors who have contracts with more than one HMO. Doctors work out of their own offices.

- **Point of Service (POS)**—an option that can be offered by any type of HMO. If patients use doctors in their HMO network, and if referrals are made only by the primary care physician, only nominal fees are charged. If patients use doctors outside their HMO network the cost is higher.

- **Physician-Hospital Organization (PHO)**—organized groups of doctors affiliated with a particular hospital who provide services to patients enrolled in their plan as they would in an HMO.

FIGURE 12.5 Types of Managed Care Plans

Source: Joanne Levine, *Working With People,* 9th Edition (Upper Saddle River: Pearson, 2013).

Many physicians believe that the quality of care has gotten worse under managed care. Some have joined unions, and others have formed networks to negotiate contracts with managed care. Still others have stopped taking HMO patients. Hospitals say they are squeezed by slow and low payments from HMOs and cuts to Medicare. Many have had to cut staff. Nurses complain that hospitals are often so short staffed that patient care is seriously compromised. One study found that nearly 70 percent of nurses worry about inadequate staffing levels.[120]

Managed care plans generally gatekeep the access to specialists for consumers. These plans do this by pressuring primary physicians to not refer or by limiting specialist care to one or two visits. Some managed care plans are reluctant to cover costly procedures or experimental treatments, especially those relating to cancer. Still other plans refuse to pay for medical care that clients receive while out of state, even if it was required in an emergency. Some enrollees complain that managed care forces them to use only primary care physicians, hospitals, and specialists that are on an approved list, which restricts their freedom of choice. And some managed care operations do not provide the same level of benefits as Medicare, especially when it comes to home health care, physical therapy, and nursing home care.[121] Critics also note that the size of managed care operations has led to greater bureaucratization and impersonality.[122]

During the late 1990s, many HMOs were in financial trouble and the industry posted $1.25 billion in net losses in 1998. To compensate, HMOs raised premiums, cut services, or many left the business. Several large managed care companies across the country went bankrupt, leaving state officials and consumers scrambling to find replacement coverage. From the mid-1990s onward, the health insurance market consolidated at a rapid pace. Between 1995 and 2001 there were over 350 mergers involving health insurers and managed care organizations. The result is that more than half of all commercially insured Americans are now covered by the 10 largest health insurers.

Managed care companies are boxed in to a degree. Specifically, they cannot reprise their 1990s' role as gatekeepers whereby they restricted care to boost the bottom line. Regulations on the state and federal levels have dampened that idea, and after bad publicity in the 1990s, managed care companies became somewhat more timid by becoming more flexible and paying for more care. Instead of gatekeeping, these companies simply pass along premium hikes plus a small percentage for profits. In short, instead of cutting costs, managed care companies simply pass on rate hikes. On the other hand, they cannot survive indefinitely by simply passing along high rate hikes each year. Once their role of belt-tightening and providing affordable health care is lost, the justification for managed care companies is called into question.

This suggests that in some degree the proponents are correct. For example, the per capita growth in health care expenditures was 2.7 percent in 1994, dropping from 5 percent in the 1980s and early 1990s (before managed care had gained a strong foothold). Per capita national expenditures on health care were $3,510 in 1994, only $100 more than in 1993 and half the increase of 1992 to 1993.

The Underinsured

The U.S. medical system provides high quality care for most people in the upper and upper-middle classes, who are protected by adequate health insurance. Although most Americans are covered by private insurance plans, gaps in private health insurance may include high deductibles and co-payments, limits on the length of hospital stays, dollar limits on payments to hospitals and physicians, exclusion of certain laboratory tests, refusal of coverage for office visits and routine health care,

noncoverage for mental health services, refusal of coverage to persons who are found to be in poor health when applying for insurance, and a lack of coverage for dental and eye care. Because privately purchased health insurance has become almost unaffordable, the availability of health insurance may be a major factor in an individual's job search or decision to continue in a job.[123] Moreover, employers may be reluctant to hire people with high-risk conditions, because of the negative effect on their insurance premiums. Finally, one of the most dramatic gaps is the frequent failure of some private health insurance plans to cover catastrophic medical costs—those costs that could reduce a middle-class family to "medically indigent" status within only a few months.

Reforming U.S. Health Care

The American health care system is partly driven by ideological values. Primary among these is whether health care access should be a right or a privilege. Conservatives believe that access to health care is a privilege that must be earned through past or present labor force participation. Some—but not all—Democrats believe that health care should be a universal right that is not tied to labor force participation. Progressives argue that health care should be a birthright granted to all citizens.

An important issue in the health care debate is the role of the private market. Conservatives support the privatization and commercialization of health care and believe that medical care should be lodged squarely in the private marketplace. They argue that medical institutions and drug companies should be free to establish the prices of health care and medical goods. In addition, they believe that medical care is like other commodities in that it benefits from increased competition, which lowers prices and increases quality. Conversely, government regulation of health care is seen as leading to inefficiencies, lower quality, poorer service and higher prices. While some liberals believe that the private marketplace is the proper venue for

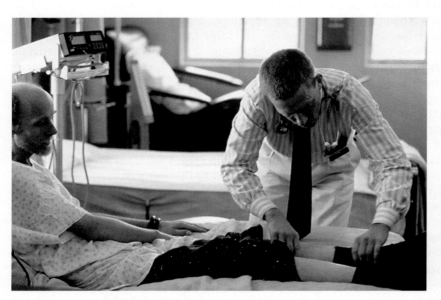

According to a Rand study, not all people with HIV are treated equally. Among adults with HIV, women receive inferior care compared to men, as do African Americans and Hispanics compared to non-Hispanic whites.

Source: David Weintraub/Science Source/Photo Researchers, Inc.

health care delivery, they also recognize that it is a commodity that does not respond to market conditions in the same way as other commodities. For example, if a person is in cardiac arrest, it is unlikely that they will shop around for the best hospital prices. Likewise, most patients facing serious surgery will not choose a surgeon based on price point. These liberals believe that the health care marketplace must be regulated by government to ensure quality, price, and access.

More progressive thinkers argue that health care is too important to be left to the vicissitudes of the market. For them, health care must be removed from the context of a market where decisions are based solely on economics. For these thinkers, health care must be free or heavily subsidized at the point of access, universal in its coverage, and administered and controlled by government.

During the last 40 years, most proposals to reform or transform U.S. health care have fallen into three basic categories: (1) removing health care from the marketplace, (2) maintaining the private health care system while providing universal coverage through national health insurance, and (3) incremental reforms designed to soften the abrasive features of the system.

National Health Service

The most radical proposal for reforming the U.S. health care system involved the creation of a National Health Service (NHS), similar to the British National Health Service. Proposed in the mid-1970s, the NHS would have established health care as a right of citizenship and provided free and comprehensive health care coverage, including diagnostic, therapeutic, preventive, rehabilitative, environmental, and occupational health services. To reduce the maldistribution of medical services, the NHS would have provided free medical education in return for required periods of service in medically underserved areas.[124] The goal of the NHS was universal health care and the elimination of private profit in health care.

Supporters argued that an NHS would allow for the coordination of health services and reduce profiteering by corporations. Moreover, the experience of other countries demonstrates that a system incorporating strict budgeting, nationalization, and elimination of profit arrests the growth of health care costs and, in the end, is less expensive than a privatized system.

National Health Insurance

Single-Payer System Another proposal for restructuring U.S. health care as a single-payer system was the National Health Care Act of 1992. Similar to the Canadian model, states would have had responsibility for ensuring the delivery of health services, for paying all providers, and for planning in accordance with federal guidelines. Although this plan would have allowed private medicine, the act would have discontinued private health insurance coverage.[125] Supporters claimed that the act would immediately reduce health care spending by up to 18 percent, and that a single-payer approach would reduce the fraud endemic to a multiple-payer system.[126]

Another strategy to restructure the U.S. health care system is national health insurance (NHI). According to Paul Starr, the United States was on the brink of establishing national health insurance several times during the twentieth century, but each time, factors unique to the United States' political and social institutions prevented its adoption.[127] For example, NHI plans began to proliferate in the 1930s as part of Roosevelt's New Deal, but the idea was abandoned because of the strident opposition of the AMA (originally a supporter of NHI) and the fear that its inclusion would jeopardize passage of the 1935 Social Security Act. Former president Harry Truman took up the NHI in the days following World War II, but by that time most middle-class and unionized workers were covered by private insurance plans. Moreover, the AMA again set its powerful lobbying machine into motion, this time equating national health insurance with socialized medicine and communism.[128]

The most recent incarnation of NHI occurred in the Health Security Act that was proposed by former president Bill Clinton in 1993. Although the proposed act was not an NHI per se, it contained important components of national insurance. Under the proposed plan all citizens and legal immigrants would get a card guaranteeing them a comprehensive lifelong package of health care benefits, including inpatient and outpatient medical care, prescription drugs, dental and vision care, long-term care, mental health services, and substance abuse treatment. Coverage would be continuous regardless of employment status. All participants would buy into large purchasing pools called Health Care Alliances. Charges for low-income self-insurers would be based on a sliding scale and those on public assistance would have their fees paid by Medicaid. Employers would pay

80 percent of the benefit package and workers the additional 20 percent.

The bill was doomed almost from its inception. Almost immediately, the Health Insurance Association of America (HIAA) broadcast $2 million worth of "Harry and Louise" commercials attacking the act as rationing health care under socialized medicine. Small business lobbyists argued that the employer costs would bankrupt thousands of small companies. Observers put the price tag on defeating the act at $100 million.[129]

Liberal critics of NHI plans charge that they modify payment mechanisms rather than encourage major changes in the health care system. Although NHI schemes would equalize the ability of patients to pay, they would not improve the accessibility or the quality of services. Furthermore, most NHI proposals call for coinsurance (copayments) in amounts that many poor people cannot afford.[130] Contrary to some critics, NHI schemes are not socialized medicine since hospitals and physicians would remain private, and most NHI plans preserve a major role for private insurance companies.

Incremental Reform

Incremental health care reform is often more acceptable to the general public and legislators than sweeping reforms. This approach has generally focused on rectifying the more troubling aspects of the private health care system and on fine-tuning public health care programs.

One conservative approach to incremental health care reform is based on individual medical savings accounts (MSA), a form of self-insurance whereby individuals purchase high-deductible health insurance while setting aside pretax dollars to pay for their medical expenses. Opponents of MSAs argue that these plans benefit only the healthy and wealthy, leaving those with less money and more health problems behind in an increasingly costly insurance pool.

Other reforms have been enacted on state levels. In Hawaii, employers are required to insure employees who work more than 20 hours a week.[131] A Health Rights program in Minnesota extends health care coverage to all non-covered, low-income residents and charges them on a sliding-scale basis. Under then Governor Mitt Romney, Massachusetts enacted health care legislation in 2006 that required nearly every resident of the state to obtain a state-government-regulated minimum level

of health care insurance coverage. The bill provided free health care insurance for residents earning less than 150 percent of the poverty threshold (and a partial subsidization for those earning up to 300 percent of the poverty threshold) who do not receive Medicaid. The legislation also incorporated tax penalties for those failing to obtain an insurance plan. The Massachusetts act formed the basis of the 2010 Patient Protection and Affordable Care Act, the most expansive piece of social legislation enacted in decades.

The Patient Protection and Affordable Care Act (P.L. 111-148)

On March 23, 2010, Barack Obama signed into law the 2,000 page Patient Protection and Affordable Care Act (ACA). This legislation was incremental—yet in some ways also comprehensive—and was based on an NHI model that required everyone to be covered by a health care plan. In particular, the legislation extended coverage to the 32 million people in 2010 without health insurance coverage. The ACA contained the following features:

- **Enrollment and Employer Requirements:** The ACA requires most U.S. citizens and legal residents to have health insurance. Almost everyone in 2014—with the exception of some low-income people—must purchase health insurance or face a $695 annual fine. Those without health insurance will pay a tax penalty of the greater of $695 a year up to a maximum of three times that amount ($2,085) per family or 2.5 percent of household income. The penalty will be increased annually after 2016 by a cost-of-living adjustment. Exemptions are granted for financial hardship, religious objections, American Indians, those without coverage for less than three months, undocumented immigrants, incarcerated individuals, those for whom the lowest cost plan option exceeds 8 percent of their income, and those with incomes below the tax filing threshold. Companies with more than 200 employees are expected to automatically enroll them in a health insurance plan. Employees may opt out of coverage. While technically there is no employer mandate, businesses with more than 50 employees must provide health insurance or pay a fine of $2,000 per worker each year if any of their workers receives federal subsidies to purchase health insurance.

- **Cost and Funding:** According to the Congressional Budget Office (CBO), the ACA is expected to cost $940 billion over 10 years, while reducing the deficit by $143 billion in the first 10 years, and $1.2 trillion in the subsequent decade. The ACA will be partly paid for by the Medicare Payroll tax on investment income. Beginning in 2018, insurance companies will pay a 40 percent excise tax on high-end insurance plans worth more than $27,500 for families or $10,200 for individuals. Dental and vision plans are exempted in the total cost of a family's plan.
- **Health Insurance Exchanges (HIE):** The un-insured and self-employed would purchase insurance through state-based HIEs. Separate exchanges would be created in 2014 for small businesses to purchase coverage. The Secretary of Health and Human Services will set up a new website to make it easy for people in any state to seek out affordable health insurance options. The website will also include information for small businesses. Illegal immigrants will not be permitted to purchase health insurance in the exchanges, even if they pay with their own money.
- **Subsidies:** Low-income individuals and families (i.e., those with incomes between 100 and 400 percent of the poverty line) who purchase health insurance in an exchange will be eligible for subsidies if (1) they are ineligible for Medicare and Medicaid and (2) they are not covered by an employer. There is a sliding scale and cap for how much enrollees will have to contribute to their premiums. Businesses with fewer than 50 employees will receive tax credits covering up to 50 percent of employee premiums. The bill also establishes a temporary program to help reduce the cost to companies that provide early retiree health benefits for those aged 55–64 years.
- **Regulation of the Health Insurance Industry:** (1) By 2014, all lifetime caps on insurance coverage will be banned, as will annual caps; (2) insurance companies cannot deny children coverage based on a pre-existing condition; (3) insurers will be prohibited from denying coverage to anyone with a pre-existing condition in 2014; (4) insurers must allow children to stay on their parent's insurance plans until age 26; (5) rescissions (arbitrarily cutting off

consumers with expensive medical conditions) will be prohibited, and insurers will no longer be able to drop consumers when they become seriously ill; (6) greater transparency will be required as insurers must reveal their overhead costs; (7) any new plan must implement a customer appeals process for coverage and claims; (8) new plans must include free checkups and other preventative care; (9) new screening procedures will help curb fraud and waste; and (10) nonprofit Blue Cross organizations will be required to maintain a medical loss ratio (i.e., money spent on procedures over incoming money) of 85 percent or higher to take advantage of IRS tax benefits.
- **Public Health:** Chain restaurants will be required to provide a nutrient content disclosure statement alongside menu items.
- **Medicare:** The ACA closes the Medicare prescription donut hole by 2020. Medicare payment protections will be extended to small rural hospitals and other health care facilities with a small number of Medicare patients.
- **Medicaid:** Starting in 2014 the bill expands Medicaid to all individuals under age 65 with incomes up to 133 percent of the poverty line. The federal government will pay 100 percent of costs for covering newly eligible individuals through 2016, and they will be guaranteed a package that provides essential health benefits. Illegal immigrants are ineligible for Medicaid.[132]
- **Abortion:** No health care plan is required to offer abortion coverage. States could pass legislation choosing to opt out of offering abortion coverage through the exchange. No federal funds can be used to pay for abortions except in the case of rape, incest, or the health of the mother.[133]

Opponents took the issue to the U.S. Supreme Court, specifically focusing on the constitutionality of the ACA's "individual mandate"—the part of the bill that requires the purchase of health insurance.[134] On October 28, 2012 the U.S. Supreme Court finally delivered its long-anticipated verdict on the constitutionality of the ACA. Overall, the Court upheld the ACA. Of particular importance, the Court's decision left in place the individual mandate. Also retained were Health Care Exchanges (designed to offer cheaper health care plans); the requirement that insurers cover the children of those they insure up to age 26 (affected about 2.5 million people in 2012 from age 19 to 25); the requirements around insuring pre-existing medical conditions; and the rule that firms with more than 50 or more full-time employees must provide health care coverage or face fines. Despite upholding most of the ACA, the Court ruled that the federal government could not require states to expand their Medicaid coverage. In effect, it struck down the provision that permitted the federal government to remove existing Medicaid funding from states that refuse to participate in the expansion of Medicaid to formerly non-covered groups.[135]

Comparative Analysis: Health Care in Canada, The United Kingdom, and Australia

Rooted in "American exceptionalism" (i.e., the belief that the United States is so unique that policies outside its borders have little relevance), many U.S. citizens and policymakers miss the opportunity to learn from approaches other nations employ to organize their health care systems. This section briefly explores health care systems in Canada (a single-payer system), Great Britain (National Health Service), and Australia (a hybrid public–private system).

The Canadian Health Care System

In 1984, Canada passed the Canada Health Act (Medicare), a publicly-funded nationwide federal/ provincial health insurance system that is privately delivered and free at the point of access.[136] Although British Columbia, Alberta, and Ontario require health care premiums, the act prohibits provinces from denying health services due to financial inability to pay premiums. While each province is responsible for administering its own health care plan, each plan is essentially universal and comprehensive, covering all residents for inpatient and outpatient hospital and physician services. Six major principles underlie the Canada Health Act:

- **Public Administration:** All administration of provincial health insurance must be carried out by a public authority and be nonprofit and subject to audits.
- **Comprehensiveness:** All approved hospital and physicians' services must be covered, including medical and hospital care, mental health ser-

vices, and prescription drugs for those over age 65 and for those with catastrophic illnesses. In addition to the mandated requirements, provinces typically provide additional services such as physiotherapy, dental coverage, and prescription medicines.
- **Universality:** Every provincial resident must be covered. All insured residents must be entitled to—and receive—the same level of health care. There must be free medical care at the point of access and services must contain no financial barriers.
- **Portability:** Residents who relocate to a different province or territory are entitled to coverage from their home province during a minimum waiting period. This also applies to residents who leave the country.
- **Accessibility:** All insured persons must have reasonable access to health care facilities. All health care providers must receive reasonable compensation for the services they provide.
- **Freedom of Choice:** A Canadian is free to choose his or her provider. After obtaining health coverage, the beneficiary registers with a primary care physician.[137]

In addition to public providers, Canada has many private clinics that offer specialized services. The major draw for these clinics is the reduced wait time for voluntary surgeries and procedures, such as MRIs. Private clinic costs are often covered by private insurance plans, which typically pick up around 80 percent of the bill. Some Canadians worry that private clinics will lead to a two-tiered health system that relegates the poor to an inferior public sector.

Unlike the U.S., the Canadian system is grounded in universal entitlement rather than being linked to employment. Except for people covered by other federal programs such as the military, all 33 million Canadian residents are eligible for provincial health insurance, regardless of their employment status. Canada's Medicare system, however, does not include prescription medication, dental or home health care.[138]

General practitioners (GPs) make up more than 50 percent of the physicians in Canada and provide most of the nation's health care. Specialists are used only if a referral is received from the GP. Although patients may choose their primary care physician, the choice is contingent upon whether the physician has openings for new patients. Patients also use the hospital in which the physician has admitting privileges. Although covered health care is free at the point of access, some elements that are not covered include out-of-hospital drugs, dental care, eyeglasses, physical therapy, and chiropractic care not ordered by a medical doctor.

Contrary to some misconceptions, the Canadian health care system is not socialized medicine; instead, it is based on a social insurance model that mixes public funds with private health care delivery.[139] Approximately 67 percent of Canada's population elect to buy private insurance coverage that contains extra benefits.[140] The basis of Canada's single-payer model is the idea that provincial government functions as a single-source payer of health care with a centralized locus of control. Private physicians' fees are negotiated between the provincial governments and the medical associations. The salaries of physicians in Canada are generally lower than their U.S. counterparts.

There are more than 1,250 hospitals in Canada, of which 57 percent are run by religious orders or nonprofit organizations. Hospital reimbursements are made on a global prospective basis. In other words, hospitals operate on a negotiated but fixed yearly budget. As such, they must stay within the budgetary allotment granted by the province regardless of the number of patients seen in a year.[141]

Canada's Medicare system is funded by a mixture of federal and provincial funds. Federal funds are directed to the provinces in the form of block grants and transfer payments. The provinces obtain funds to operate the medical system from general revenue taxes and, in the case of Alberta and British Columbia, from employer-based insurance premiums. Provinces that charge premiums provide exemptions or subsidies for the aged, the unemployed, and the indigent.

Critics of Canadian health care point to numerous problems facing the system, including less than adequate funding, increasing per capita health care costs, increased demand for services, and the high cost of technology. Taken together, this has made cost containment the number one issue facing the Canadian health care system.

Some critics have charged that Canada's prospective global budgeting system for hospitals has caused health care rationing. They argue that excessively long waiting lists exist for elective surgeries, rushed medical procedures lead to inaccuracies in diagnosis and treatment, the widespread use of cheaper medical materials, and hospitals are not investing in technology or capital improvements. Critics also charge that prioritizing illnesses into "urgent," "emergent," and "elective" categories causes artificial queues for treatment.[142] Accordingly, health care cuts are having a dramatic effect on Canada's medical system.[143]

Canada's health care system is the subject of much political controversy and debate in the United States. Some question the ability of the system to deliver timely treatment and contain costs. Although in the minority, this group often advocates the adoption of a market system similar to the United States.

In 2008, Canada spent only US $4,079 per capita on health care costs in comparison to the $7,538 spent by the United States.[144] Despite these lower expenditures, the World Health Organization ranks Canada above the United States in the performance of their health care system, with the overall health of Canadians being ranked 35th and Americans 72nd. Despite lower health care expenditures, life expectancy in Canada was two-and-a-half years longer in 2006 than in the United States. Infant and child mortality rates are also higher in the United States.[145] One indicator of the success of Canada's health care system is that a majority of Canadians are generally satisfied with it and show no inclination of giving it up. According to a 2010 Harris/Decima poll, Canadians prefer their own health care system over the U.S. system by a margin of 10 to 1 (82 percent versus 8 percent). Seventy percent of Canadians are either fairly satisfied, or very satisfied, with their system.[146]

The United Kingdom's National Health Service

The direct inspiration for the British National Health Service was a 1944 white paper written by Sir William Beveridge, which maintained that a "comprehensive system of health care was essential to any scheme for improving living standards."[147] After initial resistance from the British Medical Association, the National Health Service Act took effect in 1948. In the words of the act, the aim was to promote "the establishment of a comprehensive health service designed to secure improvement in the physical and mental health of the people . . . and the prevention, diagnosis and treatment of illness."[148] The principle of freedom of choice was upheld in that people could either use the NHS or seek outside doctors. Doctors were guaranteed that there would be no interference in their clinical judgment, and specialists were free to take private patients while participating in the service. The NHS was based on a tripartite system: (1) hospital service with specialists; (2) general medical doctors, dentists, and eye doctors that are maintained on a contractual basis; and (3) prevention and support systems, provided by local health departments.

The NHS is currently the world's largest publicly-funded health service, and it employs more than 1.7 million people, including 120,000 hospital doctors; 40,000 GPs; 400,000 nurses; and 25,000 ambulance staff. On average, the NHS serves 1 million patients every 36 hours. Each GP sees on average 140 patients a week. The NHS Act does not prohibit private medicine, and a small percentage of NHS hospital beds are reserved for private patients. GPs and specialists are permitted to treat private patients while working in the NHS. Moreover, affluent patients are permitted to purchase private health insurance and private care. The major advantages of private care are more attractive hospital rooms and quicker service for elective surgery. About 10 percent of Britons currently have some form of private health insurance, which businesses often provide as a fringe benefit for upper-level management.[149]

The backbone of the NHS is the GP, and every patient in Britain is registered with one. GPs are paid by the NHS on the basis of an annual capitation (per-person) fee for each registered patient. They have wide professional latitude and equip their own office, hire staff, and can choose to work singly, in pairs, in groups, or in a government health center. Roughly half of a GP's income comes from capitation payments, with the rest made up of allowances for services such as contraceptive advice and immunization. Since the role of the GP is to provide primary medical care, they are forbidden to restrict their practice to any special client group. Individuals can register with any GP provided he or she is willing to accept them. GPs see almost 75 percent of their registered patients at least once a year; and because mobility is relatively low in Britain, many people retain the same GP for long periods of time.[150]

The second tier of the British health care system is the physician consultant (specialist). Most referrals to consultants—except for accidents or emergency care—are made through GPs. Although employed by the government and under contract to a public hospital, a physician specialist is allowed a small private practice. In effect, patients in the community are served by GPs, whereas in the hospital they are under the care of specialists. Similar to the United States, NHS specialists are accorded greater prestige and remuneration.[151]

The NHS is funded from general taxes, with the proceeds divided among regional health authorities that plan local health services. The regions, in turn, divide their money among districts that pay for hospitals through global prospective budgets. Health services under the NHS are comprehensive, with free hospital and primary medical care. However, there are patient charges for adult dentistry, eyeglasses, and a small charge for prescriptions. Drug prices are agreed upon between the health department and the pharmaceutical industry according to a specified pricing formula based on company profits. In addition, government subsidies for medical education lower students' direct educational costs.[152]

Several criticisms have been leveled against the NHS, especially in the early 2000s. These included poor sanitary conditions that led to outbreaks of antibiotic-resistant infections, cost overruns on hospital construction, the growth of "health tourism" (people traveling to the United Kingdom to use the NHS without cost), long waiting times for elective surgeries (urgent surgeries are promptly done), and the non-availability of some treatments due to perceptions of poor cost-effectiveness. According to the 2010 Commonwealth survey, 21 percent of British participants reported waiting 4 months or more for an elective procedure, while 19 percent reported waiting 2 months or more to see a specialist.[153] Another criticism leveled against the NHS is that hospitals receive nothing extra for efficiently treating more patients at less cost, therefore they have little incentive to improve efficiency.[154]

Still another criticism of the NHS is that its funding is not based on the medical needs of consumers, but on how much the British treasury believes it can afford to spend on health care. The result is de facto health care rationing. Consumers also complain of long waits in GP offices and hospital buildings that are in poor repair. Other critics charge that despite government efforts, there are serious shortages of doctors in certain areas of Britain. Expenditures and resources under the NHS also seem to be slanted toward hospitalization rather than primary, first-level care. Critics complain about the lack of accountability of doctors and about strong unions that have supported restrictive practices and fought attempts to privatize support services.

Much of the reporting on the NHS in the U.S. press has emphasized its flaws. Despite the criticisms, the British people continue to use the NHS in large numbers, and it appears to be serving the majority of the British population as well as, and in some ways better than, the U.S. health care system. For instance, per capita health care expenditures in 2006 were only 8.3 percent of Britain's GDP compared to 15.3 percent for the United States. Much of this lower cost is attributable to the success of GPs in keeping down hospital admission rates and to the relatively low administrative costs of the NHS. Most health indicators in the United Kingdom, such as life expectancy and infant mortality rates, are equivalent to or better than those in the costlier U.S. health care system.

The Australian Health Care System

The Australian health care system is a hybrid public–private system. Introduced in 1984, Australia's Medicare system provides universal health care and subsidized pharmaceuticals for all citizens. The Medicare system was predicated on the idea that all Australians should contribute to the cost of health care according to their ability to pay. As such, it is financed by a progressive income tax and an income-related Medicare levy.[155] As a supplement to Medicare, Australians are strongly encouraged to purchase private health insurance, which in 2010 could cost up to $300 a month for a family at top-level coverage. In 2010, approximately 50 percent of Australians had private health insurance to gain access to private hospitals and to receive services not covered by Medicare.[156] Private health insurance only covers hospital care and some supplemental services such as eyeglasses, minor dental, chiropractic, physiotherapy, and so forth.

The publicly-funded Medicare system provides comprehensive benefits such as consultation fees for doctors, including specialists; medical tests like X-rays, MRIs, and pathology tests; eye tests performed by optometrists; most surgical and therapeutic procedures; and some surgical procedures performed by approved dentists. From 2006, mental health services paid for by Medicare have broadened to include services to families and individuals.

One can enter an Australian hospital either as a public or private pay (using health insurance) patient. Public hospital patients are not charged for care and treatment by attending physicians or specialists, or aftercare by the treating doctor. However, the treatment they receive is from doctors and specialists nominated by the hospital. Those admitted to a public or private hospital as a private patient (i.e., using private health insurance) have a choice of doctors.[157]

Medicare does not cover most dental examinations and treatment (except for children); ambulance services; home nursing; acupuncture (unless part of a doctor's consultation); glasses and contact lenses; hearing aids and other appliances; prostheses; medicines (except those subsidized by the Pharmaceutical Benefits Scheme, which covers most classes of medicines); and cosmetic surgery.

Criticism leveled against Medicare is similar to that directed at the British NHS—namely, long waits for elective surgery as a public patient (private patients have little or no wait), inefficiencies, staff shortages, and underfunding.[158] The 2010 Commonwealth Fund survey found that 18 percent of Australian participants waited 4 months or more for an elective procedure, and 28 percent waited 2 months or more to see a specialist, which is comparable to the waiting periods in the United Kingdom.[159] Other criticisms involve copayments and gaps in services, such as dental coverage. Despite these criticisms, Australians seem to be pleased with their system and their health indicators are positive (i.e., they have one of the longest life expectancies in the world). Only 8 percent of the 2010 Commonwealth Fund survey participants experienced difficulty paying their medical bills within the last year, and 76 percent of Australian participants were confident that if they were seriously ill they would receive the best care.[160]

While the U.S. health care system is vastly more expensive than other Western countries, its public health statistics are roughly equivalent to—and in some cases inferior to—that of countries such as Britain, Canada, and Australia. For affluent or middle-class Americans with good health insurance, the U.S. health care system provides some of the best medical care in the world. And the United States is unequaled when it comes to complex medical procedures involving sophisticated equipment and technology. Unlike the long queues for elective surgery in the United Kingdom, Canada, and Australia, the wait for surgeries, tests, and other procedures is relatively short in the United States. Finally, U.S. physicians are among the best trained in the world. However, the emphasis on costly equipment and technology does not come without a price. A medical approach that emphasizes disease treatment over primary care and preventive medicine usually results in good care, but for fewer people. Health care systems that emphasize personal and primary care, accessibility, and free or inexpensive services typically reach more people. Hence, the Canadian, British, and Australian systems distribute health resources more equitably than the U.S. system.

Conclusion

The American health care system raises important questions. What is the U.S. government's responsibility for providing health care to all its citizens? How much high-tech medicine can society realistically afford? How should U.S. medical resources be allocated? What, if any, limitations on personal freedom are permissible in the name of promoting health and preventing disease? These and other questions require thoughtful answers.

The U.S. health care system is facing an acute crisis based partly on the failure of the marketplace to curb health care costs, the system's overreliance on medical technology at the expense of primary care, huge administrative costs, and the large number of working families unable to afford health insurance. Moreover, compared to industrialized countries with less-costly health care systems, the expensive U.S. system is not resulting in greater longevity, lower rates of infant mortality, or other indicators of improved public health.

The United States is one of the few industrialized countries without a universal health care system. Moreover, it is also one of the few industrialized nations where medical expenses can cause poverty. At minimum, comprehensive health care reform should incorporate principles that include (1) universality (making health care a right rather than a privilege); (2) removing health care from the marketplace (or at least subjecting it to stricter government oversight); (3) arresting the rise in pharmaceutical prices by creating a national formulary that negotiates for the best price; (4) assuring that the quality and accessibility of health care is not dependent on income; (5) placing more emphasis on providing accessible primary care over specialized care; and (6) limiting administrative costs.

Accessible health care should be a universal right for all U.S. citizens, not a privilege to be purchased or earned through workplace participation.

DISCUSSION QUESTIONS

1. In 2012, U.S. health care expenditures were more than $2.5 trillion a year. This cost has risen dramatically over the past 25 years in terms of the amount spent, and the percentage GDP. What factors have driven up health care costs, and how can they be controlled?
2. Medicare has experienced large increases in costs. What are the major factors contributing to this steep rise?
3. Some critics argue that the costs of Medicare and Medicaid cannot be brought under control without radically reforming the entire health care system. They argue that incremental reforms have only a minimal impact on the rise in federal and state health care expenditures. Are they correct?
4. Evidence of the effectiveness of cost-controlling mechanisms, such as DRGs, has been mixed. Critics charge that not only has the DRG system failed to substantially reduce health care costs, but it has also led to a reduced level of patient care. Is the DRG system successful?
5. Many critics argue that America is experiencing a severe health care crisis. Describe the main characteristics and symptoms of that crisis.
6. Some health care analysts are calling for radical reform in the U.S. health care system. Many of them insist that the nation's free market health system should be replaced by a more cost-effective and comprehensive approach. Assuming that these analysts are correct, which of the health care systems described in this chapter would be the best model for the United States? Why?
7. Why has the United States not developed a health care system that is universal and publicly funded like those of its industrialized counterparts?
8. Anyone who watches television has probably seen at least one advertisement for the newer sleep aids such as Lunestra, Roxerem, Ambien, and Sonata. Many drugs have their own website offering discounts or even free products. What do you think of aggressive marketing for new medications by pharmaceutical firms? How does this information affect the confidence that you have in federal oversight of the prescription drug industry?

NOTES

1. "New York Times / CBS News Poll," February 23–27, 2007.
2. U.S Census Bureau, "Income, Poverty, and Health Insurance Coverage in the United States: 2010," September 2011. Retrieved Feb 2012, from www.census.gov/prod/2011pubs/p60-239.pdf
3. Health Care Financing Administration, "President Clinton Announces Approximately 2.5 Million Children

Have Enrolled in the State Children's Health Insurance Program, Praises the Decline in Uninsured, Urges Congress To Expand Coverage, Unveils New Funds for Outreach" (Washington, DC: Health Care Financing Administration, 2000).

4. Terri Combs-Orme, "Should the Federal Government Finance Health Care for All Americans?: Yes," in Howard Jacob Karger and James Midgley (eds.), *Controversial Issues in Social Policy* (Boston: Allyn & Bacon, 1993).

5. Irving J. Lewis and Cecil G. Sheps, *The Sick Citadel* (Boston: Oelgeschlager, Gunn, and Hain, 1983), p. 16.

6. J. Hadley and J. Holahan, "The Cost of Care for the Uninsured: What Do We Spend, Who Pays, and What Would Full Coverage Add to Medical Spending?", 2004. Retrieved July 2008, from www.kff.org/uninsured/upload/The-Cost-of-Care-for-the-Uninsured-What-Do-We-Spend-Who-Pays-and-What-Would-Full-Coverage-Add-to-Medical-Spending.pdf

7. W.K. Kirzinger, R.A. Cohen & R.M. Gindi, "Healthcare Access and Utilization Among Young Adults Aged 19-25: Early Release of Estimates from the National Health Interview Survey, January – September, 2011," Center for Disease Control and Prevention, May 2012. Retrieved June 2012 from http://www.cdc.gov/nchs/data/nhis/earlyrelease/Young_Adults_Health_Access_052012.pdf

8. National Coalition on Health Care, "Health Insurance Coverage."

9. Hadley, J and Holahan, J. 2004, "The Cost of Care for the Uninsured: What Do We Spend, Who Pays, and What Would Full Coverage Add to Medical Spending?". Retrieved July 2008 from http://www.kff.org/uninsured/upload/The-Cost-of-Care-for-the-Uninsured-What-Do-We-Spend-Who-Pays-and-What-Would-Full-Coverage-Add-to-Medical-Spending.pdf

10. Centers for Medicare and Medicaid Services, "Brief Summaries of Medicare and Medicaid," November 1, 2011. Retrieved May 2012 from http://www.cms.gov/Research-Statistics-Data-and-Systems/Statistics-Trends-and-Reports/MedicareMedicaidStatSupp/downloads//2011BriefSummaries.pdf

11. U.S Census Bureau, "Income, Poverty, and Health Insurance Coverage in the United States: 2010," September 2011. Retrieved Feb 2012, from www.census.gov/prod/2011pubs/p60-239.pdf

12. Kaiser Family Foundation, "Health Costs and Budgets," Retrieved June 2012 from http://www.statehealthfacts.org/comparecat.jsp?cat=5&rgn=6&rgn=1

13. C. P. Pandya, "Study: Health Insurance Premiums Rising Much Faster Than Average Wages," *The New Standard* (September 28, 2004), p. 3.

14. M. Bihari, "Laid Off? COBRA Insurance May Be An Option for Healthcare Coverage," *About.com Health Insurance*, April 14, 2010. Retrieved June 2012 from http://healthinsurance.about.com/od/healthinsurancebasics/a/COBRA_basics.htm

15. Sumner A. Rosen, David Fanshel, and Mary E. Lutz (eds.), *Face of the Nation 1987* (Silver Spring, MD: NASW, 1987), p. 75.

16. U.S. Census Bureau, "Income, Poverty, and Health Insurance Coverage in the United States: 2006."

17. U.S Census Bureau, "Income, Poverty, and Health Insurance Coverage in the United States: 2010," September 2011. Retrieved Feb 2012, from www.census.gov/prod/2011pubs/p60-239.pdf

18. Centers for Medicare & Medicaid Services, "Brief Summaries of Medicare and Medicaid," November 1, 2007. Retrieved July 2008, from www.cms.hhs.gov/MedicareMedicaidStatSupp/downloads/07BriefSummaries.pdf

19. Centers for Medicare and Medicaid Services, "Brief Summaries of Medicare and Medicaid," November 1, 2011. Retrieved May 2012 from http://www.cms.gov/Research-Statistics-Data-and-Systems/Statistics-Trends-and-Reports/MedicareMedicaidStatSupp/downloads//2011BriefSummaries.pdf

20. Centers for Medicare & Medicaid Services, "Brief Summaries of Medicare and Medicaid," November 1, 2007. Retrieved July 2008, from www.cms.hhs.gov/MedicareMedicaidStatSupp/downloads/07BriefSummaries.pdf

21. Centers for Medicare and Medicaid Services, "Brief Summaries of Medicare and Medicaid," November 1, 2011. Retrieved May 2012 from http://www.cms.gov/Research-Statistics-Data-and-Systems/Statistics-Trends-and-Reports/MedicareMedicaidStatSupp/downloads//2011BriefSummaries.pdf

22. Ibid.

23. Centers for Medicare and Medicaid Services, "Brief Summaries of Medicare and Medicaid," November 1, 2011. Retrieved May 2012 from http://www.cms.gov/Research-Statistics-Data-and-Systems/Statistics-Trends-and-Reports/MedicareMedicaidStatSupp/downloads//2011BriefSummaries.pdf

24. Centers for Medicare and Medicaid Services, "Brief Summaries of Medicare and Medicaid," November 1, 2011. Retrieved May 2012 from http://www.cms.gov/Research-Statistics-Data-and-Systems/Statistics-Trends-and-Reports/MedicareMedicaidStatSupp/downloads//2011BriefSummaries.pdf

25. Centers for Medicare and Medicaid Services, "Brief Summaries of Medicare and Medicaid," November 1, 2011. Retrieved May 2012 from http://www.cms.gov/Research-Statistics-Data-and-Systems/Statistics-Trends-and-Reports/MedicareMedicaidStatSupp/downloads//2011BriefSummaries.pdf

26. See Families USA, "Understanding the New Medicare Prescription Drug Benefit," The Medicare Road Show, Washington, D.C., Spring 2004; Kaiser Family Foundation, "The Medicare Prescription Drug Law," March 2004, retrieved November 2004 from www.kff.org/medicare/loader.cfm?url=/commonspot/ security/getfile.cfm&PageID=33325; and Egyptian Area Agency

on Aging, "Medicare Prescription Drug Benefit,"
Cartersville, IL, May 20, 2004, retrieved November 2004
from www.egyptianaaa.org/MedicareDrugBill.htm.

27. Michael Scherer, "Medicare's Hidden Bonanza," *Mother Jones* (March/April 2004), p. 11.

28. Centers for Medicare and Medicaid Services, "Brief Summaries of Medicare and Medicaid," November 1, 2011. Retrieved May 2012 from http://www.cms.gov/Research-Statistics-Data-and-Systems/Statistics-Trends-and-Reports/MedicareMedicaidStatSupp/downloads//2011BriefSummaries.pdf

29. Centers for Medicare and Medicaid Services, "Brief Summaries of Medicare and Medicaid," November 1, 2011. Retrieved May 2012 from http://www.cms.gov/Research-Statistics-Data-and-Systems/Statistics-Trends-and-Reports/MedicareMedicaidStatSupp/downloads//2011BriefSummaries.pdf

30. Centers for Medicare & Medicaid Services, "Brief Summaries of Medicare and Medicaid", November 1, 2007. Retrieved July 2008 from http://www.cms.hhs.gov/MedicareMedicaidStatSupp/downloads/07BriefSummaries.pdf

31. Centers for Medicare and Medicaid Services, "Brief Summaries of Medicare and Medicaid," November 1, 2011. Retrieved May 2012 from http://www.cms.gov/Research-Statistics-Data-and-Systems/Statistics-Trends-and-Reports/MedicareMedicaidStatSupp/downloads//2011BriefSummaries.pdf

32. Centers for Medicare and Medicaid Services, "Brief Summaries of Medicare and Medicaid," November 1, 2011. Retrieved May 2012 from http://www.cms.gov/Research-Statistics-Data-and-Systems/Statistics-Trends-and-Reports/MedicareMedicaidStatSupp/downloads//2011BriefSummaries.pdf

33. Centers for Medicare and Medicaid Services, "Brief Summaries of Medicare and Medicaid," November 1, 2011. Retrieved May 2012 from http://www.cms.gov/Research-Statistics-Data-and-Systems/Statistics-Trends-and-Reports/MedicareMedicaidStatSupp/downloads//2011BriefSummaries.pdf

34. Centers for Medicare and Medicaid Services, "Brief Summaries of Medicare and Medicaid," November 1, 2011. Retrieved May 2012 from http://www.cms.gov/Research-Statistics-Data-and-Systems/Statistics-Trends-and-Reports/MedicareMedicaidStatSupp/downloads//2011BriefSummaries.pdf

35. Centers for Medicare and Medicaid Services, "Brief Summaries of Medicare and Medicaid," November 1, 2011. Retrieved May 2012 from http://www.cms.gov/Research-Statistics-Data-and-Systems/Statistics-Trends-and-Reports/MedicareMedicaidStatSupp/downloads//2011BriefSummaries.pdf

36. Centers for Medicare and Medicaid Services, "Brief Summaries of Medicare and Medicaid," November 1, 2011. Retrieved May 2012 from http://www.cms.gov/Research-Statistics-Data-and-Systems/Statistics-Trends-and-Reports/MedicareMedicaidStatSupp/downloads//2011BriefSummaries.pdf

37. Social Security Administration, "A Summary of the 2012 Annual Social Security and Medicare Trust Fund Reports," Last Revised June 4, 2012. Retrieved June 2012 from http://www.socialsecurity.gov/OACT/TRSUM/index.html

38. David E. Rosenbaum, "Gloomy Forecast Touches Off Feud on Medicare Fund," *New York Times* (June 6, 1996), pp. A1 and B14.

39. For a good historical analysis of the Medicare program, see Theodore R. Marmor, *The Politics of Medicare* (Chicago: Aldine, 1973).

40. Centers for Medicare & Medicaid Services, "Brief Summaries of Medicare and Medicaid."

41. U.S Census Bureau, "Income, Poverty, and Health Insurance Coverage in the United States: 2010," September 2011. Retrieved Feb 2012, from www.census.gov/prod/2011pubs/p60-239.pdf

42. Centers for Medicare and Medicaid Services, "Brief Summaries of Medicare and Medicaid," November 1, 2011. Retrieved May 2012 from http://www.cms.gov/Research-Statistics-Data-and-Systems/Statistics-Trends-and-Reports/MedicareMedicaidStatSupp/downloads//2011BriefSummaries.pdf

43. Centers for Medicare and Medicaid Services, "Brief Summaries of Medicare and Medicaid," November 1, 2011. Retrieved May 2012 from http://www.cms.gov/Research-Statistics-Data-and-Systems/Statistics-Trends-and-Reports/MedicareMedicaidStatSupp/downloads//2011BriefSummaries.pdf

44. Centers for Medicare and Medicaid Services, "Brief Summaries of Medicare and Medicaid," November 1, 2011. Retrieved May 2012 from http://www.cms.gov/Research-Statistics-Data-and-Systems/Statistics-Trends-and-Reports/MedicareMedicaidStatSupp/downloads//2011BriefSummaries.pdf

45. Ibid.

46. Centers for Medicare and Medicaid Services, "Brief Summaries of Medicare and Medicaid," November 1, 2011. Retrieved May 2012 from http://www.cms.gov/Research-Statistics-Data-and-Systems/Statistics-Trends-and-Reports/MedicareMedicaidStatSupp/downloads//2011BriefSummaries.pdf

47. Nina Bernstein, "With Medicaid, Long-Term Care of Elderly Looms as a Rising Cost, "*New York Times,* September 6, 2012, B6.

48. Centers for Medicare and Medicaid Services, "Brief Summaries of Medicare and Medicaid," November 1, 2011. Retrieved May 2012 from http://www.cms.gov/Research-Statistics-Data-and-Systems/Statistics-Trends-and-Reports/MedicareMedicaidStatSupp/downloads//2011BriefSummaries.pdf

49. American Association of Retired Persons, "Average Daily Cost for Nursing Home Care by State, 2001," 2004. Retrieved November 2004 from http://www.aarp.org/bulletin/longterm/Articles/a2003-10-30-dailycost.html.

50. Social Security Administration, "Medicaid."

51. See U.S Census Bureau, "Income, Poverty, and Health Insurance Coverage in the United States: 2010," September 2011. Retrieved February 2012, from www.census.gov/prod/2011pubs/p60-239.pdf; and Centers for Medicare and Medicaid Services, "Brief Summaries of Medicare and Medicaid," November 1, 2011. Retrieved May 2012 from http://www.cms.gov/Research-Statistics-Data-and-Systems/Statistics-Trends-and-Reports/MedicareMedicaidStatSupp/downloads//2011BriefSummaries.pdf

52. See Children's Defense Fund, *A Children's Defense Budget,* p. 109; and Barbara Wolfe, "A Medicaid Primer," *Focus* 17, no. 3 (Spring 1996), pp. 1–6.

53. Kaiser Family Foundation, "State Health Facts." Retrieved July 2008, from www.statehealthfacts.org

54. Centers for Medicare and Medicaid Services, "Brief Summaries of Medicare and Medicaid," November 1, 2011. Retrieved May 2012 from http://www.cms.gov/Research-Statistics-Data-and-Systems/Statistics-Trends-and-Reports/MedicareMedicaidStatSupp/downloads//2011BriefSummaries.pdf

55. Kaiser Family Foundation, "Number of Children Ever Enrolled in the Children's Health Insurance Program (CHIP) FY2011," April 19, 2012. Retrieved June 2012 from http://www.statehealthfacts.org/comparemaptable.jsp?ind=871&cat=4

56. Medicaid, "Children's Health Insurance Program," Retrieved June 2012 from http://www.medicaid.gov/Medicaid-CHIP-Program-Information/By-Topics/Childrens-Health-Insurance-Program-CHIP/Childrens-Health-Insurance-Program-CHIP.html

57. Medicaid, "Children's Health Insurance Program Financing," Retrieved June 2012 from http://www.medicaid.gov/Medicaid-CHIP-Program-Information/By-Topics/Financing-and-Reimbursement/Childrens-Health-Insurance-Program-Financing.html

58. U.S Department of Health and Human Services, "Connecting Kids to Coverage – Continuing the Progress: 2010 CHIPRA Annual Report," 2011. Retrieved June 2012, from http://www.insurekidsnow.gov/professionals/reports/chipra/2010_annual.pdf

59. Kaiser Family Foundation, "Determining Income Eligibility in Children's Health Coverage Programs: How States Use Disregards in Children's Medicaid and SCHIP," May 2008. Retrieved July 2008, from www.kff.org/medicaid/upload/7776.pdf

60. U.S Department of Health and Human Services, "Connecting Kids to Coverage – Continuing the Progress: 2010 CHIPRA Annual Report," 2011. Retrieved June 2012, from http://www.insurekidsnow.gov/professionals/reports/chipra/2010_annual.pdf

61. Kentucky Farm Bureau, "Summary of Master Tobacco Settlement," April 1, 1999. Retrieved 2001 from www.kyfb.org/FactTobSett040199.htm

62. Centers for Disease Control and Prevention, "State Tobacco Settlement and Tax Revenues and Tobacco Control Funding Appropriations After the Master Settlement Agreement – United States, 1998 – 2010," Morbidity and Mortality Weekly Report, 61, no. 20 (25th of May 2012), pp. 370–374.

63. Centers for Disease Control and Prevention, "State Tobacco Settlement and Tax Revenues and Tobacco Control Funding Appropriations After the Master Settlement Agreement – United States, 1998 – 2010," *Morbidity and Mortality Weekly Report,* 61, no. 20 (May 25, 2012), pp. 370–374.

64. U.S Department of Health and Human Services, "Preventing Tobacco Use Among Youth and Young Adults: A Report of the Surgeon General," Atlanta, G.A, 2012. Retrieved June 2012, from http://www.cdc.gov/tobacco.

65. U.S Census Bureau, "Income, Poverty, and Health Insurance Coverage in the United States: 2010," September 2011. Retrieved Feb 2012, from www.census.gov/prod/2011pubs/p60-239.pdf

66. U.S Department of Health and Human Services, "Preventing Tobacco Use Among Youth and Young Adults: A Report of the Surgeon General," Atlanta, G.A, 2012. Retrieved June 2012, from http://www.cdc.gov/tobacco.

67. James Grubel, "New Australia Smoking Law Bans Brand Labels," *Canberra Times,* November 10, 2011, p. 2.

68. Adam Cresswell, "Most Extreme Anti-smoking Laws Planned for NSW," *The Australian,* February 22, 2012, p. 3.

69. Centers for Medicare and Medicaid Services, "Brief Summaries of Medicare and Medicaid," November 1, 2011. Retrieved May 2012 from http://www.cms.gov/Research-Statistics-Data-and-Systems/Statistics-Trends-and-Reports/MedicareMedicaidStatSupp/downloads//2011BriefSummaries.pdf

70. U.S. House of Representatives, *Overview of Entitlement Programs: 1996 Green Book.*

71. Centers for Medicare and Medicaid Services, "Brief Summaries of Medicare and Medicaid," November 1, 2011. Retrieved May 2012 from http://www.cms.gov/Research-Statistics-Data-and-Systems/Statistics-Trends-and-Reports/MedicareMedicaidStatSupp/downloads//2011BriefSummaries.pdf

72. U.S. House of Representatives, *Overview of Entitlement Programs: 1996 Green Book.*

73. HHS, Centers for Medicare and Medicaid Services, "National Health Expenditures Aggregate, Per Capita Amounts, Percent Distribution, and Average Annual Percent Change, by Type of Expenditure: Selected Calendar Years 1960 – 2010," Retrieved June 2012 from http://www.cms.gov/Research-Statistics-Data-and-Systems/Statistics-Trends-and-Reports/NationalHealthExpendData/downloads/tables.pdf

74. B.B. Blanchfield, J.L. Heffernan, B. Osgood, R.R. Sheehan, G.S. Meyer, "Saving Billions of Dollars and Physicians' Time by Streamlining Billing Practices," *Health Affairs,* 29, no. 6 (June 2010), pp. 1248–1254.

---

75. Linda Chiem, "Average Hospital Stay: 5 days, $22,596," *Pacific Business News*, October 26, 2008, p. 8.

76. Centers for Medicare and Medicaid Services, "Brief Summaries of Medicare and Medicaid," November 1, 2011. Retrieved May 2012 from http://www.cms.gov/Research-Statistics-Data-and-Systems/Statistics-Trends-and-Reports/MedicareMedicaidStatSupp/downloads//2011BriefSummaries.pdf

77. Stanton Peele, "Is Health Care Inflation Inevitable? What Are the Consequences?" *The Huffington Post*, December 17, 2010. Retrieved December 18, 2010 from, http://www.huffingtonpost.com/stanton-peele/why-do-health-care-costs-_b_797807.html

78. OECD, *Health at a Glance, 2011: OECD Indicators*, 6th edition, "Health Expenditure Per Capita," November 23, 2011. Retrieved June 2012, from http://www.oecd-ilibrary.org/docserver/download/fulltext/8111101ec060.pdf?expires=1338963876&id=id&accname=guest&checksum=12587EFD6C4FCD74F3D7A2CECCE6D50F

79. OECD, *Health at a Glance, 2011: OECD Indicators*, 6th edition, "Health Expenditure in Relation to GDP," November 23, 2011. Retrieved June 2012, from http://www.oecd-ilibrary.org/docserver/download/fulltext/8111101ec061.pdf?expires=1338963221&id=id&accname=guest&checksum=5CB99C4E2B94EFC115F9792641B03E9C

80. Gerard Anderson and David Squires, The Commonwealth Fund, Measuring the U.S. Health Care System: A Cross-National Comparison, June 20, 2010. Retrieved December 18, 2010 from, http://www.commonwealthfund.org/Content/Publications/Issue-Briefs/2010/Jun/Measuring-the-US-Health-Care.aspx

81. OECD, *Health at a Glance*, 2011: OECD Indicators, 6th edition, "Health Status," 23rd of November 2011. Retrieved June 2012 from http://www.oecd-ilibrary.org/social-issues-migration-health/health-at-a-glance-2011_health_glance-2011-en

82. Anderson & Squires, op cit.

83. Ibid.

84. U.S. House of Representatives, *1996 Green Book,* p. 995.

85. S.Langel, "Averting Medical Malpractice Lawsuits: Effective Medicine or Inadequate Cure?" *Health Affairs,* 29, no. 9 (September 2010), pp. 1565–8.

86. M.J. Hall, C.J. DeFrances, S.N. Williams, A. Golosinskiy & A. Schwartzman, "National Hospital Discharge Survey: 2007 Summary,"*National Health Statistics Report*, 29 (October 26, 2010). Retrieved June 2012 from http://www.cdc.gov/nchs/data/nhsr/nhsr029.pdf

87. HHS, Centers for Medicare and Medicaid Services, "National Health Expenditures Aggregate, Per Capita Amounts, Percent Distribution, and Average Annual Percent Change, by Type of Expenditure: Selected Calendar Years 1960 – 2010," Retrieved June 2012 from http://www.cms.gov/Research-Statistics-Data-and-Systems/Statistics-Trends-and-Reports/NationalHealthExpendData/downloads/tables.pdf

88. Department of Health and Human Services, Centers for Medicare and Medicaid Services, National and Health Expenditure Data, October 6, 2010. Retrieved on December 18, 2010 from, http://www.cms.gov/Research-Statistics-Data-and-Systems/Statistics-Trends-and-Reports/NationalHealthExpendData/index.html?redirect=/nationalhealthexpenddata/

89. B.B. Blanchfield, J.L. Heffernan, B. Osgood, R.R. Sheehan, G.S. Meyer, "Saving Billions of Dollars and Physicians' Time by Streamlining Billing Practices," *Health Affairs*, 29, no. 6 (June 2010), pp. 1248–1254.

90. HHS, Centers for Medicare and Medicaid Services, "National Health Expenditures Aggregate, Per Capita Amounts, Percent Distribution, and Average Annual Percent Change, by Type of Expenditure: Selected Calendar Years 1960 – 2010," Retrieved June 2012 from http://www.cms.gov/Research-Statistics-Data-and-Systems/Statistics-Trends-and-Reports/NationalHealthExpendData/downloads/tables.pdf

91. HHS, Centers for Medicare and Medicaid Services, "Hospital Care Expenditures Aggregate, Percent Change, and Percent Distribution, By Source of Funds: Selected Calendar Years 1970–2010," Retrieved June 2012 from http://www.cms.gov/Research-Statistics-Data-and-Systems/Statistics-Trends-and-Reports/NationalHealthExpendData/downloads/tables.pdf

92. American Hospital Association, "Rising Demand, Increasing Costs of Caring Fuel Hospital Spending," Press Release, February 19, 2003. Retrieved November 2004 from http://www.aha.org/aha/hospitalconnect/search/pressrelease.jsp?dcrpath=AHA/Press_Release/data/PR_030219_Costs&domain=AHA

93. HHS, Centers for Medicare and Medicaid Services, "National Health Expenditures Aggregate, Per Capita Amounts, Percent Distribution, and Average Annual Percent Change, by Type of Expenditure: Selected Calendar Years 1960 – 2010," Retrieved June 2012 from http://www.cms.gov/Research-Statistics-Data-and-Systems/Statistics-Trends-and-Reports/NationalHealthExpendData/downloads/tables.pdf

94. Health Care Financing Administration, "Actuarial Products, N.H.E. Projections, Table 2." Retrieved 2001 from http://www.hcfa.gov/stats/NHE-Proj

95. Myrle Croasdale, "High Medical School Debt Steers Life Choices for Young Doctors," *AMA News* (May 17, 2004), pp. 2–5.

96. Medscape, Web MD, "Medscape Physician Compensation Report, 2012 Results." Retrieved June 2012 from http://www.medscape.com/features/slideshow/compensation/2012/public]

97. C. Rampell, "How Much Do Doctors in Other Countries Make?" *Economix* (of July 15, 2009). Retrieved June 2012, from http://economix.blogs.nytimes.com/2009/07/15/how-much-do-doctors-in-other-countries-make/

98. M.G. Laugesen & S.A. Glied, "Higher Fees Paid to US Physicians Drive Higher Spending for Physician Services

Compared to Other Countries," *Health Affairs*, 30, no. 9 (September 2011), pp. 1647–1656.

99. M.G. Laugesen & S.A. Glied, "Higher Fees Paid to US Physicians Drive Higher Spending for Physician Services Compared to Other Countries," Health Affairs, 30, no. 9 (September 2011), pp. 1647–1656.

100. Myrle Croasdale, "High Medical School Debt Steers Life Choices for Young Doctors," *AMA News* (May 17, 2004), p. 6.

101. Parija Kavilanz, "Family doctors: An endangered breed." CNNMoney.com, July 18, 2009. Retrieved September 2011 from, http://money.cnn.com/2009/07/16/news/economy/healthcare_doctors_shortage/index.htm

102. Jay Greene, "Primary Care Matches Down Again; Fourth Year of Decline Worries Some," *AMA News* (April 9, 2001), p. 16.

103. Kaiser Family Foundation, "Primary Care Health Professional Shortage Areas (HPSAs), 2012," Retrieved June 2012 from http://statehealthfacts.org/comparemapreport.jsp?rep=112&cat=8

104. HHS, Centers for Medicare and Medicaid Services, "National Health Expenditures Aggregate, Per Capita Amounts, Percent Distribution, and Average Annual Percent Change, by Type of Expenditure: Selected Calendar Years 1960 – 2010," Retrieved June 2012 from http://www.cms.gov/Research-Statistics-Data-and-Systems/Statistics-Trends-and-Reports/NationalHealthExpendData/downloads/tables.pdf

105. Kaiser Family Foundation, Prescription Drug Costs, 2010. Retrieved December 18, 2010 from, http://www.kaiseredu.org/Issue-Modules/Prescription-Drug-Costs/Background-Brief.aspx4

106. OECD, Health at a Glance, 2011: *OECD Indicators*, 6th edition, "Pharmaceutical Expenditure," November 23, 2011. Retrieved June 2012, from http://www.oecd-ilibrary.org/docserver/download/fulltext/8111101ec063.pdf?expires=1339060722&id=id&accname=guest&checksum=56D1F8A317632B6C642401622A715E10

107. Katherine van Wormer, *Social Welfare: A World View* (Chicago: Nelson-Hall, 1997), p. 412.

108. Kaiser Family Foundation, Prescription Drug Costs, 2010. Retrieved December 18, 2010 from http://www.kaiseredu.org/Issue-Modules/Prescription-Drug-Costs/Background-Brief.aspx

109. Marcia Angell, The Truth About the Drug Companies: How They Deceive Us and What to Do About It (New York: Random House, 2004); and Marc-Andre Gagnon and Joel Lexchin, "The Cost of Pushing Pills: A New Estimate of Pharmaceutical Promotion Expenditures in the United States," PLoS Med, January 3, 2008 5(1). Retrieved December 19, 2010 from, http://www.plosmedicine.org/article/info:doi/10.1371/journal.pmed.0050001

110. T. Hemphill, "Extraordinary Pricing of Orphan Drugs: Is it a Socially Responsible Strategy for the U.S. Pharmaceutical Industry?" *Journal of Business Ethics*, 94

(2010), pp. 225–242. Retrieved June 2012, from http://search.proquest.com/pqrl/docview/733013947/1374FCC14026AE182E5/1?accountid=14723

111. R. Bala & P. Bhardwaj, "Detailing vs. Direct to Consumer Advertising in the Prescription Pharmaceutical Industry," *Management Science*, 56, no. 1 (January 2010), pp. 148–160. Congressional Budget Office, "Promotional Spending for Prescription Drugs," Economic and Budget Issue Brief, 2nd of December 2009. Retrieved June 2012 from http://www.cbo.gov/sites/default/files/cbofiles/ftpdocs/105xx/doc10522/12-02-drugpromo_brief.pdf

112. United States Government Accountability Office, Prescription Drugs: Improvements Needed in FDA's Oversight of Direct-to-Consumer Advertising, GAO Report to Congressional Requesters, Washington, DC, November 2006.

113. L. Mulligan, "You Can't Say That on Television: Constitutional Analysis of a Direct to Consumer Pharmaceutical Advertising Ban," American Journal of Law and Medicine, 37, no. 2/3 (2011), pp. 446-467. Retrieved June 2012 from http://search.proquest.com/docview/896358037/13753DFD2FF7766661C/13?accountid=14723

114. John H. Goddeeris and Andrew J. Hogan, "Nature and Dimensions of the Problem." In John H. Goddeeris and Andrew J. Hogan (eds.), *Improving Access to Health Care: What Can the States Do?* (Kalamazoo, MI: W. E. Upjohn Institute for Employment Research, 1992), pp. 14–15.

115. Quoted in Marie A. Caputi and William A. Heiss, "The DRG Revolution," *Health and Social Work* 3, no. 6 (June 1984), p. 5.

116. Kaiser Family Foundation, "Total HMO Enrollment, July 2010," Retrieved June 2012 from http://www.statehealthfacts.org/comparemaptable.jsp?cat=7&ind=348

117. McVicar, "Drug Costs Go Up but Coverage Comes Down."

118. McVicar, "Drug Costs Go Up."

119. C. Schoen, R. Osborn, D. Squires, M.M. Doty, R. Pierson & S. Applebaum, "How Health Insurance Design Affects Access to Care and Costs, By Income, In Eleven Countries," *Health Affairs*, 29, no. 12 (2010), pp. 2323-2334

120. Nancy McVicar, "Medical Care Is There—If You Can Afford It," *Sun-Sentinel* (February 24, 2000). Retrieved 2001, from www.sun-sentinel.com/news/daily/detail/0,1136,27500000000104840,00.html

121. Ellyn E. Spragins, "Simon Says, Join Us," *Newsweek* (June 19, 1995), pp. 55–58.

122. Thomas H. Ainsworth, *Live or Die* (New York: Macmillan, 1983), p. 89.

123. W. Greenberg, "Elimination of Employer-Based Health Insurance." In R. B. Helms (Ed.), *American Health Policy: Critical Issues for Reform* (Washington, DC: AEI Press, October 1992), pp. 1–4.

124. Ronald Dellums et al., Health Services Act (H. R. 2969) (Washington, DC: U.S. Government Printing Office,

1979). For a good summary of the act, see Waitzkin, *The Second Sickness*, pp. 222–226.

125. "Summary of S. 2817, The National Health Care Act of 1992," *NASW-LA News* 16, no. 5 (September/October 1992), p. 2-4.

126. Thomas Daschle, Rima Cohen, and Charles Rice, "Health Care Reform: Single-Payer Models," *American Psychologist* 48, no. 3 (March 1993), pp. 265–267.

127. Paul Starr, *The Social Transformation of American Medicine* (New York: Basic Books, 1984).

128. Ibid.

129. Douglas Frantz, "Lobbyists, Interest Groups Begin Costly Health Care Battle," *Los Angeles Times* (May 24, 1993).

130. Waitzkin, *The Second Sickness*, p. 218.

131. Barbara Wolfe, "A Medicaid Primer," Focus 17, no. 3 (Spring 1996), pp. 1–6.

132. E. Belmont, C.C. Haltom, D.A. Hastings, R.G. Homchick, L. Morris et al, "A New Quality Compass: Hospital Boards' Increased Role Under the Affordable Care Act," *Health Affairs*, 30, no. 7 (July 2011), pp. 1282-9. See also Stephen Gorin, "The Affordable Care Act: Background and Analysis," *Health and Social Work*, 36, no. 2 (May 2011).

133. C. Schoen, R. Osborn, D. Squires, M.M. Doty, R. Pierson & S. Applebaum, "How Health Insurance Design Affects Access to Care and Costs, By Income, In Eleven Countries," *Health Affairs*, 29, no. 12 (2010), pp. 2323-2334.

134. D.B. Gardner, "The Future of the Affordable Care Act: Will We Abandon Healthcare Reform?" *Nursing Economics*, 30, no. 1 (January/February 2012), pp. 40-41; 49.

135. Josh Levs, "What the Health Care Ruling Means to You," CNN, June 28, 2012. Retrieved June 29, 2012 from http://edition.cnn.com/2012/06/28/politics/supreme-court-health-effects/index.html?iid=article_sidebar

136. Denise Callaway, "Canadian Health Care: The Good, the Bad, and the Ugly," *Health Insurance Underwriter* (October 1991), pp. 18–35.

137. Jonathan Rakich, "The Canadian and U.S. Health Care Systems: Profiles and Policies," *Hospital and Health Services Administration* 36, no. 1 (Spring 1991), pp. 26–27.

138. Cathy Schoen, Robin Osborn, David Squires, Michelle Doty, Roz Pierson, and Sandra Applebaum, "How Health Insurance Design Affects Access to Care and Costs, By Income, In Eleven Countries," *Health Affairs*, 29, no. 12 (2010), pp. 2323-2334.

139. Rakich, "The Canadian and U.S. Health Care Systems," p. 32.

140. Schoen, et al., op cit. "How Health Insurance Design Affects Access to Care and Costs, By Income, In Eleven Countries."

141. Jonathan Rakich, "The Canadian and U.S. Health Care Systems: Profiles and Policies," *Hospital and Health Services Administration* 36, no. 1 (Spring 1991), pp. 26–27.

142. Robert Moffitt, "Should the Federal Government Finance Health Care for All Americans?: No," in Howard Jacob Karger and James Midgley (eds.), *Controversial Issues in Social Policy* (Boston: Allyn & Bacon, 1993).

143. Felipe Nieves, "Canadians Satisfied with Health Care, Despite Complaints, Polls Find," *Cleveland.com*, July 21, 2009. Retrieved December 20, 2010 from http://www.cleveland.com/nation/index.ssf/2009/07/canadians_satisfied_with_healt.html

144. Schoen, et al, "How Health Insurance Design Affects Access to Care and Costs, By Income, In Eleven Countries."

145. Karen Davis, Cathy Schoen, Stephen Schoenbaum, Michelle Doty, Alyssa Holmgren, Jennifer Kriss, and Katherine Shea, "Mirror, Mirror on the Wall: An International Update on the Comparative Performance of American Health Care," The Commonwealth Fund, May 15, 2007, vol. 59, New York.

146. Nieves, op cit., "Canadians Satisfied with Health Care, Despite Complaints, Polls Find."

147. Ruth Levitt, *The Reorganised National Health Service* (London: Croom Helm, 1979), p. 17.

148. National Health Service, About the NHS. Retrieved December 20, 2010 from, http://www.nhs.uk/NHSEngland/thenhs/about/Pages/overview.aspx

149. Schoen, et. al., op cit. "How Health Insurance Design Affects Access to Care and Costs."

150. Victor Sidel and Ruth Sidel, *A Healthy State* (New York: Pantheon Books, 1983).

151. Seidel, op cit.

152. "Nye Bevan's Legacy," *The Economist* (July 6, 1992), p. 12.

153. Schoen, et al., op cit. "How Health Insurance Design Affects Access to Care and Costs, By Income, In Eleven Countries."

154. "Nye Bevan's Legacy," op cit.

155. Australian Government, Medicare Australia, About Medicare, 2008. Retrieved June 10, 2008, from www.medicareaustralia.gov.au/public/register/index.jsp

156. Schoen, et al., op cit. "How Health Insurance Design Affects Access to Care and Costs, By Income, In Eleven Countries."

157. Australian Government, op cit., Medicare Australia.

158. Australian Government, op cit., Medicare Australia, About Medicare, 2008. Retrieved June 10, 2008, from www.medicareaustralia.gov.au/public/register/index.jsp

159. Schoen, et al., "How Health Insurance Design Affects Access to Care and Costs."

160. Schoen, et al., "How Health Insurance Design Affects Access to Care and Costs."

CHAPTER 13

Mental Health and Substance Abuse Policy

Source: Piotr Marcinski/Shutterstock

This chapter reviews the provision of mental health and substance abuse services to people with serious impairments. Before the emergence of the community mental health movement, states were solely responsible for the care of their mentally disturbed residents. When the movement to improve mental health services through federal assistance to the states stalled, many who suffered from serious mental illness were left without care. This lack of adequate care was made worse by a series of legal decisions that reinforced the civil rights of mental patients while requiring the states to provide adequate services. As a result of these developments, many former mental patients are now living on the streets or in squalid single-room-occupancy hotels. While a second generation of psychoactive drugs promised to stabilize former patients, adverse side effects made drugs unpopular among patients. During the past three decades, the proliferation of psychoactive drugs resulted in several scandals and calls to regulate the industry more rigorously. In 1996, mental health advocates were encouraged by passage of the Mental Health Parity Act, which mandated that employers offer employees mental health care benefits that were comparable to physical health care benefits. Despite this incremental reform, problems associated with chronic mental illness, as well as with alcohol and drug abuse, have become more prevalent. The lack of adequate support for substance abuse prevention and treatment efforts, coupled with the economic collapse of inner-city neighborhoods, has left many urban areas subject to unprecedented levels of street violence and social deterioration.

Despite the nation's abysmal record in mental health and substance abuse, American psychiatry largely determined the methods for intervening in mental disorders, primarily through the *Diagnostic and Statistical Manual (DSM)*, a publication of the American Psychiatric Association. Although the reliability of the *DSM* has been challenged frequently, it remains a system for classifying emotional disorders, if only because of the absence of more valid competitor. As shown in Table 13.1, the lifetime prevalence of psychiatric disorders varies significantly from country to country.

It is notable that among these nations, the United States not only leads with respect to types of disorders but their comorbidity as well.

Mental Health Reform

Begun early in the twentieth century, the National Association for Mental Health (NAMH) pioneered efforts to provide social support and treatment for the mentally ill. NAMH was frequently critical of the custodial institutions operated by state governments. For instance, during the Progressive Era, the eugenics movement contributed to the institutional abuses that were condemned by NAMH. Proponents of eugenics argued that mentally impaired patients often suffered from hereditary deficiencies that should be prevented by sterilization. Adherents of eugenics were less concerned about the civil rights of individual mental patients than they were about the future of civilization—the fact that some patients might object was merely an inconvenience. In such instances, eugenicists obtained court permission to sterilize patients without their consent. Approved by the Supreme Court in the 1927 case *Buck v. Bell*,

TABLE 13.1 Percentage Prevalence of Psychiatric Disorders

Lifetime estimates	Brazil	Canada	Germany	Mexico	Netherlands	Turkey	USA
Any anxiety	17.4	21.3	9.8	5.6	20.1	7.4	25.0
Any mood	15.5	10.2	17.1	9.2	18.9	7.3	19.4
Any substance	16.1	19.7	21.5	9.6	18.7	0.0	28.2
Any disorder	36.3	37.5	38.4	20.2	40.9	12.2	48.6
One disorder	21.2	21.2	25.5	14.8	23.0	7.9	21.3
Two disorders	8.8	9.3	8.1	4.0	9.3	3.0	13.1
Three disorders +	6.3	7.0	4.8	1.4	8.6	1.3	14.3

Source: WHO International Consortium in Psychiatric Epidemiology, "Cross-National Comparisons of the Prevalences and Correlates of Mental Disorders," Bulletin of the World Health Organization, 2000, 78(4): 417.

in which the critical determination of Carrie Buck's social degeneracy was made by a social worker, 65,000 Americans would ultimately be sterilized involuntarily.[1] Many patients, of course, lacked the mental capacity to comprehend sterilization and had no idea that the surgical procedures to which they were subjected would terminate their ability to reproduce.

The issue of mental health attracted even wider public attention during World War II, when approximately one in every four draftees was rejected for military service because of psychiatric or neurological problems.[2] In response to public outcry about mental health problems immediately after the war, Congress passed the Mental Health Act of 1946, which established the National Institute of Mental Health (NIMH). Accompanying the Mental Health Act was an appropriation for an exhaustive examination of the mental health needs of the nation. In 1961, NIMH released *Action for Mental Health,* a report that called for an ambitious national effort to modernize the U.S. system of psychiatric care.[3]

Action for Mental Health was a utopian vision of mental health care, the idealism of which coincided perfectly with a set of extraordinarily propitious circumstances. First, the postwar economy was booming, and, with cutbacks in military expenditures, a surplus existed that could be tapped for domestic programs. Second, a new generation of drugs—psychotropic medications—showed promise of being able to stabilize severely psychotic patients who before had been unmanageable. Third, literature was emerging that was critical of the "total institution" concept of the state hospital and implied that non-institutional—and, presumably, community—care was better. Finally, because of his experience with mental retardation as a family problem, a sister who was seriously impaired after a lobotomy, former president John F. Kennedy was supportive of programs that promised to improve mental health care.[4]

These political and social circumstances did not go unnoticed by Dr. Robert H. Felix, a physician who had grown up with the Menninger family in Kansas and had developed a sharp critique of the state mental hospital as an institution for the care of emotionally disturbed patients. Felix was later to become director of NIMH. A primary architect of the community mental health movement, Felix was able to draw on his extensive experience in the Mental Hygiene Division of the U.S. Public Health Service as well as on the breadth of professional and political contacts that three decades of public service afforded.[5] Felix's objective was as simple as it was radical. Through the community mental health movement, Felix would use federal legislation to reform the archaic state mental hospitals. The laws that enabled NIMH to reform mental health care were the Community Mental Health Centers Acts of 1963 and 1965.

The Community Mental Health Centers Acts

Under the propitious circumstances of the postwar era, the first Community Mental Health Centers (CMHC) Act was passed by Congress and signed by President Kennedy on October 31, 1963. The enactment of CMHC legislation was not, however, without obstacles. To allay the American Medical Association's fears that the act represented socialized medicine, the CMHC Act of 1963 appropriated funds only for construction purposes. It was not until 1965, when the AMA was reeling from governmental proposals to institute federal health care programs for the aged and the poor, that funds were authorized for staffing CMHCs. Advocates of the CMHC Acts of 1963 and 1965 maintained that a constant target of the legislation was "to eliminate, within the next generation, the state mental hospital, as it then existed." The strategy of the mental health leadership and its allies was to "de-monopolize" the state role in the provision of mental health services and to attempt to establish a triad of federal, state, and local support for mental health services. At this time, federal bureaucrats planned to blanket the whole country with comprehensive community mental health services. Their intention was not to federalize the total program through its financing, but to obtain a degree of control through the resulting federal regulations and standards.[6]

The philosophical basis for transferring mental health care from the state hospital to the community was borrowed from public health, which had developed the concept of prevention. Proponents of community mental health presumed that services provided in the community would be superior to the warehousing of patients in state institutions. According to the CMHC Acts, the United States was to be divided into catchment areas, each with a population of 75,000 to 200,000 persons.[7] Eventually, NIMH planned a CMHC for each catchment area, some 2,000 in all.[8]

Programmatically, each CMHC was to provide all essential psychiatric services to the catchment area: inpatient hospitalization, partial hospitalization, outpatient services, 24-hour emergency services, and consultation and education for other service providers in the community. Soon after initial passage of the CMHC Act, child mental health as well as drug abuse and alcoholism services were added to the array of services provided. To assure that patients were not lost between programs within the CMHC network, case management was included, whereby every case was assigned to one professional who monitored the patient's progress throughout treatment. Financially, NIMH provided funding to disadvantaged catchment areas through matching grants over an eight-year cycle. At the end of the cycle, the catchment area was supposed to assume financial responsibility for the CMHC.[9] With this framework, mental health reformers believed that the CMHC was an effective alternative to the state hospital.

Deinstitutionalization

Enthusiasm for community mental health reform ebbed when a series of circumstances that were beyond the control of the CMHC architects began to subvert the movement. By the end of Carter's presidency, 691 CMHCs received federal assistance. With the Omnibus Budget and Reconciliation Act of 1981, however, the Reagan administration collapsed all mental health funding into a block grant available to states for any mental health services they deemed fundable. As a result, the designation of CMHCs for direct receipt of federal funds ceased in 1981.[10]

In the meantime, however, many states had planned to shift responsibility for the mentally ill to the CMHCs. In fact, the community mental health movement had proved a timely blessing for officials in states where the maintenance of archaic state hospitals was an increasing economic burden. As states discharged patients from state institutions, they realized immediate savings. By the end of the 1990s, 93 percent of the state psychiatric beds that had existed in 1955 were lost to deinstitutionalization.[11]

Deinstitutionalization was further confounded by a series of judicial decisions in the mid-1970s that enhanced the civil rights of mental patients while at the same time requiring states to provide them with treatment. In *Wyatt v. Stickney*, Alabama

District Court judge Frank Johnson ruled that the state of Alabama was obliged to provide treatment to patients in state hospitals, a judgment with which the state subsequently failed to comply. Shortly thereafter, in *Donaldson v. O'Connor*, the Supreme Court determined that "the state could not continue to confine a mentally ill person who was not dangerous to himself or others, who was not being treated, and who could survive outside the hospital." Finally, in *Halderman v. Pennhurst*, the Third District Court established that institutionalized patients deserved treatment in the "least restrictive alternative."

As a group, these rulings had a profound effect on institutional care for patients with mental impairments. Only persons dangerous to themselves or others could be hospitalized involuntarily. For those hospitalized, involuntarily or otherwise, states were obliged to provide adequate treatment in the manner that was least restrictive to the patient. These decisions promised to be enormously costly to state officials who were trying to curb mental health expenditures. To comply with the court decisions, states would have to pump millions of dollars into the renovation of institutions that had been slated for closure. The solution, in many instances, was to use a narrow interpretation of *Donaldson* to keep emotionally disturbed people out of state institutions. In other words, judicial decisions, coupled with the fiscal concerns of state officials, provided a convoluted logic that served to justify first emptying state hospitals of seriously disturbed patients and then requiring the manifestation of life-threatening behavior for their rehospitalization. If people were not hospitalized in the first place, the states bore no obligation to provide the adequate, but expensive, treatment demanded by *Wyatt*. The criteria for hospitalization specified the most serious self-destructive behaviors; once admitted, however, patients were stabilized as quickly as possible and then discharged. As a result, those in greatest need of mental health services—patients who were seriously mentally ill—were often denied the intensive care they needed. The consequences for the mentally ill were substantial. In his interpretation of the legal decisions influencing mental health services, Alan Stone, a psychiatrist and a professor at Harvard Law School, observed that the true symbol of the Supreme Court *Donaldson* decision was a bag lady.[12] Thus, legal decisions favoring the mentally ill often proved illusory; in the name of enhancing the human rights of people with mental illness—but with no corresponding improvement in services—they offered those people nothing more than the right to be insane.[13]

The Revolving Door

The shortfall of the community mental health movement, states' transfers of patients from mental hospitals, judicial decisions assuring patients of their civil rights, and the deinstitutionalization movement, all combined to leave tens of thousands of former mental patients adrift. Although some former mental hospital patients were able to deal with community agencies in order to obtain mental health care, many of the seriously mentally ill were left to themselves.[14] By the late 1970s some 40,000 poor, chronically ill mental patients had been "dumped" in New York City. The 7,000 on the Upper West Side of Manhattan represented "the greatest concentration of deinstitutionalized mental patients in the United States."[15] Former patients presented such problems, that special units of nursing homes were designated for them. In 2002, the *New York Times* reported that "hundreds of patients released from state psychiatric hospitals in New York in recent years are being locked away on isolated floors of nursing homes, where they are barred from going outside on their own, have almost no contact with others and have little ability to contest their confinement."[16] Of the 5,000 residents of homes, 946 had died between 1995 and 2000: "some residents died roasting in their rooms during heat waves. Others threw themselves from rooftops, making up some of at least 14 suicides in that . . . period. Still more, lacking the most basic care, succumbed to routinely treatable ailments, from burst appendices to seizures."[17] By authorizing special homes for mental patients, state officials had effectively replaced large state institutions with a dispersed network of small private ones.

New York was not alone in routinizing the neglect of those who had resided in institutions. In 1999, Katherine Boo investigated the care of residents with mental retardation who lived in group homes in the District of Columbia. During the 1990s, 350 incidents of theft, abuse, neglect, and molestation of residents had been reported, yet not a single fine had been levied against the companies that operated the group homes. Worse, during the late 1990s, 53 residents had died in incidents related to substandard care; of these, three received only a cursory review by the District or the federal government.[18] Eventually, it was discovered that the deaths of 116 group home residents with mental retardation had never been investigated, resulting in a series of lawsuits by families of the residents.[19] For her muckraking series on the subject, Boo was awarded a Pulitzer Prize.

Meanwhile, resources for state mental hospitals dwindled, leaving patient care uncertain. In an attempt to manage patients more cost-effectively, state mental institutions relied more heavily on

The high incidence of readmissions for psychiatric hospital patients is a chronic problem in mental health care.

Source: Jim Noelker/The Image Works

psychoactive medication, sometimes with disastrous consequences. A nationwide review of deaths attributed to psychoactive medication revealed that 142 psychiatric patients had died between 1988 and 1998 as a result of institutional abuses; 33 percent of the deaths were attributed to asphyxiation and 26 percent to cardiac problems. More than one-fourth of the patients who died were children.[20]

The Psychopharmacological Scandal

As state hospitals converted from long-term custodial care to short-term patient stabilization, psychotropic medication became a routine form of treatment. But the psychopharmacological revolution, though congruent with the relatively orderly march toward deinstitutionalization in the late 1960s, actually exacerbated the psychiatric chaos of two decades later. Shown to stabilize psychotic patients until interpersonal treatment methods could be employed, the major tranquilizers—Prolixin, Thorazine, Haldol, and Stelazine, to name a few—seemed clinically indicated within the controlled environment of the hospital. In a community setting, however, psychotropic medication became problematic. Once stabilized on major tranquilizers, patients frequently found the side effects of the medication—dry mouth, nervousness, torpor, lactation in women, and impotence in men—unacceptable and stopped taking the medication.

Yet, without medication such patients frequently decompensated, and without the regular supervision of psychiatric personnel, patients disappeared into inner-city ghettos or rural backwaters, adding to an already growing homeless population. A Housing and Urban Development (HUD) census of the homeless revealed that 62 percent had problems with alcohol abuse, 58 percent with drugs, and 57 percent with mental health.[21]

In the absence of mental health care, increasingly desperate former mental hospital patients turned to petty crime to gain income, thus clogging local courts. Commenting on the surge in arrests of the mentally ill, one mental health worker became exasperated: "These people are forced to commit crimes to come to the attention of the police and get help."[22] By 2000, the Justice Department reported that 283,800, or 16 percent, of inmates in local and state correctional facilities suffered from mental disorders[23] and another 550,000 were on parole.[24]

In 2003, Human Rights Watch reported that U.S. prisons contained three times more psychiatric patients than mental hospitals. This institutional mismatch had come to the point that the largest psychiatric facility in the nation was the Los Angeles County Jail which held 3,400 mentally ill inmates; second was New York's Rikers Island with 3,000 mentally ill inmates.[25]

As a result, reformers altered judicial policy by creating special courts to deal with nonviolent offenders who had mental disorders. Paralleling special drug courts that had emerged in several metropolitan areas during the 1990s to contend with nonviolent drug abusers, the mental health court concept was advocated by the National Alliance on Mental Illness (NAMI) as well as the National Mental Health Association.[26] In 2000, Congress passed America's Law Enforcement and Mental Health Project Act. The Mental Health Courts Grant Program subsequently supported the creation of 23 mental health courts in 2002 and 14 more in 2003. By the end of 2004, a consortium of mental health advocacy organizations reported that 99 mental health courts were operating.[27] Federal funding lagged behind the initiative, however; for 2012, only $4.4 million in federal funds was available for special courts dealing with mental health and substance abuse problems.[28]

Meanwhile, a second generation of psychoactive medication was being aggressively marketed to the middle class by the pharmaceutical industry. Psychopharmacologists viewed the brain as the focus of their work, discerning those chemicals that altered mood and temperament, testing dosages of new preparations, and evaluating their effects on a larger array of disorders. The Food and Drug Administration validated the biomedical model by approving psychoactive medications through Randomized Clinical Trials (RCTs) that had been conducted by the drug companies.

By century's end, biomedical psychiatry might have been wedded to talk therapy of psychoanalysts, had not managed care intruded into American health care. Health care inflation, increasing by double digits prompted reformers to advocate for greater efficiencies at the same time focusing on prevention of illness, virtues that were evident in health maintenance organizations which spread across the nation subscribing tens of millions of members. The possibility of a psychiatric ideal, wedding psychopharmacology with psychoanalysis, was precluded as health insurance companies pared reimbursements to hospitals and clinics, cutting the number of patient sessions that would be paid for as well as their value, in process reducing the revenue of mental health providers. Biomedical psychiatrists who could demonstrate relatively quick patient improvements benefitted from a harsh regime of accountability, compared to psychoanalysts whose method was more protracted. As cost considerations came to dominate American health care, biomedical psychiatrists were encouraged to abbreviate their sessions further, effectively minimizing talking therapy in favor of dispensing medication.[29] The reorganization of psychiatry by managed care instructed mental health professionals that the real money was in short-term psychopharmacology. This, of course, didn't prohibit patients from seeking care from psychoanalysts, but they would have to pay out of pocket. Since only a small slice of mental patients had such resources, mainstream psychiatry became biomedical almost exclusively, the 15-minute medication session dominating the field.

The ascendance of the biomedical model was facilitated by the publication in 1980 of the *DSM III*, which replaced the ambiguous Freudian descriptions of 83 mental disorders of the previous edition with a behavioral classification system of 265 diagnoses. Each diagnosis listed behaviors which, if added in sufficient numbers, would justify a psychiatric label. As critics would contend, this is medicine determined not by etiology, but by committee. "Not only did the *DSM* become the bible of psychiatry, but like the real Bible, it depended a lot on something akin to revelation," observed Marcia Angell, former editor of *The New England Journal of Medicine*, "There are no citations of scientific studies to support its decisions."[30] By 1994, the *DSM IV* had expanded to 297 disorders; at 886 pages the "manual" was so large that the American Psychiatric Association (APA) and the National Institute of Mental Health (NIMH) convened a group assigned to simplify the *DSM V* through a numerical system that also included new evidence from neurobiology and genetics, a "paradigm shift." When it was learned that the drafting group had been sworn to secrecy about its work, a complaint by Dr. Robert Spitzer, who was largely responsible for earlier versions of the *DSM,* resulted in the termination of the venture. Spitzer's critique of a broadening of categories in the *DSM V* was sharp: the consequence "would be a wholesale imperial medicalization of normality that will trivialize mental disorder and lead to

a deluge of unneeded medication treatment—a bonanza for the pharmaceutical industry but at a huge cost to the new false positive 'patients' caught in the excessively wide DSM-V net."[31] Unfazed, the APA published the *DSM IV-TR* (text revised) in 2000, including 365 diagnoses.[32]

By then, American psychiatry had become a virtual subsidiary of the drug companies, Big Pharma. In 1987, Eli Lilly introduced the first blockbuster psychoactive drug, Prozac, and received approval by the FDA in 1994 to market the drug for depression and bulimia in 1996, resulting in annual sales of $2.6 billion, one-fourth of the firm's revenues. [33] An SSRI (selective serotonin reuptake inhibitor), Prozac proved so successful that similar antidepressants, such as Paxil, Zoloft, and Celexa were soon introduced. In approving new drugs, the FDA only requires two clinical trials demonstrating a drug's efficacy; however, the approval process was fraught with deceit. Upon discovering that 40 percent of the clinical trials for SSRIs had been withheld from public view, psychologist Irving Kirsch used the Freedom of Information Act to obtain the results of all of the clinical trials for antidepressants, which revealed that "82 percent of the response to medication had also been produced by a simple inert placebo," an almost insignificant difference of two points on the 51-point Hamilton depression scale, insignificant for clinical purposes."[34]

Even more alarming is the failure of the psychopharmacological industry to demonstrate the chemical process by which SSRIs actually worked, since biomedical research failed to show the causal effect. The "chemical imbalance" theory, a simplification holding that deficiencies of chemicals in the brain cause diagnosable disorders, is fundamental to antidepressants. Absent the causal process, the SSRIs enjoy the same status of aspirin, a remedy for symptom management. As behavioral pediatrician Lawrence Diller observes, "Aspirin fixes headaches, yet no one claims that headache sufferers have an 'aspirin deficiency'"[35]

All this would be an exercise in psychopharmacological frivolity, except for the quite real side effects attributed to SSRIs. "Symptoms of serotonin syndrome include restlessness, hallucinations, loss of coordination, a racing heart, rapid changes in blood pressure, fever, nausea, vomiting, and diarrhea," noted Kirsch, "SSRIs can provoke an agitated restless state called akathisia, which some people describe as feeling like jumping out of their skin. It is often in this state that people on SSRIs become violent and aggressive towards themselves and others"[36] In the absence of confirmatory research, the biomedical model of psychiatry was sold to the public by Big Pharma in collaboration with the APA. In order to expedite marketing, drug companies went beyond the usual method, relying on detail reps, by hiring psychiatrists to promote their products. The employment of "hired guns" by drug companies became systematized through "key opinion leaders," KOLs, many from prestigious academic centers[37]. Among the most celebrated was Dr. Joseph Biederman at Massachusetts General Hospital who, along with Timothy Wilens and Thomas Spencer, raked in $4.2 million over seven years from drug companies, but reported only a fraction of that to their universities. Biederman and Wilens were later reprimanded for their conduct. The self-serving circle between psychiatry and the psychopharmacological industry was closed in more pedestrian ways: 56 percent of the drafters of the *DSM V* reported significant income from drug companies.[38] Some critics of the psychiatric sell-out were less charitable: psychiatrist E. Fuller Torrey suggested that "the present system is approaching a high-class form of prostitution."[39]

Psychiatrists failing to get the message directly from colleagues would likely find the evidence of drug efficacy in research studies published in professional journals. A 1999 lawsuit against Pfizer revealed that the company had hired Current Medical Directions (CMD) to write articles favorable to its blockbuster drug, Zoloft. CMD paid ghostwriters to draft articles, located psychiatrists to sign them, then published the pieces in prestigious journals, such as the *American Journal of Psychiatry* and the *Journal of the American Medical Association*. Ultimately, the CMD articles comprised a majority of all research on Zoloft published between 1998 and 2000. As Carlat observed, "for at least one antidepressant, the bulk of medical literature was literally written by the drug company that manufactured the drug."[40]

Covering all bases, the psychopharmacological industry also made substantial contributions to organizations advocating for the mentally ill. Organizations, such as the National Alliance on Mental Illness (NAMI), not only appreciated philanthropy from drug companies because it addressed chronic budget shortfalls but also because the biomedical model promised to destigmatize mental disorders. With the biomedical model

ascendant early in the 1990s, NAMI joined with NIMH to educate the public about how chemical imbalances caused mental disorders. Between 1993 and 1996, eighteen drug companies contributed $11.7 million to NAMI. In 2009 alone, one company, Eli Lilly, contributed $551,000 to NAMI, $465,000 to the National Mental Health Association, $130,000 to an ADHD advocacy organization, and $69,250 to a suicide prevention organization.[41] In exchange for corporate beneficence, mental health advocacy organizations validated an explanation for mental disorders that could be corrected by medication, just like other diseases, in the process providing moral support to the psychopharmacological industry.

If American psychiatry has become captive to the biomedical model, other countries have flirted with the idea only to reject it. Whitaker cites a region of Finland, western Lapland, which has adopted an alternative to psychopharmacology in caring for the seriously mentally ill. Five years after receiving "open dialogue therapy," 73 percent of 75 patients (30 schizophrenics) were working or in school while only 20 percent were on disability. Whitaker reports that "Only two or three new cases of schizophrenia appear each year in western Lapland, a 90 percent drop since the early 1990s."[42]

Children's Mental Health

Reductions in federal funding, a cut of $29 million for 2013, for children's mental health occur at a time when psychiatric care for children is at a crisis point. The FDA does not require RTCs for medication unless it is specifically intended for children, and no clinical trials are targeted at minority children. As a result, a common practice in psychiatry is to prescribe medication "off-label" for children; in other words, psychoactive drugs approved for adults are often prescribed for children at lower doses. Researchers have long debated the value of Ritalin, which is often prescribed for children with Attention Deficit Hyperactivity Disorder (ADHD), for example.[43] More recently, atypical antipsychotics, such as Risperdal, have been prescribed for ADHD, a problem not only for which the medication was not approved, but which caused side effects, such as weight gain and permanent muscular tics.[44] Indeed, the adverse effects of SSRIs when prescribed off-label to children were associated with suicides at twice the number in the control group, resulting in "a black box" warning for Celexa, an SSRI produced by Forest Pharmaceuticals, a drug company fined $313 million by the Justice Department in 2010 for irresponsible off-label marketing to children.[45] By 2008, 60 percent of antipsychotic medication was prescribed "off-label" often to children for such problems as anxiety, sleep disorders, ADHD, and behavioral problems.[46]

Off-label prescriptions for children came under the scrutiny of child welfare advocates when it became evident that foster children were being administered high doses of psychoactive medication. A study of children on Medicaid revealed that foster children were often prescribed powerful antipsychotics such as Risperdal, Seroquel, and Zyprexa, drugs that were intended to treat schizophrenia.[47] Subsequently, the Government Accountability Office conducted a study of foster children in five states and found that four times as many foster children received antipsychotic medications compared to non-foster children. Not only were foster children prescribed higher doses, but they also received multiple prescriptions. In some cases, children under age 1 received antipsychotic medication.[48]

Meanwhile researchers documented an 80 percent increase in autism during the previous decade.[49] Increasing prevalence of autism raised questions about diagnosis, and planners for the *DSM V* suggested an umbrella classification, Autism spectrum disorder that incorporated classic autism, Asperger syndrome, and pervasive developmental disorder not otherwise specified.[50] Exactly how such ambiguous developmental disorders among children will be addressed in the Affordable Care Act remains to be seen.

Mental Health and Substance Abuse Funding

The Substance Abuse and Mental Health Services Administration (SAMHSA) of the Department of Health and Human Services oversees the federal Alcohol, Drug Abuse, and Mental Health block grants. Since 1981, all mental health expenditures have been in block grants to states. By using a block grant strategy, the federal government removed the power from federal agencies and transferred it to the individual states. Since the creation of mental health block grants, federal funding for mental health and substance abuse services has increased to $3.4 billion for 2013, $142 million less than

for 2012.[51] It is important to recognize how funding has shifted during the past two decades: While private funding for mental health services had diminished, state and local funding has imploded, leaving Medicaid and Medicare primary sources of revenues. Substance abuse services, on the other hand, continue to rely heavily on state and local revenues (see Tables 13.2 and 13.3).

TABLE 13.2 Distribution of Mental Health Expenditures, %

Source	1986	2003	2006	2014
Private				
Out of pocket	18	14	14	12
Private insurance	21	24	24	26
Other private	7	3	4	3
Public				
Medicare	6	7	11	11
Medicaid	16	26	24	27
Other federal	6	4	3	1
Other state & local	26	21	20	16

Source: "Projections of National Expenditures for Mental Health Services and Substance Abuse Services, 2000–2014," U.S. Department of Health and Human Services, Substance Abuse and Mental Health Services Administration, Washington, DC: 2008, p. 21.

TABLE 13.3 Distribution of Substance Abuse Expenditures among Payers, %

Source	1986	2003	2008	2014
Private				
Out of pocket	14	8	8	6
Private insurance	30	10	9	7
Other private	6	5	5	4
Public				
Medicare	4	4	4	5
Medicaid	10	18	18	20
Other federal	7	15	14	14
Other state & local	29	40	42	45

Source: "Projections of National Expenditures for Mental Health and Substance Abuse Services, 2000–2014," U.S. Department of Health and Human Services, Substance Abuse and Mental Health Services Administration, Washington, DC, 2008, p. 32.

Static funding has prompted innovation in service delivery. An example of how a capitation method of payment could be used in mental health service delivery was the integrated mental health (IMH) concept pioneered in New York State and Philadelphia. Capitated mental health care under IMH would have three major features: First, current categorical grants—Medicaid, Supplemental Security Income, Food Stamp Program, local funding—would be aggregated into a common fund from which capitation "premiums" would be paid. Second, a nonprofit planning and coordination agency would be established to oversee mental health care and in so doing negotiate contracts with providers, monitor performance, and evolve innovative programs. Third, particularly high-usage clients would be targeted for provision of less costly services in order to generate surpluses for less-intensive services.[52]

Static funding provided the rationale for subsidizing private treatment innovations in substance abuse, such as Phoenix House. Established in 1967, Phoenix House has not only expanded to over 120 locations across the country, but has introduced electronic medical records in compliance with the Affordable Care Act. Of particular interest to Phoenix House has been PTSD experienced by military veterans. Because addictive substances evolve over time, Phoenix House has been diligent about tracking them.[53]

Parity for Mental Health Care

In 1996, Congress delighted mental health advocates by agreeing on legislation establishing parity for mental health care. Effective January 1, 1998, employers with more than 50 employees who offer any health insurance coverage must include mental health benefits that are comparable to physical health benefits.[54] The consequences of legislatively mandating parity in mental health coverage were immediately disputed. Opponents warned of significant increases in health insurance premiums and the likelihood that employers would eliminate mental health coverage in order to dodge the parity mandate.[55] Defenders, on the other hand, minimized the implications for premium increases, noting that mental illness was, for the first time, being interpreted as a physiological disorder.

An evaluation of the Mental Health Parity Act released by the General Accounting Office in May 2000 tempered the enthusiasm of mental health advocates. Although 86 percent of employers surveyed were in compliance with the legislation, most—87 percent—had altered employee benefits so that mental health benefits were more restrictive. Significantly, only 3 percent reported that compliance had resulted in increased costs and none had dropped mental health coverage altogether in response to mandated mental health parity.[56] Achieving parity in mental health may have been an important development in social policy, but its provisions were quite modest. Parity was predicated on employment so it did nothing for those who were not in the labor market; moreover, because it applied only to employers with more than 50 workers, its provisions were evaded by small employers. Thus, parity did little for those with mental illness who were not working, and even less for those hired by small businesses.

Parity for mental health care may have marked the end of the downsizing of mental health care, yet much remained to be done. Providing essential mental health services for poor people who evidence severe psychological disorganization remains a primary challenge to mental health advocates, since resources remained inadequate for the task at hand. With the passage of the Affordable Care Act, mental health parity loomed once again as an issue in health care policy. In formulating rules for mental health care, the Obama administration argued for equality of reimbursement, which antagonized health insurers who understood the Mental Health Parity Act as only assuring equal access to services. Mental health advocates, on the other hand, contended that failure to provide adequate payment for care left many of those with health insurance unable to find a provider.[57]

Post-Traumatic Stress Disorder

A decade of war in Iraq and Afghanistan resulted in serious mental health problems among returning veterans. Unlike the Vietnam conflict, the prevalence of post-traumatic stress disorder (PTSD) was significantly higher,[58] although this was disputed by psychiatrist Sally Satel who contended that "a culture of trauma has blossomed," largely attributable to bonuses for veterans with PTSD.[59] More disturbing, the incidence of suicide among members of the uniformed services, particularly the Army, had increased, peaking at 164 in 2011.[60] Mental health

TABLE 13.4 Mental Health Disorders among Returning Soldiers

Type of Disorder		Return from Iraq (%)	Three to six months later (%)
Interpersonal conflict	Active duty	3.5	14
	Reserves	4.2	21.1
Post-traumatic stress disorder	Active duty	11.8	16.7
	Reserves	12.7	24.5
Depression	Active duty	4.7	10.3
	Reserves	3.8	13
Overall mental health disorder	Active duty	17	27.1
	Reserves	17.5	35.5

Source: Ann Scott Tyson, "Troops' Mental Distress Tracked," *Washington Post* (November 17, 2007), p. A3.

analysts reached an alarming conclusion: Not only were mental health disorders among returning soldiers delayed, but they were more prevalent among reservists (Table 13.4). Increases in war trauma coincided with loss of mental health personnel within the uniformed services, about 10 percent between 2003 and 2006. In response, Congress authorized $600 million for enhanced mental health services for veterans.[61] To prevent PTSD and related disorders, military researchers introduced "battlemind debriefing and training" to a random sample of platoons, then evaluated soldiers post-deployment. Soldiers who had participated in "battlemind" showed lower incidence of PTSD, depression, and sleep disorders than those in the control group.[62]

While mental disorders among soldiers garnered more attention, services to other populations lagged. Speaking for many civilians, Pete Earley, an award-winning author whose son was diagnosed with mental illness, advocated for better inpatient care: "What is missing in our system today are modern, long-term treatment facilities where the chronically mentally-ill can receive good medical attention and, if necessary, can live safely until they can be moved to less restrictive facilities."[63] Similarly, Andrew Solomon called for a network of university-based research centers that would study mental disorders, such as depression.[64] Building on the adoption of mental health parity, Art Levine advocated for "parity-plus," expanding mental health care through a five-part strategy: implement mental health parity, promote proven treatments for mental illness, fund patients not programs, provide early screening for children, and encourage mainstream activities such as work.[65] A half-century after the

community mental health movement, the question of mobilizing mental health advocates around a coherent, comprehensive reform remained.

Substance Abuse

Mental health services are often associated with substance abuse. Human service professionals in direct services are familiar with clients who have chosen to anesthetize themselves from stress or misery with alcohol, tobacco, and other substances. Individuals' psychological problems are of course compounded by reliance on such substances, and these problems not only affect the families of substance abusers but also become more severe when addiction is manifested. Ordinarily, addiction is associated with alcohol and drugs, and less often with tobacco. Substance abuse has become an important area of public policy, not only because of the necessity for appropriations for treatment programs but also because of the enormous costs that substance abuse extracts from society. As these costs have escalated, substance abuse policy has attained a higher profile in domestic affairs.

The interaction of emotional difficulties, alcoholism, and substance abuse is reflected in social welfare policy and has been institutionalized at SAMHSA. The consolidation of categorical grants into a federal block grant program under SAMHSA reflected the preference of many human service professionals for preventive programs that apply generically to all forms of substance abuse. What is the logic in having separate preventive programs for tobacco, alcohol, and illegal drugs when effective prevention programs can be developed for all of them?

Alcohol Abuse

Americans steadily increased their consumption of alcohol from the end of World War II until the 1980s, when drinking began to decrease. By 2013, average per capita consumption was a little more than 2.3 gallons of wine, 1.5 gallons of spirits, and 20.7 gallons of beer a year.[66] However, that amount was not evenly distributed throughout the population. One-third of the adult population abstains from alcohol consumption, one-third of people who do drink consider their consumption to be light, and the remaining third are considered moderate to heavy drinkers. The 2006 National Survey on Drug Use and Health revealed that 57 million Americans were binge drinkers on occasion and that 17 million were heavy drinkers.[67] These statistics are directly related to serious social problems. Forty-eight percent of all convicted criminals used alcohol just before committing a crime, and 64 percent of offenses against public order are alcohol related.[68] Yet, substance abuse services are often not available for drinkers who are subsequently incarcerated. Substance abuse services were available at 93.8 percent of federal correctional facilities but at only 60.3 percent of state prisons, 33.5 percent of jails, and 36.6 percent of juvenile facilities.[69] Perhaps the most significant adverse consequence of alcohol consumption is highway accidents. The tragic death toll on U.S. highways provoked not only the establishment of Mothers Against Drunk Driving (MADD) but also the demands for stronger penalties for drunk drivers and public education campaigns to dissuade people from drinking while driving. This combination of motivators seemed to have a positive effect: Between 1982 and 1986, the number of inebriated drivers involved in fatal accidents dropped significantly. By 2006, the percentage of people aged 12 and over who drove under the influence dropped to 12.4 percent, down from 14.2 percent in 2002.[70]

Among the most pernicious effects of alcohol consumption is fetal alcohol syndrome (FAS), a physiological and mental deformation in infants caused by their mothers' ingestion of alcohol during pregnancy. The National Institutes of Health estimated in 1990 that the incidence of FAS among children of heavy-drinking women was as high as 25 per 1,000 births, and that the annual cost of coping with the disorder was almost one-third of a billion dollars.[71] In 2012, the Pine Ridge Reservation sued several American brewing companies which distributed beer at outlets in Whiteclay,

Nebraska, adjacent to the reservation in order to reduce incidents of FAS, drunk driving fatalities, and alcohol related homicides.[72]

Drug Abuse

By contrast with alcohol abuse, the prevalence of drug abuse is more difficult to ascertain because the use of controlled substances—the focus of drug abuse—is illegal. It appears that general drug abuse has begun to decline after peaking during the 1979–1980 period. In 2006, almost 20.4 million Americans reported use of illicit drugs, a significant decrease from the 25 million abusers estimated in 1979 (see Table 13.5). Among younger Americans aged 12 to 17, drug abuse has been declining (from 11.6 percent in 2002 to 9.8 percent in 2006); drug abuse by young adults aged 18 to 25 remained static (from 20.2 percent in 2002 to 19.8 percent in 2006).

Types of illegal substances vary considerably. Next to marijuana, cocaine is the most prevalent illicit drug, accounting for 1.5 million users; heroin is far less prevalent with 323,000 addicts.[73] Even if heroin is less prevalent, it remains a major problem if only because of the health problems associated with its use: As many as 25 percent of people who contract AIDS in this country are intravenous drug users (IDUs).[74] A haunting scenario takes shape: IDUs can no longer be thought of solely as tortured souls in the slow process of self-destruction; they have become transmitters of an epidemic that promises to be as costly as it is deadly.

The federal response to illicit drug use has been twofold, involving both interdicting the supply of illegal substances and reducing the demand

TABLE 13.5 Types of Illegal Substances

Type of Substance	Millions of Users
Illicit drugs	22.6
Marijuana	17.4
Psychotherapeutics	7.0
Cocaine	1.5
Hallucinogens	1.2
Inhalants	0.7
Heroin	0.2

Source: http://www.samhsa.gov/data/NSDUH/2k10NSDUH/2k10Results.htm

TABLE 13.6 Location of Substance Abuse Treatment

Location	Numbers (thousands)
Self-help group	2,334
Outpatient rehabilitation	1,689
Outpatient mental health center	999
Inpatient rehabilitation	986
Hospital inpatient	731
Private doctor's office	653
Emergency room	467
Jail or prison	342

Source: http://www.samhsa.gov/data/NSDUH/2k10NSDUH/
2k10Results.htm

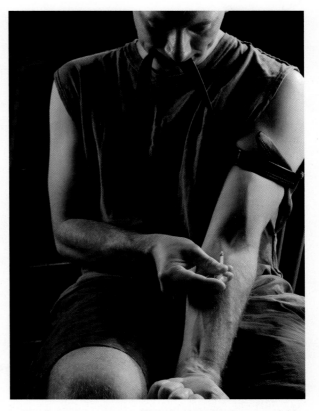

The federal response to illicit drug use has been twofold: cutting off the supply of illegal substances and reducing the demand through treatment and public education.

Source: ejwhite/shutterstock

through treatment and public education. Government strategies have oscillated wildly between the interdiction and prevention approaches. Before Ronald Reagan came to power, federal policy emphasized treatment and public education, assuming that these strategies would diminish demand. During the early 1970s, for example, two-thirds of federal appropriations for drug abuse were for treatment and education. A decade later, however, supply interdiction had superseded demand reduction as the prime strategy, consuming 80 percent of federal drug funds. Illegal drug use is considered in greater detail in Chapter 14.

In the absence of major prevention initiatives, intervention strategies focus on treatment (Table 13.6). Generally, employees with generous health insurance have been able to gain ready admission to drug abuse treatment programs. The poor, by contrast, have found treatment available irregularly, often through self-help groups. Treatment eludes large numbers of substance abusers. In 2006, over one million youth aged 12 to 17 would have received substance abuse treatment had it been available.[75]

Although treatment lags behind demand, research continues to demonstrate the wisdom of investing in rehabilitation. Columbia University's Center on Addiction and Substance Abuse has reported that 32.3 percent of Medicaid hospitalization days were due to neonatal complications attributed to substance abuse. Cardiovascular and respiratory disorders associated with substance abuse accounted for another 31.4 percent of Medicaid hospitalization

days. Significantly, when substance abuse was noted as a secondary diagnosis, the length of hospitalization doubled.[76] A comprehensive investigation of substance abuse treatment programs in California claimed savings of $7 for every $1 dollar in program costs. "Treatment is a good investment!" affirmed the California director of alcohol and drug programs. In a 1997 review of drug use treatment, SAMHSA reported that 12 months after treatment, illicit drug use dropped significantly: 48.2 percent for users of a primary drug (e.g., marijuana), 50.8 percent for crack, 54.9 percent for cocaine, and 46.6 percent for heroin.[77] As is often the case with addiction services, the subsequent question of long-term abstinence has not been thoroughly evaluated.

Conclusion

Mental health and substance abuse policies have been complex in part because they have addressed behaviors that are not well understood. Compounding this have been major policy disputes that have made it more difficult to reach a consensus about optimal programming. Mental health care has been compromised by a fundamental disconnect in American social welfare policy: Should responsibility for the aberrant rest with the federal government or the states? Since the 1980s, mental health care has been devolved to the states; yet, the states have been unwilling to pick up the costs for an adequate array of mental health services. Moreover, the aftermath of deinstitutionalization is still evident in the prevalence of homelessness and substance abuse. Substance abuse services have been compromised by a different disconnect: Should the focus be on treatment or interdiction? Since the advent of the War on Drugs, the emphasis has been on law enforcement, resulting in underinvestment in treatment. Advocates of the mentally ill and addicts were heartened with the passage of the Mental Health Parity Act, however, further expansion of mental health and substance abuse services through the Affordable Care Act has yet to be determined.

DISCUSSION QUESTIONS

1. Click on Congress.org and identify a mental health or substance abuse policy that is of interest to you. Are the provisions of the policy adequate? What could be done to make services more effective?

2. In the early 1980s, funding for community mental health centers (CMHCs) was converted to mental health block grants. To what extent did your community develop CMHCs? What has happened to them since the 1980s? What priorities have been established through the mental health block grant system? How has this changed mental health services in your community?

3. The misuse of psychoactive medication has been implicated in several undesirable consequences. Have side effects of psychoactive medications become a significant problem among mental health patients in your community? If so, what is being done to prevent it? Are more or fewer mental patients going through the "revolving door"?

4. The effects of substance abuse on innocent people present difficult policy dilemmas for decision makers. What policies could be put in place to prevent infants being born with FAS or AIDS? How could the rights of mothers be protected? What should be the role of human service professionals in such cases?

5. Prevention and treatment of substance abuse vary from locality to locality. What has your community done to dissuade young people from substance abuse?

Have these initiatives been successful? According to what indicators?

6. What resources has your community committed to dealing with substance abuse? Have these resources been adequate? Which organizations support or oppose increasing treatment for substance abuse?

NOTES

1. Nell Painter, "When Poverty Was White," *New York Times,* March 25, 2012, p. SR4.

2. Walter Trattner, *From Poor Law to Welfare State* (New York: Free Press, 1974), p. 175.

3. Joint Commission on Mental Illness and Health, *Action for Mental Health* (New York: Basic Books, 1961).

4. David Mechanic, *Mental Health and Social Policy* (Englewood Cliffs, NJ: Prentice Hall, 1969), pp. 59–60.

5. Henry Foley, *Community Mental Health Legislation* (Lexington, MA: D. C. Heath, 1975), pp. 13–14.

6. Ibid., pp. 39–40.

7. National Institute of Mental Health, *Community Mental Health Center Program Operating Handbook* (Washington, DC: U.S. Department of Health, Education, and Welfare, 1971), pp. 2–6.

8. Foley, *Community Mental Health Legislation,* p. 126.

9. The description of CMHCs is derived from the *Community Mental Health Centers Policy and Standards Manual,* 1988; see *Community Mental Health Centers Program Operating Handbook,* 1989.

10. Bernard Bloom, *Community Mental Health* (Monterey, CA: Brooks/Cole, 1977), pp. 46–56.

11. E. Fuller Torrey and Mary Zdanowicz, "Deinstitutionalization Hasn't Worked," *Washington Post* (July 9, 1999), p. A29.

12. Alan Stone, *Law, Psychiatry, and Morality* (Washington, DC: American Psychiatry Press, 1984), pp. 116–117.

13. Jean Isaac Rael, "'Right' to Madness: A Cruel Hoax," *Los Angeles Times* (December 14, 1990), p. E5.

14. Uri Aviram, "Community Care of the Seriously Mentally Ill," *Community Mental Health Journal* 26, no. 1 (February 1990), pp. 23–31.

15. Peter Koenig, "The Problem That Can't Be Tranquilized," *New York Times Magazine,* (May 21, 1978), p. 15.

16. Clifford Levy, "Mentally Ill and Locked Up in New York Nursing Homes," *New York Times* (October 6, 2002), p. A1.

17. Clifford Levy, "For Mentally Ill, Death and Misery," *New York Times* (April 28, 2002), pp. 1, 34.

18. Katherine Boo, "Forest Haven Is Gone, But the Agony Remains," *Washington Post* (March 14, 1999); "Residents Languish; Profiteers Flourish," *Washington Post* (March 15, 1999).

19. Katherine Boo, "U.S. Probes DC Group Homes," *Washington Post* (May 4, 1999); Marcia Greene and Lena Sun, "Deaths Put DC Group Home Firm under Scrutiny," *Washington Post* (May 18, 2000).

20. Joseph Sacks, John Phillips, and Gordon Cappelletty, "Characteristics of the Homeless Mentally Disordered Population in Fresno County," *Community Mental Health Journal,* (Summer 1987), p. 114.

21. "Homeless in America: A Statistical Profile," *New York Times* (December 12, 1999), p. WK3.

22. Hector Tobar, "Mentally Ill Turn to Crime in a Painful Call for Help," *Los Angeles Times* (August 26, 1991), p. A1.

23. Edward Walsh, "16% of State, Local Inmates Found Mentally Ill," *Washington Post* (July 12, 1999), p. A6.

24. Kari Lydersen, "For Jailed Mentally Ill, a Way Out," *Washington Post* (June 28, 2000), p. A3.

25. Sally Satel, "Out of the Asylum, into the Cell," *New York Times* (November 1, 2003), p. A29.

26. "Mental Health Courts," National Mental Health Association. Retrieved October 7, 2004, from http://www.nmha.org

27. "Survey of Mental Health Courts," NAMI. Retrieved October 7, 2004, from http://nami.org

28. http://www.samhsa.gov/grants/2011/ti_11_010.aspx

29. Gardiner Harris, "Talk Doesn't Pay, so Psychiatry Turns Instead to Drug Therapy," *New York Times,* March 6, 2011, p. A1.

30. Marcia Angell, "The Illusions of Psychiatry," *New York Review of Books,* July 14, 2011, p.20.

31. Daniel Carlat, *Unhinged: The Trouble with Psychiatry* (New York: Free Press 2010), p. 65.

32. Angell, op cit., p. 20.

33. Marcia Angell, *The Truth about the Drug Companies* (New York: Random House, 2005), p 82.

34. Irving Kirsch, *The Emperor's New Drugs* (New York: Random House), p. 28.

35. Lawrence Diller, *The Last Normal Child* (Westport, CT: Praeger, 2006), pp. 9–10.

36. Kirsch op. cit: pp. 152–153.

37. Robert Whitaker, *Anatomy of an Epidemic* (New York: Crown, 2010), pp. 322–325.

38. Angell, op cit., p. 22.

39. Whitaker, op cit., p. 278.

40. Carlat, op. cit., p. 115.

41. Whitaker, op cit., pp. 280, 327.

42. Whitaker, op cit., pp. 336–343.

43. Alan Sroufe, "Ritalin Gone Wrong," *New York Times,* January 29, 2012, p. SR1.

44. Gardiner Harris, "Use of Antipsychotics in Children Is Criticized," *New York Times,* November 19, 2008

45. Natasha Singer, "Forest, Maker of Celexa, to Pay $313 Million to Settle Marketing Case," *New York Times,* September 15, 2010.

46. Sandra Boodman, "They're Not Psychotic," *Washington Post,* March 13, 2012, p. E1.

47. Benedict Carey, "Drugs Used for Psychosis Go to Youths in Foster Care," *New York Times,* November 21, 2011, p. A11.

48. "Foster Children: HHS Guidance Could Help States Improve Oversight of Psychotropic Prescriptions," (Washington, DC: GAO, 2011).

49. David Brown, "Autism Rate Rises Nearly 80 Percent in a Decade," *Washington Post,* March 30, 2012, p. A1.

50. Benedict Carey, "New Autism Rule Will Trim Many, A Study Suggests," *New York Times,* January 20, 2012, p. A1.

51. http://files.www.cmhnetwork.org/media-center/blog/samhsa-fy-2013-budget-proposal-not-a-good-day-for-childrens-mental-health/budget-brief-fy2013.pdf

52. A. P. Schinnar, A. B. Rothbard, and T. R. Hadley, "Opportunities and Risks in Philadelphia's Capitation Financing of Public Psychiatric Services," *Community Mental Health Journal* 25, no. 4 (Winter 1989), pp. 257–258.

53. http://www.phoenixhouse.org/

54. Helen Dewar and Judith Havemann, "Conferees Expand Insurance for New Mothers, Mentally Ill," *Washington Post* (September 20, 1996), p. A1.

55. Stuart Auerbach, "The Cost of Increased Coverage," *Washington Post Weekly* (September 30–October 6, 1996), p. 19.

56. "Mental Health Parity," (Washington, DC:General Accounting Office, May 10, 2000).

57. Robert Pear, "Fight Erupts Over Rules Issued for 'Mental Health Parity' Insurance Law," New York Times, May 10, 2010, p. A15

58. Benedict Carey, "Review of Landmark Study Finds Fewer Vietnam Veterans with Post-Traumatic Stress," *New York Times* (August 18, 2006), p. A11; and Rick Weiss, "Few Vietnam Vets Are Found to Have Stress Disorder," *Washington Post* (August 18, 2006), p. A3.

59. Sally Satel, "For Some, the War Won't End," *New York Times* (March 1, 2006), p. A25.

60. Elisabeth Bumiller, "Suicides Among Active-Duty Soldiers Hit Record," *New York Times,* January 20, 2012, p. A11.

61. Ann Scott Tyson, "Pentagon Report Criticizes Troops' Mental-Health Care," *Washington Post* (July 16, 2007), p. A2.

62. Amy Adler, Paul Bliese, Dennis McGurk, Charles Hoge, and Carl Castro, "Battlemind Debriefing and Battlemind Training as Early Intervention with Soldiers Returning from Iraq," *Journal of Consulting and Clinical Psychology,* 77,5, 2009.

63. Pete Earley, *Crazy* (New York: Berkley Books, 2006), p. 356.

64. Andrew Solomon, "Our Great Depression," *New York Times* (November 17, 2006), p. A31.

65. Art Levine, "Parity-Plus: A Third Way Approach to Fix America's Mental Health System" (Washington, DC: Progressive Policy Institute, 2005), p. 4.

66. http://yourlife.usatoday.com/health/story/2011–11–16/US-drinking-up-but-tastes-norms-vary-from-state-to-state/51248776/1

67. 2006 National Survey on Drug Use and Health" (Washington, DC: SAMHSA, 2006), p. 10.

68. *Alcohol and Health: Sixth Special Report to the U.S. Congress* (Washington DC: Department of Health and Human Service, 1987), p. 13.

69. "1997 Survey of Correctional Facilities" (Washington, DC: SAMHSA, 1997).

70. "2006 National Survey of Drug Use and Health," p. 10.

71. "1997 Survey of Correctional Facilities," pp. 140, 139.

72. Timothy Williams, "At Tribe's Door, A Hub of Beer and Heartache," *New York Times,* March 6, 2012, p. A1.

73. Department of Health and Human Services, *Compulsory Treatment of Drug Abuse* (Washington, DC: U.S. Government Printing Office, 1989), p. 58.

74. Carl Leukefeld and Frank Tims, "An Introduction to Compulsory Treatment for Drug Abuse: Clinical Practice and Research," in *Compulsory Treatment of Drug Abuse: Research and Clinical Practice* (Rockville, MD: Department of Health and Human Services, 1988), p. 2.

75. "2006 National Survey of Drug Use and Health, Detailed Tables," p. 35.

76. Center on Addiction and Substance Abuse, *The Cost of Substance Abuse to America's Health Care System* (New York: Center on Addiction and Substance Abuse, 1993), pp. 33, 42.

77. *National Treatment Improvement Evaluation Study* (Washington, DC: SAMHSA, 1997).

CHAPTER 14

Criminal Justice

Source: Joe Sohm/The Image Works

This chapter provides an overview of crime and corrections in the United States, beginning with the history of U.S. criminal justice. Chapter sections explore the roles of various governmental jurisdictions in criminal justice; recent data on crime and justice expenditures; important developments and issues that include juvenile justice, the underclass and crime, the War on Drugs, the "new penology"; and the future of criminal justice in this country.

All societies respond to norm-defying behavior through sanctions, although there is considerable variation among the penalties that societies apply to specific behaviors. In Western cultures, irrational deviance is usually understood as a mental health matter, whereas anormative behavior on the part of a rational actor falls under the purview of law enforcement. In either case, deviance is of interest to human service professionals because clients often engage in anormative activity. Deviance is also an issue of social justice, because poor people and minorities of color are disproportionately represented among those incarcerated in mental or correctional institutions.

History of U.S. Criminal Justice

Modern criminal justice in the United States can be traced to the faith in social science that originated in the West in the eighteenth century. Before the advent of classical criminology, justice was predicated on vengeance: Illegal acts brought the wrath of authority on the deviant. In premodern societies in which deviance was understood to be a product of evil influences, vicious and barbaric methods were justified as ways to exorcise Satan or to maintain archaic social structures. Thus, mutilation, torture, and capital punishment were often employed, sometimes in grotesque public displays, in order to rid society of malevolent influences.

Modern criminology dates from the Age of Enlightenment in the eighteenth century and its notion that humankind was capable of producing the methods for its own perfectibility. The radical jurist and philosopher Jeremy Bentham (1748–1832) contended that scientific methods could be the vehicle for "the rational improvement of the condition of men." Accordingly, Bentham successfully advocated a series of reform laws in Great Britain, including several pertinent to penal institutions.[1] In the United States, Cesare Beccaria applied Bentham's utilitarian philosophy to corrections, arguing that crime could

be measured in its severity, that prevention was more important than punishment, that the purpose of punishment was deterrence (not revenge), and that incarceration should segregate prisoners so as not to exacerbate lawlessness.[2] Liberal, humanistic values in criminal justice can thus be traced to the earliest thinkers in criminology.

Nevertheless, the early American colonists imported traditional European thinking about crime and its control. Jails were a fixture of all settlements of any size, and justice was often swift and uncompromising. In 1776, in response to the dungeons that typified colonial America, the Quakers established the Philadelphia Society for Alleviating the Miseries of Public Prisons.[3] During the following decades, institutional reformers such as Dorothea Dix sought to make jails and almshouses more humane. Unfortunately, the reformer's accomplishments were often subverted. An influx of immigrants, many of whom were unable to adjust to the American experience, became incarcerated in mental and correctional institutions. The American ethos of rugged individualism left little room for compassion, particularly when adults were concerned.

Midway through the nineteenth century, an unlikely pioneer in U.S. corrections emerged. In 1841 a Boston shoemaker, John Augustus, negotiated an arrangement with the courts to use his own money in order to supervise petty criminals, post bail, and report to the courts on the offenders' rehabilitation. The services provided by Augustus were less expensive than prison, and many of his charges seemed to benefit from rehabilitation. Thus, a modest shoemaker began what was to become a nationwide system of probation.[4] Some early criminologists sought more direct applications of emerging sciences to the study of crime. The Italian psychiatrist Cesare Lombroso, for example, proposed the existence of a "criminal type," a construct of inferior intelligence, exaggerated physical features, and a taste for amoral activities, including tattooing! The idea that a criminal could be physiologically identified, and criminal behavior was genetically transmitted subsequently preoccupied some criminologists. For example, in 1913 Charles Goring studied English convicts, and during the 1920s Earnest Hooton evaluated American criminals; both concluded that prisoners were "organically inferior" to their law-abiding compatriots.

The notion of a genetic origin of deviant behavior was popularized by the eugenics movement before World War II. Proponents of natural selection, some of them esteemed scientists and jurists, convinced state legislators to pass legislation allowing for involuntary sterilization of "mental defectives." By the mid-1950s, more than 58,000 mental patients and convicts had been forcibly sterilized.[5] The practice of involuntary sterilization abated during the Civil Rights movement when it became recognized that many of the victims were women and minorities of color. The suggestion that crime was organically determined generated a firestorm of criticism during the 1960s when it was pointed out that an increasing number of criminals were minorities of color, the same populations that had been victimized by discriminative social policies. In 2012, two North Carolina lawmakers introduced legislation that would compensate each of the 7,600 residents who had been involuntarily sterilized in the state with $50,000.[6]

The Criminal Justice System

While all nations manage deviance through incarceration, they vary considerably with respect to frequency. Table 14.1 shows that the incarceration rate per 100,000 population is far higher in the United States than that of virtually all other countries. Notably, most developed nations have incarceration rates that are a fraction of that of the United States. Among the nations of the world, the incarceration rate of the United States is second only to that of Russia. Russia imprisons 687 inmates per 100,000 population; the United States imprisons 682. The rates for other nations are strikingly lower: South Africa 321, Canada 115, France 90, and Japan 39.[7]

The U.S. criminal justice system is similar to education and mental health programs in that states and localities provide a significantly larger portion of services than the federal government. The Constitution, of course, reserves public functions to the states unless they are ceded to the federal government; in the case of criminal justice, this means that state and local government expenditures exceed those of the federal government by a factor of four.[8] Between 1980 and 2003 criminal justice expenditures increased 417.5 percent.[9] Moreover, there was considerable variation in state expenditures. In 2007, for example, the per capita cost of criminal justice in the District of Columbia was $1,373; that of nearby West Virginia was $412.[10]

TABLE 14.1 Incarceration Rates, Select Countries

Country	Rate/100,000 Population
Japan	62
Sweden	78
Ireland	78
France	88
Germany	95
South Korea	97
Italy	102
Canada	107
China	118
Australia	126
Spain	145
United Kingdom	145
Brazil	191
Mexico	196
Israel	209
South Africa	335
Cuba	447
Russian Federation	607
United States	738

Source: Christopher Hartney, "US Rates of Incarceration: A Global Perspective," Research from the National Council on Crime and Delinquency (November 2006), p. 2.

The last decades of the twentieth century witnessed a boom in prison construction, a development that drew the wrath of opponents of incarceration. Prison is an expensive way to manage deviants, costing $22,000 on average per inmate annually.[11] Since states pay most of the costs for incarceration, prisons vie with schools for funding, a competition that is decidedly skewed. "While the state government of Virginia spends upward of $70,000 per year to incarcerate each child in a juvenile prison," noted critics of imprisonment of juvenile offenders, "it contributes only about $3,400 to provide for the education of that child."[12] Such disparities have led liberals to argue for greater funding of education and youth services as a way to prevent incarceration, and some conservatives have come to appreciate

TABLE 14.2 Crime and Crime Rates, by Type of Offense: 1980 to 2009, thousands

Year	Total	Murder	Rape	Robbery	Assault	Property
1980	1,345	23	83	566	673	12,064
1985	1,328	19	88	498	723	11,103
1990	1,820	23	103	639	1,055	12,655
1995	1,799	22	97	581	1,099	12,064
2000	1,425	16	90	408	912	10,183
2005	1,391	17	94	417	862	10,175
2009	1,318	15	88	408	807	9,321

the enormous expense of a criminal justice system in which prisons are dominant. Between 1995 and 2003, state correctional budgets increased by 50 percent, primarily because of prison construction and maintenance, leading several states to revise more punitive sentencing practices, such as mandatory minimums, "three strikes" provisions, and abolishing parole.[13] (See Table 14.2 for categories of crime and crime rates.)

In the criminal justice system, the disposition of offenders varies, not just by jurisdiction, but by type of offense. Those who have not been convicted of violent offenses and who have no previous criminal record are likely to be granted probation. Those who have been convicted of offenses under local or state jurisdiction may be jailed or imprisoned in facilities that have often been determined to violate minimal humane standards of care. Federal convicts, on the other hand,

may be incarcerated in prisons that are qualitatively better, some of which have a decidedly pleasant ambiance. Having served time for good behavior, many prisoners earn early release and go on parole, during which time they must report regularly to a supervising officer. These various statuses are depicted in Table 14.3.

Prisons have been a signal concern in criminal justice, both because of the cost of incarceration and because of what imprisonment rates say about the preponderance of serious precipitating offenses. The United States passed a benchmark coinciding with the new millennium in 2000, when 2 million people were behind bars.[14] In this population, gender and race emerge prominently: Roughly 90 percent of inmates are men[15] and two-thirds are minorities of color. Virtually half of all inmates are African American;[16] in 2002 about 12 percent of African American men between ages 20 and 34

TABLE 14.3 Adults on Probation, in Jail or Prison, or on Parole

Year	Total	Probation	Jail	Prison	Parole
1980	1,840,400	1,118,097	182,288	319,598	220,438
1985	3,011,500	1,968,712	254,986	487,593	300,203
1990	4,348,000	2,670,234	403,019	743,382	531,407
1995	5,335,100	3,077,861	499,300	1,078,541	679,421
2000	6,437,400	3,826,209	613,534	1,316,333	723,898
2005	7,045,100	4,166,757	740,770	1,448,344	780,616
2009	7,225,800	4,203,967	760,400	1,524,523	819,308

Source: U.S. Census Bureau, *Statistical Abstract of the United States,* 2010 (Washington, DC: U.S. GPO, 2012), p. Table 348.

years were behind bars.[17] In light of the fact that two-thirds of inmates return to prison within a few years of release,[18] recidivism poses an enormous burden on the African American community.

Traditionally, crimes have been classified as they result in personal injury or damage to property. As a result of efforts to reduce blatant discriminatory behavior, hate crimes can add to punishment adjudicated for crimes against persons and property. Hate crimes are classified in five groups, those motivated by race, religion, sexual orientation, ethnicity, and disability. For 2010, the Federal Bureau of Investigation reported 7,690 hate crime offenses, and classified them as follows: 47.3 percent were racially motivated; 20.0 percent were motivated by religious bias; 19.3 percent resulted from sexual-orientation bias; 12.8 percent stemmed from ethnicity/national origin bias; 0.6 percent were prompted by disability bias. (See Table 14.4.)

Juvenile Justice

Juvenile justice is a significant feature of U.S. criminal justice for several reasons. Young deviants are good candidates for becoming adult deviants, in which case they become subject to the adult criminal justice system. Because the majority of adult offenders were also known to the juvenile justice system, it stands to reason that diverting youngsters from juvenile crime may well keep them out of the adult criminal justice system. From a crime prevention standpoint, reaching young people early, when their understanding of themselves in relation to social norms is still being formed, is a more plausible strategy than attempting to intervene with adult offenders, who have a less malleable sense of themselves vis-à-vis social institutions.

The first institution for juvenile delinquency was the New York City House of Refuge established in 1825. Massachusetts followed suit with a facility for boys established in 1847 and one for girls in 1854.[19] Institutional care for adolescent deviants remained virtually unchanged until the 1960s, when critics of warehousing children advocated for community alternatives. In 1972, Congress passed the Juvenile Justice and Delinquency Prevention Act, a measure that intended, in part, to remove children who were "status offenders" from the more serious deviants who had actually committed felonies or violent crimes. According to Jerome Miller, a youth service advocate, the act

TABLE 14.4 Hate Crimes by Category, 2006

Bias Motivation	Incidents	Victims
Race	*4,000*	*5,020*
Anti-White	890	1,054
Anti-Black	2,640	3,332
Anti-American Indian	60	75
Anti-Asian/Pacific Islander	181	239
Anti-Multiple Races	229	320
Religion	*1,462*	*1,750*
Anti-Jewish	967	1,144
Anti-Catholic	76	86
Anti-Protestant	59	65
Anti-Islamic	156	208
Anti-Other Religion	124	147
Sexual orientation	*1,195*	*1,472*
Anti-Male Homosexual	747	913
Anti-Female Homosexual	163	202
Anti-Homosexual	238	307
Anti-Heterosexual	26	29
Anti-Bisexual	21	21
Ethnicity	*984*	*1,305*
Anti-Hispanic	576	619
Anti-Other	408	486
Disability	*79*	*95*
Anti-Physical	17	21
Anti-Mental	62	74
Total	*7,722*	*9,652*

Source: FBI, *Hate Crime Statistics*, http://www.fbi.gov/ucr/hc2006/table1.html.

ultimately failed. However, it gave impetus to the activities of those who were proponents of noninstitutional care for delinquents.

In 1969, Miller assumed the directorship of the Massachusetts Division of Youth Services (DYS), a position that was to become symbolic of correctional reform in the United States. A social worker, Miller had been an officer in the U.S. Air Force, had trained in the Menninger Clinic, and had earned a doctorate at Catholic University. His initial plan, to seek incremental reforms in Massachusetts, faded as the structural flaws of state juvenile justice became more apparent. Staff routinely resorted to within the contemporary urban milieu, the new penology became an instrument of racial and class oppression, as Miller and Alexander have contended.

It could be argued that in the United States, prisons have historically served as institutions of last resort for incorrigible populations that have proved difficult to socialize. In that respect, the large numbers of African Americans who dominate the prisons today are little different from the Irish or Italian immigrant inmates who disproportionately populated correctional facilities decades ago. If there is a qualitatively different aspect to contemporary corrections, however, it lies in the merging of systems management with the rapid expansion of the correctional corporations. The fundamental difference between the old, government-maintained penology and the new, corporate-managed penology is that the latter has a financial stake in an expanding correctional market, whereas the incentives under the old penology were such that the state attempted to limit criminal justice expenditures.

Thus, an analysis of corrections produced by Steven Donziger for the National Criminal Justice Commission targeted the emerging "prison-industrial complex." According to Donziger, the prison-industrial complex consisted of an "iron triangle" of "government bureaucrats, private industry leaders, and politicians who work together to expand the criminal justice system."[72] In the United States, in 1996, there were 21 companies with annual revenues exceeding $250 million, managing some 88 prisons in which 50,000 inmates were incarcerated—a 20-fold increase in the number of inmates managed by for-profit correctional firms since 1984.[73] The passage of the "three strikes" legislation targeting repeat offenders, the War on Drugs, and the consequences of the sentencing guidelines provided the prison-industrial complex with a more-than-adequate supply of inmates. Because most inmates were nonviolent offenders, incarceration in the minimum- and medium-security facilities that were favored by for-profit firms proved ideal. Contrasted to the archaic prisons typical of the old penology, the facilities managed by for-profit firms were not only more adequate with regard to basic amenities, but they were also more likely to provide educational and other services as methods to maintain a compliant population.

Although crime has fallen, incarceration rates remain high in large part because of prosecutorial procedures. The professionalization of the police has removed them from the very communities they are sworn to protect; in earlier periods Irish cops patrolled Irish neighborhoods and Italian cops patrolled "Little Italy," but this historical process did not occur with respect to the African American community where police officers did not emerge from it organically. In order to reduce the cost of jury trials, prosecutors offer plea bargains to miscreants at the same time admonishing them that insisting on their constitutional rights will likely result in a much stiffer sentence, in the process attaining high conviction rates.[74] Forced confessions, admissions of guilt under duress, have been disputed by DNA evidence in 24 percent of 289 sentences reviewed by the Innocence Project.[75] The entire system is so flawed that Supreme Court Justice John Paul Stevens wrote: "criminal statutes have limited the discretionary power of judges and juries to reach just decisions in individual cases, while the proliferation and breadth of criminal statutes have given prosecutors and the police so much enforcement discretion that they effectively define the law of the street."[76]

The get-tough mindset that typified corrections during the 1990s was shaken when increasing numbers of inmates were exonerated from crimes for which they had been convicted. In 1992, Barry Scheck and Peter Neufeld started the Innocence Project, reviewing convictions in light of recent developments in DNA technology. By 2012, the Innocence Project marked the release of 300 wrongfully convicted inmates. Of those released, 187 were African Americans, and their average length of incarceration was 13.6 years; yet, only 60 percent have been compensated for their wrongful convictions.[77]

Civil rights loomed large in the Innocence Project because a disproportionate number of inmates scheduled for execution were minorities of color. Because most wrongful convictions were based on questionable confessions and evidence, police departments began to videotape confessions and take precautions to retain DNA evidence.[78] Despite such exonerations, the prison-industrial complex remained intact.

What moral indignation failed to accomplish with respect to an overbuilt and costly prison system, the Great Recession achieved. Financially distressed state and local governments reconsidered their commitments to incarceration, primarily because of the costs involved. The Pew Charitable Foundation calculated that a day in prison cost $79 compared to $3.50 per day for probation or parole. Texas, the leader in executions among the states, projected the need for 8 prisons costing $1 billion if alternatives were not found.[79] In an attempt to reduce costs, Arizona instituted a $25 fee for visitors of inmates, which critics charged was a hardship, especially for those traveling from out-of-state."[80] Riverside County, California Supervisors announced a plan to charge inmates for their incarceration, expected to generate $8 million from their stay.[81]

While government attempted to maintain high rates of incarceration, problems became evident, especially when institutional capacity was exceeded by the number of inmates. About 4.5 percent of state and federal inmates reported being raped while incarcerated, most often by fellow inmates.[82] Two administrators of a remote Texas youth correctional facility routinely rousted residents from their rooms at night in order to rape them, the reports of youth prompting retaliation when uncovered by the perpetrators.[83] By 2005, 44 states had build "super-max prisons" in order to jail the most incorrigible offenders, many placed in solitary confinement which permitted only an hour each day outside a bleak cell.[84] At any given time between 25,000 and 100,000 prisoners are held in solitary confinement, sometimes for months if not years, a disposition that is twice as costly as routine incarceration. Finally, get-tough sentencing has resulted in tens of thousands of inmates residing in prisons well into their senior years, posing the extra costs associated with nursing home care for age-related conditions such as dementia.[85]

Conclusion

Because criminal justice has such profound implications for individuals and their communities, advocates continue to press for reform. After three decades of more rigorous policing, higher incarceration rates, and longer sentences, the cost of corrections has come to crowd-out such governmental obligations as public education and physical infrastructure. Consequently, reduced governmental revenues have caused public officials to seek more cost effective methods of crime control. Not surprisingly, liberal reformers have seen this as an opportunity to restore a measure of rehabilitation within a system that has focused on punishment. Massachusetts, for example, has attempted to reduce the stigma of crime by limiting employers' access to records on misdemeanors to 5 years and felonies to 10 years

at the same time providing protection to those who hire someone who commits a future crime.[86]

Predictably, some reformers have proposed more humane facilities for inmates. Norway's Halden Prison, designed by Henrik Hoilund, resembles a college dormitory with individual rooms that include kitchenettes, complemented by a gym that includes a climbing wall.[87] In Austria, Josef Hohensinn designed Loeben prison similarly in order to provide inmates with a more normal, home-like environment where inmates' rooms are arranged in 15-unit clusters around a common kitchen, with extensive educational and recreational facilities.[88] While the adoption of European reforms is unlikely in the United States, reformers have seized on opportunities to make correctional facilities more congruent with the needs of detainees. The Karnes County Civil Detention Center in Texas, for example, is an immigrant detention facility that more resembles a school than a prison, replete with a gym, library, computers with internet access, a medical center, and sports areas for soccer, basketball, and volleyball.[89] Aesthetic considerations aside, humanizing corrections so that it is more congruent with community reintegration of inmates remains a primary challenge for advocates of prison reform.

DISCUSSION QUESTIONS

1. Navigate to the Congress.org website, identify legislation related to criminal justice, and trace its implications for social welfare. Has the policy been effective? What are its costs? How might it be made more adequate?
2. Crime varies considerably in terms of both the nature of offenses and the characteristics of offenders. How prevalent is crime in your community? What are the primary offenses? Who are the offenders?
3. State and local governments vary regarding the management of juvenile delinquency. Does your community have a juvenile court? Are its deliberations open to the public? What are the usual offenses that bring a youth to juvenile court?
4. Many communities are building new correctional facilities. Is your community upgrading corrections? To what extent do new facilities reflect the new penology? Are for-profit correctional firms active in your state? If not, should they be? Should they be allowed to contract to manage probation and parole?
5. Legalization of drugs has become a heated issue. What are the implications of drug legalization for substance abuse programs? How could drug legalization be structured in your state? How would substances be taxed? How would tax revenues from legalization be allocated?

6. In many poor urban communities, drug-related street violence has escalated to unprecedented heights. How has your community balanced resource allocations for supply interdiction versus resources for demand reduction? To what extent is substance abuse treatment available to inmates in local correctional facilities? Have specific neighborhoods in your community organized to contain and reduce drug trafficking? Which agencies have supported such initiatives?

7. As the War on Drugs has failed to live up to its promise, more attention has been focused on prevention, particularly among children. What models have agencies in your community adopted to prevent substance abuse among kids? How much money has been allocated for prevention programs? What is the track record of the prevention programs adopted in your community?

8. How prevalent are hate crimes in your community? Is there any attempt to organize initiatives encouraging citizens to become more tolerant? Are victims of hate crimes in your community encouraged to take advantage of victim assistance benefits?

9. To what extent are social workers involved in community reentry activities? Does the local chapter of the National Association of Social Workers have a position on reentry programs? If not, what should it consist of? How would you encourage NASW to take up a reentry initiative?

NOTES

1. *Encyclopedia of Sociology* (Guilford, CT: Dushkin Publishing Group. 1974).
2. D. Stanley Eitzen and Doug Timmer, *Criminology* (New York: John Wiley, 1985), pp. 15–16.
3. Phyllis Day, *A New History of Social Welfare* (Englewood Cliffs, NJ: Prentice Hall, 1989), p. 181.
4. Ibid., p. 182.
5. Jerome Miller, *Search and Destroy: African-American Males in the Criminal Justice System* (New York: Cambridge University Press, 1996), p. 207.
6. http://www.newsobserver.com/2012/02/01/1821721/lawmakers-hold-meeting-on-nc-sterilization.html, downloaded February 8, 2012.
7. "Behind Bars," *Washington Post* (June 3, 2000), p. A9.
8. http://bjs.ojp.usdoj.gov/content/pub/pdf/jeeus03.pdf, downloaded February 8, 2012.
9. http://bjs.ojp.usdoj.gov/content/pub/pdf/jeeus03.pdf, downloaded February 8, 2012.
10. http://www.census.gov/compendia/statab/2012/tables/12s0345.pdf, downloaded February 8, 2012.
11. "The Growing Inmate Population," *New York Times* (August 1, 2003), p. A22.
12. Andrew Block and Virginia Weisz, "Choosing Prisoners over Pupils," *Washington Post* (July 6, 2004), p. A19.
13. John Broder, "No Hard Time for Prison Budgets," *New York Times* (January 29, 2003), p. WK5.
14. Nation's Prison Population Climbs to over 2 Million," *Washington Post* (August 10, 2000), p. A4.
15. U.S. Census Bureau, *Statistical Abstract of the United States*, 1999 (Washington, DC: U.S. Government Printing Office, 1999), p. 231.
16. David Masci, "Prison-Building Boom," *Issues in Social Policy* (Washington, DC: Congressional Quarterly, 2000), p. 138.
17. Fox Butterfield, "Prison Rates among Blacks Reach a Peak, Report Finds," *New York Times* (April 7, 2003), p. A11.
18. "The Price of Prisons," *New York Times* (June 26, 2004), p. A26.
19. Day, A New History of Social Welfare, p. 180.
20. Jerome Miller, *Last One over the Wall* (Columbus, OH: Ohio State University, 1991), p. 222.
21. Denise Gottfredson and William Barton,"Deinstitutionalization of Juvenile Offenders," *Criminology* 31, no. 4 (1993), pp. 98–117.
22. James Q. Wilson and John DiIulio, Jr., "Crackdown," *The New Republic* (July 10, 1989), p. 54.
23. Rhonda Cook, "Georgia's Prison Boot Camps Don't Work, Study Says," *San Diego Union Tribune* (May 8, 1994), p. A32.
24. "Connecticut Suspends Gang-Riddled Youth Boot Camp," *San Diego Union Tribune* (June 12, 1994), p. A6.
25. Doris Mackenzie et al., "Boot Camp Prisons and Recidivism in Eight States," *Criminology* 33, no. 3 (1995), p. 78.
26. "Residential Treatment Programs: Concerns Regarding Abuse and Death in Certain Programs for Troubled Youth" (Washington, DC: Government Accountability Office, 2007), p. i.
27. Diana Schemo, "Report Recounts Horrors of Youth Boot Camps," *New York Times* (October 11, 2007), p. A19.
28. Margaret Talbot, "The Maximum Security Adolescent," *New York Times Magazine* (September 10, 2000), p. 42.
29. Michael Tonry, "Treating Juveniles as Adult Criminals," *American Journal of Preventive Medicine* (2007), 32, no. 48, p. S3.
30. Mosi Secret, "States Prosecute Fewer Teenagers in Adult Courts," *New York Times*, March 6, 2011, p. A4.
31. Michelle Alexander, *The New Jim Crow* (New York: New Press, 2010), p. 13.
32. Adam Gopnik, "The Caging of America," *New Yorker*, January 30, 2012, pp. 72–73.
33. Donna St. George, "Black Students are Arrested more Often, Data Reveal, *Washington Post*, March 6, 2012, p. A1; Tamar Lewin, "Black Students Punished More, Data Suggests," *New York Times*, March 6, 2012, p. A1.
34. Heather Ann Thompson, "Criminalizing Kids," *Dissent Magazine*, Fall 2011, p. 3.
35. "Miranda Rights for Children," *Washington Post*, August 29, 2011, p. A14.
36. Erica Goode, "Many in U.S. Are Arrested by Age 23, Study Finds," *New York Times*, December 19, 2011, p. A15.

37. U.S. Census Bureau, *Statistical Abstract of the United States*, 2002, p. 193.
38. Mathea Falco, *Winning the Drug War* (New York: Priority Press, 1989), pp. 26–27.
39. Falco, *Winning the Drug War*, p. 29.
40. Barry Bearak, "A Room for Heroin and HIV," *Los Angeles Times* (September 27, 1992), p. A18.
41. U.S. Census Bureau, *Statistical Abstract of the United States*, 2002, pp. 191, 193.
42. Christopher Jencks, "Deadly Neighborhoods," *The New Republic* (June 13, 1988), p. 18; Juan Williams, "Hard Times, Harder Hearts," *Washington Post* (October 2, 1988), p. C4.
43. Louis Sahagun, "Gang Killings Increase 69%, Violent Crime up 20% in L. A. County Areas," *Los Angeles Times* (August 21, 1990), p. B8.
44. Jesse Katz, "County's Yearly Death Toll Reaches 800," *Los Angeles Times* (January 19,1993), p. A23.
45. Gabriel Escobar, "Slayings in Washington Hit New High, 436, for 3rd Year," *Los Angeles Times* (November 24, 1990), p. A26.
46. Claude Brown, *Manchild in the Promised Land* (New York: Macmillan, 1965); and Claude Brown, "Manchild in Harlem," *New York Times* (September 16, 1984), p. 16.
47. Miller, *Search and Destroy*, pp. 7–8.
48. Ibid., p. 99.
49. William Bennett, John DiIulio Jr., and John Walters, *Body Count* (New York: Simon and Schuster, 1996), p. 56.
50. Ibid., p. 105.
51. Ibid., p. 27.
52. Ibid., pp. 175–176.
53. Jim Wallace, "With Unconditional Love," *Sojourners* (September–October 1997).
54. William Julius Wilson, *When Work Disappears* (New York: Knopf, 1996), p. 238.
55. Juan Williams, *Enough* (New York: Crown, 2006), pp. 220, 222.
56. Ethan Nadelmann, "The Case for Legalization," *Public Interest* 92 (1988), pp. 3–17.
57. James Jacobs, "Imagining Drug Legalization," *The Public Interest* 101 (Fall 1990), pp. 27–34.
58. Kate Zernike, "A Drug Scourge Creates Its Own Form of Orphan," *New York Times* (July 11, 2005), p. A1.
59. Mathea Falco, *The Making of a Drug-Free America* (New York: Priority Press, 1989), p. 100.
60. Michael Specter, "Getting a Fix," *New Yorker*, October 17, 2011, p. 36.
61. Jessica Gresko, "Crack-Cocaine Offenders Are Eligible for Reduced Sentences," *Washington Post*, July 1, 2011, p. A16.
62. http://bjs.ojp.usdoj.gov/content/pub/pdf/cpus10.pdf
63. U.S. Census Bureau, *Statistical Summary of the United States* (Washington, DC: U.S. Census Bureau, 1995), Table 349.
64. U.S. Census Bureau, *Statistical Abstract of the United States*, 1999, p. 231.
65. Department of Justice, Annual Report of the Attorney General of the U.S., 1995.
66. U.S. Census Bureau, *Statistical Abstract of the United States*, 2002, p. 204.
67. U.S. Census Bureau, *Statistical Abstract of the United States*, 1999, p. 233.
68. Malcolm Feeley and Jonathan Simon, "The New Penology," *Criminology* 30, no. 4 (1992), p. 452.
69. Miller, Last One over the Wall, p. 76.
70. Feeley and Simon, "The New Penology," p. 455.
71. Mary Flaherty and Joan Biskupic, "Justice by the Numbers," *Washington Post Weekly* (October 14–20, 1996), p. 88.
72. Steven Donziger, "The Prison-Industrial Complex," *Washington Post* (March 17, 1996), p. C3.
73. Ibid., p. C3.
74. Richard Oppel, Jr., "Sentencing Shift Gives New Clout to Prosecutors," *New York Times*, September 26, 2011, p. A1.
75. David Shipler, "Why Do Innocent People Confess?" *New York Times*, February 26, 2012, p. SR6.
76. John Paul Stevens, "Our 'Broken System' of Criminal Justice," *New York Review of Books*, November 10, 2011, p. 56.
77. The Innocence Project "Facts on Post-Conviction DNA Exonerations" http://www.innocenceproject.org/Content/Facts_on_PostConviction_DNA_Exonerations.php
78. Keith Richburg, "States Seek Less Costly Substitutes for Prison," *Washington Post*, July 13, 2009, p. A1.
79. Erica Goode, "Inmate visits Now Carry Added Cost in Arizona," *New York Times*, September 5, 2011, p. A10.
80. *New York Times*, December 12, 2012, p. A14.
81. "Rape in Prison," *Washington Post*, June 24, 2009, p. B24.
82. "Rape in Prison," *Washington Post*, June 24, 2009, p. B24.
83. David Kaiser and Lovisa Stannow, "The Rape of American Prisoners," *New York Review of Books*, March 11, 2010, p. 16.
84. "Erica Goode, "Rethinking Solitary Confinement," *New York Times*, March 11, 2012, p. A1.
85. Pam Bellick, "Life, With Dementia," *New York Times*, February 26, 2012, p. A1.
86. Alfred Blumstein and Kiminori Nakamura, "Paying a Price, Long After the Crime," *New York Times*, January 10, 2012, p. A21.
87. http://www.dailymail.co.uk/news/article-1277158/Halden-Prison-Inside-Norways-posh-new-jail.html
88. Jim Lewis, "Behind Bars . . . Sort Of," *New York Times Sunday Magazine*, June 14, 2009, pp. 48-52.
89. Kirk Semple and Tim Eaton, "Detention for Immigrants That Looks Less Like Prison," *New York Times*, March 14, 2012, p. A30.

CHAPTER 15

Child Welfare Policy

Source: Jack.Q/Shutterstock

This chapter examines the evolution of child welfare policy in the United States. Child protective services, foster care, adoption, and Head Start have been the focus of child welfare policy since the 1960s. The devolution of welfare to the states through the Personal Responsibility and Work Opportunity Reconciliation Act (PRWORA) of 1996 has introduced questions about the prospects of poor children whose mothers are entering the labor market.

In American social welfare, the condition of children is inextricably linked to the status of their families. Because the United States has failed to establish a family policy that ensures basic income, employment, and social service supports to parents, parents frequently have difficulty in caring for their children. As families are less able to care for their children, the demand for child welfare services escalates. According to six variables presumed to define the well-being of children, the United States ranks second to last among industrialized countries, as shown in Table 15.1.

The low ranking of the United States can be attributed to two factors: the high incidence of poverty among American children and the absence of universal health care for their families. One-fifth of children in the United States live in poverty, a condition that is associated with inadequate nutrition and shelter.[1] In addition, one-third of children lack access to health care due to absence of health insurance.[2] By contrast, nations ranking higher than the United States make more financial benefits available to families, and health care is universal providing all children access to health care.

In the United States, child welfare services are often controversial because they sanction the intervention of human service professionals in family affairs that are ordinarily assumed to be private matters and the prerogative of parents. This dilemma places extraordinary demands on child welfare professionals, who are mandated to protect the best interests of the child while not intruding on the privacy of the family.[3] Recently, this conundrum has become more pronounced: Advocates for child welfare services demand more programs, but conservative, traditionalist groups attempt to cut programs that they see as designed to subvert the family. Ironically, much of this argument could be defused if the United States adopted a family policy that helped parents care for children more adequately, thus reducing the need for the more intrusive child welfare interventions. For the moment,

TABLE 15.1 Ranking Child Well-Being in Developed Nations

Nation	Ranking
Netherlands	4.2
Sweden	5.0
Denmark	7.2
Finland	7.5
Spain	8.0
Switzerland	8.3
Norway	8.7
Italy	10.0
Ireland	10.2
Belgium	10.7
Germany	11.2
Canada	11.8
Greece	11.8
Poland	12.3
Czech Republic	12.5
France	13.0
Portugal	13.7
Austria	13.8
Hungary	14.5
United States	18.0
United Kingdom	18.2

Source: http://www.unicef-irc.org/publications/pdf/rc7_eng.pdf

however, the introduction of a comprehensive family policy is unlikely, leaving services to children fragmented.

History of U.S. Child Welfare Policy

Although many states established orphanages during the eighteenth century, current child welfare policy in the United States has its origins in the 1870s.[4] The large number of child paupers led Charles Loring Brace, founder of New York's Children's Aid Society, to move thousands of children from deleterious urban conditions in New York City to farm families in the Midwest. Eventually, criticism of Brace's methods, which were divisive

Child welfare policy in the United States began in the 1870s. An early program led by Charles Loring Brace, founder of New York's Children's Aid Society, moved thousands of children from deleterious urban conditions in New York City to farm families in the Midwest. Under intense criticism, this program would later be replaced with programs that were less divisive to family and community.

Source: NMPFT/Kodak Collection/SSPL/The Image Works

Prevention of Cruelty to Children was established.[7] By 1922, 57 societies for the prevention of cruelty to children had been established to protect abused youngsters.[8]

Child welfare proved an effective rallying issue for Progressives, who advocated intervention on the part of the federal government. In 1909, James E. West, a friend of former president Theodore Roosevelt and later head of the Boy Scouts of America, convinced Jane Addams and other welfare leaders to attend a two-day meeting on child welfare. This first White House Conference on Children focused attention on the plight of destitute families, agency problems with the boarding out of children, and the importance of home care. One significant product of the White House Conference on Children was the call to establish a federal agency to "collect and exchange ideas and information on child welfare." With an initial appropriation of $25,640, the U.S. Children's Bureau was established in 1912 under the auspices of the Department of Commerce and Labor.[9]

Because of the economic circumstances of poor families, child labor emerged as a primary concern of early child welfare advocates. The absence of public relief meant that families were compelled to work at whatever employment might be available. Children worked full shifts in coal mines and textile mills; women labored in sweatshops. Neither group was protected from dangerous or unhygienic working conditions. Before the Great Depression, welfare advocates could boast of a series of unprecedented initiatives designed to improve the conditions of poor families in the United States. The Children's Bureau Act of 1912 established a national agency to collect information on children. The Child Labor Act of 1916 prohibited the interstate transportation of goods manufactured by children. The Maternity and Infancy Act of 1921 assisted states in establishing programs that dramatically reduced the nation's infant and maternal mortality rates. Yet, these hard-won successes were constantly at risk of being subverted. The Supreme Court ruled the Child Labor Act unconstitutional in 1918, and the Maternity and Infancy Act was terminated in 1929 when Herbert Hoover and

of family and community, contributed to more preventive approaches to children's problems. By the beginning of the twentieth century, most large cities had children's aid societies that practiced "boarding out" of children (the payment of a fee for child rearing) to sponsors in the community.[5] The boarding out of children until adoption (except in the case of children with disabilities, who were unlikely to be adopted) was the forerunner of today's foster care and adoption programs in the United States.

Protective services for children began with one of the more unusual incidents in U.S. social welfare. In 1874, a New York church worker, Etta Wheeler, discovered that an indentured 9-year-old child, Mary Ellen, was being tied to a bed, whipped, and stabbed with scissors. On investigating what could be done for Mary Ellen, Wheeler spoke with the director of the New York Society for the Prevention of Cruelty to Animals (NYSPCA) on behalf of the child. Although it was subsequently misreported that intervention on behalf of Mary Ellen was predicated on her status as an animal, rather than as a child, a careful review of the case indicated that Mary Ellen's case was adjudicated consistently with legal precedents involving abused children.[6] The following year, the New York Society for the

Congress refused further appropriations.[10] Child and family welfare initiatives remained unsuccessful until the Social Security Act of 1935 ushered in an array of welfare policies.

The Social Security Act of 1935 addressed child welfare in two of its provisions. Title IV introduced the Aid to Dependent Children program, which provided public relief to needy children through cash grants to their families. Cash benefits were to be authorized and overseen by welfare caseworkers who were also to provide social services to welfare families. Title V reestablished Maternal and Child Welfare Services (which had expired in 1929) and expanded the mandate of the Children's Bureau, whose goal was now to oversee a new set of child welfare services "for the protection and care of homeless, dependent, and neglected children, and children in danger of becoming delinquent."[11] Significantly, both family relief and child welfare services were to be administered by the states through public welfare departments. As a result, as of 1935 the provision of child welfare services shifted largely from the private, voluntary sector to the public, governmental sector.

Since 1935, the state and federal governments have shared responsibility for social services provided to families, but the role of the federal government has changed with respect to income maintenance benefits to poor families. From 1935 until 1996, federal and state government shared the funding and administration of the Aid to Families with Dependent Children (AFDC) program. With devolution of public assistance to the states through the 1996 PRWORA, however, the federal government limited its role to one of funding and limited oversight. PRWORA instituted a block grant program, Temporary Assistance for Needy Families (TANF), which is primarily under the control of state government. Consistent with the residual conception of welfare, primary responsibility for children rests with their parent(s), with state intervention as a backup. Ominously, since the inception of PRWORA a significant number of states had reduced TANF appropriations for transition to work, assistance to the poorest families, transportation aid, and cash assistance. Thirty-two states had restricted eligibility, instituted waiting lists, and reduced payments for child care, and four states had reduced support of teen pregnancy prevention programs.[12] Thus, although PRWORA has contributed to a sharp drop in welfare rolls, reduced support for children and youth may imperil their futures. The long-term prospects of child welfare are also problematic. Open-ended entitlements for the elderly—Social Security, Medicare, and Medicaid—are likely to squeeze discretionary funding, resulting in lower appropriations for child welfare. In 1960 federal funding for elders eclipsed that for children by 2 percent; by 2017 the gap is projected to increase to 31.5 percent.[13]

Protective Services for Children

Through the Social Security Act, states proceeded to develop services to children independent of one another and within the relatively loose specifications of the act. In the absence of a centralized authority that would ensure standardized care throughout the United States, child welfare services varied greatly from state to state and even within states. In the two decades following the passage of the Social Security Act, child welfare services had become established within American social welfare, but with a high degree of fragmentation.

In the 1960s, the status quo in child welfare was upset by increasing reports of child abuse and neglect. A pediatrician, C. Henry Kempe, identified nonaccidental injuries to children as the "battered child syndrome." As more states began to address the problem, child welfare advocates built a compelling case for a national standard for child protective services. This lobbying led to the passage of the Child Abuse Prevention and Treatment Act (CAPTA) of 1974, which established the National Center for Child Abuse and Neglect within the Department of Health and Human Services and presented a model statute for state child protective programs. All 50 states eventually enacted the model statute that, among its provisions, specified the following:

- A standard definition of child abuse and neglect
- Methods for reporting and investigating abuse and neglect
- Immunity for those reporting suspected injuries inflicted on children
- Prevention and public education efforts to reduce incidents of abuse and neglect

As a result of these national standards, the National Center for Child Abuse and Neglect was able—for the first time—to report trends in child abuse and the need for protective services for children. Alarmingly, the data collected by the National Center revealed a dramatic increase in reports of child abuse; these more than doubled between 1976 and 1986, when reports of child abuse numbered 2 million.[14] Reports of child abuse continued to climb through the mid-1980s, while at the same time expenditures for child protective services were decreasing.[15]

Increases in child abuse reports and decreases in expenditures led to a crisis in child welfare services. The magnitude of this crisis was mapped in 1987 by Douglas Besharov, an authority on child welfare policy:

> Of the 1,000 children who die under circumstances suggestive of parental maltreatment each year, between 30 and 50 percent were previously reported to child protective agencies. Many thousands of other children suffer serious injuries after their plight becomes known to authorities. . . . Each year, about 50,000 children with observable injuries severe enough to require hospitalization are not reported.[16]

The rapid deterioration of child welfare services led children's advocates to call for more funding of social services. But proposals for increased support for child welfare services did not go unchallenged. Ambiguity in the definition of what constituted child abuse and neglect had contributed to incidents in which child welfare workers appeared to disregard parental rights in their eagerness to protect children. Further distracting public attention from child maltreatment, during the 1980s some family therapists suggested that therapy could "recover memories" of childhood abuse. By the end of the decade, showcase trials of child day care providers, teachers, clergy, and parents resulted in a series of convictions based on incidents that had been previously forgotten but were later retrieved during clinical treatment. Later, appeals raised questions about the veracity of allegations, the "recovered memory" movement came under scrutiny, and virtually all of the perpetrators convicted in earlier trials would be reversed on appeal.[17]

While academics, policy wonks, and therapists debated definitional, ideological, and clinical aspects of child maltreatment, child protective services deteriorated. New York City's child welfare services became the focus of scrutiny in the cases of a series of children who died despite having been active child protection cases: Jeffrey Harden in 1992,[18] Elisa Izquierdo in 1995, and Nadine Lockwood in

1996. An investigation into the Child Welfare Administration showed the magnitude of agency failure: in a fifth of the reported cases, workers failed to interview all of the children in the family; in two out of five cases, workers ignored previous reports of child abuse; almost one-fifth of cases were closed despite the risk of future abuse. Following the exposé, then-mayor Rudolph Giuliani announced plans to restructure child welfare in the city.[19] Despite the appointment of a new commissioner of children's services, Nicholas Scoppetta,[20] a subsequent report found that 40 percent of abused and neglected children were returned home and mistreated again.[21] Reform would prove elusive in New York City, however. In September 2011, a 4-year-old girl weighing 18 pounds died, despite the provision of children's services.[22] In an unprecedented response, the Brooklyn district attorney indicted a child welfare worker and his supervisor for criminally negligent homicide for failing to protect the child.[23] Efforts to make child protection more accountable by state statute requiring openness of cases involving child fatalities, foundered on the shoals of the child welfare bureaucracy: An investigation by the *New York Times* revealed that the state's Office of Child and Family Services had been working to keep cases involving child fatalities secret.[24] Nor were other cities spared. The District of Columbia's Child and Family Service Agency (CFSA) had been so mismanaged that it was placed under a court-appointed receiver. After several years, the staff was upgraded until virtually all were MSWs; yet, the agency continued to show serious performance problems,[25] chief among them being high caseloads and high turnover.[26] In 2001, the death of a 23-month-old African American infant due to child abuse led reporters from the *Washington Post* to investigate other child deaths. Within a year, reporters had identified the outline of a rather imposing iceberg: Their research revealed that between 1993 and 2001, 229 children had died as a result of maltreatment in the District of Columbia, but the deaths had gone without proper investigation on the part of the Metropolitan Police Department and Department of Child and Family Services.[27] In 2009, Bonita Jacks was found with the bodies of her four children, whom she would later be found guilty of murdering; several child welfare workers were dismissed for failing to protect the Jacks children.[28] In Florida, a 5-year-old Miami girl in foster care, Rilya Wilson, had been missing for 15 months; yet, Florida child welfare workers were unable to locate her.[29] Although the head of the Florida family service agency admitted that the performance of child welfare workers was "appalling," she had no explanation for the whereabouts of the 374 other foster children the state was unable to locate.[30] Florida child welfare workers replicated the performance of those who had been encountered by reporters elsewhere: Rather than admit the extent of problems in children's services, workers used confidentiality as an excuse to avoid public accountability. Years after the exposé, Rilya Wilson is yet to be found.[31]

In January 2003, the decomposing body of 7-year-old Faheem Williams was found in a Newark basement; his two brothers had been locked in a nearby room, "emaciated and with burn scars on their bodies."[32] Although Williams had been an active protective services case with the New Jersey Division of Youth and Family Services (DYFS), multiple agency errors failed to save him. Subsequently, the *New York Times* obtained case records on 17 children that documented the deaths of four children and "the sometimes brutal, prolonged abuse of 13 more."[33] As the *Times* would learn, the culture at DYFS conspired to expose children to risk. Rather than redoubling efforts to protect maltreated children, child welfare workers were so intent on closing cases that they often took shortcuts, contravening agency policy and state law. In a grim parody of street slang, workers came to refer to the rush to eliminate cases as "drive-by closings." For years, DYFS used confidentiality to avoid public scrutiny.[34] Though the expose of DYFS brought the agency's defensive practices to light, it did little to correct for its malfeasance. Within a year of the Williams tragedy, Matthew Calbi was beaten to death by his mother, despite four investigations of the family during the previous two years.[35]

Tragically, the deaths of children due to abuse and neglect were not a local problem but one that had become nationwide. During Congressional testimony, an official of the Government Accountability Office suggested that 1,770 child fatalities in 2009 was an inaccurate number; a more likely figure was 2,400, concluding that "little has changed in 40 years."[36] In rating the child homicide rates for industrial nations, a British researcher concluded that the child fatality rate of the United States was double that of the second most lethal nation for children, Australia.[37] The rate of reported as well as confirmed cases of abuse and neglect in the United States was more than double that of the

United Kingdom or Canada.[38] The systematic failure of child welfare led Marcia Robinson Lowry to establish Children's Rights, a legal advocacy organization that, by 2010, had sued more than a dozen states for their failure to protect and serve maltreated children.[39]

Regardless of increases in injury and death to children due to abuse and neglect, child welfare professionals were embracing new approaches to serving at-risk families: family preservation and kinship care. Initially demonstrated in the late 1970s through the Homebuilders program, family preservation called for the provision of intensive services for a brief period, usually six weeks, by a worker assigned four to six cases. Services provided ranged from crisis intervention to home repair to child day care—all intended to stabilize the family and prevent out-of-home placement of a child. Family preservation was greeted enthusiastically by child welfare professionals because of the multiple benefits it offered. Foremost, by keeping a family intact, this approach avoided out-of-home placement of a child who had been abused or neglected. Because of the high cost of out-of-home placement, family preservation thus offered financial benefits: The cost of mounting a family preservation program was quickly recovered through savings from the reduction in out-of-home placements. Finally, in valuing family unity over child removal, family preservation allied child welfare agencies with conservative traditionalists who placed family rights over those of children.

The relationship between family preservation and child protective services was oblique but nonetheless consequential. Child welfare professionals understood family preservation as a preventive strategy that could preclude the most dramatic disposition of child protective services, out-of-home placement. As family preservation captured the allegiance of child welfare professionals, the focus on child protection began to lapse. Even as fatalities due to child abuse mounted, children's advocates pressed for policy changes focusing on family preservation. Consequently, when the 1993 Clinton economic package was passed, it included $930 million for family support and preservation services over five years, but only a footnote reference to child protective services.[40] After a decade, family preservation had been incorporated into child welfare through the Promoting Safe and Stable Families program, budgeted at $505 million annually;[41] yet, failure to intervene effectively on behalf of maltreated children contributed to Child Protective Services CPS scandals that erupted across the United States.

Despite policies intended to ameliorate child abuse, the number of confirmed cases of maltreated children climbed steadily, more than quadrupling from 10 per 1,000 in 1976 to 47 in 1996.[42] In 2006, 3.6 million children were alleged to have been maltreated; two-thirds of those were investigated, and 905,000 were determined to have been victims of abuse or neglect. This computed to an incidence rate of child maltreatment of 12.1 per 1,000 children. Children are much more likely to have been neglected than abused. For 2008, the rate of maltreatment was 10.3. Thus, 71 percent of maltreated children had been victims of neglect and 16 percent had been abused. Approximately 9 percent had been sexually abused, and 7 percent were psychologically abused.[43] Girls (10.8 per 1,000 children) were more likely to have been maltreated than boys (9.7 per 1,000 children). Although the majority of abused children were white, African American children were disproportionately overrepresented at 16.6 per 1,000 children. The vast majority of perpetrators were parents.[44] In 2008, the federal Administration on Children and Families (ACF) released an assessment of the performance of the states with respect to seven basic outcomes central to child welfare, the Child and Family Services Reviews (CFSRs). Not one state was able to assure that maltreated children had a permanent and stable living arrangement; not one state was in compliance with regard to families having improved their ability to care for their children; and only one state demonstrated that it adequately met a child's physical and mental health needs. As a result of their poor performance, states risked losing millions of dollars in federal funds; California was penalized $9.0 million.[45] But, there was little reason to expect dramatic improvement in state compliance with the seven standards Reeling from the worst fiscal crisis in a half-century, many states reduced funding for child welfare services.[46] Regardless, states were expected to mount Program Improvement Plans (PIPs), which would chart how the states would address CFSR deficiencies. States were given two years to address CFSR deficits or suffer funding penalties in relation to the number of measures in noncompliance.[47] A second round of CFSR reviews involving 32 states revealed that half had failed to address adequately all of the

child welfare outcomes expected of them.[48] Inadequate resources for child welfare affected the capacity of local agencies to address their mandated responsibilities. For decades the Annie E. Casey Foundation had invested tens of millions of dollars in children's services, identifying and supporting model programs across the nation. Unfortunately, the exemplary programs it subsidized remained just that, isolated from the mainstream and failing to catalyze system-wide reforms. In 2003, the Foundation identified a significant impediment to progress, the human services workforce:

> Human services is reaching a state of crisis. Frontline jobs are becoming more and more complex while the responsibility placed on workers remains severely out of line with their preparation and baseline abilities. Many are leaving the field while a new generation of college graduates shows little interest in entering the human services sector. Millions of taxpayer dollars are being poured into a compromised system that not only achieves little in the way of real results, but its interventions often do more harm than good. It is clear that frontline human services jobs are not attracting the kinds of workers we need, and that regulations, unreasonable expectations, and poor management practices mire workers and their clients in a dangerous status quo.[49]

Efforts to improve the quality of services to maltreated children, often uncoordinated with previous reforms, have shown little evidence that they are effective, thus contributing to the disarray of child welfare. The costs of inferior care of vulnerable children are uncertain; however, court settlements against child welfare agencies reveal that the penalties are not insignificant. In 2010, the District of Columbia agreed to pay $10 million for failing to prevent the permanent brain damage of a child whose foster mother shook him.[50]

Poorly substantiated professional ideologies, such as family preservation, invite legal jeopardy for practitioners when children are harmed. The qualified immunity of child welfare workers established through DeShaney v. Winnebago County Department of Social Services (1989) was successfully challenged in *Currier v. Doran* (2001) in which child welfare workers were found liable when their actions "created the danger" that harmed a child. *Currier* has momentous implications for child welfare professionals. Foremost,

TABLE 15.2 Federal Funding for Child Welfare, Foster Care, and Adoption (in millions of dollars)

Year	IV-B Child Welfare	IV-B/2 Safe & Stable Families	IV-E Foster Care	IV-E Independent Living	IV-E Adoption
1986	198	—	605	—	55
1987	223	—	793	45	74
1988	239	—	891	45	97
1989	247	—	1,153	50	111
1990	253	—	1,473	60	136
1991	274	—	1,819	70	175
1992	274	—	2,233	70	220
1993	295	—	2,547	70	272
1994	295	60	2,607	70	325
1995	292	150	3,050	70	411
1996	277	225	3,114	70	485
1997	292	240	3,692	70	590
1998	291	255	3,704	70	697
1999	292	275	4,012	70	843
2000	292	295	4,255	140	1,012
2001	292	305	4,395	140	1,201
2002	292	375	4,523	140	1,342
2003	290	404	4,485	182	1,463
2004	289	404	4,524	185	1,561
2005	290	404	4,541	187	1,703
2006	287	454	4,439	186	1,823
2007	287	454	4,422	186	1,920
2008	282	428	4,451	185	2,039

"social workers who blatantly fail to heed warning signs of abuse or potential abuse will not be protected from liability."[51] But *Currier* has much broader implications. Workers cannot claim that high caseloads due to agency underfunding provide an excuse for negligence. Moreover, supervisors are legally liable if their "deliberate indifference" to clients' welfare is reflected in their failure to adequately train subordinates.[52] Thus, *Currier* underscores the need for child welfare professionals to demand adequate resources in order to meet their obligations to provide adequate care for at-risk children.

Child fatalities reflected systemic flaws that subverted child well-being. Children's Rights, a New York based legal advocacy organization, sued child welfare agencies in several states, litigating consent decrees that promised to improve services to children by reducing caseloads, increasing the number of professional workers, and improving data systems.[53] Meanwhile, federal funding for child welfare steadily increased as shown in Table 15.2. Because the funding requirements for different titles vary, federal child welfare funding has become a convoluted arrangement that provides incentives to states that are often contradictory. Preserving families, funded through Title IV-B, is counterpoised with Title IV-E that funds foster care. Because Title IV-E is an open-ended entitlement, there is an implicit incentive for states to place children in foster care, if they wish to maximize federal revenues. Thus, simplifying federal funding for child welfare while supporting programs that benefit maltreated children remains a top priority for reform.

Foster Care for Children

When parents are unable to care for their children, foster care is often used to provide alternative care. There is an important relationship between child protective services and foster care: Foster care is primarily a service for victims of child abuse; more than half of children in foster care were placed there by child protective service workers. The second most prevalent reason for child foster care is the "condition or absence of the parent," accounting for about 20 percent of foster care placements.[54]

As in the case of protective services, foster care for children was not coordinated under the provisions of the Social Security Act. States adopted separate policies and, unfortunately, took few measures to monitor children in foster care. During the early 1960s, a series of studies began to document a disturbing development: Rather than being a temporary arrangement for child care, foster care had become a long-term experience for many youngsters, with 70 percent of children in foster care for more than one year.[55] Not only had states planned poorly for the reunification of children with their original families, but in many instances child welfare agencies lost track of foster care children altogether. In response to the deterioration of children's services, "permanency planning" became a central feature of the Adoption Assistance and Child Welfare Act (AACWA) of 1980.

Permanency planning is "the systematic process of carrying out, within a brief time-limited period, a set of goal-directed activities designed to help children live in families that offer continuity of relationships with nurturing parents or caretakers and the opportunity to establish lifetime relationships."[56] AACWA was an ambitious effort, and one expert heralded it as making it "possible to implement at state and local levels a comprehensive service delivery system for children."[57] As a result of permanency planning, the number of children in foster care plummeted. In 1971, 330,400 children were in foster care; by 1982 the number had dropped to 262,000, a reduction of 20.7 percent.[58] Welfare workers swiftly removed children from foster care and reunited them with their biological families under the rationale that community support services would assist parents.

Tragically, inadequate resources sometimes created a vicious circle: When biological parents received few support services, they were less able to care for their children, thereby contributing to the need for child protective services. In the absence of intensive support services, permanency planning for many children meant a revolving door—placement in foster care, reunification with the biological parent(s), and then a return to foster care. In large measure, the permanency planning movement faltered because of lack of support services to families. Not long after the passage of AACWA, Ronald Rooney observed prophetically that "if the promise of permanency planning is to be realized, those who allocate funds must provide money for a continuum of services that are delivered from the point of entry into foster care and include programs designed to prevent the removal of children from their homes."[59] By the late 1980s, with permanency planning beset with multiple problems, foster care was an unreliable way of serving many of the most endangered children in the United States. Since 1995, about 500,000 children have been in foster care, almost twice the number a decade before.[60]

With passage of the Family Support and Preservation Program in 1993, authorizing $930 million to prevent out-of-home placement of abused and neglected children, policymakers gave priority to family preservation to prevent foster care placements.

Several issues have emerged to dampen enthusiasm about foster care as a solution for children from very troubled families. Too often, foster care has emerged as the catalyst of family dramas that become the grist of journalistic accounts of a child welfare system that "is infected with mistrust, backbiting and second-guessing," hardly the ambience that builds public confidence. One reporter summarized his impression of child welfare:

> As soon as a complaint is received, a virtual industry of social workers, lawyers, judges and administrators goes to work, and no matter how pure the intentions are, the process often deteriorates into chaos. A central goal of child welfare is permanence and stability for the child, but cases routinely become so mired in complications, and legalities, and indecision, and nastiness, and the necessity of trying to understand a specific moment of horror in the larger context of societal issues, that the focus can shift from the search for permanence to the mere passage of time. Months pass. Years pass. Rather than resolution, there is drift, so much that nationally, on average a third of the children entering foster care will be there in excess of two years, creating, instead of stability, an ambiguity that can be damaging.[61]

Increasing demand for foster parents and homosexual rights collided in a controversy about the suitability of gays and lesbians as parents. A Texas child welfare supervisor ordered the removal of a foster child from a lesbian foster parent, arguing that the state's antisodomy statutes defined homosexual households as unacceptable.[62] An Arkansas judge ruled a state ban on placing foster children with families having a gay member as unconstitutional.[63] Yet, the U.S. Supreme Court refused to sort out conflicting state policies, letting stand a Florida prohibition on adoption by same-sex parents.[64] The *Washington Post*'s Colbert King undoubtedly spoke for many when he observed, "I couldn't care less what those [foster] parents look like as long as they are strong in themselves and are giving that kid the sense of security, belonging, and love that every child on this earth needs."[65]

Although a desirable outcome for children in foster care would be reunification with biological parents better able to care for them, about 25,000 foster children simply age out of care each year. Their prospects are often grim. A 1998 study of "graduates" of foster care revealed that 37 percent had not graduated from high school, 18 percent had been incarcerated, and 12 percent had been homeless.[66] A subsequent study of children who have aged out of foster care in the Northwest revealed that, within the 12 months prior to being interviewed, 20 percent had a major depressive episode, 12 percent suffered from alcohol and drug dependence, and 25 percent were diagnosed with posttraumatic stress disorder.[67] A study of former foster children from the Midwest found that six of ten boys had been convicted of a crime while three-fourths of women were on public assistance. "We took them away from their parents on the assumption that we as a society would do a better job of raising them," observed researcher Mark Courtney, "We've invested a lot of money and time in their care, and by many measures they're still doing very poorly."[68] In 1999, the Foster Care Independent Living Act provided funding for education and employment services for children who were aging out of foster care; foster youth were entitled to vouchers worth up to $5,000 per year for higher education, for example.[69]

In 2008, President George W. Bush signed Fostering Connections to Success and Increasing Adoptions Act, the most extensive child welfare reform in three decades. Among its provisions were guardianship payments to relatives of children in foster care, tribal access to federal child welfare funding, and an extension of benefits to foster children until age 21 providing they are in school or working. Despite its emphasis on maintaining family integrity, the Act budgeted only $15 million annually for Family Connection grants.[70] Promoted by advocacy organizations, such as the Children's Defense Fund and the Center for Law and Social Policy, Fostering Connections attempted to keep siblings together within the network of their biological family, citing impressionistic evidence that this was superior to traditional foster care.[71] Due to delays in reporting data, it will be years before evidence of the value of kinship care appears.

Despite increases in child welfare funding to encourage innovations, such as permanency planning, family preservation and kinship care, there is little evidence of the efficacy of these initiatives. Two child fatality researchers concluded "The vast majority of state policy that is enacted is not evaluated for effectiveness. Child welfare policy is no exception. The child welfare profession is especially susceptible to ideological movements that are implemented without the checks and balances of research and evaluation."[72] Unlike health care and welfare reform, randomized controlled trials in child welfare are a rarity: "there is not a single intervention that has generated a published peer-review article based on a study in which they accepted referrals from a child welfare agency, randomly assigned them to a treatment condition, and evaluated the outcome," concluded leading researchers in the field.[73] Equally troubling is the absence of research on child well-being.[74] Instead of assessing the benefits of children's services across several variables, the field has been content to use "avoidance of harm" as a standard of effectiveness. In the absence of such research, child welfare interventions are apt to prove ineffective. Indeed, a study of abused children revealed that child protective services intervention resulted in no improvement of families who were visited by a child welfare professional compared to a control group that received no intervention, except that the mothers in the intervention group were more likely to be depressed.[75] Thus, data collection on child welfare programs and field research on program performance are woefully inadequate.

Adoption

From the standpoint of permanency planning, adoption has become an important child welfare service. In the early 1980s, the Children's Bureau noted that 50,000 "hard-to-adopt" children were waiting for homes. Many of these children were of minority origin, had disabilities, or were older and had been in foster care for several years; subsidized adoption proved cost-effective, costing 37 percent less than foster care.[76] Because such children posed a financial burden for adoptive parents, the Adoption Assistance and Child Welfare Act of 1980 provided subsidies to adoptive parents. In 1983, 6,320 children were being subsidized each month at a cost of $12 million.[77] Between 1995 and 2002, the number of agency-involved adoptions virtually doubled from 25,693 to 50,950, respectively.[78] Through the Fostering Connections Act, the number of foster care adoptions approached 54,000, in part due to incentives provided to states: $4,000 for each foster child adopted, and $8,000 per foster child over age 9.[79]

Still, adoption is not without controversy. Because children come from a variety of racial and cultural groups, questions have been raised about transcultural adoption. Should agencies give consideration to maintaining the cultural identity of children placed for adoption by finding them homes in their birth culture? This question was at the heart of the Indian Child Welfare Act of 1978. Native Americans were disturbed that "25 to 35 percent of all American Indian children [were] separated from their families and placed in foster homes, adoptive homes, or institutions."[80] The fact that 85 percent of such placements were in non-Indian families and left the children "without access to their tribal homes and relationships" raised the specter of partial cultural genocide.[81] To reinforce the cultural identity of Native American children, the Indian Child Welfare Act provided for:

> minimal Federal standards for the removal of Indian children from their families and the placement of such children in foster or adoptive homes which will reflect the unique values of Indian culture, and for assistance to Indian tribes in the operation of child and family service programs.[82]

Equally important, the Indian Child Welfare Act established tribes, rather than state courts, as the governing bodies responsible for Indian foster children. Despite efforts to maintain the cultural identity of Native American children, the American Civil Liberties Union investigated the South Dakota Department of Social Services for placing Indian children with white families.[83]

A similar argument for culturally appropriate placement of children was advanced during the 1980s by the National Association of Black Social Workers (NABSW). Noting a high percentage of African American children placed with white families, NABSW contended that cross-racial adoptions deprived individual children of their racial identity and would eventually result in a degree of cultural genocide for the African American community. Research on cross-racial adoption, however, consistently found that African American children did not suffer adverse consequences from growing up in white families. In 1996, former president Clinton signed legislation forbidding interference by organizations, except by Indian tribes, in child placement for reasons based on race.[84] Although provisions to reinforce the cultural identity of children have unquestionable merit in a pluralistic society, the circumstances of many racial and cultural minorities leave the implementation of such policies in doubt.[85] Without basic health, education, and employment supports, many minority families are likely to have difficulty adopting children. For example, the number of African American children available for adoption far outstrips the number of African American families able to adopt children, despite the fact that African American families "adopt at a rate 4.5 times greater than white or Hispanic families."[86] The most recent data available show that African American children are significantly more likely to be waiting for adoption than are white or Hispanic children (see Table 15.3).

Changes in family composition further cloud the picture. The pool of adoptive families has diminished with the increase in the number of female-headed households. The combination of low wages for

TABLE 15.3 Race/Ethnicity of Children Waiting to Be Adopted and Adopted, 2001 (in percentages)

Race/Ethnicity	Waiting Children	Adopted Children
White	32	38
African American	42	35
Hispanic	11	16
Two or more races	2	3
Other	2	2
Unknown	4	5
Missing data	6	0

Source: House Ways and Means Committee, *Overview of Entitlement Programs*, 2004 (Washington, DC: U.S. GPO, 2004), p. 11–125.

women and a shortage of marriageable men means that mothers are encouraged to maintain small families, not to expand them through adoption. To some extent this problem will be mitigated by the Fostering Connections Act which provides payment to guardians of foster children.

In 2008, the Fostering Connections to Success and Increasing Adoptions Act was signed by former president George W. Bush in order to help extended families care for children who had been maltreated. In addition to identifying extended family members who could care for children about to be placed in care, the Fostering Connections Act provided them with guardianship payments since they served as de facto foster parents. Moreover, Fostering Connections provided states with incentives to find adoptive homes for older and disabled children. Grants were made available for Family Group Decision Making in order to strengthen extended families. And, for the first time, Native American tribes had direct access to federal child welfare funding.

Head Start

In response to concerns about the lack of educational preparation of poor children, Head Start was incorporated in the Economic Opportunity Act of 1964. The first Head Start programs were established in poor communities a year later. Intended to compensate for a range of deficits displayed by poor children, Head Start offered health and dental screening, nutrition, and socialization experiences in addition to preschool academic preparation. Of the Great Society programs, Head Start was one of a few that captured the imagination of the nation. Despite wide public support, however, participation in Head Start was somewhat uneven. Significantly, it was not until 1995 that the enrollment of Head Start eclipsed that of 1966; today, fewer than half of eligible children participate in the program.[87]

During the 1980s, when government assistance to the poor was reduced, many poor families dispatched both parents to the labor market to stabilize family income, and this increased the need for Head Start. Even the Deficit Reduction Act of 1990, which held spending for most social programs in check, provided for modest increases in Head Start.[88] In large measure, this funding reflected a growing appreciation that Head Start was a proven investment in human capital. Award-winning author Sylvia Ann Hewlett noted that "Head Start ($3,000 a year per child) is much less expensive than prison ($20,000 a year per inmate)."[89] The 1996 welfare reform act, which required recipients of family cash assistance to participate in the labor market, increased Head Start enrollments even further.

Since its inception, Head Start has largely become a pre-kindergarten program for the minority poor. In 2007, Head Start spent $6.9 billion to serve 908,412 children; 51 percent of children enrolled were age 4 and 35 percent were age 3; 31 percent were African American, 34 percent were Hispanic, 4 percent were American Indian, and 2 percent were Asian. Twelve percent of Head Start children have disabilities.[90] Few dispute the value of Head Start programming for at-risk children.

Emerging Issues in Child Welfare

Changes in the economic and social circumstances of families in the United States have broadened the scope of the issues that traditionally defined child welfare policy. Of these changes, three are likely to

Day care for children has become more important as more and more parents with children work.

Source: oliveromg/Shutterstock

shape child welfare in the future: day care, maternal and child health, and teenage pregnancy.

Day Care

Day care for children has risen in importance as more and more parents with children work. In 1998, families in which both parents worked exceeded more than half of all married couples with children, up from 33 percent in 1976.[91] At the same time, the number of working mothers with young children has skyrocketed; in 1947, only 12 percent of mothers with children under age six worked outside the home, but by 2002 this became 64.1 percent.[92] The need for child day care is felt both by middle-income families, in which both parents work in order to meet the income requirements of a middle-class lifestyle, and by low-income families, in which a parent is encouraged or required to participate in a welfare-to-work program. Yet, the child care available is often unreliable, expensive, and of questionable quality.

The primary programs assisting parents with child care are the federal dependent care tax credit, the child care tax credit, the Child Care and Development Block Grant (CCDBG), and Title XX. The largest federal child care program, CCDBG, allocated $5.0 billion in 2008 to states for care of low-income children. The dependent care tax credit allows families to deduct $3,000 for one child or $6,000 for two children spent on child day care for a given year; the child care tax credit of $1,050 per child ($2,100 total) is refundable and phased out with increased income. Unfortunately, only a small portion of the child care tax credit is refundable, allowing poor families a cash refund for child care expenses. Under Title XX states are able to purchase day care for poor families; but as of 2001, for example, only $129 million, or 7.6 percent, of the $1.7 billion in Title XX funds was expended for child care.[93]

Maternal and Child Health

Maternal and child health has emerged as an issue among child welfare advocates as younger, poor women give birth to low-birth-weight babies who have received inadequate prenatal care. Low birth weight is a concern because such infants have a higher incidence of developmental disabilities, some of which are permanent and eventually require institutional care. Low birth weight in minority infants is of particular concern because it relates to lack of adequate prenatal care.

The primary federal program to enhance prenatal care for low-income families is WIC, the Special Supplemental Nutrition Program for Women, Infants, and Children. Under WIC, low-income pregnant and nursing women and their young children are eligible for food coupons through which they may obtain especially nutritious foods. Even though the WIC program would seem a logical method for addressing the low-birth-weight problem of infants born to poor women, participation in the WIC program is not at desirable levels. Nationwide, only about half of the people financially eligible to participate in WIC do so.[94] In 2011, WIC served 9 million women and infants at a total program cost of $2 billion, or about $46.67 per recipient.[95] Important health care programs have served children, such as Medicaid and the State Child Health Insurance Program (SCHIP). Like many welfare programs, these have not proved ideal. Medicaid reimburses health care providers who agree to the programs' procedures and payments; but if providers refuse to accept Medicaid, the benefit is reduced to symbolic value.[96] Restrictive eligibility provisions introduced by the 2006 Deficit Reduction Act required beneficiaries to produce a birth certificate or passport in order to retain Medicaid. Because the parents of many children, especially immigrants, were unable to produce the necessary documentation, tens of thousands of children were deleted from Medicaid.[97] During discussions of health care reform, children's advocates insisted that SCHIP be reauthorized separately in order to assure its continuance regardless of the outcome of health reform; thus SCHIP will continue until 2015 in its current form, allowing states to extend Medicaid or fashion an independent program to provide health care to low-income children.[98] Among the most important provisions of the 2010 Affordable Care Act is the inclusion of $1.5 billion over five years for nurse home visiting, an empirically tested program through which professional nurses meet with young mothers to assist them through pregnancy and care of their infants.[99] The nurse home visiting initiative is especially important in light of the increasing number of unmarried mothers, in 2007 numbering 1.7 million.[100]

Teen Pregnancy

The Guttmacher Institute reported that the teen pregnancy rate for 2005 had declined 41 percent from its highest in 1990, but had increased 3 percent in 2006.[101] Thus, childbearing among very young women remains a compelling social problem.

Problems relating to maternal and infant health are exacerbated by the sharp rise in the numbers of adolescent females having children. Out-of-wedlock births became an important family issue in the 1980s, when the incidence of unwed motherhood increased so rapidly that by 1983 half of all nonwhite births were outside of marriage.[102] In 2001, the number of births per 1,000 unmarried women was 43.8 for women of all races, 68.2 for African American women, 87.8 for Hispanic women, and 27.5 for non-Hispanic white women.[103] Even though the absolute number of births to teenagers declined between 1973 and 1991, the decline in the total number of adolescent females meant that the teen pregnancy rate was increasing substantially.[104]

Childbearing among very young unmarried women poses a serious problem for public policy for two basic reasons. First, teenage mothers are more likely to drop out of school and thus fail to gain skills that would make them self-sufficient. Adolescent mothers, particularly those who are African American or Hispanic, are apt to have less command of these basic skills. Poor skill development represents an especially critical problem when the skills in question involve parenting. Second, teenage mothers are more likely to depend on welfare, the benefits of which are at levels lower than the actual cost of raising children. This combination of inadequate skill development and dependence on public welfare presents the specter of poor teenagers bearing poor children in an endless cycle of hopelessness. The consequences are particularly tragic for the children, who have little prospect of escaping the poverty trap. Reductions in the numbers of working African American and Hispanic males who are marriageable means that many of these children have little hope that their mother will marry and thus pull them out of poverty, which had been the most prevalent way for mothers to become independent of public welfare.[105] The loss of buying power of the income support provided by Aid to Families with Dependent Children (AFDC; now TANF) has meant that public assistance does not provide an adequate economic base for poor children.[106]

Conclusion

After a half century of federal legislation, many child welfare advocates have become pessimistic about the care provided to youngsters in the United States. Hopes for using the family as the primary institution for child welfare have faded in the absence of economic and social supports to keep families intact. The 1996 imposition of welfare time limits casts a long shadow over poor families. Although by the end of the twentieth century, some of the benefits of unprecedented prosperity and low unemployment began to trickle down to the poor, the economic crisis that began in 2008 has left many welfare and working poor families struggling even more. Aside from stimulus funding, the Obama administration has introduced no new initiatives in child welfare. In apparent deference to Congressional conservatives, the Obama administration proposed a 2012 budget that reduced allocations to child welfare programs by 6.7 percent. Table 15.4 illustrates the various allocations.

TABLE 15.4 2012 Child Welfare Budget Allocations (in percentages)	
Payments to states for foster care	−17.5
Promoting Safe and Stable Families	
Mandatory	−6.9
Discretionary	−34.0
Abandoned Infant Assistance	−8.7
Adoption Awareness	−100
Child Abuse Prevention and Treatment Act	−8.2
Child Welfare Services	−8.7
Mentoring Children of Prisoners	−100
Adoptions incentives	+634.1
Adoption opportunities	+36.1
Child welfare training	+244.7
Community Services Block Grant	+3.6

Source: Children's Budget 2011 (Washington, D.C.: First Focus, 2012).

Federal cuts in child welfare spending focused efforts on the states. Unfortunately, the Great Recession adversely affected state budgets, resulting in cuts in services to children and their families, especially those among minorities. Since 1996 states have been able to seek waivers from the federal government, essentially permitting replication of experiments in welfare reform. However, while many states have received child welfare waivers, the results have been disappointing. Eleven waivers were terminated or failed to produce expected outcomes, while ten generated weak findings. Ultimately, only five waivers yielded strong results; three in implementing guardianship, one in flexible funding, and another in substance abuse.[107] Thus, state waivers remain a largely unrealized vehicle for child welfare reform.

DISCUSSION QUESTIONS

1. Using the Congress.org website, identify a child welfare policy of interest to you. How has programming changed? Have budget appropriations been adequate to address the problem? What could be done to make the policy more effective?

2. Much of child welfare—protective services, foster care, and adoptions—is funded through a complex array of categorical programs. How does your welfare department optimize reimbursement through these funding sources? As a result of reimbursement systems, what are the priorities for children's services? How would you reconcile discrepancies between categorical funding priorities and community needs?

3. Maintaining the cultural identity of minority children who receive foster care and adoption services is a heated issue in child welfare. When there are too few minority families for the children needing foster care and adoption, what should be the policy of the welfare department be in placing minority children? How consistent is your answer with current child welfare policy in your community?

4. Providing preschool programs for children is an increasingly important issue as more mothers enter the workforce. How adequate is day care provision in your community? Who is responsible for the oversight of day care? To what extent are the needs of low-income families considered in day care arrangements? What percentage of families eligible for Head Start actually participate in this program in your community?

5. Among health-related child welfare concerns are infant mortality and low birth weight. How do the statistics in your community compare with the state and national incidence of these two important indicators of child welfare? What are the incidences of infant mortality and low birth weight for children of teenage and minority mothers in your community?

What plans does your community have for improving the health status of infants of minority and low-income families?

6. What is the plausibility of reforming child welfare by instituting a child support enforcement and assurance program, consolidating existing services under a Children's Authority, or mounting a home visiting program? If you favor one of these, how would you convince the public that it constitutes real child welfare reform?

7. *Currier* holds child welfare workers liable in the event a child is harmed. To what extent have child welfare workers in your community become aware of this judicial decision? How could it be used to empower child welfare workers?

NOTES

1. http://www.nccp.org/topics/childpoverty.html
2. http://www.familiesusa.org/resources/publications/reports/one-out-of-three-kids-without-health-insurance.html
3. Dale Rusakoff, "Assessing an Ambiguous Threat: Parents," *Washington Post* (January 19, 1998), p. A1.
4. Walter Trattner, *From Poor Law to Welfare State* (New York: Free Press, 1974), p. 100.
5. Ibid., pp. 106–107.
6. Sallie Watkins, "The Mary Ellen Myth," *Social Work* 35 (November 1990), p. 503.
7. Diana DiNitto and Thomas Dye, *Social Welfare* (Englewood Cliffs, NJ: Prentice Hall, 1987), p. 153.
8. Kathleen Faller, "Protective Services for Children," *Encyclopedia of Social Work*, 18th Ed. (Silver Spring, MD: NASW, 1987), p. 386.
9. Trattner, *From Poor Law to Welfare State*, pp. 181, 183.
10. Trattner, *From Poor Law to Welfare State*, p. 186.
11. Axinn and Levin, *Social Welfare*, pp. 224–228.
12. Sharon Parrott and Nina Wu, "States Are Cutting TANF and Child Care Programs" (Washington, DC: Center on Budget and Policy Priorities, 2003), pp. 1–2.
13. Adam Carasso, C. Eugene Steuerle, and Gillian Reynolds, *Kids' Share 2007* (Washington, DC: Urban Institute, 2007), pp. 3, 8.
14. Barbara Kantrowitz et al., "How to Protect Abused Children," *Newsweek* (November 23, 1987), p. 68.
15. Faller, "Protective Services for Children," pp. 387, 389.
16. Douglas Besharov, "Contending with Overblown Expectations," *Public Welfare* (Winter 1987), pp. 7–8.
17. William Claiborne, "Child Sex Ring or Witch Hunt: Charges Divide Town," *Washington Post* (November 14, 1995), p. A1; "A Northwest Town's Nightmare Continues," *Washington Post Weekly* (June 24–30, 1995), p. 31; and Lela Costin, Howard Karger, and David Stoesz, *The Politics of Child Abuse in America* (New York: Oxford University Press, 1996).
18. Douglas Besharov with Lisa Laumann, "Child Abuse Reporting," *Society* (May/June 1996), p. 43.
19. David Stoesz and Howard Karger, "Suffer the Children," *Washington Monthly* (June 1996), p. 20.

20. Dale Russakoff, "Protector of N.Y. City's Children Knows the System Well," *Washington Post* (December 19, 1996), p. A3.

21. Rachel Swarns, "Court Experts Denounce New York's Child Agency," *New York Times* (October 22, 1997), p. A19.

22. N.R. Kleinfield and Mosi Secret, "A Bleak Life, Cut Short at 4, Harrowing from the Start," *New York Times*, September 9, 2011, p. A1

23. Mosi Secret, "Child Welfare Workers Face Homicide Charge," *New York Times*, March 24, 2011, p. A27; Jennifer Gonnerman, "The Knock at the Door," *New York Magazine*, September 11, 2011.

24. Jo McGinty, "State Keeps Death Files of Abused Children Secret," *New York Times*, February 29, 2012, p. A20.

25. LaShawn Williams, "A Progress Report" (Washington, DC: Center for the Study of Social Policy, March 7, 2000).

26. Sari Horwitz and Scott Higham, "Foster Care Case-loads 'Horrible,'" *Washington Post* (March 27, 2000), p. A1.

27. Sari Horwitz, Scott Higham, and Sarah Cohen, "'Protected' Children Died as Government Did Little," *Washington Post* (n.d.).

28. http://www.cbsnews.com/2100-201_162-3699125.html

29. Sue Pressley, "5-year-old Missing 15 Months, and No One Noticed," *Washington Post* (May 4, 2002), p. A1.

30. Carol Miller, "Miami Welfare Workers Held Off Notifying Police of Missing Child," *Washington Post* (May 6, 2002), p. A3.

31. Dana Canedy, "Two Years after Girl Disappeared, Little Has Changed in Florida Agency," *New York Times* (January 19, 2003), p. 18.

32. Matthew Purdy, Andrew Jacobs, and Richard Jones, "Life behind Basement Doors," *New York Times* (January 12, 2003), p. A1.

33. Richard Jones and Leslie Kaufman, "New Jersey Shows Failures of Child Welfare System," *New York Times*. Retrieved April 15, 2003, from http://www.nytimes.com

34. Richard Jones and Leslie Kaufman, "Foster Care Secrecy Magnifies Suffering in New Jersey Cases," *New York Times* (May 4, 2003), pp. 1, 32.

35. Richard Jones, "For Family of Beaten Boy, Tears, Not Finger-Pointing," *New York Times* (August 20, 2003), p. 1.

36. Brown, "Child Fatalities," Congressional testimony, July 12, 2011.

37. Costin, Karger, and Stoesz, *The Politics of Child Abuse in America*.

38. Jane Waldfogel, *The Future of Child Protection: How to Break the Cycle of Abuse and Neglect* (Cambridge, MA: Harvard University Press, 1998).

39. Children's Rights, downloaded February 14, 2011.

40. Costin, Karger, and Stoesz, *The Politics of Child Abuse in America*.

41. House Ways and Means Committee, *Overview of Entitlement Programs, 2004* (Washington, DC: U.S. GPO, 2004), p. 11–15.

42. Miringoff, *Social Health*, p. 75.

43. House Ways and Means Committee, *Overview of Entitlement Programs, 2004*, pp. 11-75–11-77.

44. http://www.cdc.gov/ViolencePrevention/pdf/CM-DataSheet-a.pdf

45. *Children's Budget 2011* (Washington, DC: First Focus, 2012).

46. Robert Pear, "U.S. Finds Fault in All 50 States' Child Welfare Programs, and Penalties May Follow," *New York Times* (April 26, 2004), p. A17.

47. *Improving the Performance and Outcomes of Child Welfare* (Washington, DC: Center for the Study of Social Policy, 2003).

48. http://democrats.waysandmeans.house.gov/media/pdf/111/s11cw.pdf

49. Annie E. Casey Foundation, *The Unsolved Challenge of System Reform* (Baltimore: 2003), p. 2.

50. Henri Cauvin, "D.C. to Pay Abused Boy $10 Million," *Washington Post*, November 9, 2010, p. B4.

51. Daniel Pollack and James Marsh, "Social Work Misconduct May Lead to Liability," *Social Work 9, 4* (October 2004), p. 611.

52. Ibid., p. 611.

53. http://www.childrensrights.org/reform-campaigns/results-of-reform/

54. Theodore Stein, "Foster Care for Children," *Encyclopedia of Social Work*, 18th ed. (Silver Spring, MD: NASW, 1987), pp. 641–642.

55. Ibid., p. 643.

56. Anthony Maluccio and Edith Fein, "Permanency Planning: A Redefinition," *Child Welfare* (May–June 1983), p. 197.

57. Duncan Lindsey, "Achievements for Children in Foster Care," *Social Work* (November 1982), p. 495.

58. House Ways and Means Committee, *Overview of Entitlement Programs*, 2004, pp. 11-86–11-87.

59. Ronald Rooney, "Permanency Planning for All Children?" *Social Work* (March 1982), p. 157.

60. *Overview of Entitlement Programs*, (Washington, DC: U.S. GPO, 2008), Table 11.5.

61. David Finkel, "Now Say Goodbye to Diane," *Washington Post Magazine* (May 4, 1997), pp. 10–11.

62. Sam Verhovek, "Homosexual Foster Parent Sets Off a Debate in Texas," *New York Times* (November 30, 1997), p. 20.

63. David Hammer, "Arkansas Foster Child Law Stricken," *Washington Post* (December 30, 2004), p. A5.

64. Charles Lane, "Gay-Adoption Ban in Florida to Stand," *Washington Post* (January 11, 2005), p. A4.

65. Colbert King, "What Every Child Needs," *Washington Post* (March 11, 2000), p. A19.

66. House Ways and Means Committee, *Overview of Entitlement Programs*, 2004, pp. 11-50–11-51.

67. Peter Pecora, "Improving Family Foster Care: Findings from the Northwest Foster Care Alumni Study" (Seattle: Annie E. Casey Foundation, 2005).

68. Erik Eckholm, *New York Times*, April 7, 2010, p. A17.

69. House Ways and Means Committee, *Overview of Entitlement Programs*, 2004, p. 11–48.

70. *Overview of Entitlement Programs* (Washington, DC: U.S. GPO, 2008), pp. 11-221–11-223.

71. http://www.clasp.org/admin/site/publications/files/0347.pdf

72. Emily Douglas and Sean McCarthy, "Child Maltreatment Fatalities," *Journal of Social Policy*, 10, 2011, p. 139.

73. Fred Wulczyn, Richard Barth, Ying-Ying Yuan, Brenda Harden, and John Landsverk, *Beyond Common Sense*, (New Brunswick, N.J.: Transaction Books, 2005), p. 155.

74. http://www.soc.duke.edu/~cwi/

75. Nicholas Bakalar, "Child Abuse Investigations Didn't Reduce Risk, A Study Finds," *New York Times*, October 10, 2010, p. D3.

76. Elizabeth Cole, "Adoption," *Encyclopedia of Social Work*, 18th ed. (Silver Spring, MD: NASW, 1987), p. 70.

77. House Ways and Means Committee, *Overview of Entitlement Programs*, 1985 (Washington, DC: U.S. Government Printing Office, 1985), p. 494.

78. House Ways and Means Committee, *Overview of Entitlement Programs*, 2004, p. 11–124.

79. *Overview of Entitlement Programs* (Washington, DC: U.S. GPO, 2008), p. 1–88.

80. Ronald Fischler, "Protecting American Indian Children," *Social Work* (September 1980), p. 341.

81. Evelyn Lance Blanchard and Russell Lawrence Barsh, "What Is Best for Tribal Children?" *Social Work* (September 1980), p. 350.

82. Fischler, "Protecting American Indian Children," p. 341.

83. http://www.nativetimes.com/news/federal/6304-aclu-to-probe-if-sd-breaks-child-protection-laws

84. Spencer Rich, "Wage Bill Includes Provisions Intended to Increase Adoptions," *Washington Post* (August 10, 1996), p. A4.

85. Patricia Hogan and Sau-Fong Siu, "Minority Children and the Child Welfare System," *Social Work* (November–December 1988), pp. 312–317.

86. Cole, "Adoption," p. 70.

87. Children's Defense Fund, *The State of America's Children*, 1991 (Washington, DC: Children's Defense Fund, 1991), p. 44.

88. Paul Leonard and Robert Greenstein, *One Step Forward: The Deficit Reduction Package of 1990* (Washington, DC: Center on Budget and Policy Priorities, 1990), p. 34.

89. Sylvia Ann Hewlett, *When the Bough Breaks* (New York: HarperCollins, 1992), p. 300.

90. *Overview of Entitlement Programs* (Washington, DC: U.S. GPO, 2008, Tables 15-33 and 15-34).

91. "Two-Income Families Now a Majority," *Richmond Times-Dispatch* (October 24, 2000), p. A3.

92. House Ways and Means Committee, *Overview of Entitlement Programs*, 2004, p. 9–2.

93. House Ways and Means Committee, *Overview of Entitlement Programs*, 2004, p. 10–9.

94. Miringoff and Miringoff, *The Social Health of the Nation*, p. 52.

95. http://www.fns.usda.gov/pd/wisummary.htm

96. Denise Grady, "Children on Medicaid Shown to Wait Longer for Care," *New York Times* (June 16, 2011), p. A27.

97. Robert Pear, "Lacking Papers, Citizens Are Cut from Medicaid," *New York Times* (March 12, 2007), p. A1.

98. http://www.ncsl.org/issues-research/health/childrens-health-insurance-program-overview.aspx

99. http://www.hhs.gov/news/press/2010pres/07/20100721a.html

100. Rob Stein and Donna St. George, "Number of Unwed Mothers Has Risen Sharply in the U.S.," *Washington Post*, May 14, 2009, p. A6.

101. http://www.guttmacher.org/pubs/USTPtrends.pdf

102. Michael Novak (ed.), *The New Consensus on Family and Welfare* (Washington, DC: American Enterprise Institute, 1987), p. 135.

103. House Ways and Means Committee, *Overview of Entitlement Programs*, 2004, p. M-3.

104. U.S. House of Representatives, *1998 Green Book*, p. 1245.

105. William Julius Wilson, "American Social Policy and the Ghetto Underclass," *Dissent* (Winter 1988), pp. 80–91.

106. David Ellwood, *Poor Support: Poverty and the American Family* (New York: Basic Books, 1988), p. 58.

107. Shadi Houshyar, "Title IV-E Waivers," *First Focus* (Washington, DC: 2011), p. 3.

Housing Policies

Source: John Nordell/The Image Works

A house represents more than a mere address of domicile in America: It is the primary asset of most American families and a significant expenditure. On average, Americans spend 34 percent of their annual income on housing.[1] Homeownership appears to result in more stability since renters are 2.7 times more likely to relocate in a given year than homeowners.[2] The stability encouraged by homeownership may also be a prerequisite to the development of neighborhood identity, involvement in local social networks, and the engagement with local institutions and organizations that strengthen social support. However, with the advent of the housing market bust and the 2007 recession, the difficulties in owning and protecting an existing home from foreclosure have become more prominent.

Most of the recent attention on housing has focused on the middle class. Yet, housing problems affect millions of Americans. Persistent problems include a lack of low-income affordable housing, a large inventory of dilapidated and dangerous housing, and high numbers of homeless people. Although housing discussions have frequently focused on homelessness, finding and maintaining adequate and affordable housing is also problematic for people on public assistance, for the working poor, and for a large section of the middle class. This chapter discusses federal housing programs directed toward homeownership and examines housing problems in the United States, with particular emphasis on low-income housing, affordability, homelessness, and proposals for housing reform.

Overview of Housing Legislation

Federal housing legislation began in 1937. As Figure 16.1 illustrates, this legislation developed into a tangle of laws that often evolved in conflicting directions. In 1990, Congress passed the Cranston-Gonzales National Affordable Housing Act, which authorized housing-related block grants to state and local governments. The goals of the 1990 legislation included: (1) decentralizing housing policy by allowing states to design and administer their own housing programs; (2) using nonprofit sponsors to help develop and implement housing services; (3) linking housing assistance more closely with social services; (4) facilitating home ownership for low- and moderate-income people; (5) preserving existing federally subsidized housing units; and (6) initiating cost sharing among federal, state, and

local governments and nonprofit organizations.[3] This act also introduced the HOME investment partnerships block grant program, the Homeownership and Opportunity for People Everywhere (HOPE) program, and the national home ownership trust demonstration. Key HUD (the Department of Housing and Urban Development) programs to increase the stock of affordable housing include:

1. **The HOME program** expands the number of affordable housing for low- and very low-income families by providing grants to state and local governments. Participating jurisdictions use their grants to finance housing programs that meet local needs. Jurisdictions have flexibility in designing their local HOME programs within HUD and legislative guidelines. They may also use their HOME funds to help renters, new homebuyers, or existing homeowners.
2. **The SHOP program** funds nonprofit organizations to buy home sites and develop or improve the infrastructure needed for sweat equity so that low-income families can purchase homes. The program is designed to attract national and regional nonprofit organizations with experience in using volunteer labor to build housing (i.e., Habitat for Humanity).
3. **The HOPE program** is designed to facilitate home ownership by low income families through the sale of publicly owned or held homes to current residents or other low-income households. HOPE also includes efforts to combine social services with housing assistance for households of the elderly and disabled, who would otherwise be unable to live independently.[4]
4. The linkage between housing and social services was strengthened by **the Family Sufficiency Program** that called for public housing authorities (PHAs) to help residents obtain coordinated social services to assist them in gaining employment. Participating families must complete these programs or risk losing their housing assistance. In return, as a participant's income increased, the money that would normally go toward a higher rent (calculated at 30 percent of income) was set aside in a special escrow account to be used for the purchase of a home. The legislation also included modest funds to create "Family Investment Centers" that provided social services in or near public housing projects.[5]

The Housing Act of 1937	The United States had no national housing policy prior to the Housing Act of 1937. The objective of the act was to: "provide financial assistance to the states and political subdivisions thereof for the elimination of unsafe and unsanitary housing conditions, for the eradication of slums, for the provision of decent, safe and sanitary dwellings for families of low income, and for the reduction of unemployment and the stimulation of business activity, to create a United States Housing Authority and for other purposes."
The Housing Act of 1949 (Amended 1937 Act)	This amendment called for federal money for slum clearance and urban redevelopment and for the creation of a public authority charged with building and administering low-income housing units. Specifically, this bill required each locality to develop a plan for urban redevelopment that contained provisions for "predominantly residential dwellings." The wording of this bill was interpreted by localities to mean that only one-half of new construction was to be devoted to low-income housing.
Housing Act of 1954 (Amended the 1949 Act)	"Urban development" was changed to urban renewal, and localities were required to submit a master plan for removing urban blight and for community development. The act removed the requirement that new federally subsidized urban construction be "predominantly residential," clearing the way for massive slum clearance projects. It also allowed localities to more easily lease or sell land and to avoid the construction of public housing. Through renewal projects, localities tried to revitalize inner cities by attracting middle- and upper-income families at the expense of displaced poor families. From 1949 to 1963, urban renewal projects removed about 243,000 housing units and replaced them with 68,000 units, of which only 20,000 were for low-income families.
The Demonstration Cities and Metropolitan Development Act (Model Cities)	Passed in 1966 as part of President Lyndon Johnson's War on Poverty, the act focused on deteriorated housing and blighted neighborhoods. The Model Cities legislation promised to "concentrate public and private resources in a comprehensive five-year attack on social, economic, and physical problems of slums and blighted neighborhoods." The Model Cities Act and virtually all neighborhood development acts were superseded by the Housing and Community Development Act of 1974.
The Housing and Community Development Act of 1974	This wide-ranging bill included provisions for urban renewal, neighborhood development, model cities, water and sewer projects, neighborhood and facility grants, public facilities and rehabilitation loans, and urban beautification and historic preservation. Although spending priorities were determined at the national level, communities were required to submit a master plan, including specific references to their low-income housing needs.
Home Mortgage Disclosure Act (HMDA)	This act focused on mortgage redlining. Advocates argued that a major cause of community deterioration was a "lending strike," or redlining, by financial institutions. Redlining is defined as "an outright refusal of an insurance company, bank, or other financial institution to provide its services solely on the basis of the location of a property." The term is derived from the practice of marking in red the area on a map avoided by insurance or financial institutions. As a result, families seeking to purchase a home in a redlined neighborhood may be denied a mortgage, insurance, or other necessary services. In 1976, President Gerald Ford signed the Home Mortgage Disclosure Act, which required virtually every bank or savings and loan association to annually disclose where it made its loans.

FIGURE 16.1 Historical Highlights of Pre-1990 Housing Legislation

Community Reinvestment Act (CRA) of 1977	Broader than the HMDA, the CRA established the principle that each bank and savings institution has an obligation to make loans in every neighborhood of its service area. Virtually all lending institutions are covered under the CRA, and the law requires the federal government to annually evaluate the performance of each lending institution. Primary enforcement involves control by federal regulatory agencies over new charters, bank growth and mergers, relocations, and acquisitions. Only a handful of the CRA challenges result in punitive action against lenders. The power of the act rests with the ability of community groups to win concessions from lending institutions, usually in the form of negotiated settlements.

Sources: Quoted in Charles S. Prigmore and Charles R. Atherton, *Social Welfare Policy: Analysis and Formulation* (Lexington, MA: D. C. Heath, 1979), pp. 146–147; Robert Morris, *Social Policy of the American Welfare State,* 2nd edition. (New York: Longman, 1985), p. 131; Barbara Habenstreit, *The Making of America* (New York: Julian Messner, 1971), p. 46; Richard Geruson and Dennis McGrath, *Cities and Urbanization* (New York: Praeger, 1977), pp. 6–7; National Training and Information Center, *Insurance Redlining: Profits v. Policyholders* (Chicago: NTIC, 1973), p. 1.

FIGURE 16.1 (Continued)

In 1998, former president Clinton signed the Quality Housing and Work Responsibility Act of 1998 (QHWRA), in some ways the housing equivalent of the 1996 PRWORA. In line with the PRWORA, the federal government devolved its responsibility as the primary agent for publicly assisted housing to 3,400 semiautonomous local PHAs. With input from public housing residents, these strengthened PHAs determine rents, admissions policies, and what (if any) social services are provided. The QHWRA also ties workforce participation into housing benefits. For example (1) PHAs can consider prospective tenants' employment history in the admissions decision; (2) TANF recipients who fail to fulfill their work requirement can lose Section 8 or public housing benefits; and (3) PHAs are encouraged to recruit "good" working-class families to act as role models for welfare-dependent families (the legislation has decreased the percentage of public housing units earmarked for very low-income families from 75 to 70 percent). The QHWRA also mandates that low-income tenants take personal responsibility for moving into better living conditions (e.g., a single-family home).[6]

On February 17, 2009, President Obama instituted the American Recovery and Reinvestment Act of 2009 to soften the impact of the recession on the economy and employment. Specially, Congress provided the Department of Transportation and the Department of Housing and Urban Development $61.7 billion in additional funding. HUD used its portion of the funds to build and renovate housing infrastructure, thus stimulating the construction industry and boosting employment. HUD also provided targeted homeless and low-income groups with affordable housing options. By early 2010, HUD had assisted 357,808 low-income people and developed/rehabilitated 188,184 units. A further $1.5 billion was used to provide emergency and short-term accommodation for homeless families.[7]

The Federal Government and Low-Income Housing Programs

Housing is a fixed cost that is often paid before food, clothing, and health care bills.[8] For poor families, the precious little that remains after a rent or mortgage payment is used to buy food and other necessities for the remainder of the month. The important impact of housing costs on family finances has fueled the federal government's involvement with low- and non-low-income housing programs. In response to the problems of finding affordable housing and homeowner mortgage struggles, the Obama administration in 2009 allocated $230 billion of federal funds to homeownership programs and $60 billion for affordable rental housing programs.[9] However, federal funding declined for the HOME and Community Block Grant programs in 2010.[10]

Table 16.1 provides an overview of key HUD programs.

TABLE 16.1 Overview of HUD's Major Grant, Subsidy, and Loan Programs

- **Affordable Housing Programs (HOME Investment Partnerships—see below)** was funded at $4 billion in 2009.[11] From 1992 to 2007, more than 600 communities have completed more than 834,000 affordable housing units, including 352,000 for new homebuyers. In addition, 186,000 tenants have received direct rental assistance. HOME Investment Partnership Grants provide assistance to renters, existing home owners, and first-time homebuyers, build state and local capacity to carry out affordable housing programs, and expand the capacity of nonprofit community housing organizations to develop and manage housing. The Housing Opportunities for Persons with AIDS provides affordable housing and related assistance to persons with HIV/AIDS. The Homeless Programs consists primarily of grants to public and private organizations and agencies to establish comprehensive systems for meeting the needs of homeless people.
- **Affordable Housing Trust Fund:** is a $1 billion trust to support local governments in creating, renovating and maintaining affordable housing options for low-income homeowners.[12]
- **Brownfields Redevelopment** provides competitive economic development grants for qualified Brownfields (i.e., the cleanup and economic redevelopment of contaminated sites) projects.
- **Community Development Block Grants (CDBG)** was funded at about $4.5 billion in 2009. CDBGs are provided to units of local government and states for the funding of local community development programs that address housing and economic development needs, primarily for low- and moderate-income persons.
- **Demolition and Revitalization of Severely Distressed Public Housing (HOPE IV)** makes awards to public housing authorities on a competitive basis to demolish obsolete or failed developments or to revitalize, where appropriate, sites upon which these developments exist.
- **Empowerment Zones/Enterprise Communities (EZ/EC)** is designed to create self-sustaining, long-term development in distressed urban and rural areas. The program uses a combination of federal tax incentives and flexible grant funds to reinvigorate declining communities.
- **Fair Housing Assistance Program (FHAP)** provides grants to state and local agencies that administer fair housing laws that are equivalent to the Federal Fair Housing Act.
- **Fair Housing Initiatives Program (FHIP)** provides funds competitively to private and public entities to carry out local, regional and national programs that assist in eliminating discriminatory housing practices and educate the public and housing providers on their fair housing rights and responsibilities.
- **Government National Mortgage Association (Ginnie Mae).** Through its mortgage-backed securities program, Ginnie Mae facilitates the financing of residential mortgage loans by guaranteeing the timely payment of principal and interest to investors of privately issued securities backed by pools of mortgages insured or guaranteed by FHA, the Department of Veterans Affairs, and the Rural Housing Service. The Ginnie Mae guarantee gives lenders access to the capital market to originate new loans.
- **Homeless Assistance Grants** provides funding to break the cycle of homelessness and to move homeless persons and families into permanent housing. This is done by providing rental assistance, emergency shelter, transitional and permanent housing, and supportive services to homeless persons and families.
- **Housing Opportunities For Persons With AIDS** (HOPWA) is designed to provide states and localities with resources and incentives to devise long-term comprehensive strategies for meeting the housing needs of persons living with HIV/AIDS and their families.
- **Indian Community Development Block Grant** assists Native Alaskans and Indians in building or purchasing homes on Trust Land, rehabilitating houses and improving community infrastructure and job opportunities. In FY2011, more than $130 million was provided in funding for 84 projects.[13]
- **Indian Housing Block Grant** provides Native Americans and Indians with assistance in building, purchasing or rehabilitating their homes. In FY2011, $654 million was provided in funding to assist 6,286 families.[14]
- **Making Home Affordable Program:** Homeowners can change their loans to lower-cost options and or take fixed-rate mortgages to lock in interest rates. The federal government provided $75 billion in funds as incentives for mortgage brokers and homeowners to participate in 2009.[15] The program aims for mortgage repayments to remain at or below 31 percent of homeowners' income, thus alleviating the cost burden for homeowners.[16]

TABLE 16.1 (*Continued*)

- **Mutual Mortgage Insurance (MMI) program:** This program aims to assist low and medium income people in entering the housing market through insuring mortgages for lenders. If homeowners default on these government insured loans, the Federal Housing Administration provides the mortgage payment owed.[17]

- **Neighborhood Stabilization Program:** $2 billion in funds that is used to rehabilitate and sell abandoned and foreclosed houses.[18]

- **Office of Lead Hazard Control** is authorized to make grants to states, localities, and Native American tribes to conduct lead-based paint hazard reduction and abatement activities in private low-income housing.

- **Public and Indian Housing (PIH) Grants and Loans** was funded at about $3.9 billion in FY2011. Public Housing Operating Subsidies are financial assistance programs provided for project operations to assist approximately 1.2 million units. Public Housing was established by the U.S. Housing Act of 1937 and is restricted to households whose incomes are too low to find suitable private housing.[19] The income of most families in public housing is less than 25 percent of the area median income and about one-half rely primarily on public assistance (TANF, SSI, and General Assistance) for their income; the other half rely on earned incomes, pensions, or Social Security. Residents pay 30 percent of their monthly adjusted income on rent. Public housing is concentrated in high poverty areas.

- **Section 202/811 Capital Grants** was funded at less than $1 billion in 2007. The program is designed to provide funds for the construction and long-term support of housing for the elderly and persons with disabilities. Advances are interest-free and do not have to be repaid, providing the housing remains available for low-income persons for at least 40 years.

- **Tax Incentives for Homeowners:** First Homebuyers will receive $8,000 in tax credits that only need to be repaid if the home is owned for less than three years.[20]

- **The Home Affordable Refinance Program (HARP)** Homeowners will also be able to refinance their homes providing that the cost of the mortgage is not more than 125 percent of their house's value and the mortgage is with Fannie Mae or Freddie Mac.[21] Furthermore, the loan to value ratio (LTV) must be 80 percent.[22] To ameliorate financial losses on mortgage guarantees, the government has provided subsidies to Fannie Mae and Freddie Mac, thus taking on most of the risk involved in the lending for this program. The total in subsidies as of September 2009 was $96 billion.[23] As of early 2012, HARP's eligibility criteria has been revised, lowering credit approval scores and income limits and raising LTV ratios in order to reach more distressed homeowners.[24] Included in these loan guarantee programs are the *Indian Housing Block Grant, Federal Guarantees for Financing Tribal Housing Activities, Public and Indian Housing/Indian Loan Guarantee Program,* and *Loan Guarantees for Native Hawaiian Housing Block Grants.* These provide guaranteed loans to Native Americans, Indians, and Hawaiians for the purchase, rehabilitation, and refinancing of homes.[25]

- **The Homelessness Prevention Fund:** As part of the 2009 American Recovery and Reinvestment Act, $1.5 billion was provided by Congress to fund the Homelessness Prevention and Rapid Rehousing Program (HPRP) for a duration of three years. The program targets at-risk families and individuals, providing financial assistance for rent, utilities and moving costs. The program also focuses on shifting homeless people into more permanent housing situations.[26]

- **The Housing Choice Voucher Program** (Section 8 Rental Assistance) is HUD's largest program. The Section 8 program is based on a voucher system that allows low-income tenants (50 percent or less of the area median income) to occupy existing and privately owned housing stock. The voucher covers the difference between a fixed percentage of a tenant's income (30 percent) and the fair market rent of a housing unit. The HUD subsidy goes to the local PHA, which then pays the landlord, provided that the unit meets quality standards. Contract terms for subsidies last for from five to fifteen years. About half of Section 8 is project-based, meaning that tenants have to live in specific apartments. The other half is tenant-based, allowing tenants to take their subsidies and move. Section 8 also provides funds for new construction and for substantial and moderate rehabilitation of existing units. Only a minority of eligible applicants are served, and most are on a waiting list when they apply. In 2009, Congress provided $16 billion for rent subsidies.[27]

TABLE 16.1 (*Continued*)

- **The Office of Rural Housing and Economic Development** (FmHA Section 502) was established to ensure that HUD has a comprehensive approach to rural housing and rural economic development issues. The office funds technical assistance and capacity-building in rural, under-served areas, and provides grants for Indian tribes, state housing finance agencies, and state economic development agencies to pursue strategies designed to meet rural housing and economic development needs. Section 502 makes low interest loans available for home purchases in rural areas.

Sources: Various documents downloaded from U.S. Department of Housing and Urban Development, http://www.hud.gov and the Catalog of Federal Domestic Assistance, http://www.cfda.gov/.

Apart from HUD-administered programs, there is also the Low Income Housing Tax Credits (LIHTC). Created by the Tax Reform Act of 1986, the LIHTC was as a way for the federal government to encourage the development of affordable housing without having to allocate direct federal expenditures. Apartments supported by the LIHTC cannot be rented to anyone whose income exceeds 50 percent of the area median income and, the maximum rent charge is set at 30 percent of income.[28] Between 1992 and 2009, an average of 1,386 projects and nearly 103,000 units were placed into service each year.[29] These housing units provided affordable housing options for working families, seniors, homeless people, and those with special needs.[30] As of 2011, the LIHTC has assisted in the production of 1.6 million housing units since its inception.[31] This has been accomplished by providing investors in eligible affordable housing developments with a dollar-for-dollar reduction in their federal tax liability. The LIHTC now accounts for most new affordable apartment production.[32]

Despite its importance, governmental assistance for housing was never provided as an entitlement to all households that qualify for aid. Unlike income maintenance programs such as SSI and the former AFDC, housing programs are not automatically provided to all eligible applicants. Congress appropriates funds yearly for various new commitments which can extend to 30 years.[33] Because funding levels are usually low, only a portion of eligible applicants actually receives assistance.[34] Demand for affordable housing significantly outweighs supply. Despite the approximately 10 million extremely low-income renter households that required housing in 2009, only 3.6 million affordable housing units were available to meet the demand.[35] Moreover, more than 10 million households earning less than $15,000 a year pay more than 50 percent of their income on housing.[36]

Relatively low levels of funding have been earmarked for housing programs. This low funding level has also resulted in long waiting lists for public housing and Section 8 vouchers.[37] NLIHC data shows that waiting lists for public housing and rental assistance vouchers far surpass anticipated availability of affordable units.[38] (See Figure 16.2.) The cumulative shortfall in capital improvement funding reached approximately $26 billion in 2012 and underfunding has resulted in the demolition and dispossession of over 150,000 units in the last 15 years due to deterioration and insufficient maintenance.[39,40] In 2006, more than 70 percent of households under the poverty line were not served by public housing; in 2008 less than one-third of renters with incomes of less than 30 percent of the median local income received public housing assistance.[41]

For many families, the cost of housing represents the single largest expenditure in the household budget.

Source: Andy Dean Photography/Shutterstock

Section 8*	Public Housing
• Section 8 Housing Choice Voucher Program served over 2 million people; however, 200,000 vouchers authorized by Congress were not used, partly due to insufficient funding.	• Public housing was home to 2.3 million seniors, people with disabilities, and low-income families with children.
• More than 324,000 seniors relied on Housing Choice Vouchers for affordable housing, representing 16 percent of all Section 8 households. Twenty-three percent of Section 8 seniors were 80 years or older. The median annual income for an elderly household in Section 8 was $8,550 and 90 percent relied on Social Security or Supplemental Security payments as their primary source of income.	• Thirty-one percent of public housing residents were seniors; more than 400,000 seniors relied on public housing and supportive services; 27 percent of public housing's seniors were 80 years of age or older. The median annual income for an elderly household in public housing was $8,250 and 72 percent of seniors relied on Social Security payments as their primary source of income.
• Section 8 recipients included almost 400,000 households in which one or more members had a disability, representing 22 percent of all voucher households. Almost 40,000 Section 8 households had a child with a disability.	• Thirty-two percent of all public housing residents (400,000 households) were disabled. Almost 18,000 public housing households had a child with a disability.
• Sixty-one percent of all Section 8 households were families with children. More than 2.4 million children lived in Section 8, representing over 50 percent of all residents. Almost 50 percent of households with children obtained their primary income from wages, with the average income being $11,390.	• About 1.2 million children lived in public housing, representing 43 percent of all public housing residents.
	• Only 19 percent of families with children rely primarily on welfare; half of families with children obtain their primary source of income from wages.

*Section 8 information based on data gathered between 2007 and 2009.

Sources: Center on Budget and Policy Priorities, *Policy Basics: Introduction to Public Housing,* (Washington DC: Center on Budget and Policy Priorities, 17th of December, 2008). Retrieved July 2012 from http://www.cbpp.org/files/policybasics-housing.pdf; B. Sard & W. Fischer, *Preserving Safe, High Quality Public Housing Should Be a Priority of Federal Housing Policy,* (Washington DC: Center on Budget and Policy Priorities, 8th of October 2008). Retrieved July 2012 from http://centeronbudget.org/files/9–18–08hous.pdf; Center on Budget and Policy Priorities, *Introduction to the Housing Voucher Program,* (Washington DC: Center on Budget and Policy Priorities, 15th of May 2009). Retrieved July 2012 from http://www.cbpp.org/files/5–15–09hous.pdf. Council of Large Public Housing Authorities, *Quick Facts on Public Housing* (Washington, DC: Author, 2004).

FIGURE 16.2 Characteristics of Section 8 Recipients and Residents in Public Housing, 2008

Issues in Housing Policy

The equity in home ownership is the cornerstone of wealth for most U.S. families; however, the housing bust and subprime mortgage crisis have had widespread consequences for homeowners. Since 2006, over $7 trillion in home equity (the difference between the mortgage balance and the home's market value) has been lost, and home prices on average have declined by 33 percent.[42] As of 2011, the average homeowners' equity—the mortgage balance as a proportion of the home's market value—was 62 percent.[43] In January 2012, the Federal Reserve Board reported that 12 million homeowners had mortgages that were "underwater"; in other words, the value of their home was less than the remaining mortgage debt. This equates to more than one in five mortgaged homes and increases the likelihood of foreclosure.[44] For the first time since the Federal Reserve began record keeping in 1945, home equity represents the smallest share of household net wealth.[45]

Spotlight 16.1

THE DEPARTMENT OF HOUSING AND URBAN DEVELOPMENT

Established in 1965, the Department of Housing and Urban Development (HUD) offers various programs to increase homeownership, support community development, and increase access to affordable housing free from discrimination. To learn more about HUD and its many programs, visit its website at http://www.hud.gov.

The United States spends less on housing assistance than any other Western industrial nation. Not only does the United States fail to adequately assist poor people with housing, but most housing subsidies benefit the nonpoor. For example, individuals can deduct interest on up to $1 million in mortgage indebtedness, plus interest on another $100,000 in home equity loans. The home-mortgage deduction is the third-largest single

"tax expenditure" behind the deductions companies take for contributions to pension plans and health care premiums.[46] The richer the home owner is, the better the deal. More than 80 percent of the major tax incentives for housing go to the top 20 percent of Americans, while less than 5 percent go to the bottom 60 percent.[47] In 2009, the mortgage interest deduction cost the federal government $100 billion.[48]

Nearly half of all families with mortgages receive no housing tax benefit at all. Since the mortgage cutoff of $1 million is much higher than the cost of a basic home, the bulk of the subsidies end up encouraging families who would have bought a home anyway to buy a larger house and/or to borrow more against it.[49]

Trends in U.S. Housing

The following are some highlights of the often contradictory U.S. housing trends:

- The overall U.S. homeownership rate in early 2012 was 65.4 percent, which is the lowest rate since 1997.[50]
- Home sales and the value of residential construction reached new highs in 2003[51] but have declined significantly since 2006.[52] In 2007, the median sales price for a single-family existing home was $236,393; by 2011, that had decreased to $166,200.[53] When broken down, the differences in home ownership between races is stark and has been exacerbated by the recent recession. In early 2012, the non-Hispanic white homeownership rate was 73.5 percent compared to less than 50 percent for black and Hispanic households.[54] Despite increases in homeownership rates for minorities during the housing boom, the housing bust has resulted in black homeownership rates decreasing by 4.3 percent between 2004 and 2011, which is nearly double the decline in white

homeownership rates. The homeownership rate gap between whites and blacks is now higher than in 1994.[55]
- Renters represent a disproportionate share of the severely cost-burdened. In 2008, 8.7 million renter households spent 50 percent or more of their income on rent, an increase from 8.3 million in 2007 and 6.2 million in 2000.[56] By 2010, 10.7 million renters were severely cost-burdened.[57]
- Houses are larger than in the past. The size of newly constructed single-family homes rose from a median of 1,595 square feet in 1980 to 2,267 square feet in 2011, nearly a 30 percent increase.[58]

Problems in Home Ownership

Beginning in the 1970s, many people were forced to spend a higher percentage of their income on housing than they could reasonably afford. Some of these people became so financially overextended that they were vulnerable to mortgage default or eviction—or lacked the necessary cash to purchase other necessities.

Between 1967 and 2004, the median income for first-time home buyers rose from $28,011 to $54,500, while the median home price went from $56,466 to $168,500. In 1967, the average annual mortgage payment was $3,400; by 2004 it had risen to roughly $12,000.[59] The price increase of single-family homes is even sharper when not adjusted for inflation. In 1970, the average new single-family home was $26,600; in 2007 it cost $218,900.[60] In early 2012, the average price of a new home was $274,200 and the average price of an existing home was $204,600.[61] The median price of housing also varies widely by city and region. For example, from 1985 to 2007 the median price for an existing single-family home in Los Angeles County went from $119,000 to $528,000, dropping down to $460,000 in early 2008.[62] This decline in house value has had a significant impact on homeowners, particularly minority groups. Hispanic homeowners in particular have experienced the largest decline in home equity; a median decrease of 51 percent between 2005 and 2009.[63]

As a result of these and other factors, more homeowners are struggling with the ongoing cost of owning a home, especially if they have a mortgage and/or are in a low-income bracket. In fact, servicing a mortgage is directly related to housing affordability. For example, 94 percent of homeowners in the lowest income bracket with mortgages experienced a severe cost burden. This contrasts with only 44.2 percent of homeowners in the same income bracket, but without a mortgage. Even when examining the expenditure of low- to middle-income homeowners (those earning between $30,000 and $44,999), there is a significant difference in housing affordability, with 25 percent of low- to middle-income mortgaged homeowners experiencing a severe cost burden compared to less than 1 percent of low- to middle-income homeowners without a mortgage.[64] Overall, of the 20.2 million households that experienced a severe cost burden in 2010, 9.5 million were homeowners.[65]

Homeownership and the Subprime Mortgage Crisis

The subprime mortgage industry imploded in 2007, and hundreds of subprime mortgage lenders have shut down or gone bankrupt since then. Although there are still some subprime mortgage lenders, most have tightened their lending criteria and borrowers are required to have a higher level of qualification compared to pre-2007 levels.

Even mainstream financial institutions felt the impact as Countrywide, formerly the nation's largest mortgage lender, was sold to Bank of America in 2007 for the fire sale price of $4 billion. Only a year earlier Countrywide had been worth $27 billion. The subprime crisis also affected Wall Street brokerages that invested in these loans, with reverberations felt from Tokyo to London to Sydney. The losers and the amounts they lost in 2007 were staggering. Merrill Lynch faced $14 billion in mortgage-related write-offs; Citigroup wrote off $19 billion; UBS $13.5 billion; and Morgan Stanley $9.4 billion.[66] Why did millions of families sign up for mortgage loans that were likely to end in failure and foreclosure? Homeownership has become an important rite of passage in U.S. society. Most Americans view it as a ticket to the middle class and the best choice for everyone, everywhere, and at all times. It is assumed that the more people who own their homes, the more robust the economy, the stronger the community, and the greater the collective and individual benefits.

For the most part, this is an accurate picture: Homeowners gain a foothold in the housing market that until recently had the appearance of an almost infinite price ceiling. Others enjoy important tax benefits. Owning a home is often cheaper than renting. Most important, homeownership builds equity and assets for the next generation by promoting forced savings. According to the National Housing Institute's Winton Picoff and Sheila Crowley, the median wealth of low-income homeowners is 12 times higher than that of renters with similar incomes.[67] Less tangibly, homeownership is a status symbol that supposedly distinguishes winners from losers.

Homeownership may also have positive effects on family life. Ohio University's Robert Dietz found that owning a home contributes to household stability, social involvement, environmental awareness, local political participation and activism, good health, and a low crime rate. According to Dietz, homeowners are better citizens, are healthier both physically and mentally, and have children who achieve more and are better behaved than those of renters.[68]

Johns Hopkins University researchers Joe Harkness and Sandra Newman looked at whether homeownership benefits kids even in distressed neighborhoods. Their study concluded that "Home ownership in almost any neighborhood is found to benefit children. . . . Children of most low-income renters would be better served by programs that help their families become homeowners in their current neighborhoods instead of helping them move to better neighborhoods while remaining renters."[69] The study was unable to determine whether owning a home leads to positive behaviors or whether owners are already predisposed to those behaviors.

Faith in the benefits of home ownership—along with low interest rates and a plethora of governmental incentives—produced a surge in the number of low-income homeowners. In 1994 former president Bill Clinton set, and eventually surpassed, a goal to raise the nation's overall home ownership rate to 67.5 percent by 2000. By the early 2000s, there were 71 million U.S. homeowners representing close to 68 percent of all households. By 2003, 48 percent of African American households were homeowners, up from 34.5 percent in 1950. Much of this gain has been among low-income families.[70] This hyper housing market came with a stiff price. From 1997 to 2006, the typical American home price increased by 124 percent. From 1981 to 2001 the national median home price ranged from 2.9 to 3.1 times the median household income; by 2006 it reached unsustainable 4.6 percent. In 2008, Americans owed about $13 trillion in mortgages, more than a 50 percent jump in just seven years.[71] While home ownership has undeniable benefits, many low-income families find that the burdens can sometimes outweigh the positives.

The recession and the subprime mortgage crisis contributed to the decline in the housing market, resulting in mortgage delinquency and foreclosure rates reaching record highs by 2009.[72] Foreclosure rates were particularly high in areas where subprime mortgages were concentrated. Low-income, minority communities had the highest foreclosure rate, estimated at over 8 percent between 2007 and 2008. Higher income minority areas had a median rate of over 4 percent during this period.[73] One study found that 42 percent of existing homes sold in 2008 were sold at a loss (defined as below the original price of the home, below the remaining mortgage balance or both). By the end of 2009, a staggering 14.41 percent of mortgage owners were either in foreclosure or had defaulted by at least one payment.[74] In particular, foreclosure rates for subprime adjustable rate mortgages increased from 22.6 percent of all foreclosure loans in 2004 to a peak of 43.5 percent in 2007.[75] By 2012, delinquency and foreclosure rates had slightly declined due to a somewhat stronger economy. The percentage rate of forced sales due to foreclosure or short sales (selling a property below the remaining balance of a mortgage) also declined, from 39 percent of all homes in the early 2011 to 33 percent in early 2012.[76]

The Downside of Homeownership

Low-income families are vulnerable to wide-ranging risks when purchasing a home, including:

- Affordable housing is often rundown and expensive to maintain.
- Affordable neighborhoods are often economically distressed with few jobs, few services, high crime rates, and poor schools. Houses appreciate slowly (if at all) in these neighborhoods.
- Subprime mortgages for low-income home buyers have high interest rates and high fees.
- Low-income home buyers often work in unstable and recession-sensitive jobs. Slight employment interruptions can mean losing a home.

Taken together, these factors make home buying a far riskier proposition for low-income families than for middle- and upper-income households.

Contrary to popular myth, home ownership is not an automatic hedge against rising housing costs. Too often, low-income families pay inflated prices for homes beset with major structural or mechanical problems masked by cosmetic repairs.

Apart from maintenance and repair costs, home ownership expenses also include property taxes and insurance. Average home insurance premiums rose nationally by 62 percent from 1995 to 2005.[77] Despite the drop in home values—which should translate into lower homeowners' insurance rates—rates went up from 7 to 17.6 percent in 23 states from 2009–2010, stayed the same in nine states, and dropped in only seven states.[78] Low-income home owners in distressed neighborhoods are especially hard hit by high insurance costs. According to one study, 92 percent of large insurance companies run credit checks on potential customers, which then translates into insurance scores used to determine whether the company will insure an applicant, and if so, what they will cover and how much they will charge. Those with poor or no credit are denied coverage, and those with limited credit pay high premiums.[79] Credit scoring may explain why homeowners in minority neighborhoods are less likely to have home insurance, more likely to have policies that provide less coverage, and pay more for similar policies than their white counterparts.

With few cash reserves, low-income families are a heartbeat away from financial disaster if they lose their jobs, if their property taxes or insurance rates rise, or if expensive repairs are needed. These families often have no cushion for emergencies.

According to HUD, between 1999 and 2001 the only group whose housing conditions worsened included low- and moderate-income home owners. The National Housing Conference reported that in 2005, about 50 percent of working families with critical housing needs were homeowners.[80]

Most people who purchase a home believe they will live there for a long time and will benefit from secure and stable housing. This is not the case for many low-income families. A 2005 study found that from 1976 to 1993, 36 percent of low-income homeowners gave up or lost their homes within two years, and 53 percent exited within five years. Very few low-income families bought another house after returning to renting.[81] Another study reached similar conclusions. Following a national sample of African Americans from youth in 1979 to middle age in 2000, the researchers found that 63 percent owned a home at some point, but only 34 percent still did in 2000.[82]

Home ownership can also limit financial opportunities. A 1999 study found that states with the highest home ownership rates also had the highest unemployment rates. The report concluded that home ownership may constrain labor mobility because the high costs of selling a house make unemployed homeowners reluctant to relocate to find work.[83]

Special tax breaks are touted as a key selling point in deciding to become a homeowner. But, if mortgage interest and other expenses come to less than the standard deduction ($11,400 for joint filers in 2010), there is no tax advantage to home ownership. This is one reason why only 34 percent of taxpayers itemize their mortgage interest, local property taxes, and other deductions. The mortgage deduction primarily benefits those in high-income brackets who need to shelter their income; it has little value to low-income homeowners.

Finally, home ownership promised growing wealth as housing prices in various parts of the United States soared from the late 1990s until 2007. However, homes bought by low-income families generally do not appreciate as rapidly as middle-income housing. For instance, Reid's longitudinal study survey of low-income minority homeowners from 1976 to 1994 found that they realized a 30 percent increase in the value of their homes after 10 years; middle- and upper-income white homeowners enjoyed a 60 percent jump.[84]

Spotlight 16.2

THE ROOTS OF THE SUBPRIME HOUSING CRISIS: THE BRAVE NEW WORLD OF HOME LOANS

The new home loan products that were marketed widely in recent years to low- and moderate-income families were generally adjustable rate mortgages (ARMs) with some kind of twist. Here are a few "creative" mortgage options:

- *Option ARMs* are loans whereby borrowers could choose which of three or four different fluctuating payments they would make. (A) Full (principal + interest) payment based on a 30-year or 15-year repayment schedule. (B) Interest-only payment that does not reduce the loan principal or build homeowner equity. Borrowers who paid only interest for a period of time soon faced a big jump in the size of their monthly payments, and some were forced to

refinance or lose their home. Refinancing only works if the home has appreciated in value or a substantial part of the mortgage has been paid off. If the home's value had remained stagnant or decreased (negative equity), it could not be refinanced because little or no money can be drawn out.

The minimum payment may be lower than one month's interest. If that occurs, the shortfall is added to the loan balance and results in "negative amortization," whereby over time, the principal goes up, not down. Eventually the borrower may have an "upside down" mortgage, whereby the debt is greater than the market value of the home. When a negative amortization limit is reached, the borrower suddenly has to start paying the real bill.

Option ARMs started with a temporary super-low teaser interest rate and low monthly payments that allowed borrowers to qualify for "more house" than they could afford. Because the low monthly payment was insufficient to cover the real interest rate, they suddenly faced a sudden sharp increase in monthly payments.

- *Balloon loans* were written for a five- to seven-year term during which time the borrower paid either interest plus principal each month or, in a more predatory form, interest only. At the end of the short loan term, the borrower either paid off the entire loan balance (i.e., a balloon payment), refinanced, or walked away from the home. Balloon mortgages are known as "bullet loans" because if the loan comes due during a period of high interest rates, it is like getting a bullet in the heart. About 10 percent of all subprime loans were balloon mortgages.

Balloon loans were sometimes structured with monthly payments that failed to cover the interest, much less pay down the principal. Although the borrower made regular payments, the loan balance increased each month. Many borrowers were unaware that they had a negative amortization loan until they had to refinance.

- *Shared appreciation mortgages (SAMs)* were fixed-rate loans for up to 30 years that had easier credit qualifications and lower monthly payments than conventional mortgages. In exchange for a lower interest rate, the borrower relinquished part of the future value of the home to the lender. Interest rate reductions were based on how much appreciation the borrower was willing to give up. SAMs discouraged "sweat equity" because the homeowner receives only a fraction of the appreciation resulting from any improvements. The nature of these loans has been likened to sharecropping.
- *Stated-income loans* are aimed at borrowers who do not draw regular wages but live on tips, Casual cash jobs, commissions, or investments. Often called "liar loans" in the trade, these loans did not require W-2 forms or other standard wage documentation. The trade-off was higher interest rates.
- *No-ratio loan.* The debt–income ratio (the borrower's monthly payments including the planned mortgage divided by monthly income) was a standard benchmark used by lenders to determine how large a mortgage they would write. In return for a higher interest rate, no-ratio loans abandon this benchmark. These loans were aimed at borrowers with complex financial lives or those who were experiencing divorce, the death of a spouse, or a career change.

It should be noted that not all negative equity is bad. One of the newer variations of refinancing endorsed by HUD is a reverse mortgage for senior citizens, called Home Equity Conversion Mortgage (HECM). This program unlocks the equity the elderly have built up in their property. Homeowners aged 62 or older can borrow against the value of their property. They receive payments from lenders monthly, in a lump sum or as a line of credit. The size of the reverse mortgage is determined by the borrower's age, the interest rate, and the value of the home. The older the homeowner, the larger the percentage of a home's value they can borrow. For example, a 65-year-old owner can borrow up to 26 percent of a home's value, a 75-year-old up to 39 percent, and an 85-year-old up to 56 percent. The amount owed increases over time, but no payment is due until the end of the loan term. When the loan term expires, the total loan amount plus interest is due in full. This lump sum payment is usually paid by selling the property. No repayments are required while a borrower lives in the home, and the monthly income is tax free.

Luckily, most of the questionable loans ignominiously died when the subprime market crashed in 2007. However, when the credit market is stabilized, they could reappear again in various forms.

Source: Howard Karger, Shortchanged: *Life and Debt in the Fringe Economy*. San Francisco, CA: Berrett-Koehler, 2005.

Tricky Mortgages

Buying a home is the largest purchase most families will make in their lifetimes and the biggest expenditure in a family budget. Real estate assets represent about one-third of the net worth of U.S. households.[85] Real estate transactions are also the most fraught with danger, especially for low-income families. The primary reason for this is the large gap between high home prices and the stagnant income of millions of working-class

TABLE 16.2 Average U.S. Housing Prices, Mortgage Rates, and Median Family Income in Non-Inflation Adjusted Dollars: Selected Years

Period	New SF Homes*	Existing SF Homes	Mortgage Rates	Median Family Income	Cost of Existing SF Home as Proportion of Income
1970	$26,600	$25,700	8.35%	$9,867	2.5.
1975	42,600	39,000	9.21	13,719	2.9.
1980	76,400	72,800	12.95	21,023	3.5.
1985	100,800	86,000	11.74	27,735	3.1
1990	149,800	118,600	10.04	35,353	3.4
1995	158,700	139,000	7.85	40,612	3.5
2000	201,100	179,400	8.02	50,733	4.4
2004	263,100	186,500	5.83	54,061	4.3
2007	299,700	255,300	6.50	61,173	5.3
2010	228,801	178,564	4.89	61,313	3.45
2011	227,200	166,200	4.67	60,831	3.20

*SF=Single Family.

Source: Based on data from U.S. Department of Housing and Urban Development, U.S. Housing Market Conditions (Washington, DC: HUD, Office of Policy Development and Research, 2nd Quarter 2004 and 2007); The Harvard Joint Center for Housing Studies, The State of the Nation's Housing: 2007, retrieved November 2007 from http://www.jchs.harvard.edu/publications/markets/son2007.pdf; The Harvard Joint Center for Housing Studies, The State of the Nation's Housing 2012, 14th of June 2012. Retrieved June 2012 from http://www.jchs.harvard.edu/sites/jchs.harvard.edu/files/son2012_bw.pdf; and U.S. Department of Housing and Urban Development, U.S. Housing Market Conditions: Historical Data (Washington, DC: HUD, Office of Policy Development and Research, 1st Quarter 2012). Retrieved June 2012 from http://www.huduser.org/portal/periodicals/ushmc/spring12/USHMC_1q12_historical.pdf.

Americans. (See Table 16.2.) Despite the current drop in housing prices, stagnant or contracting incomes still do not support current home prices. Even lower mortgage interest rates are largely neutralized by high property taxes, higher insurance premiums, and rising utility costs. Housing costs operate like a shell game: Low interest rates and high housing prices lead to higher property taxes and high home insurance costs. High interest rates and lower home prices lead to lower taxes and lower home insurance costs. At the end of the day, what matters the most are the total monthly housing expenses, which may or may not be different under different scenarios.

The disparity between stagnant incomes and formerly rising housing prices was made possible by "creative financing." The mortgage industry had developed creative schemes to (temporarily) squeeze buyers into homes they could not afford. This sleight of hand required imaginative and risky financing for both buyers and financial institutions. It also helped usher in the subprime crisis, the housing market bust, and the global financial crisis.

Most of the new mortgage products were subprime mortgages offered to people whose problematic credit, lack of assets, or low income dropped them into a lower lending category. Subprime mortgages had interest rates ranging from a few points to 10 points or more above the market rate, plus onerous loan terms. Until the crash, the subprime market had created more than $2.7 trillion in risky loans from 2000 to 2007.[86,87]

Before the collapse, the rate of return for subprime lenders was nothing short of spectacular. *Forbes* claimed that subprime lenders could realize returns up to six times greater than the best-run banks.[88] In the past there were two main kinds of home mortgages: fixed-rate loans and adjustable rate mortgages (ARMs). In a fixed-rate mortgage, the interest rate stays the same throughout the 15- to 30-year term of the loan. In a typical ARM, the interest rate varies over the course of the loan, although there is usually a cap. Both kinds of loans traditionally required borrowers to provide thorough documentation of their finances and a down payment of between 5 and 20 percent of the purchase price.

Adjustable rate mortgages were unable to push enough low-income families into the housing market and to keep home sales buoyant. To meet this challenge, the mortgage industry created "affordability" products with names like "no-ratio loans," "option ARMs," and "balloon loans," which doled out money to people who never fully understood the risk in these complicated loans. New mortgage options allowed almost anyone to secure a mortgage, regardless of his or her capacity for repayment.

Low-income homebuyers faced other costs as well. For instance, predatory lenders often required borrowers to carry credit life insurance, which pays off a mortgage in the event of a homeowner's death. This insurance was frequently sold by the lender's subsidiary or a company that pays the lender a commission. Despite low payouts, lenders charged high premiums for this insurance. As many as 80 percent of subprime loans included prepayment penalties for paying off a loan early, which locked borrowers into a loan by making it difficult to sell the home or refinance with a different lender. Other borrowers discovered that their mortgages had "call provisions" that permitted the lender to accelerate the loan term even if payments were current. Lenders inflated closing costs by charging outrageous document preparation fees; billing for recording fees in excess of the law; and by "unbundling" (closing costs are padded by duplicating charges included in other categories).

Mortgage products were often sold by mortgage brokers who acted as finders or "bird dogs" for lenders. Largely unregulated, mortgage brokers lived off loan fees. Borrowers paid brokers a fee to help them secure a loan. Brokers also received kickbacks from lenders for referring a borrower, and many steered clients to lenders that paid the highest kickbacks rather than those offering the lowest interest rates. Closing documents used arcane language to hide these kickbacks. Some hungry brokers found less-than-kosher ways to make their sale, including fudging paperwork, arranging for inflated property appraisals, or helping buyers find cosigners who had no intention of guaranteeing the loan.

Realizing that closer regulation of the mortgage industry was needed, the HUD RESPA reform was created in 2008. This changed disclosure requirements for mortgage lenders, with the aim of reducing loan fees and assisting homebuyers in making fully informed decisions when choosing mortgages. The Good Faith Estimate (GFE) was simplified and standardized so that all mortgage lenders had to use the same form and provide the same information on the full cost of a loan. This allowed homebuyers to compare loans across the board. Fees on title and settlement services were capped at no more than a 10 percent increase in total and included on the GFE. Loan fees were not permitted to rise once a borrower had locked in an interest rate. The goal was to increase competition between lenders who would lower fees in an effort to close more loans, thus ultimately benefiting the homebuyer.[89] Additional Truth In Lending (TILA) disclosures in 2009 and further strengthening of the GFE in January 2010 aimed to further support the aims of RESPA. Unfortunately, the damage to low-income buyers had already been done.[90] Almost 3 million homeowners (one in 45 households) received at least one foreclosure notice in 2009. By 2010, lenders foreclosed on about 100,000 homes a month (around 1 million for the year), the highest number ever recorded. More than 4.5 million U.S. homes were lost to foreclosure from 2007 to 2010, and by 2010 the sale of foreclosed properties accounted for 25 percent of all home sales.[91,92,93]

According to the *New York Times,* there were three distinct foreclosure waves: (1) speculators who deserted their property due to plunging real estate prices, (2) borrowers whose low or introductory interest rates expired and were reset much higher, and (3) mortgages held by creditworthy people who lost their jobs in the economic downturn.[94] Although foreclosures decreased by 8.5 percent between 2010 and early 2012, this still equates to a substantial number of families losing their homes.[95]

The federal government has tried to limit foreclosures. Under the Home Affordable Modification Program (HAMP), the government initially allocated $75 billion for sustainable mortgage modifications designed to reach 3–4 million homeowners by 2012. By April 2010, HAMP made 1.5 million offers resulting in 695,000 temporary and 295,000 permanent mortgage repayment modifications. However, the Treasury Department estimated that 40 percent of those households would redefault. The federal government also allocated $6 billion to the Neighborhood Stabilization Program to deal with foreclosed properties, and another $2.1 billion to housing finance agencies in states hardest hit economically.[96]

Evidence emerged in 2010 that the foreclosure process used by many banks was marked by sloppy record keeping and fraudulent activity, which is highlighted by "robo-signing," whereby frazzled and minimally qualified bank employees signed off on hundreds of foreclosures a day based on forged or non-reviewed documents. By 2011, the foreclosure abuse investigations and the ensuing scandal led to a slowdown of bank-initiated foreclosures. In 2012, the federal government and big banks and lenders reached a $26 billion settlement that provided relief to nearly 2 million current and former homeowners. Unfortunately, that settlement will only help a modest number of delinquent homeowners facing foreclosure. Interestingly, the Obama administration did not support a national freeze on evictions, fearing that it would hurt an already shaky banking industry.[97,98]

Given these considerations, homeownership may not be a cure-all for low-income families who earn low wages and have poor prospects for future income growth. According to economist Dean Baker, given that mortgage delinquencies and foreclosures are at record levels among low-income households, millions of people would be better off today remaining renters.[99]

Problems in Finding Affordable Rental Housing

Rents follow similar trajectories as other market commodities. As more people entered the housing market through subprime loans and easy credit, the demand for rentals softened and rental prices dropped in some areas.[100] As credit has tightened, and since the advent of the subprime mortgage crisis, fewer people can become homeowners and foreclosures led to some homeowners becoming renters again. This increases rental demand, resulting in housing shortages and higher prices. In 2011, all metro areas bar one (Las Vegas) experienced increases in rent, with San Francisco leading with a double digit rent rise, and some parts of the Northeast (New York and Boston); South (Austin); and West (Denver) reporting increases of between 3 and 5 percent.[101,102] Moreover, nearly 8.8 million households still live in inadequate units.

If finding affordable housing is difficult for poor and moderate-income homeowners, it has reached crisis proportions for extremely low-income (ELI) renters. ELI renters are those who earn 30 percent or less of the Area Median Income (AMI). Very low-income (VLI) renters are those who earn between 30 to 50 percent of the AMI.[103]

The standard benchmark for "affordability" is that households should pay no more than 30 percent of their after-tax income on housing. Those paying between 30 and 50 percent have moderate cost burdens; households paying more than 50 percent have severe cost burdens. There were about 7 million VLI renter households in 2009, and approximately 2 million had severe cost burdens. Of the 10 million ELI renter households, over 6.4 million had severe cost burdens. Hence, more than half of the poorest households spend more than 50 percent of their earnings on rent.[104]

The number of households with low incomes has increased at a time when affordable rental housing is decreasing. Rising unemployment led to a 7 percent increase in VLI renter households between 2007 and 2009. At the same time, the number of VLI-affordable vacant housing units declined by 370,000 which led to a rent increase. Housing availability is even worse for ELI renter households. In 2009, there were approximately 6 million affordable rental houses for the 10 million ELI households. In central cities, there were only 34 housing units per 100 ELI renter households.[105]

Affordability pressures are likely to increase since wages in many low-wage jobs are insufficient to cover (at 30 percent of income) even a modest one-bedroom apartment in many parts of the country.[106,107]

Rising rental costs and the failure of many ELI and VLI renters to receive rental assistance also affects the amount of rent these households can afford. In 2009, only 34 percent of ELI renter households received rental assistance.[108,109]

When poor households live in unaffordable housing they often pay for it by spending less on other necessities such as heat, food, clothing, and health care. Some of these families find themselves in a "heat or eat" situation. Low-income, severely cost-burdened families with children spend half as much on clothes, two-fifths as much on health care, and three-fifths as much on food as families living in affordable housing.[110]

Severe housing problems are related to the dwindling supply of affordable unsubsidized housing units available to very low-income households.

Losses of units to either rising rents or demolition have intensified the housing problems of VLI renters who receive no rent subsidies. Adding to the pressures on these households is the cost of supplying new affordable housing. Restrictive regulations and public resistance to high-density development make it difficult to replace or add lower-cost units.[111,112]

Even though the LIHTC program has been provided with further funding and creates approximately 100,000 subsidized houses every year, this is not meeting the increasing demand for affordable housing. Between 2001 and 2010, the number of low-income households earning $15,000 or less grew by 2.2 million, while the number of affordable rental houses available to this demographic declined by 470,000. What this equates to is a widening gap between supply and demand; in 2001 8.1 million low-income renters competed for 5.7 million affordable houses, leaving a gap of 2.4 million. By 2010, the number of low-income households was over 10 million and the gap between affordable housing had more than doubled to 5.1 million.[113,114]

Several other factors have converged to deplete low-income housing stock, including the commercial renovation of central-city downtown areas. Developments consisting of new office buildings, large apartment complexes, shopping areas, and parking lots often replace low-income housing bordering on downtown areas. Traditionally affordable (and often rundown) apartment buildings, cheap single room occupancy (SRO) hotels, rooming houses, and boardinghouses are razed as new office buildings and shopping malls are erected. Displaced longtime residents are forced to find housing in more expensive neighborhoods, to double up with family or friends, or to become homeless.

The loss of SROs has exacerbated the homeless problem. SROs were home to many poor people (including those suffering from substance abuse and mental illnesses) who were not living in public or subsidized housing. But between 1970 and the mid-1980s, an estimated 1 million SRO units were demolished. San Francisco lost 43 percent; Los Angeles lost more than 50 percent; New York lost 87 percent; and Chicago experienced the total elimination of its SRO housing units and hotels. These demolitions left many poor persons homeless, particularly those suffering from mental illness and substance abuse.[115]

Gentrification

According to George Sternlieb and Jones Hughes, "a new town may be evolving in-town."[116] This new town, or "gentrified" neighborhood, is a major component of the urban renaissance taking place in many U.S. cities. Attracted by old houses or lofts amenable to restoration; good transportation facilities; and close proximity to employment and artistic, cultural, and social opportunities, young professional and white-collar workers have begun to resettle the poor, aging, and usually heavily minority sections of central cities in the process called **gentrification.** As part of the process, upscale condos are built, houses are rehabbed, dusty lofts are modernized and sold for small fortunes, and trendy candlelit restaurants and boutiques replace minimarts and used furniture stores. Critics argue that a valuable piece of city real estate is being cleansed of its working-class residents.

Although the renovation of central-city areas, such as New York's SoHo district, often makes a neighborhood more attractive (and potentially a tourist attraction), the effect on the poor population can be devastating. As more homes are renovated, the price of surrounding housing increases. Landlords find it an opportune time to sell their former rental properties for a high price. Even though low-income homeowners will receive a high price for their homes, they may not find suitable places to relocate. As neighborhoods become more affluent, property taxes rise, thus creating a burden on existing low-income homeowners. Previously affordable rental housing undergo large rent increases as neighborhoods become more desirable, thereby driving out older and poorer residents. Moreover, as baby boomers age, the justification for living in the suburbs—good schools and safe neighborhoods for their children—is eclipsed by the stress of long commutes and highway gridlock. Large numbers of couples without children are increasingly opting to move closer to work and cultural amenities.

The conversion of apartment buildings into condominiums represents another threat to low-income renters. As a consequence of tax breaks and income shelters, previously affordable rental housing is rapidly being converted into condominiums. Whether initiated by tenants or by developers, condominium conversion represents serious depletion of good quality rental stock. Because units in these conversions may cost upwards of $100,000 or much more, low-income tenants can rarely afford the benefits of condominium living, and although long-term renters are sometimes offered a separation fee when a building undergoes conversion, this may barely cover the costs of moving, much less make up the difference between current rent and a higher alternative rent.

Overcrowded and Deficient Housing

Problems of overcrowding and structural inadequacy affect a significant number of U.S. households. HUD defines a housing unit as overcrowded if there is an average of more than one person per room. According to this definition, almost 3 million households live in overcrowded conditions, sometimes as a result of families doubling up to avoid becoming homeless.[117] In 2009, HUD reported that almost 9 million households were living in inadequate housing units; 5.2 million of these were homeowners, and 3.7 million were renters. HUD classifies inadequate housing as seriously inadequate if it has severe physical deficiencies like no hot water, electricity, or a toilet, or it lacks a bathtub or shower.[118]

Lead paint is one of the principal problems in units needing rehabilitation. The Centers for Disease Control and Prevention notes that lead poisoning is one of the most common and devastating environmental diseases that affects young children, causing developmental and behavior problems. Children are exposed to lead poisoning by living in older homes with peeling, chipping, and flaking paint. Because low-income families often occupy poorly maintained older homes, their children are four times more likely to have lead poisoning than children in high-income families.[119]

Other Factors Affecting Housing

Another problem affecting affordable housing is property taxes—the heart of local revenues. The escalating costs of providing governmental services have resulted in significant increases in property taxes, which landlords generally pass along to renters in the form of higher rents. In response, many states have tried to reduce property tax burdens for low-income households. The most common form of property tax relief occurs through circuit breaker programs. A typical circuit breaker is activated when taxes exceed a specified proportion of a home owner's income, and in some states, low-income households are sent a yearly benefit check that covers all or part of the property taxes they paid. Circuit breaker programs for low-income renters operate in a similar manner. Typically, a portion of the rent paid by a low-income household is considered to represent the property tax passed on by the landlord and is thus refunded by the state or local government. Although circuit breakers provide relief, they are often restricted to the elderly or disabled.[120]

Housing costs are also aggravated by high utility rates. Nationwide, the average family in 2011 paid about $2,000 in utility bills, although that number reached more than $3,500 in parts of the Northeast and Midwest. Low-income consumers spend anywhere from 13 to 44 percent of their total household income on utilities, whereas average-income Americans spend only 4 percent.[121] Increases in home energy bills disproportionately affect the poor, and in some cases, lead to utility shutoff.[122] In 2007, about 1.2 million households had their utilities shut off.

To mitigate the effects of the federal deregulation of oil prices and the large oil price increases of the 1970s, Congress passed the Low-Income Home Energy Assistance Program (LIHEAP) in 1981. This legislation permits states to offer three types of assistance to low-income households: (1) funds to help eligible households pay their home heating or cooling bills, (2) allotments for low-income weatherization, and (3) assistance to households during energy-related emergencies. States are required to target LIHEAP benefits to households with the lowest incomes and the highest energy costs relative to income and family size. In 2010, total LIHEAP funding was $5.1 billion, and the program served roughly 8.7 million households who received an average grant of $456, enough to cover 47 percent of the cost of home heating. It is estimated that less than 20 percent of eligible families receive LIHEAP assistance.[123] Housing discrimination—another barrier facing the poor—can take the form of racial discrimination or discrimination against families with children. Although illegal, racial discrimination in housing is still prevalent. In addition, many landlords and real estate agents refuse to rent to families with children. Even when these families find housing, they are often required to pay higher rents, provide excessive security deposits, or meet qualifications not required of renters without children.[124] Discrimination against families with children continues despite its ban by Congress in 1988.[125]

Homelessness

Homelessness represents both a simple and a complex problem. For one, the homeless are not a homogeneous group. Homelessness for some individuals is a lifestyle choice, the freedom to roam without being tied down to one place. For others, particularly those with mental illness or chronic alcoholism, homelessness reflects the failure of an overburdened public mental health system. For others, homelessness is rooted in cuts in federally subsidized housing programs and in the cost/income squeeze of the housing market. Finally, large numbers of people are homeless because public assistance benefits have failed to keep pace with the cost of living. Despite different causes, homelessness is tied to poverty.

The actual number of homeless people in the United States is difficult to ascertain. First, the definition of homelessness varies from study to study, and different methods for counting the homeless yield different results. Second, many of the homeless are "hidden" because they live in campgrounds, automobiles, boxcars, caves, tents, boxes, and other makeshift housing. Or, the homeless may temporarily live with family members or friends. Most studies count people who are homeless in a given community by tracking people who use the services of soup kitchens and shelters.[126]

Third, the homeless population is often undercounted in federal surveys for fiscal reasons: If the true extent of homelessness were acknowledged, local, state, and federal authorities would have to target more services and funds for this population.[127] The U.S. Department of Housing and Urban Development reported that in 2011, 400,000 individuals and 236,000 persons in families were homeless on any given night.[128] The 2010 Annual Homeless Assessment Report (AHAR) further reports that between October 2009 and September 2010, there were 1.59 million people who used a shelter or emergency/transitional housing.[129] It is difficult to gauge the true extent of homelessness on the streets, given that most estimates are based on point-in-time counts (the number of homeless people counted in one night) or the annual number of homeless people who use shelters and other crisis accommodation.

Characteristics of the Homeless Population

Homelessness has been a long-standing problem in most urban areas, propelled onto center stage by media images of bag ladies, the mentally ill, chronic alcoholics, street people, and uprooted families. These images make for interesting copy, but popular stereotypes obscure both the extent and true nature of the problem. The homeless are generally the poorest of the poor. They include single-parent families and, increasingly, two-parent families. They are often people who work but earn too little to afford housing. They are women and children escaping from domestic violence. They are runaway youngsters or "throw-away kids." They are unemployed people—some who are looking for work, and some who have never worked. The homeless include retired people on small fixed incomes, many of whom have lost their cheap SRO hotel rooms to gentrification; school dropouts; drug addicts; disabled and mentally ill people lost in a maze of outpatient services; those who have worn out their welcome with family or friends; young mothers on welfare

Spotlight 16.3

THE NATIONAL COALITION FOR THE HOMELESS

The National Coalition for the Homeless (NCH) was established to end homelessness in America. To that end, this organization engages in public education, policy advocacy, and grassroots organizing. The work of NCH is focused in the following four areas: housing justice, economic justice, health care justice, and civil rights. To learn more about NCH, go to its website at http://www.nationalhomeless.org.

Homelessness in America is both a simple and complex problem.

Source: Jon Le-Bon/Shutterstock

who are on long waiting lists for public housing; and families who have lost their overcrowded quarters.[130]

The prevalence of homelessness in families increased during the recession and reflects the impact of the declining economy on those struggling to make ends meet. Longitudinal data in the 2009 AHAR report notes that homeless families (considered as households) increased by 30 percent from 2007 to 2009. As the recession resulted in widespread job losses, family support networks struggled with their own problems of unemployment and income loss, and were less able to provide for their relatives and friends. Overcrowding in houses increased as more families "doubled up" to keep costs low, leaving less room for others requiring transitional housing.[131]

According to HUD, the homeless population has the following characteristics:

Race. While African Americans represented 12.4 percent of the total U.S. population in 2008, they made up 39 percent of the sheltered homeless population.

Geographic spread. While homelessness exists in all American communities, over half of all homeless people are in California, Florida, Nevada, Texas, Georgia, and Washington.

Rural homelessness. The rural homeless tend to live in cars, double up, or live in grossly substandard housing. Most are married, white, working females, often with families.

Frequency. The Annual Homeless Assessment Report found that on a single night in 2009, 643,067 people were homeless. Of those, only 63 percent were in shelters. Thirty-seven percent of the homeless were part of family groups; the other 67 percent were individuals. Emergency shelters or transitional housing programs were used by 1.6 million people in 2009. For the 2008–2009 school year, public schools reported over 956,000 homeless students, a 20 percent increase from 2007 to 2008.

Families. Families experiencing homelessness are usually headed by a single woman in her late 20s with two children, one or both of whom are under 6 years of age. Families experiencing homelessness have very low incomes, less access to housing subsidies than housed low-income families, and have weaker social networks unable to provide help.

Among homeless mothers with children, more than 80 percent had previously experienced domestic violence, including financial abuse that left them with poor credit and limited resources. Emergency domestic violence shelters typically limit stays to 90 days or less to ensure sufficient beds for those in imminent danger. On a single day in 2009, 65,000 adults and children nationwide sought services for domestic violence; however, domestic violence programs provided emergency shelter and housing to only 32,000 adults and children.

Children in homeless families have a high rate of chronic and long-term health problems. School-age homeless children are more likely than children in the general population to have emotional problems and manifest aggressive behavior. They also exhibit poorer academic performance. The rate of foster care placement is highest for the children of women with at least one episode of homelessness.

Unaccompanied youth. Young people often leave home due to severe family conflict, which may include physical and/or sexual abuse. Some youth become homeless when they leave foster care or residential facilities (e.g., they are runaways, aged out, or discharged). According to HUD, unaccompanied youth at minimum make up 2.2 percent of the sheltered homeless population (about 22,700 people). Other sources suggest that about 110,000 youth live on the streets (or in other public places), in cars, and in abandoned buildings. About 53,000 un-accompanied youth are supported through school-based programs. Some teenage boys are separated from their families due to shelter policies that force older adolescent males to be housed in adult shelters.

Individual adults. In 2009, 63 percent (983,835) of those accessing shelters and transitional housing programs were individual adults, and three-quarters were men. Forty-three percent of sheltered single adults had a disability and 13 percent were veterans. This reflects the growing population of older (over age 50) homeless adults. Single individuals who experience long-term homelessness have high rates of mental illness and/or substance abuse disorders. Chronic homelessness is strongly correlated with alcohol abuse, schizophrenia, and other mental health problems.

Veterans. According to the Veteran's Administration (VA), the number of veterans experiencing homelessness has been rapidly declining due to an increased effort to serve this population. In 2009, the VA estimated 107,000 homeless veterans on any given night.[132]

Trends in Homelessness

As noted earlier, homelessness and poverty are inextricably linked. Because poor families have limited resources that only cover a portion of their basic needs, they are forced to make difficult choices between housing, food, clothing, or health care. Housing costs absorb the greatest percentage of a poor family's income, which can leave them only a paycheck away from living on the streets if faced with a crisis. Families who have moved from welfare to work under the 1996 welfare reform law are not doing as well as projected (see Chapter 11) due to inadequate work supports and low wages. Moreover, the five-year TANF lifetime cap may lead to even greater numbers of homeless people in coming years, especially in the wake of the recession.[133] Indeed, the impact of the recession, particularly in terms of home foreclosures and the rising unaffordability of rents, has been linked to homelessness.[134]

Lack of affordable health care can cause many struggling families to spiral into homelessness when a serious illness or injury causes extended absence from work, job loss, or depletion of savings to pay for health care. Mental illness and drug and alcohol addiction also play a role. The increasing number of mentally ill homeless individuals is not entirely due to the deinstitutionalization of mentally ill patients from mental hospitals; rather, homelessness results because mentally ill people experience difficulty in accessing supportive housing along with treatment services. People who are both poor and addicted also face a high risk of homelessness.[135]

Domestic violence has been linked to homelessness. Specifically, many poor women are forced to choose whether to stay in an abusive relationship or become homeless. Several studies demonstrate the contribution of domestic violence to homelessness, particularly among families with children. A 2003 survey of ten U.S. locations found that 25 out of 100 homeless women had experienced physical abuse in the last 12 months. A 2004 Los Angeles study found that 34 percent of homeless women in California had experienced domestic violence in the past 12 months, and of those, 58 percent had left their housing situations because of it. The stigma of domestic violence can also provide a barrier to finding affordable housing: a 2005 New York study found that 27.5 percent of housing providers would not rent to a person who had been a victim of domestic violence. Overall, anywhere between 22 and 57 percent of homeless women cite domestic violence as the primary reason for their homelessness.[136] Being unable to find affordable housing and having a low-income increase the likelihood that women will stay in violent relationships or return to their violent partners. A 2003 study in Fargo, North Dakota, found that 44 percent of homeless women had previously stayed in violent relationships because they had "nowhere else to go".[137]

Homeless youth (typically runaways) is a persistent problem. An Urban Institute report estimated that the number of runaway youth alone, many who are homeless, could be anywhere between 1.6 million to 2.8 million.[138] Many homeless youth run away because of physical or sexual abuse, strained relationships, addiction of a family member, and parental neglect. In one study, more than half of the youth in shelters reported their parents either told them to leave or knew they were leaving but did not care.[139] According to U.S. government agencies, 17 to 35 percent of homeless youth had reported being sexually abused and up to 60 percent had been physically abused prior to leaving home. In another study, 50 percent of homeless youth reported being physically abused and 39 percent reported being sexually abused at home.[140] A history of foster care has also been correlated with becoming homeless at an early age and remaining so for a long period of time. Some youth living in residential placements become homeless after discharge—they are too old for foster care and leave with no housing or income support. Emancipation from foster care can be another risk factor for homelessness, as youth in this group lack the fiscal means and social networks to support themselves.[141] Many homeless adolescents find that survival on the streets requires exchanging sex for the necessities. In turn, they are at a greater risk for contracting AIDS/ HIV. Studies suggest that the HIV prevalence rate for homeless youth may be between 3 to 30 times higher than for other adolescents.[142,143]

Attempts to Address Homelessness

On July 22, 1987, former president Ronald Reagan signed the McKinney-Vento Homeless Assistance Act into law which created more than 20 separate programs to be administered by nine federal agencies. Some highlights of the Act include:

- Emergency Shelter Grants Program (ESGP). This program provides formula (block grant) funding for emergency shelter and essential services.
- Supportive Housing Demonstration Program (SHDP). This program funds a variety of grants for transitional and permanent housing, particularly for homeless families and those with special needs or handicaps.
- Section 8 Moderate Rehabilitation for Single-Room Occupancy Dwellings. This program provides funding to owners of SRO housing in the form of rental assistance payments on behalf of homeless individuals, in conjunction with the rehabilitation of the facility. The program provides permanent housing for previously homeless tenants.
- Shelter Plus Care. Congress added this program to HUD in 1990. Funds are awarded for rental assistance. Grantees must match the value of rental assistance with an equal value of supportive services. The target population is homeless persons living on the streets or in emergency shelters with severe mental illness, chronic substance abuse problems, or AIDS.
- Supplemental Assistance for Facilities to Assist the Homeless. This program funds projects that meet the immediate and long-term needs of the homeless, as well as projects already receiving funds under ESGP and SHDP. The flexible range of assistance permits program expansion, capital improvement, and startup of new, needed supportive services.
- Single Family Property Disposition Initiative. Created in 1983, this program provides the HUD secretary broad legislative authority to dispose of single-family properties. It was broadened in 1985 to allow HUD to sell or lease foreclosed single-family properties to nonprofit organizations, or to state or local governments to provide temporary shelter for homeless persons. In 1992, it was recognized as a McKinney initiative. Given the recent run of foreclosures on residential and commercial properties, this program provides nonprofits with the opportunity to use the housing crisis to further expand low-income housing stock.

In 1990, Congress amended the McKinney-Vento Act to remove requirements that kept homeless children from attending school, including proof of immunization, former school records, and proof of residency.[144]

The 2010 plan to end homelessness prepared under the auspices of the Interagency Council for the Homeless provides a set of objectives aimed at reducing homelessness:

(1) Provide and promote . . . leadership at all levels of government . . . to commit to preventing and ending homelessness; (2) strengthen the capacity of public and private organizations by increasing knowledge . . . to . . . end homelessness; (3) provide affordable housing to people experiencing or most at risk of homelessness; (4) provide permanent supportive housing to prevent and end chronic homelessness; (5) increase meaningful and sustainable employment for people experiencing or most at risk of homelessness; (6) improve access to mainstream programs and services to reduce people's financial vulnerability to homelessness; (7) integrate primary and behavioral health care services with homeless assistance programs and housing to reduce people's vulnerability to . . . homelessness; (8) advance health and housing stability for youth aging out of systems such as foster care and juvenile justice; (9) advance health and housing

stability for people experiencing homelessness who have frequent contact with hospitals and criminal justice; and (10) transform homeless services to crisis response systems that prevent homelessness and rapidly return people . . . to stable housing.[145]

Housing First is an alternative approach to the current system of emergency shelter/transitional housing. It is premised on the belief that homeless families are more open to interventions and social service after they are in their own housing, rather than while living in a temporary or transitional facility. This model is grounded in the view that with permanent housing, distressed families can regain the control over their lives that they lost on becoming homeless. In contrast to traditional emergency programs, Housing First (1) helps homeless families move quickly and directly into affordable rental housing in residential neighborhoods and (2) provides each family six months to a year of individualized, home-based social services support after the move in order to help families transition into stability.[146]

Homelessness cannot be eradicated without basic changes in federal housing, income support, social services, health care, education, and employment policies. Benefit levels for these programs must be made adequate; the erosion of welfare benefits must be stopped; residency and other requirements that exclude homeless persons must be changed; and programs (including outreach) must be made freely available to the homeless and the potentially homeless. Moreover, a real solution to the homeless problem must involve the provision of permanent housing for those who are currently or potentially homeless. Federal programs and legislation should be coordinated and expanded to provide decent, affordable housing, coupled with needed services, for all poor families. Finally, both the states and the federal government should intervene directly in the housing market by controlling rents, increasing the overall housing stock, limiting speculation, and providing income supports.

Housing Reform

The housing crisis faced by low-income people has led to numerous suggestions for housing reform. Some conservative critics argue that low-income housing assistance should be abolished, thereby allowing the law of supply and demand to regulate rents and, eventually, to drive down prices. Free market economic philosophy suggests that as rents increase, demand will slacken, and rents will eventually drop. Another argument is that government intervention in housing should occur only by stimulating production of rental housing through financial incentives such as tax breaks to builders, entrepreneurs, and investors. If rental housing is made more profitable, more units will be built, and the increase in the housing stock will lower prices. Some liberal critics contend that because housing is a necessity and the demand is relatively inelastic, marketplace laws should not be allowed to dominate. The 1995 National Low-Income Housing Coalition plank continues to remain relevant:

- Guarantee housing assistance to people who need it
- End homelessness by linking housing with services to support recovery and self-sufficiency
- Provide a permanent and adequate supply of affordable housing
- Preserve and improve federally assisted affordable homes for people with low incomes
- Provide the opportunity for resident control of housing
- Preserve neighborhoods and end displacement (i.e., gentrification)
- End economic and racial segregation through affirmative housing programs and the enforcement of fair housing laws
- Reform federal tax laws to give priority to aiding people with the greatest housing needs
- Provide the financing needed to preserve, build, and rehabilitate housing.[147]

Much of the housing innovation in recent years has come from the nonprofit sector. There are now more than 2,000 nonprofit housing groups that have built or renovated more than half a million housing units, most of them since 1990. Although nonprofit housing organizations are having an important impact on the country's housing problem, they have limitations. For example, many of the housing groups focus their attention on the "less needy"—those with incomes at 50 percent of the median. This occurs partly because no one group knows how to house large numbers of the poorest people, especially those on public assistance. If the poorest are grouped together too tightly, neighborhoods may collapse. If they are spread out in the suburbs, the new neighbors complain. Perhaps more importantly, the scope and pace of building or renovating under nonprofits is inadequate to meet the need—nonprofits build or renovate about 50,000 units a year, and at that rate it would take a century to house the millions of families with rent burdens.[148]

Housing in an International Context

The impact of the global economic crisis on housing has been felt differently in various countries. For instance, Germany's housing market was relatively unaffected due to its low home ownership rate (43 percent), extensive public housing, and few subsidies for home buyers. The UK housing boom was similar to the U.S. in terms of relying on self-documented (i.e., liar) loans and heavy investor (called buy-to-let) lending in real estate. However, the fallout was lighter in the United Kingdom since government intervention was swifter and provided more help to banks and borrowers.

Ireland's boom and bust housing market closely paralleled what had happened in the United States. At its high point in 2006, the Irish housing boom was so intense that the number of houses exceeded the number of Irish families. This housing mania was fed by massive capital inflows from UK and European banks coupled to low interest rates. The crash of the Irish housing market was stunning.[149] By mid-2010 house prices in Ireland had fallen by 35 percent and approved loans by 73 percent compared with mid-2007. By early 2012, Dublin's house prices had dropped 56 percent (apartment prices by 62 percent) from its peak in 2007.[150]

Spain's highly inflated housing market was partially driven by foreign demand for vacation homes. Nevertheless, Spanish property prices dropped by 41.7 percent between 2006 and 2011. In the first three months of 2012 home prices dropped almost 13 percent.[151] The strength of China's economy in the financial crisis helped protect its housing market and that of its Asian trading partners. Japan's long-term problems with deflation and economic stagnation shielded the housing market. In other words, Japan's stagnant economy precluded a similar housing boom like in Ireland, the United Kingdom, and Spain. Although Australia's housing market flattened in parts of the country, its strong trade with China, robust mineral exports, a stable banking system, fiscal surplus, and the rapid stimulus packages enacted by the federal government helped soften the blow. Canada's regulated banking and financial sector kept it from

participating in some of the riskier ventures of the U.S. banks, including massive subprime lending.[152]

U.S. and European Cities

First-time U.S. visitors to European cities are often struck by several things. For one, European cars are smaller, which is understandable given that the average price of gasoline in the European Union's 27 (EU-27) member nations was $8.44 a gallon (double that of the United States) in April 2012. Visitors also notice that city streets are narrower (having been built before the advent of automobiles) and are often more congested. Public transportation is omnipresent and convenient, especially when compared to post-car American cities like Phoenix, Houston, Dallas, and Denver. Housing is denser than in most newer U.S. cities. Visitors also notice that European homes and apartments are typically smaller than in the United States and often are not centrally air conditioned. Appliances, such as refrigerators and washing machines, are also smaller. If European homes have a clothes dryer (many do not) it is generally smaller than one found in a typical American home.[153]

Europe's limited use—at least when compared to the United States—of energy-intensive appliances is partly driven by the cost of electricity. In 2011, electricity cost 23 cents a kilowatt hour in the European Union compared to 11 cents in the United States.[154] Lifestyle choices combined with cheap energy partly explains why the United States consumed 18 metric tons of CO_2 emissions (carbon dioxide emissions from burning fossil fuels and manufacturing cement) per capita in 2008 compared to 5.3 tons in Sweden, 8.5 in the United Kingdom, 9.6 in Germany, 5.9 in France, 7.2 in Spain, and 7.4 tons in Italy.[155]

Most European cities also lack the large rental-only apartment complexes found in the American South, Midwest, and West. Rental housing in the United States is typically in multifamily structures, often built exclusively for that purpose rather than for individual ownership. These complexes can be large, sometimes encompassing 500 or more rental apartments. This differs from Europe where apartments tend to be individually owned.

Comparison of U.S. and European Housing

As noted above, European housing tends to be smaller than in the United States (see Table 16.3). For instance, the floor area and room sizes in new UK homes are the smallest in Europe—the average

TABLE 16.3 Post 2003 New Construction Housing Sizes (in square feet)

United States	2,300
Australia	2,217
Denmark	1,475
France	1,216
Spain	1,044
Ireland	947
United Kingdom	818

Source: BBC News Magazine, "Room to Swing a Cat? Hardly," August 15, 2009. Retrieved August 2012 from, http://news.bbc.co.uk/2/hi/uk_news/magazine/8201900.stm

room size is 170 square feet, compared to 289.5 square feet in France. Newly built British homes are less than half the size of homes in the United States and Australia.[156]

New homes and apartments built after 2003 illustrate the dramatic differences in housing sizes between U.S. and European homes.

In 2007, 27 percent of the EU-27 population lived in owner-occupied homes with an outstanding loan or mortgage; close to half (46.5 percent) lived in a free and clear owner-occupied home.[157] In contrast, U.S. home owners have high levels of indebtedness. Out of 76 million U.S. homeowners in 2009, only 31 percent owned their homes free and clear. Most Americans buy their first home in their mid-thirties with the goal of paying off the mortgage by retirement age. In turn, most accomplish that goal: 76 percent of those age 65 and over own their homes free and clear. Through 1995, more than 50 percent of homeowners had their home paid off by age 55. However, in the current recession half of all homeowners will not be able to pay off their homes until they reach age 65. This has important implications for labor market participation and for the feasibility of early retirement.[158] By having their home paid off, Europeans are better protected against economic vicissitudes.

Another difference is the mortgage instruments used in Europe and the United States. Of the existing 52 million U.S. mortgages in 2009, about 40 million were 25–30 year fixed-rate mortgages and only 2 million were adjustable rate. In contrast, more than 80 percent of home mortgages in Spain, Ireland, and elsewhere in Europe were variable rate.[159]

The preponderance of variable rate mortgages is also true for Australia. Fixed-rate mortgage

options are only offered for the first one to five years of the mortgage. Most large Australian banks review mortgage interest rates monthly, thereby making borrowers instantly vulnerable to inflationary changes. Even a small interest rate change can have a significant impact on family finances. For instance, the monthly mortgage payment on a $300,000 loan with a 6 percent interest rate is $1,798. Increasing that interest rate to 6.5 percent adds another $100 a month to that payment. Australian mortgage borrowers are even more vulnerable because most mortgage payments are automatically debited from their bank accounts. As a result, borrowers are never certain of what their mortgage payment will be from month to month.

In contrast, the dominant U.S. model is a 30-year fixed term mortgage that protects borrowers from rapid rate hikes. Also unlike some European banks, U.S. lenders do not typically charge mortgage prepayment fees (penalties), and they hold a large number of mortgages that are secured only by the property and not the borrower's other assets.

Still another difference is that the U.S. mortgage market is dominated by lenders that originate and hold loans for only a short period of time before reselling them to the secondary investment market. In Europe, mortgage banks hold their loans in a portfolio and raise funds by selling mortgage bonds. Since European lenders retain their loans, they need to be more careful about who qualifies compared to U.S. lenders who quickly sell off their loans to other financial entities. The cavalier lending attitude promoted by the quick sale of mortgages was partly responsible for the subprime mortgage meltdown and the global financial crisis.[160]

There is also a difference in the type of dwellings that house European and U.S. populations. In 2009, 42 percent of the EU-27 population lived in flats, 34 percent in detached houses, and 23 percent in semi-detached houses. Almost three-quarters (74 percent) of the EU-27 population lived in owner-occupied dwellings while 13 percent lived in rental homes, and 13.5 percent in subsidized or free housing.[161] By comparison, close to 80 percent of all new U.S. households live in single-family houses. As Joel Catkin points out, two major drivers of economic change—the millennial generation (born between 1983 and 2003) and immigrants—both prefer suburban, single-family houses. This is especially true in Sunbelt cities where immigrant centers tend to be in suburban rather than inner-urban areas. Studies show that the majority of the millennial generation—even more than their parents—identify their ideal residential location as the suburbs.[162]

Despite the American dream of owning a single-family home, construction of multifamily units is growing faster than detached single-family homes. From 2010 to 2011, permits for structures with five or more units rose 60 percent compared to 24 percent for single-family homes. While much of new construction is for rental-only properties, many developments are also built as owner-occupied units.[163] Should this trend continue, the growth of owner-occupied units will bring the United States closer to a European model that stresses apartments over detached single-family homes.

Public Housing

The Europeans use the term "social housing" to refer to public or publicly-subsidized housing. Social housing in the European Union is characterized by a wide variety of approaches among its member states. While most social housing is rent-based, some countries allow the property to be bought by tenants. For instance, social housing recipients in the United Kingdom can assume shared ownership whereby they buy a share of the dwelling and pay rent on the rest. Social housing in Greece, Spain, and Cyprus is only available for sale.[164]

One of the primary differences between U.S. and European housing policy is the availability of publicly assisted housing. In the United States, this would be either public housing or HUD subsidized units. There are approximately 1.2 million U.S. households living in public housing units managed by 3,300 HUD-funded local housing agencies. All told, there about 5.5 million HUD subsidized housing units out of a total inventory of 41 million rental properties. Hence, roughly 13 percent of the U.S. rental stock is publicly subsidized. Put another way, 4 percent of the total 130 million U.S. housing units is publicly subsidized or assisted.[165]

By comparison, social housing accounts for 32 percent of the total housing stock in the Netherlands, 23 percent in Austria, 19 percent in Denmark, and 18 percent in the United Kingdom. Even more telling, Austria's social housing stock totals 56 percent of the total available rental stock. Social housing stock as a percentage of the total rental stock is high in other European nations as well: Denmark (51 percent); Finland (53 percent); France (44 percent); Hungary (53 percent); Netherlands (75 percent); Poland (64 percent); Slovakia

(87 percent); Sweden (48 percent); and the United Kingdom (54 percent). America's commitment to publicly-subsidized housing pales in contrast to most of the EU-27 countries.

Despite its problems, the U.S. housing sector displays considerable strength in a number of areas. For one, America's competitive mortgage market is more consumer-friendly than the European market which locks borrowers into risky variable rate mortgages. Facing inflation, variable rate mortgages will inevitably rise higher and faster than salaries, leaving homeowners with financial uncertainty. The U.S. housing market also performs well in home ownership rates, where more than 64 percent of families own their homes. This rate is on par with the EU-27 and considerably higher than Germany's low home ownership rate. U.S. tax policies, such as mortgage interest rate deductions, help make home ownership more affordable for a larger number of families. While U.S. housing sector policies effectively help middle class families purchase and stay in their home, they do not reflect adequate support for public and subsidized housing, especially when compared to many European countries.

Conclusion

The housing crisis is a structural problem based on the failure of incomes to keep pace with housing costs; an overdependence on credit to build and buy houses; and a profit-making system that drives home ownership, development, and management. In contrast to many European nations, states and the federal government have failed to actively intervene in the housing market. This lackluster performance is illustrated by the failure to build enough high quality public housing units, by not offering greater subsidies for low-income home ownership, and by not adequately protecting poor families from predatory mortgage lending practices. Until the housing crash of 2007—which arguably functioned as a dramatic but necessary market correction—profit and speculation drove up the price of rental and residential property faster than income growth. As a profit is made by each link in the housing chain (real estate agents and developers, lenders, builders, materials producers, investors, speculators, landlords, and home owners), renters and home buyers pay the costs. Put another way, the cost of every rental unit or home reflects the profits made by every party that has directly or indirectly come into contact with that property even before it was even built.

The provision of adequate low- and moderate-income housing is an important challenge in modern society. The poor have difficulty finding decent affordable housing; blue-collar workers and the lower-middle class are caught in the cost/income squeeze and are having a hard time buying and holding onto their homes. In an economic downturn, this "affordability squeeze" has resulted in increased mortgage foreclosures, high rates of property tax and delinquency defaults, evictions and homelessness, more overcrowding and doubling up of families, decreases in the consumption of other important necessities, deteriorating neighborhoods, increased business failures, higher rates of unemployment in the building trades, and the collapse of several large financial institutions.

Past and current government programs have had limited impact on the affordable housing crisis. Current housing programs are underfunded, fragmentary, and are often without clear or focused goals. Because the federal government has been viewed as an arbiter of last resort, some housing advocates contend that the government has the responsibility to ensure that adequate housing becomes a right rather than a privilege, and that healthy, sound, and safe neighborhoods become a reality.

An adequate housing policy for the United States must address cost burden, overcrowding, and housing quality. It must also provide opportunities for true housing choice and an end to the discriminatory practices that have led to de facto housing segregation. The nation will not have achieved the 1949 housing goal of "a decent home and suitable living environment for every American family" until all households live in adequate housing located in safe neighborhoods.

DISCUSSION QUESTIONS

1. The history of federal housing programs and policies has been marked by evolving priorities. Describe the dominant trends in federal housing policy from 1937 and show how they led to the current housing policies. What is the current direction of federal housing policy?
2. Describe the major shortcomings in federal low-income housing policy and discuss alternative policies to rectify these problems.
3. Home ownership is important because it can lead to asset growth. For example, a renter has nothing to show for a long-term rental except rental receipts.

In contrast, a poor family that owns a home will have a major asset after paying off their mortgage. What are some of the obstacles standing in the way of homeownership for the poor? What policies can best help these families overcome the barriers?
4. Propose federal or state policies that might help poor families find affordable rental housing.
5. Homelessness has been described as simply a manifestation of poverty. Others contend that its roots are psychological, and it should be treated as a social service problem. Where do you stand on the issue?
6. Several proposals have been developed around homelessness. Which of these (or combination thereof) have the best chance for success?
7. Should housing be viewed as a right or a privilege?

NOTES

1. Committee of Appropriations, House of Representatives, *Departments of Transportation, and Housing and Urban Development, and Related Agencies Appropriations Bill, 2011*, Report 111-564, 111th Congress, 2nd Session, 26th of July 2010. Retrieved June 2012 from http://www.clpha.org/uploads/HR5850-CmteRpt111-564Hse07-26-10.pdf
2. "Historical Census of Housing Movers," U. S. Census Bureau, 2000. Retrieved April 9, 2007 from http://www.census.gov/hhes/www/housing/census/historic/movers.html
3. Edward B. Lazere, Paul A. Leonard, Cushing N. Dolbeare, and Barry Zigas, *A Place to Call Home: The Low-Income Housing Crisis Continues* (Washington, DC: Center on Budget and Policy Priorities and Low-Income Housing Information Service, December 1991), pp. 45–47.
4. National Training and Information Center, *Insurance Redlining, Profits v. Policyholders* (Chicago: NTIC, 1973), p. 1.
5. National Training and Information Center, Insurance Redlining, Profits v. Policyholders (Chicago: NTIC, 1973), pp. 52–53.
6. Center for Community Change, "Solutions," 1999. Retrieved December 29, 2000, from http://www.communitychange.org/pahcrisis2.html
7. Committee of Appropriations, House of Representatives, *Departments of Transportation, and Housing and Urban Development, and Related Agencies Appropriations Bill, 2011*, Report 111-564, 111th Congress, 2nd Session, 26th of July 2010. Retrieved June 2012 from http://www.clpha.org/uploads/HR5850-CmteRpt111-564Hse07-26-10.pdf
8. Joint Center for Housing Studies of Harvard University, *The State of the Nation's Housing* (Cambridge, MA: Harvard University, 2003), p. 22.
9. Congressional Budget Office, *Overview of Federal Support for Housing 1*, 3rd of November 2009. Retrieved June 2012 from http://heinonline.org

10. The Harvard Joint Center for Housing Studies, *The State of the Nation's Housing 2012*, 14th of June 2012. Retrieved June 2012 from http://www.jchs.harvard.edu/sites/jchs.harvard.edu/files/son2012_bw.pdf

11. Congressional Budget Office, "Overview of Federal Support for Housing 1," 3rd of November 2009. Retrieved June 2012 from http://heinonline.org

12. N.K. Kutty & G.D. Squires, "Shelter From the Storm: The Multi-Dimensional Housing Crisis," New Labor Forum (Fall 2009), pp. 37-46, 118-119. Retrieved July 2012 from http://search.proquest.com/pqrl/docview/237229321/137DA28C457176BAA03/16?accountid=14723

13. Catalog of Federal Domestic Assistance, Indian Community Development Block Grant Program, Retrieved July 2012 from https://www.cfda.gov/?s=program&mode=form&tab=step1&id=97f025f256b79be5093ae8efa705b810

14. Catalog of Federal Domestic Assistance, Indian Housing Block Grants, Retrieved July 2012 from https://www.cfda.gov/?s=program&mode=form&tab=step1&id=97bf33a9c23e9fcc29bfffc861fcb275

15. Congressional Budget Office, "Overview of Federal Support for Housing 1," 3rd of November 2009. Retrieved June 2012 from http://heinonline.org

16. N.K. Kutty & G.D. Squires, "Shelter From the Storm: The Multi-Dimensional Housing Crisis," New Labor Forum (Fall 2009), pp. 37-46, 118-119. Retrieved July 2012 from http://search.proquest.com/pqrl/docview/237229321/137DA28C457176BAA03/16?accountid=14723

17. Congressional Budget Office, "Overview of Federal Support for Housing 1," 3rd of November 2009. Retrieved June 2012 from http://heinonline.org

18. Congressional Budget Office, "Overview of Federal Support for Housing 1," 3rd of November 2009. Retrieved June 2012 from http://heinonline.org

19. Catalog of Federal Domestic Assistance, Public and Indian Housing, Retrieved July 2012 from https://www.cfda.gov/?s=program&mode=form&tab=step1&id=e3fadc17ec79b0e9c2139cf95b940a13

20. N.K. Kutty & G.D. Squires, "Shelter From the Storm: The Multi-Dimensional Housing Crisis," New Labor Forum (Fall 2009), pp. 37-46, 118-119. Retrieved July 2012 from http://search.proquest.com/pqrl/docview/237229321/137DA28C457176BAA03/16?accountid=14723

21. N.K. Kutty & G.D. Squires, "Shelter From the Storm: The Multi-Dimensional Housing Crisis," New Labor Forum (Fall 2009), pp. 37-46, 118-119. Retrieved July 2012 from http://search.proquest.com/pqrl/docview/237229321/137DA28C457176BAA03/16?accountid=14723

22. The Harvard Joint Center for Housing Studies, The State of the Nation's Housing 2012, 14th of June 2012. Retrieved June 2012 from http://www.jchs.harvard.edu/sites/jchs.harvard.edu/files/son2012_bw.pdf

23. Congressional Budget Office, "Overview of Federal Support for Housing 1," 3rd of November 2009. Retrieved June 2012 from http://heinonline.org

24. The Harvard Joint Center for Housing Studies, The State of the Nation's Housing 2012, 14th of June 2012. Retrieved June 2012 from http://www.jchs.harvard.edu/sites/jchs.harvard.edu/files/son2012_bw.pdf

25. Catalog of Federal Domestic Assistance, Office of Public and Indian Housing, Retrieved July 2012 from https://www.cfda.gov/?_page_back=1

26. U.S. Department of Housing and Urban Development, The 2010 Annual Homeless Assessment Report to Congress, June 2011. Retrieved June 2012 from http://www.hudhre.info/documents/2010HomelessAssessmentReport.pdf

27. Congressional Budget Office, "Overview of Federal Support for Housing 1," 3rd of November 2009. Retrieved June 2012 from http://heinonline.org

28. U.S. Department of Housing and Urban Development, *New Low-Income Housing Tax Credit Property Data Available: Summary*, September 2011. Retrieved June 2012 from http://www.huduser.org/Datasets/lihtc/topical9509.pdf

29. U.S. Department of Housing and Urban Development, *New Low-Income Housing Tax Credit Property Data Available: Summary*, September 2011. Retrieved June 2012 from http://www.huduser.org/Datasets/lihtc/topical9509.pdf

30. U.S. Department of Housing and Urban Development, *Low-Income Housing Tax Credits: About the LIHTC Database*, Last revised September 22, 2011. Retrieved June 2012 from http://www.huduser.org/portal/datasets/lihtc.html#data

31. J.M. Quigley, "Rental Housing Assistance," *Cityscape: A Journal of Policy Development and Research*, 13, no. 2 (2011), pp. 147 – 158. Retrieved June 2012 from http://www.huduser.org/portal/periodicals/cityscpe/vol13num2/Cityscape_July2011_rental_housing_4.pdf

32. U.S. Department of Housing and Urban Development, *New Low-Income Housing Tax Credit Property Data Available: Summary*, September 2011. Retrieved June 2012 from http://www.huduser.org/Datasets/lihtc/topical9509.pdf

33. U.S. Department of Housing and Urban Development, *New Low-Income Housing Tax Credit Property Data Available: Summary*, September 2011. Retrieved June 2012 from http://www.huduser.org/Datasets/lihtc/topical9509.pdf

34. Congressional Budget Office, "Overview of Federal Support for Housing 1," 3rd of November 2009. Retrieved June 2012 from http://heinonline.org

35. U.S. Department of Housing and Urban Development, *Evidence Matters: A Spotlight on Rental Market Research*, Spring 2011. Retrieved June 2012 from http://www.huduser.org/portal/periodicals/em/spring11/highlight2.html

36. The Harvard Joint Center for Housing Studies, *The State of the Nation's Housing 2012*, 14th of June 2012. Retrieved June 2012 from http://www.jchs.harvard.edu/sites/jchs.harvard.edu/files/son2012_bw.pdf

37. National Low-Income Housing Coalition, *NLIHC's Comments to FDIC on Proposed Changes to the Community Reinvestment Act* (Washington, DC: NLHIC September 20, 2004).

38. National Low-Income Housing Coalition, *NLIHC's Comments to FDIC on Proposed Changes to the Community Reinvestment Act* (Washington, DC: NLHIC September 20, 2004).

39. U.S. Department of Housing and Urban Development, "Congress Authorizes the Rental Assistance Demonstration (RAD)," *HUD Public Housing Management E-Newsletter*, 3, issue 1 (January 2012).

40. National Coalition for the Homeless, "Why are People Homeless?" June 1999, retrieved December 29, 2000, from http:/nch.ari.net; see also Laura Waxman, *A Status Report on Hunger and Homelessness in America's Cities: 1995* (Washington, DC: U.S. Conference of Mayors, 1995); and Children's Defense Fund, *The State of America's Children,* 1991 (Washington, DC: Children's Defense Fund, 1991).

41. J.M. Quigley, "Rental Housing Assistance," *Cityscape: A Journal of Policy Development and Research*, 13, no. 2 (2011), pp. 147 – 158. Retrieved June 2012 from http://www.huduser.org/portal/periodicals/cityscpe/vol13num2/Cityscape_July2011_rental_housing_4.pdf

42. Board of Governors of the Federal Reserve System, *The U.S. Housing Market: Current Conditions and Policy Considerations*, 4th of January 2012. Retrieved July 2012 from http://media.oregonlive.com/finance/other/housing-white-paper-20120104.pdf

43. The Harvard Joint Center for Housing Studies, *The State of the Nation's Housing 2012*, June 14, 2012. Retrieved June 2012 from http://www.jchs.harvard.edu/sites/jchs.harvard.edu/files/son2012_bw.pdf

44. Board of Governors of the Federal Reserve System, *The U.S. Housing Market: Current Conditions and Policy Considerations*, 4th of January 2012. Retrieved July 2012 from http://media.oregonlive.com/finance/other/housing-white-paper-20120104.pdf

45. The Harvard Joint Center for Housing Studies, *The State of the Nation's Housing 2012*, 14th of June 2012. Retrieved June 2012 from http://www.jchs.harvard.edu/sites/jchs.harvard.edu/files/son2012_bw.pdf

46. Jason Furman, End the Mortgage-Interest Deduction! Why the Left Should Embrace the Bush Tax Commission's Most Radical Proposal, *Slate*, November 10, 2005. Retrieved March 20, 2008, from http://www.slate.com/id/2130017

47. Daniel Gross, "Location, Location—Deduction. The Mortgage-Interest Deduction Costs Taxpayers Billions, but It Won't Go Away Anytime Soon," *Slate*, April 14, 2005. Retrieved March 20, 2008, from www.slate.com/id/211673

48. Mark Robyn, Study Finds the Mortgage Interest Deduction to Be Ineffective at Increasing Ownership, Tax Foundation, October 1, 2010. Retrieved January 2011 from, http://www.taxfoundation.org/blog/show/26762.html

49. Jeff Schneppe, "10 Big Tax Breaks for the Rest of Us," *MSN Money*, 2004. Retrieved November 2004 from http://moneycentral.msn.com/content/Taxes/Taxshelters/P75680.asp

50. The Harvard Joint Center for Housing Studies, *The State of the Nation's Housing 2012*, June 14, 2012. Retrieved June 2012 from http://www.jchs.harvard.edu/sites/jchs.harvard.edu/files/son2012_bw.pdf

51. Joint Center for Housing Studies of Harvard University, *The State of the Nation's Housing,* 2003. Retrieved November 2004 from http://www.jchs.harvard.edu/publications/markets/son2004.pdf

52. Donald Haurin, Christopher Herbert, and Stuart Rosenthal, "Home ownership Gaps among Low-Income and Minority Households," *Cityscape 9*, no. 2, 2007, pp. 26–35.

53. The Harvard Joint Center for Housing Studies, *The State of the Nation's Housing 2012*, 14th of June 2012. Retrieved June 2012 from http://www.jchs.harvard.edu/sites/jchs.harvard.edu/files/son2012bw.pdf

54. Department of Housing and Urban Development, *U.S. Housing Market Conditions: First Quarter 2012*, May 2012. Retrieved June 2012 from http://www.huduser.org/portal/periodicals/ushmc/spring12/USHMC_1q12.pdf

55. The Harvard Joint Center for Housing Studies, *The State of the Nation's Housing 2012*, 14th of June 2012. Retrieved June 2012 from http://www.jchs.harvard.edu/sites/jchs.harvard.edu/files/son2012_bw.pdf

56. R. Collinson & B. Winter, "U.S. Rental Housing Characteristics: Supply, Vacancy, and Affordability," *HUD PD&R Working Paper 10-01*, January 2010. Retrieved June 2012 from http://www.huduser.org/Publications/PDF/FinalReport_Rental_Housing_Conditions_Working_Paper.pdf

57. The Harvard Joint Center for Housing Studies, *The State of the Nation's Housing 2012*, June 14, 2012. Retrieved June 2012 from http://www.jchs.harvard.edu/sites/jchs.harvard.edu/files/son2012_bw.pdf

58. The Harvard Joint Center for Housing Studies, *The State of the Nation's Housing 2012*, June 14, 2012. Retrieved June 2012 from http://www.jchs.harvard.edu/sites/jchs.harvard.edu/files/son2012_bw.pdf

59. Joint Center for Housing Studies of Harvard University, *The State of the Nation's Housing,* pp. 28–31.

60. U.S. Department of Housing and Urban Development, *Evidence Matters: A Spotlight on Rental Market Research,* Spring 2011. Retrieved June 2012 from http://www.huduser.org/portal/periodicals/em/spring11/highlight2.html

61. Department of Housing and Urban Development, "U.S. Housing Market Conditions: First Quarter 2012," May 2012. Retrieved June 2012 from http://www.huduser.org/portal/periodicals/ushmc/spring12/USHMC_1q12.pdf

62. See U.S. Census Bureau, *Statistical Abstract of the United States,* 1991 (Washington DC: U.S. Government Printing Office, 1991), pp. 715–717; and MSNBC, "SoCal Median Home Price Falls To $408,000," KNBC-TV, March 13, 2008.

Retrieved March 23, 2008, from http://www.msnbc.msn.com/id/23614434

63. The Harvard Joint Center for Housing Studies, *The State of the Nation's Housing 2012*, 14th of June 2012. Retrieved June 2012 from http://www.jchs.harvard.edu/sites/jchs.harvard.edu/files/son2012_bw.pdf

64. The Harvard Joint Center for Housing Studies, *The State of the Nation's Housing 2012*, 14th of June 2012. Retrieved June 2012 from http://www.jchs.harvard.edu/sites/jchs.harvard.edu/files/son2012_bw.pdf

65. The Harvard Joint Center for Housing Studies, *The State of the Nation's Housing 2012*, June 14, 2012. Retrieved June 2012 from http://www.jchs.harvard.edu/sites/jchs.harvard.edu/files/son2012_bw.pdf

66. E.S. Belsky & N. Richardson, *Understanding the Boom and Bust in Non-Prime Mortgage Lending*, The Harvard Joint Center for Housing Studies, September 2010. Retrieved July 2012 from http://www.jchs.harvard.edu/sites/jchs.harvard.edu/files/ubb10-1.pdf

67. Winton Picoff and Sheila Crowley, "Rental Housing for America's Poor Families: Farther Out of Reach Than Ever," National Low Income Housing Coalition (2002). Available at http://www.nlihc.org/oor20029

68. Robert Dietz, Estimation of Neighborhood Effects in the Social Sciences: An Interdisciplinary Literature Review, URAI Working Paper No. 00–03, Urban and Regional Analysis Initiative, Ohio State University January 1, 2001

69. Joseph Harkness & Sandra Newman, "Effects of Home ownership on Children: The Role of Neighborhood Characteristics and Family Income," *Economic Policy Review* 9, no. 2 (June 2003), p. 51.

70. Howard Karger, "The Homeownership Myth," *Dollars & Sense*, 270, Spring (March/April & May/June 2007), pp. 2–11.

71. Bankrate.com, "Countrywide, the Mortgage Mess and You," August 17, 2007. Retrieved March 12, 2008, from MSNMoney, http://articles.moneycentral.msn.com/Banking/HomeFinancing/CountrywideTheMortgageMessAndYou.aspx?page=all

72. L.A. Fennell and J.A. Roin, "Controlling Residential Stakes," *The University of Chicago Law Review*, 77, no. 1 (Winter 2010), pp. 143-176.

73. E.S. Belsky & N. Richardson, *Understanding the Boom and Bust in Non-Prime Mortgage Lending*, The Harvard Joint Center for Housing Studies, September 2010. Retrieved July 2012 from http://www.jchs.harvard.edu/sites/jchs.harvard.edu/files/ubb10-1.pdf

74. L.A. Fennell and J.A. Roin, "Controlling Residential Stakes," *The University of Chicago Law Review*, 77, no. 1 (Winter 2010), pp. 143-176.

75. E.S. Belsky & N. Richardson, *Understanding the Boom and Bust in Non-Prime Mortgage Lending*, The Harvard Joint Center for Housing Studies, September 2010. Retrieved July 2012 from http://www.jchs.harvard.edu/sites/jchs.harvard.edu/files/ubb10-1.pdf

76. Department of Housing and Urban Development, *U.S. Housing Market Conditions: First Quarter 2012*, May 2012. Retrieved June 2012 from http://www.huduser.org/portal/periodicals/ushmc/spring12/USHMC_1q12.pdf

77. Howard Karger, *Shortchanged: Life and Debt in the Fringe Economy* (San Francisco: Berrett-Koehler), 2005.

78. Homeinsurance.com, "Average 12-Month Home Insurance Rates," October 2010. Retrieved January 2011 from, http://homeinsurance.com/rates-in-your-state/

79. Howard Karger, *Shortchanged: Life and Debt in the Fringe Economy* (San Francisco: Berrett-Koehler), 2005.

80. National Housing Coalition, "The Housing Landscape for America's Working Families, 2007." NHC, Washington, DC, August 2007.

81. Carolina Katz Reid, "Studies in Demography and Ecology: Achieving the American Dream? A Longitudinal Analysis of the Home ownership Experiences of Low-Income Households," University of Washington, CSDE Working Paper No. 04-04, 2004.

82. Donald Haurin & Stuart Rosenthal, "The Sustainability of Home ownership: Factors Affecting the Duration of Home Ownership and Rental Spells," Office of Policy Development & Research, U.S. Department of Housing and Urban Development, 2005; and Donald Haurin and Stuart Rosenthal, "The Influence of Household Formation on Home ownership Rates Across Time and Race," Office of Policy Development & Research, U.S. Department of Housing and Urban Development, 2005.

83. Richard Green and Patric Hendershott, "Homeownership and Unemployment in the U.S." *Urban Studies*, 38, no. 9, pp. 1509–1520, 2001.

84. Carolina Katz Reid, "Studies in Demography and Ecology: Achieving the American Dream? A Longitudinal Analysis of the Home ownership Experiences of Low-Income Households," University of Washington, CSDE Working Paper No. 04-04, 2004.

85. Kathleen Howley, "Americans Selling Homes See Prices Go Below Mortgage," February 13, 2008. Retrieved March 12, 2008, from www.bloomberg.com/apps/news?pid=20601109&refer=home&sid=aaKqieyMLwnc

86. E.S. Belsky & N. Richardson, *Understanding the Boom and Bust in Non-Prime Mortgage Lending*, The Harvard Joint Center for Housing Studies, September 2010. Retrieved July 2012 from http://www.jchs.harvard.edu/sites/jchs.harvard.edu/files/ubb10-1.pdf

87. Ibid.

88. Ibid. Karger, *Shortchanged*, op cit.

89. Department of Housing and Urban Development, *U.S. Housing Market Conditions: First Quarter 2012*, May 2012. Retrieved June 2012 from http://www.huduser.org/portal/periodicals/ushmc/spring12/USHMC_1q12.pdf

90. E.S. Belsky & N. Richardson, *Understanding the Boom and Bust in Non-Prime Mortgage Lending*, The Harvard Joint Center for Housing Studies, September 2010. Retrieved July 2012 from http://www.jchs.harvard.edu/sites/jchs.harvard.edu/files/ubb10-1.pdf

91. *Wall Street Journal,* "Foreclosure Rates Surge in Third Quarter," November 1, 2007. Retrieved March 12, 2008 from, http://blogs.wsj.com/developments/2007/11/01/foreclosurerates-surge-in-third-quarter.

92. See Les Christie, Record 3 Million Households Hit with Foreclosure in 2009, *CNN Money,* January 14, 2010. Retrieved January 2011 from, Z01_http://money.cnn.com/2010/01/14/real_estate/record_foreclosure_year/

93. See Realty-Trac Staff, Foreclosure Activity Decreases 21 Percent in November, RealtyTrac, December 16, 2010. Retrieved January 2011 from, http://www.realtytrac.com/content/press-releases/foreclosure-activity-decreases-21-percent-innovember-6251

94. *New York Times,* Foreclosures (2012) Robosigning and Mortgage Servicing Settlement, April 2, 2012, p. A15.

95. The Harvard Joint Center for Housing Studies, *The State of the Nation's Housing 2012,* 14th of June 2012. Retrieved June 2012 from http://www.jchs.harvard.edu/sites/jchs.harvard.edu/files/son2012_bw.pdf

96. The Harvard Joint Center for Housing Studies, *The State of the Nation's Housing 2012,* June 14, 2012. Retrieved June 2012 from http://www.jchs.harvard.edu/sites/jchs.harvard.edu/files/son2012_bw.pdf

97. *The New York Times,* Foreclosures (2012) Robosigning and Mortgage Servicing Settlement, April 2, 2012, p. A15.

98. Ibid.

99. Dean Baker, "The Housing Bubble: A Time Bomb in Low-Income Communities?" Shelterforce Online, Issue #135, May/June 2004, http://www.nhi.org/online/issues/135/bubble.html

100. Joint Center for Housing Studies of Harvard University, 2004.

101. The Harvard Joint Center for Housing Studies, *The State of the Nation's Housing 2012,* 14th of June 2012. Retrieved June 2012 from http://www.jchs.harvard.edu/sites/jchs.harvard.edu/files/son2012_bw.pdf

102. The Harvard Joint Center for Housing Studies, *The State of the Nation's Housing 2012,* 14th of June 2012. Retrieved June 2012 from http://www.jchs.harvard.edu/sites/jchs.harvard.edu/files/son2012_bw.pdf

103. U.S. Department of Housing and Urban Development, Evidence Matters: A Spotlight on Rental Market Research, Spring 2011. Retrieved June 2012 from http://www.huduser.org/portal/periodicals/em/spring11/highlight2.html

104. U.S. Department of Housing and Urban Development, Worst Case Housing Needs 2009: Report to Congress, 2009. Retrieved June 2012 from http://www.huduser.org/portal/Publications/pdf/WorstCaseNeeds2009Summary.pdf

105. U.S. Department of Housing and Urban Development, Worst Case Housing Needs 2009: Report to Congress, 2009. Retrieved June 2012 from http://www.huduser.org/portal/Publications/pdf/WorstCaseNeeds2009Summary.pdf

106. The Harvard Joint Center for Housing Studies, The State of the Nation's Housing 2012, June 14, 2012. Retrieved June 2012 from http://www.jchs.harvard.edu/sites/jchs.harvard.edu/files/son2012_bw.pdf

107. Joint Center for Housing Studies of Harvard University, 2004.

108. U.S. Department of Housing and Urban Development, *Worst Case Housing Needs 2009: Report to Congress,* 2009. Retrieved June 2012 from http://www.huduser.org/portal/Publications/pdf/WorstCaseNeeds2009Summary.pdf

109. National Low Income Housing Coalition (NLIHC), *Out of Reach 2003,* (Washington, DC: NLIHC, 2003).

110. The Harvard Joint Center for Housing Studies, *The State of the Nation's Housing 2012,* 14th of June 2012. Retrieved June 2012 from http://www.jchs.harvard.edu/sites/jchs.harvard.edu/files/son2012_bw.pdf

111. U.S. Department of Housing and Urban Development, *Finding 2: The Stock of Rental Housing Affordable to the Lowest Income Families Is Shrinking and Congress Has Eliminated Funding for New Rental Assistance since 1995,* HUD. Retrieved November 2004 from http://www.huduser.org/publications/affhsg/worstcase/finding2.html

112. U.S. Department of Housing and Urban Development, *Finding 2: The Stock of Rental Housing Affordable to the Lowest Income Families Is Shrinking and Congress Has Eliminated Funding for New Rental Assistance since 1995,* HUD. Retrieved November 2004 from http://www.huduser.org/publications/affhsg/worstcase/finding2.html

113. The Harvard Joint Center for Housing Studies, *The State of the Nation's Housing 2012,* 14th of June 2012. Retrieved June 2012 from http://www.jchs.harvard.edu/sites/jchs.harvard.edu/files/son2012_bw.pdf

114. The National Coalition for the Homeless, "Facts About Homelessness, People Need Affordable Housing." Retrieved November 2004 from http://www.nationalhomeless.org/facts/housing.html

115. National Coalition for the Homeless, "Why Are People Homeless?" NCH Fact Sheet #1, June 1999. Retrieved December 2000 fromhttp://nch.ari.net

116. George Sternlieb and James W. Hughes, "Back to the Central City: Myths and Realities." In George Sternlieb et al. (eds.),*America's Housing* (New Brunswick, NJ: Rutgers University, Center for Urban Policy Research, 1980), p. 173.

117. Habitat for Humanity, "U.S. Affordable Housing Statistics" (Washington DC: Author, 2000); and Joint Center for Housing Studies at Harvard University, *The State of the Nation's Housing: 2000.*

118. P. Emrath & H. Taylor, "Housing Value, Costs, and Measures of Physical Adequacy," *Cityscape: A Journal of Policy Development and Research,* 14, no. 1 (2012), pp. 99–126. Retrieved June 2012 from http://www.huduser.org/portal/periodicals/cityscpe/vol14num1/Cityscape_Mar2012_hsg_values.pdf

119. See National Low-Income Housing Coalition, *NLIHC Background on Housing Issues;* and Environmental Protection Agency, "Shut the Door on Lead Poisoning," EPA November 2, 2004. Retrieved November 2004 from http://www.epa.gov/lead

120. Ibid., pp. 43–44.

121. Carol Biedrzycki, "Residential and Low-Income Electric Customer Protection," Texas Ratepayers' Organization to Save Energy, Inc. Retrieved December 2000, from http://www.ncat.org/liheap/pubs/txreport.htm

122. Center on Budget and Policy Priorities, *Smaller Slices of the Pie* (Washington, DC: CBPP, November 1985), p. 33.

123. National Energy Assistance Directors' Association, States Project Massive Cuts in LIHEAP Under Senate Appropriations Bill, November 29, 2010. Retrieved January 2011 from, http://www.neada.org/communications/press/2010-11-29.pdf

124. Senator Paul Wellstone.

125. Children's Defense Fund, *The State of America's Children, 1992* (Washington, DC: Children's Defense Fund, 1992), p. 38.

126. E.S. Belsky & N. Richardson, *Understanding the Boom and Bust in Non-Prime Mortgage Lending*, The Harvard Joint Center for Housing Studies, September 2010. Retrieved July 2012 from http://www.jchs.harvard.edu/sites/jchs.harvard.edu/files/ubb10-1.pdf

127. Quoted in Diana M. DiNitto, *Social Welfare: Politics and Public Policy* (Boston: Allyn & Bacon, 1995), p. 87.

128. The Harvard Joint Center for Housing Studies, *The State of the Nation's Housing 2012*, June 14, 2012. Retrieved June 2012 from http://www.jchs.harvard.edu/sites/jchs.harvard.edu/files/son2012_bw.pdf

129. U.S. Department of Housing and Urban Development, *The 2010 Annual Homeless Assessment Report to Congress*, June 2011. Retrieved June 2012 from http://www.hudhre.info/documents/2010HomelessAssessmentReport.pdf

130. The National Coalition for the Homeless, *Facts about Homelessness*.

131. U.S. Department of Housing and Urban Development, *The 2009 Annual Homeless Assessment Report to Congress*, June 2010. Retrieved June 2012 from http://www.huduser.org/publications/pdf/5thHomelessAssessmentReport.pdf

132. Interagency Council on Homelessness, Opening Doors: Federal Strategic Plan to Prevent and End Homelessness 2010. Retrieved January 2011 from, http://www.usich.gov/PDF/Opening-Doors_2010_FSPPreventEndHomeless.pdf

133. See National Coalition for the Homeless, "Domestic Violence and Homelessness," April 1999, retrieved November 2004, from http://www.nationalhomeless.org/domestic.html; and Institute for Children and Poverty, *Homes for the Homeless—Ten Cities 1997–1998*, Homes for the Homeless and Institute for Children and Poverty, New York, 1999.

134. N.K. Kutty & G.D. Squires, "Shelter From the Storm: The Multi-Dimensional Housing Crisis," *New Labor Forum* (Fall 2009), pp. 37-46, 118-119. Retrieved July 2012 from http://search.proquest.com/pqrl/docview/237229321/137DA28C457176BAA03/16?accountid=14723

135. See National Coalition for the Homeless, "Domestic Violence and Homelessness," April 1999, retrieved November 2004 from http://www.nationalhomeless.org/domestic.html; and Institute for Children and Poverty, *Homes for the Homeless—Ten Cities 1997–1998*, Homes for the Homeless and Institute for Children and Poverty, New York, 1999.

136. National Law Center on Homelessness and Poverty, *Some Facts on Homelessness, Housing and Violence Against Women*, Retrieved June 2012 from http://www.nlchp.org/content/pubs/Some%20Facts%20on%20Homeless%20and%20DV.pdf

137. National Law Center on Homelessness and Poverty, *Some Facts on Homelessness, Housing and Violence Against Women*, Retrieved June 2012 from http://www.nlchp.org/content/pubs/Some%20Facts%20on%20Homeless%20and%20DV.pdf

138. M. Pergamit, "On the Lifetime Prevalence of Running Away from Home," *The Urban Institute of Policy Research*, April 2010. Retrieved June 2012 from http://www.urban.org/url.cfm?ID=412087

139. See National Coalition for the Homeless, "Homeless Youth," April 1999, retrieved November 2004, from http://www.nationalhomeless.org/youth.html; Institute for Health Policy Studies, *Street Youth at Risk for AIDS: 1995* (San Francisco: University of California, 1999); and National Association of Social Workers, *Helping Vulnerable Youths: Runaway and Homeless Adolescents in the United States* (Washington, DC: NASW, 1992).

140. J.P. Edidin, Z. Ganim, S.J. Hunter & N.S. Karnik, "The Mental and Physical Health of Homeless Youth: A Literature Review," *Child Psychiatry and Human Development*, 43 (2012), pp. 354-375. Retrieved July 2012 from http://www.springerlink.com/content/e4682w0567qq3248/fulltext.pdf?MUD=MP

141. J.P. Edidin, Z. Ganim, S.J. Hunter & N.S. Karnik, "The Mental and Physical Health of Homeless Youth: A Literature Review," *Child Psychiatry and Human Development*, 43 (2012), pp. 354–375. Retrieved July 2012 from http://www.springerlink.com/content/e4682w0567qq3248/fulltext.pdf?MUD=MP

142. J.P. Edidin, Z. Ganim, S.J. Hunter & N.S. Karnik, "The Mental and Physical Health of Homeless Youth: A Literature Review," *Child Psychiatry and Human Development*, 43 (2012), pp. 354–375. Retrieved July 2012 from http://www.springerlink.com/content/e4682w0567qq3248/fulltext.pdf?MUD=MP

143. See National Coalition for the Homeless, "Homeless Youth," April 1999, retrieved November 2004 from http://www.nationalhomeless.org/youth.html; Institute for Health Policy Studies, *Street Youth at Risk for AIDS: 1995* (San Francisco: University of California, 1999); and National Association of Social Workers, *Helping Vulnerable Youths: Runaway and Homeless Adolescents in the United States* (Washington, DC: NASW, 1992).

144. National Low-Income Housing Coalition, *1996 Advocate's Resource Book* (Washington, DC: NLIHC, 1996

145. Interagency Council on Homelessness, Opening Doors: Federal Strategic Plan to Prevent and End Homelessness 2010. Retrieved January 2011 from, http://www.usich.gov/PDF/Opening-Doors_2010_FSPPreventEndHomeless.pdf

146. Tanya Tull, "The 'Housing First' Approach for Families Affected by Substance Abuse," The Source (National Abandoned Infants Assistance Resource Center), 13, no. 1 (Spring 2004).

147. See National Low-Income Housing Coalition, NLIHC Background on Housing Issues; and National Low-Income Housing Coalition, *1995 Advocate's Resource Book* (Washington, DC: NLIHC, 1995).

148. See National Low-Income Housing Coalition, NLIHC Background on Housing Issues; and National Low-Income Housing Coalition, *1995 Advocate's Resource Book* (Washington, DC: NLIHC, 1995).

149. Shashank Bengali, "Housing Developments, Many of Them Empty, Alter the Pastoral Landscape and Cost the Builders Dearly," *Maine Sunday Telegram*, June 10, 2012, p. 15.

150. Conor Pope, "Dublin House Prices Fell 4% Last Month as Rate of Decline Hit Two-year High," *The Irish Times*, February 29, 2012, p. 2.

151. Laura Quintana, "Spanish Property Prices Dropped by 41.7% Between 2006 and 2011," Catalan News Agency, April 30, 2012. Retrieved August 2012 from, http://www.catalannewsagency.com/news/business/spanish-property-prices-dropped-417-between-2006-and-2011.

152. Ashok Bardhan, Robert Edelstein, and Cynthia Kroll, A Comparative Context for U.S. Housing Policy: Housing Markets and the Financial Crisis in Europe, Asia, and Beyond, Bipartisan Policy Center, April 2012. Retrieved August 2012 from, http://www.scribd.com/doc/90364427/A-Comparative-Context-for-U-S-Housing-Policy-Housing-Markets-and-the-Financial-Crisis-in-Europe-Asia-and-Beyond

153. Elisabeth Rosenthal, "What Makes Europe Greener than the U.S.?, Environment 360, Yale University, September 28, 2009. Retrieved August 2012 from, http://e360.yale.edu/feature/what_makes_europe_greener_than_the_us/2193/

154. Bruce Mountain, Electricity Prices in Australia: An International Comparison. A report to the Energy Users Association of Australia, CME, March 2012, Melbourne, Australia.

155. The World Bank, CO2 Emissions (Metric Tons per Capita), nd. Retrieved August 2012 from, http://data.worldbank.org/indicator/EN.ATM.CO2E.PC

156. BBC News Magazine, "Room to Swing a Cat? Hardly," August 15, 2009. Retrieved August 2012 from, http://news.bbc.co.uk/2/hi/uk_news/magazine/8201900.stm

157. European Commission, Housing Statistics (October 2011 data), Eurostat. Retrieved August 2012 from, http://epp.eurostat.ec.europa.eu/statistics_explained/index.php/Housing_statistics

158. U.S. Census Bureau, Table 998. Mortgage Characteristics – Owner-Occupied Units: 2009. Retrieved August 2012 from, http://www.census.gov/compendia/statab/2012/tables/12s0998.pdf

159. Richard Green, Has the Variable Rate Mortgage Saved the European Mortgage Market? Wall Street Pit, April 23, 2012. Retrieved August 2012 from, http://wallstreetpit.com/91384-has-the-variable-rate-mortgage-saved-the-european-mortgage-market

160. Adrian Coles and Judith Hardt, Mortgage Markets: Why US and EU Markets Are So Different, International Union for Housing Finance, nd. Retrieved August 2012 from, http://www.housingfinance.org/uploads/Publicationsmanager/Europe_coles_hardt.pdf

161. European Commission, Housing Statistics (October 2011 data), Eurostat. Retrieved August 2012 from, http://epp.eurostat.ec.europa.eu/statistics_explained/index.php/Housing_statistics

162. Joel Catkin, Don't Bet Against the (Single-Family) House, *Forbes*, February 28, 2012.

163. Peter Coy, Apartment Nation: Trend to Multi-Family Housing Continues, *Bloomberg Business Week*, March 20, 2012. Retrieved August 2012 from, http://www.businessweek.com/articles/2012-03-20/apartment-nation-trend-to-multi-family-housing-continues

164. CECODHAS *Housing Europe Review 2012. The Nuts and Bolts of European Social Housing Systems*, October 2011. Retrieved August 2012 from, http://www.housingeurope.eu/www.housingeurope.eu/uploads/file_/HER%202012%20EN%20web2_1.pdf

165. U.S. Department of Housing and Urban Development, HUD's Public Housing Program, nd. Retrieved August 2102 from, http://portal.hud.gov/hudportal/HUD?src=/topics/rental_assistance/phprog; see also U.S. Census Bureau, Statistical Abstract of the United States: 2012, Table 982. Total Housing Inventory for the United States: 1990 to 2010. Washington, DC.

CHAPTER 17

The Politics of Food Policy and Rural Life

Source: The Image Works

How can a nation as affluent as the United States allow food insecurity (i.e., poverty-related insecurity around the lack of access to food) and even starvation to occur? Food policy in the United States is marked by important contradictions. In 2010, 35.5 million people lived in households that were unsure where their next meal was coming from.[1] Of that number, almost 17 million were children, or 22.5 percent of all U.S. children. The policies related to the production and distribution of food form an important part of the U.S. welfare state. For example, over the course of a year an estimated one in four Americans participates in at least one of the 15 food assistance programs administered by the U.S. Department of Agriculture (USDA). Expenditures for these 15 food assistance programs totaled $103 billion in 2011.[2] This chapter examines the federal response to hunger and the government's attempts to distribute foodstuffs to the poor. Topics include the Supplemental Nutrition Assistance Program (SNAP) (formerly called Food Stamps), WIC and other food programs, U.S. farm policy, the plight of farmworkers in the United States, and the overall problems of food production and distribution. Although the issues around food may initially seem disparate, they are tied together in a complex mosaic that is fundamental to the well-being of the nation.

The Contradictions of American Food Policy

Food policy in America is marked by notable contradictions. Despite food insecurity, 36 percent of U.S. adults and almost 17 percent of U.S. children and adolescents are obese.[3] About 68 percent of adult Americans are either obese or overweight.[4] That is not surprising since Americans spend more money on fast food than on higher education, personal computers, computer software, and new cars.[5] The Centers for Disease Control and Prevention (CDC) labels the obesity problem an epidemic.

Prevalence rates for both obesity and overweight are higher in lower socioeconomic groups, indicating a link between income and inexpensive fast food options that have poor nutritional value.[6] In fact, some of the most food-insecure households have the highest rate of obesity.

The impact of obesity on America's healthcare system is also growing. In 1998, the estimated medical costs of obesity were $78.5 billion; by 2008 it had reached $147 billion.[7] Directly and indirectly, obesity costs the United States $117 billion a year

and results in 39 million lost work days. Three-fourths of the $1.4 trillion the United States spends on health care is to treat chronic illnesses, many of which are tied to obesity and being overweight.[8]

Obesity, overweight, and fast food diets are bringing the nation's steady rise in life expectancy to a grinding halt. The CDC predicts that 29 million Americans will be diagnosed with diabetes in 2050 compared with about 11 million in 2003. Twenty years ago, the United States led the world's longevity league. That is no longer true today.[9]

The widespread impact of being obese and overweight on all areas of life is not always apparent. For example, childhood obesity has emerged as a cost to the workforce. Specifically, since many employers insure dependents as well as the workers themselves, the medical conditions of obese children are paid for by employers. A study on a large U.S. corporation found that that the average health insurance claim for an obese child was $2,907 per capita in 2008 compared to $10,789 for children with type 2 diabetes.[10] In addition, parents of obese children with associated medical conditions will also have increased absentee rates as they stay home to care for their children.[11]

With an annual 2011 budget of approximately $148 billion,[12] the U. S. Department of Agriculture (USDA) is responsible for distributing more federal resources than DHHS spends outside of Medicare and Medicaid. Almost 46 percent of the USDA budget is comprised of means-tested food and nutrition programs; however, the balance is largely commodity price supports ($19.7 billion), soil conservation programs ($2.0 billion), crop insurance ($7.2 billion), export credit guarantees ($2.4 billion), rural development of utilities, housing, and businesses ($14.9 billion), and natural resource and environmental protection ($7.5 billion).[13]

Commodity price supports, conservation programs, crop insurance, and export credit guarantees are largely direct financial subsidies to the 2.1 million farms in America. However, these subsidies are not supporting the small, family owned and operated farms so frequently mentioned in Congressional appeals for more funding. A recent study shows that large-scale commercial farms receive the greater share of commodity payments.[14] In response to this monopoly, an income cap for commodity payments was instituted which specifically targeted large farms, but its efficacy has been dubious, and the USDA proposed that stricter measures be applied to the income cap.[15] To put this into perspective, the USDA manages around $18 billion in subsidies that are justified in support of what may be less than half a million family farms.[16] In comparison, TANF provides approximately $15 billion[17] to provide income security to an average of 4 million recipients with incomes below the poverty line.[18]

Hunger in the United States

Hunger exists in the United States, but unlike the stereotype of emaciated Third World children, it typically occurs in subtle ways. For example, poor Americans may eat only once a day or skip meals for several days; they may be subject to chronic malnutrition; women may deliver low-birth-weight babies; and babies may be at risk from high infant mortality rates. Crossing age, race, and gender lines, hunger in the United States affects children, the elderly, the unemployed and the underemployed, the homeless, people with disabilities, and both two-parent and single-parent families. The single common thread connecting these diverse groups to the problem of hunger is poverty.

The USDA measures the continuum of food security and insecurity using the following criteria:

- *High food security households* report no problems or anxieties around accessing adequate food.
- *Marginal food security households* have occasional problems or anxiety around accessing adequate food. However, their intake of quality food is not substantially reduced.
- *Low food security households* have reduced quality and variety in their diets, but the quantity of food intake and normal eating patterns are not substantially disrupted.
- *Very low food security households* exhibit disrupted or reduced eating patterns of one or more family members in a given year because of the lack of money or benefits.[19]

Cheap and plentiful food is an American tradition, which partly explains why so many Americans over the age of 25 are overweight.[20] Americans spend a smaller percentage of their income on food than any other nation, and we feed much of the world with our surplus (the value of U.S. agricultural exports totaled almost $116 billion in 2010).[21] Moreover, food has become cheaper. In 1963, the average American family spent 20 percent of their income on food; by 2010 it was only 10 percent. Consumers, retailers, restaurants, and farmers throw away one-quarter of the U.S. food stock (almost 100 billion pounds of edible food) each year.[22]

Yet in 2010, 14.5 percent (17.2 million) of U.S. households were food insecure. Households are classified by the USDA as food secure, food insecure without hunger, or food insecure with hunger (i.e., if one or more household members were hungry at some time during the year because the household could not afford enough food). Women and children make up about three-fourths of this population. Adults were food insecure in about half of the food insecure households. However, 8.3 percent of households with children had one or more children who were food insecure at some time during the year. In 0.8 percent of households with children, one or more of the children experienced the most severe food-insecure condition measured by USDA—very low food security, irregular meals, and food intake below levels considered adequate. Food pantries and emergency kitchens (soup kitchens) helped close that gap by feeding approximately 17.4 million people in 2010.[23]

Children who are denied an adequate diet are at a greater risk of not reaching their full potential as individuals. Undernourished youngsters have trouble concentrating and bonding with other children and are more likely to suffer illnesses resulting in school absences. Compared to adequately nourished children, they consistently perform more poorly on standardized tests and are at a major risk of dropping out of school. Studies have also shown that even mildly undernourished children may potentially suffer brain, cognitive, and psychological impairment that, if not corrected, can be irreversible. Teenagers who are food insufficient are more likely to have seen a psychologist, have been suspended from school, and have difficulty getting along with other teenagers. Food insufficiency is also associated with increased risk of suicide in teenagers.[24] Research conducted by the Center on Hunger, Poverty and Nutritional Policy at Tufts University found compelling evidence that improved nutrition can modify and even reverse these effects.

The following data provides a snapshot of America's hungry in 2009–2010.

- Of the total U.S. households, 85.3 percent (100.8 million) were food secure.
- In 2010, the average daily prevalence of very low food security was between 800,000 to 1.2 million households, and children went hungry in 46,000 to 56,000 homes.[25]
- At some time during 2009, 14.7 percent (17.4 million) of U.S. households were food insecure; low food security was observed in 9 percent (10.6 million) of U.S. households; and very low food security was observed in 5.7 percent (6.8 million) of households.

- In 2009, 9 million children (12 percent of children) lived in households with food insecurity; 988,000 (1.3 percent of U.S. children) lived in households with very low food security.
- Some groups with rates of food insecurity are much higher than the national average (14.7 percent): Households with incomes below the official poverty line (43 percent); households with children; those headed by a single woman (36.6 percent); black households (24.9 percent); and Hispanic households (26.9 percent).
- Households with children had nearly twice the rate of food insecurity (21 percent) as those without (11 percent). Among households with children, married-couple families had the lowest rate of food insecurity (15 percent).
- Food insecurity was higher for households in metropolitan areas (17 percent) than in nonmetro areas (14 percent). Regionally, food insecurity was highest in the South (16 percent) and West (15 percent), intermediate in the Midwest (14 percent), and lowest in the Northeast (12 percent).[26]
- Almost 60 percent of food-insecure households in 2010 had participated in one or more of Federal food and nutrition assistance programs—the National School Lunch Program, the Supplemental Nutrition Assistance Program (SNAP—previously called Food Stamps), and the Special Supplemental Nutrition Program for Women, Infants, and Children (WIC).[27]
- About 23 percent of food-insecure households obtained emergency food from a food pantry at some time during the year, and 3 percent ate one or more meals at an emergency kitchen.[28]

The extent of hunger and food insecurity is reflected in the number of people seeking food from emergency food providers, such as food pantries and soup kitchens. Food pantries, shelters, soup kitchens, and other emergency food providers serve at least 23 million people a year.[29]

Governmental Food Programs

The politics of food—or the way food is distributed in U.S. society—is complex. Like all resources in a free market society, food is a commodity that is bought and sold. In a pure market sense, those who cannot afford to purchase food are unable to consume it. Left to the caprice of the marketplace, many poor people would face malnutrition or even starvation. This problem is particularly acute in an urban environment, where most people lack gardening skills and have little or no access to land. Providing the poor with food is a redistributive function of the welfare state.

SNAP (Formerly Called Food Stamps): A Description of the Program

The current Supplemental Nutrition Assistance Program (SNAP—formerly called Food Stamps) was originally enacted by the U.S. Congress in 1964. Food stamps increase the nutritional value of a low-income household's home food supply by 20 to 40 percent and households that participate spend more and acquire more food than nonparticipating low-income households.[30]

The federal government funds 100 percent of SNAP benefits, with federal and state governments sharing 50 percent of administrative costs. Although administered by the USDA, state and local welfare agencies qualify applicants and provide them with Electronic Benefit Transfer (EBT) cards, which are the sole method of benefit delivery. Recipients are given an allotment based on family size and income, with eligibility requirements and benefits determined at the federal level (see Table 17.1), which can then be used at participating SNAP retail stores. SNAP eligibility is based on a means test (see Figure 17.1). For example, the gross

TABLE 17.1 U.S. Maximum Monthly SNAP Allotments, October 2011 to September 2012

Household Size	Maximum Allotment Level (48 states and DC)
1	$200
2	$367
3	$526
4	$668
5	$793
6	$952
7	$1,052
8	$1,202
Each additional person	+$150

Source: U.S. Department of Agriculture, Food and Nutrition Service, Supplemental Nutrition Assistance Program: How Much Could I Receive?, Last Updated April 11, 2012. Retrieved August 2012 from http://www.fns.usda.gov/snap/applicant_recipients/BEN.HTM.

Assets and Income

Calculating eligibility: Households may have no more than $2,000 in countable resources, such as a bank account ($3,000 if at least one person in the household is age 60 or older, or is disabled). Certain resources are not counted.

The gross monthly income of most households must be 130 percent or less of the federal poverty guidelines. For example, gross income includes all cash payments to the household, with a few exceptions. The gross income standard requirement is waived if an elderly or disabled person is part of the household.

The net monthly income must be 100 percent or less of federal poverty guidelines. Net income is figured by adding all of a household's gross income, and then taking a number of approved deductions for child care, some shelter costs and other expenses. Households with an elderly or disabled member are subject to the net income test, but can include other deductions such as medical costs. If the elderly or disabled are in a separate household, they are subject to the gross monthly income at 165 percent of the poverty level.

Countable assets include bank accounts, certificates of deposits, investments, and valuable artwork, antiques, and other valuables.

Countable assets do not include:

- Homesteaded property that the claimant intends to return to if they are in a nursing home, or property occupied by a spouse, siblings, minor child, or disabled child of any age.

- Personal effects and household goods up to $2,000.

- As of October 2008, all education and retirement savings accounts are not included as countable assets.

- One automobile of unlimited value if used for employment (long distance travel, not daily commute), medical purposes, or as the family home. The SNAP program currently exempts any vehicle whose equity value is less than $1,500. For other vehicles, SNAP rules count either the fair market value over $4,650 or the equity value, whichever is greater. Some states use their TANF rules to determine vehicle eligibility, so these federal rules can vary from state to state.

Countable income does not include:

- Allowed deductions such as a 20 percent deduction from earned income; a standard deduction of $141 for households with one to three members (higher for some larger households), and a dependent care deduction when needed for work, training, or education. As of October 1, 2009, there is no longer a cap restricting the amount of deductions claimed for each dependent.

- Medical expenses for elderly or disabled members that are more than $35 for the month if they are not paid by insurance or someone else.

- Legally owed child support payments.

- Shelter costs for homeless households of $143 (some states only).

- Excess shelter costs that are more than half of the household's income after the other deductions. Allowable costs include the cost of fuel to heat and cook with, electricity, water, telephone, rent or mortgage payments, household insurance, and taxes on the home. (Some states allow a set amount for utility costs instead of actual costs.) The amount of the shelter deduction cannot be more than $459 unless one person in the household is elderly or disabled.

Legal Immigrants and Rules of Work

A person must be a U.S. citizen, a member of a small group of certain non-citizens, or an eligible non-citizen to qualify for food stamps.

Citizenship/Alien Status

- The 2002/2008 Farm Bill restores SNAP eligibility to most legal immigrants that have lived in the country for 5 years; or are receiving disability related assistance or benefits, regardless of entry date; or are children regardless of entry date.

- Certain non-citizens such as those admitted for humanitarian reasons and those admitted for permanent residence are also eligible for the program. Eligible household members can receive SNAP benefits even if there are other members of the household that are not eligible.

FIGURE 17.1 SNAP Eligibility and Benefit Guidelines, 2010

- Non-citizens that are in the U.S. temporarily, such as students, are not eligible.

- A number of states have their own programs to provide benefits to immigrants who do not meet the regular SNAP eligibility requirements.

Work

With some exceptions, able-bodied, non-disabled adults must register for work, accept suitable employment, and take part in an employment and training program to which they are referred by the SNAP office. Failure to comply with these requirements can result in disqualification from the program. In addition, able-bodied adults between 18 and 49 who do not have any dependent children can receive SNAP benefits only for 3 months in a 36 month period unless they work or participate in a workfare or employment and training program other than job search or are participating in a drug or alcohol rehabilitation program. Between April 1, 2009 and September 30,

2010, the ARRA Act suspended this time limitation for non-disabled persons without dependents.

Benefits

An individual household's SNAP benefit amount is adjusted according to the Thrifty Food Plan based on household location, and is equal to the maximum allotment for that household's size, less 30 percent of the household's net income. Households with no countable income receive the maximum allotment. The 2008 Farm Bill increased minimum monthly benefits for one and two person households to 8% of the maximum benefit for a one person household. The average monthly benefit was $287 per household in FY2010.

Source: E. Eslami, K. Filion & M. Strayer, *Characteristics of Supplemental Nutrition Assistance Program Households: Fiscal Year 2010,* Nutrition Assistance Program Report no. SNAP-11-CHAR (September 2011), U.S. Department of Agriculture, Food and Nutrition Service, Office of Research and Analysis. Retrieved August 2012 from http://www.fns.usda.gov/ora/menu/Published/snap/FILES/Participation/2010Characteristics.pdf.

FIGURE 17.1 (Continued)

monthly income of most households who apply must be 130 percent or less of the federal poverty guidelines.[31] Recipients originally had to pay a set price (depending on family size and income) for their stamps. For example, some families or individuals could purchase $75 worth of food stamps for $35; the difference between the cost and the face value of the stamps was called a "bonus." This system proved unwieldy because many poor people could not afford to purchase stamps. When purchase requirements were dropped in 1977, the participation rate rose by 30 percent.[32]

SNAP: Who Is in the Program, and What Does It Cost?

In 2011, almost 45 million people participated in the SNAP program at a cost of $75 billion.[33] (See Table 17.2.) This represented a significant increase from 2000 when only 17 million people received SNAP benefits. This increase is partly fueled by high jobless rates, states improving access to low-income populations (including legal immigrants), and better outreach.[34] Nevertheless, only about half of all eligible people receive SNAP benefits.[35] Contrary to the myths surrounding SNAP, the program

is targeted toward those most in need. Data from 2009–2010 illustrate that:

- The average SNAP household in 2011 received a monthly SNAP benefit of $284 and had a gross monthly income of $734. In 2009, less than 10 percent of SNAP households received public assistance, and more than 29 percent had earnings. About 24 percent of SNAP households received Supplemental Security Income (SSI), and 22 percent received Social Security. Only 14 percent of households were above the poverty line and nearly 18 percent had no cash income. On average, SNAP households had $101 in countable resources and a majority (78 percent) had no countable resources.[36]

- In 2010, the average SNAP household size was 2.2 people, and recipients were largely children, elderly or disabled: Most SNAP households (76 percent) contained a child under age 18, an elderly person (age 60 and over), or a disabled nonelderly person.[37] In 2009, working-age women represented 28 percent of the caseload; working-age men only 16 percent.[38]

The National School Lunch Program is a federally assisted meal program that provides lunches to school-age children.

Source: Fotokostic/Shutterstock

farm prices and input/output costs.[55] In 1942, Congress established the price support levels at 90 percent of parity, and from 1942 to 1953, average prices paid to farmers were at 90 to 100 percent of parity, thereby raising market prices, ensuring a secure income for farmers, reducing the need for excessive debt, and encouraging stabilization in the price of grain. By the end of World War II, powerful corporations, academics, and free traders had begun to wage war on the farm parity program. Soil conservation, supply management, and parity were characterized as socialist ideas that interfered with a free market economy. Grain companies called for lower prices to help foreign sales, arguing that expanded exports and food aid programs would compensate farmers for lower commodity prices.

The small farmer eventually lost to this powerful coalition, and farm parity was terminated in 1953. As a result, the purchasing power of farm income decreased even as exports rose. In 1952, net farm income was greater than total farm debt; by 1983 net farm income was less than farm interest payments.[56]

Family farming embodies many of America's most cherished values—hard work, independence, strong family life, and close-knit communities. For many rural families, farming is a way of life. Working the land—often a legacy handed down from parents or grandparents—creates a commitment to place and family heritage.[57] This psychological connection

to farming means that many farmers see themselves as farmer–caretakers. Hence, financial failure not only leaves farmers with a sense of personal failure, but also with shame for having failed their heritage. Reverend Paul Tidemann, a Lutheran minister who studied the 1980s farm crisis reported that "The loss of a farm . . . is not the same as a loss of a job. It signals the loss of a personal and family connection to the land. It prompts a sense of betrayal, in many cases, of generations of farmers, past, present, and future."[58]

Governmental Farm Policies

In 2002, former president George W. Bush signed the Farm Security and Rural Investment Act, which governed federal farm programs until 2008. The bill altered the farm payment program and introduced counter-cyclical farm income support; expanded conservation land retirement programs; emphasized on-farm environmental practices; relaxed rules to make more borrowers eligible for federal farm credit assistance; restored food stamp eligibility to legal immigrants; added various commodities to those requiring country-of-origin labeling; and introduced provisions on animal welfare. One of the more contentious issues in the bill was mandatory country-of-origin labeling for meat and other foods, something which was not implemented.[59] The 2008 Farm Bill (a continuation from 2002) has ensured that counter-cyclical farm income support and other farm subsidy and conservation plans continued.[60]

A new farming bill was introduced in 2012 to replace the 2008 bill that had expired. If passed, the bill promises to:

- Eliminate direct payments. Farmers would no longer be paid for crops they are not growing.
- Increase risk management coverage by strengthening and expanding access to crop insurance.
- Consolidate and streamline existing programs.
- Increase accountability in SNAP by curtailing the abuse and misuse of benefits.
- Invest in research to help commercialize new agricultural innovations.
- Spur advancements in bio-energy production.

Spotlight 17.2

THE NATIONAL FARMER'S UNION

The National Farmer's Union is a general farm organization that represents farmers and ranchers in the United States. The goal of this organization is to sustain and strengthen family farm and ranch agriculture. To learn more about this organization, go to its website at www.nfu.org.

American Farm Bureau

The American Farm Bureau is an independent non-governmental, non-partisan, and non-sectarian organization representing agricultural producers at all levels. To learn more about this organization, go to its website at http://www.fb.org/

The United Farm Workers Association

The United Farm Workers Association (UFW) represents the interests of farm workers throughout the United States. To learn more about this organization, go to its website at **www.ufw.org**.

- Help family farmers sell locally by increasing support for farmers' markets and the creation of food hubs to connect farmers to community-based consumers.
- Extend rural development initiatives to help communities upgrade the infrastructure and stimulate small business growth.[61]

Biofuels, Fracking, and Farming

Biofuel production (ethanol) has been a boon to the American farmer. Touted as a greener alternative to gasoline, ethanol can be made from corn, barley, wheat, sugar cane, or beet. Proponents argue that ethanol is a clean-burning renewable energy source that can help the U.S. reduce its energy reliance on foreign oil. By 2011, about 25 percent of the nation's grain crops and corn went into ethanol production for cars.[62]

Critics argue that biofuel crops, such as corn, are grown with the help of fossil fuels in the form of fertilizers, pesticides and the gasoline needed for farm equipment. One estimate is that corn needs 30 percent more energy than the finished fuel it produces. Another problem is the land required to produce it. Still others estimate that the grain needed to make enough ethanol to fill the gas tank of a 4×4 is sufficient to feed a person for a year. Critics argue that this biofuel production is helping to usher in worldwide food shortages. Other critics have questioned the role fertilizer is playing in climate change, claiming that using fertilizer on biofuel crops will be emitting enough nitrous oxide (more than 296 times more powerful heat trapping gas than CO_2) to eliminate all the carbon savings biofuels produce.[63]

While biofuels are more carbon dioxide neutral than fossil fuels, the UN warns that land use, food supply and water supply issues can be problematic in biofuel production. The dangers of biofuels involves the loss of biodiversity as forests are cleared to grow crops for ethanol, the exacerbation of water shortages, the distortion of food prices, and the competition with local food production. By 2012, increased biofuel production from corn coupled with reduced crop yields due to drought, had dramatically raised the price of corn in many developing countries to record levels, thereby leading to increased political instability.

The thirst for energy has also led to various kinds of high impact carbon extractions, such as hydraulic fracturing or "*fracking*." Fracking is the process of drilling deep wells and injecting water, sand, and proprietary chemicals into them at a high pressure in order to fracture shale rocks to release the natural gas inside. Horizontal fracking uses a mixture of almost 600 chemicals (many of them proprietary and carcinogenic) and 1 to 8 million gallons of water for each frack job. After fracking, the water becomes contaminated and must be either cleaned or disposed of.

Fracking industry officials and supporters claim that the process is safe, environmentally responsible, and the key to energy self-sufficiency. They point to Canada, which has been using fracking techniques for 35 years with little record of pollution or major environmental impacts. Supporters point to North Dakota, which has a booming economy, a budget surplus, and the lowest unemployment rate of any U.S. state. They also point to how fracking has driven down natural gas prices so low that power plants are using natural gas instead of dirty coal.[64]

Critics point to the potential environmental impacts, including contamination of ground water, risks to air quality, the migration of gases and chemicals to the surface, contamination from spills, and the deleterious health effects associated with fracking. For instance, during fracking, methane gas and toxic chemicals leach out from the system and contaminate nearby groundwater. Contaminated well water is then used for drinking water for farms and nearby cities and towns. Reports have surfaced of cases of respiratory and neurological damage due to contaminated water. The waste fluid is left in open air pits to evaporate, releasing harmful compounds into the atmosphere, creating acid rain and ground level ozone. For these and other reasons hydraulic fracturing has come under scrutiny, with some countries suspending or banning it.[65] Fracking has an important impact on farming since it often occurs on prime farmland.

The Face of U.S. Farming

The following highlights important trends in U.S. agriculture:

- *The changing landscape of U.S. farming.* Of all the U.S. occupations, farming is facing the greatest decline, albeit that is dependent on the size of the farming operation. As of 2010, there were about 2.2 million farms in the United States, which is a slight increase from the 2 million farms in 2006. However, it is a significant decrease from the nearly 4 million farms in 1960.[66] Between 1998 and 2010, the number of small farms decreased by about 49,000 while the number of larger farms (those earning more than $250,000 annually) increased by roughly the same amount.[67]

Of the 2.2 million U.S. farms in 2007, only one million showed a positive net cash income from the farm operation. Newer small farms tend to have more diversified production, fewer acres, lower sales, and younger operators who also work off-farm.[68] In short, small family farms often rely on outside income from other occupations in order to supplement their household income. Moreover, approximately 45 percent of small family farms are categorized as residential/lifestyle (hobby farms) and 18 percent as retirement farms. Some of the reasons behind the decline in farming become clear given that small family farms made up 88 percent of all U.S. farms in 2007. Conversely, large farms have the competitive edge and are more economically viable than the large number of small farms. This explains why farming is declining while agricultural output and value (particularly exports) are increasing.[69]

- *Farm incomes.* In 2010, the average family farm received only 13 percent ($10,031) of its household income ($77,169) from farm sources, with the remaining 87 percent coming from off-farm employment or income. About 73 percent of off-farm income for the average farm operator household in 2010 came from other sources, such as wages and nonfarm businesses. Hence, farming has played an increasingly smaller role in determining the well-being of small farm households. Those farmers who remain on their land often face the prospect of working off the farm just to stay on the land.[70]
- *The graying of U.S. farms.* The average age of the U.S. farmer is 58 (in 2007, 30 percent of principal farm operators were 65 years or older), and more than half of all current farmers are likely to retire within the next decade. Less than 5 percent of farmers are under the age of 35. This raises the question of whether there is a younger generation ready to replace older farmers once they retire. There appears to be conflicting perspectives on whether the ageing of farmers is a problem. However, older farmers who own large commercial farms often have younger generations of children to inherit the farm once they retire. Nevertheless, the reality is that farmers aged 35 years or younger declined from 16 percent in 1982 to 5 percent in 2007.[71]
- *Consolidation and control.* In 2009, 60 percent of family farms had gross sales of less than $10,000 and accounted for only 2 percent of agricultural production. Conversely, the 10 percent

of family farms that grossed at least $250,000 a year accounted for 80 percent of the value of production. Nearly half of all U.S. land is farmland (more than 1 billion acres) and by 1990, 4 percent of landowners held 47 percent of it. In California, the nation's largest agricultural producer, 3 percent of California farms controlled 60 percent of the market. Nationwide the figures were similar—7 percent of U.S. farms received 60 percent of the net cash farm income in 1992.[72]

- *Women and farming.* By 2007, nearly 30 percent more women were principal farm operators than in 2002. Ownership and control in U.S. agriculture contains distinct gender bias. Despite the fact that the number of female farmers more than doubled between 1982 and 2007, women only comprised 14 percent of U.S. farms in 2007. Women tend to own smaller farms; the average size of properties held by men is one-third larger than farms held by women.[73] As such, 78 percent of female farmers operated farms that earned less than $10,000 a year.[74]
- *Rural health and food quality.* Many rural residents are exposed to excessive odors from factory farms and often suffer from nausea, vomiting, coughing, and headaches. In extreme cases, people living near factory farms have developed neurological diseases and women have suffered from miscarriages as a result of water and air contamination. Employees working inside factory farms have died from exposure to manure lagoons. The factory farms' extreme confinement and increased levels of production of animals intensify the opportunity for contamination of meat and poultry with bacteria, such as Escherichia coli and Salmonella. Crowded livestock conditions lead to a reliance on antibiotics to maintain animal health, and more than 70 percent of all antibiotics consumed in the United States are fed to healthy farm animals. This indiscriminate use of drugs has contributed directly to the evolution of antibiotic-resistant bacteria that the American Medical Association considers an impending public health crisis.[75]

In April 2012, the U.S. Food and Drug Administration (FDA) issued non-binding industry guidelines containing two primary recommendations. First, farmers and ranchers should restrict the use of antibiotics to cases where drug intervention is necessary for farm animal health. The FDA considers antibiotics used for growth promotion or to increase efficiency in feed requirements as inappropriate uses of the drug. Second, antibiotics should be administered under the continual supervision of veterinarians.[76]

- *Farm subsidies.* From 1995 to 2009 the largest and wealthiest top 10 percent of farm program recipients received 74 percent of all farm subsidies with an average total payment over 15 years of $445,127 per recipient. In turn, the bottom 80 percent of farmers received an average total payment of just $8,682 per recipient. Sixty-two percent of U.S. farmers did not receive any subsidy payments.[77]
- *Efficiency.* Because they often farm small acreages using greater crop diversity and careful management of natural resources, family farmers are more efficient than large, industrialized food producers. Moreover, per unit costs for agricultural production are no better in larger commercial operations than in family farms. Factory farms add many real costs, such as increased use of fossil fuels, environmental damage, health threats, and threats to the safety of the food supply. Because they often farm small acreages using greater crop diversity and careful management of natural resources, family farmers are more efficient than large, industrialized food producers. Moreover, the per unit cost for agricultural production is no better in larger commercial operations than in family farms. Factory farms add many real costs, such as increased use of fossil fuels, environmental damage, health threats, and threats to the safety of the food supply.[78]

Farmworkers

The efforts of millions of farmworkers are essential to the multibillion-dollar U.S. fruit and vegetable industry. Because agricultural production depends on the influx of seasonal labor, each year anywhere between 800,000 to just over 1 million farmworkers leave their homes to follow the crops.[79] The wages and conditions they labor under are in many cases scandalous.

In 2011, the U.S. Crop industry was worth $204 billion.[80] Most crop industry produce is cultivated by hand through the labor of America's farmworkers. While some Americans assume that farmworker poverty results in lower food prices, Eric Schlosser notes that "Maintaining the current level of poverty among migrant farmworkers saves the average American household (just) $50 a year."[81]

Thousands of migrant farmworkers risk death and incarceration each year by crossing the U.S.–Mexico border. In the blistering Arizona heat, 14 immigrants died in 2001 after smugglers abandoned them. In 2003, 17 immigrants, including a 5-year-old boy, died of dehydration in the back of an abandoned truck in Texas. Despite the danger, illegal immigration rates have soared. And as of 2009, roughly half of all crop farmworkers were illegal immigrants.[82]

As of 2010, just over one million year-round and seasonal migrant workers worked in the U.S. a number that is declining each year.[83] About two-thirds are immigrants, of whom approximately 68 percent are from Mexico. Roughly 45 percent of all farmworkers are hired for the full year, with the remainder being seasonal and part-year workers.[84] The following represents an overview of U.S. farmworkers based on data gathered between 2005 and 2010.

- *Demographics*. Sixty-one percent of all farmworkers (crop and livestock, year-round and seasonal) were U.S. citizens in 2010. The average age of farmworkers was 35, and 32 percent were over the age of 44. Around 84 percent of farmworkers were men and 54 percent were married.[85]

- *Education and language*. Eighty-one percent of farmworkers spoke Spanish, and 24 percent reported they could speak English well. In turn, 70 percent of farmworkers said they couldn't speak English at all or could speak English only a little. Twenty-six percent of farmworkers had not completed grade 12.[86]

- *Labor and conditions*. Due to the seasonal nature of their work and the illegal or temporary status of migrants, farmworkers (even year-round workers) are particularly vulnerable to exploitation through poor working conditions.[87] In 2006, only 39 percent of farmworkers were covered by Unemployment Insurance. They were also prone to under-employment, and on average, they only spent 66 percent of the year working on the farm. Employer provided health insurance was also rare; only 8 percent of farmworkers claimed that they were insured, a number that declined to 5 percent for seasonal workers.[88]

- *Wages and poverty*. Growers employed 79 percent of farmworkers while labor contractors employed the remainder. Farmworkers had an average of 12 years of U.S. farm experience; 41 percent had worked more than 10 years. On average, they were employed with their current farm employer for four and a half years and 60 percent had only seasonal work. The average farmworker worked about 42 hours a week and 79 percent were paid by the hour. They earned between $10,000 and $12,499 and had a total family income between $15,000 and $17,500—30 percent had family incomes below the poverty line.[89]

According to the USDA, non-supervisory farm laborers received an hourly wage of $10.22 in 2010; however, this includes year-round as well as seasonal workers and is comparable to the hourly wage of maids and housekeepers ($10.17).[90] These low wages are particularly striking since the largest 1.5 percent of U.S. farms employ more than half of the farm labor. Archer Daniels Midland, the world leader in the production of soy meal, corn, wheat, and cocoa, reaped $4 billion in operating income in 2011. Dole, the world's largest producer of fresh fruit, vegetables, and cut flowers made $38 million in 2011.

- *Use of social services*. Despite the fact that many crop farmworkers qualify for Medicaid and SNAP, the migratory nature of seasonal work (travelling across state lines) makes it difficult for farmworkers to be approved since states vary in their eligibility criteria.[91] In 2006, only 15 percent of migrant and seasonal farmworkers used Medicaid, 11 percent used WIC, and 8 percent used SNAP.[92] In 2005, only 2 percent of farmworkers reported that they were receiving Social Security benefits.[93]

- *Housing*. Although rural housing programs to improve farmworker housing conditions are becoming more prevalent, farmworkers still often live in substandard accommodations. In 2008, a North Carolina study found that 89 percent of migrant labor camps had more than one Migrant Housing Act violation for that state, and that 78 percent of participants felt that their habitation was overcrowded. A 2007 California study in the Coachella Valley found that 30 percent of migrant farmworkers lived in unsuitable habitats (i.e., sleeping rough, in vehicles, or in garages).[94]

Farmworkers are also particularly susceptible to the effects of occupational workplace health and safety violations. These workers frequently come into contact with pesticides containing dangerous chemicals that can harm both the worker and their family. A 2006 study on California farmworkers found that many were experiencing acute symptoms of pesticide poisoning, including headaches, nausea, eye irritation, and muscle weakness. Long-term exposure to pesticides can result in chronic health conditions including cancer, memory disorders, and depression. Many employers fail to ensure that farmworkers receive adequate occupational health and safety education, and/or they fail to provide proper safety equipment and procedures. In another Californian study, 92 percent of 213 farmworkers were found to have pesticide contaminants in their urine.[95]

Farmworkers are also often exposed to long hours in the sun without adequate hydration and sun protection, exacerbating the risks of heat stress, heat stroke and melanoma. A 2005 survey found that 20 percent of farmworkers had no access to drinking water while working. Farm tools and machinery also present risks of injury and death, with 2,165 farmworkers dying as a result of tractor accidents between 1992 and 2001.[96]

The number of farmworkers that need housing often exceeds the available housing units. In addition, migrant farmworkers face barriers in obtaining private housing. For example, rural communities may not have enough rental units available, or they may be unwilling to rent to migrant farmworkers because they cannot provide deposits, qualify for credit checks, or make long-term rental commitments.[97]

Education is also problematic for migrant farmworkers. Constant mobility makes it hard for the children of farmworkers to complete their education. Children who move often are two and a half times more likely to repeat a grade than children who are stationery. Changing schools is emotionally difficult, and youngsters are more likely to drop out of school if they change schools four or more times. Educators who work with migrant children say that 55 percent of these children graduate nationwide. Migrant children also face intense economic pressure to drop out of school.[98]

The poverty experienced by migrant families requires that all able family members work. In fact, agriculture is the only industry that allows workers under age 16: The Fair Labor Standards Act sets age 12 as the legal limit for farm work, with exemptions available for children as young as 10 or 11. It has been estimated that almost 432,000 children aged 12 to 17 years old work on farms, although many children work "off the books" if they are under age, or use their parent's Social Security number.[99]

Since children work and play in areas where chemicals are sprayed and machinery is present, they are exposed to the same occupational hazards as adults. Because of their lower weight and higher metabolism, children are more susceptible to the effects of toxic chemicals than adults. One study found that 48 percent of children had worked in fields still wet with pesticides; 36 percent had been sprayed either directly or indirectly (by drift); and farm operators had sprayed 34 percent of the children's homes in the process of spraying nearby fields.[100] Moreover, injuries involving tools and machinery and exploitative working conditions are also common for child farmworkers. A 2002 Human Rights Watch Study found that children as young as 12 often worked 14 hours a day during peak harvest season times. Between 1992 and 2000, 42 percent of all work fatalities for youth were attributed to the agricultural industry, and between 1995 and 2002, 907 children died on farms.[101]

As a result of the exposure to pesticides, farmworkers frequently suffer stomach ailments, headaches, rashes, burns, and other toxic chemical-related problems. Many die from environmentally caused cancer, and too often workers' babies are born with severe birth defects. Many families must sleep, bathe, and cook near the fields where they work and have no option but to use water that may be contaminated with toxic chemicals.[102] The following illustrates some of the health and safety problems faced by America's farmworkers.

- One study found that about 34 percent of migrant children were infected with intestinal parasites and/or suffered severe asthma, chronic diarrhea, vitamin A deficiency, chemical poisoning, or continuous bouts of otitis media leading to hearing loss. Other commonly reported health problems included lower height or weight, respiratory disease, skin infections, and undiagnosed congenital and developmental problems.
- Water-related parasitic infections afflict migrant farmworker adults and children on average 59 times more often than the general population.
- Death rates from influenza and pneumonia are as much as 20 percent and 200 percent higher, respectively, for farmworkers than the national average.
- In one CDC study, 44 percent of farmworkers had positive tuberculosis (TB) tests.
- It is estimated that as few as 42 percent of female farmworkers receive prenatal care

during the first trimester of pregnancy, even though many migrant pregnancies are classified as high risk with multiple indicators. The infant mortality rate among migrant farmworkers is 125 percent higher than in the general population.[103]

In the 1960s, the conditions faced by farmworkers led to the creation of the United Farm Workers union (UFW) in California, a movement led by the charismatic Cèsar Chávez. At its peak in the 1970s, the UFW had about 120,000 workers under contract, and between 1966 and 1980 it obtained two 40 percent wage increases in the grape industry, among other gains. But during the 1980s, contracts began to expire and successive Republican administrations stacked the California Agricultural Labor Relations Board with pro-industry members, effectively gutting the law that had created the board. In the midst of a hostile political climate and internal differences, the UFW went into a membership slump. By 2011, the UFW had only about 27,000 members under contract.[104]

Farm labor contractors hire 20 percent of farmworkers nationwide and 40 percent in California. The 1980s saw the rise of independent labor contractors as key players in the farm industry. Hired by growers, these middlemen round up laborers and deliver them to the fields. Contractors pay less than growers, offer few benefits, and provide little job security. They also have a reputation for mistreating farmworkers and cheating them in wages. Contractors shield large growers from labor actions and legal claims, distancing them from the actual hiring of workers.[105] If a judgment comes down against a labor contractor, the contractor often vanishes or puts the businesses into bankruptcy, only to emerge in a new place or under a new name. The labor subcontracting system is an important obstacle to improving the welfare of farmworkers. One issue being pressed by farmworker activists is the creation of legislation that would make growers legally responsible for their workers, regardless of whether they use contractors.

Issues in American Farming

There are a number of important issues affecting U.S. farming, including the corporatization of agriculture, genetic engineering, global trade, food safety, local selling, organic farming, sustainable agriculture, and climate change.

The Corporatization of American Farming

U.S. family farms are rapidly being replaced by corporate farms. Corporate agriculture is a system whereby the farm owner, the farm manager, and the farmworker are different people. This system represents a dramatic shift from family farms, where the individual farmers make the decisions. Industrial agriculture encourages large-scale, highly specialized farms where uniformity is emphasized over quality. Large-scale agriculture contains significant environmental risks. For example, hogs produce three times the waste of humans, and the 500,000 pigs housed in Smithfield Foods Utah subsidiary generate more fecal matter each year than the 1.5 million inhabitants of Manhattan. Jeff Tietz estimates that Smithfield's total waste discharge of 26 million tons a year would fill four Yankee Stadiums.[106]

Corporatization leads to closed markets where prices are fixed not by open, competitive bidding but by negotiated contracts. Small volume producers are discriminated against in price or other terms of trade. Moreover, in traditional food markets, 91 cents of every dollar spent on food goes to suppliers, processors, middlemen, and marketers, most of whom are not based in the community. As such, less than 10 cents of each dollar goes directly to the farmer.[107]

An integral part of corporate farming is vertical integration, whereby agricultural corporations control all aspects of production, including raising, owning, slaughtering, and marketing livestock or agricultural products. One example is ConAgra, the largest distributor of agricultural chemicals in North America and one of the largest fertilizer producers in the world. ConAgra's gross revenues were just over $13 billion in 2012. In 2007, the company owned more than 100 grain elevators, 2,000 railroad cars, and 1,100 barges. It was the largest of the three corporations that mill 80 percent of North America's wheat. ConAgra was also the largest turkey producer and the fourth largest broiler producer, producing its own poultry feed as well as other livestock feed. The company hired growers to raise its birds and then processed them in their facilities. This poultry was then purchased as fryers, under the name of Butterball, or in further processed foods such as TV dinners and pot pies under the label of Banquet, Marie Callender's, or Healthy Choice. ConAgra also owns 62 well-known brand names such as Act II Popcorn, Award Cuisine, Banquet, Blue Bonnet, Chef Boyardee, Chun King, David Sunflower Seeds, Egg Beaters, Fernando's,

Facts About Corporate Agriculture

- By 2007, the largest 12 percent of farms generated 84 percent of all U.S. farm output.

- In 2005, the top 10 commercial seed companies controlled more than 50 percent of the world's commercial seed sales. This was an increase of 17 percent in only two years.

- The top 10 biotech companies control 75 percent of world biotech crop sales. This is also an increase of 50 percent in two years.

- Among pesticides manufacturers, the top six companies account for 70 percent of the global market.

- The top ten pesticide manufacturers control 84 percent of the pesticide market.

- Among agrochemical companies, the top ten control 80 percent of global sales.

- In the vegetable seed market, one corporation dominates: Monsanto. It controls 31 percent of bean seed sales, 38 percent of cucumber seed sales, 34 percent of hot pepper sales, 29 percent of sweet pepper sales, 23 percent of tomato seed sales, and 25 percent of onion seeds.

- As of 2004, Monsanto accounted for 88 percent of the total land acreage producing genetically modified (GM) seeds: 91 percent of GM soybean lands; 97 percent of GM maize lands; 63.5 percent of GM cotton lands; and 59 percent of canola.

- Among grocery retailers, one company, Wal-Mart, is four times the size of its nearest competitor in terms of food sales, and bigger than the combined sales of the next four leading retailers.

Sources: The International Forum on Globalization, "The Rise and Predictable Fall of Globalized Industrial Agriculture", 2007. Retrieved July 2008 from http://www.ifg.org/pdf/ag%20report.pdf; R.A. Hoppe & D.E. Banker, "Structure and Finances of U.S. Farms: Family Farm Report, 2010 Edition", Economic Information Bulletin, no. 66 (July 2010), U.S. Department of Agriculture, Economic Research Services. Retrieved from http://www.ers.usda.gov/media/184479/eib66_1_.pdf

FIGURE 17.3 Facts About Corporate Agriculture

Fleischman's, Gulden's, Healthy Choice, Hebrew National, Hunt's, Jiffy Popcorn, Kid Cuisine, La Choy, Libby's, Manwich, Marie Callender's, Move Over Butter, Orville Redenbacher's, PAM, Parkay, Patio, Peter Pan, Ranch Style, Reddi-Whip, Rosarita, Slim Jim, Swiss Miss, Van Camp's, Vogel Popcorn, Wesson, and Wolf Brand Chili.[108] The extent of corporate agriculture is illustrated in Figure 17.3. Many smaller farmers who cannot participate in "vertical integration" are forced out of business because they have no place to sell their products.

Genetic Engineering

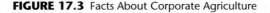

Genetic engineering, which sparked a global controversy since its introduction in 1995, is the manipulation of specific genes that are moved from one species to another to create a trait that did not previously exist. For example, crops such as corn have been engineered to contain pesticides in every cell of the plant. As a result, these crops are not registered as food and are actually considered pesticides.[109] While the Food and Drug Administration claims genetically modified (GM) products are safe, there has been no thorough analysis of their long-term effects. Moreover, GM products are not labeled as such in the United States.

In contrast, the European Union recognizes the consumers' right to information and since 1997 has made labeling of GM food mandatory for products that consist of GMO or contain GMO, and products derived from GMO if there is still GM DNA or protein present.[110] As of 2012, no GM crops were grown commercially in New Zealand. Any GM food imported into New Zealand would require approval under the Hazardous Substances and New Organisms Act (HSNO Act). Any GM food sold in New Zealand and Australia must be labeled 'genetically modified' if it contains DNA or protein from a GM source or they have altered characteristics.[111] However, Australia's labeling laws are porous, and some GM products are not required to be labeled. Interestingly, Most European consumers have shied away from buying GM-labeled products.[112]

Critics argue that GM crops are increasingly threatening the biodiversity in the seed supply and making crops more vulnerable to disease outbreaks and pest infestations. Two multinational companies, Monsanto and DuPont, dominate the U.S. seed industry.[113]

Farmers buy GM seeds based on promise of lower costs and higher yields, but they often find additional costs in veterinary bills, medications, unstable markets, and extra pesticides. Specifically, farmers that buy GM seeds enter into a contract that dictates how and when the crop can be grown. This contract also forbids the farmer to save any seeds, which is contrary to traditional farming practices. Many farmers have been sued for allegedly saving seeds, while neighboring farmers whose crops have been contaminated by GM pollen drift have been sued by Monsanto for unknowingly possessing GM seeds.[114]

Global Trade

The global trade in food has emerged as a serious threat challenging family farmers in the United States and around the world. Agricultural free trade agreements, like the North American Free Trade Agreement (NAFTA)—which linked the economies of the United States, Mexico, and Canada—promote agricultural trade with little regard to its impact on local communities and family farmers. As a result, several countries, including the United States, have been flooded with cheap food imports that have caused small farmers to lose their local markets, and family farmers worldwide have been forced off their land. In turn, this "food dumping" has weakened local food production.[115]

Since the passage of NAFTA in 1994, family farmers in all three countries have felt the negative impacts of a free trade agreement designed to benefit agribusiness. In the United States, 100,000 family farmers were forced out of farming between 1996 and 2001. During that same period, Canada lost 11 percent of its family farms.[116] NAFTA and other trade liberalization policies have dramatically increased rural poverty and hunger in Mexico. Between 1992 and 2002, the number of rural Mexicans living in extreme poverty grew from 36 to 52 percent. Almost two million subsistence farmers were pushed off their land and migrated to export factories, maquiladoras, or to fields and cities in the United States. NAFTA critics estimate that as many as 15 million more Mexican farmers—one in six—could be displaced.[117] Despite the issues associated with global free trade, the export industry is big business. In 2009, the Obama administration announced a series of aggressive export strategies (called the National Export Initiative) to strengthen domestic agricultural profits and employment. The goal was to double U.S. exports by 2014. Farm exports reached a new record high of $137.4 billion in 2011.[118]

Food Safety

Food safety has become a troubling concern for many Americans. In January 2009, the Peanut Corporation of America issued one of the largest food recalls in history for peanut products containing salmonella. The tainted peanuts caused eight deaths and more than 500 illnesses in 43 states. The recall included 2,100 products from more than 200 companies. In June 2009, Nestlé recalled 300,000 cases of refrigerated cookie-dough because of E. coli contamination. Kraft Foods recalled almost 53,000 pounds of Oscar Mayer/Louis Rich Chicken Breast Strips after listeria bacteria was detected. The next month, an additional 2.8 million pounds of chicken were recalled. The largest recall of beef in U.S. history occurred in February 2008 when Hallmark recalled 143 million pounds of beef. The recall occurred after a video showed the slaughterhouse mistreating cows and allowing unhealthy cattle to be slaughtered without an inspection. In 2011, Cargill recalled 36 million pounds of ground turkey because of possible contamination by a drug-resistant strain of salmonella. The company then recalled another 185,000 pounds of meat due to the same contamination risk. In 2006, 205 people were stricken (five died) by E. Coli after eating contaminated spinach from a central California farm. Two Iowa egg-producers recalled 550 million eggs in 2010 after 1,500 cases were contaminated by salmonella. The FDA believed that the contaminated eggs were linked to unsanitary farm conditions and the small size of the chicken cages.[119] All of the major food contamination episodes arose as a result of large-scale corporate manufacturing or mass production farming.

Mad Cow Disease (Bovine Spongiform Encephalopathy, or BSE), is a neurological disease that affects cattle by attacking the brain and central nervous system. It is believed that cattle become infected with BSE by eating feed that contains remnants of other infected cattle. Humans can become infected with a BSE-like illness, called Creutzfeldt Jakob Disease (CJD) by eating meat from infected cows. There is no known cure for CJD and cooking at high temperatures or treating meat with radiation is not effective in preventing the disease. Because organic livestock producers adhere to strict feed requirements, which exclude animal by-products in the feed, it is believed that BSE is absent in this kind of meat.[120] As a result of Mad Cow disease, some consumers have become wary of purchasing and eating beef.

Local Selling

Because many small farmers cannot compete directly with agribusiness, they are realizing the importance of selling their products locally. Between 2008 and 2011, farmers' markets increased by 54 percent, and in 2011, they numbered over 7,200. Community Supported Agriculture (CSA) programs that encourage local residents to buy produce directly from family farms have been driven by the "Know Your Farmer, Know Your Food" (KYF) program initiated by the Obama administration.[121] A map displays farmers markets across the United States, with specific addresses and information on each market. A search engine enables consumers to search for local markets in their ZIP and area code.[122] Farmers can now sell more easily to schools through the Farm to School Team, which helps navigate through administrative "red tape," thereby assisting more farmers to participate in programs such as the school meal program.[123] For more information, visit the Know Your Farmer, Know your Food website at www.usda.gov/KnowYourFarmer/.

Organic Farming

Started by family farmers, the organic movement is the fastest growing sector of American agriculture. In 2011, organic sales in retail stores increased by 9.5 percent, totaling more than $31 billion. In 2010, organic agriculture had a 4.2 percent share of the U.S. retail food sales market. Overall, the number of certified organic operators increased by 1,109 from 2009 to 2011, which represented more than a 6 percent increase.[124] The trend toward organics and less processed food has created confusion for consumers who are unsure of what the various labels mean (see Figure 17.4). Throughout the 1990s and into the twenty-first century, large agricultural corporations have increased their participation in organic farming, which has raised questions as to whether the values of these mega companies conflict with those of organic farming, a local movement that began primarily to improve people's access to natural, chemical-free produce. In fact, corporations have been criticized for exploiting what was originally a local niche market, as smaller competitors struggle to compete with large corporations that are jumping on the organic bandwagon. Often, large retailers like Walmart who undercut local retailers will source low-integrity factory-farmed organic products.[125]

Sustainable Agriculture

The environmental challenges facing the United States are greater than at any time in the nation's history. Global environmental threats such as climate change; stratospheric ozone depletion; and the loss of biological diversity (through the accelerated extinctions of species), forests, and fish stocks are affecting all countries regardless of their stage of economic development.

The definition of sustainable development proposed by the 1987 United Nations Brundtland Commission stated that **sustainable development** must "meet the needs of the present without compromising the ability of future generations to meet their own needs."[126]

Sustainable development theories also address the crisis of farmland mismanagement in the United States and abroad. Farming and related activities are the foundation of the U.S. food and fiber industry, which provides jobs for 17 percent of the workforce and contributes more than $1 trillion to the GNP. Moreover, the 1 billion acres of land in agricultural production is responsible for feeding, clothing, and housing 312 million people in the United States and millions more abroad. Yet, every minute, the United States loses 2 acres of productive farmland to urban sprawl—shopping malls, housing subdivisions, and the like. Since the first Earth Day in 1970, the United States has lost more than 40 million acres of farmland to development. Net cropland losses between 1992 and 1997 alone covered an area the size of Maryland.[127]

Urbanization is a leading cause of cropland loss. The spread of roads, buildings, and industrial parks consumes precious farmland. Cropland is also lost because of the depletion or diversion of irrigation water. In many water-scarce areas, water is supplied from nonrenewable aquifers. If farmers deplete the water stock, or if it is siphoned off by large cities, agricultural land will either be abandoned or become less productive. Although irrigated land accounts for only 16 percent of all cropland worldwide, it supplies 40 percent of the world's grain.[128]

What the Food Labels Mean

- *Organic:*   Regulated by the USDA, the National Organic Standards assure that food products contain at least 95 percent organic ingredients and that no synthetic growth hormones, antibiotics, pesticides, biotechnology, synthetic ingredients, or irradiation were used in production or processing. Organic labels can be found on produce, dairy, meat, processed foods, condiments, and beverages.

- *Fair trade:*   Fair trade standards are enforced by the Fairtrade Labeling Organization International (FLO). Fair trade products are produced in accordance with several guidelines. For example, workers must receive decent wages; and housing, health, and safety standards must be adhered to. Workers must have the right to join trade unions, and child or forced labor is prohibited. Crops must also be grown, produced, and processed in an environmentally friendly manner. Fair trade standards have been established for coffee, tea, cocoa, honey, bananas, orange juice, and sugar. Some producers have established alternative fair trade-type labels. Most are little more than marketing pitches.

- *Free farmed:*   This certification program was created by the American Humane Association in 2000 to ensure that animals raised for dairy, poultry, and beef products are treated in a humane manner. These guidelines ensure that livestock have access to clean and sufficient food and water as well as a safe, healthy living environment.

- *Feel good buying (not certified):*   Some meat and dairy products are now being marketed as hormone free. In dairy products, this means that the farmer has chosen not to inject their cows with the artificial growth hormone called rBGH. On beef products, this label indicates that the animal was raised without growth hormones or steroids.

- *Raised without antibiotics:*   This meat and dairy label indicates that the animal was raised entirely without the use of low-level and/or therapeutic doses of antibiotics.

- *GE free, non-GMO:*   Food products that use GE Free or Non-GMO labels are regulated by individual companies, distributors, or processors. Often, the companies require certification or affidavits from farmers that the materials were not genetically modified in any way.

- *All natural:*   There is no universal standard or definition for this claim.

- *Free range:*   This label claims that a meat or poultry product (including eggs) comes from an animal that was raised in the open air or was allowed to roam. However, the regulations do not specify how much of each day animals must have access to fresh air. In poultry, the USDA considers five minutes adequate exposure to be considered free range. In beef, the use of the label is completely unregulated or standardized.

Source: Adapted from Farm Aid, Inc., "Issues in Farming," 2004. Retrieved November 2004 from www.farmaid.org/site/PageServer?pagename=info_facts_global. Used by permission.

FIGURE 17.4 What the Food Labels Mean?

Each year, the United States loses almost 3 billion tons of topsoil to wind and water erosion. As many as 1 billion tons wash into nearby waterways, carrying away natural nutrients and the fertilizers and pesticides contained in the soil.[129] This erosion damages water quality, fish and wildlife habitat, and recreational opportunities. Moreover, the use of fertilizers, toxic chemicals, and fuel strains already tight farm budgets.[130]

The impressive success of the agricultural revolution that began in the 1960s has led to a complacent attitude toward cropland loss. Specifically, some people believed that farm yields were rising so quickly that they more than compensated for the loss of arable land. However, by 1984 the growth in crop yields had slowed down. At the same time, the amount of productive U.S. cropland per person fell to less than one-sixth the size of a soccer field.[131] The shrinking supply of cropland combined with the slowing of yield increases comes on the heels of the largest projected increase in food demand in history. In 25 years, farmers will be required to feed 2.2 billion more people than today; yet most governments continue to allow fertile land to be developed or washed away by erosion.[132]

In an ecological context, sustainable development promotes a process whereby natural resources are replenished and future generations continue to have adequate resources to meet their needs.[133] Some groups use sustainable development to designate a radical restructuring of society around environmental development and economic growth. Others simply use sustainable development to signal a change in attitudes and emphasis. These different approaches are sometimes labeled "dark green strategies" versus "light green strategies."[134]

Climate Change

Despite the skepticism of the American right, climate change has become an accepted fact among the vast majority of scientists and much of the general public. For some, environmental consciousness was bolstered by Al Gore's documentary, *An Inconvenient Truth.*

The effects of climate change in the United States and elsewhere is striking. The earth is warming, and its average temperature has risen by 1.4°F over the past century. It is projected to rise another 2 to 11.5°F over the next hundred years. Even small changes in the average temperature can result in large and potentially dangerous shifts in climate and weather. For instance, the first eight months of 2012 were the warmest of any year on record in the contiguous U.S.; 2012 has been the third hottest summer since record-keeping began in 1895. Each of the last 15 months has seen above-average temperatures, something that has never happened before in the 117 years of the U.S. record. This was followed by a severe drought in parts of the Midwest and Texas.[135] By August 2012, Arctic sea ice broke the record low set in 2007, and has dropped below 1.5 million square miles. That represents a 45 percent reduction in the area covered by sea ice compared to the 1980s and 1990s, and may be unprecedented in human history. The extent of sea ice that melted by mid-2012 was equivalent to the size of Canada and Alaska combined.[136]

The destruction wreaked by climate change is not limited to the United States alone. In 2012, a deadly drought was causing suffering for more than 12.5 million people in 13 countries in the Eastern Horn of Africa region.

Climate change is causing rising sea levels, dramatic glacial retreat, arctic shrinkage exceeding even some of the most aggressive computer projections, significant slowing of the ocean circulation that transports warm water to the North Atlantic, and altered patterns of agriculture (prolonged droughts punctuated by extreme flooding). Other predicted effects include extreme weather events (hurricanes, cyclones, floods, intense droughts), an expansion of tropical diseases as subtropical areas heat up, and drastic economic changes including starvation as marginal crop lands become deserts. Overall, the consequences of global warming result from one of three changes: rising sea levels, higher local temperatures, and changes in rainfall patterns.

Lastly, climate change is having a major impact on farming and food production. The greenhouse effect—a naturally occurring phenomenon—is the way the atmosphere traps part of the sun's heat and stops it from going back into space. It makes the earth warm enough for life, and without it, the earth would be about 86°F colder. Although global warming is a common term used to describe these changes, climate change is a better descriptor since some areas may in fact cool. Global warming also describes other effects such as rising sea levels and wilder weather.[137]

Many scientists believe that increased emissions of greenhouse gases have contributed to the rise in global temperatures and sea level. These scientists maintain that we are adding dangerously to the natural greenhouse effect as the gases from industry and agriculture—chiefly carbon dioxide, methane, and nitrous oxide—trap more solar heat. Indeed, the average global surface temperature has risen in the last 100 years, and scientists say the earth is warming faster than it has in the last thousand years.[138]

The Kyoto Protocol is a global treaty on tackling climate change. It commits industrialized nations to reduce their emissions of six greenhouse gases by an average of 5.2 percent below their 1990 levels within a decade. Scientists say it would take carbon cuts of 60 percent or more to prevent dangerous climatic instability, so Kyoto is only a modest start. The United States pollutes more, absolutely and per head, than any other country. Its greenhouse emissions have risen by more than 13.1 percent from 1990 to 2002, despite the Kyoto commitment to reduce them by 6 percent.[139]

In 2001, the Bush administration rejected the Kyoto Protocol claiming that the agreement was fatally flawed because it excluded developing nations, such as China and India. Bush maintained that forcing U.S. businesses to reduce their emissions while letting companies in those countries off the hook would cost American jobs. Of all the industrialized Western nations (and the 191 ratifiers), only the

United States has refused to sign the Kyoto Protocol. Despite the U.S. rejection, the Kyoto accord took effect in 2005 as a result of Russia's ratification. Key provisions of the Kyoto Protocol are set to expire in December 2012. The future of Kyoto looks bleak. Canada has already exited it, Japan and Russia have said they will not continue, and the United States never joined. Developing nations such as China, India, and Brazil are not bound by its targets. Australia and New Zealand sit on the fence.[140]

The other strategy employed to slow the effects of climate change has centered on a carbon tax. A carbon tax is designed to tax the carbon emissions of large and small industrial producers and polluters. The intent is to drive the price of these emissions so high that it will spur on the growth and adoption of less expensive alternative energy sources. As carbon emissions become more highly taxed, other energy sources become more attractive, and with greater production and development, prices invariably come down. For instance, the average price of solar panels (per watt) has already dropped 97 percent from 1975 to 2012.

Part of this strategy also involves an emissions trading scheme based on carbon credits. A carbon credit is a term for any tradable permit that allows a plant to emit one ton of carbon dioxide or another greenhouse gas. Specifically, each plant is given (often generous) free permits—i.e., carbon credits or Certified Emissions Reductions (CER)—to meet their emission targets. Targets are based on a proportion (somewhere around 90 percent) of a plant's historic emissions level. Companies can trade or buy CERs from other companies or even other countries. These carbon credits became a commodity that is traded in a kind of carbon exchange.[141] For instance, a company can buy a cheap CER from a developing country for $4 and sell it back to another company or country for $12.[142] However, the ultimate goal is carbon reduction.

Conclusion

The production, distribution, and consumption of food have historically been rooted in political economy. Through various forms of legislation, the U.S. government has traditionally responded to the needs of diverse groups that have an interest in food—farmers, consumers, the poor or their advocates, food distributors, grain traders, and the Third World and wealthier countries that depend on U.S. food production.

The federal government has responded to these interests by creating a patchwork quilt of policies and programs. One of the most important is SNAP, an ingenious strategy that helps keep food affordable for low-income consumers, helps stabilize farm prices, slows down agricultural surpluses by subsidizing consumption, and allows food retailers and distributors to increase their profits by ensuring a volume of subsidized consumers. The nation's food problems persist, however. These problems, which are serious for many poor people and farmers, have reached crisis proportions for others—including the very poor, farmworkers, and marginal farmers. Tragically, many farmers in the United States now profit from food stamps not because the program helps them control surplus farm goods but because it provides them with coupons redeemable in food. It is a sad commentary when the producers of food are unable to purchase what they grow.

DISCUSSION QUESTIONS

1. WIC and the SNAP program are similar in many respects. What are the specific differences between them? Is it necessary for WIC to be a separate program?
2. Serious questions exist as to the effectiveness of U.S. food programs for the poor. What alternatives, if any, exist to the current matrix of food programs that make up the nutritional safety net?
3. American farming has historically been economically volatile. For example, farming was reasonably good in the 1970s, after which it descended into a depression in the early and mid-1980s. What programs and policies might help stabilize U.S. farming?
4. Climate change and sustainability are two sides of the same coin. Some critics question climate change as pseudo-science while others see it as the most pressing issue facing civilization. How valid are these arguments?
5. The problem of how to deal fairly with farmworkers in the United States is both difficult and chronic. What are some possible solutions for promoting equity and fairness for farmworkers in this country?
6. Proponents of biofuels see it as a potential solution to America's energy dependency on imports. Supporters argue that the production of ethanol would decrease the foreign trade imbalance, eliminate agricultural surpluses, reduce agricultural subsidies, and lower the emission of hydrocarbons that contribute to global warming. Are they right?

NOTES

1. A. Coleman-Jensen, M. Nord, M. Andrews, S. Carlson, *Household Food Security in the United States in 2010*, U.S Department of Agriculture, Economic Research Services Report No. 125 (September 2011). Retrieved August 2012 from http://www.ers.usda.gov/media/121076/err125_2_.pdf

2. U.S. Department of Agriculture, Economic Research Service, "The Food Assistance Landscape: 2011 Annual Report," *Economic Information Bulletin,* no. 93 (March 2012). Retrieved August 2012 from http://www.ers.usda.gov/media/376910/eib93_1_.pdf

3. C.L. Ogden, M.D. Carroll, B.K. Kit & K.M. Flegal, "Prevalence of Obesity in the United States, 2009-2010," *NCHS Data Brief*, no. 82 (January 2012). Retrieved August 2012 from http://www.cdc.gov/nchs/data/databriefs/db82.pdf

4. American Heart Association, Overweight in Children, June 10, 2010. Retrieved January 2011 from, http://www.heart.org/HEARTORG/GettingHealthy/Overweight-in-Children_UCM_304054_Article.jsp; and Centers for Disease Control and Prevention, Obesity and Overweight, June 18, 2010. Retrieved from, http://www.cdc.gov/nchs/fastats/overwt.htm

5. Eric Schlosser, *Fast Food Nation* (New York: Perennial, 2002), p. 3.

6. G.K. Singh, M. Siahpush, R.A. Hiatt & L.R. Timsina, "Dramatic Increases in Obesity and Overweight Prevalence and Body Mass Index Among Ethnic-Immigrant and Social Class Groups in the United States, 1976-2008," *Journal of Community Health*, 36, no. 1 (February 2011), pp. 94-110. Retrieved August 2012 from http://search.proquest.com/pqrl/docview/837474166/abstract/138DC3374C27224D49B/1?accountid=14723

7. E.A. Finkelstein, J.G. Trogdon, J.W. Cohen & W. Dietz, "Annual Medical Spending Attributable to Obesity: Payer And Service Specific Estimates," *Health Affairs,* 28, no. 5 (September/October 2009), pp. 822-831. Retrieved August 2012 from http://content.healthaffairs.org/content/28/5/w822.full.pdf+html

8. United Health Foundation, *America's Health: State Health Rankings, 2004 Edition*, 2004. Retrieved November 2004, from www.unitedhealthfoundation.org/shr2004/commentary/obesity.html

9. Robin McKie, "Lifespan Crisis Hits Supersize America," *Observer* (September 19, 2004), p. 2.

10. M.J. Sepulveda, F. Tait, E. Zimmerman and D. Edington, "Impact of Childhood Obesity on Employers," *Health Affairs,* 29, no. 3 (March 2010), pp. 513-521. Retrieved August 2012 from http://content.healthaffairs.org/content/29/3/513.full?sid=dde863bc-6bfc-4143-a1a2-83c5e1546020

11. M.J. Sepulveda, F. Tait, E. Zimmerman and D. Edington, "Impact of Childhood Obesity on Employers," *Health Affairs,* 29, no. 3 (March 2010), pp. 513-521. Retrieved August 2012 from http://content.healthaffairs.org/content/29/3/513.full?sid=dde863bc-6bfc-4143-a1a2-83c5e1546020

12. U.S. Department of Agriculture, *2012 Budget Summary and Annual Performance Plan,* March 2011. Retrieved August 2012 http://www.fsa.usda.gov/Internet/FSA_File/fy12budsum.pdf

13. U.S. Department of Health and Human Services, *2012 President's Budget for HHS: HHS Budget in Brief,* February 2011. Retrieved August 2012 from http://www.hhs.gov/about/budget/fy2012/fy2012bib.pdf

14. E.J. O'Donoghue, R.A. Hoppe, D.E. Banker, R. Ebel, K. Fuglie, P. Korb et al, "The Changing Organization of U.S. Farming," *Economic Information Bulletin*, no. 88 (December 2011), U.S. Department of Agriculture, Economic Research Services. Retrieved August 2012 from http://www.ers.usda.gov/media/176816/eib88_1_.pdf

15. U.S. Department of Agriculture, *2012 Budget Summary and Annual Performance Plan,* March 2011. Retrieved August 2012 http://www.fsa.usda.gov/Internet/FSA_File/fy12budsum.pdf

16. U.S. Department of Agriculture, *2012 Budget Summary and Annual Performance Plan,* March 2011. Retrieved August 2012 http://www.fsa.usda.gov/Internet/FSA_File/fy12budsum.pdf

17. U.S. Department of Health and Human Services, Administration for Children and Families, *Summary of Federal TANF Expenditures in 2011,* 16th of May 2011. Retrieved August 2012 from http://www.acf.hhs.gov/programs/ofa/data/2011fin/table_c1a.pdf

18. U.S. Department of Health and Human Services, Administration for Children and Families, *TANF: Total Number of Recipients,* 3rd of April 2012. Retrieved August 2012 from http://www.acf.hhs.gov/programs/ofa/data-reports/caseload/2011/2011_recipient_tan.htm

19. USDA, Food Security in the U.S.: Measurement, September 4, 2012. Retrieved September 2012 from, http://www.ers.usda.gov/topics/food-nutrition-assistance/food-security-in-the-us/measurement.aspx

20. CNN, "Poll: Most Americans Older than 25 Are Overweight," March 5, 2002. Retrieved November 2004 from http://archives.cnn.com/2002/HEALTH/03/05/obesity.poll

21. United States Census Bureau, 2012 Statistical Abstract, National Data Book, June 27, 2012. Retrieved September 2012 from,http://www.census.gov/compendia/statab/cats/agriculture.html

22. U.S. Department of Agriculture, "Household Food Security in the United States, 2006," November 2007. Retrieved July 2008, from www.ers.usda.gov/Publications/ERR49/ERR49_ReportSummary.pdf

23. Mark Nord, "Food Insecurity in Households with Children Prevalence, Severity, and Household Characteristics," ERS Report Summary, U.S. Department of Agriculture, September 2009; and A. Coleman-Jensen, M. Nord, M. Andrews, S. Carlson, *Household Food Security in the United States in 2010*, U.S Department of Agriculture, Economic Research Services Report No. 125 (September 2011). Retrieved August 2012 from http://www.ers.usda.gov/media/121076/err125_2_.pdf

24. See Katherine Alaimo, Christine M. Olson, and Edward A. Frongillo, "Food Insufficiency and American School-Aged Children's Cognitive, Academic and Psychosocial Development," *Pediatrics* 108 (2001), pp. 44–53; and Katherine Alaimo, Christine M. Olson and Edward A. Frongillo, "Family Food Insufficiency, but Not Low Family Income, Is Associated with Dysthymia and Suicide Symptoms in Adolescents," *Journal of Nutrition* 132 (2002), pp. 719–725.

25. A. Coleman-Jensen, M. Nord, M. Andrews, S. Carlson, *Household Food Security in the United States in 2010*, U.S Department of Agriculture, Economic Research Services Report No. 125 (September 2011). Retrieved August 2012 from http://www.ers.usda.gov/media/121076/err125_2_.pdf

26. USDA, Food Security in the U.S.: Measurement, September 4, 2012. Retrieved September 2012 from, http://www.ers.usda.gov/topics/food-nutrition-assistance/food-security-in-the-us/measurement.aspx

27. A. Coleman-Jensen, M. Nord, M. Andrews, S. Carlson, *Household Food Security in the United States in 2010*, U.S Department of Agriculture, Economic Research Services Report No. 125 (September 2011). Retrieved August 2012 from http://www.ers.usda.gov/media/121076/err125_2_.pdf

28. A. Coleman-Jensen, M. Nord, M. Andrews, S. Carlson, *Household Food Security in the United States in 2010: Statistical Supplement*, U.S. Department of Agriculture, Economic Research Services Administrative Publication no. 057 (September 2011). Retrieved August 2012 from http://www.ers.usda.gov/media/120995/ap057.pdf

29. Mark Nord, "Food Insecurity in Households with Children Prevalence, Severity, and Household Characteristics," ERS Report Summary, U.S. Department of Agriculture, September 2009.

30. Food Action Research Council, "Food Stamp Program," October 22, 2004. Retrieved November 2004 from http://www.frac.org/html/federal_food_programs/programs/fsp.html

31. U.S. Department of Agriculture, Economic Research Service, "The Food Assistance Landscape: 2011 Annual Report," *Economic Information Bulletin,* no. 93 (March 2012). Retrieved August 2012 from http://www.ers.usda.gov/media/376910/eib93_1_.pdf

32. Food Action Research Council, "Food Stamp Program," October 22, 2004. Retrieved November 2004, from www.frac.org/html/federal_food_programs/programs/fsp.html

33. U.S. Department of Agriculture, Economic Research Service, "The Food Assistance Landscape: 2011 Annual Report," *Economic Information Bulletin,* no. 93 (March 2012) Retrieved August 2012 from http://www.ers.usda.gov/media/376910/eib93_1_.pdf

34. U.S. Department of Agriculture, Economic Research Service, "The Food Assistance Landscape: 2011 Annual Report," *Economic Information Bulletin,* no. 93 (March 2012). Retrieved August 2012 from http://www.ers.usda.gov/media/376910/eib93_1_.pdf

35. Food Action Research Council, "Food Stamp Program," October 22, 2004. Retrieved November 2004 from www.frac.org/html/federal_food_programs/programs/fsp.html

36. Joshua Leftin, Andrew Gothro, and Esa Eslami, Characteristics of Supplemental Nutrition Assistance Program Households: Fiscal Year 2009, U.S. Department of Agriculture, Food and Nutrition Service, Office of Research and Analysis. Retrieved January 2011 from, www.fns.usda.gov/ora

37. E. Eslami, K. Filion & M. Strayer, *Characteristics of Supplemental Nutrition Assistance Program Households: Fiscal Year 2010*, Nutrition Assistance Program Report no. SNAP-11-CHAR (September 2011), U.S. Department of Agriculture, Food and Nutrition Service, Office of Research and Analysis. Retrieved August 2012 from http://www.fns.usda.gov/ora/menu/Published/snap/FILES/Participation/2010Characteristics.pdf

38. Joshua Leftin, Andrew Gothro, and Esa Eslami, Characteristics of Supplemental Nutrition Assistance Program Households: Fiscal Year 2009, U.S. Department of Agriculture, Food and Nutrition Service, Office of Research and Analysis. Retrieved January 2011 from, www.fns.usda.gov/ora.

39. M. Nord & M. Prell, *Food Security Improved Following the 2009 ARRA Increase in SNAP Benefits*, U.S. Department of Agriculture, Economic Research Services Report No. 116 (April 2011). Retrieved July 2012 from http://www.ers.usda.gov/media/127913/err116.pdf

40. U.S. Department of Agriculture, Economic Research Service, "The Food Assistance Landscape: 2011 Annual Report," *Economic Information Bulletin,* no. 93 (March 2012). Retrieved August 2012 from http://www.ers.usda.gov/media/376910/eib93_1_.pdf

41. Illa Tennison, "WIC Policy Analysis," unpublished paper, School of Social Work, University of Missouri–Columbia, 1987, p. 5.

42. U.S. Department of Agriculture, Food and Nutrition Service, *Nutrition Program Fact Sheet: WIC – The Special Supplemental Nutrition Program for Women, Infants and Children,* Last Updated August 2011. Retrieved August 2012 from http://www.fns.usda.gov/wic/WIC-Fact-Sheet.pdf

43. U.S. Department of Agriculture, Economic Research Service, "The Food Assistance Landscape: 2011 Annual Report," *Economic Information Bulletin,* no. 93 (March 2012) Retrieved August 2012 from http://www.ers.usda.gov/media/376910/eib93_1_.pdf

44. U.S. Department of Agriculture, Food and Nutrition Service, *Nutrition Program Fact Sheet: WIC – The Special Supplemental Nutrition Program for Women, Infants and Children,* Last Updated August 2011. Retrieved August 2012 from http://www.fns.usda.gov/wic/WIC-Fact-Sheet.pdf

45. U.S. Department of Agriculture, Food and Nutrition Service, *Nutrition Program Fact Sheet: WIC – The Special Supplemental Nutrition Program for Women, Infants and*

Children, Last Updated August 2011. Retrieved August 2012 from http://www.fns.usda.gov/wic/WIC-Fact-Sheet.pdf

46. U.S. Department of Agriculture, Food and Nutrition Service, "Nutrition Assistance Programs" February 6, 2000. Retrieved January 2001 from www.fns.usda.gov/fns

47. See U.S. House of Representatives, *1992 Green Book,* p. 1688; and Kristin Cotter, "Texas WIC: Strategy for Outreach Policy," unpublished paper, Graduate School of Social Work, University of Houston, Houston, TX, Fall 1996.

48. See Second Harvest, "Hunger in America, 2001," retrieved November 2004 from www.secondharvest.org/site_content.asp?s=81

49. U.S. Department of Agriculture, Food and Nutrition Service, "How WIC Helps," May 15, 2000. Retrieved December 2001 from www.fns.usda.gov/wic/CONTENT/howwichelps.htm

50. Douglas J. Besharov, "We're Feeding the Poor as If They're Starving," American Enterprise Institute, Washington, DC, December 2002.

51. U.S. Department of Agriculture, Economic Research Service, "The Food Assistance Landscape: FY2011 Annual Report," *Economic Information Bulletin,* no. 93 (March 2012) Retrieved August 2012 from http://www.ers.usda.gov/media/376910/eib93_1_.pdf

52. See Second Harvest, "Hunger in America, 2001," retrieved November 2004 from www.secondharvest.org/site_content.asp?s=81

53. See Second Harvest, "Hunger in America, 2001," retrieved November 2004 from www.secondharvest.org/site_content.asp?s=81; and U.S. Conference of Mayors, "Hunger and Homelessness Survey," December 2003, retrieved October 2004 from www.usmayors.org/uscm/hungersurvey/2003/onlinereport/HungerAndHomelessnessReport2003.pdf

54. Feeding America, Hunger in America: Key Findings, 2012. Retrieved September 2012 from, http://feedingamerica.org/hunger-in-america/hunger-studies/hunger-study-2010/key-findings.aspx

55. United States Department of Agriculture, "History of Agricultural Price Support and Adjustment Programs, 1933–84," *Bulletin No. 485* (Washington, DC: Economic Research Service, 1984), pp. 8–9.

56. Steve Little, "Parity: Survival of the Family Farm." Unpublished paper, School of Social Work, University of Missouri–Columbia, 1986, pp. 8–9.

57. Mermelstein, "Criteria of Rural Mental Health Directors," pp. 5–6.

58. Quoted in John M. Herrick, "Farmers' Revolt! Contemporary Farmers' Protests in Historical Perspective: Implications for Social Work Practice," *Human Services in the Rural Environment* 10, no. 1 (April 1986), p. 9.

59. Anuradha Mittal, "Giving Away the Farm: The 2002 Farm Bill," *Backgrounder* 8, no. 3 (Summer 2002), p. 1.

60. U.S. Department of Agriculture, *Fact Sheet: Direct and Counter-Cyclical Payment (DCP) Program,* December 2008. Retrieved August 2012 from http://www.usda.gov/

61. U.S. Representative Debbie Stabenow, Chairwoman's Summary of the 2012 Farm Bill Committee Print, April 20, 2012. Retrieved September 2012 from, http://www.ag.senate.gov/newsroom/press/release/2012-farm-bill-committee-print

62. Gregory Lamb, "Biofuels Show Promise, But Also Present Problems," *The Christian Science Monitor,* May 10, 2007, p. 6; and Claudio Langone, Brazilian Ministry of the Environment, United Nations Commission on Sustainable Development, 14th Session, United Nations, New York, May 10th and 12th, 2006.

63. Ibid.

64. Halah Touryalai, "Fracking is Misunderstood, It's the Key to Energy Self-Sufficiency," *Forbes,* May 21, 2012, p. 18.

65. Natural Resources Defense Council, "Risky Well Drilling Threatens Health, Water Supplies," 2010. Retrieved September 2012 from, http://www.nrdc.org/energy/gasdrilling/; and Josh Fox, Gasland, 2010. Retrieved September 2012 from, http://www.gaslandthemovie.com/

66. U.S. Department of Agriculture, Economic Research Services, *Table: U.S. and State Level Data, 1850-2010: Number of Farms,* U.S. and State Farm Income and Wealth Statistics Data Set, Last Updated May 5, 2011. Retrieved from http://www.ers.usda.gov/data-products/farm-income-and-wealth-statistics.aspx#27514

67. U.S. Department of Agriculture, Economic Research Services, *Table: Value Added and Number of Farms By Farm Size Class (Measured by Value of Output), 1991–2010,* U.S. and State Farm Income and Wealth Statistics Data Set, Last Updated 13th of February, 2012. Retrieved from http://www.ers.usda.gov/data-products/farm-income-and-wealth-statistics.aspx#27514

68. USDA, Census of Agriculture Shows Growing Diversity in U.S. Farming, February 4, 2009. Retrieved January 2011 from, http://www.usda.gov/wps/portal/usda/usdahome?contentidonly=true&contentid=2009/02/0036.xml

69. R.A. Hoppe & D.E. Banker, "Structure and Finances of U.S. Farms: Family Farm Report, 2010 Edition", *Economic Information Bulletin,* no. 66 (July 2010), U.S. Department of Agriculture, Economic Research Services. Retrieved from http://www.ers.usda.gov/media/184479/eib66_1_.pdf

70. E.J. O'Donoghue, R.A. Hoppe, D.E. Banker, R. Ebel, K. Fuglie, P. Korb et al, "The Changing Organization of U.S. Farming,"*Economic Information Bulletin,* no. 88 (December 2011), U.S. Department of Agriculture, Economic Research Services. Retrieved August 2012 from http://www.ers.usda.gov/media/176816/eib88_1_.pdf

71. E.J. O'Donoghue, R.A. Hoppe, D.E. Banker, R. Ebel, K. Fuglie, P. Korb et al, "The Changing Organization of U.S. Farming,"*Economic Information Bulletin,* no. 88 (December 2011), U.S. Department of Agriculture, Economic Research Services. Retrieved August 2012 from http://www.ers.usda.gov/media/176816/eib88_1_.pdf

72. Christine Ahn, Melissa Moore, and Nick Parker, "Migrant Farmworkers: America's New Plantation Workers," *Backgrounder* 10, no. 2 (Spring 2004), pp. 2–11.

73. E.J. O'Donoghue, R.A. Hoppe, D.E. Banker, R. Ebel, K. Fuglie, P. Korb et al, "The Changing Organization of U.S. Farming,"*Economic Information Bulletin,* no. 88 (December 2011), U.S. Department of Agriculture, Economic Research Services. Retrieved August 2012 from http://www.ers.usda.gov/media/176816/eib88_1_.pdf

74. E.J. O'Donoghue, R.A. Hoppe, D.E. Banker, R. Ebel, K. Fuglie, P. Korb et al, "The Changing Organization of U.S. Farming,"*Economic Information Bulletin,* no. 88 (December 2011), U.S. Department of Agriculture, Economic Research Services. Retrieved August 2012 from http://www.ers.usda.gov/media/176816/eib88_1_.pdf

75. See U.S. Department of Agriculture, "2002 Census of Agriculture," Retrieved December 2004, from www.nass.usda.gov/census/census02/volume1/us/index1.htm; U.S. Department of Agriculture, "Farms and Land in Farms," February 2004, retrieved June 2004, from http://usda.mannlib.cornell.edu/reports/nassr/other/zfl-bb/fmno0204.txt; U.S. Department of Agriculture, "2002 Census of Agriculture;" U.S. Department of Agriculture, "Income, Wealth, and the Economic Well-Being of Farm Households," ERS Agricultural Economic Report No. AER812, July 2002, retrieved May 2004, from www.ers.usda.gov/publications/AER812; U.S. Department of Agriculture, "Structural and Financial Characteristics of U.S. Farms: 2001," Family Farm Report, ERS Agriculture Information Bulletin No. 768, May 2001, retrieved April 2004, from www.ers.usda.gov/publications/aib768; Farm Aid, "Factory Farms: The Worst of Industrial Agriculture, 2004," retrieved November 2004, from www.farmaid.org/site/PageServer?pagename=info_facts_factory; Andrew Nelson, *From a Lifestyle to a Business, Small Farming in Transition: A Case Study Analysis of Small Farming in the Upper Midwest,* unpublished paper; Larry Keller, "Family Farming: An Endangered Career," CNN.com, October 30, 2000, retrieved October 2001, from http://fyi.cnn.com/2000/fyi/news/10/30/family.farms; Center for Rural Affairs, "Corporate Farming and Industrialization"; Farm Aid, "Family Farm Numbers," 2000, retrieved October 2001, from www.farmaid.org/org/farm/facts.asp; Farm Aid, "Factory Farming," 2000, retrieved December 2001, from www.farmaid.org/org/farm/factory.asp; and Farm Aid, "Questions and Answers," 2000, retrieved December 2001, from www.farmaid.org/org/farm/q_a.asp

76. U.S. Department of Health and Human Services, Food and Drug Administration, *Guidance for Industry: The Judicious Use of Medically Important Antimicrobial Drugs in Food-Producing Animals,* Report no. 209, April 13, 2012. Retrieved August 2012 from http://www.fda.gov/downloads/AnimalVeterinary/GuidanceComplianceEnforcement/GuidanceforIndustry/UCM216936.pdf

77. T.K. White & R.A. Hoppe, "Changing Farm Structure and the Distribution of Farm Payments and Federal Crop Insurance," *Economic Information Bulletin*, no. 91 (February 2012), U.S. Department of Agriculture, Economic

78. Sustainable Table, Family Farms, nd. Retrieved January 2011 from, http://www.sustainabletable.org/issues/familyfarms; Farm Aid, "Factory Farms: The Worst of Industrial Agriculture, 2004," retrieved November 2004, from www.farmaid.org/site/PageServer?pagename=info_facts_factory; "Factory Farming," 2000, retrieved December 2001, from www.farmaid.org/org/farm/factory.asp; USDA, Census of Agriculture Shows Growing Diversity in U.S. Farming, op cit.; Environmental Working Group, Farm Subsidy Database, 2010. Retrieved from, http://farm.ewg.org/region.php?fips=00000&regname=UnitedStatesFarmSubsidySummary; and USDA, Economic Research Service, Farm Household Economics and Well- Being: Beginning Farmers, Demographics, and Labor Allocations, November 30, 2010. Retrieved from, http://ers.usda.gov/Briefing/WellBeing/demographics.htm

79. U.S. Department of Agriculture, Economic Research Service, *Farm Labor: Background,* Last Updated July 23, 2012. Retrieved August 2012 from http://www.ers.usda.gov/topics/farm-economy/farm-labor/background.aspx#Numbers

80. T. Park, M. Ahearn, T. Covey, K. Erickson, J. M. Harris, J. Ifft, C. McGath, M. Morehart, S. Vogel, J. Weber, and R. Williams, *Agricultural Income and Finance Outlook,* Economic Research Service Report AIS-91, U.S. Department of Agriculture, December 2011. Retrieved August 2012 from http://www.ers.usda.gov/media/246635/ais-91_3-1-12.pdf

81. Eric Schlosser, *Reefer Madness: Sex, Drugs, and Cheap Labor in the American Black Market,* (Houghton Mifflin Company, 2003), p. 56.

82. U.S. Department of Agriculture, Economic Research Service, *Farm Labor: Background,* Last Updated July 23, 2012. Retrieved August 2012 from http://www.ers.usda.gov/topics/farm-economy/farm-labor/background.aspx#Numbers

83. U.S. Department of Agriculture, Economic Research Service, *Farm Labor: Background,* Last Updated July 23, 2012. Retrieved August 2012 from http://www.ers.usda.gov/topics/farm-economy/farm-labor/background.aspx#Numbers

84. U.S. Department of Agriculture, Economic Research Service, *Farm Labor: Background,* Last Updated July 23, 2012. Retrieved August 2012 from http://www.ers.usda.gov/topics/farm-economy/farm-labor/background.aspx#Numbers

85. U.S. Department of Agriculture, Economic Research Service, *Farm Labor: Background,* Last Updated July 23, 2012. Retrieved August 2012 from http://www.ers.usda.gov/topics/farm-economy/farm-labor/background.aspx#Numbers

86. National Center for Farmworker Health, Inc., *Farmworker Health Factsheet: Facts about Farmworkers,* August 2012. Retrieved August 2012 from http://www.ncfh.org/docs/fs-Facts%20about%20Farmworkers.pdf

87. National Center for Farmworker Health, Inc., *Farmworker Health Factsheet: Facts about Farmworkers*, August 2012. Retrieved August 2012 from http://www.ncfh.org/docs/fs-Facts%20about%20Farmworkers.pdf

88. National Center for Farmworker Health, Inc., *Migrant and Seasonal Farmworker Demographics,* 2009. Retrieved August 2012 from www.ncfh.org/

89. National Center for Farmworker Health, Inc., *Farmworker Health Factsheet: Facts about Farmworkers*, August 2012. Retrieved August 2012 from http://www.ncfh.org/docs/fs-Facts%20about%20Farmworkers.pdf; National Center for Farmworker Health, Inc., *Migrant and Seasonal Farmworker Demographics,* 2009. Retrieved August 2012 from www.ncfh.org/

90. U.S. Department of Agriculture, Economic Research Service, *Farm Labor: Background,* Last Updated July 23, 2012. Retrieved August 2012 from http://www.ers.usda.gov/topics/farm-economy/farm-labor/background.aspx#Numbers

91. National Center for Farmworker Health, Inc., *Farmworker Health Factsheet: Facts about Farmworkers*, August 2012. Retrieved August 2012 from http://www.ncfh.org/docs/fs-Facts%20about%20Farmworkers.pdf

92. National Center for Farmworker Health, Inc., *Migrant and Seasonal Farmworker Demographics,* 2009. Retrieved August 2012 from www.ncfh.org/

93. National Center for Farmworker Health, Inc., *Farmworker Health Factsheet: Facts about Farmworkers*, August 2012. Retrieved August 2012 from http://www.ncfh.org/docs/fs-Facts%20about%20Farmworkers.pdf

94. National Center for Farmworker Health, Inc., *Farmworker Health Factsheet: Facts about Farmworkers*, August 2012. Retrieved August 2012 from http://www.ncfh.org/docs/fs-Facts%20about%20Farmworkers.pdf

95. National Center for Farmworker Health, Inc., *Occupational Health and Safety,* 2009. Retrieved August 2012 from www.ncfh.org/

96. National Center for Farmworker Health, Inc., *Occupational Health and Safety,* 2009. Retrieved August 2012 from www.ncfh.org/

97. See V. A. Wilk, *The Occupational Health of Migrant and Seasonal Farmworkers in the United States* (Washington, DC: Farmworkers Justice Fund, 1985); Juan Ramos and Celia Torres, "Migrant and Seasonal Farm Workers," *Encyclopedia of Social Work,* 18th ed. (Silver Spring, MD: NASW, 1987), p. 151; and National Center for Farmworker Health, *Facts about America's Farmworkers* (Washington, DC: National Center for Farmworker Health, 1996).

98. Wilk, *Occupational Health.*

99. National Center for Farmworker Health, Inc., *Child Labor,* 2009. Retrieved August 2012 from www.ncfh.org/

100. Margaret Reeves, Anne Katten, and Martha Guzman, "Fields of Poison, 2002: California Farmworkers and Pesticides," United Farmworkers, 2003. Retrieved August 2004, from www.ufw.org

101. National Center for Farmworker Health, Inc., *Child Labor,* 2009. Retrieved August 2012 from www.ncfh.org/

102. Gary Huang, "Health Problems among Migrant Farmworkers' Children in the U.S." ERIC Digests, January 1, 1993. Retrieved December 1999 from www.ed.gov/databases/ERIC_Digests/ed357907.html

103. Ibid.

104. Gosia Wozniacka, "United Farm Workers Fight Dwindling Membership," *Press Democrat,* April 20, 2011, p. A8.

105. Ahn, Moore, and Parker, "Migrant Farmworkers: America's New Plantation Workers."

106. Jeff Tietz, "Boss Hog," *Rolling Stone,* December 14, 2006, pp. 85–102.

107. Stewart Smith, "Farming Activities and Family Farms: Getting the Concepts Right," Presentation to the Joint Economic Committee Symposium, Agricultural Industrialization and Family Farms: The Role of Federal Policy, Washington DC, October 1992.

108. ConAgra, Products, 2012. Retrieved September 2012, from www.conagrafoods.com

109. Farm Aid, "Genetic Engineering," 2004. Retrieved November 2004 from www.farmaid.org/site/PageServer?pagename='info_facts_genetic

110. European Union, GM Food and Feed – Labelling, 2012. Retrieved September 2012 from, http://ec.europa.eu/food/food/biotechnology/gmfood/labelling_en.htm

111. Ministry for the Environment, What Genetically Modified Foods are Sold in NZ?, 2012. Retrieved September 2012 from, http://www.mfe.govt.nz/issues/organisms/about-gm/food.html

112. Joel Dyer, "Monsanto's Point of No Return," *Boulder Weekly,* August 30, 2012. Retrieved September 2012 from, http://www.boulderweekly.com/article-9613-monsantos-point-of-no-return.html

113. Farm Aid, "Genetic Engineering," 2004. Retrieved November 2004, from www.farmaid.org/site/PageServer?pagename='info_facts_genetic

114. Ibid.

115. Farm Aid, "Issues in Farming," 2004. Retrieved November 2004 from www.farmaid.org/site/PageServer?pagename=info_facts_global

116. Ibid.

117. Ahn, Moore, and Parker, "Migrant Farmworkers: America's New Plantation Workers."

118. U.S. Department of Agriculture, *USDA Accomplishments 2009-2011: Trade,* Retrieved August 2012 from http://www.usda.gov/documents/Results-Trade.pdf

119. Businessinsurancequotes.org, 10 Biggest Food Recalls in U.S. History, 2011. Retrieved September 2012 from, http://www.businessinsurance.org/10-biggest-food-recalls-in-u-s-history/

120. Farm Aid, "Genetic Engineering," 2004.

121. U.S. Department of Agriculture, *USDA Accomplishments 2009-2011: Local and Regional Food Systems,* Retrieved August 2012 from http://www.usda.gov/documents/Results-Local.pdf

122. U.S. Department of Agriculture, *Know Your Farmer, Know Your Food Compass Map,* Retrieved August 2012 from http://www.usda.gov/maps/maps/kyfcompassmap. htm

123. U.S. Department of Agriculture, *USDA Accomplishments 2009-2011: Local and Regional Food Systems,* Retrieved August 2012 from http://www.usda.gov/documents/ Results-Local.pdf

124. U.S. Department of Agriculture, *USDA Accomplishments 2009-2011: Organic Agriculture,* Retrieved August 2012 from http://www.usda.gov/documents/Results-Organic-Agriculture.pdf

125. D. Jaffee & P.H. Howard, "Corporate Cooptation of Organic and Fair Trade Standards," *Agriculture and Human Values,* 27 (2010), pp. 387–399. Retrieved August 2012 from http://search.proquest.com/docview/81528256 1/138EA4131AA6C09E071/19?accountid=14723

126. The Council on Sustainable Development, "Sustainable America: A New Consensus," 1995. Retrieved December 1998 from www.whitehouse.gov/WH/EOP/pcsd/info/ highlite.html

127. American Farmland Trust, "Farming on the Edge: Sprawling Development Threatens America's Best Farmland," 2003. Retrieved June 2004 from www. farmland.org/farmingontheedge/downloads. htm#foodchart

128. Ibid.

129. Richard Magleby, "Agricultural Resources and Environmental Indicators: Soil Management and Conservation," No. AH722, February 2002. Retrieved August 2004 from www.ers.usda.gov/publications/arei/ ah722/arei4_2/DBGen.htm

130. American Farmland Trust, "Why Save Farmland?" 1996. Retrieved January 6, 2001, from http://farm.fic.niu.edu/ aft/aftwhysave.html

131. American Farmland Trust, "What's Happening to America's Agricultural Resources?" 1996. Retrieved January 6, 2001, from http://farm.fic.niu.edu/aft/ aftwhathap.html

132. Ibid.

133. Katherine van Wormer, *Social Welfare: A World View* (Chicago: Nelson-Hall, 1997).

134. James Midgley, *Social Development: The Development Perspective in Social Welfare* (London: Sage, 1995).

135. Deborah Zabarenko, "In U.S., 2012 So Far is Hottest Year on Record," *Chicago Tribune,* September 10, 2012, P. B6.

136. Huffington Post, "Arctic Ice Melt Could Mean More Extreme Winters For U.S. And Europe," September 12, 2012. Retrieved September 2012 from, http://www. huffingtonpost.com/2012/09/12/arctic-ice-melt-extreme-weather_n_1878833.html

137. BBC News, "Global Climate Change, A Changing World," 2001. Retrieved July 2003 from http://news.bbc.co.uk/ hi/english/static/in_depth/sci_tech/2000/climate_change/ impact/default.stm

138. See Stevenson Swanson, "States May Lead Action against Global Warming, Manufacturers Reduce Emissions; Local Policies Try to Bypass Bush Stance," *Chicago Tribune* (November 14, 2004), p. 8A; and Juliet Eilperin, "Cool to Global Warming, Bush Administration Challenges Evidence, Tries to Keep Council from Endorsing Plans to Curb Climate Change," *Washington Post* (November 8, 2004), p. 10.

139. Swanson, "States May Lead Action against Global Warming."

140. The United Nations Framework on Climate Change, The Kyoto Protocol, 2012. Retrieved September 2012, from http://unfccc.int/kyoto_protocol/items/2830.php; Giles Parkinson, "EU Link Smarter than it Looked," *The Australian,* September 14, 2012, p. 9.

141. Giles Parkinson, "EU Link Smarter Than It Looked," *The Australian,* September 14, 2012, p. 9.

142. Tristan Edis, "Climate Spectator: How Polluters Can Cream the Scheme," *Business Spectator,* September 5, 2012, Retrieved September 2012 from, http://www. businessspectator.com.au/bs.nsf/Article/Australian-carbon-trading-scheme-pd20120905-XTW44?opendocument &src=rss

CHAPTER 18

The American Welfare State in International Perspective

Source: AP Wide World Photos

Various models have evolved to depict the comparative levels of development of nations. In recent times, a three-part classification has enjoyed extensive use: a First World, consisting of the industrial nations of the capitalist West; a Second World, made up of the communist nations that constructed political economies as an alternative to the market-dominated First World; and a Third World, comprising nations that were former colonies of the First World and later achieved independence, often through revolutions of liberation. This tri-part formulation became prevalent after World War II as the Cold War intensified. Many developing nations adopted the slogans of revolution, if not outright insurrection, in order to shed the influences of First World colonial nations. The Second World viewed the Third World as a theater of independence, an arena in which the exploitation of capitalism would be summarily ended, and the colonized nations would be brought into the communist sphere of influence. On the defensive, the First World deployed foreign aid, technical assistance, cultural exchange, and, on occasion, diplomatic subterfuge to neutralize Second World incursions into the Third World. In several regions—Central America, Southeast Asia, and sub-Saharan Africa—the First and Second Worlds recruited insurgents who acted as their surrogates, engaging the opposition in armed conflict at considerable cost in arms and human life.

With the fall of the Berlin Wall in 1989, the Three-World formulation lost utility. Foremost, the collapse of the Soviet Union and its Warsaw Pact satellites halved the scale of the Second World. The remaining communist nations—the People's Republic of China, Vietnam, North Korea, and Cuba—posed little immediate threat to the First World and were unlikely to serve as models for Third World nations. At the same time, some nations of the Third World had been transformed substantially from their colonial era status. Several Arab nations, despite feudal forms of governance, had prospered through oil exports, achieving levels of income that mirrored those of industrial nations. And despite the absence of natural resources, a handful of nations in Southeast Asia—Hong Kong, South Korea, Taiwan, and Singapore—experienced such consistently high levels of growth that they became known as the "Four Tigers." Tragically, many Third World nations lost ground. By the end of the millennium, several of the nations of sub-Saharan Africa and Southeast Asia were significantly less developed than they had been a generation earlier,

when they achieved independence from the First World. Nations such as Cambodia, Bangladesh, Afghanistan, Somalia, and Sierra Leone had lost so much capital, their infrastructure had deteriorated to such an extent, and their polity had become so unstable that development analysts began to speculate about the emergence of a Fourth World. Further confounding the prospects of Fourth World nations, the end of the Cold War led the affluent industrial nations of the First World, particularly the United States, to expend relatively less on foreign aid than they had during the Soviet threat.

Typologies of Welfare States

The welfare states of the industrialized West vary structurally. With his colleague Charles Lebeaux, Harold Wilensky sought to summarize the differences between the European and American welfare states by constructing a typology of social welfare systems. The typology contrasts residual welfare with institutional welfare. The residualist approach is concerned with providing a minimal safety net for the poorest sections of the population rather than catering to the population as a whole. Residualists argue that people can enhance their well-being through their own efforts, through the help of families or neighbors, by purchasing services on the market, or by obtaining help from voluntary organizations.[1] They point out that in the United States people make effective use of nongovernmental agencies, and that international comparisons should not be limited to government social programs. They also point out that although the United States may lag behind other developed nations in public welfare provision, people enjoy exceptionally high standards of living and unequaled opportunities. This is why the country remains a magnet for immigrants from all over the world—people who come not to receive government handouts but to share the American dream. Wilensky and Lebeaux believed that social policy in the United States is essentially residualist in nature. On the other hand, the institutional approach, which typifies European social welfare, seeks to provide a variety of social programs for the whole population and to combine economic and social objectives in an effort to enhance the well-being of all.[2]

British social philosopher Richard Titmuss agreed that the residual approach typified social welfare in the United States and that an institutional approach was dominant in Europe. However,

Titmuss noted that some countries did not fall into the residual and institutional dichotomy. For this reason, he added a third category to the typology, which he called the industrial performance model. He believed that this approach characterized social policy in the former Soviet Union and communist Eastern European countries.[3]

Several subsequent attempts have been made to construct typologies of welfare states that go beyond Wilensky and Lebeaux's twofold category. One of the first was by Norman Furniss and Timothy Tilton, who provided a threefold classification that encompassed what they called the "positive state," the "social security state," and the "social welfare state." The United States exemplified the first, Britain the second, and Sweden the third.[4]

Canadian writer Ramesh Mishra, who has written extensively about international social welfare, retained the twofold approach developed by Wilensky and Lebeaux, but he stressed the efforts of some countries to forge strong alliances among government, labor, and business in order to reach a consensus on social welfare issues. This approach is known as *corporatism*. In corporatist societies, social welfare is integrated into the economy and other institutions of society. Countries such as Sweden, Austria, and Australia are typical of the corporatist approach. Mishra used the term *integrated welfare state* to connote the corporatist approach. On the other hand, Britain and the United States were noncorporatist in that they did not integrate social and economic policy or seek to forge a consensus around welfare issues. For this reason, Mishra called them *differentiated welfare states*. Mishra was one of the first writers to suggest that Britain was not, as Titmuss believed, like the rest of Europe but rather more like the United States in its approach to social welfare.[5]

Gosta Esping-Andersen's typology also recognized the corporatist type when classifying welfare states. However, Esping-Andersen grouped countries somewhat differently from Mishra. In addition to the corporatist category (Italy, Japan, France, and Switzerland), Esping-Andersen identified two other types—the liberal welfare state (Australia, Britain, and the United States) and the social democratic welfare state (Austria, the Netherlands, and the Scandinavian countries).[6]

Although the typologies differ, they use similar criteria when classifying countries. All emphasize government social programs and neglect the role of voluntary organizations and other nonstatutory activities in social welfare. Although the typologies

are intended to classify countries for analytic purposes, it is clear that they give expression to beliefs about the desirability of the role of government in social welfare. Analysts who favor extensive government involvement in social welfare have represented countries with extensive public programs more favorably in the typologies than countries that do not place as much emphasis on government involvement. For this reason, it is not surprising that most of the typologies depict the United States negatively in comparison to European welfare states.

American Exceptionalism

The apparent unwillingness of the United States to emphasize government social welfare programs has been described by Edwin Amenta and Theda Skocpol as "welfare exceptionalism."[7] These authors also summarized explanations of the country's reluctance to create an institutional European-style welfare state. One such explanation is that the racial, ethnic, and religious diversity of the United States has prevented the emergence of a comprehensive welfare state. In European nations, people are more united and have a stronger sense of civic responsibility; in contrast, the pursuit of separate interests by a great number of different groups in the United States militates against the emergence of a single national system of provision that caters to all citizens.

Another explanation is based on the country's high degree of political decentralization that impedes the emergence of strong central political institutions. Combined with a high degree of diversity, the tradition of federalism in which the states assume much responsibility for social welfare, creates cleavages in U.S. society that effectively prevents the emergence of a strong, centralized, and comprehensive welfare state. It has also been noted that the United States does not have a long tradition of bureaucratic government that can support centralized welfare programs. Some have claimed that this is because of the absence of a feudal tradition. Developing this idea, others have pointed to the unique role of the courts in policymaking in this country, the separation of the executive and legislative branches, and the role of powerful political interest groups—all of which impede the emergence of a strong, federal welfare state. Another factor is the role of individualism in the United States, which is fundamentally antithetical to the collectivist assumption underlying the welfare state. It has also been argued that trade unions are weaker in the United States than in Europe and that the political left, which has played a major role in the emergence of the European welfare states, has not been strong in the United States.

Although the notion of welfare state exceptionalism offers interesting insights into social policy in the United States, it can be criticized. For example, the idea that the United States is a welfare laggard is based largely on a comparison of social programs, such as health insurance and family allowances. The absence of these programs is usually emphasized by those claiming that the United States does not have a comprehensive welfare state. Although it is true that government health care and family income maintenance programs are poorly developed in the United States, the role of indirect support for families through tax relief and tax deductions for medical expenses is often ignored, as is the significance of Medicare and state and local health care programs. Jacob Hacker evaluated the extent to which private sector health and welfare benefits effectively augmented public social programs, concluding that the inclusion of the private sector put the United States on par with European welfare states. On public benefits alone, the United States expended 17.1 percent of gross domestic product (GDP), less than half that of Denmark's 37.6 percent. An analysis of after-tax public and private social welfare expenditures showed a different picture, however; the United States expended 24.5 percent of GDP compared to Denmark's 24.4 percent.[8] Thus, the United States is different from other advanced nations with respect to social welfare provision because of its reliance on the private sector.

In addition, the United States has excelled in other social fields. Historical research reveals that in the late nineteenth century, the United States was ahead of other Western countries in developing income maintenance programs for veterans and for women with children. At the turn of the century, no other industrializing country had introduced mother's pensions, and none came as close to creating a "maternal" rather than "paternal" welfare state.[9] During the nineteenth century, the United States led the world in the development of public education; and it still compares favorably with many other countries in terms of access to education, particularly at the tertiary (college and university) level. Comparative studies have also shown that when particular social programs such as retirement pensions are compared, the United States fares quite well.[10]

Another problem is that comparisons between Europe and the United States are often characterized by strong personal biases. For example, a strong pro-British bias pervades Titmuss's writings. He has been criticized for presenting his arguments in a way that ensures the moral superiority of the institutional welfare state model.[11] It is also apparent that the European countries have widely varied welfare systems and that not all European welfare states are centralized, comprehensive, or highly activist. Studies of welfare policies in other parts of the world have also shown the U.S. welfare state in more favorable terms. For example, unlike the United States, Australia did not until recently have a universal Social Security system, and it relied extensively on means-tested social programs.[12] Nevertheless, it is difficult to reach the conclusion that the United States is one of the world's welfare

During the nineteenth century, the United States led the world in the development of public education. Today it still compares favorably well with many other countries in terms of access to education, particularly at the college and university level.

Source: Pearson Education/PH College

leaders. Despite its extensive educational and Social Security provisions, the country does not compare favorably to the other industrial nations in the extent, comprehensiveness, or coverage of its welfare system. In fact, its position has deteriorated in recent years as social programs were retrenched since the Reagan administration.

The Welfare State in Transition

As a result of the globalization of capital, welfare states—however they are classified—have made structural adjustments to remain competitive. Welfare states grew steadily during the relatively stable economic period of the 1950s to the early 1970s; however, by the mid-1970s, most industrial economies began to experience high inflation, high rates of unemployment, sluggish economic growth, and unacceptably high levels of taxation. During this difficult period, Western governments were forced to reassess their overall economic strategies, including the resources allocated to welfare activities. Hence, beginning in the early 1970s, most Western governments either cut welfare programs or arrested their growth.[13]

All Western nations are experiencing a crisis rooted in the need to compete in a new global economy.[14] According to conservative policy analysts, national survival in the new economic order can be achieved only if government cuts costs and becomes more efficient. In addition, these analysts argue for the creation of government policies that encourage the accumulation of the capital necessary for investment, industrial modernization, and corporate growth. Conservatives maintain that this precondition for economic survival is possible only when government freezes or lowers personal and corporate tax rates. The subsequent loss of tax revenue, however, often results in heavy governmental debt, cuts in all services (including social services), a deterioration of the infrastructure, and myriad social problems. The general emphasis on efficiency and profitability also leads to industrial reorganization, which in turn leads to rapidly changing production technologies that displace workers and result in plant closures and downsizing. Thus, the effects of conservative policy changes are exacerbated as cuts in governmental services coincide with the increased demand for social services by victims of global economic changes. In other words, Western industrial nations face a two-pronged assault on the welfare state: (1) the impact of the global economy on government spending and (2) an increase in the use of social services by workers dislocated by global economic changes.[15]

Western industrialized nations pursued liberal social policies after World War II.[16] In the United States, most presidents following Franklin D. Roosevelt tolerated—and in some cases even promoted—a liberal social welfare agenda. Although the general belief in the United States was that people should adjust to the market rather than the other way around, the social consensus also dictated that the nation should strengthen human capital in order to make people more economically competitive.[17] Thus, social welfare programs were developed to increase human capital through education, employment, health, and housing. The belief was that as human capital increased, the dependent person (or at least his or her children) would eventually be able to compete in a free market. For those who could not compete because of serious deficits (such as disabilities or old age), a system of social insurance or public assistance was developed to ensure a minimum level of subsistence. Thus, the dual focus of the welfare state was (1) to create programs to increase human capital and (2) to create programs to subsidize people unable to participate in the workforce. Even conservative presidents like Richard Nixon acquiesced to this welfare consensus.

But a more conservative welfare consensus emerged during the 1980s. This new consensus called for (1) making welfare benefits conditional on employment and other norms; (2) transforming open-ended entitlements to discretionary programs; (3) containing the growth of the governmental sector while retaining (in curtailed form) fundamental programs that affect the elderly and the working poor; (4) replacing government with other institutions, such as families and community-based organizations; and (5) contracting out services and benefits to the private sector. In effect, ideologues of the new right argued that the liberal welfare state was a failed social experiment.[18] During the 1990s, the conservative critique of the welfare state, introduced first by Margaret Thatcher in the United Kingdom and Ronald Reagan in the United States, prompted a reassessment of public welfare within liberal circles, with the result that Bill Clinton and Tony Blair (nominal liberals) essentially continued the conservative vector in social policy. Most recently, the implications of this trend have been explored by Anthony Giddens, who contends that this represented a "third way" in British social policy.[19] In the United States, Neil Gilbert observed the emergence of an "enabling state," which conditions social welfare benefits on participation in mainstream activities, particularly work.[20]

By the end of the twentieth century, it was evident that the welfare state was on the wane. "Across all of Europe and North America, the social democratic century has come to an end," observed Alan Wolfe. He further noted:

> Solidarity, social citizenship, the gift relationship, and the difference principle—as all of them representing formulations of the idea that those who live in a society are obligated to insure the welfare of everyone else—are terms bandied about in academic circles, but they no longer make much of an appearance in real politics.[21]

Retrenchment of the welfare state produced political crises in Europe and the United States. Economic instability shook the European Union when several member countries, particularly Greece, Spain, and Iceland, were encumbered with debt far beyond what their economies could sustain. "The deficit crisis that threatens the euro has also undermined the sustainability of the European standard of social welfare, built by the left-leaning governments since the end of World War II."[22] Austerity measures provoked street demonstrations as citizens faced sharp reductions in their living standards. In the United States, citizen disenchantment with the status quo assumed two forms. First, an indignant group fearful of government debt and overreach formed the Tea Party. A loose amalgam of groups forswearing ideological identity, the Tea Party, was nonetheless funded by wealthy conservatives who, liberal critics alleged, orchestrated a Right-wing agenda. During the 2010 midterm elections, Republican candidates aligned with the Tea Party won enough Congressional offices to subvert the centrist tactics of the leadership of both political parties. At the other end of the ideological continuum, commemorating the tenth anniversary of the September 11, 2001 attacks against the World Trade Center, progressive militants began camping out in a church-owned lot near Wall Street. Announcing that they represented the 99 percent of Americans who had been disadvantaged by the 1 percent who were wealthy, Occupy Wall Street (OWS) spawned similar counter-demonstrations in cities across the country. Unlike the Tea Party, OWS has failed to craft an agenda with sufficient specificity to propose legislation or sponsor candidates for election. Regardless, both insurgencies have contempt for the status

quo: "the Tea Party and Occupy Wall Street both rage against a financial elite that stumbled into a ruinous recession—and then got bailed out by a Washington elite that's in hock to special interests."[23] Such political convulsions will probably continue as First World nations confront the reality that budget commitments to welfare state benefits may no longer be sustainable given the tax burden they require.

Ranking National Development

Various frameworks have been proposed to gauge the progress of nations. Among the first was the Gini coefficient, a figure denoting the extent to which the distribution of income diverges from perfect equality. Critics of the Gini coefficient cite the limitations of a portrait of development that is based solely on income. Other indicators, such as longevity, education, opportunity, and environment, should be included, they claim. Although this argument has obvious merit, defenders of the Gini coefficient cite its value when the disparity between the rich and poor has become such a chasm. By way of illustration, 1 billion people survive on less than $1 per day; yet, "the assets of the world's 358 billionaires exceed the combined annual incomes of countries with 45 percent of the world's people."[24]

The Human Development Index

Since 1990, the United Nations has published the Human Development Index (HDI) as a ranking of the development of nations. The HDI is a composite of three variables: life expectancy, educational attainment, and income. A nation's HDI score, an average of the sum of the three variables, has a maximum possible value of 1. In constructing the HDI, researchers arbitrarily designated the 47 nations with HDI scores above .793 as very high in human development (see Table 18.1). Nations classified as high, between .698 and .783, numbered 48, while the 47 nations between .522 and .698 were noted as medium. The 46 countries below .522 were identified as low in human development.

The HDI demonstrates that nations with somewhat lower incomes are nonetheless able to sustain longevity and mount educational programs. Cuba's per capita GDP is one-fourth percent that of Saudi Arabia, yet Cubans enjoy greater longevity and more educational opportunity than Saudis. Still, the HDI is a less than optimal classification. An important qualification is that nations evidence significant

TABLE 18.1 Human Development Index

HDI Rank	Human Development Index (HDI) Value	Life Expectancy at Birth (Years)	Mean Years of Schooling (Years)	Expected Years of Schooling (Years)	Gross National Income (GNI) Per Capita (Constant 2005 PPP$)
	2011	2011	2011[a]	2011[a]	2011
VERY HIGH HUMAN DEVELOPMENT					
1. Norway	0.943	81.1	12.6	17.3	47,557
2. Australia	0.929	81.9	12.0	18.0	34,431
3. Netherlands	0.910	80.7	11.6[b]	16.8	36,402
4. United States	0.910	78.5	12.4	16.0	43,017
5. New Zealand	0.908	80.7	12.5	18.0	23,737
6. Canada	0.908	81.0	12.1[b]	16.0	35,166
7. Ireland	0.908	80.6	11.6	18.0	29,322
8. Liechtenstein	0.905	79.6	10.3[c]	14.7	83,717[d]
9. Germany	0.905	80.4	12.2[b]	15.9	34,854
10. Sweden	0.904	81.4	11.7[b]	15.7	35,837
11. Switzerland	0.903	82.3	11.0[b]	15.6	39,924
12. Japan	0.901	83.4	11.6[b]	15.1	32,295
13. Hong Kong, China (SAR)	0.898	82.8	10.0	15.7	44,805
14. Iceland	0.898	81.8	10.4	18.0	29,354
15. Korea, Republic of	0.897	80.6	11.6[b]	16.9	28,230
16. Denmark	0.895	78.8	11.4[b]	16.9	28,320
17. Israel	0.888	81.6	11.9	15.5	25,849
18. Belgium	0.886	80.0	10.9[b]	16.1	33,357
19. Austria	0.885	80.9	10.8[b]	15.3	35,719
20. France	0.884	81.5	10.6[b]	16.1	30,462
21. Slovenia	0.884	79.3	11.6[b]	16.9	24,914
22. Finland	0.882	80.0	10.3	16.8	32,438
23. Spain	0.878	81.4	10.4[b]	16.6	26,508
24. Italy	0.874	81.9	10.1[b]	16.3	26,484
25. Luxembourg	0.867	80.0	10.1	13.3	50,557
26. Singapore	0.866	81.1	8.8[b]	14.4[e]	52,569
27. Czech Republic	0.865	77.7	12.3	15.6	21,405
28. United Kingdom	0.863	80.2	9.3	16.1	33,296
29. Greece	0.861	79.9	10.1[b]	16.5	23,747
30. United Arab Emirates	0.846	76.5	9.3	13.3	59,993
31. Cyprus	0.840	79.6	9.8	14.7	24,841
32. Andorra	0.838	80.9	10.4[f]	11.5	36,095[g]
33. Brunei Darussalam	0.838	78.0	8.6	14.1	45,753

(Continued)

TABLE 18.1 (*Continued*)

HDI Rank	Human Development Index (HDI) Value	Life Expectancy at Birth (Years)	Mean Years of Schooling (Years)	Expected Years of Schooling (Years)	Gross National Income (GNI) Per Capita (Constant 2005 PPP$)
34. Estonia	0.835	74.8	12.0	15.7	16,799
35. Slovakia	0.834	75.4	11.6	14.9	19,998
36. Malta	0.832	79.6	9.9	14.4	21,460
37. Qatar	0.831	78.4	7.3	12.0	107,721
38. Hungary	0.816	74.4	11.1[b]	15.3	16,581
39. Poland	0.813	76.1	10.0[b]	15.3	17,451
40. Lithuania	0.810	72.2	10.9	16.1	16,234
41. Portugal	0.809	79.5	7.7	15.9	20,573
42. Bahrain	0.806	75.1	9.4	13.4	28,169
43. Latvia	0.805	73.3	11.5[b]	15.0	14,293
44. Chile	0.805	79.1	9.7	14.7	13,329
45. Argentina	0.797	75.9	9.3	15.8	14,527
46. Croatia	0.796	76.6	9.8[b]	13.9	15,729
47. Barbados	0.793	76.8	9.3	13.4[h]	17,966
HIGH HUMAN DEVELOPMENT					
48. Uruguay	0.783	77.0	8.5[b]	15.5	13,242
49. Palau	0.782	71.8	12.1[i]	14.7	9,744[j,k]
50. Romania	0.781	74.0	10.4	14.9	11,046
51. Cuba	0.776	79.1	9.9	17.5	5,416[l]
52. Seychelles	0.773	73.6	9.4[m]	13.3	16,729
53. Bahamas	0.771	75.6	8.5[m]	12.0	23,029[n]
54. Montenegro	0.771	74.6	10.6	13.7[h]	10,361[o]
55. Bulgaria	0.771	73.4	10.6[b]	13.7	11,412
56. Saudi Arabia	0.770	73.9	7.8	13.7	23,274
57. Mexico	0.770	73.9	7.8	13.7	11,412
58. Panama	0.768	76.1	9.4	13.2	12,335
59. Serbia	0.766	74.5	10.2[b]	13.7	10,236
60. Antigua and Barbuda	0.764	72.6	8.9[h]	14.0	15,521
61. Malaysia	0.761	74.2	9.5	12.6	13,685
62. Trinidad and Tobago	0.760	70.1	9.2	12.3	23,439[p]
63. Kuwait	0.760	74.6	6.1	12.3	47,926
64. Libya	0.760	74.8	7.3	16.6	12,637[q]
65. Belarus	0.756	70.3	9.3[r]	14.6	13,439
66. Russian Federation	0.755	68.8	9.8	14.1	14,561
67. Grenada	0.748	76.0	8.6	16.0	6,982
68. Kazakhstan	0.745	67.0	10.4	15.1	10,585

TABLE 18.1 (*Continued*)

HDI Rank	Human Development Index (HDI) Value	Life Expectancy at Birth (Years)	Mean Years of Schooling (Years)	Expected Years of Schooling (Years)	Gross National Income (GNI) Per Capita (Constant 2005 PPP$)
69. Costa Rica	0.744	79.3	8.3	11.7	10,497
70. Albania	0.739	76.9	10.4	11.3	7,803
71. Lebanon	0.739	72.6	7.9m	13.8	13,076
72. Saint Kitts and Nevis	0.735	73.1	8.4	12.9	11,897
73. Venezuela, Bolivarian Republic of	0.735	74.4	7.6b	14.2	10,656
74. Bosnia and Herzegovina	0.733	75.7	8.7r	13.6	7,664
75. Georgia	0.733	73.7	12.1r	13.1	4,780
76. Ukraine	0.729	68.5	11.3	14.7	6,175
77. Mauritius	0.728	73.4	7.2	13.6	12,918
78. Former Yugoslav Republic of Macedonia	0.728	74.8	8.2r	13.3	8,804
79. Jamaica	0.727	73.1	9.6	13.8	6,487
80. Peru	0.725	74.0	8.7	12.9	8,389
81. Dominica	0.724	77.5	7.7m	13.2	7,889
82. Saint Lucia	0.723	74.6	8.3	13.1	8,273
83. Ecuador	0.720	75.6	7.6	14.0	7,589
84. Brazil	0.718	73.5	7.2	13.8	10,162
85. Saint Vincent and the Grenadines	0.717	72.3	8.6	13.2	8,013
86. Armenia	0.716	74.2	10.8	12.0	5,188
87. Colombia	0.710	73.7	7.3	13.6	8,315
88. Iran, Islamic Republic of	0.707	73.0	7.3	12.7	10,164
89. Oman	0.705	73.0	5.5m	11.8	22,841
90. Tonga	0.704	72.3	10.3b	13.7	4,186
91. Azerbaijan	0.700	70.7	8.6m	11.8	8,666
92. Turkey	0.699	74.0	6.5	11.8	12,246
93. Belize	0.699	76.1	8.0b	12.4	5,812
94. Tunisia	0.698	74.5	6.5	14.5	7,281
MEDIUM HUMAN DEVELOPMENT					
95. Jordan	0.698	73.4	8.6	13.1	5,300
96. Algeria	0.698	73.1	7.0	13.6	7,658
97. Sri Lanka	0.691	74.9	8.2	12.7	4,943
98. Dominican Republic	0.689	73.4	7.2b	11.9	8,087
99. Samoa	0.688	72.4	10.3m	12.3	3,931s

(*Continued*)

TABLE 18.1 (*Continued*)

HDI Rank	Human Development Index (HDI) Value	Life Expectancy at Birth (Years)	Mean Years of Schooling (Years)	Expected Years of Schooling (Years)	Gross National Income (GNI) Per Capita (Constant 2005 PPP$)
100. Fiji	0.688	69.2	10.7[b]	13.0	4,145
101. China	0.687	73.5	7.5	11.6	7,476
102. Turkmenistan	0.686	65.0	9.9[l]	12.5[h]	7,306
103. Thailand	0.682	74.1	6.6	12.3	7,694
104. Suriname	0.680	70.6	7.2[r]	12.6	7,538
105. El Salvador	0.674	72.2	7.5	12.1	5,925
106. Gabon	0.674	62.7	7.5	13.1	12,249
107. Paraguay	0.664	72.5	7.7	12.1	4,727
108. Bolivia, Plurinational State of	0.663	66.6	9.2	13.7	4,054
109. Maldives	0.661	76.8	5.8[b]	12.4	5,276
110. Mongolia	0.653	68.5	8.3	14.1	3,391
111. Moldova, Republic of	0.649	69.3	9.7	11.9	3,058
112. Philippines	0.644	68.7	8.9[b]	11.9	3,478
113. Egypt	0.644	73.2	6.4	11.0	5,269
114. Occupied Palestinian Territory	0.641	72.8	8.0[m]	12.7	2,656[k,t]
115. Uzbekistan	0.641	68.3	10.0[r]	11.4	2,967
116. Micronesia, Federated States of	0.636	69.0	8.8[l]	12.1[u]	2,935[v]
117. Guyana	0.633	69.9	8.0	11.9	3,192
118. Botswana	0.633	53.2	8.9	12.2	13,049
119. Syrian Arab Republic	0.632	75.9	5.7[b]	11.3	4,243
120. Namibia	0.625	62.5	7.4	11.6	6,206
121. Honduras	0.625	73.1	6.5	11.4	3,443
122. Kiribati	0.624	68.1	7.8	12.1	3,140
123. South Africa	0.619	52.8	8.5[b]	13.1	9,469
124. Indonesia	0.617	69.4	5.8	13.2	3,716
125. Vanuatu	0.617	71.0	6.7	10.4	3,950
126. Kyrgyzstan	0.615	67.7	9.3	12.5	2,036
127. Tajikistan	0.607	67.5	9.8	11.4	1,937
128. Vietnam	0.593	75.2	5.5	10.4	2,805
129. Nicaragua	0.589	74.0	5.8	10.8	2,430
130. Morocco	0.582	72.2	4.4	10.3	4,196
131. Guatemala	0.574	71.2	4.1	10.6	4,167
132. Iraq	0.573	69.0	5.6	9.8	3,177

TABLE 18.1 (*Continued*)

HDI Rank	Human Development Index (HDI) Value	Life Expectancy at Birth (Years)	Mean Years of Schooling (Years)	Expected Years of Schooling (Years)	Gross National Income (GNI) Per Capita (Constant 2005 PPP$)
133. Cape Verde	0.568	74.2	3.5[i]	11.6	3,402
134. India	0.547	65.4	4.4	10.3	3,468
135. Ghana	0.541	64.2	7.1	10.5	1,584
136. Equatorial Guinea	0.537	51.1	5.4[r]	7.7	17,608
137. Congo	0.533	57.4	5.9	10.5	3,066
138. Lao People's Democratic Republic	0.524	67.5	4.6	9.2	2,242
139. Cambodia	0.523	63.1	5.8	9.8	1,848
140. Swaziland	0.522	48.7	7.1	10.6	4,484
141. Bhutan	0.522	67.2	2.3[r]	11.0[u]	5,293
LOW HUMAN DEVELOPMENT					
142. Solomon Islands	0.510	67.9	4.5[i]	9.1	1,782
143. Kenya	0.509	57.1	7.0	11.0	1,492
144. São Tomé and Principe	0.509	64.7	4.2[i]	10.8	1,792
145. Pakistan	0.504	65.4	4.9	6.9	2,550
146. Bangladesh	0.500	68.9	4.8	8.1	1,529
147. Timor-Leste	0.495	62.5	2.8[i]	11.2	3,005
148. Angola	0.486	51.1	4.4[r]	9.1	4,874
149. Myanmar	0.483	65.2	4.0	9.2	1,535
150. Cameroon	0.482	51.6	5.9	10.3	2,031
151. Madagascar	0.480	66.7	5.2[i]	10.7	824
152. Tanzania, United Republic of	0.466	58.2	5.1	9.1	1,328
153. Papua New Guinea	0.466	62.8	4.3	5.8	2,271
154. Yemen	0.462	65.5	2.5	8.6	2,213
155. Senegal	0.459	59.3	4.5	7.5	1,708
156. Nigeria	0.459	51.9	5.0[r]	8.9	2,069
157. Nepal	0.458	68.8	3.2	8.8	1,160
158. Haiti	0.454	62.1	4.9	7.6[u]	1,123
159. Mauritania	0.453	58.6	3.7	8.1	1,859
160. Lesotho	0.450	48.2	5.9[b]	9.9	1,664
161. Uganda	0.446	54.1	4.7	10.8	1,124
162. Togo	0.435	57.1	5.3	9.6	798
163. Comoros	0.433	61.1	2.8[i]	10.7	1,079
164. Zambia	0.430	49.0	6.5	7.9	1,254

(*Continued*)

TABLE 18.1 (*Continued*)

HDI Rank	Human Development Index (HDI) Value	Life Expectancy at Birth (Years)	Mean Years of Schooling (Years)	Expected Years of Schooling (Years)	Gross National Income (GNI) Per Capita (Constant 2005 PPP$)
165. Djibouti	0.430	57.9	3.8[r]	5.1	2,335
166. Rwanda	0.429	55.4	3.3	11.1	1,133
167. Benin	0.427	56.1	3.3	9.2	1,364
168. Gambia	0.420	58.5	2.8	9.0	1,282
169. Sudan	0.408	61.5	3.1	4.4	1,894
170. Côte d'Ivoire	0.400	55.4	3.3	6.3	1,387[p]
171. Malawi	0.400	54.2	4.2	8.9	753
172. Afghanistan	0.398	48.7	3.3	9.1	1,416
173. Zimbabwe	0.376	51.4	7.2	9.9	376[n]
174. Ethiopia	0.363	59.3	1.5[i]	8.5	971
175. Mali	0.359	51.4	2.0[b]	8.3	1,123
176. Guinea-Bissau	0.353	48.1	2.3[r]	9.1	994
177. Eritrea	0.349	61.6	3.4	4.8	536
178. Guinea	0.344	54.1	1.6[w]	8.6	863
179. Central African Republic	0.343	48.4	3.5	6.6	707
180. Sierra Leone	0.336	47.8	2.9	7.2	737
181. Burkina Faso	0.331	55.4	1.3[r]	6.3	1,141
182. Liberia	0.329	56.8	3.9	11.0	265
183. Chad	0.328	49.6	1.5[i]	7.2	1,105
184. Mozambique	0.322	50.2	1.2	9.2	89.8
185. Burundi	0.316	50.4	2.7	10.5	368
186. Niger	0.295	54.7	1.4	4.9	641
187. Congo, Democratic Republic of the	0.286	48.4	3.5	8.2	280
REGIONS					
Arab States	0.641	70.5	5.9	10.2	8,554
East Asia and the Pacific	0.671	72.4	7.2	11.7	6,466
Europe and Central Asia	0.751	71.3	9.7	13.4	12,004
Latin America and the Caribbean	0.731	74.4	7.8	13.6	10,119
South Asia	0.548	65.9	4.6	9.8	3,435
Sub-Saharan Africa	0.463	54.4	4.5	9.2	1,966
Least Developed Countries	0.439	59.1	3.7	8.3	1,327
World	0.682	69.8	7.4	11.3	10,082

Notes:

[a]Data refer to 2011 or the most recent year available.

[b]Updated by HDRO based on UNESCO (2011) data.

TABLE 18.1 (*Continued*)

cAssumes the same adult mean years of schooling as Switzerland before the most recent update.

dEstimated using the purchasing power parity (PPP) and projected growth rate of Switzerland.

eCalculated by the Singapore Ministry of Education.

fAssumes the same adult mean years of schooling as Spain before the most recent update.

gEstimated using the PPP and projected growth rate of Spain.

hBased on cross-country regression.

iBased on data on years of schooling of adults from household surveys from World Bank (2010).

jBased on UNESCAP (2011) and UNDESA (2011) projected growth rates.

kBased on unpublished estimates from the World Bank.

lPPP estimate based on cross-country regression; projected growth rate based on ECLAC (2011) and UNDESA (2011) projected growth rates.

mBased on UNESCO (2011) estimates of education attainment distribution.

nBased on PPP data from IMF (2011).

oBased on EBRD (2011) and UNDESA (2011) projected growth rates.

pBased on World Bank (2011b).

qBased on OECD and others (2011) and UNDESA (2011) projected growth rates.

rBased on data from UNICEF (2000–2010).

sBased on ADB (2011) projected growth rate.

tBased on UNESCWA (2011) and UNDESA (2011) projected growth rates.

uRefers to primary and secondary education only. United Nations Educational, Scientific and Cultural Organization Institute for Statistics estimate.

vBased on ADB (2011) and UNDESA (2011) projected growth rates.

wBased on data from ICF Macro (2011).

DEFINITIONS

Human Development Index (HDI): A composite index measuring average achievement in three basic dimensions of human development—a long and healthy life, knowledge, and a decent standard of living. See *Technical note 1* for details on how the HDI is calculated.

Life expectancy at birth: Number of years a newborn infant could expect to live if prevailing patterns of age-specific mortality rates at the time of birth stay the same throughout the infant's life.

Mean years of schooling: Average number of years of education received by people ages 25 and older, converted from education attainment levels using official durations of each level.

Expected years of schooling: Number of years of schooling that a child of school entrance age can expect to receive if prevailing patterns of age-specific enrolment rates persist throughout the child's life.

Gross national income (GNI) per capita: Aggregate income of an economy generated by its production and its ownership of factors of production, less the incomes paid for the use of factors of production owned by the rest of the world, converted to international dollars using purchasing power parity (PPP) rates, divided by midyear population.

GNI per capita rank minus HDI rank: Difference in rankings by GNI per capita and by the HDI. A negative value means that the country is better ranked by GNI than by the HDI.

Nonincome HDI: Value of the HDI computed from the life expectancy and education indicators only.

MAIN DATA SOURCES

Column 1: HDRO calculations based on data from UNDESA (2011), Barro and Lee (2010b), UNESCO Institute for Statistics (2011), World Bank (2011a), UNSD (2011), and IMF (2011).

Column 2: UNDESA (2011).

Column 3: HDRO updates of Barro and Lee (2010b) estimates based on UNESCO Institute for Statistics data on education attainment (2011) and Barro and Lee (2010a) methodology.

Column 4: UNESCO Institute for Statistics (2011).

Column 5: HDRO calculations based on data from World Bank (2011a), IMF (2011), and UNSD (2011).

variations internally that are not registered by the national HDI score. Ordinarily, national capitals, industrial cities, and ports elevate a nation's HDI score; rural and remote areas have a depressive effect. Although the "medium" developing nations rank higher than those ranked "low," the rural areas of the "medium" HDI-scoring nations tend to parallel those nations that rank lowest.

The Fourth World

To address important issues related to social progress, the United Nations developed other indices to assess national development. A Human Poverty Index incorporates nations' percentages of people not expected to reach age 40, percentages of illiterate adults, the resources nations have available in the form of health services and safe water, and percentages of underweight children under age 5. A general indicator of entrenched poverty is the percentage of a nation's population living on less than $1.25 per day. Table 18.2 ranks nations according to the percentage of their population living on less than $1.25 per day.

That so many remained in abject poverty despite global prosperity prompted a rigorous debate about development efforts in the Fourth World. Jeffrey Sachs proposed a global strategy for ending

poverty by 2025, expanding on the United Nations' Millennium Development Goals. Sachs suggested a range of minimum standards:

- Primary education for all children
- Adequate nutrition for vulnerable populations
- Access to antimalarial bed nets
- Access to potable water and sanitation
- A half kilometer of paved road per 1,000 population
- Access to cooking fuels and stoves that reduce indoor pollution

Adopting the United Nations' expectation that developed nations dedicate 0.7 percent of gross national product (GNP) for foreign aid, Sachs calculated that ending global poverty by 2025 could cost $124 billion.[25] The agenda set forth by Sachs received notoriety once it was endorsed by Bono and other celebrities.

Within a year, another developmental economist, William Easterly, published a rebuttal to "the Plan," the attempt by elite planners, such as Sachs, from developed nations to dictate the route to prosperity for citizens in developing nations. "The Big Plans are attractive to politicians, celebrities, and activists who want to make a big splash, without the Western public realizing that those plans at the top are not connected to the reality at the bottom," Easterly wrote. Too often, Easterly argued, the best of intentions on the part of experts from the West are sabotaged by circumstances of "the Rest," citing antimalarial mosquito nets that are diverted to the black market where they are sold for wedding veils and fishing nets.[26] Instead of planners formulating, implementing, and evaluating development projects from afar, Easterly stated a preference for "searchers," development experts whose ideas spring organically from the circumstances of indigent populations. "The aid agencies would be forced to act as social entrepreneurs, trying to offer innovative services that would prove attractive to the poor."[27]

Inevitably, the debate degenerated into an ideological polemic with liberals favoring Sachs and conservatives supporting Easterly; an unfortunate development because both had valid points to make with respect to traditional development strategies. A more strategic analysis by Paul Collier appeared in 2007. Collier contended that the bottom billion should be the focus of aid because of four traps: chronic civil conflict, the discovery of natural resources, being geographically landlocked, and having corrupt governance. Under these

TABLE 18.2 Top Ten Nations with Population Living on Less Than $1.25 per Day

Rank	Nation	% Living on Less Than $1.25/day
1	Liberia	83.7
2	Burundi	81.3
3	Rwanda	76.8
4	Malawi	73.9
5	Tanzania	67.9
6	Madagascar	67.8
7	Nigeria	64.4
8	Zambia	64.3
9	Central African Republic	62.8
10	Swaziland	61.9

Source: Adapted from United Nations, Multidimensional Poverty: http://hdr.undp.org/en/media/HDR_2011_EN_Table5.pdf, downloaded January 25, 2012.

circumstances, neither Sachs's nor Easterly's strategies are likely to address the needs of the most impoverished people on the planet. Massive aid from developed nations becomes a spoil for corrupt and inept governments of developing nations and local projects are insufficiently coordinated or funded to rise to the scale necessary to reverse protracted poverty. Instead, Collier calls for a series of international charters—a social contract on development—agreements between donor nations and developing nations which structure development:

- A charter for natural resources designed to optimize transparency in extraction contracts, even out economic fluctuations, and set aside revenues for future generations
- A charter for democracy that would not only assure fair elections but would also institute the civil institutions necessary for checks and balances in decision making
- A charter for budget transparency that would identify how funds are to be appropriated as well as track the outcomes of expenditures
- A charter for postconflict situations that would establish institutions and procedures for the reconciliation of disputes
- A charter for investment that would preclude populist dictators from confiscating private holdings

In addition to development charters, Collier concedes that innovations are necessary to aid the most destitute, such as "independent service authorities," an alternative network of basic services for the poor.

> The authority would be a wholesale organization for purchasing basic services, buying some from local governments, some from nongovernmental organizations (NGOs), such as churches, and some from private firms. It would finance not just the building of schools and clinics but also their day-to-day operations. Once such an organization was put into place, managed jointly by government, donors, and civil society, both donors and government would channel money through it.[28]

So configured, such an authority would be similar to an airport or port authority in a developed nation.

Few would dispute the validity of Sachs's contention that the developed world could contribute more for development, or Easterly's insistence on projects that have immediate relevance for the poor;

Collier provides an essential third component of reform: infrastructure. The reassessment of development accounts, at least in part, for the Millennium Challenge Account initiative launched by the George W. Bush administration. Initially budgeted at $5 billion per year, those developing countries that meet minimal standards of good governance are eligible for special assistance. During a 2008 trip to Tanzania, Bush announced one of the largest grants, $698 million over five years, primarily for schools, roads, and utilities.[29] Unfortunately, Congressional reluctance to fund the initiative has left it between $1.2 billion and $1.8 billion—insufficient to realize its objectives.[30] Subsequent military incursions into Iraq and Afghanistan subtracted from U.S. development efforts. Jeffrey Sachs criticized the Obama administration for spending $100 billion for fighting the Taliban in Afghanistan, yet appropriating only $10 billion for the poorest in Africa.[31]

Capability Poverty

The idea that development is a multifaceted phenomenon has eclipsed a more circumscribed notion based on simple economic parameters. Using the HDI as a basis, development researchers began to evolve a more inclusive and dynamic understanding of authentic progress and to promulgate the idea of "capability poverty." The philosophical rationale for capability poverty was stated fully by Amartya Sen, who noted two profound historical truths: There are no records of famine within democratic societies, nor are there instances of wars waged between them. Rather, these most severe events can be attributed to nondemocratic decision making that excludes large groups of people, who then bear the brunt of flawed policies. Sen's contention that freedom was a precondition of development, not a byproduct to be enjoyed long after industrialization, earned him the Nobel Prize in economics in 1998.

The capability approach to development advocates "the expansion of the 'capabilities' of persons to lead the kind of lives they value—and have reason to value," Sen proposed, "Greater freedom enhances the ability of people to help themselves and also to influence the world, and these matters are central to the process of development."[32] Logically, however, deprivation of elemental requirements of survival subverts the possibility of full social participation, as do inadequate institutions that deny education, health, and recreation to subgroups. In constructing

Among the 10 elements of a capability approach is play—
enjoying activities that are entertaining and rejuvenating.

Source: saurabhpbhoyar/Shutterstock

his argument for a "support-led process," Sen di-
verged with proponents of an economic model in
which health, education, and labor benefits were
viewed as being secondary. He contended that:

> [T]he success of the support-led process as a route
> [to development] does indicate that a country
> need not wait until it is much richer (through
> what may be a long period of economic growth)
> before embarking on rapid expansion of basic
> education and health care. The quality of life can
> be vastly raised, despite low incomes, through an
> adequate program of social services. The fact that
> education and health care are also productive in
> raising economic growth adds to the argument
> for putting major emphasis on these social ar-
> rangements in poor economies, without having to
> wait for "getting rich" first.[33]

Sen's path-breaking work was soon elaborated
by his colleague, Martha Nussbaum. In *Women*

and Human Development, Nussbaum states the
philosophical rationale for an absolute standard
of social justice for the most chronically oppressed
among the world's poor: women. "The core idea is
that of the human being as a dignified free being
who shapes his or her own life in cooperation and
reciprocity with others, rather than being passively
shaped or pushed around by the world in the manner of a 'flock' or 'herd' animal," contends Nussbaum. "A life that is really human is one that is
shaped throughout by these human powers of practical reason and sociability."[34] Thus, optimal development is not only freedom from want but also
the full enjoyment of a range of social and political
opportunities. Nussbaum lists 10 elements of a capability approach to development (see Figure 18.1).

So formulated, the capability approach to development provides a blueprint for achieving and
maintaining progress. This approach is particularly
compelling in an era of rapid international changes
attributable to shifts in capital, production, and labor.
"Especially in an era of rapid economic globalization,
the capabilities approach is urgently needed to give
moral substance and moral constraints to processes
that are occurring all around us without sufficient
moral reflection," Nussbaum concludes. "It may be
hoped that the capabilities list will steer the process
of globalization, giving it a rich set of human goals
and a vivid sense of human waste and tragedy, when
choices are pondered that would otherwise be made
with only narrow economic considerations in view."[35]

Among the most compelling issues in international social welfare has been the status of women.
Notably in traditional, rural cultures, women's
opportunities have been circumscribed, but their
options have also been attenuated in wealthy, industrialized nations. In this respect, the United Nations
calculated the extent to which nations optimize opportunities for women. Unlike most components of
development, women's status does not necessarily
parallel national prosperity. This has been particularly evident within the Arab world where women
do not enjoy the same opportunities as their sisters
in other nations. For example, the Gender Empowerment Measure of Saudi Arabia (.254), Egypt
(.263), and Yemen (.129) is approximately half the
HDI ranking of comparable nations.[36]

Thus, empowering women generates significant
development outcomes. Improving the economic,
educational, and health of women is associated
with a 25 percent reduction in the mortality rate of
children since 1990,[37] and a fourfold drop in the
maternal death rate since 1980.[38] When multiple

1. **Life.** Being able to live to the end of a human life of normal length; not dying prematurely, or before one's life is so reduced as to be not worth living.

2. **Bodily Health.** Being able to have good health, including reproductive health; to be adequately nourished; to have adequate shelter.

3. **Bodily Integrity.** Being able to move freely from place to place; to be secure against violent assault, including sexual assault and domestic violence; having opportunities for sexual satisfaction and for choice in matters of reproduction.

4. **Senses, Imagination, and Thought.** Being able to use the senses, to imagine, think, and reason—and to do these things in a "truly human" way, a way informed and cultivated by an adequate education, including, but by no means limited to, literacy and basic mathematical and scientific training. Being able to use imagination and thought in connection with experiencing and producing works and events of one's own choice, religious, literary, musical, and so forth. Being able to use one's mind in ways protected by guarantees of freedom of expression with respect to both political and artistic speech, and freedom of religious exercise. Being able to have pleasurable experiences and to avoid non-beneficial pain.

5. **Emotions.** Being able to have attachments to things and people outside ourselves; to love those who love and care for us, to grieve at their absence; in general, to love, to grieve, to experience longing, gratitude, and justified anger. Not having one's emotional development blighted by fear and anxiety. (Supporting this capability means supporting forms of human association that can be shown to be crucial in their development.)

6. **Practical Reason.** Being able to form a conception of the good and to engage in critical reflection about the planning of one's life. (This entails protection for the liberty of conscience and religious observance.)

7. **Affiliation.**

   A. Being able to live with and toward others, to recognize and show concern for other human beings, to engage in various forms of social interaction; to be able to imagine the situation of another. (Protecting this capability means protecting institutions that constitute and nourish such forms of affiliation, and also protecting the freedom of assembly and political speech.)

   B. Having the social bases of self-respect and non-humiliation; being able to be treated as a dignified being whose worth is equal to that of others. This entails provisions of non-discrimination on the basis of race, sex, sexual orientation, ethnicity, caste, religion, and national origin.

8. **Other Species** Being able to live with concern for and in relation to animals, plants, and the world of nature.

9. **Play.** Being able to laugh, to play, to enjoy recreational activities.

10. **Control over One's Environment.**

   A. **Political.** Being able to participate effectively in political choices that govern one's life; having the right of political participation, protections of free speech and association.

   B. **Material.** Being able to hold property (both land and movable goods), and having property rights on an equal basis with others; having the right to seek employment on an equal basis with others; having the freedom from unwarranted search and seizure. In work, being able to work as a human being, exercising practical reason and entering into meaningful relationships of mutual recognition with other workers.[39]

FIGURE 18.1 The Central Human Capabilities

development strategies were engaged in a small Kenyan village as part of Jeffrey Sachs's Millennium Village initiative in Africa, the child mortality rate dropped 30 percent.[40]

At the national level, female representation in the legislature is likely to generate pro-family policies. While 16.8 percent of Congressional seats are occupied by women, the national legislatures of other countries are more likely to be held by women: Sweden, 46.4 percent; South Africa, 44.5 percent; Cuba, 43.2 percent; Germany 32.6 percent; China, 21.3 percent; Britain, 19.5 percent; France 18.9 percent, but only 16.8 percent in the United States.[41]

International Aid

Historically, intergovernmental transfers have accounted for most foreign aid, although other intermediaries are being employed with increasing frequency. The recent performance of the industrialized nations demonstrates several trends in international aid. Foremost, nations with the largest economies, notably Japan and the United States, lag behind smaller industrialized nations with respect to the percentage of GNP committed to international aid. The Scandinavian welfare states have consistently demonstrated international citizenship superior to that of the more laissez-faire economies. Compounding this pattern has been a downward trend in allocations for international aid. Since 1990, international aid from national governments dropped only to rebound in response to the adverse effects of the global recession on developing nations; for 2010 development aid totaled $129 billion, an increase of 6.5 percent over 2009.[42] Since government developmental aid has been uneven over the decades, reliance has increased on private NGOs and on quangos (quasi-NGOs) such as the World Bank, the International Monetary Fund (IMF), and regional development banks. Although the United States is the largest donor, not only is its percent GNP allotted to international aid the lowest among industrialized nations, but that ratio has roughly halved since the mid-1980s (see Table 18.3).

TABLE 18.3 Net Official Development Assistance Disbursed, as a Percentage of Gross National Income, 2010 and 2005

Rank	Nation	Total (millions)	% of GNP 2010	% of GNP 2005
1	Norway	$ 4,582	1.10	.94
2	Luxembourg	399	1.09	.82
3	Sweden	4,527	.97	.94
4	Denmark	2,867	.90	.81
5	Netherlands	6,351	.81	.82
6	Belgium	3,000	.64	.53
7	United Kingdom	13,763	56	.47
8	Finland	1,335	.55	.65
9	Ireland	895	.53	.42
10	France	12,916	.50	.47
11	Spain	5,917	.43	.27
12	Switzerland	2,295	.41	.44
13	Germany	12,723	.38	.36
14	Canada	5,132	.33	.34
15	Australia	3,849	.32	.25
16	Austria	1,199	.32	.52
17	Portugal	648	.29	.24
18	New Zealand	353	.26	.27
19	United States	30,154	.21	.22
20	Japan	11,045	.20	.28
21	Greece	500	.17	.17
22	Italy	3,111	.15	.29
23	Korea	1,168	.12	—

Source: Adapted from http://www.oecd.org/dataoecd/54/41/47515917.pdf, downloaded January 27, 2012.

Global Capital

The foundation for global markets was laid after World War II with an international agreement for currency stabilization and debt financing that was negotiated at Bretton Woods, New Hampshire. The Bretton Woods agreement established the IMF, an international agency accountable to its member nations. With the expansion of capital to overseas markets during the 1960s, the IMF initiated a program of Special Drawing Rights (SDRs) or loans that encouraged expansionary policies in developing nations. This program, however, collided with the acute economic contraction of the 1970s due to the oil embargo, driving much of the developing world into severe debt. Subsequent IMF policies to restructure debt payments have stressed "conditionalities," or internal economic reforms, often requiring controversial reductions in domestic spending for health, education, and related social programs.

The World Bank, also accountable to its member nations, provides resources to enhance infrastructure, initially through the International Bank for Reconstruction and Development (IBRD). Following the dramatic success of the Marshall Plan that rebuilt postwar Europe, the World Bank instituted the International Development Association (IDA) in 1960 to redirect activities to developing nations. Focusing on the poorest nations, World Bank aid is often in the form of credits, long-term loans that are interest-free.[43]

Both the IMF and World Bank presume that international markets will be a means for development, a strategy that, although markedly successful for industrialized nations, has been less so for developing nations. With the demise of state socialism, international markets have, nonetheless, become the primary means for economic growth of the Third World. Two entities have facilitated this growth: The General Agreement on Tariffs and Trade (GATT), established in 1947, enjoyed only modest success in reducing tariffs until 1967, but in that year, impediments against international trade were cut drastically. Moreover, in 1995 the World Trade Organization (WTO) was created to accelerate the emergence of global markets, augmenting GATT. Since then, membership in GATT/WTO has increased dramatically. Between 1980 and 1999 the number of GATT member nations increased from 85 to 134. Globalization has accelerated with the increasing flow of private capital into developing nations. Indeed, although direct foreign investment slowed subsequent to the global recession, in 2010 it totaled over $360 billion, more than twice direct government aid.[44]

The Future

Although the unprecedented expansion of global markets has furthered economic growth internationally, the benefits have not been evenly distributed. During the last decades of the twentieth century, the per capita GDP of the most-developed one-third of nations increased significantly; in contrast, that of the middle-third dropped from 12.5 to 11.4 percent, and that of the lowest-third fell from 3.1 to 1.9 percent. "Such findings are of great concern," observed authors of the World Bank's development report, "because they show how difficult it is for poor countries to close the gap with their wealthier counterparts."[45] Thus, in 2000 Millennium Development Goals (MDGs) were established, providing benchmarks against which to measure development objectives. Approaching 2015, the number of people subsisting on less than $1.25 per day is expected to fall to 883 million, significantly less than 1.4 billion in 2005. In addition, targets for the provision of primary education for both genders as well as the availability of safe drinking water are about to be reached. On the other hand, health and sanitation objectives are unlikely to be achieved. Significantly, the MDG strategy has not been even throughout the developing world; much of these accomplishments are due to unprecedented development in China and India, while the nations of sub-Saharan Africa continue to fall behind.[46]

Specific initiatives have defined international development during the past half-century, while others are emergent: Microcredit, introduced with the founding of the Grameen Bank in the late 1970s, enjoyed wide popularity in following decades, earning its founder, Muhammad Yunus the 2006 Nobel Peace Prize. Using social collateral in the form of group lending and adherence to a moral code, the 16 decisions, Grameen not only loaned $11.5 billion dollars to 3.7 million poor families in 2010, but achieved a repayment rate exceeding 96 percent. Early in its inception, over several loan cycles most Grameen borrowers were able to invest in business activities that, however modest, allowed them to escape poverty.[47]

Three decades later, however, cracks were evident in the microcredit façade. Having pioneered the lending model, Grameen was imitated by nonprofits that transferred microcredit to Africa and Latin America, in the process demonstrating that the scale of the nascent capital market of the world's poorest communities exceeded $60 billion. By 2011, commercial lenders, such as the Indian company SKS Microcredit, were becoming publicly traded corporations, generating millions of dollars in profits for owners and investors.[48] Meanwhile, a chorus of critics alleged that microcredit loans carried interest rates that many borrowers were unable to repay, sometimes exceeding 100 percent annually; as a result microcredit borrowers took out additional loans to service existing loans.[49] In Bangladesh, Yunus antagonized the government by threatening to form a political party, and the Prime Minister accused Grameen of laundering a $100 million grant from Norway.[50] Threatened by government regulation of microcredit and borrowers' withholding payments, microcredit organizations vowed to reinvent themselves to serve their clientele in a manner that was responsible and accountable. "We created microcredit to fight the loan sharks," Yunus said, "we didn't create microcredit to encourage new loan sharks."[51]

Field experiments, considered the gold standard of research in the First World, have only recently been introduced in developing countries, largely due to the insistence of Esther Duflo and Abhijit Banerjee who co-founded MIT's Abdul Latif Jameel Poverty Action Lab (J-PAL) in 2003. One of Duflo's earliest experiments involved absentee teachers in India, a chronic problem which undermined student learning. Duflo randomly assigned 120 schools to one of two groups; in the test group teachers were photographed with their students before and after each school day by using a tamper proof camera and a control group with no changes. Teacher pay was adjusted for attendance. At the end of the experiment, teachers in the test group were half as likely to be absent from school.[52] In 2005 Duflo examined activities of Spandana, an Indian microcredit lender. When Spandana announced plans to expand into 52 neighborhoods in Hyderabad, a matched set of 52 neighborhoods was identified. More than a year later, Duflo's team interviewed 7,000 residents, evaluating in detail their economic circumstances. Duflo concluded that microcredit was not for every poor household; while some used loans as intended to start-up businesses, others used the money to purchase consumable goods, effectively worsening their poverty since they had to repay the loan. Duflo and Banerjee identified two circumstances in which the standard microcredit model was ill-advised: borrowers who were able to operate independently from a lending group, and those who were not positioned to begin immediate repayment of loans. Ultimately, the researchers concluded that economic stability was a precursor for microcredit success. "A sense of stability may be necessary for people to be able to take the long view," they observed, "A steady and predictable income makes it possible to commit to future expenditure and also makes it much easier and cheaper to borrow now."[53]

The "Robin Hood Tax," first proposed by Nobel Laureate James Tobin in 1974 would tax currency transactions, the revenue from which would be used to finance development efforts.[54] A spot tax on financial trading languished until the global recession in the late 2000s, when economic inequality became more obvious internationally. Demonstrators against cuts in social welfare benefits in the European Union as well as the United States contended that a Robin Hood tax could produce a measure of economic equity.[55]

Supporters noted that Britain, Hong Kong, and Singapore had instituted a tax on financial transactions ranging from $10 to $50 per $10,000. By the end of 2011, prime ministers of Germany, Italy, and France announced support for the concept, and Bill Gates proposed to the G20 nations a modest tax that would generate $48 billion annually. Leaders of the United States and the United Kingdom were ambivalent, however, suspecting that any such tax would place adopting countries at an economic disadvantage unless the tax were in effect internationally.[56]

Technological innovations have attempted to replicate the astounding success of the Green Revolution of the 1970s in increasing the world's food supply by introducing scientific and economic innovations to developing nations. Toward the end of 2011, for example, GlaxoSmithKline, funded by the Bill and Melinda Gates Foundation, announced that a new antimalarial drug had proven successful on half of children to whom it had been administered.[57]

In 2009, the Indian government appointed Nandan Nilekani, the wealthy founder of Infosys, to manage the Aadhaar identity system through which 1.2 billion Indians will have fingerprints and iris scans encoded on an identity card that will allow access to such government services as drivers' licenses and welfare benefits. Reversing traditional caste methods for establishing identity, the Aadhaar card will promote equality among all Indians in the process advantaging the poorest.[58]

In the mid-1990s Santiago Levy, undersecretary of finance in Mexico, conducted an experiment that asked the poor if they preferred continuing a traditional surplus food program or receipt of cash tied to specific conditions. When the results showed the poor preferred conditional cash, Levy convinced the government to establish *Oportunidades*, through which low-income households go to a local bank to receive cash in order to purchase consumer needs. The cash conversion was not only welcomed by low-income Mexicans, but the model was imported by New York Mayor Michael Bloomberg as Opportunity New York where low-income households are given cash incentives for constructive activities, such as holding a job and participating in child care.[59] Among the most intriguing of technological applications has been the introduction of companies that are hybrids between traditional for-profit ventures and nonprofits committed to social welfare. In *Building Social Business*, Grameen founder Yunus proposed the "social business" as a model to generate capital, develop products, and market them to low-income consumers, including yogurt and shoes.[60]

Similarly, Vinod Khosla, billionaire and co-founder of Sun Microsystems, established an initiative to promote socially responsible business activities in India, such as Moksha Yug Access a milk collection, cooling, and distribution company.[61]

In each of these examples, new technological applications are furthering development efforts by government as well as the nonprofit and commercial sectors, all congruent with the "social entrepreneurship" model of change.

Conclusion

Nations vary developmentally both as individual entities and as clusters. Thus, the United States is more developed than Niger, just as the countries of the industrialized West are more affluent than those of sub-Saharan Africa. At the same time, countries and regions influence one another, contributing to the dynamism of international relations. A common tendency in the West has been to regard the welfare states of North America and Western Europe as ideals to which the developing nations should aspire.

Yet, a series of events challenged this assumption. First, since the 1980s the welfare states of the West have retrenched, reducing their fiscal commitments to social programs. Second, among developing nations, subgroups have emerged. The oil embargo of the 1970s highlighted a small group of nations, the oil-exporting countries, which have comparatively high per capita income despite relatively low industrialization. Another subgroup consists of Southeast Asian nations that have prospered by aggressively pursuing capitalist strategies of development. As for the nations of sub-Saharan Africa: Most of them are worse off today than when they achieved independence during the 1960s, a tragedy that has been exacerbated by the HIV/AIDS epidemic. Third, international development agencies, such as the United Nations and the IMF, have begun to explore alternative scenarios to prosperity—scenarios, such as sustainable development[62]—that are often contrary to the alienating individualism and narcissistic consumption characteristic of the traditional welfare state.

A world in which inequality and strife contribute to social instability poses enormous challenges for human service professionals, with respect to both direct services and development theory. Social workers who have served in the Peace Corps have an immediate appreciation for the intractability of problems in the Third and Fourth Worlds, of course. But immigrants seeking better opportunities in developing nations are presenting new problems to human service workers in industrialized nations. Social workers in the United States, for example, are confronted with human trafficking, undocumented workers, and refugee families in increasing numbers.[63] As James Midgley advised, addressing such problems requires strategies that focus on human capital, social development, and self-sufficiency—interventions that are not commonly taught in First World schools of social work.[64]

DISCUSSION QUESTIONS

1. What are the limitations of the Human Development Index in measuring a nation's development?
2. Is examining a nation's material conditions the best way to evaluate social development? If not, what other indicators should be used?
3. What are the main reasons that Fourth World countries are less developed now than before they achieved independence?
4. Which welfare state typology provides the best explanation for the development of welfare states?

5. Compared to those of other nations, is the U.S. welfare state really "exceptional"? Why or why not?
6. In the light of international data, how important is foreign aid to development relative to private capital?
7. Select a developing nation and investigate the adequacy of its social infrastructure. What is the level of provision of welfare, health, and education services? How does it compare to the benefits and services of the United States?

NOTES

1. See Martin Rein and Lee Rainwater (eds.), *Public/Private Interplay in Social Protection* (Armonk, NY: M.E. Sharpe, 1986); Sheila Kamerman, "The Mixed Economy of Welfare." *Social Work* 29 (1983), pp. 5–11; David Stoesz, "A Theory of Social Welfare," *Social Work* 34 (1989), pp. 101–107; Neil Gilbert and Barbara Gilbert, *The Enabling State: Modern Welfare Capitalism in America* (New York: Oxford University Press, 1989); and Richard Rose, "Common Goals but Different Roles: The State's Contribution to the Welfare Mix," in R. Rose and R. Shiratori (eds.), *The Welfare State East and West* (New York: Oxford University Press, 1986), pp. 13–39.
2. Harold Wilensky and Charles Lebeaux, *Industrial Society and Social Welfare* (New York: Russell Sage Foundation, 1965).
3. Richard M. Titmuss, *Social Policy: An Introduction* (London: Allen and Unwin, 1971).
4. Norman Furniss and Timothy Tilton, *The Case for the Welfare State* (Bloomington, IN: Indiana University Press, 1977).
5. Ramesh Mishra, *The Welfare State in Crisis* (Brighton, England: Wheatsheaf Books, 1984).
6. Gosta Esping-Andersen, *Three Worlds of Welfare Capitalism* (Cambridge, England: Polity Press, 1990).
7. Edwin Amenta and Theda Skocpol, "Taking Exception: Explaining the Distinctiveness of American Public Policies during the Last Century," in Francis C. Castles (ed.), *The Comparative History of Public Policy* (New York: Oxford University Press, 1989), pp. 292–333.
8. Jacob Hacker, *The Divided Welfare State* (New York: Cambridge University Press, 2002), pp. 13–14.
9. Theda Skocpol, Protecting Soldiers and Mothers: The Political Origins of Social Policy in the United States (Cambridge, MA: Harvard University Press, 1992).
10. In 1975 Harold L. Wilensky noted that the United States "allocates a larger fraction of its total welfare spending to pensions that any of the twenty two richest nations [in the world]." However, more recent expenditure data from the Organization for Economic Cooperation and Development (OECD) show that while pension expenditures remain comparatively high, the United States is by no means a world leader. See Harold L. Wilensky, *Welfare State and Equality* (Berkeley, CA: University of California Press, 1975), p. 105; and OECD, Social Expenditure, 1960–1990, retrieved from www.oecd.org

11. Robert Pinker, *The Idea of Welfare* (London, Heinemann, 1979).
12. M. A. Jones, *The Australian Welfare State: Growth Crisis and Change* (Sydney, Australia: Allen and Unwin, 1980); and Terry Carney and Peter Hanks, *Social Security in Australia* (Melbourne: Oxford University Press, 1994).
13. Howard Glennester and James Midgley (eds.), *The Radical Right and the Welfare State* (London: Wheatsheaf Books, 1991).
14. See Barry Bluestone and Bennett Harrison, *The Deindustrialization of America* (New York: Basic Books, 1982); Samuel Bowles, David Gordon, and Thomas E. Weisskopf, *Beyond the Wasteland* (Garden City, NY: Anchor Press, 1983); Bennett Harrison and Barry Bluestone, *The Great U-Turn* (New York: Basic Books, 1988); Robert Reich, *Tales of a New America* (New York: Times Books, 1987); and Lester C. Thurow, *The Zero-Sum Solution* (New York: Simon and Schuster, 1985).
15. Wim Van Oorschot, Michael Opielka, and Birgit Pfau-Effinger, *Culture and Welfare State* (Edward Elgar: Northampton, MA, 2008).
16. See Charles Atherton, "The Welfare State: Still on Solid Ground," *Social Service Review* 63 (Fall 1989), pp. 167–179; and Joel Blau, "Theories of the Welfare State," *Social Service Review* 63 (March 1989), pp. 226–237.
17. Atherton, "The Welfare State."
18. Martin Anderson, "Welfare Reform," in Peter Duignan and Alvin Rabushka (eds.), *The United States in the 1980s* (Stanford, CA: Hoover Institution, 1980), pp. 145–164; George Gilder, *Wealth and Poverty* (New York: Basic Books, 1981); Lawrence Mead, *Beyond Entitlement* (New York: Free Press, 1986); and Charles Murray, *Losing Ground* (New York: Basic Books, 1984).
19. Anthony Giddens, *The Third Way* (London: Polity Press, 2000).
20. Neil Gilbert, *Transformation of the Welfare State* (New York: Oxford University Press, 2002).
21. Alan Wolfe, "Paths of Dependence," *The New Republic* (October 14, 2002), p. 41.
22. Steven Erlanger, "Crisis Threatens Liberal Benefits of European Life," *New York Times,* May 23, 2010, p. A1.
23. David Ignatius, "The Global Discontent," *Washington Post* (October 16, 2011), p. A27.
24. Jeffrey Sachs, *The End to Poverty* (New York: Penguin, 2005), pp. 266–293.
25. William Easterly, *The White Man's Burden* (New York: Penguin, 2006), p. 17.
26. Ibid., p. 379.
27. Paul Collier, *The Bottom Billion* (New York: Oxford University Press, 2007), p. 119.
28. Peter Baker, "Pride in Obama Aside, Tanzanians Praise Bush," *Washington Post,* February 18, 2008, p. A10.
29. "The Millennium Challenge," *Washington Post* (July 16, 2007), p. A14.

30. Neil MacFarquhar, "U.N. Poverty Goals Face Accountability Questions," *New York Times,* September 19, 2010, p. 14.

31. Amartya Sen, *Development as Freedom* (New York: Knopf, 1999), p. 18.

32. Ibid., pp. 48–49.

33. Martha Nussbaum, *Women and Human Development* (New York: Cambridge University Press, 2000).

34. Ibid., pp. 78–80.

35. http://hdr.undp.org/en/media/HDR_20072008_GEM.pdf, downloaded January 25, 2012.

36. Celia Dugger, "Global Number of Early Childhood Deaths Falls Below 9 Million for First Time," *New York Times,* September 10, 2009, p. A6.

37. David Brown, "Maternal Death Rates Drop Around the World," *Washington Post,* April 14, 2010, p. A10.

38. Jeffrey Gettleman, "Shower of Aid Brings Flood of Progress," *New York Times,* March 9, 2010, p. A9.

39. Ibid., p. 105.

40. Rama Lakshmi, "Indian Bill on Legislative Seats for Women Advances, *Washington Post,* March 10, 2010, p. A13.

41. http://www.oecd.org/document/49/0,3746,en_2649_34447_46582641_1_1_1_1,00.html, downloaded January 27, 2012.

42. Michael Todaro, *Economic Development* (New York: Pearson, 1994), pp. 476–481.

43. World Bank, *Entering the 21st Century* (Washington, DC: World Bank, 2000), pp. 6–7.

44. http://www.oecd.org/document/8/0,3746,en_2649_34529562_40930184_1_1_1_34529562,00.html, downloaded January 27, 2012.

45. World Bank, Entering the 21st Century, p. 18.

46. http://web.worldbank.org/WBSITE/EXTERNAL/EXTDEC/EXTGLOBALMONITOR/EXTGLOMONREP2011/0,,contentMDK:22882843~pagePK:64168427~piPK:64168435~theSitePK:7856232,00.html, downloaded January 27, 2012.

47. http://www.grameen-info.org/index.php?option=com_content&task=view&id=453&Itemid=527, downloaded January 27, 2012.

48. Stephanie Strom and Vikas Bajaj, "Wealth and Controversy in Microlending," *New York Times,* July 30, 2010, p. B1.

49. Neil MacFarquhar, "Many Borrowers of Microloans Now Find the Price Is Too High," *New York Times,* April 14, 2010, p. A1.

50. Bajaj, "15 Years In, Microcredit Has Suffered a Black Eye," *New York Times,* January 6, 2011, p. B3.

51. MacFarquhar, "Many Borrowers," p. A1.

52. Ian Parker, "The Poverty Lab," *The New Yorker,* May 17, 2010, p. 30.

53. Banerjee and Esther Duflo, *Poor Economics* (New York: Public Affairs, 2011), p. 229.

54. http://www.triplepundit.com/2011/11/tobin-tax-debate/, downloaded January 30, 2012.

55. Michael Greenberg, "Zuccotti Park: What Next?" *New York Review of Books,* December 8, 2011, p. 14.

56. Steven Greenhouse and Graham Bowley, "The Robin Hood Tax," *New York Times,* December 7, 2011, p. B1.

57. Donald McNeil, Jr., "Scientists See Promise in Vaccine for Malaria," *New York Times,* October 19, 2011, p. A4.

58. Lydia Polgreen, "Scanning 2.4 Billion Eyes, India Tries to Connect Poor to Growth," *New York Times,* September 2, 2011, p. A1.

59. Tina Rosenberg, "A Payoff Out of Poverty?" *New York Times Magazine,* December 25, 2008.

60. Muhammad Yunus, *Building Social Business* (New York: Public Affairs, 2010).

61. Vikas Bajaj, "In Capitalism, Sun's Co-Founder Sees a Pathway to Help the Poor," *New York Times,* October 6, 2010, p. B1.

62. World Bank, *Sustainable Development in a Dynamic World* (Washington, DC: Author, 2003).

63. Lynne Healy, *International Social Work* (New York: Oxford University Press, 2001).

64. James Midgley, *Professional Imperialism* (London: Heinemann, 1981); and James Midgley, *Social Development* (London: Sage, 1995).

INDEX

Note: Page numbers followed by f denote figures; t, tables.